AF761135

The Historical Analysis of China's State Capital

Wu Taichang, Wu Li et. al.

Translated by Song Ying, Chen Juebin, Li Zhaohui

Paths International Ltd

中国社会科学出版社
CHINA SOCIAL SCIENCES PRESS

Contents

Overview

This book aims at describing and analyzing the historical evolution of state capital in China. Starting from the national intervention of the economy and the direct management of industry and commerce in the feudal era (this part can be viewed as the pre-history of state capital) and running through the entire modern China and the new China, this book inspects the changes and characteristics of China's state capital over the past two thousand years, so as to probe into China's actual national conditions and the status, role and evolution of state capital. In commenting on the Populist economists' research on the development of Russian capitalism, Lenin pointed out, "Some of us tend to portray the essence of the issue of the fate of Russian capitalism as such: what seems to be of great significance is the speed (i.e., how quickly capitalism develops?). In fact, the question of how and from where it develops (i.e. how was the economic system in pre-capitalism in Russia?) is of much greater significance. The most serious mistake of Populist economics is that it gives incorrect answers to these two questions.[1] The slow and tortuous development of China's capitalism is related to the long-term continuation of China's feudal economy. Similarly, the emergence and development of socialism in China are closely related to the two factors mentioned above. China's socialism was established on the basis of the old

1 *Complete Works of Lenin*, Vol. 3, Development of Russian Capitalism, p. 343, People's Publishing House, 1984.

semi-feudal and semi-colonial systems with insufficient development of capitalism and relatively backward productivity. It takes a long time to get rid of the old system and establish and improve the new system. This is the national conditions of the primary stage of socialism. National conditions reflect tradition. Tradition can be criticized and transformed, but it cannot be cut off. To do so is like trying to leave the earth by pulling one's hair. Given the ancient and modern knowledge, we know that Chinese characteristics lie in China's national conditions and traditions.

1. China's Feudal Social and Economic Structure and National Economic Functions

Karl Marx pointed out: "The unique economic form of extracting unpaid surplus labor from direct producers determines the relationship between domination and subordination, which is directly generated from production itself and has a decisive reaction to production. However, the whole structure of the economic system produced by the relations of production itself, as well as its unique political structure, are based on the above-mentioned economic forms. At any time, we are always in a direct relationship between the owner of the production conditions and the direct producer, in which any form of such relationship naturally corresponds to the mode of labour and to a certain stage of development of the productive forces of the labour. We try to find the deepest secret and the hidden foundation for the whole social structure, thus for the political form of sovereignty and dependence, and in short, for any particular form of state at that time. [1] There is no doubt that the development of China's feudal society has its own characteristics, which can only be clarified through the analysis of China's feudal economic structure guided by the general law of human social development by Marxism, proceeding from the facts of China's feudal society and the comparative study of the feudal system with other countries and regions. Here we should neither proceed from individual principles, nor replace the analysis

1 *Das Kapital*, Vol. 3, pp. 891-892, People's Publishing House, 1975.

of essence with simple phenomenal comparison, nor substitute comparison with analogy to rigidly create a world "center" and force the reality of Chinese feudal society to the "model". For example, China has not completed its feudalization; its feudal society has been stagnating for a long time; there exists a "super-stable structure"; or at the end of the feudal society in China, it is impossible for the capitalist factors to develop; and the theory of "exogenous cause" of capitalism in China. Those discussions are generally related to the simplified research methods mentioned above, which deviates from the reality of Chinese society and the general principles of Marxism.

The development of China's feudal economy can be roughly divided into two stages. First, the stage of lordship economy, roughly from the Western Zhou Dynasty to the end of the Spring and Autumn Period. Second, the stage of landlord economy, from the Warring States Period to the Qing Dynasty. This stage can be further divided into two periods. Before the middle of the Tang Dynasty, the aristocratic landlord economy occupies the dominant position, with more traits of serfdom. And the later stage (after the middle of the Tang Dynasty) is the typical mature landlord economy. This second stage is the main difference between China and other feudal countries in Europe. Generally, feudal countries either did not experience this stage of development (such as Germany and Russia), or this stage came into being at the same time with capitalism (or perhaps a little successively) in the period of the collapse of the lordship economy, so they did not develop sufficiently and were gradually excluded and replaced by the capitalist mode of production (Britain and France can be regarded as typical of such countries), with the maximum duration of about 300 years. Only in China, this stage has lasted for more than 2000 years. This stage has been fully developed without the challenge of new production modes and has achieved a typical independent form. We will focus on the analysis of the basic characteristics of the socio-economic structure at this stage.

In the feudal economic form, agriculture is the main productive sector of society, so the land system is of course the basic elements, or core elements, of social and economic structure. The land system in the second stage of Chinese feudal society is quite complex, and it has the following characteristics.

(1) Private ownership of land coexists with state ownership of land, with private ownership of land occupying a dominant position; landlord ownership of land coexists with ownership of small plots of land owned by self-employed peasants, with landlord ownership of land occupying a dominant position. In the early days of the second stage, aristocratic landlord ownership, commoners landlord ownership, state land ownership and self-farming ownership coexist, with aristocratic landlord ownership having comparative advantages. As a supplement to landlord ownership, state ownership and self-farming ownership also have a certain scale. In the later stage, although landlord ownership, state ownership and self-farming ownership still exist side by side, state-owned land relatively decreased, and a large number of self-employed farmers turned into tenants, with landlord ownership having an absolute advantage.

(2) Because of the diversity of the land system, the conditions for decentralization and mobility of land ownership are mature, and land can be freely traded within a reasonable range. On the other hand, the feudal land ownership system in China lacks a strict hierarchical structure (the later, the more so). The economic status and economic identity of all social classes and strata can remain unchanged, with land being regarded as the symbol of social wealth and class status. These two points lead to the combination of land rent, profit and interest, forming the economic ties of landlords, businessmen and usurers, intensifying land annexation, and promoting the bankruptcy of small-scale peasant economy and the development of large-scale land ownership.

(3) Countries and landlords generally do not operate agriculture directly, but rent land to small tenants to operate separately. China's tenants enjoy relative freedom compared with the serfs under the monarchy (of course, they still retain the personal dependence on the landlords to varying degrees, and the more serious the dependence is the earlier it is), but the combination of the tenants and the land is unstable, lacking economic security and competing with each other.

This on the one hand improves the productivity of social labor, and deepens the cruelty of landlord exploitation on the other hand. Land rental and taxation of land surplus products strengthens the domination of the landlord class and its country, worsening the economic status of small farmers. Decentralized small-scale agriculture is basically a simple reproductive structure.

The inexorable result of the diversity of land system and the decentralization of land management is that the feudal landlord ownership system in China cannot form the complete manor economic system under the feudal lordship economic system. Small farmers who produce by themselves not only produce the agricultural products they need, but also produce part of the industrial products they need daily. This self-sufficient small-scale agriculture and family handicraft industry are intertwined. The combined production structure became the cell organization of Chinese feudal economy and the special manifestation of natural economy in the second stage of Chinese feudal society. On the other hand, the basic characteristics of the agricultural-industrial integration of small-scale peasant economy in China are "combination of farming and weaving". The scope of self-sufficiency is mainly limited to food and clothing. A considerable part of the supply of means of production (such as production tools) and means of livelihood depends on exchange and market. The surplus labor occupied by feudal landlords is mainly grain rent, and very few industrial and agricultural products. Their consumption depends more on market. Considering the geographical constraints of textile raw materials and regional product production, the incompleteness of this natural economy is more obvious.

Therefore, as a necessary supplement to the feudal landlord economy, the production of small commodities in urban and rural areas can exist and be highly developed in the second stage of Chinese feudal society. At the same time, commerce, especially entrepot trade, based on the small-scale peasant economy and the production of small commodities, which are scattered but have a large population, has also been prosperous and developed, thus constituting a special phenomenon after the loss of typical natural economy in the second stage of

Chinese feudal society. This kind of commodity economy, accompanied by the landlord economy, has limited independence and still maintains its dependence and subordination to the feudal natural economy to a certain extent. However, the development of commodity economy is ultimately the result of social productive forces and the expansion of social division of labor and exchange. The landlord economy, which represents a higher labor productivity than the lordship economy, enables the typical natural economy to change. It needs the development of small commodity production and commerce as its supplement. The natural economy and commodity economy are interdependent and supplementary to each other, which enlarges the economic foundation of the second stage of Chinese feudal society. It is on this basis that the centralized state system in Chinese feudal society was established and developed.

Karl Marx pointed out that "the national division of labor and the diversity of domestic exchanges" ... "are the only possible basis for establishing a unified management system and a unified legal system".[1] Previous discussions on China's centralized feudal state system came to the conclusions of either that the landlord economy is its basis, or that the small-scale peasant economy is its basis (this view is totally wrong). And still some other conclusions are combinations of the two arguments. All agree that the natural economy is the basis of the centralized state, while ignoring the role of commodity economic development in its formation, or even denying the difference between commodity economy and natural economy and equating the two. Certain political systems and forms of state are always the result of economic development. The development of world history has proved that it is impossible for a centralized state system to emerge in a purely natural economic form characterized by a feudal lordship economic system. For example, the centralized state system that once flourished in European slavery era ceased to exist in the feudal natural economy era of the Middle Ages; Charles the

1 *Complete Works of Marx and Engels*, Vol. 10, Revolutionary Spain, People's Publishing House, 1964, p. 462.

Great attempted to establish the monarchy centralization system in the Frankish kingdom where the feudal lordship economy held a dominant position, but he did not succeed; after the establishment of the feudal monarchy, the centralization system of the Byzantine Empire gradually disappeared; in Asia, Japan tried to imitate the Han system, but after more than a thousand years, it failed to establish a centralized state. Let's look at other obvious examples. During the Wei, Jin and Southern and Northern Dynasties, the centralized system declined several times because the aristocratic landlords turned into feudal lords; the early and late stages of the second stage of Chinese feudal society showed the difference in the development and stability of the centralized state system because of the different degrees of maturity of the landlord economy and the development of the commodity economy.

This book will not discuss the whole process of the formation and development of the centralized state system in Chinese feudal society, nor does it deal with other aspects of the system. Here we only focus on the economic functions of the centralized feudal state and its profound impact on the social and economic structure. According to Marx's exposition of the state function of "Ancient Oriental", under certain conditions, the ancient state can have some economic function. [1] Of course, China is different from India and other countries. It is not because of the influence of geographical environment that a centralized feudal country is established. As we have already analyzed above, China's centralized state system is built on the basis of the highly developed landlord economy and the related commodity economy. It is the product of the high development of feudal civilization. In the second stage of Chinese feudal society, more developed productivity and extensive social and economic ties made the centralized feudal countries have more complete and developed economic functions than India and other countries. This kind of economic function involves not only being engaged

1 *Complete Works of Marx and Engels*, Vol. 9, The Rule of Britain in India, People's Publishing House, 1964, p.143.

in public water projects because of the need for joint irrigation as in India and other countries. Although the feudal China also engaged in the construction of water projects on a large scale, but also engaged in the construction of public works such as transportation and national defense. But these are not the core of their economic functions. The economic functions of China's centralized feudal state are manifested in three aspects: firstly, it is engaged in the construction and management of public works such as hydraulic engineering, transportation and national defense; secondly, it interferes in social reproduction through taxation and various economic policies; and thirdly, it is directly engaged in handicraft, commerce and agriculture.

Regarding the first point, there is no need for further explanation that this is a logical act of the centralized state. But it should be emphasized that the construction and management of public works requires a great deal of human, material and financial resources. It accounts for a considerable proportion of the national expenditure and plays an extremely important role in the development of social economy. The second and third points are interrelated. Marx said, "On the basis of any mode of production, commerce will promote the production of surplus products that are to be exchanged in order to increase the enjoyment of producers (in this case, the owner of products) or to store money; therefore, commerce makes production more and more productive for exchange value", "commerce more or less plays the role of disintegration to the various existing forms of production organizations that mainly produce use value."[1] In the second stage of Chinese feudal society, the expansion of social division of labor and the development of commodity economy continuously promoted the prosperity of the landlord economy. However, the development of small commodity production and commerce as a supplement to the feudal landlord economy objectively negated the natural economy. Its excessive development would inevitably endanger the foundation of the landlord economy and shake the foundation of the centralized

1 *Das Kapital*, Vol. 3, People's Publishing House, 1975, pp. 364, 371.

feudal state, which is beyond the pale for the landlord class. Therefore, the feudal regime intervened in social reproduction through taxation and various economic policies, trying to restrain the development of commodity economy, in order to consolidate the root of landlord class rule. All dynasties took "Emphasizing Agriculture and Restricting or Despising Industry and Commerce" as the center of their economic policies. They advocated rewarding farming and weaving, and restrained the development of commercial capital and its disintegration to the small-scale peasant economy by imposing heavy commercial taxes, restricting the business activities of businessmen and depreciating the social status of businessmen. But the development of commodity economy is the embodiment of social productive forces. This economic power cannot be arbitrarily inhibited by some economic policy of feudal countries. Therefore, "today's law belittles businessmen, but businessmen already become rich; it respects farmers, but farmers are still poor!" [1] It is a true portrayal of the development of history. It is in this contradictory movement of natural economy and commodity economy that the third economic function of the centralized feudal state has been highly developed.

As early as the Zhou Dynasty, the government-run handicraft industry has been in existence in the form of labor slavery as compared with serfdom. At that time, it mainly produced supplies for feudal nobles and military supplies, and was a typical form of natural economy. By the Han Dynasty, important changes had taken place in government-run handicraft industry. Production activities were no longer limited to the production of non-profit self-used industrial products and military supplies, but gradually expanded to the production of profitable important products related to the national economy and people's livelihood, such as salt making, iron smelting and other mining, currency casting, shipbuilding, etc. The scale of operation was getting larger and larger, and the production organization

1 *Han Shu* (*The Book of Han Dynasty*), Vol. 24, Shi Huo Zhi I, Zhonghua Book Company, 1962.

was getting more and more compact. The centralized feudal state monopolized the production of important industrial products. The first intention was to increase fiscal revenue, and expand the economic power of the centralized state. The second was to restrain the development of commodity production and consolidate the landlord economy. The latter was more important. As stated in *On Salt and Iron*, "Today's policy on salt and iron is not only for profit, but also for the sake of emphasizing agriculture and restricting industry and commerce, cracking down on factions, and banning extravagance. … In the past, powerful people monopolized the profits from natural resources, mining iron and casting, and making salt from sea water. They could gather as many as more than a thousand people, mostly of whom were people in exile. Those people left their homes and gathered together in remote and backward places to commit treacherous and fraudulent business, thus forming cliques. This led to really baneful influence."[1]

At the same time, the economic activities of the feudal society also extended to the commercial sector. The state set up such commercial organizations such as Jun Shu (Tribute Equalization Organization), Ping Zhun (Commodity Prices Stabilizing Organization) and Chang Ping Cang (Food Prices Stabilizing Organization) With its strong economic power and super-economic political power, it established a national commercial network based in the capital. It implemented monopoly system for some important commodities, maintained considerable control over circulation and market, and make huge profits during the process. It can be seen that the policies of "Emphasizing Agriculture and Restricting or Despising Industry and Commerce" in feudal countries differed in the actual implementation process. They restrained only private industry and commerce, while the development of government-run industry and commerce was entirely in line with the interests of the landlord class. All this is to consolidate the dominant position of the landlord economy. This is the result of institutional

1 Huan Kuan, Annotated by Wang Li: *Annotations on Salt and Iron*, Vol. 1, Revival of Ancient Times VI, Zhonghua Book Company, 1992, pp. 78-79.

choice. While intervening in and regulating social reproduction with economic policies, the feudal state also used economic means, that is, to provide safeguards for the existing economic and social system in the form of direct participation in business activities, which should be called institutional innovation.

The economic function of the feudal regime to directly engage in industrial and commercial activities was continuously developed and improved in the Tang and Song Dynasties and later generations. The scope and scale of industrial and commercial activities were further expanded. The internal division of labor and production technology reached a rather high level, which constituted an important aspect of the prosperity of the feudal economy in China. Government-run industry and commerce is different from general commodity economy in essence, but it has the external characteristics of commodity economy. It is the result of the evolution of economic structure in the second stage of China's feudal society and a special mixed economy resulting from the variation of natural economy. The development of government-run industry has restricted the market of folk handicraft industry, especially urban handicraft industry, and blocked the transformation of commercial capital into industry. At the same time, the development of government-run commerce has further strengthened the control of feudal landlord economy over urban and rural handicraft industry, restrained the development of commercial capital, weakened its disintegration effect on small-scale peasant economy, reducing it to the state of having to rely on the landlord economy. The government-run agriculture is dominated by the station farm system, and its military and political role is naturally important. However, the scale and influence of the system in the past dynasties are different, and its share in the total economic volume is small, so it will not be discussed in this chapter. As an integral part of the social and economic structure in China's feudal society, a buffer between natural economy and commodity economy, and an economic force, government-run industry and commerce further strengthened the economic foundation of the landlord economic system and consolidated the centralized feudal state system. Therefore, the status and role of government-run industry and commerce in the economic structure of China's feudal society can never be ignored. In the early period of the past dynasties, the governance was clean, the policy was fair, the ability of the state to participate in, intervene and regulate the economy was strong, and the society was in the stage of rise and development as a whole; but in the middle and late period, the hierarchy tended to corrupt, the ability of the state to participate in, intervene and regulate the economy was continually weakened, and even the phenomenon of reverse regulation appeared. The government became the "plunderer", intensified the bankruptcy of the small-scale peasants and other working class, promoted the merger from the powerful, the stagnation and recession of the economy. These being combined with the natural disasters and man-made misfortunes, the social contradictions gradually intensified. All these showed that the feudal dynasty was doomed for peasant uprising and dynasty change. China's feudal society experienced this tortuous ascendancy and development in this periodical change. Of course, the negative impact of this turbulent change of dynasties on economic and social development is also obvious.

2. The Development of China's Feudal Economy and Capitalism

"When reaching a certain level, the existence and development of merchant capital becomes by itself the historical premise of the development of capitalist mode of production".[1] It can be said that since the Tang and Song Dynasties, the material conditions for the emergence of this historical precondition have already appeared in the social and economic structure of China's feudal society. Before the Ming Dynasty, there were some incidental and early records of capitalist relations. Scholars generally believe that after the mid-Ming Dynasty, there has been an obvious germination of capitalist relations in Chinese feudal society. But after all, the germination refers only to the scattering of a mode of production in the old social and economic structure. Strictly speaking, it does not constitute an independent stage of development of the new mode of production. Karl Marx

1 *Das Kapital*, Vol. 3,, People's Publishing House, 1975 p. 365.

said: "The economic structure of capitalist society originates from the economic structure of feudal society. The disintegration of the latter liberates the elements of the former."[1] Although Chinese capitalism burgeoned early, the disintegration of feudal economic structure was extremely slow. Why? Any mode of production is historically temporary, so the so-called "super-stable structure" is of course not based on history and logic. Under the influence of the development of productive forces, once a new production relationship comes into being, its potential cannot be deterred. How long can the old mode of production last? On the one hand, it depends on the solidity of its internal structure; on the other hand, it depends on its temporary inclusiveness of the new mode of production. China's feudal social and economic structure has its unique features in the above-mentioned two aspects and their relationship, so the disintegration was slow and blocked the development of capitalist mode of production.

The disintegration of the feudal economic structure is generally reflected from the role of commercial capital. The commerce in the feudal society of China is quite prosperous and developed, but its disintegration of the old mode of production is not proportional to its degree of development. As Marx has analyzed, "the development of merchant capital itself is not enough to promote and explain the transition from one mode of production to another", "The extent to which it disintegrates the old mode of production depends, first of all, on the solidity and internal structure of these modes of production. Besides, where does this disintegration process lead? In other words, what new production mode will replace the old one depends not on commerce, but on the nature of the old one."[2] The development of commercial capital in China's feudal society has two distinct characteristics. The first is its parasitism to the small-scale peasant economy and the production of small commodities. And the second is its dependence on the landlord economy. In China's feudal landlord economy, social products as

1 *Das Kapital*, Vol. 1, People's Publishing House, 1975, p. 783.
2 *Das Kapital*, Vol. 3, People's Publishing House, 1975, pp. 366, 371.

commodities entering the circulation field can be divided into the following categories: (1) necessary products of individual peasants who combine agriculture with industry (self-cultivating peasants have some surplus products); (2) products of independent handicraftsmen; (3) feudal land rent; (4) products of later folk handicraft workshops; (5) government-run handicraft products; (6) State taxation (including taxes from state-owned land and some products). Workshop handicraft industry belongs to capitalist management. The latter two categories have nothing to do with the activities of non-governmental commercial capital, and we will not discuss them. From the first three categories, we can see that the main providers of social commodities are individual peasants and independent handicraftsmen. Peasants are not direct commodity producers. They sell and exchange some of their essential products in order to obtain different use values. They "didn't have to raise the market price of land products to the level of yielding average profits to them, as in the normal capitalist mode of production, let alone to a degree of fixed form of land rent that exceeds the balance of average profits. Therefore, it is not necessary to raise the market price to the same level as the value or production price of other products. [1] On the other hand, although the independent handicraftsmen as small commodity producers are different from farmers, their production motivation is not pursuing surplus value. Their products enter circulation mainly for the exchange of other essential products. Their production structure is also limited and simple, just like the small-scale peasant economy.

Commercial capital with a broad base of these two has developed independently in the product exchange of the underdeveloped community, and has achieved a dominant position in the industry. It has encroached on most of the peasants and independent craftsmen through fraud and buying cheap and selling dear, and deprived them of most and even all of the surplus products (here, it refers to the remaining part after the feudal landlord and the political power's plunder). For the tenant farmers, their necessary products were directly encroached on. Although

1 *Das Kapital*, Vol. 3, People's Publishing House, 1975, pp. 908-909.

the development of commerce and commercial capital leads to the exchange value of production and the total amount of production is increasing, it is hard for most producers to improve their economic status. And some of their conditions will even deteriorate, making them further controlled by the feudal landlords and commercial capital. According to Karl Marx, there are two ways of transition from feudal production mode to capitalism. And of the two, it is probably very difficult for this "real revolutionary road"[1] of "producers turning to businessmen and capitalists" to form in front of the independent small commodity producers in Chinese feudal society, let alone the individual peasants as a result of the combination of agriculture and industry. Cottage industry in natural economy is the strongest fortress to resist capitalist production mode. However, because of the dependence of commercial capital on the landlord class, the transition of the other way of "businessmen directly dominating production" is extremely difficult and slow. In the second stage of China's feudal society, owing to the characteristics of the land system, a trinity of landlords, businessmen and usurers was formed. There was a certain accommodation between commercial capital and the landlord economy. Commercial profits were absorbed by the land in large numbers. The result was, of course, not to promote the development of commodity economy, but to promote land annexation and the development of large-scale land ownership. In short, the dependence of commercial capital on the landlord economy and its accommodation with the landlord economy greatly weakened the disintegration of commercial capital on the feudal economic structure. Engels said: "Businessmen are a revolutionary element in a society that has stagnated in the past as a result of heredity... Now that businessmen have come to this world, they should be the starting point for change in this world. But they were not self-awakened revolutionaries; on the contrary, they were closely linked with the world. The medieval businessman was by no means an individualist. Like all his

1 *Das Kapital*, Vol. 3, People's Publishing House, 1975, p. 373.

contemporaries, he was essentially a member of the community."[1] It seems that commercial capital in the second stage of Chinese feudal society, as an element of revolution, cannot be overestimated for its role of the disintegration of the feudal economic structure, but it is relatively competent as a well-behaved member of the feudal community. This is what we should pay full attention to when comparing the different characteristics of the transition from feudal economy to capitalism between China and the West.

The above is one aspect of the ruggedness of China's feudal social and economic structure, and the other is the role and influence of the feudal state's economic functions. In the process of feudal economy development, the most positive aspects of industrial production form are urban handicraft industry and rural independent handicraft industry. Their development and transition to a larger scale, more developed division of labor and more cooperative factory handicraft industry mark the dawn of capitalism. As mentioned above, due to the parasitic exploitation of commercial capital, it is difficult for independent handicraft industry in urban and rural areas to make the transition to workshop handicraft industry. Here we must further emphasize the restrictions of the activities of government-run industry and commerce on its development.

The obstacles of government-run handicraft industry to the development of independent handicraft industry in urban and rural areas are mainly manifested in two aspects: the control of labor force and the restriction of market. Before the mid-Tang Dynasty, the labor force of the government-run handicraft industry, except for the official servants and prisoners, was mostly unpaid. Most of them were soldiers, craftsmen and men doing all kinds of corvee for the feudal government. During this period, the government-run industry mainly adopted the form of labor service. From the mid-Tang Dynasty to the mid-Ming Dynasty, the nature of government-run industrial labor gradually transitioned from corvee service system to labor service system. The dependence of handicraftsmen on

1 Addendum to Vol. 3 of *Das Kapital*, People's Publishing House, 1975, p. 1019.

feudal regime was weakened compared with the previous period. However, through the establishment of the household registration system, the state immobilized the industrial labor force, making the independent handicraftsmen in urban and rural areas the reserve force of government-run handicraft industry. This national household registration system of labor force hinders the normal development of economic activities of independent handicraftsmen. The service places of craftsmen are generally far away from their homeland. It takes two to three months to go back and forth. Especially after the harassment and exploitation by officials, the official handicraftsmen get little income left, which means they work almost free of charge. The feudal restraint of government-run handicraft industry on the labor force of folk handicraft industry is a serious obstacle to the development of independent handicraft industry in urban and rural areas.

It is also obvious that the government-run handicraft industry restricts the development of folk handicraft industry in the market. Since the Qin and Han Dynasties, China has established a unified centralized feudal state, but in the dominant natural economy, local small markets and regional markets are still the main market players. Although the national market of important products which can provide more opportunities for the development of handicraft industry has existed for a long time, it is basically monopolized by the government-run industry and commerce. Even the market for industrial consumer goods (especially luxury goods) that the ruling class needs has also been greatly reduced by the self-sufficiency of the government-run handicraft industry. Thus, the independent handicraft industry in urban and rural areas can only compete for the limited local market with the rural family handicraft industry in natural economy. The expansion of the market is the premise of the development of commodity production. The existence of government-run handicraft industry has greatly limited the market of independent handicraft industry in urban and rural areas, making its operation scale correspondingly narrow. The progress of production technology and productivity are slow, and the transformation of commercial capital into industry is more difficult. The role of government-run commerce should also be discussed here. By monopolizing important commodities, government-run commerce not only inhibits the development of private commercial capital and weakens its disintegration of natural economy, but also prevents the infiltration and impact of private handicraft industry on the national market, further strengthens the control of feudal state over private handicraft industry, and ensures the dominant position of government-run industry. In addition, the government-run business controls and monopolizes international trade and inhibits the expansion of the market, the negative effect of which on the development of private industry and commerce cannot be underestimated. European capitalist production relations first appeared in shipping, textile and mining industries, mainly because these production sectors have a global impact on social and economic development. It is easy to open up markets in these sectors, and it is most likely to achieve breakthroughs in productivity in these sectors. In China, besides the above three industries, ceramic and shipbuilding are also sectors with national significance and high productivity. But before the mid-Ming Dynasty, because the government-run handicraft industry occupied a dominant position in industrial production, the higher productivity of the above-mentioned sectors was not mainly reflected in the independent handicraft industry in urban and rural areas, but in the official handicraft industry, which was the fundamental reason why the large-scale handicraft workshops rarely appeared in the independent handicraft industry in urban and rural areas.

In the overall process of social and economic development, various economic forces interact with each other. All we have discussed is just one aspect of the problem. On the other hand, the government-run handicraft industry itself is also a productive force. As an economic force, it also has a positive significance for the development of the whole social economy. By virtue of the huge manpower, material and financial resources centralized by the feudal state, the government-run industry can engage in large-scale public engineering construction and handicraft production. The expansion of production scale leads to the development of division of labor and cooperation, which leads to the continuous progress of production technology and the improvement of productivity. At the same time, the dissemination of more advanced production technologies and tools in the government-run workshops stimulates and promotes the development of private handicraft industry. It should be noted that the development of production and economic prosperity in China's feudal society are closely related to the economic activities. Since the mid-Ming Dynasty, with the development of productive forces, the social and economic links have become wider, the market has further expanded, and the independent handicraft industry in urban and rural areas has acquired certain opportunities for development. The number of handicraft workshops employing more workers for large-scale production activities has gradually increased, so the capitalist factors have begun to grow slowly. The development of folk workshops handicraft industry and the emergence of a large number of employed labor have intensified the conflicts between handicraftsmen and the feudal regime. Their class struggle to get rid of the fetters of feudalism has also developed day by day. The escape, slack working and deliberate depreciation of product quality of the workers in official workshops, together with the evasion of rotation, resistance to taxes, strikes, 'illegal mining', and even riots by independent handicraftsmen in urban and rural areas, all have shown that the exploitation mode of the industrial servitude system in the government-run handicraft industry has increasingly become the shackles of the development of productive forces. The development and competition of the handicraft industry in the folk workshops gradually weakened the original comparative advantage of the productivity level of the government-run handicraft industry. Because of the craftsmen's struggle and the chronic problems in management, the production cost of the government-run workshops increased sharply and the quality of the products declined continuously, which forced the feudal dynasty to further change the labor system of the government-run industry and gradually narrow the business scope of the government-run industry. After Chenghua years in the Ming Dynasty, the craftsmen in the government-run industry gradually used silver to replace corvee. The government used the silver collected to hire the craftsmen, or to buy directly from the market. The registration system of the craftsmen existed only in name.

The state's control over the industrial labor force weakened, and the government-run industry that have prospered for several dynasties began to decline. In the early Qing Dynasty, the system of craftsmen was abolished by decree. And in the second year of Yongzheng Dynasty (1724), the system of the craftsmen becoming government officials was abolished. Since then, the government-owned industry, whose business scope has been greatly reduced, has generally adopted the system of free recruitment. The dependence of craftsmen on the feudal regime has been greatly relaxed, which is an important symbol of the further development of the relationship between workshop handicraft industry and capitalism. It can also be seen that the development of productive forces must always break through the obstacles of the original economic relations.

We can further illustrate the inclusiveness of China's feudal economic structure to the capitalist mode of production in a certain period from the economic function of the feudal state. The capitalist era began in the period of workshop handicraft industry. The development of workshop handicraft industry promoted the separation between handicraft industry and agriculture, accelerated the speed of the deprivation of small farmers and handicraftsmen of their means of production, opened up the domestic market for capitalism and created the premise for further development. However, Karl Marx also emphasized that "the workshop handicraft industry can neither control the whole social production nor transform it fundamentally. Workshop handicraft industry, as an economic artwork, towers over the broad foundation of urban handicraft industry and rural household industry. When the narrow technological foundation of the workshop handicraft industry develops to a certain extent, it comes in contradiction with the production needs created by it itself.[1] "The real period of workshop handicraft industry did not cause fundamental changes. ...Only big industry has provided a solid foundation for capitalist agriculture with machinery, deprived most rural residents of their means of production thoroughly, completely separated agriculture from

1 *Das Kapital*, Vol. 1, People's Publishing House, 1975, p. 407.

rural household handicraft industry, and eradicated the foundation of rural household handicraft industry - spinning and weaving. Only in this way can it conquer the whole domestic market for industrial capital. "[1] Therefore, while acknowledging the role of workshop handicraft industry in the disintegration of feudal production mode, we should also realize that the independence of workshop handicraft industry is limited. Its development does not necessarily lead to the collapse of the old system immediately. Under certain conditions, the old production mode can accommodate it. The degree of tolerance varies in different countries due to the distinctive characteristics of feudal economic structure. Looking from the history of world capitalism, workshop handicraft industry is also a transitional period, which can be completed under bourgeois regime or feudal regime. For example, the development of the workshop handicraft industry in Britain and France is generally synchronous, but the French bourgeois revolution is nearly 150 years later than that in Britain. And it took place under the influence of the British Industrial Revolution. And China's feudal economic structure is inclusive of the capitalist mode of production with the nature of workshop handicraft industry, because the role of the feudal state's economic function this inclusiveness becomes more prominent.

China's feudal society has a high level of material civilization. On the one hand, its economic structure is stable; on the other hand, it is also flexible and can accommodate a higher level of productivity. Government-owned industry is an integral part of the feudal economy, but as an economic force, it represents a higher productivity, and its impact on the whole social economy is the objective reality. As far as the level of productivity is concerned, there is no difference between the government-run industry and the workshop handicraft industry. What they differ from each other is only the economic form of occupying the surplus labor. Any change in production relations is always the result of the development of productive forces to a certain extent. Therefore, in order to

1 *Das Kapital*, Vol. 1, People's Publishing House, 1975, pp. 816-817.

thoroughly break away from the old economic relations, the handicraft industry of non-governmental workshops must create higher productivity than the state-run industry. From the mid-Ming Dynasty to the early Qing Dynasty, we haven't observed such a situation. From the mid-Qing Dynasty to the Opium War, the handicraft industry of the folk workshops had developed rapidly. In some production sectors, it had a dominant position compared with the government-run industry, but the productivity level it represented was not enough to completely break through the original mode of production, and the feudal economic structure could still accommodate it to a certain extent.

Before the Opium War, China's feudal economic structure began to disintegrate slowly and capitalism developed to a certain extent. But the development of private industry has not yet reached the level of a period of workshop handicraft industry. Even if we assume that there is no invasion of foreign capital, there is still doubt as to whether China's private industry could develop independently into the period of workshop handicraft industry and complete the transition to free capitalism. Although the government-run industry gradually lost its dominant position in some industrial sectors after the mid-Qing Dynasty, it was still irreplaceable in some sectors as the material basis of the feudal economy. At the same time, the feudal state strengthened financial measures and policy intervention, and continued to maintain social and economic control through the activities of the government-run business and the cultivation of privileged businessmen. It was very difficult for the non-governmental industry to get rid of the influence of the economic functions of the feudal state and developed independently. Moreover, there are no insurmountable obstacles between the government-run industry and the capitalist workshop handicraft industry. There have been many important changes in the labor system and commodity production of the government-run industry. Especially after the Yongzheng years, the government-run industry generally adopted the labor system of free recruitment and pay according to the value of work. Although this cannot be said to be a fundamental change, it can at least be seen as a precursor and preparation for the transition from government-run industry to capitalist national workshop handicraft industry. The transition from feudal society to capitalism is fundamentally different from the transition from capitalist society to socialism. The former does not require a radical change in the nature of the regime as a sign of the transformation of production relations. Therefore, there is no basis for denying the transformation of government-run industry into the workshops of capitalist countries by the feudal nature of the regime. We should take the basic form that the owner of the means of production occupies the surplus labor of the direct producers as the symbol to measure the change of the nature of the production relations of government-run industry. As mentioned earlier, various economic forces interact with each other in the process of social and economic development. After the mid-Qing Dynasty, under the influence of non-governmental workshop handicraft industry and other social and economic forces, the government-run industry tended to decline on the one hand, and transformed to the capitalist mode of operation on the other hand. According to the available data, before the Opium War, the government-run industry had adopted a large number of capitalist employment and management systems in mining, mintage, weaving and other sectors, which can be regarded as the initial form of China's national capitalism. This is also the institutional choice for the feudal regime to adapt to the development of productive forces.

In short, according to the normal process of China's social and economic development, China's capitalist development is totally different from that of other Western countries, such as Britain and France. For those countries, national capitalism and non-governmental capitalism go hand in hand at the beginning, completing the transition of the period of workshop handicraft industry and the transformation of the feudal economic structure to the capitalist economic structure. Without the typical stage of free capitalism, it entered the stage of monopoly accompanying the emergence of modern industry. This is determined by the inherent characteristics of China's feudal socio-economic structure. However, history cannot be assumed. In the late Qing Dynasty, the corruption of the feudal regime, the decline of management ability, the lack of system and policy innovation ability, and the deviation from the world trend have become serious obstacles to economic and social development, even lacking in the ability to maintain national security. It is an indisputable historical fact that the feudal regime lagged behind and lost its territory and sovereignty. Drastic social change is inevitable.

3. Development, Expansion and Collapse of State Capital in Modern China

Since the Opium War, the invasion of foreign capital diverted China from its normal social-economic development path. China entered an era of turmoil, characterized with accelerated disintegration of the feudalist system and transition towards a semi-colonial and semi-feudal society. Under the influence of advanced productivity from overseas, China's economic development skipped the phase of handicraft workshops and entered directly the early stage of modern machinery. This was also the period for the development of the three basic capitalist production relations, namely foreign capital, state capital and national capital.

Among the three basic forms of capitalism in modern China, foreign capital dominated. However, around the Opium War, because of the lack of competitiveness of foreign commodities, foreign capital penetrated China market mostly by opium smuggling, coolie trafficking, arms trade, real estates speculation and war. Commodity trade was limited, let alone capital flow. This period of colonization was characterized with primitive accumulative exploitation. By the 1860s, the completion of the Industrial Revolution and the common use of machinery in major western capitalist powers led to decreasing cost and enhanced competitiveness, coupled with unfair treaties and changes in China market, greatly promoted the export of foreign commodities into China.Foreign capital quickly monopolized China trade and dominated China market by establishing trade firms and compradors. By the end of the 19th century, capitalism took the new form of imperialism and the Sino-Japanese War of 1894-1895 marked the beginning of capital export in China by foreign capital. Then, foreign industrial trusts and financial consortia invested heavily in China's industries, and gradually dominated such backbone industries as transportation, resources, energy and textile. At the meantime, by expanding capital export through government loans, imperialist powers controlled China's finance and other economic lifelines. Compared to the slow growth of Chinese capital, foreign capital expanded much faster. To a certain degree, foreign capital, as an economic force, somewhat sped up the breakup of the feudal economic system and promoted capitalism. However, foreign capital developed in China through economic invasion and seriously hindered the development of Chinese capital, though the main obstacle is China's domestic problems.

China's state capital and national capital clearly descended from the seeds of capitalism before the Opium War. For example, national capital had its root in folk handicraft workshops. However, commodity dumping by foreign capital somehow disrupted the development of traditional handicraft workshops, especially the farmer household-based textile industry in China. According to *The History of Capitalism Development in China*[1], of the 32 traditional Chinese handicraft trades, after the Opium War, seven disappeared, ten managed to survive while the other 15 developed and transited to machine-based production. As for the dozens of trades where capitalism took its roots in the early Qing Dynasty, only cloth grinding and tobacco cutting were replaced by their respective foreign equivalents, while all the other trades survived with nine mechanized. This is the mainstream of national capitalism.

Extensive work has been done on the development, status and roles of foreign capital and national capital in modern China. The following chapter shall focus on the birth, development and roles of modern state capital in China, which is very particular in the development of capitalism in China.

State monopoly capitalism is a variation of modern capitalism. When laissez-faire capitalism was replaced by monopoly capitalism or imperialism, the innate

1 Xu Dixin and Wu Chengming, ed., *History of Capitalism in China*, The People's Publishing House, 1985.

contradictions capitalism, instead of mitigating or disappearing, aggravated unprecedentedly. Monopoly capitalism could no longer maintain its ruling position relying on its own economic forces while private ownerships could no longer accommodate productivity growth. This mandated the direct use of state apparatus to sustain power while intensifying the exploitation of laborers within and without. Consequently, "as the official representative of capitalism, the state had to play the role of the leader of production", which led to the transition from regular monopoly to state monopoly. The state, the "ideal general capitalist", through state economy and comprehensive intervention into social-economic activities, favored monopoly capitalism in national redistribution so as to strengthen the rule of monopoly capitalists and postpone the decay of capitalism. In short, state monopoly capitalism came into being and developed as an inevitable consequence of the aggravation of innate contradictions and social crises of imperialism and the socialization of production. It, to a certain degree, mitigated social contradictions and expanded the room for capitalist development. Enhanced state intervention and regulation capabilities symbolized system maturation in the way similar to feudal development in China.

However, the Chinese state capitalism obviously did not follow the same path of development. Unique in its background and development path, the Chinese state capitalism must be understood and analyzed in the broad sense of state monopoly capitalism. The Chinese state capitalism did not originate from production centralization or socialization, but decentralization and underdeveloped capitalism. Its origin could be traced to capitalism prior to the Opium War. Therefore, primitive state capital in China was not characterized with monopoly, social-economic disintegration and turmoil as a result of the invasion of foreign capital seriously undermined the feudal regime. The Qing government, as the last resort, tried "to learn the technologies of the barbarians" in the 1860s by introducing advanced western production methods and investing in and developing modern enterprises in order to maintain its tumbling rule, a movement known in history as the "Westernization Movement". These westernized modern enterprises descended from government-controlled businesses, a primitive form of state capitalism and was intended by their founders to secure the old feudal economic structure. However, productivity overgrew the feudal system and these westernized modern enterprises led to the full transition from feudal state-controlled businesses to state capitalism. Civilian or military, enterprises founded by the Qing government were all based on unpaid labor and therefore capitalist in nature. These were the primary forms of state capitalism in China.

These westernized modern enterprises were based on not production centralization but relatively centralized production. Therefore, they were still feudal in nature and to a large extent dependent on foreign capital. However, though primitive and imperfect, this kind of state capitalism somehow played the role of balancing and resisting foreign capital invasion. The development of state capitalism during the transition of China's economic structure was historically inevitable. In China, modern capitalist industries did not descend from handicraft workshops as a result of productivity breakthrough in certain leading sectors, but developed by introducing and transplanting advanced western productivity for the purpose of "self-empowerment" by focusing on heavy industries in general and military industry in particular. Around the Opium War, the primitive accumulation of capitalism in China was rather slow with the government capturing most surplus value through taxation while folk capital lacked the necessary resources to develop heavy industry based modern economy. Moreover, national defense was in essence the responsibility of the government. So, the development of modern enterprises starting from the heavy industry fell on the shoulder the Qing government, whether it chose to or not. In practice, because the Qing government's advocacy of using western technologies was aimed at maintaining the old feudal system by incorporating capitalist production into the feudal system and because of the corruption and incompetence of officials in charge, most westernized enterprises, troubled by poor management and low effectiveness, hardly finished capital accumulation and therefore failed to promote the development of capitalism in China.

In terms of the birth of state capitalism, Japan and China shared some common ground, (Of course, the two countries differed in economic structure. Moreover, modern state capitalism developed earlier in China because of its tradition in government controlled industries, which also created greater inertia.) in spite of the diametrically different achievements. The pre-Meiji Reform Japan faced many similar challenges as China did around the Opium War. In the 1870s, the Japanese government founded the first modern enterprises to stand own its own feet. Later, in the 1880s, all of these state enterprises except military ones were transferred to the private sector to promote and support private ownerships-based capitalism, and in the meantime state enterprises also kept growing at a remarkable rate. After the Sino-Japanese War of 1894-1895, in order to support its invasion and expansion, state economy kept growing in Japan. In the 1930s and 1940s, military state monopoly capitalism established its dominance in Japan. In a sense, capitalism developed in Japan by means of state capitalism and overseas aggression.

In retrospect, in countries like China and Japan where capitalism had developed before the invasion of foreign capital, the birth and development of state capitalism as a first response to advanced foreign productivity was no accident. State capitalism in China and Japan appeared earlier than state capitalism and even general monopoly capitalism in western countries, because state capitalism was the inevitable choice for countries like China during economic structural transition. Therefore, it is biased to argue that the Chinese state capitalism as the state capitalism prototype for underdeveloped countries and that the birth and development of the Chinese state capitalism was influenced by state monopoly capitalism in other countries.

After the Sino-Japanese War of 1894-1895, the frail and corrupt feudal regime, nothing but a tool in imperialists' hands, was totally incapable of leading social-economic development. As a halfway capitalist revolution, the Revolution of 1911 overthrew the Qing government and ended imperialists' willful control of China, but was not thorough with anti-imperialism and anti-feudalism. The Northern Warlords, representing rich landlords and comprador capitalists and supported by imperialists, took helm of the state. As a result, state capital was more and more controlled by compradors and dependent on foreign capital. In spite of all these, state capital did develop during this period in forms of official-merchant joint venture or merchant management with official support. In the process, bureaucrat capital took shape and started to develop.

Engels once said, "Compared with all other classes once in power, the bourgeoisie has one feature: a turning point in its development, beyond which its tightened power means lead to not only further increase in capital but also decrease in political power. Waiting behind the capitalists are the proletariat."[1] The May Fourth Movement in 1919 was such a turning point in China. The spread of Marxism and the victory of the October Revolution showed the Chinese people the socialist path. The rise and booming of proletariat revolution pushed imperialists, big bourgeoisie and landlords to gang up to strengthen their rule, suppress people's revolution, monopolize social-economic policies and prevent the old system from bankruptcy. The development of the Kuomintang (the KMT) state monopoly capital marked their choice and efforts to sustain the semi-colonial and semi-feudal economic structure. The KMT monopoly capital targeted not at imperialism (though anti-Japanese in a sense), but, with the support of imperialists, at jeopardizing the New Democratic Revolution lead by the Communist Party of China (the CPC). The KMT betrayed Sun Yat-sen's political and economic ideals and paths and violated his original intention about developing state capitalism. The KMT state monopoly capital was the product of underdeveloped industry in China and in turn suffocated industrial development. It originated in the lack of development under the semi-colonial and semi-feudal system and hindered China from social-economic development. The development and expansion of the KMT state monopoly marked the primitive accumulation of sale in the history of capitalism development in China. However, the exploitation and accumulation

1 Preface to the Second Edition of Farmers' War in Germany, *The Complete Works of Marx and Engels*, Vol.16. The People's Publishing House, 1964, p. 451.

in the process put the Chinese people, including the middle class, in unbearable suffering. After the victory of the Anti-Japanese War, corruption, speculation and hyper-inflation devastated social productivity especially in agriculture and medium-small industry and led to the collapse of economy.

The KMT state monopoly capital and bureaucrat capital once were used interchangeably. Research mandates distinguishing the two. To be fair, the KMT state monopoly capital did contribute to economic development and the victory of the Anti-Japanese War and the work done by the people in the government deserved recognition. Therefore, the failure of the KMT was not the failure of state capital. The real evil was bureaucrat capital as a product of the combination of power and capital and of corruption in the KMT government. Bureaucrat capitalist groups and families as represented by the Kong and Song families were the tumors in the KMT regime and the most evil forms of capital. The disastrous effect had to be taken by the KMT regime and the KMT state monopoly capital. In this sense, the KMT regime died from corruption.

These previous paragraphs have focused on the economic transition to capitalism, especially the development of state monopoly capital. However, capitalism was still underdeveloped in China, accounting for only a small portion in the social industrial structure, while the feudal economic system sustained. Such a situation was attributed to the special realities in China's semi-colonial and semi-feudal system. After the Opium War, China's natural economy based on small farming and household handicraft further disintegrated and the domestic market expanded. This created the conditions for capitalism development. Though household handicrafts was waning and commercial agriculture started to develop, China's feudal land ownerships did not change with landlords' continued control of the rural areas. The disintegration of natural economy in rural China happened mostly because of the influx of foreign products. Because of the feudal economy's resilience to accommodate a relatively high level of productivity, foreign capital in practice faced great resistance from the existing economic system, only to find parasitic exploitation by taking advantage of the old system much easier.

Therefore, foreign capital did not aim to end feudalism and develop capitalism in China. Instead, bureaucrats and feudal authorities, compradors and the existing usury system all became foreign capital's tools to exploit Chinese farmers and craftsman, dominate China market and expand economic aggression, even during capital export stage.

Heavily feudal in nature, state capital was interdependent with landlord economy and spared no effort to maintain the obsolete feudal system. As Lenin said, the nature of state capitalism decides the nature of the regime. From the Qing government to the KMT government, from westernized modern enterprises to the KMT state monopoly capital, feudalism remained intact when the contradiction between capital and feudalism was alleviated by semi-feudal state capital. The preservation of feudalism in China was mainly attributed to the combination between political power and state capital. National capital played the most positive role among the three main forms of capital in modern China. However, it never became an independent economic force, but depended on foreign capital and state capital and maintained strong bond with feudalism. National capital on one hand stood opposite to feudalism and on the other had a vested interest in feudalism, with the latter being the mainstream. The operation of national capital, to a large extent, depended on feudal power and exploitation system when landlords were also capitalists at the same time. Putting national capital and state capital together does not negate their differences or deny the dual character of national capital and bourgeoisie (though in terms of its revolutionary potential, national bourgeoisie were far more anti-imperialist than anti-feudal), but highlights its dependent status in the semi-colonial and semi-feudal system. National capital played some positive roles in social-economic development, but did not represent the future, which constituted its common ground with state capital. It is just because of this that the national bourgeoisie could not lead China's democratic revolution but played the role of a potential ally to the revolutionary forces.

In a word, the trinity of foreign capital, domestic capital and feudalism constituted the basic feature of semi-colonial and semi-feudal China. As a result, capitalism in China started from a very fragile foundation. Although imperialist invasion and capitalism development sped up the disintegration of natural economy, feudalism managed to sustain in rural areas and farmers had to strive for self-sufficiency. The disintegration went through a slow and painful process. The economic and production structure did not experience fundamental transformation until the liberation of the whole country, but stayed feudal and semi-natural. In the mean time, the market did not expand much and even shrank during the 1930s and 1940s. Moreover, because of the prolonged existence of feudalism, the disintegration of natural economy failed to created opportunities for capitalism in rural China. Instead, it led to the bankruptcy of landlord ownerships and rural economy, the exhaustion of rural finance and the decrease of farmers' purchasing power. This is the root cause of the difficulty in developing domestic market and the constant market crises in the agricultural China with a low level of capitalism development. Chinese farmers' deteriorating economic conditions and extreme poverty created adequate conditions for the New Democratic Revolution. Bankrupt farmers, unable to find employment in capitalist mass production, became the most reliable ally to the proletariat and a backbone force in the Chinese revolution.

The post-Opium War development of capitalism in China demonstrated that the trinity economic structure facilitated the imperialists' economic expansion and political control in China, instead of favoring domestic capital, especially national capital. Suppressed by imperialism from without and state capital and feudalism from within, national capital faced unprecedented challenge. The final demise of the semi-colonial and semi-feudal economy proved that semi-feudal capitalism was doomed.

In the history of capitalism development in China, the Sino-Japanese War of 1894-1895 was a demarcation line. In the imperialist period, with the deepening of colonization, China had lost the external environment for capitalist development and the independent development of capitalism in China was impossible. Furthermore, after the war, the trinity economic structure solidified and as result lost its ability to regulate and adjust itself. None of the three forms of capital was powerful enough to breach feudalism. Neither state capital nor national capital could take up the responsibility of ending imperialist control and suppression. Capitalism was impossible for the semi-colonial, semi-feudal China.

The KMT state monopoly capital further intensified various contradictions in the semi-colonial, semi-feudal society and therefore was doomed to failure. However, the high productivity level achieved prepared the necessary material conditions for the transition from the New Democratic Revolution to the Socialist Revolution. This is the only way for China to transfer from semi-colonialism and semi-feudalism to socialism. To embark on a healthy road of social-economic development and to liberate productivity necessitate destroying the semi-colonial, semi-feudal economy, a mission that could only be fulfilled by the proletariat. The New Democratic Revolution and the Socialist Revolution under the leaderships of the proletariat were the only way out for China, as has been proven by history. This institutional choice ushered China into a new stage in state capital development.

4. Experience of and Lessons from the Development and Operation of State Capital in the Planned Economy

Chinese economy and society embarked on a new track after the People's Republic of China was established in 1949. State-owned capital and state-owned economy of considerable size was formed quickly while the national economy recovered under the new regime, which turned its focus to large-scale economic construction in 1953. Under the general economic guideline for the transitional period, state capital grew further in both size and control power through socialist reforms of agriculture, handicraft industry, capitalist industry and commerce as well as continual transfer of agricultural surplus through "price scissors", thus ensuring the establishment of a socialist economic system. However, despite our success in establishing a relatively independent and comprehensive industrial system within a short time with the help of state capital and securing in a way a guarantee for national security, our neglect of the law of value and market and our lack of advanced management resulted in substantial fluctuations in economic operation, serious imbalances in industrial structure and imbalances and waste in resources allocation. This adverse situation served as the backdrop for the reform and opening-up policy.

4.1. Formation of PRC's state capital

The rapid establishment and development of state-owned economy was a necessary choice for CPC (the Communist Party of China) and the new regime to recover national economy and realize the transition from New Democracy to Socialism. After four years of confiscation of the Kuomintang government's legacy of state-owned enterprises and bureaucrat capital enterprises, the basic industries of PRC were initially formed with a framework for central and local industries, based on which a state-owned economy capable of controlling the national economy and people's livelihood was established. Part of the state-owned economy was based on the public sector of the Revolution Districts and was mainly concentrated in finance and trade, while the transfers from the Soviet Union, foreign countries and other sources formed another part. These are the initial sources of the state capital of PRC.

PRC adopted the policy of "use, limit, reform" for private capitalist economy in urban and rural areas in the economic recovering period, when state capitalism began to develop as a form of cooperation between state-owned capital and private capital. State capitalism was further specified in CPC's "General Guidelines for the Transitional Period" in 1953 as the form to complete the socialist reformation of capitalist industry and commerce, whereby the latter was transformed to state-owned enterprises through "joint state/public-private ownership", thus turning private capital into state-owned capital. The reform lasted until the end of 1956.

The reform is a creative application of Marxist-Leninist theories to the realities of China by CPC. The conflict between the proletariat and the bourgeoisie was resolved peacefully through the "redemption policy", the capitalist enterprises were transformed into socialist ones, and the industrialists and businessmen were now socialist workers. Social productivity was greatly promoted rather than damaged in the institutional reform. The main source of the assets of state-owned enterprises, of course, was state investment. In the "public-private ownership" reform, private capital shares were valued in total at RMB 2.4 billion, while budgetary state investment for the First Five-Year Plan alone amounted to RMB 53.12 billion, and to 58.85 billion if counting extrabudgetary investment, 24.5 times of all the private shares. It can be seen that this reform, with its grand scale and far-reaching influence, did not constitute mprise the main source of state-owned enterprises and their assets, even though it annihilated the capitalist private ownership of production materials; however, it provided institutional foundation for subsequent centralized surplus and resource allocation. State capitalism should be seen as the basic form for PRC's socialist reforms, and should play a long-term role. This should shed some light on our appreciation of the national conditions of the primary state of socialism, and many mistakes in our measures resulted from our failure to grasp this, which were divorced from reality as all levels of governments were too eager for success after the completion of the socialist transformation. It is a pity to give up prematurely the market role of state capitalism and put undue stress on the pureness of the socialist system and the planned management of the government.

4.2. Expansion of state capital

The overall objective of China's economic development in the period of planned economy was to realize industrialization and establish a socialist system as soon as possible. Both the Second Plenary Session of the Seventh Central Committee of CPC in March 1949 and the First National CPPCC (Chinese People's Political Consultative Conference) in September 1949 established the basic policy of prioritizing the development of heavy and chemical industries and state-owned economy. After the basic completion of the socialist transformation in 1956, the ownership structure of China was basically composed of the state-owned economy and the collective economy; China's industrialization, on the other hand, was mainly promoted by government investment, thus forming a mechanism for the sustained expansion of state capital.

In March 1950, China implemented the "unified financial and economic" system, and the central government's investment gradually became the dominant form of investment. By the end of 1952, China had basically completed the task of national economic recovery, and the first five-year national economic plan began in 1953. At the end of the First Five-Year Plan, the government invested 58.85 billion yuan in infrastructure, 82% of which was directly managed by the central government and 18% by local governments. Under the policy of prioritizing the rapid development of heavy industry, government investment in this period was mainly concentrated on industry. Machinery manufacturing, especially national defense industry, was the focus of heavy industry, and the 156 key projects sponsored by the Soviet Union were the core projects. From 1958 to 1960, the national infrastructure investment totaled 10.7 billion yuan, yet a large part of it did not transform into real productivity, resulting in serious difficulties in the national economy in the early 1960s. Just as the national economy turned onto a sound development track after adjustments from 1961 to 1965, from 1966-1976 the government investment centered on accelerating the development of heavy industry and inland industry. A new round of investment surge was launched in 1976, but caused fluctuations in the national economy with its unrealistically speedy construction of projects and introduction of foreign equipment and technology. The value of fixed assets of state-owned enterprises increased by 18.7 times from RMB 24.06 billion in 1952 to RMB 448.82 billion in 1978, with an annual growth rate of 12.4%.

A considerable part of the state capital formed in the planned economy period was extracted from agriculture through "price scissors" between industrial and agricultural products. Before the reform and opening-up, the government converted nearly 300 billion yuan from agriculture into fiscal revenue and state capital, with the difference between the market price and unified purchase and sales prices obtained by the state at RMB 280 billion, and an additional RMB 19.428 billion from the difference between the agricultural tax revenue and the agriculture supporting fund.

4.3. Management mechanism and operation of state-owned economy

From 1949 to 1978, China's state-owned enterprises were state-owned and government-run both in name and in fact. State-owned enterprises were divided into those directly under the central government operated and managed by the central ministries and headquarters, and those operated and managed by local governments of provinces, cities and counties. However, in the era of planned economy with constant changes to its system, neither central nor local enterprises had autonomy in operation and management and they became practically affiliates of the government.

A highly centralized operation and management system was certainly not suited to the development of productivity, considering China's weak industrial foundation, relatively underdeveloped and unbalanced productivity, and the vast number of state-owned enterprises with huge differences in technology, equipment, and management. Explorations into reforming the management system had always been carried out within the planned economy, and had achieved some successes, such as democratic management, management of public-private joint ventures, the formulation and implementation of the "Angang Constitution" (Charter of Anshan Iron and Steel Company), trial of the Trust system, and division of rights and liabilities between the central and local governments. Nonetheless, these reforms happened too frequently and were all oriented towards central-local power division, which could only be self-defeating as they never challenged the unitary public ownership or the system of planned economy, even though they aimed to mobilize the initiatives of both the central and local governments and make decision-making at the central level less rigid. On the other hand, excessive decentralization did not come with the necessary restraints, and an over-zealous mood for quick economic results arose in the "anti-rightist" and anti-"anti-rash advance" movements. All these contributed to fluctuations and chaos in economic operations. The essential problem is that the enterprises were never considered the key player in solving the problems, no matter how power was divided or how the management system was reformed; the price paid for neglecting the law of value and market rules was a swing between unitary centralization and chaotic decentralization.

The profit growth of state-owned enterprises between 1949 and 1978 was featured by drastic fluctuations, with the growth rate sometimes rising to over 80% and sometimes falling to below zero, but overall the trend was downward. The labor productivity of state-owned enterprises presented similar fluctuations, rising continually during the economic recovery and the First Five-Year Plan, turning to a sharp decline in the late 1950s, picking up during the three-year adjustment period, then falling again in the 1960-1970s, and finally beginning to recover between 1976 and 1980. Besides, productivity differed vastly between different enterprises. A large number of state-owned enterprises suffered unreasonable losses in the 1960-1970s, some of which remained in the red even in 1977 and 1978.

4.4. Historical contributions of state capital

The historical contributions made by state capital and state-owned economy in promoting the development of Chinese economy could be seen in the following aspects.

First, state-owned enterprises served as the major drive for China's industrial development and laid the economic foundation for the socialist system. China's industry developed at an amazing speed from 1948-1978, which was largely attributable to the continual massive investment from the government. The state-owned industrial enterprises not only had a growth rate equal to that of the whole industry, but also a faster growth speed, making it the leading growth factor.

Second, a series of large projects were constructed. The greatest advantage of the planned economy was that it could pool a large number of resources within a short time and invested them on key projects, thus forming productivity rapidly. Between 1953 and 1980, 3,531 large and medium projects were constructed with national investment, among which 2,324 were industrial projects, accounting for 65.8% of the total number, while transportation, post and telecommunication came up second, with 493 projects accounting for 14% of the total number. Of the industrial projects mechanical and power engineering projects occupied the largest share. These key projects greatly promoted China's productive and technical capacity and served as strong economic foundation for the reform and opening-up policy.

Third, the development of the state-owned economy optimized China's regional economic layout. The rapid development of state-owned industrial enterprises not only increased the percentage of industry in the economic makeup, but also improved the regional layout of China's industry, contributing most noticeably to the extraordinary growth in the industrial capacity of Western China. In terms of industrial output, the ratio of coastal regions to inland regions was 69.4:30.6 in 1952, which changed to 60.9:39.1, with the inland output increasing nearly 9 percent; in terms of light and heavy industries output, the ratio of coastal regions to inland regions in light industry changed from 71.5:28.5 in 1952 to 64.5:35.5 in 1978, signaling a 7 percent growth in inland regions; in terms of product makeup, some basic industries focusing on raw material production were gradually relocated from the coastal regions to the inland regions during the planned economy period, resulting in a considerable number of raw materials being produced inland in 1980. All these were credited to state capital.

4.5. Internal conflicts in the operation of state capital

In the planned economy period, the excessive expansion of state capital and the rigid management mode of the state-owned economy greatly reduced the operational efficiency of state capital, and the conflicts within the system became increasingly prominent.

(1) Excessive expansion of state capital and the ensuing "crowding out effect". The development of state capital was necessary for a country with an extremely underdeveloped economy and a large population as it could effectively solve the shortage of capital and promote the national economy through developing state-owned economy, but it was not a panacea for all enterprises at different development levels. The nationalization of existing private capital while developing state capital, especially while reforming the capitalist industry and

commerce, was actually excluding and "crowding out" other types of capital, most important of which were small-and-medium sized enterprises with features fit for private management. Notwithstanding private capital's lack of proper orientation and its disregard of principles in pursuit of profits, we cannot deny its efficiency in operation. What's more, the stimulation and constraints of competition were lost when there was only one type of capital in the market of a country, which hindered the capital holders from making right decisions and improving gradually the efficiency of capital operation. In this sense, the dissolution of the planned economy is an inevitable outcome of the capital's failure to accrue reasonable returns.

(2) Rigid management system of the state-owned economy and the huge transaction costs. The management system of the state-owned economy during the planned economy period had always been a distribution and redistribution of power between central and local governments despite a few reforms, while the enterprises never had autonomy in operation or management. Management of the state-owned economy was delivered top-down through planned quota. Under the "vertical management" system, state-owned enterprises were managed systematically by functional departments of the government, and could only contact other enterprises through these departments as there were no communication channel between enterprises. Likewise, under the "horizontal management" system, state-owned enterprises were managed by local governments and could only realize any contact with any other enterprises through the governments. There was obviously a rigid side to both systems, which caused huge transaction costs in the management of the state-owned economy as well as wastes in social resources.

(3) Conflict between the highly concentrated management and the law of value. One of the core elements of a planned-economy dominated by state capital is that the price is decided by the government, which is clearly in conflict with the inherent requirements of the law of value. Besides, a society-wide unified pricing and accounting is practically impossible even though it may be theoretically

possible since products and services vary vastly in reality. Any rough unified accounting outcome achieved at great costs would be either outdated or greatly devalued as it was inapplicable.

(4) Expansion of state capital and the imbalance of the economic structure. There were reasons for the expansion of state capital in the planned economy period, but excessive expansion would be hazardous for the balance of the economic structure. During the end of 1950s, state capital grew at flying speeds, ignoring the intrinsic connections between sectors and areas in the economy and seriously upsetting the balance of the economic structure, and the imbalance became more severe from 1966 to 1976 due to massive investment on the third front industries. Another consequence of the excessive expansion of state capital was the continual imbalance between the accumulation rate and the consumption rate, with the former always kept at a high level while the latter at a very low level. Such long-term imbalance in the economic structure caused huge waste in the country's human, material, and financial resources, and adversely impacted the operation and efficiency of the macro-economy.

(5) Unreasonable governance and operational framework of the state-owned economy. The State-owned economy was endowed with many responsibilities in the planned economy period, including not only developing economy and providing the country with returns, but also social functions such as employment, social welfare for the employees, and even national security and urban development. Too many goals made it rather difficult to assess the performance of the managers, who could easily find excuses from other fronts for the poor management.

The SOEs' incentive mechanism presented another difficulty in planned management, as there were differences between some specific interests of the SOEs and those of the nation, even though no essential conflicts. Out of the needs for easy management, the SOEs would try to take as many resources as possible, negotiate with the government for reduced quota, and raise the income and welfare of the employees as much as possible. As for the restraint mechanism,

SOEs were actually like children to the government, as they were owned by the government, and the restraint therefore could only be "soft". As much as the government tried to manage the SOEs through planned quotas, the SOEs would never be punished for failing to achieve them, as they were all eating from the same big pot. The same goes for employees, who found no motivation under the egalitarian income distribution system as they would earn the same whether they did a good job or a bad one. Under such a mechanism, the SOEs lacked the incentive for operation, management, and accounting, which means they couldn't make reasonable use of the existing productivity to achieve maximum economic outcome, nor could they create as much new productivity as possible with as little human and materialized labor costs. This explains why it had always been so hard to improve the production efficiency of SOEs.

(6) Conflict between the dominance of state capital and the multiple forms of ownership. Public ownership in the planned economy period included both ownership by the whole people and, within a certain scope, collective ownership by some people, which means that proper material interests must be utilized to motivate their productivity; on the other hand, however, any distribution of power under the dominance of state capital would be considered as weakening the foundation of the socialist economy. Consequently, there would be no ground for the emergence of more flexible forms of enterprise organization.

All the above reasons combined to call for a stop to the unsustainable low efficiency of the national economy, and served as mature conditions for a complete reform of the old system unfit for the needs for developing productivity. This book focuses on discussions of the state-owned economy and does not concern much about agriculture, rural areas, and farmers. It needs to be emphasized that farmers' interests were somewhat infringed as economic development in this period relied mainly on high accumulation, which made it difficult to narrow the gap between farmers and workers and the rural and urban areas and served to strengthen the traditional dual economic structure. The three rural issues had become the weak link in the socialist economic system and structure, restraining economic development and impacting the stability of the system. It is exactly where the reform should begin.

5. Reform and Development of State Capital since the Reform and Opening-up Policy

The Third Plenary Session of the Eleventh Central Committee of the CPC sounded the trumpet for the reform and opening-up policy. Based on the achievements of the rural reform implemented earlier, a series of reforms and explorations were carried out in the early 1980s, focusing on invigorating the SOEs and aiming to change the control methods, improve their operational efficiency and enhance their competitiveness. Starting from the early 1990s, as the state-owned economy adapted to the gradual establishment of the socialist market economy and insisted on the principles of adjustment and reorganization while adhering to the guideline of developing what should be developed, withdrawing what should be withdrawn, doing what should be done while leaving others alone, the management system of state capital was reformed comprehensively, which in turn further strengthened the influence and control of the state-owned economy. After more than 30 years of unremitting efforts, the for-profit state capital has undergone significant changes in its operational form, operational efficiency and basic functions, which are highlighted in its closer proximity to the requirements of market rules, more flexible and autonomous operation, and better capacity in fulfilling its functions such as exerting influence and control on the national economy, making up for market failures and "inducing" the market.

5.1. Reform the SOE system and improve the micro-efficiency of state capital

Expanding the autonomy of SOEs conforms with the inherent logic of improving operational efficiency and carrying out market reform and was actually where the reform history started. In October 1978, Sichuan provincial government took the lead in granting certain autonomy to some industrial and commercial SOEs and officially opened the curtain for SOE reform. Such practices of "decentralization of power and transfer of profits" quickly spread to almost all

SOEs, and soon the economic responsibility system and the policy of "tax for profits" followed, facilitating the transition even though they were short-lived. In 1984, The Decision of the Central Committee of the Communist Party of China on the Economic System Reform passed at the Third Plenary Session of the Twelfth Central Committee of CPC proposed that the ownership and management rights of SOEs could be separated, based on which some SOEs created the contracted management responsibility system. The system, which soon became the main stream model for SOE reforms with Chinese characteristics, delineated the responsibilities, rights, and interests of both the state and the enterprise following the principle of the separation of ownership and management, ensuring the enterprise's autonomy in management and finances without infringing on its public ownership. Compared with the previous "decentralization of power and transfer of profits", the contracted management responsibility system was concerned with more fundamental problems of the SOE system such as the separation between the government and the enterprise and legalization of the enterprise's autonomy, yet it failed to systematically overcome the drawback of unclear ownership of SOEs; the reform of the basic ownership of the SOEs was now an inevitable item on CPC's agenda.

The Fourteenth Congress of the CPC held in October 1992 made it clear that the goal of China's economic system reform was to establish a socialist market economy system; as enterprises are the basic economic units and the main competitive agents on the market, their central position on the market must be re-established under the socialist market economy. Against this backdrop, some enterprises began to explore reforms for multiple forms of ownership with the aim to establish a modern enterprise system, most important of which was the stock-holding system.

5.2. Implement strategic re-structuring of the state-owned economy and improve the social benefits of state capital.

Even though considerable progresses had been made in establishing a modern enterprise system for SOEs, there were no essential improvement to the state-owned economy in general with the losses expanding in scale and rising in amount within independently accounting industrial SOEs; contrarily, the non-state-owned economy took on a momentum for development. In response to this, the central government proposed in the early 1990s policies to strategically restructure the state-owned economy, that is, to strengthen control on the big SOEs and give more autonomy to the small ones, and to make advances or withdrawals when necessary, so that the overall state-owned economy can be developed. For the big SOEs and corporations, the policy of "reforming, restructuring, transformation, and strengthening management" was carried out to boost their development, while for the small and medium-sized ones multiple forms were adopted to invigorate them; in important industries and key areas, the control and influence of the state-owned economy must be strengthened, while in others either advances or withdrawals could be made with the focus placed more on improving the social benefits of state capital.

Although the vast majority China's SOEs were small enterprises, the big and medium-sized SOEs, despite their smaller number, were central to the national economy; controlling and developing these "key minorities", therefore, could consolidate the dominance of public ownership, bring into play the leading-role of the state-owned economy, effectively influence and inspire the development of a large number of small and medium-sized enterprises, and better help enterprises in distress, all of which could be achieved by improving their capacity and scale effect and making them the key market player through establishing a modern enterprise system, optimizing their capital structure, speeding up technological renovation and strengthening internal management. For the small and medium SOEs which were large in number and scattered about in different industries and areas, more open and flexible policies should be adopted, for example, mergers, joint-ventures, leases, joint-stock cooperatives or sale in some cases. Hence the term "strengthen control on the big SOEs and give more autonomy to the small ones".

In the process of developing big SOEs, state capital gradually shifted from its old material form to the more negotiable form of securities, as the SOEs entered the capital market and became state-owned listed companies. Such an advanced form of state capital reflects its latest trend for development and also marks the maturing of China's socialist market economy.

As the guideline for SOE reform changes from "decentralization of power and transfer of profits" to innovation of enterprise system and from developing each individual enterprise to invigorating the entire state-owned economy, strategic restructuring of the state-owned economy in its industry layout became an inevitable choice. In the beginning of the year 2001, the central government announced officially the restructuring of the state-owned economy in 196 industries, with the state-owned industry maintaining absolute or near-absolute monopoly in 15 of them, some control in 35 of them, and withdrawing from the other 146 which were only averagely competitive. In 2004, based on the status quo and the adjustment goal of SOEs, SASAC (State-owned Assets Supervision and Administration Commission of the State Council) further divided the industries into three categories and seven areas according to which SOEs were restructured. On December 18, 2006, the General Office of the State Council forwarded the Guiding Opinions of the SASAC about Promoting the Adjustment of State Capital and the Restructuring of State-owned Enterprises, which stipulates clearly that seven major industries will be controlled by the state-owned economy. For central SOEs in the military industry, important resources exploitation such as oil and natural gas, and infrastructure such as the power grid and telecommunication, state capital must have sole proprietorship or absolute controlling shares; for important subsidiaries and central enterprises in civil aviation and shipping, state capital must hold absolute controlling shares; for central enterprises in downstream products management in the petrochemical industry and value-added services in the telecommunication industry, further steps should be taken in the reforms to attract non-public and foreign capital and promote diversity in investors and ownership. Meanwhile, for key enterprises in fundamental and pillar industries, the state-owned economy should maintain strong control, including equipment manufacturing, automobile, electronic information, construction, iron and steel, nonferrous metals, chemical industry, survey and design, and science and technology, where the percentage of state capital should be reduced while the influence and pull of the state-owned economy should be strengthened. Among these industries, in mechanical equipment, automobile, electronic information, construction, iron and steel and nonferrous metals, central enterprises need to become the key enterprises and leading models with state capital holding absolute controlling shares or conditional controlling shares; for central enterprises in the science, technology and design industries responsible for important tasks such as common research for the industry and conversion of technological achievements, state capital should hold controlling shares.

The SOE reform has taken another step and a series of policies and measures have been adopted since the promulgation of Decision of the CCCPC on Some Major Issues Concerning Comprehensively Deepening the Reform at the Third Plenary Session of the Eighteenth CPC Central Committee. To name a few, in August 2015 CCCPC and the State Council jointly issued Guiding Opinions on Deepening State-Owned Enterprise Reform and in the next month Opinions of the State Council on Development of an Economy of Mixed-Ownership of State-Run Enterprises; in October of the same year, NDRC (National Development and Reform Commission), SASAC, and ministries of finance, human resources and social security jointly released Notice on Issuing the Guiding Opinions on Encouraging and Regulating the Introduction of Non-State-owned Capital into Investment Projects of State-owned Enterprises.

With the implementation of these reform policies, especially the gradual establishment of the modern enterprise system, enterprises funded by state capital have been invigorated and developed continually in its management capacity in the market system and innovation in both mechanisms and technology. Despite a significant reduction in their numbers due to restructuring, these enterprises have acquired more control and influence on national economy on higher levels instead of losing it.

5.3. Reform of the supervision and administration system of state-owned assets

The reform of the supervision and administration system of state-owned assets has gone through three stages since 1978.

The first stage is the initial establishment of the system (1978-1988). This was the time when the relationship between the government and the enterprise began to change as reforms were carried out to grant power and concede profits to enterprises and to allow the contracted management responsibility system on a large scale, while in the meantime the central government transferred power of managing enterprises under the central ministries to local governments, especially key municipalities. The over-centralized managing system was changed, and some key municipalities now had more power in the supervision and administration of state-owned assets.

The second stage is the active exploration of the system. This period was marked by the establishment of the first specialized state-owned assets management agency in Shenzhen in 1987, and then the establishment of the National State-Owned Assets Bureau by the State Council in 1988, which had partially fulfilled the functions of supervision and administration. Beijing and Shanghai followed in reform attempts and had formulated different models for supervision and administration of state-owned assets. These explorations created favorable conditions for establishing a unified national system, and the reform practices helped increase the awareness of the property rights of state-owned assets as well as set the goal that the value of these assets should be maintained or appreciated. Nonetheless, because of the explorative nature of these reforms, there were still many serious problems in the system formed during this period.

The third stage is the establishment of SASAC by the State Council and the formation of the new system for supervision and administration of state-owned assets. The National State-Owned Asset Bureau was dissolved in the latter half of 1998, and together with it administrative departments of averagely competitive industries, having their personnel and supervision responsibilities combined into one department yet leaving distribution of profits and change of state ownership in the charge of different departments. Such division of power and functions between multiple agencies led directly to the division of state ownership and reduced efficiency in the operation of state-owned assets. In 2001, state-owned assets only grew by 6.6%, and the right to the yields of state capital was neglected or even violated, resulting in the loss of tens of billions of state-owned assets; besides, as responsibilities of the government and the enterprises were not clearly defined and administration was divided, asset management was separate from personnel and business management, making it difficult to establish a traceable mechanism for ownership liabilities. In response to this situation, the Sixteenth National Congress of the CPC held in November 2002 proposed to set up a special agency responsible for the supervision and administration of state-owned assets; in March 2003, such agencies were established in both the central and local governments, finally unifying the management of personnel, business and assets. In the central government, SASAC was set up to take full charge of supervision and administration of state-owned assets, combining all the functions of the three administrative departments in the State Council; in provincial and municipal governments, SASAC's local branches were also set up. In June 2003, the State Council issued Interim Measures for the Supervision and Administration of State-Owned Assets of Enterprises, further stipulating the basic framework of the new system. In August 2015, CCCPC and the State Council jointly issued Guiding Opinions on Deepening State-Owned Enterprise Reform, proposing that the responsibilities of administrative agencies of state-owned assets would shift from managing the enterprises to managing the assets. In October of the same year, the State Council issued Several Opinions of the State Council on Reforming and Improving the State-Owned Asset Management System, and then Opinions on Strengthening and Improving the Supervision and Preventing the Loss of State-

Owned Assets.

It can be concluded that impressive progress has been made in the SOE reform, with the boundaries of state-owned assets clearly defined and the form and functions of the state-owned economy greatly changes. Still, some fundamental conflicts remain unresolved and the relationship between state capital and the socialist market system needs to be smoothened. It is for the deeper reform of SOEs and the re-adjustment of the functions of state capital.

There is huge room for adjustment in the industry layout and makeup of the state-owned economy. State capital is now dispersed in many industries and areas, with general processing, trade and commerce, and service industry making up nearly half of the numbers, where state capital should continue to withdraw. It also needs to withdraw from the segments and businesses open to competition in monopolistic industries and areas. On the other hand, there is a clear shortage of state capital in public welfare areas, which should be one of its focuses. In short, strategic restructuring of the state-owned economy remains an arduous task.

Moreover, there is still a long way to go to establish a modern enterprise ownership system in the real sense. The four major ownership systems of SOEs, including clear definition of ownership, rational allocation of ownership structure, normal circulation of property rights and effective protection of property rights income, have not yet been fully implemented. A considerable number of large SOEs, especially groups affiliated to the central government, are still solely funded by the state, with many inconsistencies in their internal organizational structure and governance structure. The contradiction between the "old three meetings" (Party committee, staff meeting, and Trade Union) retained by the old system and the "new three meetings" (shareholders' meeting, board of directors and board of supervisors) required by the modern enterprise system leads to the "internal friction" of enterprises and hence the difficulty in improving the efficiency of enterprise governance.

Thirdly, relationships between the stakeholders have not been dealt with properly during the system reform of some SOEs. Some reform measures harmed the interests of not only the investors and creditors, but also the employees; some "insiders" of SOEs embezzled greedily public funds and assets, and state-owned assets and capital are still in the danger of being lost.

Finally, the government and the enterprise, and the government and capital seem to be merged once again in the supervision and administration system of state-owned assets. Even though special agencies have been set up to fulfill these tasks, the problem that the agencies are both the referee and the player in the game needs to be solved. Therefore, total separation of the government and the enterprise is an inevitable next step in the supervision and administration of state-owned assets.

6. Current Strategic Status and Function of State Capital

After thousands of years of vicissitudes in ancient, modern and contemporary times, China's economic development has entered an unprecedented glorious period since 1978. By 2015, China had almost completed industrialization and become the second largest economy in the world, with an annual per capita income of more than 8,100 USD that ranked among the higher-middle income countries. In such a rapid process of industrialization, marketization, urbanization and globalization, state capital and its SOEs have merged into market economy and become an important player in market competition through continual reforms. Now SOEs are concentrated more in pillar and upper-stream industries concerning the national economy and people's livelihood after strategic restructuring, and state capital has transformed to a higher form through securitization. It is clearly demonstrated that the Chinese model with distinct regulatory functions of state capital has made remarkable achievements. In view of the fact that countries are learning from each other and deepening their individual development models, it is of great theoretical and practical significance that we study the functions and status of state capital in the socialist market economy, especially in the transitional economy, with reference to historical experiences of China.

On August 24, 2015, CCCPC and the State Council jointly issued Guiding Opinions on Deepening the Reform of State-Owned Enterprises, in which the latest understanding of state capital and SOE is laid out: "State-owned enterprises

("SOE") belong to the people. They represent an important force to promote China's modernization and safeguard the common interests of the people, and are the vital material basis and political foundation for the development of Party and national undertakings." In December of the same year, according to the strategic positioning of SOEs and their development goals set by CCCPC and the State Council after the 18th National Congress and in response to the needs of deepening the reform, SASAC, NDRC and the Ministry of Finance jointly issued Guiding Opinions on the Function Definition and Categorization of State-Owned Enterprises, classifying SOEs into commercial SOEs and SOEs in public welfare. According to the Guiding Opinions, "As independent market players, commercial SOEs and SOEs of public welfare nature must have business operation mechanisms that meet the requirements of the market economy. On the other hand, as SOEs under a socialist market economy, they shall conscientiously serve national strategies and take the initiative to fulfill social responsibilities." Commercial SOEs "shall engage in commercial operations in accordance with market requirements, and independently carry out production and business activities pursuant to the law primarily for the purposes of enhancing the vitality of the state-owned economic sector, amplifying the functions of state-owned capital, and preserving and increasing the value of state-owned assets, so as to achieve the survival of the fittest and orderly market entry and exit. Specifically, commercial SOEs whose primary business belongs to major industries and key fields concerning national security or national economic lifeline, or that are mainly responsible for major special project tasks shall, with the aim of safeguarding national security and national economic operation, focus on developing forward-looking strategic industries and achieve the organic unity of economic, social and safety benefits." SOEs in public welfare "shall actively introduce market mechanisms, and constantly raise the efficiency and capabilities of public services primarily for the purposes of protecting people's livelihood, serving the society at large, and providing public goods and services. The prices of necessary products or services may be subject to government regulation."

6.1. State capital as the basic tool for implementing national economic strategies

Based on historic experiences of economic development of some countries in the world, especially the developing countries, state capital and state-owned economy are irreplaceable in developing the national economy and establishing national industries. It is believed that the same irreplaceable significance and value applies for state capital and state-owned economy in market economy, which serve as a strong support for realizing China's strategic goals.

The first significance lies in the research, development, and promotion of strategic technology. Science and technology are becoming increasingly important as the world enters the era of new economy, and their development direct impacts the comprehensive strength and competitiveness of a country or region. Scientific achievements in areas such as information technology, alternative energy, space and aeronautics, nuclear technology, new materials, marine and biotechnology can fundamentally change a country's competitiveness. However, research in these areas require such a large scale of capital investment, involves such high risk, long return period, strict confidentiality, and concerns so many parties that it is impossible to be funded by private capital or carried out by non-SOEs, which means they need to depend on state capital for R&D activities. Even in some developed countries high-tech industries are developed by SOEs controlled by state capital, for example, NASA, the European Space Agency, and Airbus. Similarly, in China aerospace and nuclear technologies have gained rapid development with the help of state capital.

The second significance lies in controlling the strategic industries. Economically speaking, all strategic industries are featured by their reflection of the level of national industrialization, strong relevance to industries, and strong pull of growth over the whole economy. It goes without saying that strategic industries of a country will change with the level of economic development. State-owned capital should exert a certain degree of control on these industries to help realize national strategies, and should withdraw from those which have lost their strategic significance so that their competitive efficiency will not be influenced.

The third significance can be found in the exploitation and acquisition of strategic resources. Such resources, including land, oil, coal, iron mines, rare metal mines, and forests, are the lifeline of the national economy whose exploitation is crucial to its development, not to mention that they are also concerned with national security. State capital should obtain direct control of these resources and execute more effectively and directly the will of the nation in their exploitation and use. This is supported by experience from other countries, as SOEs occupy a considerable percentage in strategic resources industries.

6.2. State capital as policy tool for the government's macro-control

In countries with developed market economies, the main methods for macro-control are fiscal and currency polices, as their state-owned economy is not powerful enough. In China, however, the state-owned economy is an important economic force whose control and influence make it a policy tool for the government to adjust and control the economy as effective as fiscal and currency policies. It is in fact because of the policy value of state capital and the state-owned economy that China is forming a market economy model different from the western countries – the socialist market economy, which can be summarized in very simple terms as the following: the government controls and adjusts the market through policy tools such as fiscal and currency policies and the state-owned economy, which in turn guides the operation of other enterprises to fulfill the government's economic goal. It needs to be emphasized, of course, that SOEs in the socialist market economy are neutral economic organizations, which means that even though they are economic entities making profits is not their sole purpose, otherwise the SOEs would monopolize the market by drawing on the power of the government and consequently defeat the socialist market system. In short, SOEs should adhere to principles of both economic benefits and social responsibilities and practices of sustainable development to make themselves a model and benchmark for the whole society in aspects such as system construction, operation in accordance with the law, fair treatment of employees, reasonable income distribution, regulated management, resources preservation, environment protection and repaying the society.

6.3. State capital as safeguard of China's economic security

Capital can be roughly divided into physical capital and virtual capital, which will develop into physical capital market and virtual capital market under the market economy. Risks are intrinsic to the market, and as demonstrated by the history of economic development in many countries, such risks sometimes are released through a market crisis that brings a huge blow to the economy of a country and even the world, or paralyzes or bankrupts the economy within a very short time, especially the risks of the virtual capital market whose destructiveness and lethality are often beyond people's imaginations. State capital, on the other hand, can avoid or reduce to some extent the damages of economic crises by maintaining the stability and liquidity of the market while speculative capital is raising the devil, as it is by nature a reflection of the nation's and the people's will and can effective curb speculative capital. It is perfectly demonstrated by China's outstanding performance in both the Southeast Asian financial crisis in 1997 and the "financial tsunami" in America in 2008. What is more, the American government, following the nationalization of banks by some developed countries in Europe to cope with the 2008 financial crisis, became shareholders of the banks, drawing upon national strength to stabilize the violent fluctuations in the financial market. No real economy can be completely free from government intervention and participation; the only difference lies in the degree of intervention and participation.

In terms of physical capital, there is also the risk of crisis as industrial capital may suffer from structural imbalance and poor industrial upgrading. As the world's economy is increasingly globalized, multinational companies from developed countries are fighting a battle of life and death with local companies, relying on their advantages in scale, technology, and system. It would be a hard battle for survival for the physical capital of developing countries, including their national industry and strategic industries, if they did not have a mechanism to check and balance these companies, and the core of such a mechanism has to be state capital and SOEs. Only state capital can ensure the safety of the national economy and national industry by applying its scale advantage to stabilize the market, crack down on speculation, and resist sudden attacks of foreign capital once there are disturbances on the industrial capital market, for example, extreme shortage or excess of some factors or monopolization of others.

6.4. State-owned economy and structural upgrading of industries

Industries follow their intrinsic rules for development, accumulating experiences, improving themselves, and continually extending from lower to upper levels. However, history has also demonstrated the role government plays in the development of industries, and one of the measures it adopts in promoting industrial upgrading is to apply the unique functions of state capital. As is learnt from the basic principles of development economics, state capital is of considerable importance in the early stages of development as "inducing" capital, when the most effective way for development is to rely on the government to create the market using state capital so that the industrial system could be formed initially and the national and regional industrial structures upgraded, since private capital cannot accumulate enough and the virtual capital market cannot function fully in an underdeveloped economy. State capital and state-owned economy serve mostly to entice the creation of the market during the adjustment of industrial structure, and should withdraw when such market has achieved a certain scale to "induce" other areas. It needs to be pointed out that excessive interference of the government through SOEs in resource allocation will distort the prices of factor market and product market, resulting in a waste of resources and decline of economic competitiveness, which should be avoided.

6.5. State-owned economy and coordinated economic development between regions

State capital and state-owned economy have an active role to play in promoting the development of regional economy. Economically backward regions have difficulty in attracting private capital whose choice of investment regions depends on the return rate, but state capital can help improve the "hardware" of these regions and attract more private capital by investing in their public sectors, for example, infrastructure such as ports, airports, water, gas, and power supply, public transport, environmental protection facilities, and public cultural business. In as early as the planned economy period, specifically during the 1960s and 1970s, the state invested a large number of SOEs in the backward "third-front" areas, mostly mid-western inland regions of China, and greatly improved their productivity. The state continued its support of Western China through direct investment in public projects and expanded investment in SOEs after the reform and opening-up policy, especially after the central government pushed forward the "grand western development program" in 1998, leading to another big surge in the economic development of these regions.

6.6. State-owned economy and social stability

State capital and SOEs are important means for the government to implement social development policies. As carriers of social capital, state capital and state-owned economy should shoulder more social responsibilities instead of having making profits as their only goal; SOEs, on the other hand, are the means through which the government controls key living materials, deals with emergencies, and implements crisis management. Experiences from all over the world suggest that there must be a percentage of state-owned economy in industries concerned with people's daily life, for example, necessities such as food, refined oil, natural gas, and electricity, whose consumption elasticity is low. If these industries are completely run by non-state-owned economy, once a social emergency occurs, the companies may very likely ignore the interests of the country and the people as well as relevant laws and regulations in pursuit of high profits, causing huge damage to the interests of the whole society. It is therefore essential for state-owned departments to control certain percentage of living materials and resources key to socio-economic development on behalf of the state, and deal with emergencies appropriately. It is especially important for China to retain some scale of state capital and state-owned economy, as it is a big developing country in the process of a full-scale transition.

State capital and state-owned economy also have political functions in addition to their economic and social functions, playing an important part in safeguarding national sovereignty. In the increasingly globalized world, economic competition is the most essential, even though international competitions have now gone full-scale to include political, economic, cultural and other fronts. If a country cannot be economically independent and strong, it might fall subservient politically to economically developed countries, which is the basic drive why so many developing countries are eager to develop their national economy. For the stability of the government and the security of the country, the state controls the economic lifeline of the whole country through various means, including establishing SOEs, so that it can have firmly within its grasp strategic departments concerning the country's political and economic lifelines.

Furthermore, state capital and state-owned economy carry out special missions for national security in some industries which are closely related to the country's economic development as well as to its international status, prestige, and interests, and in other industries which are more concerned with national security and serve as strategic tools to safeguard the country's interests and security. In addition, state-owned industries are responsible for disseminating the country's mainstream culture and ideology. At present, the culture and media industries are controlled directly by the government, even in some developed countries, such as the government-run Public Broadcasting Service in the US, as news media industry must be strictly monitored by the government and directly controlled by it when necessary due to its nature as social public goods. In short, state capital and state-owned economy have always been the most important foundations for the socialist superstructure, as is intrinsic to the socialist system.

7. Inspirations from History

The world is now going through a period of drastic turbulences and reforms with all kinds of entangled and complex interests, yet all these interests are eventually reflected in the interests of the country and the nation, which are of a comparatively more permanent nature. In such a globalized world, individual enterprises can only have limited influence and competitiveness on the market relies more and more on the comprehensive economic strength drawn from the accumulation of many enterprises, on the comprehensive strength of a country and its support and intervention, and also on the development and participation of state capital. There is a growing trend for government intervention of and participation in economy, and China is no exception. This is actually the most obvious and most fundamental feature of the Chinese way of development, as analyzed before. The tradition of government intervention of and participation in economy has been going on in China for over two thousand years, inviting accolades and criticisms alike, which are actually comments on different aspects in different periods. Despite such comments and despite people's likes or dislikes, this tradition will continue in China. The nature, performance, and development prospects of the state-owned economy depends on the nature, performance and prospects of the regime, and when it changes from development to stagnation, or from prosperity to decline, it is usually due to some anomie in the regime or major errors in decision-making; history has a lot to teach in this respect. Now with the reform deepening, various social conflicts begin to surface and government decision, SOE performance and the image of government officials are brought more and more into the public spotlight. Under such new circumstances at home and abroad, we must sum up and keep in mind the historical experience and lessons and adhere to the reform and opening-up under the socialist market economy system by putting the people first and developing in a scientific way according to the basic national conditions of the primary stage of socialism; we should also vigorously improve economic and social management, constantly improve the legitimacy and effectiveness of state capital's intervention of and participation in economic activities. We should strive to do a good job in what we should do and what we can do so that SOEs can be well-managed and operated, and the state-owned economy and state capital will have more brilliant development prospects. It will bring good fortune to both the country and the people.

Part I

The Regulation and Direct Management of the Economy in China's Feudal Society (before 1840)

To discuss the economy of feudal society and its operation, we must first have a clear understanding of the beginning of the feudal society, as for which there are various views in the academic circles. According to the author's knowledge, they include at least the following statements: Western Zhou feudalism, Warring States feudalism, Wei and Jin feudalism, Northern and Southern Dynasties feudalism, Sui and Tang feudalism and even Song feudalism.

From an academic point of view, there are certain reasons for the above-mentioned views. However, if we conduct long-term investigations based on literature analysis and unearthed archaeological data, there will be an indelible impression. This is just like what "The Book of Songs · Xiaoya· Beishan" said, "Under the sky, which part is not the king's land; Within the Four Seas, who is not a subject of the King". Almost throughout the entire feudal society, the state-led economic system and the many economic activities directly operated by the government has always been at a critical position in the social and economic life, although the weight of this determinant has varied at different times. The size of the cultivated land and that of the population or the labor force is the most concerned content of the government in the agricultural society. This determines that the land and labor are the most important production factors at that time, and the government also allocates production resources and engages in various powerful economic management activities from these two basic aspects. Therefore, to examine the economic structure and operation of China's feudal society from the perspective of long-term and large-scale perspectives, we could admit that the Western Zhou Dynasty feudalism statement is quite reasonable.

Under such a theoretical premise, we can understand the establishment of China's feudal society, the uniqueness of China's feudal society in human history, and the irreplaceable role of China's feudal state power in the economic life.

Although Part I focuses on the Warring States, the Qin and Han dynasties and the later landlord economy, it also acknowledges that the lordship system from the beginning of the Western Zhou Dynasty to the Spring and Autumn Period is the establishment period of the feudal system, and there is an inseparable natural connection between the two.

Chapter 1

Establishment and Operation of the Feudal Landlord Economy

Feudal society in China can be divided into two stages: the lordship system and the landlord economy. Among them, the feudal landlord economy is based on the private ownership of land, mainly to implement the rent in kind of tenant farming, and is basically a mode of production decentralized by individual small agricultural production. If we look at it from this perspective, it is not unreasonable to say that the feudal society in China is dominated by the self-cultivating peasant economy. In human history, the development of feudal landlord economy in China is the most complete and typical, which has become an indisputable fact in the academic circles.

1. The Feudal Lordship Economy

The feudal society in China began with the feudal lordship system, that is, the aristocratic class occupies land and its direct producers in strict accordance with the hierarchical status. It mainly exploits the direct producers through labor rent. Under this system design, the land possession right was consistent with the administrative power and even the judicial power. The feudal lords of Chinese history generally existed in the Western Zhou Dynasty and the Spring and Autumn

Period, from about the 11th century BC to the early 5th century BC.

In the long-term slavery society in China, some rural commune organizations were retained. The rulers of the Xia Dynasty levied a certain amount of tribute on the commune. According to the "Zuo Zhuan (The Spring and Autumn Annals)", Xia Yu once asked the princes for a tribute, "Yu summoned in Tushan the feudal princes, holding jade and silk in their hands." Not only that, but even the copper used by Xia Yu to cast the tripod is also tribute by various countries: "People in distant places drew pictures of various exotic objects. All the kingdoms contributed copper for the tripod, thus the images of the various objects were cast on the tripod." In this way, the economic obligations of the various vassal states to the Xia Dynasty were relatively clear and direct from the very beginning. The economic strength and political power, or cohesion, of the Xia Dynasty were continuously strengthened, and the political symbolic significance of such tributes was greater than the actual use value.

During the Shang Dynasty, the members of the village community had the obligation to provide the rulers with the help of the farmland. In fact, these are the factors of feudal labor exploitation in the slave society. These new factors are conducive to the transformation or transition of the slave society in China to the feudal society. In fact, the feudal system of feudal lords in Western Zhou Dynasty came into being under this background.

During the Western Zhou Dynasty and the Spring and Autumn Period, the land and residents of the country were nominally owned by the King, Zhou Tianzi. This political right and its corresponding allocation of land, residents or labor force were carried out in accordance with the provisions of enfeoffment. That is to say, the emperor of the Zhou Dynasty granted the land and residents outside the Royal region to the vassals, and the vassals granted the land and residents beyond their direct jurisdiction to the ministers and doctors, who then granted the land and residents beyond their direct jurisdiction to their subordinates. At that time, this enfeoffing was carried out in accordance with the principle of patriarchal clan system or aristocratic blood relationship. According to the principle of patriarchal clan system, in the whole country, Zhou Tianzi belongs to the big clan, and the princes belong to the small clan; in the feudal state of the princes, the princes belong to the big clan, and the Qing doctor is the small clan; in the feudal land of the Qing doctor, the Qing doctor belongs to the big clan, the scholar is the small clan. This is the so-called "The Emperor of Heaven stablished a state; the princes set up a family; the Qing set up a side room; the doctor has the base clan; and the scholar has the descendants; the common merchants have their relatives; all are treated in a hierarchy."[1] It can be seen that at that time, from the Emperor to the scholar, the patriarchal or aristocratic bloodline was used as a link to maintain the rulers at all levels, forming a strictly hierarchical subordinate relationship and a possession and distribution relationship for social wealth.[2] This political structure and the distribution of social wealth are pyramidal.

In the bronze inscriptions of the Western Zhou Dynasty, there are many records of the land figures. Zhou Tianzi often gives gifts to the nobility and servants in the unit of "field". Land is obviously the most basic and important social wealth at the time. This kind of enfeoffment system is the "feudal" society recorded in ancient Chinese society, that is, the so-called "feudal state-building". This differs from the feudal society we say today, which takes the landlord economy as the premise and the small land production as the content. This is something that needs special explanation.

In terms of the land system, the Western Zhou Dynasty practiced the Nine Square-fields system. Under this system design, the land of the direct producers—the peasants, namely the private land, was no longer allocated and adjusted by the rural communes, but gradually evolved to be granted by the nobles at all levels. For the convenience of management and the practical needs of production, especially for the purpose of imposing feudal taxes and corvees on the peasants,

1 *Zuo Zhuan · Huan Gong Year II.*

2 See China Agricultural Encyclopedia: Agricultural History Vol. Editorial Committee, China Agricultural Encyclopedia Editorial Office, *China Agricultural Encyclopedia: Agricultural History*, Agricultural Publishing House, 1995, pp. 415-416.

the rulers formed "wells" as a unit according to a certain amount of land or the number of agricultural producers. A number of wells formed into a fief, a number of fiefs into a hill, a number of hills into a suburb. The direct producers under the Nine Square-fields system, the peasants, or the so-called " common people", generally live outside the castle "country" and are therefore called " savages " to distinguish them from the "nationals" living in the castle. The Nine Square-fields system was then directly related to irrigation or drainage of arable land and transport of land. What's more, these projects were quite time-consuming and were completed by the labor of the whole feudal organization, organized by the royal family and its aristocracy at that time, but not by individual producers. In this way, Zhou Tianzi and his aristocrats at all levels enjoy economic distribution power within the fiefdom. According to the documents, the common people living outside the castle at that time not only had their own land, i.e. private land, but also had their own production tools, houses and families, and operated a relatively independent family economy. The common people are engaged in unremunerated labor on the land of the lord in the form of labor rent. In this case, there is the record of "public affairs completed, and then dared to govern private affairs."[1] This is consistent with the record in the *Book of Songs*, indicating that the peasants who were the direct producers at that time not only had the obligation to work for the lord on the land, but also needed to ensure the labor on the land of the lord first, so that the peasants could arrange the production time on their private land. It is also because the main practice at that time was the labor rent, and the peasants also had a certain amount of their own land, that the direct producers' prayer for heaven is "rain on my public land, and then my private land"[2]. And the order of production in time is undoubtedly the private land first, and then the public land. Theoretically speaking, the labor leases paid by the peasants under the Western Zhou "nine squares" system accounted for about one-ninth of the total grain

1 *Mencius · Tengwen Gong,* Vol. I.

2 *Book of Songs. Xiaoya · Datian.*

production, which is what the historical record says "The Zhou dynasty practiced 'Che' taxes for every hundred mu of land, which is equal to one tenth of the production as taxes." [1] The rest were reserved for the direct producers to maintain the reproduction of simple agriculture (including certain household sideline handicrafts) and the reproduction of household population, reflecting the relatively low productivity at that time. In addition to the servant rent, the peasants under the Nine Square-fields system also have the obligation to pay for corvee and tribute for the nobility and the state. In order to ensure the control of direct producers and the acquisition of state taxation and corvee, the government clearly stipulates in the law that "Land cannot be freely transferred and traded"[2], and "Funeral and relocation do not leave the native land" [3]. The solidification of land was mainly determined by the scarcity of cultivated land resources and labor resources under the conditions of low productivity at that time. Under such a social system design, the personal dependence of the direct producers was particularly strong. That being said, in the social reality at that time, the land system was not static as stipulated, but it was transferable under certain conditions. It was common that the land began to transfer among the nobles in the mid-Western Zhou Dynasty, and it was confirmed in the Chinese bronze inscription.

Even within the territory of the lord, it was not just the natural economy, but at the beginning there are artisans who were mainly engaged in the production of handicrafts and merchants who were engaged in trafficking and commerce. As far as the Western Zhou Dynasty and the Spring and Autumn Period were concerned, the government controlled a large number of government craftsmen to engage in various handicraft production activities, while maintaining a certain number of full-time businessmen directly serving the government. The so-called "Handicraftsmen and businessmen depend on officials for food" was the basic feature of this period. In addition to satisfying the living needs of the aristocrats

1 *Mencius. Teng Wen'gong*, Vol. I.
2 *The Ritual Records. System of King.*
3 *Mencius. Teng Wen'gong*, Vol. I.

and even their extravagant consumption, a large number of artisans controlled by the government also produced weapons and coins for the government, engaged in urban construction, mausoleums and other construction projects, which was one of the important sources for the government to accumulate social wealth. In the environment of "Handicraftsmen and businessmen depend on officials for food", the size of the official handicraft industry was relatively large, which was the main body of the handicraft industry and the leading technology of handicraft industry.

The peasants under the lord system, while mainly engaged in agricultural production, also engaged in certain family sideline businesses as a necessary supplementary form of agricultural production. And in addition to the direct consumption by their own family members, these sideline products were often partly used for exchange in order to exchange needed goods, supplement life and production needs. The most typical example is the "Exchange silk with cloth" in the *Book of Songs*,[1] the handicraft barter between families. At that time, the sideline production was abundant in content. In addition to the natural division of labor and seasonal division of labor among family members, such as men tilling the farm and women weaving and farming when the sun shines and weaving when it rains, there were also things such as planting vegetables, collecting fruits, fishing and hunting. Farmers were self-sufficient, but their products were also used for a certain degree of exchange, and some of them were used for tribute.

In the Western Zhou Dynasty, although the state-owned economy was relatively developed, it was not for the royal family to control the economic lifeline. Rui Liangfu, the doctor of the King Zhou Li period, pointed out that "Profit is produced from all things, nurtured by heaven and earth. And if you want to monopolize it, there will be a lot of resentment. All things in heaven and earth must be used by everyone. How can they be monopolized? ……He who governs the world should open up a path of profit and distribute it to the people from above

1 *Book of Songs · Wei Feng· Mang*. Academic circles have different explanations for this. For example, some scholars think that "cloth" here does not refer to textiles but money.

and below, so that the people of God and all things in the world can get their due share. Even so, he worries every day for fear of incurring resentment."[1] Yan Liangfu is aiming at the discussion that the Yigong of Rongguo during the Zhou Liwang period was good at profit, but was supported by Zhou Tianzi. It can be seen that even in the social environment of the Western Zhou Dynasty when "Under the heavens, there is no land that does not belong to the royal family", its normal state is not that Zhou Tianzi and his vassal states controlled all the profits, but they allowed the private sector to engage in business and industry. Qiu Jun in the Ming Dynasty believed that after the disintegration of the Nine Square-fields system in the Western Zhou, "the field is not given out, and the people are not all farmers; the farmers are few and the eaters are more; those who can support themselves account for only three or four out of ten, but the other seven to eight out of ten would buy food." [2] If this is the situation after the Western Zhou Dynasty, I am afraid there is an exaggeration. But the facts reflected in the two aspects are unquestionable: the number of people engaged in agricultural production is decreasing, which is a real situation in the Ming Dynasty; even in the Western Zhou Dynasty, feudalism society in China is not a pure natural economy, and there are certain exchange and commodity production. This was determined by the relatively clear social division of labor at that time, that is, there were both craftsmen specialized in handicraft production and merchants mainly engaged in trafficking in the lord's fiefdoms, and the existence of the family side-line industry of farmers under the Nine Square-fields system. Because of the detailed social division of labor, there are "a hundred trades"[3] at the time. The continuous development of these factors has led to the transition of the feudal economy to the landlord economy.

1 The National Language. Zhou Language.

2 *Da Xue Yan Yi Bu*, Vol. 25, Statecraft·Regulations for Official Purchase of Grain.

3 The Rites of Zhou·Winter Officials·Book of Diverse Crafts: "There are six occupations in the country, and 'a hundred trades' is one of them." At that time, "a hundred trades" did not refer to a specific handicraft industry, but an estimate.

During the Spring and Autumn Period and the Warring States Period, as the feudal lord system was replaced by the landlord economy, the peasants who were originally in the Nine Square-fields system gradually evolved into land-holding peasants under the landlord economy. The Western Zhou Dynasty and the Spring and Autumn Period were the era of feudal monarchy in China. After the Spring and Autumn Period and the Warring States Period, with the advancement of production tools and the relative development of social productivity, especially the widespread use of iron tools and cattle farming in agricultural production, as well as the widespread emergence of water conservancy projects, the ability of the ancient Chinese people to tap natural resources has been greatly improved. Thus household-to-household self-farming became a comparatively advantageous unit of production at that time. The rent in kind has gradually replaced labor rent as an important form of rent, and the landlord economy has been gradually established and maintained for more than 2,000 years.

The characteristics of the landlord economy in China's feudal society, the focus of Section II, mainly refer to some basic features of the landlord economy in the Warring States, the Qin and Han Dynasties and the late Qing Dynasty.

2. The Operation and Structure of the Feudal Landlord Economy

As mentioned above, although the feudal society of our country has emerged since the Western Zhou Dynasty, the focus of this Section is on the feudal landlord economy from the Warring States Period, Qin and Han Dynasties until before the Opium War. Therefore, the characteristics of the feudal landlord system economy discussed here should be mainly from the Warring States Period, Qin and Han Dynasties to the end of Qing Dynasty, that is, the second stage of the Chinese feudal society as stated in the "Overview" of this book. On the basis of previous studies, the following is just a brief description of the basic characteristics of the feudal society in China's landlord economy, and the specific content will be discussed in the following discussion.

While describing the feudal social and economic structure of our country, we should not only seriously discuss the progress and changes of productive forces, but also pay attention to the relations of production at that time. Marxism holds that "the unique economic form of extracting unremunerated surplus labor from direct producers determines the relationship between domination and subordination, which is produced directly from production itself and has a decisive counteraction to production. However, the entire structure of the economic system produced by the production relationship itself, as well as its unique political structure, is based on the above-mentioned economic form. At all times, we always need to find the deepest secrets and the hidden foundation in the direct relationship between the owner of the production conditions and the direct producer – any form of this relationship is always naturally adapted to a certain stage of development of the means of labor and the productivity of the labor society – for the entire social structure, and thus for the political form of sovereignty and dependency or, in short, for any unique state form at the time." [1] For China's feudal society, the direct producer's personal attachment is a main thread running through the whole feudal society, though there are different times of strengthening and relaxing in the early and late stages. If we bypass the personal attachment of the direct producers and simply focus on the feudal society of our country, we would be nowhere near the reality. Because in the feudal society in China, "the main form of class oppression … … is not so much that the masses are deprived of land, as that their labor is possessed." [2] According to the legal provisions of feudal society since the Spring and Autumn Period and the Warring States Period in China, the landlords have no direct power to rule the peasants. Therefore, a centralized bureaucracy is needed to represent the landlord class in exercising its power to rule. Especially since the establishment of the centralized Dynasty in the Qin Dynasty, the bureaucrat system and the local county system have become the two pillars to support the centralization of power.

1 *Das Kapital*, Vol. 3, pp. 891-892, People's Publishing House, 1975.

2 Engels: Preface to the American Edition of *The Condition of the Working-class in England in 1844*, *Complete Works of Marx and Engels*, Vol. 21, p. 387, People's Publishing House, 1972.

Land rent is a common and normal expression of surplus labor in feudal society, and is "a unique economic form of extracting unremunerated surplus labor from direct producers." The change of land rent is consistent with the evolution process of personal dependence in feudal society from establishment to strengthening to relaxation, as reflected in the change of the form of rent, which experienced a process from labor rent complemented with rent in kind, to rent in kind complemented with labor rent, until rent in kind complemented with money rent (Fig. 1-1). Similarly, this development and change coincided with the division of the early and late feudal society in China. From the evolution of the land rent pattern in the feudal society of our country, it can also be seen that the commodity monetary relationship appeared quite early, and continue to be active with the development of social economy and the reduction of the direct producer's personal dependence.

labor rent complemented with rent in kind

↓

rent in kind complemented with labor rent

↓

rent in kind complemented with money rent

↓

money rent complemented with rent in kind

Figure 1-1 Schematic diagram of land rent evolution in feudal society of China

In fact, the form of land rent and its evolution here is only described in general terms. Whether in the middle or late period of the feudal society in China, rent in kind, monetary land rent and labor rent are often intertwined with each other. It is almost impossible to find a pure form of land rent in the feudal society, especially in the middle and late period of the feudal society. Even in the early stage of feudal society in China, it is quite difficult to find a pure form of land rent.

Taxation and servitude in feudal China were a form of division and transformation of part of the rent. At that time, it was roughly divided into four situations: First, the poll tax, which was mainly levied based on the number of family members and asset. There were various types in different dynasties, such as the poll tax on children and adults in the Western Han Dynasty, the household tax in the Wei, Jin, Southern and Northern Dynasties, Zu Yong Diao (land rent, silk and cloth rent, and corvee which could be replaced by silk and cloth) and household tax "based on the household population" in the Sui and Tang Dynasties, the poll tax on male adults in the two Song Dynasties, and the poll taxes and those in place of labor in the Yuan Dynasty, etc. After the Ming Dynasty, relatively great changes occurred, mainly in the form of incorporating poll tax as regular tax. The second is the land tax, or the land income tax, such as the legal 1/30 land rent rate in the Western Han Dynasty, the land rent levied by mu in the Wei, Jin, Southern and Northern Dynasties, 2 liters per mu per year for the land tax in the Tang Dynasty, and so on. At that time, the land rent was generally in kind. In the Tang Dynasty, the two-tax law stipulated that part of tax was levied in the form of money, and even the collection of silk also takes money as units of account. It was not until the Ming and Qing Dynasties that tax was levied in the form of money after discount and conversion. This obviously has the nature of currency rent. The third is corvee tax. In the Western Han Dynasty, military service and corvee were classified together and collectively called "Geng". Afterwards, there was a change, and the military service was gradually separated from the corvee. In the Sui and Tang Dynasties, there were regular corvee and miscellaneous corvee, and later corvee was converted into silk for payment, which was called "Yong". In the Song Dynasty, the corvee was renamed "Chai Yi", instead of "Yao Yi". After the Song Dynasty, there have been relatively large changes in the name and content of the corvee. But one thing is clear; that is, it has never been abolished. The fourth is property tax. Because in the feudal society, people needed to pay a certain amount of land tax, the property tax generally did not include land tax, such as the "Zi Suan" in the Western Han Dynasty, the household tax in the Tang Dynasty and so on. In addition to the four types of regular taxes and corvees above, there are various miscellaneous taxes and corvees, temporary apportions, as well as a large number of additional expropriations. The situation is different in different periods, different regions, and for different officials. And there have even been such situations when the burden of miscellaneous taxation and corvee is heavier than that of regular taxation and corvee. The background is the liveliness of the commercial economy, the improvement of productivity, the financial needs of the state and local governments, as well as the rectitude or corruption of the bureaucracy and the vision of decision-makers, etc.

With the development of the commodity economy and the continuous reduction of the direct producer's personal dependence, the state tax (taxes and corvee) has gradually changed. The main changes include: First, the status of the poll tax is declining until it is abandoned; the proportion of property tax is gradually rising, and the land tax gradually becomes the main component of the property tax. Poll tax is levied on the basis of household and then number of household members, therefore household registration becomes very important. The compilation of household registration is also very strict, and used as one of the main basis for levying taxes and corvees. At the beginning, the number of households and household members in the household registration is very important content. The premise and basis for the poll tax on children and adults in the Han Dynasty, the household tax in the Wei, Jin, Southern Dynasties, and the fixed amount tax in the Northern Dynasty are the number households, household members, and labor. In the Northern and Southern Dynasties, the Sui Dynasty and the early Tang Dynasty, the system of land equalization had been practiced for hundreds of years. According to the decree of land equalization issued at that time, which says "If you own land, you must pay the land rent", the object of government acquisition was land. But in fact, the amount of land received by the average farmer was generally insufficient, and so the land rent was still levied by the household as the main unit, that is, "according to the number of household members", regardless of land ownership. As long as they are included in household registration, they should pay regular farmland rent according to the provisions of the full amount of field according to the system of land equalization.[1] Therefore, it is quite reasonable for some scholars to say that from the ninth year of Taihe in the Northern Wei Dynasty (485 A.D.) to the early Tang Dynasty, the implementation of the centuries-old land equalization system is only nominal[2]. As for the corvee service, only the male and female adults in the household register serve a certain period time, which later changed to Yong, that is, silk and cotton can be the converted to corvee service. And even later, it developed into "two years' corvee can be converted to silk and cotton". As to the payment of silk and cloth, they can be levied with household as the unit. Since the Song Dynasty began levying poll tax, the number of household members was still retained in the household registration. But it was only when "the Law of Uniform Taxation" was adopted in the Ming Dynasty that poll tax was officially converted into land rent.[3] In the Qing Dynasty, the practice of "poll tax merged into land tax" was carried out, and the former practice of taking the household as the unit of collection was completely integrated into the land tax.

Second, changes in corvee service. In the history of our country, the corvee was mainly for the male, that is, the labor force, especially the male labor force. Actually, the corvee was the transformation of labor rent. At the beginning of feudal society, it was a direct conscription of corvee, and then gradually changed to money payment for corvee (called 'Geng' in the Western Han Dynasty and 'Yong' of Sui and Tang Dynasties). In this way, the government needs the corvee service, and then the government uses a part of the money from the collection of corvee money to hire people. The political reform of Wang Anshi in the Song Dynasty changed the law into hire conscription, and have it officially included in

1 *The Book of Wei Dynasty*, Vol. 110 Shi Huo Zhi; *The Book of Sui Dynasty* Vol. 24 Shi Huo Zhi; *Book of Tang* Vol. 48 Shi Huo Zhi; *New Book of Tang* Vol. 51 Shi Huo Zhi One.

2 Jin Baoxiang, A Study on the system of land equalization of the Northern Wei, Sui and Tang Dynasties, *A Collection of Dissertations on the History of the Tang Dynasty*, Gansu People's Publishing House, 1982.

3 *Xu Wenchang's Three Books*, Vol. 17, Kuaiji County Annals· On taxes and Corvees.

the tax system. This is relatively economical and a win-win measure for both the government and the direct service men.

Thirdly, change from paying in kind to paying in money, which is a monetary land rent or a conversion of monetary land rent. It was stipulated in the Han Dynasty that money and goods should both be levied. In the Three Kingdoms, the Jin Dynasties, the Southern and Northern Dynasties, the Sui Dynasty, and the early Tang Dynasty, taxation was mainly in the form of goods. After the implementation of the two tax laws in the middle of Tang Dynasty, the provisions were changed from paying in the form of goods to paying in the form of money, but goods of equivalent value could also be handed in instead of the money. It was a period of money and silk both used for taxation. In fact, the government collects taxation whenever it needs either in the form of money or in the form of money with equivalent value of the goods (the taxpayers earned the money by selling goods in the market). Corrupted manipulation prevailed and the taxpayers suffered a lot. In the Northern Song Dynasty, the two-tax regulations had its conversion method, and money and goods were convertible to each other, which inevitably increased the actual burden of taxpayers. In the Ming Dynasty, "the Law of Uniform Taxation" was adopted, and all taxes were paid with silver in accordance with the monetary value, which was followed ever since. Thus, money became a real means of dividing land rent, or a manifestation of monetization of land rent or monetary land rent. Gu Yanwu, a famous scholar in the Qing Dynasty, commented on "the Law of Uniform Taxation" in the book of "Merits and drawbacks of all the provinces and counties in China · Su Song":

> In the past, there were all kinds of taxes with different names, such as summer tax, autumn grain tax, poll tax, corvee, labor tax, and make-up service tax. They were levied in different times or amounts. The government officials complained about the confusion, and the taxpayers were overwhelmed with the hounding. Since Jiajing 40 years (1561), the Supervising Censor Pang Shangpeng went on a tour of inspection

> in Zhejiang province, and adopted "the Law of Uniform Taxation", which was the most convenient and straightforward. However, the rice is divided into natural rice and silver rice. Lipai levied taxes from the taxpaying households, and the county magistrate sent them to all the counties. How much is the starting point for the levy? How much should be reserved for the local expense? How many staff members should be hired? When to increase the staffing level? What should come first, and what next? What should be increased and what should be decreased? What has been absolved but still remains? What has been exempted by provincial governors but still increased? The calculation is the duty of the head of the county, the borrowing is also the duty of the head of the county. But the allocation power is in the hands of the shrewd county magistrate. This law has been implemented for over eighty years, and this is the beginning of "the Law of Uniform Taxation".

It can be seen that "the Law of Uniform Taxation" has indeed simplified the government's tax compilation and procedures, which has greatly reduced the government's operation and management costs in this respect, and also made the taxpayers' expenses relatively transparent. This also restrained the bureaucrat's back room operation to some extent, thus reducing the actual burden on the working people to a certain extent.

Fourth, simplify taxation. Although the taxation and corvee undertaken by the direct-producers in a certain period of time in the feudal society are relatively fixed, at least the law provides so. However, in the actual implementation process, the government often concoct verious pretexts and levy various new taxes due to different needs. Exorbitant taxes and miscellaneous levies spring up constantly. As for the actual operation process, it is a common phenomenon that officials at all levels feather their own nests. At the same time, the government is constantly cleaning up and simplifying it, but it soon revives and becomes complicated again. The actual burden of the taxpayers is increasing, that is, the so-called "Huang

Zongxi Law" summarized by scholars today. The general trend of feudal society in China is that the agricultural tax gradually changes from poll tax to property tax, while the property tax tends to focus on the land tax (that is, the field tax).

On the whole, there have been four relatively large reforms in China's feudal society to simplify the taxation system, which had a far-reaching impact on the social economy at that time and beyond. The first clean-up reform in the Three Kingdoms, Wei and Jin Dynasties mainly reduced the past rural taxes and corvee from seven in the Western Han Dynasty to two types --- land rent and household rent. The second reform was that in the Tang Dynasty, the Zu Yong Diao (land rent, silk nad cloth rent, and corvee which could be replaced by silk and cloth) was changed into two taxes with household tax as the main content, while the other regular taxes and miscellaneous rents was changed to household tax and local tax. No other tax should be levied beyond the two taxes. However, taxes such as Ru Se tax have been retained. The third time was "the Law of Uniform Taxation" in the middle of the Ming Dynasty. All the taxes were put together, but the poll tax was not abolished and was included in the local tax. The fourth reform was "poll tax merged into land tax" in the Qing Dynasty, which stipulated that the newborns will not be counted in for the tax, and the taxes were levied entirely according to the amount of land. The poll tax was entirely abolished. These clean-ups should be said to have received temporary effects at that time, but after a long period of time, malpractices sprang up, and various temporary taxes arose, such as the two-tax law of the Tang Dynasty, the three taxes of the late Ming Dynasty, the tax for loss of metal when casting coins (Huo Hao) in the Ming and Qing Dynasties, and the business tax for transaction in goods and transportation of goods (Li Jin) in the late Qing Dynasty. These practices expanded the tax source, and once eased the government's urgent financial situation, but it eventually ended up being a heavy burden for the working people. This is undoubtedly an excess burden of taxation and even becomes the source of the turmoil leading to the overthrow of some dynasties.[1]

The emergence of the three major economic sectors of agriculture, handicraft industry and commerce reflects the social division of labor when human productive forces have developed to a certain degree or stage. At least as early as the Qin and Han Dynasties, people have been keenly aware that "If the peasants do not produce grain, food will be scarce; if the craftsmen do not produce utensils, labor and life will be in trouble; if the merchants do not circulate, then the grain, utensils and wealth will be cut off; if the people do not develop the mountain, resources will be scarce."[2] That is, they already recognize the division of labor and the dialectical relationship among agriculture, handicraft industry, commerce and finance at that time. As far as China's entire feudal society is concerned, non-governmental and governmental agriculture, handicrafts and commerce develop at the same pace with each other. The proportion of them has changed greatly in different periods, while finance is monopolized by the government and becomes the core of the government controlling the economic lifeline. The government maintains the normal functioning of the state apparatus and the social economy and the order of its life through the collection and redistribution of financial resources. Especially in the production of official handicraft industry which concerns the national economy and the people's livelihood, in the relief of natural disasters, in the recovery of production, in the post-war recovery of production and so on, the government plays an irreplaceable role. Even so, agriculture, handicraft industry and commerce were the basic sources of wealth and the basis for maintaining the normal functioning of society.

As far as the three major economic sectors are concerned, the fundamental role of agriculture is self-evident, especially for the agriculture-oriented society. Handicraft industry is a production sector second only to agriculture and one of the basic forms of early human production activities. At the same time, handicraft

1 Ning Ke: On China's Feudal Economic Structure, *Academic Monthly*, 2006.11.

2 *Records of the Grand Historian*, Vol. 129 Biographies of Merchants quoted from Zhou Shu.

industry is the first commodity production sector in human history. Historically, the improvement of agriculture and commerce, transportation, military, science and technology, as well as the daily living standards of the people, all reflected the progress of handicraft technology at that time. Every major progress in agricultural production in China's history, such as the extensive use of iron in agricultural production, the emergence of hydraulic milling (i.e. hydraulic grain processing industry), the invention and promotion of Jiangdong plough, reflects not so much the development of agricultural technology as the improvement of handicraft technology. The improvement of handicraft technology is not only a contribution to the handicraft economy, but more importantly, it has a direct influence on the reduction of transportation costs and the improvement of economic efficiency, thus reflecting the improvement of the productivity of the whole society.In addition, the government often plays an irreplaceable role in the popularization and promotion of new agricultural production tools. Some of the local bureaucrats have played an exemplary role in their demonstration and promotion. According to "Records of the Grand Historian": The proverb warns that 'Do not go hundreds of miles away to trade firewood, and do not travel thousands of miles away to buy grain", [1] which cannot be changed at that time. But later with the improvement of handicraft technology, bridges are more widespread, the capacity and convenience of vehicles and ships are enhanced. With such continuous breakthroughs, such record of "the maximum capacity of a ship is no more than 8000-9000 Dan" in the middle and late Tang Dynasty has already been rewritten. For example, the load capacity of the famous "Auntie Yu Ship" has more than 10,000 Dan. [2] Later on, the situation was all more so. People's communication radius was constantly expanding, and the restrictions on the variety of commodity exchange was getting smaller and smaller. It was enough to understand this just by looking at the deeds of Zheng He's voyages in the Ming Dynasty before the discovery of the New

1 *Records of the Grand Historian*, Vol. 129 Biographies of Merchants.

2 *Supplement to the History of Tang Dynasty*, Vol. II.

World.The degree and type of change in the handicraft industry and the ever-changing business focus correspond to the different stages of social economic evolution. When the handicraft industry adopts a certain production structure and social form, and on this basis, its technical nature is updated, the production mode of the whole society will inevitably change from a natural economy to a commodity economy or both, or both at the same time.

In short, agriculture, handicraft industry and commerce are the three major economic sectors of ancient society. They have been a symbol of human social progress and economic development for a long period of time, and are the basic dependence of human social life and production. To discuss the social and economic operation of feudal society in China and its basic economic characteristics, we must start from the operation of the basic production sector at that time, agriculture, handicraft industry and commerce, and their mutual relations, so as to get the essentials.

3. Basic Features of China's Feudal Economy

In the entire era of the land-based economic system in China, the land system is characterized by the coexistence of private land and state-owned coexistence and the private ownership of the land or landlord economy as the main element. There is no doubt about that. As early as the late Spring and Autumn Period, countries have successively adopted a series of measures to carry out social changes. The main economic manifestations are as follows: replacing the Nine Square-fields system featured by labor rent with land area based rent system featured by rent in kind, thus breaking away from the former taxes and corvee system. The reforms of various countries have cracked down on the power of the old feudal lords, and gradually abolished the hierarchical clan enfeoffment system and the hereditary system, expanded the Mu system, and did away with the old drainage system for the Nine Square-fields system. The peasants under the feudal lord system gradually became the land-holding peasants under the landlord system, and their social status and economic status have been improved to some extent. At that time, various political powers introduced incentives to reward farming and military operation measures to varying degrees, which led to the rapid development of agricultural production and boosted the development of handicraft industry, especially the household sideline handicraft industry. Since the Warring States Period, Qin and Han Dynasties, China has established the laws and regulations of private ownership of land, making land privatization a universal social reality. To a certain extent, the government regulates the land, but even in the era of land equalization, the shortage of land is a normal situation. For example, according to the "Turfan Unearthed Documents", in the population and land record of Gaochang County, Xizhou, recorded in the 14th year of Emperor Taizong of the Tang Dynasty (640 years). [1] And this is not rare.

The basic characteristics of China's feudal economy mainly have the following characteristics:

1. Private and state-owned land coexists; 2. The government has restrictions on land trading, but land trading exists all along; 3. Tenancy system is relatively developed, especially in the middle and later period of feudal society; 4. Official handicraft industry is large in scale, involving a wide range of fields, but at the same time, household sideline handicraft industry is also active, and individual handicraft production accounts for a certain share; 5. The commodity economy is quite active in the natural economy; 6. The government controls the social economic lifeline from beginning to end, the main way of which is either to directly control some industries that are related to the national economy, or to directly operate or monopolize some economic sectors.

After the disintegration of patriarchal clan society and its entry into class society, China has experienced slave society and feudal society in the course of

1 Edited by the Ancient Documents Research Office of the State Administration of Cultural Relics, the Museum of Xinjiang Uygur Autonomous Region, and the History Department of Wuhan University: *The Unearthed Documents of Turpan*, Vol. 4, the 14th Year of the Zhenguan (64 AD), The Population and Land Record of Li Shizhu and Other Households in Gaochang County, Xizhou (2), Cultural Relics Publishing House, 1983, pp. 72-73.

the evolution of class society for thousands of years.[1] After the Warring States Period, with the establishment of the landlord economy, there appeared a large number of land-holding peasants, some of whom became private tenant peasants who lost their land and were enslaved and exploited by the landlords. Some others became registered land-holding peasants who owned small plots of land but were controlled by the state. At the same time, the state directly controlled a considerable amount of land. These official fields are either directly organized by the government, distributed to nobles, bureaucrats, or rewarded to military officers with military merits. Compared with the European medieval seignorial economy, the main characteristics of China's landlord economy are manifested in the following three aspects: First, there is a certain degree of freedom in land trading, and the variables of land concentration and dispersion are relatively large. Second, individual small-scale production agriculture and its household sideline handicraft industry are more active all along. Third, there are labor rents, rent in kind and money rent in different periods of land rent, with rent in kind as the dominating type. At the same time, there are also individual craftsmen whose household registration is controlled by the government. Their legal status is often comparable to that of businessmen, generally lower than that of peasants, but their economic status is higher than that of ordinary peasants. "If one wants to rise out of poverty and seek wealth, farming is not as good as doing craftwork, which is not as good

1 There are different opinions on the concept of feudal society in the academic circles now. One of them holds that "feudalism" is a peculiar social form in the Middle Ages of Western Europe, and that "feudalism" is different from the 'enfeoffment system' in the Western Zhou Dynasty and the 'nobility conferring' after the Qin and Han Dynasties. Therefore, it is easy to cause misunderstanding over the word 'feudal society' in China. In fact, today's concept of feudal society has become a conventional concept. Those who have the basic knowledge of Chinese history will not misunderstand it. Just like the word "cadre" borrowed from Japan in modern times, although it has no corresponding meaning with the traditional Chinese "official" and "leadership" and so on, it is widely used, so it is no longer necessary to coin a new term to replace it. Similarly, the term "economy" in common use today is also introduced from Japan, which is totally different from the meaning of "benefiting the state through economy" in Chinese ancient books, and does not cause ambiguity or confusion.

as doing business. And embroidery and literacy are not as good as trading."[1] At the latest, this became the consensus of people in the Qin and Han Dynasties. The order of income in society from low to high is as follows (Figure 1-2)

Agriculture → Handicraft → Business → Service Industry

Figure 1-2 Schematic diagram of industry income level in the feudal society

In fact, it is very difficult today to distinguish very clearly between individual craftsmen and individual small-scale farming in terms of profession and identity. Even in the era of the land equalization system in the 5th and 8th centuries[2], land equalization peasants were often required by the government to plant a certain number of mulberry, hemp or other trees, which are one of the essential raw materials for the production of household sideline handicraft industry. Likewise, a certain amount of land can be acquired by industry and commerce, which is inextricably linked to land, and land income is often a part or a necessary supplement of their normal income.[3] Studies have shown that the productivity of agriculture and handicraft industry play a better role after commodity exchange, which tends to optimize the allocation of resources. The development of commodity economy can stimulate and promote the progress of feudal productivity.[4] And this kind of resource allocation leads to a certain amount of exchange among the agricultural producers because of the different kinds of products they have. The handicraft producers have different kinds of commodities, so it is unavoidable for them to exchange certain commodities

1 *Records of the Grand Historian*, Vol. 129 Biographies of Merchants.

2 The system of land equalization in China began in the ninth year of Taihe in the Northern Wei Dynasty (485 years), and lasted for more than 300 years from the Northern Qi Dynasty, the Northern Zhou Dynasty, the Sui Dynasty and the early Tang Dynasty to the Kaiyuan period of Emperor Xuanzong.

3 *The Book of Wei Dynasty*, Vol. 110 Shi Huo Zhi; *The Book of Sui Dynasty* Vol. 24 Shi Huo Zhi; *Book of Tang* Vol. 48 Shi Huo Zhi I; *New Book of Tang* Vol. 51 Shi Huo Zhi I.

4 Ning Ke: On China's Feudal Economic Structure, *Academic Monthly*, 2006.11.

with the agricultural producers. The exchange between the agricultural producers and the handicraft producers a matter-of-course. This is the basic content of the commodity economy at that time, and it is also one of the basic conditions for the commodity economy and social and economic development at that time.

Peasants and craftsmen are the basic creators and providers of wealth in feudal society, the essential undertakers of government tax and corvee, and the main source of manpower for government-run handicraft production. Hundreds of thousands of individual small-scale production agriculture and individual craftsmen became the main body of feudal social production, which provided the possibility for the powerful rule of the state power and the government-run handicraft industry to maintain the enormous scale and advanced technology from beginning to end. It became a feature of the feudal social economy of China, and also an economic starting point after China entered the modern society, although this was greatly influence by the changes in the international and domestic social situation at that time.

Chapter 2

The Feudal State's Management of the Economy

From the perspective of the overall economic activities of the feudal society in China, the government, especially the central government, whether as manager or operator, played a very important role in the formulation and implementation of economic policies, in the regulation of macro-economy, in the direct control or management of key areas of the economy, and in the direct participation and restriction of market activities. This will inevitably affect the direction of the development of China's feudal social economy, and also have a non-negligible impact on the choice of modern social and economic operations. The following is a brief description of the government's economic management level.

1. The Macroeconomic Regulation and Control in China's Feudal Society

The handicraft industry management institutions in China's feudal society is comparatively complete. Although there have been many changes during the period, as early as the Sui and Tang Dynasties, it has formed a relatively perfect pattern of Shaofu supervisors, Jiangzuo supervisors (Note: in charge of the supervision of craftsmen of architecture, utensils and embroidery, tec.) and Junqi (Note: military weapons) supervisors, so that the government can manage, control and dispatch handicraft craftsmen scattered all over the country in a unified way, mobilize them to engage in the production of various kinds of needs at any time in the imperial court and the government office, and produce and sell salt iron, which has a decisive influence on the national economy and the people's livelihood. The administrative efficiency and the economic benefits could not be underestimated. Such a management system has been maintained for over a thousand years.

The acquisition of tax and corvee is not only the basic embodiment of the political function of the feudal society, but also the economic basis for a government to operate and consolidate, and also one of the basic premises for maintaining the social and economic order under an established system. In addition to embodying the political will of the ruling class, the government also reflects to a certain extent the responsibility and ability of macroeconomic control with the indispensable distribution and redistribution of taxation and corvee through the financial budget.

The macro-control of the government, especially the central government, is mainly manifested in the redistribution of the tax-related services that have been acquired to reflect the state's function of intervening in the social economy. The specific manifestations of this aspect are the government's provision of public goods, the supply of necessary relief materials, and the granting of grain, silk, and farmland and the exemption of taxes and corvees, and the help for disaster victims to have food and be resettled. From Li Kui's 'Ping Di' to Geng Shouchang's 'Chang Ping Cang' in the Han Dynasty, the regulation of grain has become a basic function of the government, and has continued. According to the records of Emperor Wu of the Han Dynasty:

> Shandong was flooded, and the people were so hungry that the emperor sent the envoy to open the county granary to save the poor. But this was still not enough. Then wealthy people were called upon to loan

> money, which was still not enough. Then more than 700 thousand poor people were then relocated to the west of Guanzhong or to Xin Tai Zhong, the south of Shuo Fang County. Their food and clothes were all provided by the government. The government lent the poor land and house, sent lots of envoys to protect them. The cost is too high to calculate. [1]

During the reign of Emperor Wu of the Han Dynasty, the government took some typical measures to relieve the severe flood area in Shandong Province. The measures taken by the government include the distribution of official warehouse food, loans from the rich in the name of government, dislocation of the victims, and employment creation instead of direct relief. More than 700,000 victims mainly relied on the government's relief to tide over the difficulties. After several years of efforts, it has received good economic and social benefits for stabilizing the society and successfully passing the disaster. In the face of such natural disasters, with only civilian efforts, it is difficult to achieve an ideal effect. Only by making full use of the all-powerful capacity for government to mobilize resources and coordinate of civilian forces can such an obvious effect be achieved. It can be said that the role of the feudal society in the economy has been vividly demonstrated during this disaster relief in Shandong. In fact, such a situation can be seen everywhere in China's feudal society. In the late Qing Dynasty, even in the grim situation of internal and external troubles and the financial constraints of the Qing government, the special funds allocated to the provinces and customs departments from the nine years of Guangxu (1883) included the funds for famine relief preparation, with a fixed amount of 120,000 silver. [2] It can be seen that the cost of disaster relief is an important part of the normal fiscal expenditure of the

1 Records of the Grand Historian, Vol. 30 Ping Zhun Shu.

2 See Shi Zhihong's *Statistics on the Treasury Income and Expenditure of the Ministry of Revenue in Qing Dynasty*, Fujian People's Publishing House, 2008, pp. 29-30. The specific information in this respect can be consulted from the 1965 photocopy of *The Political News* (Taiwan) published by Wenhai Publishing House.

feudal society, even in the case of a very bad social environment.

Chang Ping Granary is one of the social security systems that the government generally implements in the feudal society in China to regulate food distribution between harvest and crop failure years. The specific provisions of the grain are: "When it is a harvest year, the grain is cheap and everybody can have enough, then you buy it; when there is crop failure, the grain is expensive and not everybody can afford, then you sell it." Later, the government also brought Chang Ping Granary, Zheng Granary and Yi Granary into strict control of the government.[1] Since Yi Granary plays a very important role in the economic life of China's feudal society, it is necessary to give a brief account of the emergence of Yi Cang (Charitable Granary) or She Cang (Civil Granary) in the history of China.

The Sui Dynasty unified the whole country and ended centuries of divisive disputes between the Southern and Northern Dynasties. As a result of a long period of war, once the Sui Dynasty was established, Emperor Wen of the Sui Dynasty put the restoration of normal production and living order into a more important position. The top priority for the new Sui Dynasty was to crack down on the Chen Dynasty in the south of the Yangtze River. The government should concentrate its financial and material resources on military operations. At that time, the government was unable to engage in large-scale social relief activities, so that the relief of natural disasters would mainly rely on the people themselves to complete. Under such a special background, there has been a form of civil self-help such as the establishment of a local public welfare granary or barn. In May of the five years of Kai Huang(585 years), Zhangsun Ping, Gong Bu Shang Shu (the Minister of Industry), Xiangyang County Governor, proposed:

> The people and soldiers of Zhuzhou are advised to establish local public welfare granaries. On the day of harvest, they are encouraged to hand in millet and wheat for the granary. An official in charge of grain

1 *Six Codes of Laws in the Tang Dynasty*, Vol. 20 Changping Department.

storage will be appointed for the collection, inspection and guarantee of the quality. When there is crop failure and famine, the grain in the granary will be used for relief. From then on, Zhuzhou begins to store grains. [P]

In view of the social reality that "many counties suffer from floods and droughts, and the people suffer from famine", Zhangsun Ping "proposed that every household should hand in grains of no more than one dan each autumn. The amount handed in should be different for the rich and the poor. The grain will be stored in the lane granary for the lean years. And this is called "the Yi Cang". [2] Yicang is set up in units of traditional organization "She" to encourage members to donate grain. Its purpose is to prepare for local relief during the floods and droughts. The warehouse is managed by the head of the society "She". Because the granary is sponsored by the society, it is also known as "Social Granary". At the very beginning, Yicang played a very important role in the civilian rescue in the Sui Dynasty. The purpose of Yicang was clearly stated by Emperor Wendi of Sui Dynasty in the February decree of the 15th year of the Kaihuang Emperor (595) as follows: "This is the right place to stop the flood and drought." [3] Its purpose is definite.

To sum up, the nature of Yicang is a self-rescue form spontaneously generated by the people. Secondly, Yicang is managed by the people themselves. And thirdly, the grain in the granary can only be used for natural disaster relief, such as floods and droughts, and cannot be misappropriated. Yicang in the early Sui Dynasty received obvious economic and social benefits during the flood and drought period, and its expected goal of self-rescue was fully implemented. Historically, after the promotion of Yicang, "the county became rich, and many people rely on it." [4] It should be said that the successful rule of emperor Wendi in

1 *The Book of Sui Dynasty* Vol. 24 Shi Huo Zhi.
2 *The Book of Sui Dynasty* Vol. 46 Biography of Zhangsun Ping.
3 *The Book of Sui Dynasty* Vol. 24 Shi Huo Zhi.
4 *The Book of Sui Dynasty* Vol. 46 Biography of Zhangsun Ping.

Sui Dynasty was related to the promotion of Yicang and its high efficiency.

With the victory of the Sui Dynasty's war to pacify the South of the Yangtze River and the unification of the country, the central government gradually incorporated the granary or social granary into the unified management system of the government. In the fourteenth year of Kaihuang (594), a severe drought occurred in the northwest of the seat of the capital. Due to the impact of this disaster, "there was a widespread famine" all over the country. [1] Therefore, Emperor Wendi went to Luoyang, the east capital, and allowed the people to go to Luoyang for food to survive the disaster. At this time, Yicang or social granary is still in the private sector, and its basic function is still to implement self-rescue after the local disaster. But after the fifteenth year of Kaihuang (595 A.D.), the nature of the granary in the Sui Dynasty had undergone a great change. Emperor Wendi of the Sui Dynasty ordered the granary in the northwest region to be managed by local prefectures or counties instead of civilians, and the grain collection was also changed from the form of persuasion to a fixed amount of taxation on a household basis. In the fifteenth year of Kaihuang (595 A.D.), a February imperial edict reads as follows:

> The purpose of Yicang is to prevent the suffering from floods and droughts, but the common people do not think ahead for the future. They tend to quickly consume the grains and end up with no food in no time. And different from the rest, the northern border states, Yun, Xia, Chang, Ling, Yan, Lan, Feng, Shan, Liang, Gan, Gua and other states, all give their Yicang grains to the local government. If someone suffers from drought and lacks food, they will be provided with various seeds and also grains from the past years. [2]

1 *Zhenguan Zhengyao* Vol. 8 A debate on the rise and fall of a country, Shanghai Ancient Books Publishing House, 1978 edition, p. 256.

2 *The Book of Sui Dynasty* Vol. 24 Shi Huo Zhi.

It can be seen that the nature of the people's self-rescue in case of flood and drought has changed, and becomes an economic organization controlled by the local government. If drought and other crop failures occur, only the coarse grain and old grain in the granary will be used for relief, which means that its function has changed greatly. The granary has turned from a kind of self-rescue spontaneously organized by the local people to a governmental organization directly responsible for disaster relief and prevention. In Janurary of the sixteenth year of Kaihuang (596 A.D.), the central government further determined in the form of imperial decrees that Yicang should be unified as a social granary and was set up at the county level:

> The decree is also sent to the social granaries in Qin, Die, Cheng, Kang, Wu, Wen, Fang, Dang, Xu, Tao, Min, Wei, Ji, He, Kuo, Bin, Long, Jing, Ning, Yuan, Fu, Dan, Yan, Sui, Yin, Fu counties, and is settled in that county. [1]

At that time, the adjustment of Yicang by the central government was based on the special economic environment of Northwest China, including today's Gansu and most part of Xinjiang. Later, Yicang controlled by local government will be popularized and implemented nationwide. In February of the sixteenth year of the Kaihuang (596 A.D.), the central government further determined the specific amount of tax levied per household on social granaries:

> ... It also decrees that the upper, middle and lower level of taxes are allowed in the social granary, and that the upper-level household should pay no more than one Dan, the middle-level household no more than seven Dou, and the lower-level household no more than four Dou. [2]

1 *The Book of Sui Dynasty* Vol. 24 Shi Huo Zhi.
2 Ibid.

After the management of Yicang in Sui Dynasty was shifted to the local government, the source of its storage was guaranteed because of the collection of grain by household. Besides, its disbursement was not entirely for relief, but only as part of it, which made the national grain storage very sufficient in the Sui Dynasty. Although there were many problems in dealing with Yicang in the Sui Dynasty, the basic tenet of "building Yicang to prevent the suffering from floods and drought" was consistent on the whole.

On June 4 of the ninth year (626 A.D.) of Wude, Emperor Gaozu of the Tang Dynasty, Li Shimin of the Qin Dynasty forced his father to abdicate and he himself ascended the throne after killing his brothers. In March of the second year of Zhenguan (628 A.D.), Li Shimin "decreed to all the prefectures and counties to build Yicang"[1]. We can see from this how important it is to set up a Yicang to stabilize social and economic life! In January of the second year of Yonghui (651) during Emperor Gaozong's reign, the emperor decreed, "Last year in Guanzhong, or the Central Shaanxi Plain, there occurred locust plague. Some prefectures in our country suffered from floods or droughts, resulting in shortage of food among the people. ... In the suffering area, those who don't have enough food could be provided with food from the Pingcang and Yicang".[2] In the sixth year (811 A.D.) of Yuanhe during the reign of the emperor Xianzong, "Because people living in the capital and its environs were poor, 240,000 Dan of grain from the Changpingcang and Yicang were provided to them. The other prefectures and counties followed suit".[3] Although there is still a distinction between regular Zhengcang (Changping) and Yicang, there is no doubt that the government controls the two kinds of granaries and plays an irreplaceable role in disaster relief.

It remained so in the later years. Although in the beginning years of the Song Dynasty, Yicang was sometimes established and sometimes abandoned, it was basically institutionalized later. There were many such records as "when there

1 *Book of Tang* Vol. 2 Emperor Taizong of Tang I.
2 *Book of Tang* Vol. 4 Emperor Gaozong of Tang I.
3 *Book of Tang* Vol. 14 Emperor Xianzong of Tang I.

were floods in the prefectures and towns and the people who suffered from the disasters were provided with food from the Yicang".[1] The difference between the Song Dynasty and the Sui and Tang Dynasties was that in the Sui and Tang Dynasties it was stipulated that all the nobilities and the common people should pay a certain amount of grain to the granary for disaster relief, while in the Song Dynasty it was stipulated that the common people should pay 5% of the principal tax as the cost of the social granary or Yicang[2], which further guaranteed the source of the social granary or Yicang, and also made it one of the basic burdens of taxpayers at that time. In the Yuan Dynasty, "people in Hejian and Baoding suffered from famine, and the granary food was granted for relief. What's more, people were exempt from that year's land rent"[3]. "In the Yuan Dynasty, Yicang was established in the township community, and Changping granary was established on the county level, so that people didn't suffer from either poor or good harvest, the price of grains didn't fluctuate, and people's complexion wasn't sallow due to hunger. This can be called good following of the Han and Tang Dynasties' examples". The reason is that this is "a good method for famine relief". Therefore, we can say that the Changping granary and Yicang in the Yuan Dynasty came down in the same line from Han and Tang Dynasties. The specific situation of Changping granary and Yicang controlled by the government in the Yuan Dynasty can be known from the record of "The history of Yuan Dynasty·Shi Huo Zhi":

> According to the record, Changping granary was established in the sixth year (1269 A.D.) of Yuan Shizu. The law stipulates: When the grain

1 *History of the Song Dynasty* Vol. 35 Chronicles of Emperor Xiaozong III; *History of the Song Dynasty* Vol. 43 Chronicles of Emperor Lizong III.

2 *History of the Ming Dynasty* Vol. 214 Biography of Jin Xue Yan: "Since Yicang was established in the Tang Dynasty, all the nobilities and common people should contribute to it every year; in the Song Dynasty, one-twentieth of the civilian principal tax was taken into the social granary".

3 *History of the Yuan Dynasty* Vol. 15 Chronicles of Yuan Shizu Kublai Khan.

> is cheap in a good harvest year, the government will buy the grain at an increased price; when the grain is expensive in a poor harvest year, the government will sell the grain at a decreased price. So, in the eighth year, the granary was stored with the grain bought and that appropriated from other water transported granaries. In the twenty-third year, a strict law was adopted, and the granary was stored with the grain from taxation. And the Yicang was also established in the sixth year of Yuan Shizu (1269).The method is as follows: a granary is established in the community, presided by the community leader. In the year of good harvest, people with blood relations hand in five Dou of grain, and servants hand in two Dou. Those who don't have grains could hand in coarse grain. And in the year of poor harvest, the grain will be provided to the community people. So in the twenty-first year Xincheng flood and the twenty-ninth year famine in Dongping and other places, grain from Yicang was used in the disaster relief. In the second year of Huang Qing (1313 A.D.), the same order was repeated. [1]

In the Ming Dynasty, people still believed that "the preparation of Yicang was supposed to help the poor" [2]. This understanding is a summary of the essence of Yicang since the Sui and Tang Dynasties. In the Qing Dynasty, the government continued to maintain the Yicang and the social granary; at the same time, the private individual granary also achieved a certain degree of development. However, in the Qing Dynasty, Yicang and Shecang gradually developed some differences between them, as Fang Guancheng pointed out in his memorial to the throne in the reign of Qianlong (1736-1795):

> The Yicang and the social granary are both for the storage of grain. But the social granary is especially for the lending of grain as seed, and

1 *History of the Yuan Dynasty* Vol. 98 Shi Huo Zhi·Changping Yicang.

2 *History of the Ming Dynasty* Vol. 164 Biography of Zhang Zhao.

> the Yicang addresses both concerns of seed lending and disaster relief, with its special attention on the latter. It is better to set up a granary in the countryside but not in the city, and the storage of grain should be on the people but not the government. When there is a good harvest in autumn, people should be persuaded to hand in grain. At the end of the year, the amount of grain should be clearly reported, and there is no need to specify the detailed number of grain handed in and sent out. If the government officials are not directly in charge, the method will last long. [1]

We can see from this memorial to the throne that Yicang is mainly located in cities and towns, and is directly controlled by the government; the social granary is mainly to provide grain for grain-deficient sowers to ensure the harvest of summer and autumn. And besides the function of social granary, the most important function of Yicang is disaster relief. There is a clear division of labor between the social granary and Yicang. However, in some cases, there seems to be no difference between the two, which deserves our special attention.

In fact, before the implementation of Yicang in Sui and Tang Dynasties, the feudal government had taken similar measures to carry out social relief and resource allocation, so as to reflect the functions of the state in its economic life. As early as the fifth year (487 A.D.) of Yongming in the Southern Qi Dynasty, a September, imperial edict states: "The capital and the nearby cities provide hundreds of millions of dollars to buy grain, silk and cotton, etc. The price is lowered to benefit the common people." [2] The book " The Book of the Yuan Dynasty (Ce Fu Yuan Gui)" said in its account of the implementation of this imperial edict:

> In the Yongming years (483 - 493) of the Southern Qi Dynasty, the grain and cloth were cheap. Emperor Wu intended to set up the Changping

1 The history of the Qing Dynasty Vol. 324 Biography of Fang Guan Cheng.

2 Book of Southern Qi Dynasty Vol. 3 Chronicles of Emperor Wu.

> granary for grain storage. In the sixth year, the Emperor issued an imperial edict to call Minister Li Guizhi and others for counselling. They decide to use 50 million yuan from the national treasury to buy rice, silk, cotton, damask silk, Juan (thin, tough silk) and cloth in the capital city; Yangzhou contributed 9.1 million yuan and Southern Xuzhou 3 million yuan for the counties and cities to buy rice; Southern Yuzhou contributed 2 million yuan to buy silk, cotton, damask silk, Juan, cloth, rice, beans and wheat; Jiangzhou contributed 5 million yuan to buy rice and flax; Jingzhou contributed 5 million, Yanzhou 3 million for Juan, cotton, cloth, rice, soybeans, red beans, barley, flax, Jingzhou rice and japonica millet; Huzhou contributed 2 million to buy rice, cloth, and wax; Sizhou contributed 2.5 million, West Yuzhou 2.5 million, South Yanzhou 2.5 million, Yongzhou 5 million to buy Juan, cotton, cloth, rice; South Yanzhou also bought barley and soybeans to sell in the market.[1]

It shows that in the fifth and sixth years of Yongming, the Southern Qi government purchased large quantities of rice and cloth by setting up Changping granary.

In a word, Yicang has been valued by all levels of government since its appearance in the Sui Dynasty till Qing Dynasty. It has gradually become an economic organization controlled and operated by the government from the form of civilian disaster relief at the beginning. Although in the actual operation many officials embezzled public fund, lined their own pockets, and processed with low efficiency, it is difficult to write off the role played by the Yicang or the social granary in disaster relief and self-rescue, which reflects one of the important economic functions of the government. It should be said that the exploitation of usury capital in rural areas, such as "selling new silk in February, selling new

1 *Ce Fu Yuan Gui*, Vol. 497, Bang Ji Bu.

grain in May; curing the sores in the eyes, but cutting out the flesh in the heart"[1], is quite common in feudal society in China. And Yicang or social granary could reduce the incidence of usury. This is the main basis for our positive evaluation of the feudal social granary or Yicang, but also the reason why the government spared no effort to pay attention to it and many times personally managed it.

2. Maintain Market Order and Protect the Interests of Direct Producers and Consumers

In feudal society, the government paid close attention to the commodity price of the whole country, regarding it as a necessary condition for the government to stabilize the order of people's life and order of production, and also to a certain extent as a source of information and one of the decision bases for the government to obtain commercial profits. In terms of price control, the government has the ability to collect information accurately and comprehensively and to suppress prices economically. At the same time, it also has the ability to regulate and forcefully crack down on price hikes.

> Liu Yan, a financier in the Tang Dynasty, is a typical example of collecting price data in various places in time. According to "Book of Tang":
>
> The government established price inspecting departments and recruited at high salary those who are good at visiting and enquiring to fill up the position. They were arranged at the courier station. Thus, the fluctuation of commodity price far and near could be sent to the government. The price information of the remotest area could be obtained no later than four or five days. Therefore, the circulation and price of all kinds of commodities was in control of the government, and the government could reap huge profits. And there was no need to worry about extremely high or low prices. This is really the right tactic.[2]

1 Nie Yizhong: Sympathy for the peasants, see *Collected poetry of the Tang Dynasty* Vol. 636.

2 *Book of Tang* Vol. 123, Biography of Liu Yan.

Zi Zhi Tong Jian (A General Reflection for Political Administration) recorded as follows:

> (Liu) Yan is energetic, resourceful, flexible and tactful. He often hires at high salary those who are good at visiting about, and posts them at different courier stations, so that they could visit about and report the commodity price in different areas. Even the information about the price in the remote areas could reach the inspectors within days. Thus the price fluctuation is completely under control, and the government gets the profit and there is no need to worry about extremely high or low prices. [1]

Liu Yan's approach to price information is precious in the feudal society, although this situation is not common in other times, including other periods of the Tang Dynasty. But one thing is quite clear, that is, at any time the government, as an economic management department, attaches great importance to price and price control is one of the most basic functions of the government. What is especially commendable is that the central government has formed a relatively rigorous business information network system, which could timely gather business information. And then the departments concerned in the central government will analyze and research, so as to timely adjust the corresponding measures in the government's economy.

There were many laws and decrees regulating agriculture, handicraft industry and commerce in our feudal society, especially those promulgated in the form of imperial decrees. From these decrees, we can see that the protection of individual small-scale production agriculture was a basic national policy at that time. Even in the period of the Five Dynasties and Ten Kingdoms, although wars were frequent, there was still such policies as "those who open up land as much as 80 Mu will

1 *Zi Zhi Tong Jian (A General Reflection for Political Administration)* Vol. 226, the first year (780 A.D.) of Jianzhong during the reign of Emperor Dezong in the Tang Dynasty, the July article.

be awarded 20,000 yuan, and will be exempt for tax for five years". [1] According to records, it was quite common for the government to " urge and encourage the development of natural economy dominated by agriculture" at that time. [2] As for the era of peace, the government all the more takes measures to maintain and develop the normal social economy.

Since the middle and late Tang Dynasty, tea has been popularized in the south and north of the country and even in ethnic minority areas, thus becoming one of the seven daily necessities together with firewood, rice, oil, salt, sauce and vinegar. Nobody in the society could do without it. In this way, tea tax has become one of the important revenue source for the central government. The government attaches attention to the whole process of tea purchase, processing and distribution, and even directly manages some of the links. The circulation of tea in the Ming Dynasty was also combined with the horse trade of nomadic people in the northern region, which became one of the important means for the government to keep in touch with the minority nationalities. The nomadic people's food structure mainly consisted of meat and cheese, which decided that "People from other minority nationalities especially love cheese, and if they can't get tea, they will fall ill." Therefore, "since the Tang and Song Dynasties, tea is traded for horse, so as to check and balance Qiang and Rong minority nationalities in the western part of China". The tea-horse exchange trade plays an irreplaceable role in the political and economic life of the Tang and Song Dynasties. On the basis of the trade developed in the Tang and Song Dynasties, the tea-horse exchange trade was "especially frequent in the Ming Dynasty: there are official tea and commercial tea, and they are all stored along the border for horse trade". At that time, the "official tea was occasionally taxed, and the profit from the commercial tea was only next to that from salt trade".[3] In the Ming Dynasty, like the license

1 *Book of Tang Continued* Vol. 20 Shi Huo Zhi.

2 *Spring and Autumn of the Ten States* Vol. 90 Min Si Kong Family; *Spring and Autumn of the Ten States* Vol. 49 Biography of the King of Hou Shu.

3 *History of the Ming Dynasty* Vol. 80 Shi Huo Zhi.

for salt marketing, tea trade also needed license after the government inspection. In the Ming Dynasty, there was specialized management agencies for tea licensing and salt licensing---Pi Yan Suo (Inspection Station). One envoy and one deputy envoy were set up in the License Approval Agency to "be in charge of the inspection and license issue of tea and salt".[1] In this way, through the issue of tea and salt licenses, the government incorporate the commodities related to common people's daily life into the government's management and control. On the one hand, it raises the government's tax revenue; on the other hand, it helps to plan the production, distribution and consumption of tea and salt, so that commodities, including tea and salt, can circulate. And at the same time, it prevents individuals from hoarding for excessive profits to a certain extent. Another noteworthy effect is that it guarantees the economic contacts between the peasants in the central plains and the nomads in the surrounding areas, or rather, further strengthens the effective control of the Central Dynasty over the minority nationalities. These measures not only are conducive to maintaining the normal progress of social and economic production and social order, but also increase the government's financial revenue.

While macro-controlling the economy, the government also attaches great importance to commodity price, among which the price of grain has become the focus of the government's attention all along. Its premise is not only to protect the interests of direct producers, i.e. the peasants, but also to take into account the affordability of consumers, and at the same time to motivate businessmen to engage in business activities with certain degrees of enthusiasm. In addition, in the rural society, the production, storage and circulation of grain is one of the basic criteria for measuring the degree of prosperity of a family, a region and even a country. According to the *Yue Jue Shu (Book of Wu and Yue)· Ji Ni*, when the

1 *History of the Song Dynasty* Vol. 386 Biography of Jin Anjie, *History of the Yuan Dynasty* Vol. 22 Chronicles of Emperor Wu Zong, *History of the Ming Dynasty* Vol. 75 Records of Officials IV, *Draft of the History of the Qing Dynasty* Vol. 285 Biography of Yuan Zhouzuo`.

government collected grain from the people, "If the grain is sold at 20 Yuan per Dou, the peasants will suffer a loss, and if sold at 90 per Dou, the merchants will get no profit". Whether the peasants or the merchants will suffer a loss, it will cause negative social impact: "if the peasants suffer a loss, they will be unwilling to till the land, and if the merchants couldn't reap profit, they will not be willing to sell products". The price range of grain purchased by the government in the "Ji Ni's Plan" is: " The buying price should neither be higher than 80 Yuan per Dou, nor lower than 30". Only in this way can we achieve the social effect of "both the peasants and the merchants can gain profits". As we all know, Li Kui's famous "Ping Di" policy was based on this. Li Kui believes:

Those who are good at using economic measures to control grain prices by purchasing or selling grain with government financial power must know that there are good harvest, normal harvest, and poor harvest, ...If there is good harvest, the government will buy 300 Dan grain, leaving 100 Dan to the peasants; if the harvest is just ordinary, the government will buy 200 Dan grain; and if the harvest is poor, the government will buy 100 Dan grain. In this way, people could have enough food to eat, and the grain price remains stable. If the famine is not so serious, the government will sell the grain collected in the poor harvest year; if the famine is medium, the government will sell the grain collected in the ordinary harvest year; and if the famine is very serious, the government will sell the grain collected in the good harvest year.

The actual effect of this is that, "despite famine, floods and droughts, the grain price is not high, and the people will not flee away from the famine-stricken area, since there will be more than enough to make up for the shortage.

Therefore, in good harvest years, the government funded grain storage, and in poor harvest year, the government sold grain at a price below the market level. This is the "Ping Di" policy, which is the precedent for the later "Changping granary". Changping granary was first put forward and implemented by Geng Shouchang, the Prime Minister of agriculture during the reign of Emperor Xuan of Han Dynasty. Geng Shouchang "built granaries along the Bailing border.

When grain prices are low in the market, the government buy large amounts of the grain at a higher price, so as to benefit the peasants; when the grain prices are high, the government sell the stored grain at a lower price. And this is called the Changping granary. [1] Here Changping granary further promotes the policy of price stabilization to the border areas. Changping granary is actually a grain storage trade directly engaged by the government, and the main purpose of the government is not to make profits, but to adjust the grain prices in good or bad harvest years, which is conducive to the development of agricultural production in the border areas[2], while at the same time maintaining normal production and living order in the border areas. Changping granary was implemented by the central government as an important policy of benefiting agriculture for a long time after the Han Dynasty. Although in the process of implementation, there were often cases of officials lining their own pockets, the overall economic and social benefits of Changping granary are quite obvious.

The function of the feudal government in organizing production and developing economy in our country is relatively sound, and our previous research on this aspect is far from enough. In the period of unification and peace, the measures taken by the government in this respect need not to be overstated. Even in the period of separatist rule, the local authorities took a series of measures to increase government revenue and develop the economy. From the end of the Western Jin Dynasty to the unification of the North in the Northern Wei Dynasty, it was an important period for the North to conquer different ethnic nationalities and to strive for Sinicization or feudalization, during which period the minority authorities also attached importance to agricultural production to a certain extent, and restored and developed the social economy. For example, after the founding of the Qian Zhao (or Han Zhao), Liu Zhi, a Hun, stipulated that "no cattle should

1 *Han Shu (The Book of Han Dynasty)* Vol. 24 Shi Huo Zhi I.

2 Leng Pengfei: *Research on the Form of Commodity Economy in Ancient Chinese Society*, Zhonghua Book Company, 2002, p. 229.

be killed for sacrifices in non-clan temples, and all who violate should die"[1]. This is the protection of farming cattle, which played an important role in agricultural production. At that time, the protection of farming cattle was the protection of productive forces. Hou Zhao (or Shi Zhao), founded at the same time with Qian Zhao, in the reign of Shi Le, a Jie nationality, "strictly prohibited the northern nomadic people from insulting the Han people"[2], and "sent envoys to make an inspecting tour around the prefectures and counties to advise and encourage peasants to engage in agriculture"[3]. The "Han people" were the representative of the feudal relations of production, and the emphasis on the "Han people" undoubtedly amounts to emphasis on the feudal relations of production. Then the Xianbei Murong clan of Zhan Erqi established Qian Yan in Houzhao's old haunt. When Murong Wei came to power, the Xianbei aristocrats imitated the nobility of the Han nationality and implemented the feudal mode of production on the mainland: "they controlled many people as their tenants", resulting in "the state's household registration is less than the household controlled by the aristocrats"[4], and the landlord economy developed to a certain extent. The Qian Qin Dynasty (the Former Qin Dynasty), which was founded by the Di people with the surname of Fu in Guanzhong (the Central Shaanxi Plain), during the reign of Fu Jian, it had already been that "large tracts of land were opened up for farming, and the national treasury had enough money"[5], "from Chang'an to Zhuzhou ... all kinds of peddlers lined the streets"[6].After the battle of Fei Shui, the Hou Yan established by Murong Chui of the Xianbei national minority and the Hou Qin established by Yao Chang of the Qiang national minority formed a confrontation. When

1 *Book of the Jin Dynasty* Vol. 103 Liu Yao notes

2 *Zi Zhi Tong Jian* Vol. 91, the second year (319 A.D.) of Daxing during the reign of Emperor Yuandi in the Eastern Jin Dynasty, the November article.

3 Ibid.

4 *Zi Zhi Tong Jian* Vol. 101, the third year (368 A.D.) of Taihe during the reign of Emperor Haixigong in the Eastern Jin Dynasty, the September article.

5 *The book of Jin Dynasty*, Vol. 113 "Biography of Fu Jian".

6 Ibid.

Murong Chui was in power, "he created a legislative system, handled issues with leniency and simplicity, cleared prisons, lowered taxes and corvees, advise and encourage peasants to engage in agriculture, so the people were quite well off"[1]. When Yao Xing was in power in the Hou Qin Dynasty, "taxes at checkpoints were increased, and there were taxes on all kinds of goods such as salt and bamboo"[2].It is obvious that since Qian Qin the commodity exchange in the Central Shaanxi Plain area has not been completely sluggish or even non-existent as some scholars have described. The very existence of commodity exchange is a sign of the development of social production.[3]

In China's feudal society, the government took advantage of both the resources and information. On the one hand, it tried to keep prices down and protect the interests of the direct producers and consumers; on the other hand, the government also obtained certain benefits. There are numerous such examples in the feudal society, among which Liu Yan, the financier in the Tang Dynasty, was quite typical. In The Book of Tang Volume 123, Biography of Liu Yan, it records:

> The government established price inspecting departments and recruited at high salary those who are good at visiting and enquiring to fill up the position. They were arranged at the courier station. Thus the fluctuation of commodity price far and near could be sent to the government. The price information of the remotest area could be obtained no later than four or five days. Therefore, the price change of all kinds of commodities was being monitored by the government, and the government could reap huge profits. And there was no need to worry about extremely high or low prices. This is really the right tactic. Liu Yan only appointed those who are really capable,

1 *Zi Zhi Tong Jian* Vol. 106, the tenth year (385 A.D.) of Taiyuan during the reign of Emperor Xiaowu in the Eastern Jin Dynasty, the November article.

2 *The book of Jin Dynasty*, Vol. 118 Biography of Yao Xing.

3 Jin Baoxiang: A Study on the Land Equalization System in the Northern Dynasties, Sui and Tang Dynasties, *The Journal of Gansu Normal University*,1978.3. Quoted from *The Collected Essays of Tang History*, Gansu people's publishing house, 1982.

valuing ability and efficiency, and rectified the unhealthy tendency of the subordinate officials in their pursuit of private interests. At that time, those with power and influence asked him to pull strings for their relatives. Liu Yan complied with them but never gave them important positions. Those designated to important positions must be the most outstanding talent of that period. Therefore, more than 20 years after Liu Yan's death, Han Hui, Yuan Xiu, Pei Tian, Bao Ji, Lu Zhi and Li Heng successively took charge of the finance and tax. And they were all Liu Yan's old subordinates. His subordinates lived thousands of miles away, but they followed his instructions as if he was in front of them. And they would not cheat even when they were chatting with people. They were the first to know if there was any kind of information. If there was a matter for congratulation, they would first send the memorial to the throne. Liu Yan and other inspectors paid tribute every year with tea and tangerine in the Yangtze River and Huai River area, and all tried to be the first. Those officials with land would blockade the road to discourage them. Liu Yan often used large sums of money to beat the others.

In the process of fully collecting and utilizing commodity price information, Liu Yan showed the wisdom of politicians to deal with matters flexibly, and made a positive contribution to controlling the price of the whole country at that time. More than that, Liu Yan also trained a large number of economic reformers in practice, who also played an important role later, making Liu Yan's reform enjoy a considerable continuity.

In addition, since Qin Shi Huang (the First Emperor of Qin Dynasty), the government kept building a nationwide network of road. Although the building was mainly for the consolidation and strengthening of authoritarian centralization and military considerations, it is objectively conducive to the circulation of commodities, and has far-reaching significance for the development of social economy, the formation of land and water traffic network, and the formation of a business network with urban cities as the node. During the reign of Sui Yang Di (Emperor Yang of the Sui Dynasty), the Grand Canal connected the South and the North with the commitment of the whole nation. Although Sui Yang Di said that it was motivated by "I dreamed of the beauty of the south of the Yangtze River and the expedition to Liao was only temporary", it was in fact an objective requirement for the development of social economy, especially commodity economy. The excavation of the Grand Canal in the Sui Dynasty formed a land-and-water transportation network centered on Chang'an, the political center at that time, which had a great impact on the social economy at that time and thereafter. And the acceleration of the southward shift of China's economic center was closely related to this. On the basis of the construction in the Sui and Tang Dynasties, the world-renowned Grand Canal of Beijing (northern) and Hangzhou (southern) was further excavated. It was the earliest and longest man-made canal in the world. The Grand Canal runs through six provinces and cities, including Beijing, Hebei, Tianjin, Shandong, Jiangsu and Zhejiang. It connects the Haihe River, Yellow River, Huaihe River, Yangtze River and Qiantang River with a total length of 1,794 km. The Grand Canal of Beijing and Hangzhou has made tremendous contributions to the development of north-south traffic and the communication of socio-economic and cultural aspects between the north and the south. Such a grand project can only be achieved through the central government's planning and practical organization and implementation.

In the fifty-first year (1712) of Kangxi in Qing Dynasty, it stipulated that, " the newborns will not be counted in for the tax"[1]. This is one of the most important macroeconomic policies formulated by our country in the late feudal society, which means that the labor force as a scarce resource has been alleviated in social and economic activities, and the scarcity of land resources is further highlighted in the case of increasing population. To adapt to such a major social change,

1 *The History of the Qing Dynasty* Vol. 120 Shi Huo Zhi I.

the highest policymaker would fix the total amount of the poll tax in the whole country or a place, and the poll tax will not change even with the increase of the population. In the feudal society dominated by agricultural production in China, the reproductive capacity of the population was very strong and the trend is irreversible[1]. However, the emergence of "poll tax merged into land tax"[2] in the Qing Dynasty was a revolutionary change in the traditional society, which really meant that the labor force was no longer a scarce resource, but the scarcity of land resources became an irreversible situation at that time and in the future. This is in sharp contrast to the previous situation that "Liu Yan also believed that the increase in household would naturally lead to wider scope of tax collection. So when Liu Yan was charge of finance, he always took the people's concern as a priority"[3]. Before "the Law of Uniform Taxation", especially "poll tax merged into land tax", was implemented, a large household registration amounts to an increase in the government's tax corvee. Because of this, the government's "prioritizing the concern of the people" is to "better manage money", and to take measures to control more household registration. After the implementation of "poll tax merged into land tax", the government's revenue has no direct relationship with the household registration, but with the land directly occupied by the taxpayers and other scarce resources, that is, property. The "land right equalization movement" in modern society and the later land reform movement led by the Communist Party of China are inevitable choices against this historical background.

The management and control of the feudal government over the economy in

1 In the history of China, there are also records of the population decline, which mainly results from war and natural disasters. In some rare periods, there is also a serious phenomenon of hidden household registration caused by heavy tax and corvee service. These are special rather than normal cases in China's history.

2 *The Written Instruction from the Emperor* Vol. 73 IV, The Written Instruction from Emperor Xianzong: "... All provinces share the corvee and taxes. stalls are distributed evenly according to the original amount of grain in the county..."

3 *Zi Zhi Tong Jian* Vol. 226, the first year (780 A.D.) of Jianzhong during the reign of Emperor Dezong in the Tang Dynasty, the July article.

China is more specific and direct in some aspects, and the management of the market is a very important aspect. Although the feudal economy is an economy mainly for the purpose of its production and use value, because exchange is necessary, only the exchange between products is obviously not enough. The exchange of goods is also needed. If there is no commodity economy, the whole feudal economy is hard to run, let alone development. [1] In fact, commodity exchange in China's history appeared relatively early, and basically showed a good momentum. Although there have been many times in the history of commodity exchange depression, and even the situation of commodity exchange replaced by barter, we still need to make it clear that these are only special cases of special circumstances, such as war, but not the normal state of feudal society. That is to say, the commodity economy exists in our feudal society from beginning to end, but not something dispensable.

In this way, the government's management of the market has been put on the agenda. Commodity exchange in China's history has been existing as early as the clan society, as recorded in the Yi · Xici: "Shennong started the early market... people around the area gathered around noon at the market with their goods. They traded with each other and left after they got what they needed". Of course, the exchange at that time was a barter exchange between tribes, and was generally small in scale and limited in frequency. According to "Shang Shu · Gao Tao Mo (the History of Ancient Times · The Strategies of Gao Tao), Shun's administrative policy includes the contents of "barter with each other to exchange needed goods". This shows that as early as the time of Shun, trade has become an indispensable part of social and economic life. In class society, trade is valued and controlled by the government, and the government directly operates a certain scale of commerce to meet the direct needs of the royal family and the governments at all levels. As early as the Western Zhou Dynasty, there were merchants who served the royal family directly under the jurisdiction of Taizai, while the merchants who worked

1 Ning Ke: On China's Feudal Economic Structure, *Academic Monthly*, 2006.11.

under Situ served in the court (this was consistent with the separation of the Royal finance and the government finance in the feudal society for a long time). Among them, the merchants of the Inner Court mainly distinguished the ranks and prices of local contributions for the Royal family, and also purchased livestock, gold, silver, jewelry, textiles and other daily necessities and luxuries for the Royal family. These merchants are merchant officials serving the royal family and the government. Therefore, the "industrial and commercial food official" appeared very early in ancient China and had a profound impact on society. In the history of our country, the "market order" has undergone a process of evolution from the relevant market decrees to market administrators. In Zhou Li, there is a record of "money paid by those who violates the market order"[1]. The "market order" here clearly refers to the relevant laws and regulations about the market promulgated by the government. This situation underwent relatively great changes during the reign of Emperor Zhuangwang of Chu in the Spring and Autumn Period. At that time, "city orders" mainly appeared as market management officials.[2] In the period of Wang Mang's Xin Chao (New Dynasty), there were "East and West market orders" in the capital of Chang'an, "Market head" in Chengdu and other big cities, and then they were renamed "Sishi (market supervisor)" and so on.[3] In Wei, Jin, southern and Northern Dynasties there were also "market orders". In the Sui Dynasty, the "market order" became the subordinate of Tai Fu Qing.[4] Although there are differences in the names of market officials in different periods, they basically fulfill the duty of "Si Shi" as the chief market officer of the Pre-Qin period. The Tang Dynasty followed the system in the Sui Dynasty, and still had the "market order" as the manager of the market. But its development and changes are quite significant. It can be seen that in China's history, "city

1 *Notes and Commentaries of Zhou Li*, Vol. 15, Tax Bureau.
2 *Records of the Grand Historian*, Vol. 119 Upright Officials · Biography of Sun Shu'ao.
3 *Han Shu* (*The Book of Han Dynasty*) Vol. 24 Shi Huo Zhi Vol. II.
4 *The Book of Sui Dynasty* Vol. 26 Official rank table of civil and military officials Book I · Tai Fu Qing.

order" has gone through a process of evolution from relevant market decrees to management officials.

Before the mid-Tang Dynasty, the "market" was generally directly managed by government officials, usually referring to a regular market with specific time and space. In the Tang Dynasty and the dynasties before it, the "market" was mainly set up in the capital and the prefectures and counties throughout the whole country. The "market order" was the chief administrator of the market. He was either appointed by the central government and the corresponding local governments, or was held concurrently by local officials. In the surrounding ethnic minority areas, there established "intermarket supervisors", who are specifically responsible for business matters. The top-down state management of the market includes the Tai Fu Si, the Market Administration Department of Chang'an (Xi'an) and Dong Du (Luo Yang), the Price Stabilization Department, and other market supervision institutions above the prefecture and county level, and the officials responsible for the specific matters are the "city order". It can be seen that in the feudal society, the government attached great importance to the market and the market management was quite mature and up to standard, and has already incorporated it into the normal state management procedures.

We know that the "Sishi (market supervisor)" in the Pre-Qin period was the head of the market officials, who was in charge of the city's governance, religion, politics, punishment, measurement, prohibition, orders and other duties. The city officials under the command of the Sishi have their own respective responsibilities and clear division of labor. They include the "Zhi Ren (agents)" who are in charge of controlling the price of goods, the "Chan Ren (tax-collectors)" who collect taxes on houses, as well as the "Xu Shi" who lead the petty officials in the market. In addition, there are the "Gu Shi" who assess the commodity price, the "Si Bao" who are responsible for market order and public order, the "Si Ji" who especially inspect those who fail to comply with the market hours, and the

"Quan Fu" specially charged for the collection of municipal taxes, etc.[1] It can be seen that as early as the pre-Qin period, the market management of our country already appeared quite comprehensive. From the very beginning, the Tang Dynasty inherited the traditional practices in the history, and the responsibilities of market management were further clarified. The Tang Dynasty stipulated that the market order of the capital was "in charge of the trade among people", and his assistant, the assistant market order, had the specific responsibility of "establishing a standard, classifying products, unifying the measurements, and marking out three kinds of prices according to the quality of products (upper, middle and lower prices)"[2]. In addition, the government at that time had quite stringent regulations on the quality of goods entering the market, especially handicraft products. We can see from the basic duties of "market orders" and "associate market orders" in the Tang Dynasty that their basic duties involve managing people's transactions, balancing prices, regulating the market, assessing commodity grades, collecting taxes, and maintaining public order, etc. There were relatively clear and strict market entry and exit mechanisms. It should be said that there was already the basic management model and content of the traditional market at that time. This kind of management model can be traced back to the market official --- Si Shi --- in the pre-Qin market system. The market official system with Si Shi in charge shows that the market management has been relatively advanced, and this "direct management model" is mostly inherited by later generations.

In the feudal society, textiles were one of the main sources of national finance, and were also indispensable daily necessities for both the people and officials.

1 See in *Notes and Commentaries on the Rites in the Zhou Dynasty*, Vol. 9, entries of "Si Shi", "Zhi Ren", Chan Ren" etc. in Local officials · Si Tu II.

2 *Tong Dian* (*A general history of the system of laws and regulations*) Vol. 40 Official rank XXII· Ranks and salary V· Official ranks in the Tang Dynasty in the twenty-fifth year of Kai Yuan during the reign of Tang Xuanzong: the market orders of the two capitals (Chang'an and Dong Du) are sixth-grade officials (Rank 11); the Shu Cheng of the two capitals are eighth-grade officials (Rank 15); the governor of Du Hu Fu, Document writing clerk of Shangzhou (large-sized states), market orders and so on are nine-grade officials (Rank 18).

They can even serve as a measure of value under certain circumstances. Strict stipulation of their quality and unit scale was to ensure the interests of the direct producers and consumers, and this was also one of the necessary means to maintain normal social and economic order. This can only be achieved in feudal society by the relevant government departments. In this respect, Emperor Xiaowen of the Northern Wei Dynasty had made mandatory provisions in law. "In the old system, silk and cloth woven by the people should be two feet and two inches wide, 40 feet long as one Pi, and 60 feet long as one Duan. However, in the process of production and communication, people are often driven by interests, especially by the psychology of speculation and skillfulness, "and they gradually abused the provisions, and ignored the criteria." In the third year (473 A.D.) of Yanxing, Emperor Xiaowen of the Northern Wei Dynasty, the central government "established more stringent regulations, and commanded a uniform system as that in the past", that is, the width of textiles was uniformly set at 2 feet 2 inches, the length of each piece was 40 feet, and the length of each Duan was 60 feet. If the textiles being sold do not conform to the above provisions, the producers will be subject to different penalties according to the specific circumstances. Not only that, the relevant departments and the persons directly responsible will be subject to the same legal liability for negligence as the producers. [1] The so-called restoration of the old system here means the restoration of the feudal mode of production and the maintenance of the historical market order, which is of great significance to the acceleration of the feudalization process of the Northern Wei Dynasty.

According to the records of "Tang Hui Yao (Historical records of the systems in the Tang Dynasty)", about February of the third year (687 A.D.) of Chuigong during the reign of Empress Wu Zetian, there was the stipulation that "Shang Zhou (large States) set up market order"[2]. In December of the same year, the

1 *Book of the Wei Dynasty* Vol. 110 Shi Huo Zhi.

2 *Tang Hui Yao (Historical Records of the Systems in the Tang Dynasty)*, Vol. 69 Prefectural governor II

imperial court allowed key areas such as San Fu (Jing Zhao, Zuo Feng Yi, You Fu Feng), the Four Du Du Fu (Lu, Yi, Bing, Jing, Yang), and prefectures with a population of 40,000 or more to adjust or supplement market orders and other officials.[1] With the recovery and development of social economy, there are "market orders" not only in the Shang Zhou, but also in the Zhong Zhou (medium-sized states), Xia Zhou (small-sized states), and cities where the counties are located. In this way, local officials will inevitably increase accordingly, and the government's financial expenditure is even greater, so in the Yuan He years (806-820 A.D.) during the reign of Tang Xianzong, Prime Minister Li Jifu had asked for the reduction of officials. By September of the Sixth Year (811 A.D.) of Yuanhe, the Ministry of Officials cut and merged 808 local officials. It is clearly stipulated that "the assistant of Zhong and Xia counties (county with medium-sized and small-sized population) magistrate, as well as the city order should all be cut down"[2]. This layoff, in turn, tells us that at least by the year of Yuanhe (806-820 A.D.), local markets in such areas as Zhong and Xia counties had already set up "market orders". What is especially noteworthy is that although in 811 A.D. the "market order" had been abolished in Zhong and Xia Counties, 40 years later, in August of the fifth year (851 A.D.) of Dazhong during the reign of Tang Xuanzong, the court restored the market order in Zhong and Xia Counties, and further clearly stipulated that "Zhong County, with a household of more than 3000, there should establish one market order and two secretaries". While "those counties with a population of no more than three thousand should not set up a market official. If there is the need for market, the 3000-household requirement should be followed. The counties set up market management officials under the Zhou".[3] That is to say, until the early 9th century AD, the establishment of "market order" was

1 *Tang Hui Yao* (*Historical Records of the Systems in the Tang Dynasty*), Vol. 67 Skilled governor.

2 *Tang Hui Yao* (*Historical Records of the Systems in the Tang Dynasty*), Vol. 69 Prefectural governor II.

3 *Tang Hui Yao* (*Historical Records of the Systems in the Tang Dynasty*), Vol. 86 Market.

confined to areas with more than 3,000 households. This reflects the market development of the Tang Dynasty from one perspective. The government has certain provisions for the local setting up of markets, and these provisions from one side reflects the socio-economic development, especially the development of commodity economy, and the recognition and guidance of the government for this economic development at that time. That is to say, in a county seat of less than 3,000 households, if on a major traffic thoroughfare or in a place where the trade was already operating on a scale, it is possible to set up market management officials with a reference to the counties with 3,000 households, which means the government's recognition of its market setup. According to The Book of Tang, there established "market orders" in the Da (Big), Zhong (Medium) and Xia (Lower) Du Du Fu (the governor's Office), as well as the Shang (Upper), Zhong (Middle) and Xia (Lower) Zhou. The special status of the Da, Zhong and Xia Du Du Fu is self-evident, and the scale of population is an important yardstick in the delimitation of the Shang, Zhong and Xia Zhou. According to the Tang system, "an area with more than 40,000 households is called Shang Zhou", "more than 20,000 is Zhong Zhou", "less than 20,000 is Xia Zhou"[1]. In the feudal society, the population size was also an important basis to measure the total social economic quantity and its development in a region. Therefore, setting up "market orders" in these official markets undoubtedly showed the level of market development from one side; and whether a place set up "market orders" became another important indicator to measure the strength of market management in the Tang Dynasty.

In addition to setting up markets in the core areas, the Tang government also stipulated that in the surrounding areas, special agencies "Frontier Trade Supervisors" were set up by the court to manage the local market, and that each city should have one "Supervisor", sixth-grade officials (Rank 12); one "Assistant supervisor", eighth-grade officials. The "supervisor" is mainly in charge of the matter of "dealing with transactions with ethnic minorities on the frontier;

1 *The Book of Tang* Vol. 44 Officials III.

The position of the county magistrate is to assist the county magistrate. " From the point of view of the court's attention for commodities, the most important commodities in the frontier trade supervision should be horses, donkeys, mules, cattle, etc. The court clearly stipulated that "horses, cows, donkeys, donkeys, etc. The imperial court stipulates that "everything bought in the frontier market, including horses, camels, donkeys, cattle, etc., should be distinguished according to their quality, age, and color, and then be reported to the Zhou or Fu government it belonged to, and the government should record in writing. Tai Pu sent officials to brand the livestock. [1] These regulations have already been very specific, reflecting the importance and maturity of trade management in the surrounding areas at that time, as well as the government's emphasis on commodity exchange between the inland area and surrounding ethnic areas.

The Tang Dynasty also had overseas trade. According to the records, there was "Shi Bo Shi (Maritime Foreign Trade Envoy)" in the first year of Kaiyuan period (713-741) of the Tang Emperor Xuanzong. At first, it seemed that military officers concurrently held this position. The record in the New Book of Tang Dynasty "Shi Bo Shi, Right Wei General Zhonglang Zhou Qingli"[2] can prove this. But in the late Tang Dynasty, because "foreign ships in the South China Sea are quite convenient, and the precious goods converge", and "The old governors tried to profit from this, and all those who stayed in the South China Sea returned fully loaded." So Lu Jun "asked the supervisory officer to hold the post of Shi Bo Shi, and he himself did not intervene any more." [3] Obviously, "Shi Bo Shi" was not permanent at this time, and there were no special organization for that. However, the emergence of the "Shi Bo Shi" undoubtedly illustrated from one aspect

1 *The Six Administrative Codes in the Tang Dynasty* Vol. 22 Frontier Trade Supervisors.
2 *New Book of Tang* Vol. 112 Biography of Liu Ze.
3 *The Book of Tang* Vol. 177 Biography of Lu Jun.

that maritime foreign trade[1] had become part of the central government's direct operation, and that the central government attached great importance to overseas trade. In the Tang Dynasty, "Zhu Hu Shi (Frontier Trade Supervision)" under the supervision of Shao Fu Jian was specially responsible for this business through the handicraft industry management institutions. According to the provisions of the time, the specific duties of Zhu Hu Shi were "dealing with all kinds of transactions with the ethnic minorities on the frontier"[2]. That is to say, the Zhu Hu Shi is responsible for the trade with foreign and minority businessmen. It is precisely because of the special functions of the Shao Fu Jian that when foreign ships arrive, the government stipulates that the local government should first buy the goods in a package and then "send them to the Shao Fu Jian to select for further sale."[3] On the one hand, the emergence of Zhu Hu Shi illustrated the strengthening of the social function of the feudal society to restrict the commodity economy, which was based on the premise of restricting the development of non-governmental trade (or protecting the existence of state-operated commerce). On the other hand, this is also the objective requirement of the Tang Dynasty's opening to the outside world. It was the very fact that Tang Dynasty provided certain convenience for the activities of foreign businessmen that made the business activities of foreign businessmen in the Tang Dynasty a quite safe and profitable trade.[4] Not only in the Tang Dynasty, the situation was roughly the same in other dynasties. Shanxi businessmen, who had been in a leading position in the business of China for hundreds of years in the Ming and Qing Dynasties, spared no effort to build manors and houses in their hometown. And this is a typical example.

1 China's foreign trade in feudal society has a long history and has always been linked to the feudal society, which can be fully explained by the Silk Road which appeared no later than the period of Emperor Wudi of Han Dynasty and the subsequent rise of the Maritime Silk Road.

2 *The Book of Tang* Vol. 44 Officials III.

3 *Tang Hui Yao* (*Historical Records of the Systems in the Tang Dynasty*), Vol. 66 Shao Fu Jian.

4 Wei Mingkong, The Openness and Closure of Tang Dynasty's Foreign Policy and Its Evaluation, *Social Sciences*, 1989 (2).

It can be seen from the above about the basic situation of the market management officials set up by the Tang Dynasty from the central to the local government, from the cities to the border areas. Although the setting time of the "market order" varied, and there were also hierarchical differences in the setting place, but there is no doubt that the "market order" played an important role in the high-level market management at all levels in the Tang Dynasty.

To sum up, the market management in the Tang Dynasty mainly adopted the mode that the "market order" was especially in charge or other officials concurrently took control and standardized the market space and market exchange behavior at all levels. It makes sense that this is called the "direct management mode" by some scholars. An important feature of this direct management mode is that market officials directly manage all links of exchange, such as whether to establish a "market" and the scale and grade of the "market", which are also determined by the government. In the "market", the determination of prices, the quality of commodities, the specific location of the exchange and the time of the exchange should all be subject to national arrangements. In this mode, although the existence of the exchange place --- market --- is the result of the exchange activities, the objective development of social economy and the state's understanding of the market or market concept have not reached such a level for quite a long time, i.e. both individual businessmen and the state are trying to make use of the market in order to maximize profits by increasing or expanding exchange activities. Therefore, the market management of Tang Dynasty and its preceding dynasties all took great efforts to regulate the exchange behavior of the market, and what they valued was how to embody the state power and social laws and regulations. This management mode reflects the limitations of the market at that time. After the middle and late Tang Dynasty, the market development accelerated, and the market level obviously improved. There even appeared night markets, as well as emerging markets at different levels, such as Cao Shi market, Xu Shi market, etc., beyond the capital and the prefectures and counties. But throughout the Tang Dynasty, with the concerted efforts from his subordinate officials, the "market order" all along was the major official being directly in charge of all the links of market exchange. Whether or not there established a "market order" can be used as a measure of market development and management level.[1]

After the Tang Dynasty, the government's restrictions on the local market setup, the market operation time, residence and business areas and so on were obviously relaxed and even gradually cancelled. Instead, the government increased its service to the market, strengthened its standardization of the market as well as its tax collection on the market. It is consistent with the development of productive forces and the commodity economy.

3. Formulating a Unified Tax Policy

The Qin and Han Dynasties were an important period for the formation and development of a unified multi-ethnic centralized feudal state. This period also established the basic framework of the tax and financial system of the feudal state in the next 2,000 years.

In the economic decision-making of the government in the Chinese feudal society, people always pursue the policy of "measuring income for expenditure"[2], which has all the time been attached importance to by the general public and adhered to by the feudal society. In fact, people's understanding of this is incomplete, and one of the most important aspects is that they do not pay enough attention to its development and evolution. "Living within means" is the basic principle of government's fiscal revenue and expenditure when productivity development reached a certain stage, and it is also a basic national economic

1 See Wu Xiaoliang, An Analysis of the Change of the State Market Management Model in Tang and Song Dynasties - A Historical Review of the "Market" in the Tang Dynasty and the "Taxation" in the Song Dynasty, *China Economic History Research*, 2007 (4).

2 In *The Book of Changes*, there is already the record of "measuring income for expenditure". At the beginning of *Zhou Guan Yi Shu*, it reads: "The cost of the king's meal and clothes should all be within the means and be based on the rules." In this regard, there are similar records in *Three Kingdoms* Vol. 21 Wei Shu · Wei Ji, *Book of Song* Vol. 6 Emperor Xiaowu, *Song History* Vol. 163 Records of Officials and so on.

policy at that time. However, this basic national policy changed obviously when the two tax laws were implemented in the late Tang Dynasty. This reflects how the government changed its tax policy of "measuring income for expenditure" into "measuring expenditure to regulate income"[1]. The taxation principle of "measuring expenditure to regulate income" also had a far-reaching and direct impact on the late Tang Dynasty and later feudal society in China. It could be said that the principle of "measuring expenditure to regulate income" formulated in the middle and late feudal society of China shows foresight, which reflects the maturity of the highest decision-makers at that time in the aspect of economy, especially in taxation.

According to "The New Book of Tang Dynasty" Volume 52 "Shi Huo Zhi" II,

> Since the reign of Emperor Daizhong, the tax has been fixed on mu, and is collected in summer and autumn. To the time of Yang Yan, the Prime Minister of Emperor Dezong, the two-tax law was adopted, which stipulated that the summer taxation should not be later than June and the autumn taxation should not be later than November. Thus two-tax law aimed at measuring expenditure to regulate income. The taxation will not distinguish the head of the household and others. Everybody who lives within the household will be registered. Besides, tax collection does not depend on the number of people in each household, but only on the amount of property in each household. The business tax is one thirtieth of the profit, and all the people who live in the same household should equally share this. And the land tax depends on the amount of land already cultivated until the fourteenth year of Dali (779 A.D.). And Chu Zhi Shi (administrative supervision officials who inspect local officials, report their achievements to higher-level departments, and give suggestions for promotion or dismissal) are sent out to monitor the taxation based on the number of persons and

1 *Tang Hui Yao* Vol. 83 Rents and Taxation I.

> amount of land, and exempt the tax of those with no capacity for physical labor and no relatives to take care of as well as poor people. And officials who dare to increase the tax will be punished. The Zu Yong Diao and the laws in the Gao Zu and Tai Zong years shouldn't be lightly changed. Until then De Zong Emperor started to trust Yang Yan. There are 3.805 million old households, and based on the proportion in can be calculated that there are 3.8 million principal households and 300 thousand guest households. Thus the recorded land increased, and the actual situation of the land was obtained. Each year, more than 20 million 500 thousand Min (strings of coin) and 4 million Hu of rice are collected for provinces beyond the capital, and more than 9 million 500 thousand Min and 16 million Hu of rice are collected for the capital.

According to "Tang Huiyao" Volume 83 "Rents and Taxation", the Prime Minister Yang Yan, who was the main architect and practitioner of the two-tax laws at that time, proposed as follows to Emperor Tang Dezong in "Instruction Request Note". The so-called two-tax laws are:

This method is to abolish all kinds of servitude fees and uniformly collect one kind of tax. the first thing is to estimate the total expenditure and distribute it to everyone. The principle is to measure the expenditure (government budget) to determine the amount of tax levied.

In the first year of Jianzhong during the reign of Tang Dezong's (780 A. D.), the implementation of two-tax law has very important significance and influence in the feudal society of China, and has epoch-making significance in the history of national taxation. Thus, it is necessary to further analyze the two-tax law.

Firstly, household tax became an even more important government tax than poll tax for the first time. We all know that in the collection of taxes and corvee before the implementation of the two-tax laws, the number of persons reaching the age of servitude is the most important basis, while the adoption of household tax is relatively late. Although it already existed before the two-tax law[1], it was the first time in history that household tax was regarded as the most important source of government tax. Compared with the former principle of "measuring income for expenditure", the principle of "measuring expenditure for income" tax system seems more reasonable, because it is more in line with the social reality of frequent land concentration or transfer and the uncertain rise and fall of the rich and poor. Taxation is based on the amount of property, thus having the elements of modern tax principles. At the same time, this taxation principle further emphasizes the leading role of the government in social economy and highlights the importance of planning in the feudal society.

Secondly, for the first time, the principle of tax distribution between central and local governments has been clearly defined. After the implementation of the two-tax law, under the special circumstances of the military governor segmentation, the Tang Dynasty adopted the principle of "Some taxes are handed over to the central government, some are sent to the envoys, and some are reserved for the use of the state"[2]. That is, the central government, the local government and the envoys share the tax according to a certain proportion. In the first year of Jianzhong during the Tang Dezong's reign (780), when the two-tax law was implemented, it was clearly stipulated that "Each year, more than 20 million 500 thousand Min and 4 million Hu of rice are collected for provinces beyond the capital, and more than 9

1 According to *The Book of Sui Dynasty* Vol. 24 Shi Huo Zhi, in the Northern Qi Dynasty, "there was the establishment of nine-class households; the rich paid their taxes with money, and the poor with their labor", and this should be the time when the household tax came into being. In the eighteenth year of Emperor Wendi of Sui Dynasty (589 A.D.), "taxation was levied on households under administration". This is the continuance and development of the Northern Qi household tax. During the period of Wu Zetian in the Tang Dynasty, according to Vol. 6 of *the General Code*, Shi Huo Dian and Taxation, it was recorded that "all people under the nobility should pay taxes". At that time, household tax was already quite common. By the time of Emperor Xuanzong Tianbao in the Tang Dynasty, "the eighth-class household tax totaled 452, and the ninth-class household tax 222. Generally, the tax rate was 250."

2 *Tang Hui Yao* Vol. 83 Rents and Taxes I; *The New Book of Tang Dynasty* Vol. 169 Pei Ji.

million 500 thousand Min and 16 million Hu of rice are collected for the capital."[1] According to the regulations at that time, there was a specific proportion among the three parts. Because the specific purposes of the three parts were different, the government budget and its expenditure were calculated separately. Of course, the three-part system of government finance at that time was a special case under the circumstances of the military governor segmentation. With the re-emergence of unified centralization in the Northern Song Dynasty, this situation changed. In fact, the principle of three-part finance in Tang Dynasty could be simplified to the principle of two-part finance between central and local governments. Both Song Shi (taxation of State-owned Transportation and Savings and Observation Missions) and Liu Zhou (taxation reserved for use by local prefectures and counties) are for local expenditure, and belong to the same type of consumption. If the Jie Du Shi, i.e. the local separatist, commanded strong power, they often dominated the part of Liu Zhou in this area for themselves. If the leadership of the Jie Du Shi was not rendered ineffectual by recalcitrant subordinates, the central government will uniformly allocate its expenses. When Zhu Wen, the founder of Hou Tang, was appointed as Xuanwu, Xuanyi, Tian Ping, and Hu Guo (Protector of the State) envoys in the late Tang Dynasty, he once recruited Peidi as his staff. "For 30 years since then, four townships were commissioned to manage rents, military records, Treasury and granary, government officials, prison proceedings, rewards and punishments, funds, as well as grain transportation. And there were designated persons responsible for these."[2] Such a Jie Du Shi has undoubtedly become an expropriator of local finance. In the late Tang Dynasty, such Jie Du Shi as Zhu Wen was rather common. Nevertheless, it is a new change in the history of China to implement the principle of central and local taxation in the Tang Dynasty, which deserves our attention today.

The third is to use currency as the unit of measurement of household tax or

1 *The New Book of Tang Dynasty* Vol. 52 Shi Huo Zhi II.

2 *History of the Old Five Dynasties*, Vol. 4, Hou Liang Chronicle of Taizu.

two-tax law. The two-tax law clearly stipulated that taxpayers pay household tax, which is the basic type of tax, to the government, "according to the amount of old taxes, the number of household residents, ranking and amount of money, and the taxes are paid in summer and autumn"[1]. It can be seen that the two-tax law uses such measuring units of coin as Min, Guan, and Wen, a considerable part of which is directly surrendered in the form of money, while the remaining part can be surrendered in kind – textiles. Even the surrendered physical part is not directly calculated by the unit of measurement of textiles – Pi, Zhang, foot, inch, and so on, but is first converted into money, and money as the unit of measurement. "The amount of taxes is determined with currency, but when people pay taxes, they should also pay with silk and damask." Just because of this, people said at that time that "what is levied is not what people produce, and what people produce is not what is levied"[2]. We know that there are many kinds of textiles. Even the same kind of textile is officially classified into upper, middle and lower grades because of difference in quality. Textiles in different regions differ greatly in quality and variety, which makes it impossible for the government to set a unified standard of collecting the taxes. After the adoption of currency taxation or currency conversion taxation, the relevant government departments could have a unified and viable tax standard. This makes it more precise in terms of central government budget, revenue and expenditure. In addition, this strengthens the connection between direct producers and the market. In order to pay the two taxes, they must pass some of the products through the market. As the New Book of Tang Dynasty · Shi Huo Zhi: "Before the Dali (766-779), Ziqing, Taiyuan and Weibo iron was used for general purpose, while in Lingnan iron was mixed with gold, silver, red sand and ivory for mintage. And now people all use Huoquan coins for taxes." There are numerous examples of taxpayers exchanging money for goods after the

1 *Tang Hui Yao* Vol. 83 Rents and Taxes I.

2 *Collection of Lu Xuan Gong* Vol. 22 Averaging out Taxation to Compensate the People Article 2 "Requesting that Two-Tax Law levy in the amount of cloth and silk, not that of money".

implementation of the two-tax law, although the farmers did not do this willingly. Having said that, we should fully recognize the positive role of the two-tax law in promoting the development of commodity economy. Because of this, after the implementation of the two-tax law, the land rent pattern at that time changed greatly in the field of feudal economy; that is, the rent in kind and money rent were combined, and the proportion of money rent increased significantly. In the process of implementing money rent, there is a common phenomenon that "money is more valued than goods". The direct reason of this phenomenon is the inability of the government's money input to meet the needs of the market, which has a significant impact on the government's fiscal revenue and the burden of the direct producers. Since the implementation of the two-tax law, when taxpayers pay the taxes stipulated by the government, they either pay money directly or convert physical objects into money, which greatly increases the demand for money for circulation. It is not difficult to understand that money is more valued than goods. At that time, the magnitude of undervalue of goods was relatively large. Although the amount of tax levied by the government had not changed, the government's fiscal revenue was doubling, and the tax burden of the direct producers was also increasing. After the implementation of the two-tax law, the phenomenon that money is more valued than goods is often one of the thorny problems that financial managers in the successive dynasties spared no effort to solve, and it is also one of the social problems that ordinary people are most concerned about, and even an important source of countermeasures in imperial examinations at that time. After the implementation of the two-tax law, with the emergence of the undervalue of goods and its aggravation, "Since the implementation of two taxes, the goods were more valued than money. The value of goods was calculated and people pay with silk. Then, the lower the price, the more taxes people needed to pay. One Pi of Silk was worth 3,200 coins, but later the value of one Pi of silk was reduced to 1,600 coins, which means a great depreciation. Therefore, although the on the surface, the taxes were not increased, people in fact became even poorer". There is no doubt that the actual burden of the two-tax payers has doubled. On the other hand, officials at all levels imposed extra taxes in the actual collection process. "Official Du Zhi specified the amount of taxes and issued it to all the departments, who all increased the claimed value to pay the taxes. The imposed taxes were called Zhe Na, later renamed Jin Feng, Xuan Suo, and the name of the enforced labour service was changed from Ke Yi to Zhao Gu. This was mainly for the avoidance of criticism, and the taxes were doubled than the Dali years (766-779)"[1]. The actual burden of the direct producers increased exponentially. Originally, it was stipulated that the levy of any amount of extra money outside the two taxes was "violation of the law"[2], but it had not been actually implemented in the actual process. The levy of extra taxes has become an important source of income for the government since the late Tang Dynasty, and also a major feature of the social economy at that time.

Fourthly, change the principle of taxation from "measuring income for expenditure" to "measuring expenditure for income". The principle of "measuring expenditure for income" breaks through the traditional taxation principle and occupies an important position in the finance and economic history of China's feudal society. Because under the traditional principle of "measuring income for expenditure", the specific amount of expenditure is determined according to the actual tax revenue of the government, which keeps a general balance between fiscal revenue and expenditure. After the implementation of the two-tax law, "expenditure is measured to determine the income, and the quota is set to appropriate the money"[3]. In the Tang Dynasty, when the two-tax law was implemented, the central power was dominant. The central government adopted the method of determining the income based on the expenditure, so as to approve the central and local budgetary revenue and expenditure and their proportions,

---

1 *The New Book of Tang Dynasty* Vol. 52 Shi Huo Zhi II; Collection of Lu Xuan Gong Vol. 22 Averaging out Taxation to Compensate the People Article 2 "Requesting that Two-Tax Law levy in the amount of cloth and silk, not that of money"; *Tang Hui Yao* Vol. 83 Rents and Taxes I.

2 *Tang Hui Yao* Vol. 83 Rents and Taxes I.

3 *Collection of Yuan Zhen*, Vol. 35, On Currency and Goods.

thus providing the basis for the next year's budget. The specific meaning of the " measuring expenditure for income " after the implementation of the two tax laws is just as what Lu Zhi said, "The maximum amount of grain and taxes per year in the Da Li years (766-779) for each state is set as the two-tax quota".[1] In the first year of Jianzhong in Tang Dynasty (780), the largest amount of government expenditure in the Da Li years of Dai Zong of Tang Dynasty was taken as the total tax amount of the two-tax laws. Specifically, that is the fourteenth year of Da Li (779), and also one year before the implementation of the two-tax law, which served as the base of the income of the two taxes. In other words, the fiscal expenditure of the government in the fourteenth year of Da Li (779) was taken as the basis for the total amount of tax under the two-tax laws in the first year of Jian Zhong (780). The change from "measuring income for expenditure" to "measuring expenditure for income" can never be regarded as arbitrary reversal of the two words "income" and "expenditure". There are profound historical reasons. This is a relatively mature reflection of the tax budget in the feudal society of China. On the one hand, the government's budgetary outlays and tax revenue and expenditure are increasing significantly, which undoubtedly increases the exploitation rate, and the government's ability to control the economy is also getting stronger. On the other hand, the government limits the budget, revenue and expenditure to a "degree". That is to say, the expenditure of the previous year is used as the basis for the budget and expenditure of the current year. This is the so-called "the amount of all the taxes is based on the prior calculation". In this way, the government's arbitrariness in setting the fiscal budget, revenue and expenditure is limited, theoretically making the amount of the two taxes a constant amount, and making it viable. Especially in tax revenue, the government has completed the transition between the current year and the next year, and the transition is relatively stable. This should be said to be a sign of the maturity of tax policy in

1 *Collection of Lu Xuan Gong*, Vol. 22, Averaging out Taxation to Compensate the People Article 1 "On the Disadvantages of Two-Tax Law and the Need for Change".

the late Tang Dynasty, which occupied a very important position in the tax history and even economic history at that time and in later years.

Because the two-tax law is a very important system in the history of China, Ma Duanlin in the Song Dynasty compares in his "Comprehensive Examination of Documents · Preface" Yang Yan, the designer and implementer of the two-tax law in the Tang Dynasty, with Shang Yang in the Qin Dynasty:

The law of taxation on the land, regardless of the amount, begins with Shang Yang, while the law of taxation on the people with land begins with Yang Yan, while that of those who follow the land begins with Yang Yan.

Ma Duanlin attributed the collapse of the well-field system and labor rent to Shang Yang's reform, and the collapse of the equal-field system and the Zu Yong Diao based on it to Yang Yan's design and implementation of the two-tax law, which is quite insightful and reflects a thread of social and economic development and change in feudal society in China. Yang Yan, together with Shang Yang, is one of the important landmarks in the social and economic reform of the feudal society in China. In addition, Ma Duanlin's insightful words here reveal a very important but ignored historical fact: property tax, with land tax as the main content, replaces the poll tax, with persons reaching the tax age as the main content. The feudal government has shifted its focus on property rather than population. This change reflects the trend that the personal bondage of the direct producers was relatively reduced under the active social environment of the commodity economy at that time. After the implementation of the two-tax law in the Tang Dynasty, with the change of the content of government collection, the relative reduction of the personal bondage of the direct producers, the active commodity economy in the feudal economy, the relative popularity of craftsmen's "hiring" or "paying for servitude", the sources of raw materials for the production of government-run handicraft industry still come from collecting, tribute and other forms, but the part obtained by the government through the market is increasing obviously, and there is a growing trend. Lu Zhi in the Tang Dynasty pointed out that at that time "changing the name of the taxes and continue levying"[1], which sounds quite absolute now, but it indeed points out a momentum of the production source of government-run handicraft industry after the mid-Tang Dynasty, which is closely linked with the social change at that time. The implementation of the two-tax law in the Tang Dynasty is in line with the later "Law of Uniform Taxation" and "poll tax merged into land tax", which reflects the key change of the government in fiscal levy[2]. The series of taxation reform to a certain extent reflects the maturing trend of the government's tax policy. At the same time, because of the relatively reasonable tax policy, the government's tax sources have been further guaranteed, so that some products in the government-run handicraft industry are no longer necessarily produced in the government-run handicraft workshops, but through the market instead. For the same reason, some raw materials of government-run handicraft industry can also be obtained through market procurement.

The centralization of financial power in feudal society was an important part of the intellectual history of economic management or finance at that time. It reflected from one aspect the characteristics of the times when the supreme rulers highly strengthened centralization and tried to solve the financial crisis. The Song Dynasty inherited the trend of Tang Dynasty, there were many financial reforms, and they were carried forward by later generations, so there was a widespread theory of Tang and Song Dynasty reform in academic circles. Therefore, this paper makes a clear exposition of the idea of centralized finance in Song Dynasty on the basis of Tang Dynasty, which can be seen that the central government's functions in this respect are embodied in the later period of feudal society.

At the beginning of the founding of the Song Dynasty, in order to remove the drawbacks of military governors a series of measures were taken in the late

1 *Collection of Lu Xuan Gong*, Vol. 22, Averaging out Taxation to Compensate the People Article 1 "On the Disadvantages of Two-Tax Law and the Need for Change".

2 Yu Shenxing of the Ming Dynasty pointed out in *Bi Zhu* Vol. 12 Taxation, "Yang Yan's Two-tax law is the current Law of Uniform Taxation". In addition, Huang Jingfang of the Ming Dynasty also had similar views in Vol. 9 of *Guo Shi Wei Yi*.

Tang Dynasty and the Five Dynasties to strengthen the centralized government. "Seize their power, regulate their money and grains, and deprive them of their troops" [1], thus the local administrative power, financial power, judicial power and military power were all collected into the central government. In the second year of Qiande, Emperor Taizu of Song Dynasty (964), "It was ordered that starting from now all the counties need to send their collected taxes and silk every year to the central government beyond their expenditure" [2]. In the following year, "all the counties were ordered to contribute gold and silk to help with military expenditures, and they could not retain any. At that time, the city guarding officials passed out the order and sent for the capital officials to supervise the process. And Zhuan Yun Shi and Tong Pan (transfer envoys and general judges) were also placed. As a result, the rules became more and more precise, and thus the interests returned to the government and the local powers were reduced". [3] Especially "since the central government pacified the neighboring countries, it was rich in financial resources. But all the troops gathered in Beijing, and there was no money left in the local government. All the expenditures of the country came from the Three Departments, so the expenditure was huge".[4] In the early Song Dynasty, the Three Departments were in charge of the fiscal and taxation affairs of the whole country, while the prime minister, who was extremely powerful, had no right to give his opinion. The Northern Song Dynasty adopted the strategy of " relieve the general of his military power". On this basis, the idea of the central government to centralize financial power was very clear, and the measures were concrete and advanced. Accordingly, the economic authority of the local government was quite limited. It should be said that the Song Dynasty was one of the important periods for the further development of social and economic level in China, and the economic development created favorable conditions for the national fiscal

1 *First Draft* (*Chang Bian*), Vol. 2.
2 *First Draft* (*Chang Bian*), Vol. 5.
3 *First Draft* (*Chang Bian*), Vol. 6.
4 *First Draft* (*Chang Bian*), Vol. 34.

and taxation levy. Because of the frequent wars in the borderland areas of Song Dynasty, the huge number of domestic troops and the excessive number of officials at all levels, the government was under a huge financial pressure. In order to cope with the situation, the government took a series of measures to expand the tax sources, even to the extent of financial exhaustion for the people.[1]

From the imperial decrees and specific measures of Emperor Taizu's centralization of financial power in the early Song Dynasty, we can see that his financial ideas can be mainly described as the following: first, to transport all the precious metals such as gold and silver, coins, cloth, silk etc. to the capital, except for the necessary expenditure. Second, the central government dispatches officials to supervise local finance, and sets up Zhuan Yun Shi and Tong Pan (transfer envoys and general judges) to supervise local economy. Third, local revenue and expenditure and accounts should be submitted to the three related ministries for examination and approval. In the early Song Dynasty, the content of centralized financial power was relatively rich. Its core content was to strengthen the central financial power, weaken the financial power of local governments, and strengthen the central financial supervision over local governments.

While centralizing finance, Taizu of Song Dynasty implemented the separation of administrative, military and financial powers in order to prevent the alienation of power. The result is that although Zhong Shu is the prime minister and the chief administrative officer, he basically does not participate in the management of financial affairs. As recorded in the history book, "The central government inherited from the previous dynasties, and set up Three Departments to monitor the financial affairs. The prime minister could not anticipate."[2] Although the separation of administrative power and financial power has received the expected social effect of strengthening the central financial power and preventing the expansion of local forces, which is based on the lessons learned from the late Tang

1 Guo Xiaodong, Ed., *A Brief History of China's Finance and Taxation*, Guangdong Economic Publishing House, 1997, p.128.

2 *Notes of the government and the public since Jianyan Years* Section I, Vol. 19.

Dynasty and the Five Dynasties, this mechanism may inevitably be overshooting. And in the course of its specific operation, it also exposes some insurmountable problems, as pointed out by Fan Zhen of Zhi Jian Yuan (Advisory Department) in the Second Year of Zhihe, Renzong in the Song Dynasty (1055):

> According to the system of Zhou Dynasty, Zhong Zai (the Minister of Personnel) is responsible for the government expenditure. In the Tang Dynasty, the Prime Minister concurrently manages the transportation of salt and iron, Hu Bu (the Ministry of Revenue and Population), and the national revenue and expenditure. This case of the Prime Minister being in charge of the expenditure has existed since ancient times. Nowadays, the Zhong Shu is responsible for the civil affairs, the Shu Mi Yuan (the Privy Council) is responsible for the military issues, and the Three Departments are for the finance. Their powers are separated from each other. Therefore, the people are already poverty-stricken, but the Shu Mi Yuan continue recruiting soldiers, and the Three Departments continue levying taxes. Zhong Shu already noticed the poor situation of the common people, but it doesn't know the way to deliver the poor people by asking the Shu Mi Yuan to reduce conscript and the Three Departments to decrease the taxes. The Zhong Shu is not responsible for the amount of government expenditure...... If the Zhong Shu and the Shu Mi Yuan could deliberate the matter of conscription and taxation with the Three Departments for the purpose of measuring the income and the expenditure, then the people's burden could be lightened, and to be worthy of His Majesty's concern. This is not to make the Zhong Shu and the Privy Secretary to shoulder the responsibility of the Three Departments, but to let them know the yearly government plan to better administer the state affairs.[1]

1 *First Draft* (*Chang Bian*), Vol. 179.

In the Song Dynasty, the defects of the system of the Zhong Shu in charge of administration, the Privy Council in charge of military affairs and the Three Departments in charge of finance were fully exposed under the circumstances of the serious consumption of national power and financial difficulties in the long-term war between the Renzong Dynasty and the Western Xia Dynasty. That is, the separation of powers could not coordinate the collection of taxes and the full supply of war, but restricted each other, affected the efficiency and overall situation, and left the Northern Song Dynasty passive in the war with the Western Xia Sttus. Fan Zhen's proposal that Zhong Shu, the Privy Council must deliberate with the Three Departments about "their financial plans concerning conscription and taxation" is of profound historical background. It is intended to change the operating mechanism of the separation of administrative, military and financial powers since Taizu of the Song Dynasty as one of the necessary means to solve financial difficulties.

In the Song Dynasty, redundant officials, frequent conscription and excessive taxation appeared as early as the Song Zhenzong period. And in the Song Renzong period, the problems accumulated over the years and cannot be resolved overnight. As the First Draft (Chang Bian) points out:

> During the reign of Emperor Zhenzong, there were 912,000 soldiers altogether, and 9,785 royal clan members and officials were paid salary. After Baoyuan years (1038-1040), the conscription expanded, the imperial clan members increased, and the number of officials augmented year by year. As a result, the number of soldiers was 2.159 million, and the number of officials and clans who received salaries was 15,5443. Thus, the salaries and largess increased dramatically. In Jingde years (1004-1007), the emperor offered sacrifices to ancestors at the southern suburbs. The coins, gold, and silk totaled 6.01 million, which later increased to more than 12 million. So, the outlay was bound to be insufficient. Since Tiansheng years (1023-1032), the Emperor was all the time concerned about expenditure,

the number of people who ordered the officials to be ruled down has been counted, requesting the officials to cut the expenses several times. But some departments couldn't comply with this, and there was also the constraint of customs.Finally, nothing was changed, and the proponents were disappointed.

In the more than 20 years from Zhenzong to Renzong Baoyuan years, the number of soldiers supported by the government increased by about 137%, and the number of salaried officials increased by about 58%. The scope and rate of its growth are rare in feudal societies. And the additional grants and awards from the central government are more common. With the increasing national financial expenditure, the government was overwhelmed and couldn't make ends meet. So in this situation, it is necessary for the central government to arrange financial resources as a whole. Although the Song Dynasty somewhat overshot the mark, it did restrain the local government's enthusiasm for economic development and fiscal levy to a certain extent, which can be said to have formed a vicious cycle to a certain extent. (Sic)

In the Southern Song Dynasty, due to the further expansion of military expenditure, it is also very important to arrange financial revenue and expenditure as a whole. The idea of centralizing financial power is deeply rooted, and its main content still revolves around the Prime Minister's financial management and the unified management and supervision of and internal Treasury in the Northern Song Dynasty. For example, at the beginning of Xiaozong Qiandao years (1165-1173), some officials penetratingly pointed out that "Recently, the Prime Minister concurrently holds the position of Shu Mi Shi, which was intended for the Prime Minister to better understand the military affairs. But still the Prime Minister don't know the reason behind the income and expenditure. Therefore, we suggest that we can follow the example of the system in the Tang Dynasty, appointing the Prime Minister to lead the three departments. The Prime Minister is in charge of the income and expenditure of finance and grains, while the Ministry of Revenue and Population governs everything else.[1] The central idea here is to restore the system in which the Prime Minister were in charge of the finance before the Song Dynasty. In the fourth year of Ningzong Jiatai (1204), another minister emphasized that "finance and taxes are of fundamental importance for a country. The ministers should be informed of the financial surplus and deficiency. It is hoped that regulations could completely eradiate deception and concealment."[2] In the mid-Southern Song Dynasty, Wei Liaoweng further pointed out: "Recent reports show that the Guo Yong Shi (national expenditure envoy) has been sent out for the checking of the exact number of taxes and goods. If all the money taken from the national treasury can be strictly verified, Guo Yong Shi could regulate the expenditure, and the Can Ji Guan (advisory official) could check the truthfulness, then the national treasury money will not be abused."[3] Thus, it can be seen that the Southern Song Dynasty inherited the Northern Song Dynasty system. In the Southern Song Dynasty, it is a basic fact that the Prime Minister had no right to control the finance, and even did not know the state's fiscal revenue and expenditure. The ministers of the Southern Song Dynasty repeatedly appealed for the unification of the whole country's financial management by the prime minister, and their main purpose was to control the balance of revenue and expenditure, supervise the illegal acts of deception and concealment of revenue and expenditure, so as to open up sources and reduce expenditure, and arrange the government's fiscal revenue and expenditure as a whole to overcome financial difficulties. The centralization of financial power in the emperor severely weakened the ability of the central government to coordinate economic and social activities, and affected the normal operation of the system. Therefore, some ministers in the Song Dynasty repeatedly called for the prime minister to control the state's revenue and expenditure. In fact, what they demanded was certain restrictions on the emperor's power, which also reflected the contradiction

1 *History of the Song Dynasty* Vol. 162 Records of Officials II.

2 Ibid.

3 *Collection of Heshan* Vol. 21 Policy advice.

between the emperor and the centralized government in power arrangement.

It could be said that since the reform of Shenzong Yuanfeng (1078-1085) in the Northern Song Dynasty, great changes have taken place in the national financial and economic management institutions. Before the restructuring, the Three Departments were in charge of the national finance, and Hu Bu was only responsible for the tribute. After the restructuring of Yuanfeng, the Three Departments were abolished, and the national finance and accounting was returned to Hu Bu. Under Hu Bu, there instituted Zuo Cao and You Cao (the Left and Right Department). The job responsibilities of the former Three Departments were given to Zuo Cao, and the job responsibilities of the former Si Nong Si (Agriculture Affairs Department) were given to You Cao. Compared with the original Three Departments, the financial power of the restructured Hu Bu has been greatly reduced. Although Hu Bu is divided into Zuo Cao and You Cao, only Zuo Cao is affiliated to Hu Bu Shang Shu (minister), while You Cao is not affiliated to him. As a result, Shang Shu, the Minister of Hu Bu, and the Minister who was responsible for the Zuo Cao and You Cao affairs did not belong to the same system. Therefore, Hu Bu Shang Shu could not coordinate the allocation of the part of money and property under the control of the You Cao. That is to say, the reform of Yuanfeng is to divide up the original central financial power and take it over. More than that, there are many affairs directly related to finance and economics in the five ministries and twenty departments, as well as the nine Sis (offices in charge of imprisonment) and four Jians (supervising offices) beyond Hu Bu, many of which were originally under the responsibility of the Three Departments. Now, because they have no subordinate relationship with Hu Nu, Hu Bu has no right to interfere. Especially, Hu Bu can neither interfere with the affairs of Gong Bu (the Ministry of industry), Du Shui Bu (the Ministry of water conservancy), Jun Qi Jian (the Supervising Office of Weapons), and Jiang Zuo Jian (the Office of Building and Craftsmanship), most of which involve high expenses. In fact, Hu Bu has lost the necessary supervision and management of its expenditure. The result is that "the five Caos and Si and Jian could act on its own on money and goods issues"[1], "the other department is in charge of handling affairs, but is not concerned with the expenditure of money; Hu Bu is mainly concerned with allocating funds, regardless of whether the matter is right or not. Each party performs its own function, and its situation is no longer known to each other"[2]. In a word, after Yuanfeng's reform, Hu Bu no longer has the position of the highest financial management organization of the original Three Departments, namely, Ji Sheng (the Ministry of Accounting), whose official name is "Ji Xiang (Minister of Accounting)". Although the reformed Hu Bu is nominally the highest financial management organ in the country, its financial management power has been greatly reduced, which is unfavorable to the planning, allocation and monitoring of the extremely limited national financial resources. Therefore, Sima Guang submitted memorials to the throne on February in the first year of Yuanyou (1086) of Emperor Zhe Zong in the Song Dynasty:

> According to the ancestral system, all the money and grains, after being submitted to the Chang Ping granary, should all be turned over to the Three Departments. Every bit should be recorded in the account book. Those that are not stipulated in the regulation could not be expended without authorization. Therefore, we can know the total amount of expenditure, measure their incomes as well as expenditures, detail their advantages and disadvantages, adjust their rules and regulations, remove the excessive, and replenish the insufficient. We can easily command all the departments, Zhuan Yun Shi, and the counties... So the granary is filled up, with grains more than enough, and the people are not tired out. Both the country and family enjoy stability and harmony. Since the reform of the official system, there have been 24 divisions of six Caos in Shang Shu Sheng (the

1 *Textual Research of Books*, sequel Vol. 33, The financial power of Hu Bu in the Song Dynasty should be unified.

2 *Luancheng Collection* Vol. 41 Request for Hu Bu to Respond to the Three Departments' Case Notes.

Department of State Affairs), three Sis and three Jians, each of which has its own responsibilities. The affairs of the former three divisions have been scattered among the six Caos and the Jians and Sis. Hu Bu can't control the taxes in the whole country. The account book will not be reported to Hu Bu, therefore Hu Bu could not fully know the amount of the taxes and grains. Five Caos each had their own expenditure, and they had the right to command. Hu Bu could not control them. Therefore, Hu Bu cannot know the amount of taxes and grains in the world, and could not measure income for expenditure. Five Caos and the various divisions within it have their own ways of money management. When they apply for the approval, Hu Bu can't interfere. Today's Ministry of Hu Bu is still charge of the responsibilities of the old three divisions. Left Cao is attached to Shang Shu, but Right Cao is not. The country's wealth is divided into halves, and cannot be diverted for other use. All the wealth in the world belongs to the nation, and nobody can exclusively own it. Can anybody stretch the rules and handle it by himself? For example, if a person has money, he himself is in charge of the expenditure. If several others are allowed to share, and everyone trespasses against and take advantage over each other, will that increase the wealth? Therefore, if the rights and interests are not unified, although the country's wealth is as much as water in rivers and seas, there is also the possibility of exhaustion. Much less, people's labor and resources are limited! This is what I am deeply concerned about day in and day out. Today, even though there is not much change, I hereby propose that Shang Shu concurrently hold the positions of Left Cao and Right Cao, and the responsibilities of Shi Lang (Court Attendant) are separated. The money and goods in the responsibility of You Cao should not be withdrawn by Shang Shu without authorization from the throne. The coins, grain, gold and silk submitted by the counties should be commanded by the administrators of the Chang Ping granary. And they should also keep a monthly account and submit it to Six Caos and Si Jian in the Hu Bu. If

> they want to withdraw money and goods, they must first inform Hu Bu. If this request accords with the rules, the money or good requested will be appropriated. It is not allowed that they directly withdraw the money and goods when before the request is approved. Without permission for the HU Bu, no division should provide with either money nor goods. I propose that the money and grains formerly in the responsibility of the Three Divisions should be put in the responsibility of Hu Bu. If this would add to the burden for Hu Bu, I advise that the diverse and complicated affairs of Hu Bu be reduced, and let the idle Cao concurrently hold the post. And they are all affiliated to Hu Bu. Thus, the benefits and rights are unified. If the right person is chosen, then the wealth management problem will be solved.[1]

Sima Guang emphasizes here that the power of Hu Bu after the restructuring is much weaker than that of the Three Departments before the restructuring, and there are some insurmountable shortcomings in the management and supervision of the national finance and economics. First, before the restructuring, the Three Departments was in charge of the financial revenue and expenditure of the whole country. All accounting records are submitted for their audit, so they can control the balance of revenue and expenditure. After the restructuring, the powers of Hu Bu to control the financial revenue and expenditure has been greatly weakened. Many accounting books are no longer audited by them. Therefore, it is impossible for Hu Bu to comprehensively control the balance of revenue and expenditure. Second, before the restructuring, except for the Changping Granary under the Sinong Si (the Agricultural Division), the surplus or deficiency of money and goods were coordinated by the Three Departments; after the restructuring, the Minister of Hu Bu did not participate in the Right Cao's affairs, and the financial power was divided into two parts, so the surplus or deficiency of money and

1 *The Collected Works of Sima Guang*, Vol. 51, On the Necessity of Unified Management of Money and Grains.

goods could not be reasonably allocated. Third, before the restructuring, the Three departments had the right to examine and approve the expenditure of money and grain in various departments, and effectively controlled the expenditure beyond the provisions; after the restructuring, Hu Bu partially lost the right, resulting in the arbitrary withdrawal of money and goods by Five Caos and some departments without any supervision. In a word, after the restructuring, the functions of the Hu Bu in controlling the balance of the state's fiscal revenue and expenditure, the overall coordination of surplus and deficiency, and the audit and supervision of the use of money and goods have been greatly weakened. The abovementioned deficiency in the operational mechanism of institutions is summarized by Sima Guang as "incongruence between interests and powers". That is, poor co-operation among different branches of an administration resulted in the unreasonable allocation and serious drain of the state's financial resources, inefficiency and more difficulties in national finance.

Faced with these specific financial situations in Song Dynasty, Sima Guang put forward specific reform measures. He mainly proposed that the power of Hu Bu Shang Shu should be expanded, so that he could concurrently lead both Left and Right Caos. And the money and goods in the responsibility of Right Cao could only be administered after Shang Shu proposed to the emperor and got his consent. In this way, Hu Bu Shang Shu can coordinate the allocation and can effectively control the balance of fiscal revenue and expenditure at the macro level. Secondly, the accounts of coins, grains, gold and silk in local prefectures must be submitted to Hu Bu for examination and verification every month; if they want to withdraw, they must first submit the request to Hu Bu for approval. Through the approval in advance and supervision afterward, Hu Bu can control the expenditure right of money and goods more effectively, thus achieving the goal of saving financial expenditure, reducing management costs and improving the utilization rate of finance. Whether it is to control the balance of the state's fiscal revenue and expenditure, or to coordinate allocation between deficiencies and surplus, or to check and supervise the use of money and goods, its focus is to solve the actual financial difficulties of the government.

Shortly after Sima Guang's submission, the central government adopted his proposal, stipulating that Hu Bu Shang Shu should be responsible for both the Left and Right Cao's affairs. It can be said that the central government attaches great importance to his proposal. In July of the first year of Zhe Zong's Yuanyou (1086), "Hu Bu's words are as follows: 'The money and grain of various Prefectures, who used to be reported to the Three Divisions, were sent to the Zhuang Yun Shi for account examination yesterday; the ledger of Changping granary, which was reported to Si Nong Si Jian (Agriculture) in the past, was sent to the Ti Ju Si for account examination yesterday; and account book of Beijing warehouses, which used to be separately managed by Li Bu (the Ministry of Rites), Bing Bu (the Ministry of War), Gong Cao (the Ministry of Construction), etc., was converted to the management of Hu Bu.' From then on, the legislation proposed by Sima Guang was adopted."[1] Besides, the central government also stipulates that "military weapons, Jiang Zuo (construction), Shao Fu, Du Shui Jian, Tai Fu, Guanglusi and other places should be responsible for application, construction, repair, build, repair, planning, material purchase, money collection, mintage, etc. They should first apply for Hu Bu to examine and approve the amount, and supervise the Si Jian inspectors to assign the job to craftsmen according to their merits and limitations. If the inland waterway defense is in urgent need for materials, it should also be Hu Bu to inspect and approve"[2]. In this way, "the three inspecting departments, Du Shui (flood prevention), Jun Qi (Weapons), and Jiang Zuo (palace architecture), are all under the Li Bu and Hu Bu, so that the Hu Bu can decide its feasibility and cost, while Gong Bu (the Ministry of Works) judges its quality and speed. Since the feasibility and cost are decided by Hu Bu, it cannot shirk its responsibility for injuring the people and damaging property; since quality and speed are decided by Gong Bu, it will not escape the blame for any failure"[3].

1 *First Draft* (*Chang Bian*), Vol. 383.
2 *First Draft* (*Chang Bian*), Vol. 422.
3 Ibid.

Obviously, there is an intention to centralize financial rights. After Zhe Zong Shao Sheng of the Song Dynasty (1094-1098), there was a period of time when the Right Cao of Hu Bu was still commanded by the Right Cao Shilang, who had direct access to the ruling class. But from the Southern Song Dynasty, it basically followed Sima Guang's idea of financial centralization. Although the Hu Bu Shang Shu was not permanently established, the two Shi Langs were in charge of Left and Right Cao affairs. As for the proposal by the Jian Cha Yu Shi (Supervisory Censor) Shangguan Jun of "inspection of the warehouse by the Hu Bu and the Tai Fu Si", according to Li Tao's textual research, it is not known "whether the Court adopted his opinions or not".

From the above description, we can see clearly that the idea of centralized financial power in Song Dynasty mainly centered on three aspects: first, to coordinate the centralization and decentralization of financial management between central and local governments; second, the prime minister was in charge of the national finance, and the internal Treasury must be integrated into the unified management and supervision of financial institutions; third, the Hu Bu after the restructuring, like the Three Departments before the restructuring, had a wide range of financial management authority. It is not difficult to see that the starting point of these three aspects is relatively consistent, that is, starting from the level of institutional operation mechanism, through the centralization of financial power to achieve an effective overall allocation of national money and property, the government can maintain the balance of fiscal revenue and expenditure, prevent illegal acts on fiscal revenue and expenditure, increase income and reduce expenditure, thus solving financial difficulties. This idea of centralized financial power was of certain positive significance at that time because of redundancy of officials, soldiers, and expenditure, huge war expenditure and limited national financial revenue. However, from the specific content of these three aspects, the operability of the former two is relatively limited, and only the third point has been better implemented. In the entire Song Dynasty, the local financial power was highly concentrated in the central government. In addition to the fact that in a relatively short period of time, the accounting department and the utility department of the central government were concurrently led by the Prime Minister to control the country's wealth and taxes, save money according to the system and guard against fraud and concealment, the Prime Ministers in other times participated in some financial management and supervision, but they were regional and temporary, which seemed weak and powerless. They were basically in the condition of "the disposition, withdrawal and use of the world's financial revenue, including the emperor, court, and Hu Bu's use of money and property, are not known to each other"[1]. There has always been no unified body to manage and supervise all aspects of the expenditure. In the Song Dynasty, a considerable part of the country's money and property was stored in the internal treasury, which was directly controlled by the emperor. The purpose of the emperor's personal control of the country's large amount of money and property is to force the accounting department to rely on the imperial power to a certain extent, so as to enable the emperor to control and supervise the state's financial revenue and expenditure effectively and directly. When military expenditure, redundant official expenditure, redundant expenditure or provisional huge expenditure caused the fiscal deficit, the emperor balanced the money out of the treasury. The emperor played a significant role in adjusting finance, especially extraordinary funds, by personally controlling the wealth of the internal treasury. Because the Treasury was the key to the national finance, in order to prepare for the use of the military, the emperor of the Song Dynasty "was concerned that the accounting officials could not save the money, thus leading to the deficiency in urgent times, and so the government had to raise taxes on the people"[2]. Therefore, the number of money and goods stored in the Treasury was strictly confidential, and the court can make nothing of it. The Minister of Accounting also refused to discuss the state's fiscal revenue and expenditure. As Su Zhi said in the

1 *History of the Song Dynasty* Vol. 179 Shi Huo Zhi II·Chapter One.
2 Ibid.

Accounting Records of Yuanyou," As for the savings managed by Nei Fu and You Cao, and the storage of the world's sealed storehouses, which are not under the control of the Three Divisions, they will not be recorded in the accounting book." [1] In the thirty-second year of Gaozong Shaoxing in the Southern Song Dynasty (1162), Huang Zhong, a courtesy waiter, said, "Today, half of the taxes is incorporated into the royal property, and the officials cannot count the profit and loss." [2] It is self-evident that although the ministers of Song Dynasty emphasized from time to time that the internal Treasury should be managed and supervised by the financial institutions and the rights and interests should be unified, in fact, this requirement undoubtedly touched the power of the Supreme ruler, the emperor, to directly control and supervise the state's total revenue and expenditure. Therefore, under the premise of the continuous strengthening of the imperial power, it is difficult to achieve that goal.

In short, under the restriction of the highly intensified centralization of feudal autocracy in the Song Dynasty, the supreme power of management and supervision of finance and economics in the Song Dynasty was in the hands of the emperor. The emperor read the accounting records personally, inquired about major financial matters, tightly controlled a large amount of money and goods in the internal treasury, in order to cope with shifting events by sticking to a fundamental principle, thus adjusting the balance of the state's fiscal revenue and expenditure. When military expenditure, redundant officials and redundant expenditure caused the budget deficit and the accountants cannot make ends meet, the emperor gave them money from the treasury. The emperor monopolized power. Even when he was wise and decisive, he could not attend to all the affairs, let alone the fatuous monarch, who would certainly aggravate the financial difficulties. So in the Song Dynasty, none of the court ministers knew the total revenue and expenditure of the whole country. Even the accounting ministers "could not know the amount

1 *The Second Luancheng Collection*, Vol. 15.

2 *Zhu Wengong's Collection of Documents*, Vol. 91, Epitaph of Huang Gong, Bachelor of Duanming Palace.

of money and grain in the whole country"[1], which led to the confusion of the state finance and economy, "the management and collection not being known to all"[2]. People of insight always appeal to the prime minister to consul the state plan and to supervise the unified management of the internal treasury, but the effect is negligible. On the other hand, the emperor did not have to and could not personally inquire about the management and supervision of the daily complicated and trivial financial revenue and expenditure, so he handed it over to the central and local departments concerned. Generally speaking, the Song Dynasty's central financial consisted of the accounting department (Three Departments or Hu Bu), the internal Treasury and the imperial court, whose management and supervision are independent and mutually exclusive. Local Transport Department, Sentencing Department and Changping Department are also responsible for different financial revenues and expenditures, each of which belongs to different departments of the central government. This decentralization is conducive to the mutual restraint between departments, to prevent the loss of power to others, and embodies the principle of not allowing one department to monopolize the supervision of financial management, limited scope of responsibility and mutual restraint.

The financial management and supervision in Song Dynasty was dominated by the emperor, while the power of the officials of the relevant departments were decentralized and mutually restricted. This kind of operation mechanism includes management and supervision in the unity of opposites between centralization and decentralization, which is consistent with the strength and weakness of the military and the internal and external dimensions of politics. Of course, under the specific historical background of Song Dynasty, this mechanism has its reasonable side. In the war environment, it is difficult to make budgets and the planning is relatively weak. The emperor coped with temporary expenditures through the

1 *The Collection of Sima's Documents*, Vol. 51, The Management of Money and Grain should be Unified.

2 *History of the Song Dynasty* Vol. 179 Shi Huo Zhi II·Chapter One.

internal treasury, which is a simple and effective way.[1]

The central government of Song Dynasty, especially the emperor, firmly controlled the financial power. Another reason that cannot be ignored is that it developed and perfected the accounting system on the basis of that in the Tang Dynasty. The national tax revenue in Song Dynasty was mainly reflected in the accounting records. In almost every period, a complete accounting record was compiled. It focused on recording and assessing the financial revenue and expenditure of the whole country, analyzing and comparing the problems of fiscal and taxation management, revenue and expenditure, in order to achieve the purpose of financial management. Specifically, its analysis mainly includes income analysis, that is, that of the relationship between household registration and taxation income at that time; comparative analysis of revenue and expenditure, that is, analysis of fiscal expenditure in the year mainly on the taxation principle of basing expenditures upon the income; expenditure analysis, that is, analysis of military expenditure, salary of officials and expenditure of public construction projects in the year. In addition to these routine accounting analyses, the relevant departments also carry out special analysis of revenue and expenditure at any time at the request of the emperor. At that time, the Song Dynasty fiscal and taxation accounting report had a special name, generally known as "Zhuang", or "Zhang". The accounting report should be reported by the governments level by level, until the relevant departments of the central government. At that time, the accounting records were one of the contents of the performance appraisal of governments at all levels. If it was found that the accounting reports did not conform to the actual situation, the responsible persons would be punished to a certain extent.[2]

According to the Accounting Records, which started in the Tang Dynasty at the latest, in the second year of the reign of Tang Xianzong Yuanhe (807),

1 Fang Baozhang: On the Thought of Concentrating Financial Power in Song Dynasty. *Research on Chinese Economic History*, No. 4, 2008.

2 See Guo Xiaodong, *A Brief History of China's Finance and Taxation*, Guangdong Economic Publishing House, 1997, pp. 149-150.

Prime Minister Li Jifu wrote the National Accounting Book of Yuanhe Years, and submitted it to Emperor Xianzong. The Number of household registration, prefectures and counties, income and expenditure of each year, number of officials and number of soldiers etc. were listed in the Book, and compared with those in the period of Emperor Xuanzong Tianbao years in Tang Dynasty. To be sure, the Accounting Records of the Song Dynasty was compiled in accordance with Li Jifu's National Accounting Book. According to Volume 185 of Yuhai, there were Jingde Accounting Record, Qingli Accounting Record, Huangyou Accounting Record, Zhiping Accounting Record, Xining Accounting Record, Yuanyou Accounting Record, Xiangfu Accounting Record, Xuanhe Accounting Record, Shaoxing Accounting Record, Qiandao Accounting Record, Shaoxi Accounting Record, Qingyuan Accounting Record, etc. in the Song Dynasty. It can be seen that the Accounting Record has become an indispensable part of the economic activities of the central and local governments at that time.

These practices in the Song Dynasty were further supplemented and improved thereafter, such as the Qing Dynasty treasury as the "world's treasure trove". "All provinces submit land tax, salt, tariffs, miscellaneous taxes every year. Except for those retained for the province's expenditure, all will be to the central government". [1] As the money became a financial revenue controlled by the central government, its use includes the disaster relief mentioned earlier, and the railway funds, which are as much as 2 million Liang a year (including 1.2 million Liang raised by the treasury and 800,000 Liang shared by the provinces). [2]

4. Chinese Feudal Government's Laws and Regulations on Social Economy

The central government's laws and regulations on social economy in feudal society of China involve various aspects. Among them, the ranking of "scholar,

1 Guangxu, *Book of Classical Cases of the Qing Dynasty*, Vol. 182, Hubu·Storage · Treasury.

2 Shi Zhihong, *Statistics of Income and Expenditure of Treasury and Inventory of Hu Bu of the Qing Dynasty*, Fujian People's Publishing House, 2008, pp. 29-30.

farmer, worker and businessman", i.e. "different people have different business", and the series of supporting measures such as the government's restrictions on the political status of businessmen, the government's foster and encouragement of the self-cultivating peasant economy, and the government's policy of permitting land sale but not encouraging it. These are the full manifestation of the social functions of the feudal state to intervene in social redistribution through taxation and various economic policies. At the same time, the government's restrictions on businessmen's official career, clothing and even travel are consistent with the feudal society. [1] "Emphasizing agriculture and restraining commerce" is a basic national policy of the feudal government to regulate social economy. Under such a social background, agriculture is regarded as the "root" by the government, while industry and commerce, especially commerce, are regarded as the "end".

The government's cultivation and protection of the self-cultivating peasant economy is a basic state policy in the feudal society of China, especially so in the early period of dynasty change and the period of social reform. Its social effect is often the so-called "flourishing age" in the history. In age of the "rule of Emperor Wen Di and Emperor Jing Di" during the Western Han Dynasty, "the governance of non-interference" was implemented as measures to protect individual small producers. When Emperor Wu Di was enthroned, the grand occasion was:

> During the seventy years of Hanxing, the country experienced a peaceful period of time. The common people are self-sufficient if they don't suffer from floods and droughts. The granaries of the country are full, and the government treasury has a favorable balance. The string of money in

1 As early as the founding of the Western Han Dynasty, according to *Records of the Grand Historian*, Vol. 30 Ping Zhun Shu, it was recorded that "The world has been peaceful. Gao Zu Liu Bang forbade businessmen to ride and wear silk clothes. And they were humiliated by heavy taxation". This situation has not been seriously implemented in the actual process. In some cases, the participation of businessmen in imperial government is ubiquitous. However, as a political attitude, it can be seen all the time, at least in the decrees and legal provisions of feudal society.

the Capital Treasury is rotten and the amount of money can't be counted. [1]

It is these measures to protect the economy of individual small producers that made the accumulation of social wealth in the Han Dynasty reach a new level in history. It has laid a certain material foundation for them to pacify the Huns in the period of Emperor Wu Di in the Han Dynasty, open up the Western Regions and the Silk Road, carry out some large-scale public works, including large-scale water conservancy and urban construction, open the Silk Road with foreign political, economic and cultural links, and initially establish the basic territory of a unified centralized state.

In the Ninth Year of Taihe in Northern Wei Dynasty (485 AD.), the farmland equalization system, which was widely implemented in the Northern Qi Dynasty, Northern Zhou Dynasty, Sui Dynasty and the early Tang Dynasty, was carried out by the feudal state in the form of policies and laws to protect and cultivate the national self-farming economy as the main content of the farmland system. The "prosperity of Kaiyuan" in the period of Xuanzong in Tang Dynasty is the concrete manifestation of the full exertion of the economic potential of the self-cultivating peasants under the system of equalizing farmland.

One of the most important reasons for the appearance of a flourishing Tang Dynasty was that the government took measures to implement the system of land equalization, which made the self-farming economy develop significantly. With the collapse of the system of land equalization in the middle and late Tang Dynasty, a large number of self-employed peasants went bankrupt or ran away from the famine-stricken area, and the prosperity of the Tang Dynasty ended. The emergence of the Anshi Rebellion in the Xuanzong period of the Tang Dynasty and the subsequent Fanzhen separatist regime are good illustrations. Zhu Yuanzhang, the founding emperor of the Ming Dynasty, was born in the lower strata of society. He attached great importance to agricultural production.

1 *Records of the Grand Historian*, Vol. 30 Ping Zhun Shu.

In the twenty-fifth year of Hongwu (1392), Zhu Yuanzhang "instructed Gong Bu (the Ministry of Works) to issue documents, requesting the people to plant more mulberries and red dates. Two mu of seedlings are planted in each li, and manpower is provided from every one hundred households to carry firewood and open up wasteland. After ploughing and burning three times, seeds will be planted. When the seedlings are three feet high, they are planted separately. Every ridge (Long) is five square feet wide. Each household has 200 plants in the first year, 400 plants in the next year, and 600 plants altogether in three years. The planting process will be examined by several departments, and the number of plant will be recorded submitted to the emperor. For those violators, the whole family will be sent into exile. Kill (guilty) people in a human way, and they will not be angry even if they die".[1] In the early Ming Dynasty, the social benefits of such practices were not necessarily obvious, but the protection and attention paid by the central government to the individual small agricultural economy and its family sideline handicraft industry economy were quite manifest.

The vigor of the self-farming economy in the basic form of "men farming and women weaving" or "farming in sunny days and weaving in rainy days" ensures the government's tax and corvee fairly well, and is therefore the basis for the prosperity of the society. Some books hold that the production form of "men farming and women weaving" or "farming in sunny days and weaving in rainy days" hinders the development of social economy, especially commodity economy. This idea is biased. Because this mode of production not only is for self-sufficiency, but also has a certain function of exchange. At the same time, individual small producers also have a certain motivation to engage in commodity exchange. In the feudal society, the handicraft products produced by individual peasant households and some of the crop products they sold accumulated, which were often one of the main sources of commodity exchange in feudal society. Their contribution to the social economy at that time was undeniable. Under

1 *Notes at the End of Winter*, Vol. 10.

the influence of the state's policy of emphasizing agriculture and restraining commerce, the government advocates the social values of " Those who become rich by farming are superior, and those who become rich by doing business are inferior." Therefore, "making money by doing business, but hoarding wealth by farming"[1]. The private businessmen often have a preference for land investment[2], which has almost become the consensus of the government and general public in China for thousands of years, and even has a certain impact on today's society. But such an idea is not conducive to the concentration of social wealth, and the restrictions on land mobility after the Qin and Han Dynasties are becoming less and less. This is the so-called "Within one thousand years, 800 owners will alternately own the same piece of land ".

In the feudal society of China, the central government often held a basic idea of governing the country: leave the wealth with the people, especially in the early stage of the establishment of a new dynasty or in the period of relatively fair and clear administration. As designed by Mencius Teng Wen Gong I, when there were surplus grain and cloth, the peasants would "trade with each another". The surplus grain and cloth here refer to articles and by-products produced by individual small-scale production agriculture and their families. Besides ensuring the maintenance of simple agricultural reproduction and population reproduction, and fulfilling the tax and corvee stipulated by the government, there are still some surplus in circulation, which is very important for stabilizing the production and living conditions of the direct producers. Not only that, but it was also one of the basic conditions for feudal society to ensure economic vitality. Therefore, under the centralized system of "great unification" autocracy for a long time in China, the strength of the state is mainly reflected in the government's protection of the self-farming economy and the environment provided for the living conditions of the self-farming economy, rather than just the amount of resources allocated

1 *Records of the Grand Historian*, Vol. 129 Biographies of Merchants.

2 Refer to Wei Mingkong's Economic Functions of the State in Pre-modern China, *Academic Monthly*, No. 8, 2006.

directly by the state. On the contrary, in the Qin and Sui dynasties, the state acquired enormous wealth of national resources at the expense of the vast self-farming economy. Although it achieved unprecedented strength of the state and concentrated social wealth, it was difficult to sustain for a long time because of the lack of a strong economic and class foundation. Finally, it ended up being the short-lived dynasty providing profound lessons for the future generations.[1] In the early period of Han and Tang Dynasties, when the government seemingly adopted the rule of noninterference, it was one of the important periods in which the social economy had made great progress. At the beginning of Zhen Guan (627-649), Emperor Taizong of the Tang Dynasty said, "The rule of monarchy must first let the people live. If you harm people to provide for yourself, it is like cutting the meat on a person's thighs to fill his own stomach. Even though he is full, he will die."[2] This is a representative idea. "If the people are rich, the rulers will surely be rich."[3] It is the basic idea of the supreme decision-maker in the time of national peace and order, that is, the idea of leaving the wealth with the people, which almost became the theoretical basis for some thinkers and politicians in feudal society to oppose extravagant expropriation and excessive convergence. Under this basic idea, to govern by not interfering, to lighten the burden of the

1 Tang Taizong, with the reputation of a wise emperor, summed up the profound lessons of the short-lived Qin and Sui dynasties: "When Emperor Sui Yang Di was in power, he enslaved the people to satisfy his personal desires, collected all the treasures of the world for his personal enjoyment, selected beautiful women from all over the world for his personal pleasure, and sought exotic treasures for his personal amusement. The palace he lived in was extremely magnificent and luxurious, and the pavilions he built were grand and beautiful. This will inevitably lead to various servitude and constant warfare. In addition, outside the court, the other great powers were always ready to prey on it; within the court, the ministers were vicious and treacherous. In this way, those flattering people are bound to be successful, while those loyal and upright people are bound to die. Throughout the court, the monarchs and ministers deceived each other. It is the general trend for the masses to live in dire poverty, and it is unavoidable for the country to split up." (*Zheng Guan Zheng Yao*, Vol. 1, Jun Dao: The Way to be an Emperor)

2 *Zheng Guan Zheng Yao*, Vol. 1, Jun Dao.

3 *The Analects of Confucius*, Yan Yuan.

people and to cut down the unnecessary projects of the government are the most important ways for the top decision makers to understand the long-term stability of society from the perspective of maintaining normal production and economic order. " Everything must be done based on the fundamentals. The state takes the people as the fundamentals and the people take food and clothing as the fundamentals. In order to solve the problem of food and clothing for the common people, it is essential not to violate the agricultural time. Those who will not miss the opportunity can achieve their goals simply by being simple and quiet in front of the monarch. If you wage wars frequently, constantly going in for large-scale construction, how can you guarantee the time for farming?"[1] In the Taizong period of the Tang Dynasty, the practice of neglecting Fu and collecting wealth from the people succeeded for quite a long time. For example, during "Tang Gaozong's administration in the Yonghui years (650-655), the people enjoyed a peaceful and prosperous life, bearing similarity with that of the Zhenguan years (627-649)".[2] At the beginning of the reign of Emperor Xuanzong of Tang Dynasty, he repeatedly emphasized that "good governance in ancient times attaches great importance to sufficient food provision; if you want to enrich the country, you must first bring benefits to people".[3] Xuanzong of Tang Dynasty was able to carry it out in his later practice of governing the country, especially in the Kaiyuan period (713-741). He deeply realized that "the way to govern the country is to bring people prosperity and peace".[4] In the feudal society, the policy of "noninterference" adopted by the highest decision-makers in protecting the economy of individual small-scale production agriculture and its family sideline handicraft industry often received all kinds of social and economic benefits, which was also praised by politicians in history.

1 *Zhenguan Zhengyao*, Vol. 8 Farming.
2 *Zi Zhi Tong Jian* Vol. 199.
3 *Ce Fu Yuan Gui*, Vol. 497 Bang Ji Bu.
4 *Collection of Tang Dazhao Decrees* Vol. 74 Edict of the Ceremony of Emperor's Leading Princes to Till the Field in the 23rd Year of Kaiyuan.

In the basic state policy of emphasizing agriculture and restraining commerce in feudal society, the government adopted a method of combining encouragement and restriction on commerce, trying to make commerce develop but not affect the degree of agricultural production. On the whole, it was only one of the means by which the government regulated and controlled the economic operation, but not real attack and restriction on commerce or businessmen. In the Qin and Han Dynasties, measures were taken to involve the businessmen and businessmen in the relevant economic activities of the country, and even to absorb some of them into the ruling class. These are not individual cases.[1] And this is a common practice in the whole feudal society. The "Gao Min Qian" once adopted in the Han Dynasty was a heavy blow to the private industry and commerce. As a result, most of the people above the "middle class" went bankrupt.[2] Although it was an extreme measure to restrict and crack down on the private industry and commerce, it reflected the preference of the feudal government in the choice of policies and regulations. As for the strength and effect of the government's crackdown on the smuggling of proprietary goods, it is often directly related to the good or bad governance of officials and the determination of policymakers. During the Ming and Qing Dynasties, the tea-horse exchange was specifically controlled by the relevant government departments. During Zhu Yuanzhang's period, his son-in-law Ouyang Lun once requested 50 wagons for tea smuggling. When crossing the river in Lanzhou, Ouyang Lun was reported by the upright and outspoken inspector and was sentenced to death.[3] This is enough to show that the central government in the early Ming Dynasty is relatively powerful in cracking down on smuggling activities and implementing the policies.

In the economic functions of the feudal government, the governments of the successive dynasties have clear legal provisions on the issuance and repayment

1 *Records of the Grand Historian*, Vol. 129 Biographies of Merchants.

2 *Han Shu* (*The Book of Han Dynasty*), Vol. 24 Shi Huo Zhi II.

3 The Record of Hongwu Years during the Reign of Taizu of the Ming Dynasty, Vol. 253.

of folk usury[1]. According to Records of the Grand Historian (Shi Ji), Chronicle of Meritorious Statesmen of the Emperor Gaozu of Han Dynasty, there were many cases in the Han Dynasty of "abolishing the duke status or the nationality" because of "taking usury interest more than is allowed by the law". Many times in Tang Dynasty, the interest rate of private and government lending was regulated, and nobles and officials were not allowed to engage in usury. This is only one aspect. In fact, because of the profitability of usury, it is very common for the government to participate in usury business activities. For example, in the Sui Dynasty it stipulated that governments at all levels could issue and collect debts with "Gong Xie Qian (government money for lending)" or engage in other business activities, and their income could be used for officials' salaries, meals, candles and repair costs.[2] In the early Tang Dynasty, following the situation of Sui Dynasty, rich households were appointed to the position of "Zhuo Qian Ling Shi", and they raised debts from the government and used the money to engage in business activities for governments at all levels.[3] Originally, the government of Tang Dynasty had stipulated that the annual interest rate of government lending should not exceed 40%, but in fact, the actual restraint was relatively weak. Sometimes the interest rate of government lending was as high as 500%, which often became an intolerable tyranny for the people, and had a negative impact on the normal social and economic order. Of course, the existence of Gong Xie Qian (government money for lending) indicates its rationality to some extent. The common people are powerless in the face of inexorable disasters and diseases. Thus, usury capital such as Gong Xie Qian serves as a kind of buffer in the special environment, or its existence has a certain rationality.

1 *Tang Hui Yao*, Vol. 88 Miscellaneous Records: Emperor Xuanzong's February edict in the 26th year of Kaiyuan (728) of the Tang Dynasty "In recent years, public and private usury have made a lot of profits, which have harmed the poor, and things need to be changed. From now on, the interest of all the usury should be no more than 40 percent. And the interest of official usury should be no more than 50 percent."

2 *The Book of Sui Dynasty*, Vol. 24 Shi Huo Zhi.

3 *Tang Hui Yao* (*Historical records of the systems in the Tang Dynasty*), Vol. 91-93.

Similarly, successive governments have attached great importance to local market management. The maintenance of market order and the appointment of officials in Qin and Han Dynasties were highly valued by the central government. Another example is that in the Tang Dynasty, "according to the state and county clerk laws, there sets up an official in the Da Du Du Fu (Office of Commander in Chief), who is in charge of inner-city transactions, prohibition of crimes, and administer the general judgment of municipal affairs. There also sets up one assistant officer, being responsible for the decision of market affairs. There also sets up one Zuo, one Shi, and three Shi, who are responsible for branch inspection respectively." [1] In addition, the prefectures and counties also set up "municipal officials of Ling and Cheng, who are in charge of business and trade in the market and banning illegal acts".[2] At that time, there established the regional avoidance system, which stipulated that the local people should not act as the prefecture and county officials, so as to prevent them from using their powers to play favouritism and commit irregularities for their relatives and friends. These measures are undoubtedly reasonable to some degree. At that time, it was also stipulated that bonds must be issued for slaves and large-scale livestock trading. This kind of bond is relatively mature. As we can see from Danhuang and Turpan documents unearthed today, the bonds must indicate the names of the buyers and sellers, time, place, identity, guarantor's testimony, basic information of the slaves or livestock, and then be examined by the municipal securities issuing organs. After the bonds are signed and sealed by the officials, the securities must be delivered to the buyers. In Tang, Song, Ming and Qing Dynasties, there were clear provisions on the quality, price, specifications and commercial tax levy of commodities entering the market. It can be seen that the market at that time was quite standardized.

With the development of commodity economy, the market in China has changed a lot in history. One of the most noteworthy changes is that the early urban market

1 *Tang Hui Yao* (*Historical Records of the Systems in the Tang Dynasty*), Vol. 86 Market.
2 *Six Codes of Laws in the Tang Dynasty*, Vol. 30 Prefecture and County Officials.

was of a closed management mode. Since the middle and late Tang Dynasty, it has gradually broken the closed management mode of fixed-time and fixed-location of urban market, and formed a developing open market mode with expanding space and time. At the latest, there was a night market in the Tang Dynasty, which broke the strict rule of the early Tang Dynasty that "market opens at noon". Such themes as "The night market in Yangzhou city is busy, with thousands of lights shining on the clouds. There are women with bright makeup everywhere inside and outside the high buildings. Those pleasure-seeking tourists come in succession." and " At night, the lights on the stone bridge are like the stars shining on the Milky Way, and the masts on the cruise ships on the river outside the city are like stars in the sky." had become one of the economic life themes extolled by poets of the Tang Dynasty. In the mid and late Tang Dynasty, cities and even the capital city market "opening at noon" and "closing before sunset" have been replaced by round-the-clock markets, which have undergone great changes in space and time. At that time, shops could be set up in the residence area, and even the layout of the city had changed greatly. For example, Ya Cheng of Yang Zhou and Luocheng outside Zi Cheng had become commercial districts. The functions of the city were changing, that is, its economic functions became even more prominent. In particular, it is worth mentioning that a new trading place, Cao Shi (grass market), has emerged in places where residents are concentrated outside the city. Liu Yuxi describes in his poem "Guan Shi (Visiting the Market)" that "When the dawn cracks, people hurry to the market. When it is noon, people gather together for trade. Everybody strives to be the first. When people finish the trading, it is already sunset." In such a Cao Shi, "there are different areas for different goods, and the price is listed." As a result, new towns continue to emerge, and their economic functions outweigh their political and military functions.[1] After Song Dynasty, night market became one of the important contents of city commercial

1 Wei Mingkong: Small-scale Peasant Economy and Market in the Transitional Period of Chinese Feudal Society. *Research on Chinese Economic History*, No. 2, 1996.

market.[1] According to experts' estimates, in the late Northern Song Dynasty, there were more than 3,000 large and small cities. Although the effective ruling territory of the Southern Song Dynasty was reduced, there would be no less than 1,300 towns in its territory. Compared with the distribution density of the Tang Dynasty and its predecessors, the urban layout of the Song Dynasty and its later dynasties gradually formed a closed-net structure.[2] From Zhang Zeduan's Riverside Scene at Qingming Festival in the Song Dynasty, we can clearly view the prosperous streets both inside and outside Kaifeng at that time. It is well-known that in the Ming and Qing Dynasties, Beijing was very active in business. In addition, in Nanjing, Suzhou, Hangzhou, Guangzhou and so on, the industrial and commercial economy was quite prosperous. Especially at that time, the development of industrial and commercial towns in the whole country was very rapid. At the same time, the market trade activities in rural areas and the market in urban areas complement each other. In the Qing Dynasty, if the conservative figures of 700 rural fairs per province were used, there would be no less than 20,000 rural fairs in the whole country. In this way, a countryside market network covering all parts of the country has been formed.

In short, during the Song, Yuan, Ming and Qing Dynasties, the trend of the development of rural fairs in China was to intensify their distribution, diversify their forms and regularize their transactions, thus becoming the basic network for connecting urban and rural commodity trade and forming a larger regional market.[3] In this way, the network system of urban-rural trade in late feudal society has been formed, the radius and frequency of trade is increasing, and the development of social commodity economy has become an area of great concern to academic

1 *Record of Life in the Capital Dong Jing* Vol. 3: "Night market just closes at midnight, and in the early morning it opens again. And there are people milling about the market around the clock."

2 See Li Chuntang, New Pattern of Urban External Space of Cities in Song Dynasty, *Journal of Hunan Normal University*, No. 4, 1990.

3 Leng Pengfei: *Research on the Form of Commodity Economy in Ancient Chinese Society*, Zhonghua Book Company, 2002, pp. 301-302.

circles at home and abroad today. Even so, the development of commodity economy at that time still operated within the feudal social and economic structure, and did not have a fundamental corrosive effect on the feudal economy. If we say that the new relations of production emerged at that time, that was at best the germination of capitalism. This is our basic estimate and judgment for the later period of our feudal society.

Our feudal society's foreign trade often has a very strong political, diplomatic and even military color. In each dynasty which regards itself as the "heavenly empire", the preferences for foreign businessmen who come in the name of "paying tribute" or those who accompany the envoys are very obvious, which makes the tribute trade of foreign businessmen profitable.

During the reign of Emperor Taizong, Zhenguan years (727-649), the countries in the Western Regions rushed to send envoys to pay tribute to the Tang Dynasty. Wei Zheng, the minister, admonished Taizong, "If the merchants are allowed to come and go freely, the border people will benefit; if we treat them as guests, our country will suffer." [1] Wei Zheng first directly associates it with foreign businessmen, which really strikes home. As a matter of fact, allowing foreign businessmen to engage in private free trade in border areas is very meaningful for economic development and commodity circulation, and local residents will benefit from it. On the contrary, when foreign envoys, together with businessmen, came to pay tribute, the government of the Tang Dynasty first considered imperial facade, the protocols, safety control, and generous awards. The government of the Tang Dynasty first weighed the political benefits rather than the economic benefits, which must lead to a waste of manpower and money. Even Taizong of Tang Dynasty, known as the wise emperor of thousands of years, is no exception. In stark contrast with this, the government imposes strict restrictions on local businessmen. If we take the Tang Dynasty as an example, we can conclude that in the long time of feudal society, China implemented the basic national

1 *The Book of Tang* Vol. 71 Biography of Wei Zheng.

policy of closed up inside the country and opening up to the outside world[1], and the international trade between China and foreign countries has been in a non-corresponding relationship for a long time. Because the major concern of the foreign policy of the Tang Dynasty was political influence, and strict control of the local residents was its basic national policy, the Tang government strictly prohibited the local residents from going abroad from beginning to end, that is to say, to implement strict internal closure. The internal closure of the Tang Dynasty seriously affected the normal trade activities of the people, and also further contributed to the expansion of the complacency of the empire, which made the rulers of the Tang Dynasty keen on the "Tian Ke Han (Heavenly Khan)" status and maintain the majesty of "Tian Ke Han", which was not conducive to fully absorbing the nutrition of foreign cultures. This is in line with the "Emperor Khan" of the Sui Dynasty. In fact, the so-called relatively enlightened foreign policy of the Tang Dynasty only lingered on the point of opening up to foreigners, and it didn't and was impossible to take the key step of allowing its own people to go abroad. This is the case in the Tang Dynasty, and the situation of each dynasty after the Tang Dynasty go even further than that. The Ming and Qing Dynasties adopted the close-door policy of exclusion, which was not formulated and implemented overnight. We can clearly see its historical origin in the measures of strict closure of foreign residents in the Tang Dynasty. Therefore, it is obviously not enough to discuss the closed country in the history of China only from the Ming and Qing Dynasties. It is necessary to put it in a longer time span, at least from the Tang Dynasty, in order to have a clearer understanding. Before the 1730s, China's foreign trade had always been in an obvious superior position, but the central government still did not implement the sub-policy of opening to the outside world, which should be for profound historical reasons.

It is necessary for us to discuss the Hu Shi (Frontier trade) which had great

1 See Wei Mingkong, The Openness and Closure of Tang Dynasty's Foreign Policy and Its Evaluation, *Social Sciences*, 1989 (2).

influence on feudal society, especially the government-run economy. Hu Shi is a special form of economic communication between different nationalities or different local separatist regimes in Chinese history. Its actual content goes far beyond the scope of economy and trade. Besides economic and trade subjects, it also includes political, cultural, military, ethnic and even diplomatic aspects. Its connotation is very rich. Hu Shi has different appellations in different periods and regions in our history, including "border trade", "joint market", "market", "exchange market", "monopoly market", "monopoly market trade" and so on. Hu Shi in history includes silk and horse trade as well as tea and horse trade, which is a kind of barter between the products of agricultural people in the Central Plains and those of the nomadic peoples of the border area. The emergence of Hu Shi is actually determined by the difference in the production structure between the farming economy in the interior area and the animal husbandry economy of the minority nationalities in the border areas, which is mainly manifested in the division and complementarity of farming economy and animal husbandry economy. Whether it is the silk and horse trade as the main content at the beginning or the tea and horse trade as the main trade afterwards, the goods used by both sides of the trade, such as textiles, tea and horses, are regional. From the point of view of economic location, the trade between products with regional characteristics is relatively frequent, and the volume of trade is relatively large. At the same time, this type of trade often stimulates and drives the social production.[1] Another historical fact that cannot be ignored is that such trade often has relatively obvious economic benefits.

In fact, Tea-Horse trade market is one of the important forms of Hu Shi. Tea-horse exchange is a special form of ethnic communication that rose in Tang and Song Dynasties, developed in Ming Dynasty and declined in Qing Dynasty, and lasted for more than a thousand years. It mainly refers to the large-scale market-

1 See Kong Jingwei, Handicraft Industry and China's Economic Change: Introduction. Edited by Peng Zeyi, *Social and Economic Change in China*, China Finance and Economics Press, 1990, p. 4.

oriented trade activities of minority nationalities engaged in animal husbandry economy in Northwest China, which use horses and other livestock and animal products to exchange for tea, silk, iron and other production and living necessities with the mainland farming nationalities. Tea-horse Hu Shi is a special form of barter trade between nomadic and farming nationalities. It is a complementary type of economic exchanges and plays a very important role in the history of trade history and history of nationalities of China. It once played a very important role in flourishing the agriculture and animal husbandry economy in Northwest and southwest China, improving the production and living structure or diet structure of agricultural and animal husbandry areas, and promoting peaceful coexistence among ethnic groups. At the same time, the tea-horse market to a certain extent and within certain scopes plays the role of Jin Que, or restricting non-governmental commercial trade. This prohibition system is to seize commodities such as salt, iron, wine and tea from the private merchants, and to implement the government's monopoly of all purchases and sales. In fact, this is to turn private business into official business, so that private businessmen lose the opportunity to profiteer. Or, even if private merchants are engaged in business, they must also be under the strict control of the government. The government's control over tea in the tea-horse border market is not only due to the consideration of monopoly or allocation of such resources, but also related to national security, national functions, national interests, balanced economic development and other factors. For the Central Plains dynasty, the tea and horses border trade in the Ming Dynasty was mainly based on the pacifying policy and military considerations of the Northwest minorities, besides the widely known economic reasons. Therefore, governments at all levels make every effort to control the tea-horse market, and generally do not allow individuals to get involved in it.

However, non-governmental businessmen use tea to directly trade with ethnic minorities in private. The transaction cost is relatively low, while the rate of return is relatively high. Therefore, they spare no effort to engage in such profitable business, often ignoring the harsh law. Not only the ordinary businessmen, but also the powerful families, especially some senior officials, nobles and garrison leaders, take advantage of privileges and use bribes to participate in tea smuggling activities, which lead to rampant tea smuggling. There even appears the situation of openly armed smuggling. Therefore, tea smuggling activities in Ming Dynasty were complex and varied.

In Ming Dynasty, tea smuggling becomes more and more rampant. The direct consequence is that the normal Tea-Horse exchange market of the government is seriously damaged, or there is no horse or tea for sale or exchange in the market. Or official tea encounters poor sale. As a result, the central government's policies and decrees on Tea-Horse exchange exist in name only. Private tea is cheaper than official tea, and it can also be directly transported to minority areas, with fewer direct selling links, lower transaction costs, better service attitude, more convenience for ethnic minorities to buy or barter, and higher credibility, it is hard for the official tea to beat the competitiveness of private tea.

Throughout the Ming Dynasty, the measures to ban tea smuggling are quite complete, and the punishment of smuggling was quite stringent. But the smuggling of tea have never been fundamentally eliminated. From the emperor down to the local officials, all rack their brains to completely eradicate tea smuggling. But what is especially puzzling is that "the stricter the ban, the thicker the tea profit". This is because "where the benefits lie, the number of profit seekers is overwhelming".[1] The border trade of tea and horses in Ming Dynasty formed a strange circle in which the ban became more and more stringent and the rate of return on smuggling was higher, thus the smuggling activities became more and more rampant.

A series of policies and regulations adopted by the feudal government in China economically protected the maintenance of the normal social and economic order and became the legal safeguard for the relative coordinated development

1 *Memorial to the Emperor on the Central Shaanxi Plain* Vol. 3 Tea and Horses· For Restoring the Old System of Tea and Horse Trade to Pacify the Foreign Tribes, Article 1, *Yang Yiqing Collection* (I) Vol. 3, Zhonghua Book Company, 2001, p. 77.

of agriculture, handicraft industry and commerce, which were all based on the understanding of "the fundamental to make a country rich and powerful is farming and sericulture".[1]

The state economic function of the feudal society in China indicates that the government directly manages all aspects of the national economy and people's livelihood, making the government-run handicraft industry quite developed from beginning to end. And this is even one of the basic reasons that affect the normal social and economic life among people. At the same time, the actual economic function of the state in China's feudal society are often not consistent with the legal provisions. Among them, the government's many legal restrictions on businessmen and the historical fact that businessmen have become a powerful class economically and politically are typical examples. Although emphasizing agriculture and restraining commerce is a basic national policy in the feudal China, the social reality is "By contrast, people who engage in business get rich faster than those who engage in agriculture and handicraft".[2] As early as the Western Han Dynasty, there emerged such paradox that "today's law slights businessmen, but businessmen have already become rich and respected; it shows respect for farmers, but the farmers are poor and humble".[3] Its economic status in social life is not fully consistent with the political status of scholars, farmers, craftsmen and businessman repeatedly established by the government. In feudal society, the idea of "A good scholar will make an official" was quite common. In some areas, such as Shanxi, where Shanxi businessmen were located, there once appeared the idea of "A good scholar will make a businessman", which illustrated the actual situation of the improvement of the status of businessmen.

The function of the government in the feudal society of China is not confined to that of the politics, military and other state machines that we have repeatedly emphasized before. Its function of organizing, coordinating economic operation

1 *History of the Ming Dynasty* Vol. 77 Shi Huo Zhi.
2 *Records of the Grand Historian*, Vol. 129 Biographies of Merchants .
3 *Han Shu* (*The Book of Han Dynasty*), Vol. 24 Shi Huo Zhi I.

and allocating resources cannot be underestimated in any case. During the Qin and Han Dynasties, people already keenly realized that "If farmers do not produce grain, food will be scarce. If craftsmen do not produce utensils, labor and life will be in distress. If businessmen do not trade, then food, utensils and wealth will be cut off. If people do not develop mountains and rivers, resources will be scarce." [1] That is, they already knew fully well the dialectical relationship among agriculture, industry, commerce and finance. China's feudal society has long been in the forefront of the world economically. Sui and Tang dynasties once appeared on the world stage as "Tian Ke Han".[2] The gross product of Ming and Qing dynasties accounted for about one third of the world's total output, which has been accepted by most scholars at home and abroad. All these are inseparable from the full play of the economic functions of the state in China's feudal society.

In particular, it is worth pointing out that, despite the active commodity economy and the development of social economy, the handicraft industry and commercial activities directly operated by the government are decreasing, but the government's emphasis on economic aspects in the legal system has not relaxed but strengthened instead. For example, if we compare the Da Qing Lv (Laws in the Qing Dynasty) and the Tang Lv Shu Yi (Commentary of Criminal Law of Tang Dynasty), it will be easy to find that the former has eight more chapters than the latter. Among them, the five chapters of Gong Shi, Tian Zhai (houses and fields), Ke Cheng, Qian Zhai (money and debts), He Fang (Flood Control) may be especially designed for the social and economic life at that time, or the main content is related to social economy. This reflects a basic fact that the central government pays more and more attention to social economy. Especially important, in the late feudal period of China, the government also brought the operation and organization of economic life into the legal process to a certain extent.

1 *The Book of Zhou*, quoted in *Records of the Grand Historian*, Vol. 129 Biographies of Merchants.

2 *The New Book of Tang Dynasty* , Vol. 2 Tai Zong Ji.

Chapter 3

The Direct Management of the Economy by the Chinese Feudal Society

In China's feudal society, the government-run handicraft industry has been relatively developed all the while. On the one hand, the government-run handicraft industry produces some special articles needed by the royal family, the government and the nobles, as well as government officials. At the same time, it also engages in such special crafts as palace construction, tomb construction, the renovation of the government's office gates, the production of weapons, and the casting of coins, as well as such public facilities as bridges. Another very important aspect of handicraft industry is the government's monopoly system on salt and iron, which directly monopolizes the production and circulation of salt, iron, wine and tea. It concerns the national economy and people's livelihood, and private ownership is not allowed. Not only that, in the feudal society of China, the government also managed water conservancy construction and water transport directly, but also managed or controlled a certain amount of land directly. Even under normal circumstances, it could regulate and control land resources to a certain extent. From this point of view, the feudal government in China actually directly controlled or operated the key areas and important links of the national economy. In other words, the government controlled the operation of the economy from beginning to end. The direct management of economy by the feudal government in China is mainly manifested in the directly operated government-run handicraft industry, the direct control or management of mining, coinage, salt and iron monopoly, wine monopoly, water conservancy, transportation, urban public works and national defense construction, etc. In the financial redistribution, poverty alleviation and disaster relief are also the government's basic concern of national economy and people's livelihood.

1. Government-run Handicraft Economy

1.1. The basic situation of the government-run handicraft industry economy

The government-run handicraft industry in the feudal society of China has been relatively developed all the time. The reasons for this are very complex. Among them, the fact cannot be ignored that the earliest national ruling center in China appeared in cities, because the construction of the city and the maintenance of normal life order need the support of a variety of handicraft industries, especially the life and support of the ruling class and the army, which cannot do without handicraft production for a moment. Relatively speaking, in feudal society, the needs of the ruling class are effective demands that can be realized, including some luxury consumption. This provides the possibility for the existence and development of urban handicraft industry economy, especially the government-run handicraft industry economy.

As early as the pre-Qin period, China's handicraft industry division of labor was quite meticulous. To say the least, there were metal working, carpentry, jade working, stonemason, pottery, textile, leather, weapons manufacturing and so on. At that time, there was the saying of "Bai Gong (100 different types of workers)" [1]. The so-called "hundred workers" is actually an approximate number, which only shows the specialized division of labor and the number of craftsmen at that time.

1 *Notes to Shangshu*, Vol. 1.

It does not refer to an exact number of types of crafts. According to the book Kao Gong Ji written by the people of Qi in the late Spring and Autumn Period, the society at that time was divided into "six jobs" of Wang Gong (noblemen), Shi Da Fu (scholar-bureaucrat), Bai Gong (Craftsmen), Shang Lv (businessmen), Nong Fu (farmers) and Fu Gong (weaving, embroidery, etc.), which indicated that the handicraft producers were independent from other producers and occupied an important position in society. At that time, there were 30 specialized production departments in the government-run handicraft industry alone, according to the division of labor. "Carpentry is the seventh, gold work the sixth, leather work, coloring work and scraping work the fifth, and pottery the second". All these production departments involve transportation, production tools, weapons, musical instruments, containers, jades, leather, dyeing, construction and other industries. Each industry has a more detailed division of labor. For example, for the production of vehicles, there are not only so-called "car workers", but also "wheelers" specializing in the manufacture of wheels, as well as "carriage people" specializing in the production of carriages, as well as the "shaft people", etc. The emergence of "Bai Gong" itself was the embodiment of the relatively developed government-run handicraft industry at that time. The so-called "Gong Shang Shi Guan (industrial and commercial officers)" at that time showed that the government kept a large number of handicraft producers with special skills and professional businessmen to ensure the economic operation of the political ruling center. This also showed that the political center of the country was also the economic and cultural center, indicating that the government had excellent control and resource allocation capabilities over the social economy from the very beginning.

In fact, the government-run handicraft industry in China's history is based on the development of the folk handicraft industry, because the advanced division of labor of the folk handicraft industry undoubtedly provides sufficient labor force for the prosperity of the government-run handicraft industry, especially skilled craftsmen. At the same time, it also provides raw materials and semi-finished products for the government-run handicraft industry. In addition, although there is a tradition of technological closure among folk craftsmen to meet the needs of market competition, their technology must be unreserved for the government, which undoubtedly provides inexhaustible technical support for the government handicraft workshops. Not only that, as Sang Hongyang of the Han Dynasty said, in terms of iron production, private production is small in scale, capital is insufficient, technology and equipment are backward. And the problem of "iron does not melt and the soft and the hard do not fuse"[1] often appears, which is the conclusion drawn from the comparison with the scale advantage of the government-run handicraft industry. Moreover, the information advantages of the government-run handicraft industry at that time were incomparable to those of the private handicraft industry.

Commodity circulation existed throughout the feudal society in China, and handicraft products and their raw materials were the basic commodities in the market at that time. The government can ensure that the raw materials produced by the government-run handicraft industry are of good quality and sufficient quantity either through the market or by collecting from the people. It is precisely because government production does not take the cost into account, manpower is sufficient, craftsmen technology is comprehensive, and information is flowing relatively freely, that some major inventions are often made by the government and gradually spread to the general public. The emergence of plant papermaking technology in the Western Han Dynasty and full development of it as official handicraft industry in the Eastern Han Dynasty[2] is inevitable, which is also one of the important contributions of official handicraft industry to technology and culture.

The production of government-run handicraft industry mainly consists of two parts: one is set up directly to meet the special needs of the Supreme ruler --- the

1 *On Salt and Iron*, Vol. 6, Flood and Drought Thirty-sixth.

2 *History of the Later Han Dynasty*, Vol. 78, Biography of Cai Lun.

emperor, members of the Royal family, nobles and the feudal government, such as money-making, weaving, ceramics, repair, shipbuilding, weapons, gunpowder and coinage; the other is important national economy and people's livelihood goods. Because of the large demand and high economic benefit, the government carries out official management in order to obtain this part of benefit. This aspect includes not only necessities such as salt, wine and tea, but also raw materials such as iron, gold, silver, copper, lead and tin. The first part is set up directly to meet the special needs of emperors, nobles, governments and armies. It involves textiles, porcelain, gold and silver utensils, architecture, weapons and so on.[1] On the one hand, this is mainly about the needs of daily life and luxury goods. Its direct contribution to society and economy is not very great, or its contribution to society is indirect. However, its effect on the concentration of social wealth, especially on the creation of culture and art to enhance the international influence of the nation, cannot be ignored in any case. On the other hand, it is about the products that are related to the national economy and people's livelihood. Because of their large social demand, high profits and some relationship to national security, they are often operated directly by the government. The most common practice is that the government implements monopoly. The proportion of monopoly revenue in the whole government's financial revenue is relatively high. For example, the tax revenue of salt alone once reached about 50% of the government's financial

1 According to Vol. 21 of *Xuan De Record of Ming Xuanzong*, in the first year of Xuan De (1426), the Ministry of Works and Craftsmanship was appointed to request "every craftsman household with two or three adult men could keep one man at home; those households with four or five adult men could keep two at home; and those with more than six could keep three" in order have more men work in the official handicraft workshops. This is the basic guarantee for the workers in the government-run handicraft industry, and it is a common practice in feudal society. Before the abolition of the system of craftsman registration, the government craftsmen who fled were often "convicted" or "sent to the capital" to be forced to engage in production in the government workshop (*Records of the Zheng Tong years of Emperor Ying Zong of the Ming Dynasty*, Vol. 43, Vol. 47).

revenue in the Tang Dynasty.[1] If other monopoly content is added, its proportion in government revenue is very high. In Tang Dynasty and other periods, the situation was similar. The operation of the feudal government in this respect has a far-reaching and direct impact on the national economy and people's livelihood, and is an indispensable part of the national economy at that time.

It is precisely because the government-run handicraft industry serves the ruling class and its army first that it has good technical equipment, abundant raw materials, sufficient manpower, comprehensive technology and spacious workshop, its management belongs to the government departments at all levels. However, its products are mainly used for consumption and public facilities, but not mainly for market production. So, its production efficiency is relatively low. Next. On the other hand, due to the fact that government's production doesn't take cost into consideration, and has sufficient manpower and comprehensive craftsmanship, some major inventions are often made by the government and gradually spread to the people. Just because the government has taken a series of measures to ensure that the government-run handicraft industry has sufficient manpower and raw materials, this becomes the prerequisite for the existence and development of the government-run handicraft industry. For example, in January of the first year of Tianxing in the Northern Wei Dynasty (398), "360,000 ordinary people and officials from Six Prefectures in Shandong Province and tribes people from He Gao Li, together with more than 100,000 skillful workers were sent to the capital to serve as craftsmen"[2]. After the establishment of the Sui Dynasty, "the government began to recruit craftsmen from all over the country, and skillful craftsmen of all skills and techniques were selected to gather in the capital"[3], which were typical examples. During the middle and late Tang

1 *Zi Zhi Tong Jian* (*A General Reflection for Political Administration*) Vol. 225, the 14th year (779 A.D.) of Dali during the reign of Emperor Daizong in the Tang Dynasty, the May article: "The total income of one year is 1.2 billion, while the profit of salt accounts for more than half of it."

2 *The Book of Wei Dynasty*, Vol. 2 Chronicle of Taizu.

3 *The Book of Sui Dynasty* Vol. 46 Biography of Su Xiaoci.

Dynasty, under the general situation of government employing craftsmen, it is still stipulated that the "skillful workers" could not "pay to be exempt from corvee" to ensure the technical personnel in the government-run handicraft industry. Specifically, it is through such measures as not allowing "avoiding the important and difficult things" to guarantee that the craftsmen of the government-run handicraft workshop are "strong, skilled workers"[1]. This is not an exception, but a general rule in feudal society. Even in the later period of feudal society when the craftsmanship registration system was abolished, some special handicraft products in the government were not allowed to be produced by the common people because of their quality and technical confidentiality requirements. Although the craftsmen in the government get a certain amount of pay, they could hardly leave the official workshops at will. Their production is compulsory.

In order to organize the normal operation of the government-run handicraft industry and manage the handicraft industry production in the whole country, the government-run handicraft industry management organizations in the feudal society of China were relatively well-developed at the beginning, and gradually formed the division and cooperation mode of Shaofu supervisors, Jiangzuo supervisors (Note: in charge of the supervision of craftsmen of architecture, utensils and embroidery, tec.) and Junqi (Note: military weapons) supervisors in the Sui and Tang Dynasties, which was divided into three parts, and combined into one for convenience of government use and management as well as internal division of labor, coordination and supervision. This handicraft industry model developed further later. In the Qing Dynasty, although the government-run handicraft industry management institutions were further improved, Gong Bu (the Ministry of Industry) was set up in the early Qing Dynasty, which was the main management organization for the government to set up various projects and the government-run manufacturing industry. Under Gong Bu, Ying Shan Si, Yu Heng Si, Du Shui Si, Tun Tian Si, Zhi Zao Ku, Jie Shen Ku, Xiao Huang Ku, Zhuo

1 *Six Codes of Laws in the Tang Dynasty*, Vol. 7 Annotation.

Ling Chang, Ying Shan Suo, Wen Si Yuan, Bao Yuan Ju, Guang Ji Ku, Chai Tan Si, Tongzhou Chou Fen Zhu Mu Ju are responsible for the establishment of water conservancy and construction projects and the production and management of supplies. Among them, the handicraft industry is mainly related to Ying Shan Si, Yu Heng Si, Zhi Zao Ku, Zhuo Ling Chang and Bao Yuan Ju, etc. [1] This is only the general situation. In fact, the ownership of institutions and the changes of their responsibilities in the Qing Dynasty vary a lot. Of course, in feudal society, the overlapping of institutions, mutual restraint, inefficiency and high production costs are also obvious shortcomings.

On the whole, the main purpose of the government-run handicraft industry was not commodity production. But the government-run handicraft industry in China's history was not unrelated to the commodity economy. In fact, it played a positive role in the feudal commodity economy in a certain period of time and in certain industries, so it cannot be generalized. Although the goods produced by government-run handicraft industry organizations are mainly to meet the needs of Royal families, nobles and officials at all levels, with the continuously increasing activity of commodity economy in the feudal economic field, the connection between government-run handicraft industry and the market has been gradually strengthened. This situation became more obvious in the middle and late Tang Dynasty, especially in the Ming and Qing Dynasties.

As early as the second year of Hou Jin Tian Fu in the late Tang Dynasty (937), a decree expressly stipulated that "bronze mirrors will be cast by the government in the future and sold at the capital's stores, which can be bought by ordinary people and sold in other places"[2]. At the same time, paper and engraving prints produced by government-run handicraft workshops (such as calendars) have become common commodities in the private market. As commodities circulating in the market, the utensils produced by government workshops are very popular

1 Guangxu, *Classical Cases of Laws in the Qing Dynasty*, Vol. 20
2 *History of the Old Five Dynasties* Vol. 146 Shi Huo Zhi.

with consumers because of their high quality and sufficient quantity, which was rarely recorded in the Tang Dynasty and before. Engels pointed out that "production and exchange are two different functions. ......These two functions restrict and influence each other at every moment, so much so that they can be called horizontal and vertical coordinates of economic curves" [1]. Commodity economy exists from beginning to end in the feudal society of China and shows a continuous active trend (of course, there are often some retrogression within a certain period of time, so the trend cannot be regarded absolutely). It is historical fact beyond doubt, which constitutes one of the indispensable contents of social and economic life at that time.

There are many reasons for the development of government-run handicraft industry in China's history. The following reasons cannot be ignored in any case: private artisans guarantee the basic source of workers in government-run handicraft industry; folk handicraft industry is the inexhaustible technological source of government-run handicraft industry; government-run handicraft industry can provide the necessary handicraft raw materials through the state's ability to allocate resources; the government-run handicraft industry has the convenience to absorb foreign technology; the luxury consumption of the ruling class actually makes it possible for the government-run handicraft industry to continuously improve some of its technology. In the production of official handicraft industry in feudal society of China, government goods and wine monopoly are mainly carried out not according to the law of market value, but by administrative means as far as possible. Although the control and exploitation of craftsmen are rather harsh and the cost of management is relatively high, they utilize social resources to engage in large-scale activities such as mining, salt production and other aspects, which gives them the comparative advantage of scale that private craftsmen and private businessmen can hardly have. At the same time, state monopoly of salt

1 Engels: Anti-Dühring, *Selected Works of Marx and Engels*, Vol. 3 I, People's Publishing House, 1972, p. 186.

and iron plays an important role in preventing the rich merchants from controlling the circulation field and increasing prices without limits or monopolizing prices. In addition, the state's operation of salt and iron, to a certain extent, also provides the society with the total amount of commodities, and guarantees a certain quality of commodities, which to some extent promotes the development of commodity economy. Another basic fact that cannot be neglected is that the government controls raw materials such as salt and iron, operates large-scale handicraft production, and grasps the fiscal revenue of the whole country, which makes the governments at all levels, especially the central government, have a strong ability to regulate and control the whole feudal social and economic operation, and can often become the mainstay of social and economic operation. This aspect cannot be ignored when we evaluate the monopoly system of the feudal society in China. This is no other than one of the important contents of handicraft industry management in feudal society. Because of its special status at that time and the inconsistency between its production and operation and the general government-run handicraft industry, the salt and iron monopoly system will be specially discussed below.

1.2. The support of the government-run handicraft industry for people's livelihood

In addition to meeting the consumption of the royal family and officials and public consumption, the government-run handicraft industry also organizes the production of necessary production tools, including farm implements and water conservancy facilities within a certain period of time and a certain scope, which has a positive impact on the recovery and development of agricultural production. It is particularly worth mentioning that the role of government-run handicraft industry in promoting production technology cannot be ignored in any case.

The government has the unique advantages of controlling sufficient material resources and craftsmen. If it engages in agricultural casting, it will play an unparalleled role in promoting iron farm tools that cannot be compared by any other social forces. For example, when Emperor Wudi of Han Dynasty, Kong

Jin once "ordered the people to cast farm tools"[1], which is a typical example. According to *Hou Han Shu* (History of the Later Han Dynasty), Biography of Du Shi, Nanyang Taishou Du Shi in the Eastern Han Dynasty "designs and manufactures water drains for ironmaking and casting farm implements, so that the people feel very convenient with less effort and more benefits". [2] As recorded in *Hou Han Shu*, Biography of Ren Yan, Jiuzhen Taishou Ren Yan "asked the local people to cast farming tools and taught them to reclaim wasteland". These practices played a certain role in promoting the restoration and improvement of agricultural production at that time, especially in the promotion and demonstration role of the government in the field of agricultural machinery, which could not be replaced by any other force. The long-term use of the "two bulls lifting bars" tillage form in China's history seems to be very backward tillage today. But in the Qin, Han, Wei, Jin, Southern and Northern Dynasties, it was relatively advanced. At that time, the promotion of such advanced tillage form throughout the country was inseparable from the active implementation of governments at all levels. For this reason, Two Bulls Lifting Bars is the form of farming that lasts for the longest time and enjoys the widest popularity in China's history since the emergence of cattle farming. It is more suitable for the production scale of small-scale individual production agriculture with five family members and 100 mu of land at that time.

In agricultural production, for Northern areas, land irrigation is one of the important means to ensure food production. In this respect, the government also plays a certain role. In March of the second year of Dali, Daizong of the Tang

1 *Records of the Grand Historian*, Vol. 30 Ping Zhun Shu.

2 *Hou Han Shu*, Vol. 31, Biography of Du Shi: "Du Shi was promoted to the position of Nanyang Taishou. He was thrifty, honest and fair in his administration. He established his prestige by cracking down on violence, being good at planning, and caring for the people who served in labor. He also designs and manufactures water drains for ironmaking and casting farm implements, so that the people feel very convenient with less effort and more benefits. Ponds have also been built and land has been reclaimed extensively. Every household in the county is rich. At that time, people compared him to Zhao Xinchen. Nanyang people praised him for these deeds and said, 'There was Zhao Xinchen before, then there was Du Shi now.'"

Dynasty (767):

The government designed the waterwheel, and ordered Jing Zhao Fu to produce it and send the waterwheels to the ordinary people in Zheng and Bai Qu area, so that they could water field.[1]

The imperial court designed waterwheels, delivered them to Jing Zhao Fu for production, and irrigated the land for the people of the Central Shaanxi Plain free of charge. Such waterwheels must be relatively advanced and have a positive role in promoting agricultural production. At the same time, they also have a certain role in promoting and demonstrating waterwheels in other areas. In September of the first year of Yongle in the Ming Dynasty (1403), "the government ordered Bao Yuan Ju to cast agricultural implements"[2]. Baoyuan Bureau in Ming and Qing Dynasties was affiliated to Gong Bu (the Ministry of Industry), and was in charge of money-making. The central government makes use of the national resources and temporarily engages in the production of agricultural tools in Baoyuan Bureau, an institution that is directly controlled by the central government and is specially responsible for money-making. This shows that the state attaches great importance to agricultural production, especially the self-farming economy. It also shows that the state power has a special advantage in mobilizing the national resources. In a certain period of time and within a certain range, the government often provides this kind of production tool for the people free of charge. The government's record of the promotion of advanced production tools is endless. This is a manifestation of the state's economic function in the process of realizing the basic national policy of emphasizing agriculture, although it has not formed a relatively stable system.

The improvement and popularization of production tools are very important for the improvement of social productivity. The role of government-run handicraft industry in promoting the improvement and popularization of

1 *Tang Hui Yao* (*Historical Records of the Systems in the Tang Dynasty*), Vol. 89 Dredging and Digging

2 *History of the Ming* Dynasty Vol. 6 Biography of Emperor Cheng Zu II.

social production tools cannot be underestimated. Under the situation that the traditional self-employed operators "will not change the tools if there is no ten-fold profit" [1], the attitudes of the individual small-scale production agriculture towards improvement, especially updating, of the farming tools are generally not very positive. First, there is a serious lack of motivation for the owners of agricultural tools to change tools. Second, considering the cost, they will not eliminate old agricultural tools unless they have to. Or, in the absence of a very obvious comparative advantage, individual small-scale production agriculture will not update their farm tools. The government has an obvious demonstration and promotion role in the improvement and promotion of agricultural tools, including the use of treasury funds for this work, which cannot be replaced by any individual. However, the relevant government departments often cheat on labour and materials in the production of farm tools, mainly because some officials embezzle the public fund. As the sage in "On Salt and Iron, Flood and Drought" says, "The iron tools cast by the imperial court were mostly large ones, which were not suitable for the needs of the common people because they only wanted to increase the quantities and meet the deadline. People use all kinds of blunt or broken tools. They can't even cut the grass." Although this is what both sides of the debate said, it is not exaggeration. Nevertheless, we still have to give a positive evaluation of the government's contribution to the promotion of agricultural production tools.

The smelting and iron processing of government-run handicraft workshops are mainly to meet the needs of the government, nobles, officials and the army. Just because of this, it is only their incidental but not their main functions to provide the necessary production tools for farmers who are the direct producers. In addition, the government has many restrictions on the production and use of iron tools, the allocation and replacement of basic iron production tools are not

1 *New Preface* Vol. 9; *Chun Qiu Zhan Guo Yi Ci* (*History of the Spring and Autumn Period and the Warring States*) Vol. 23.

guaranteed. Another situation is that the government monopolized the market price after the monopoly of salt and iron, which increased the price of salt and iron. "The price of salt, iron and grain is very high, and this led to great inconvenience to the people. Poor people can only use hands or wooden tools to till the land, and eat less salt." The price of government monopolies such as salt and iron is on the high side. It is not easy for farmers to purchase and replace production tools under normal circumstances, which seriously affects the needs of normal production and daily life of ordinary people. Not only that, the government also adopted the policy of forcible sale to the people. For example, "People everywhere accused the government of controlling the salt and iron industry. The quality of the ironware was poor and the price was high. They also forced the people to buy it. "[1] The quality of the goods produced by the government is a difficult problem that the government cannot solve in the long period of feudal society. In this case, private casting is often a profitable business, even severe laws cannot fundamentally stop the existence and spread of private casting. With the increasing trend of private casting, the government gradually relaxed the restrictions on private manufacturing of farm tools. It only formulated strict policies on the supply and sale of raw materials. On the one hand, it tried to meet farmers' needs for farm tools, and on the other hand, it also cracked down on the rich merchants who hoarded goods at high prices and sold them to farmers. Another important content that cannot be neglected is that the government restricts or controls its entry into ethnic areas and foreign countries by manufacturing and selling ironware, which undoubtedly has national security considerations.

But on the whole, as Sang Hongyang of the Han Dynasty said, the government-run handicraft industry had sufficient funds and complete facilities, and the managers had rich experience and the workers had comprehensive skills, so the quality of the products was good, and "the tools were made of good iron and were easy to use"[2]. It is very obvious to see that it played an important role in the

1 *Records of the Grand Historian*, Vol. 30 Ping Zhun Shu.

2 *On Salt and Iron*, Vol. 6, Flood and Drought Thirty-sixth.

spreading of handicraft technology among the people. At the same time, it has advantages that other handicraft producers do not have.

In feudal society, the support of government-run handicraft industry for people's livelihood is an important aspect that cannot be ignored in any case. When discussing the economic functions of the government in feudal society, we should not ignore this point.

2. Government Monopoly System and Canal Transportation

2.1. Salt and iron monopoly

The monopoly system is a basic national policy pursued throughout the feudal society. One of the important events in the social economy of the Western Han Dynasty is that the government implemented the salt and iron monopoly system, which is of vital importance to the national economy and the people's livelihood. It further strengthened the central government's control over social economy, especially in key areas or industries, and affected every period after the Han Dynasty. It can be said that the design of this system has the foresight suitable for China's national conditions. Salt and iron monopoly, i.e. salt and iron official management, refers to the monopoly of salt and iron by the state power, which includes two situations: direct operation by the government or merchant operation entrusted by the government.

Salt and iron are necessities of life and raw materials in production. They are unique and difficult to replace. In addition, it has great potential for market or consumption, and the seller has the ability to monopolize the price and output of products. Secondly, there are barriers for other forces to enter the field of production or operation. In this way, the government can guarantee the basic stability of salt and iron in the field of production and circulation in economic life.

In fact, in the process of carrying out salt and iron monopoly in feudal society of China, it was not smooth sailing at the beginning. Instead, it went through a very fierce debate and even struggle. The controversy over the exclusive sale of salt and iron in the Han Dynasty is mainly reflected in the book *On Salt and Iron*, which has been retained to this day. As for the practice and theoretical controversy of the monopoly system with salt and iron as its main content, a series of financial management measures adopted by Sang Hongyang, a financier of the Western Han Dynasty, during the period of Emperor Wudi of the Han Dynasty, had a far-reaching impact on the then and future generations. Especially under the advocacy of Sang Hongyang, the government carried out the policies of salt and iron official operation (monopoly), Jun Shu (Tribute Equalization), Ping Zhun (Commodity Prices Stabilizing) and Jiu Que (Wine Monopoly). The government set up Jun Shu (Tribute Equalization) officials. Their task is to convert the annual tribute to the imperial court into a certain amount of local specialty, and collect the special goods with sufficient quantity and at relatively low price. And then they transport the goods to high-priced areas in order to exploit the difference in pricing. That's the so-called Jun Shu (Tribute Equalization) which can save the huge freight cost for local governments to transport tributes directly to the capital, and also reduce the burden of corvee to a certain extent. The Ping Zhun (Commodity Prices Stabilizing) policy is to set up a price stabilization organization in the capital, which takes the materials and funds directly controlled by the state as the basic storage. When the market price rises, it will dump the goods, while when the market price falls, it buys a lot. Its function is to stabilize the price in the capital and earn the price difference. In this way, the state can control the circulation and sale of major commodities or commodities related to the national economy and the people's livelihood through the two institutional arrangements of Jun Shu (Tribute Equalization) and Ping Zhun (Commodity Prices Stabilizing), so as to achieve the goal of "making the best of the world's goods".[1] Although these measures were criticized by many scholars at that time, they were approved by the highest decision-makers, and became the theoretical basis and model for the dynasties following the Eastern Han Dynasty to act out and follow.[2] For example, Su Shi, a famous scholar in the Northern Song Dynasty, believed that:

1 *Records of the Grand Historian*, Vol. 30 Ping Zhun Shu.

2 See Jin Wen *Review and Biography of Sang Hongyang*, Nanjing University Press, 2005.

> Since the Han Dynasty, scholars feel ashamed of talking about Shang Yang and Sang Hongyang, but the emperors accept their theories. Though the emperors do not mention their names in the open, they secretly put their theories into practice. More than that, some emperors approve their theories both in the open and secretly, hoping that the theories could succeed[1].

This comment really hits the mark. Because the economic countermeasures such as salt and iron monopoly and wine monopoly are not the expedient policy of the highest decision-maker in the feudal society of China, but the rational choice that the government has to take to solve the financial revenue problem and do not give up the control of the economic lifeline at the same time. As Wei Xiang of the Northern Song Dynasty said:

> It is true that there is nothing to gain from the insufficient state funding, and we can do nothing without it. Therefore, the profits from the trade of wine, salt, iron, and mountain and river resources are all returned to the public, and the people cannot manipulate the scarcity and excess of goods in the market to make huge profits. Since Jin, Wei, Sui and Tang dynasties, they have all followed the policy. Even when the future generations have abundant wealth, we cannot do without monopoly.[2]

This is not only the view of people in Song Dynasty, but also that of people in Yuan Dynasty, who believe that "Salt, iron and wine monopoly has not been abandoned since Han Dynasty"[3]. It can be seen that the monopoly or levy system

1 *Dongpo Zhilin* Vol. 5 Sima Qian's Two Grave Crimes.
2 *Collection of Mr. Wei*, Vol. 18 On Monopoly.
3 *Yuan Wen Lei*, Vol. 60, Yao Sui: Gong Shen Dao Bei of Zhong Shu Zuo Cheng Yao Wenxians.

of salt, iron and other commodities has been a basic national policy since the Qin and Han Dynasties. The criticism of those scholars is just a scholar's talk resulting from a lack of familiarity with the national conditions. "*Han Shu* (" Volume 24, "Shi Huo Zhi" records: In the Qin Dynasty, "the government monopolizes the benefits from mountain and river resources. ... The profits from salt and iron are twenty times those of ancient times". This points out the huge economic benefits of government control over salt and iron, which are mainly caused by price control and resource monopoly. In addition to the government's price control and resource monopoly, another important reason that cannot be ignored is that this is decided by economies of scale efficiency, which is a relative disadvantage of private handicraft owners in feudal society. Since the implementation of the salt and iron monopoly system in the Western Han Dynasty, the content of government monopoly has been expanding, although there are many times of reversals. In the third year of Emperor Wudi's reign in the Tianhan years (98 BC), the central government ordered that the government has the right to brew and operate wine, which was executed by local government officials. It was strictly forbidden for the people to brew and sell wine by themselves. The government's control over wine-making and its management rights is the "Que Gu" system. Salt and iron monopoly and Que Gu undoubtedly increase the government's financial revenue, improve the country's economic strength, but also improve the government's control of social economy. After the "Wen Jing Zhi Zhi (the enlightened administration of the Han emperors Wen and Jing)" in the Western Han Dynasty, the enhancement of social and economic strength was unprecedented. Many of political and military achievements in the period of Emperor Wudi of Han Dynasty were the historical witnesses of this situation. Because of this, the Western Han Dynasty had also abolished the monopoly of salt and iron and wine, but soon announced the resumption. In the feudal society of China, from the beginning to the end, no good policy was found to replace the salt and iron monopoly system.

Among a series of important economic measures implemented in the history of the Western Han Dynasty, in addition to the above mentioned industries, such as salt and iron monopoly and Que Gu system, which are related to the national economy and people's livelihood, measures of adjusting and stabilizing prices were also implemented, namely, the two measures of Jun Shu (Tribute Equalization)and Ping Zhun (Commodity Prices Stabilizing). In the first year of Emperor Yuanfeng (110 A.D.), with Da Si Nong Sang Hongyang taking charge, the government changed the policy that subordinate countries handed over the money and the central government used the money to buy goods from merchants to the policy that the subordinate countries pay tribute to the central government directly. This is the so-called " Referring to the practice of merchants in transporting different commodities to different regions at different times, countries far away should pay tribute with their own special products, and transport them to the central government"[1]. The government manufactures transportation tools and transports tribute directly to the capital. If the tribute is not what the central government needs, the local government sells it and turns over the proceeds to the central government. This flexible and diversified approach can not only reduce the transport costs of local governments, but also effectively prevent big businessmen from profiting from it. It is a win-win measure for the benefit of the country and the people.

The government is involved in production, circulation and consumption of some special products, which helps the government, especially the central government, control the economic lifeline and become the main body of social economy. The period of Emperor Wudi of Han Dynasty was one of the important periods of our country's traditional commerce-restraining policy. The state power adopted a series of new strategies to directly manage and control some key areas of social economy and monopolize the important industrial and commercial sectors such as salt and iron by the state, so as to meet the needs of the commodity economy of the authoritarian centralized state and strike and restrict the economic strength of the rich businessmen. As we all know,

1 *Han Shu* (*The Book of Han Dynasty*), Vol. 24 II Shi Huo Zhi II.

individual small-scale production agriculture and its family sideline handicraft industry are the smallest production units which are suitable for our traditional society. Their management costs are very low, but their economic benefits are relatively high. Therefore, they have obvious comparative advantages. The rich businessmen occupy a considerable number of producers, monopolize certain social and economic resources, and have a certain impact on the state's financial revenue and labor force, thus affecting the consolidation and strengthening of the authoritarian centralized regime. Therefore, in order to strengthen the economic foundation of the autocratic centralized regime, Emperor Wudi of Han Dynasty, with the aim of strengthening the economic foundation, began with the monopoly of salt and iron resources by the state. In the fourth year of the Yuanshou period (119 BC), Emperor Wudi boldly reinstated the big salt and iron merchants Dongguo Xianyang and Kong Jin, as well as Sang Hongyang, son of the Luoyang merchants, and commissioned them to plan the national salt and iron affairs. Sang Hongyang and others, adhering to the will of Emperor Wudi, formulated a series of concrete plans for government management of salt and iron and seriously put them into practice. The specific plan mainly includes: salt officials are set up in salt producing areas, and salt farmers are recruited to boil the salt off the water. The government controls the production process by providing the production tool of boiling salt - "Lao Pen (salt-boiling basin)". Under this regulation, salt households provide for themselves the living expenses, and the government pays salt households varying amounts of remuneration according to the number of Lao Pen. The production of salt households is under the strict control of salt officials. Salt households do not have any power to dispose of salt by themselves. Salt is uniformly allocated by salt officials and transported to all over the country for sale according to the unified plan of the government. It can be seen that the production of salt must be approved by the state, and "Lao Pen" and other production tools must be provided by the government. The salt is produced by private investment, and sold to the consumers after the unified purchase by the government. That is to say, the state controls the production process by franchising, while monopolizes the circulation field. The state becomes a double monopolist in the buyer's market and the seller's market. It monopolizes not only the production and purchase, but also the sale of salt. This ensures that the state has full control over the price of salt.

On the whole, the commodity economy in the feudal society of China presents an active trend. The commercial area is expanding and developing continuously, the radius of commodity circulation is increasing constantly, and the trend of commodity specialization is becoming more and more obvious. However, the monopoly of salt and iron resources by the government has not changed fundamentally. Moreover, the content of government monopoly is expanding, among which wine and tea often become an important part[1]. The government's monopoly commodities, first of all, come down to the acquisition and processing of raw materials for such commodities, which was the basic content of the government-run handicraft industry at that time, and also one of the important reasons for the development of the government-run handicraft industry. After the mid-Tang Dynasty, in order to ease the financial pressure, some insightful financiers began to draw on the experience of Sang Hongyang.

Salt tax is also one of the important sources of government revenue in the Tang Dynasty. The collection of salt tax in the Tang Dynasty was constantly improved, and finally a new salt monopoly system with far-reaching influence was formed. From the early Tang Dynasty until before the Xuanzong years, officials and people jointly developed salt. Private salt was not prohibited, and salt was not taxed at the same time. In the first year of Emperor Xuanzong's reign (713), the government began to levy a tax on salt, but the salt tax was relatively light at that time. Thereafter, the salt tax experienced a gradual aggravation process. In the Tianbao years during the reign of Emperor Xuanzong (742-756) and Zhide years during the reign of Emperor Suzong (756-758), taxes on salt amounted to 10 Qian

1 According to *The New Book of Tang Dynasty* Vol. 54 Shi Huo Zhi IV, tea as the official tax of the government began in the Dezong period of the Tang Dynasty when tea was popular. Wine monopoly and control vary from time to time and cannot be generalized.

per Jin (1/2 kilogram).

When Di Wuqi, a financier, was in charge, it was an important period when the salt law of the Tang Dynasty was greatly changed. In the first year of Emperor Suzong's reign (758), Di Wuqi held an important position as an envoy of salt, iron and mintage. He reviewed the situation and began a series of rectifications, including that of the salt law. Di Wiqi's rectification of salt law mainly includes setting up special supervisory institutions in salt producing areas, establishing special household registration for former salt farmers and migrants engaged in salt production, namely, Ting Hu household, which specializes in salt production, and is exempted from corvee. The salt produced by Ting Hu households is purchased by the government in full. Then the government sells the salt by adding an extra 100 Qian per Dou, making the selling price of salt 110 Qian per Dou. Under the salt monopoly system, the government made a huge profit of up to 1,000%. In other words, at that time, the government exploited Ting Hu households' labor income by as high as 90%. At that time, under the monopoly system, local governments often raised the price of salt in order to make a good profit, and the burden of consumers increased further.

After Di Wuqi, Liu Yan contributed a lot to salt law. In the first year of Bao Ying during the reign of Emperor Daizong (762), Liu Yan, as an envoy of Salt and Iron Du Zhi (national revenue and expenditure) appointed by the central government, carried out a radical reform of the salt law. In the reform of salt law, Liu Yan insisted on a win-win strategy that not only increased the government's financial revenue, but also did not increase the burden of consumers. This is the salt law that combines monopoly with taxation. Liu Yan set up salt officers in places where salt production is relatively concentrated, who purchase salt produced by salt farmers, and then resell it to businessmen with certain credibility and qualifications, who can then sell it freely. In areas where salt is not produced, salt officials are generally not set up to reduce government management costs. The Jiangling area is far from the salt producing area. Salt officials transport salt to this area and store it. If salt merchants do not come and the price of salt rises, the government sells it at a price lower than the local salt price. This not only suppresses the price of salt, which is indispensable to the people's daily necessities, but also increases the government's financial revenue. This is known as "Changping Yan" (Salt Prices Stabilizing Policy) - the government guaranteed the basic stability of salt prices in the areas under effective control. On the whole, Liu Yan's salt law has its basic form: civil production, official purchase, commercial transportation and commercial sales. [1] During the period of implementing Liu Yan's Salt Law, the government-controlled salt tax increased from 600,000 Min per year to 6 million Min at the end of Dali years during the reign of Emperor Daizhong (766-779), which accounted for about 50% of the total tax revenue at that time. Salt tax became the most important source of government finance at that time and the most important economic support to maintain the Tang Dynasty's rule under the circumstance of Fanzhen separatist regime. After Shunzhong came to power, he paid more attention to salt law and assigned Du You to the position of envoy of Salt and Iron Du Zhi, with its headquarters located in Yangzhou, where the economy was prosperous at that time[2]. This reflects the focus of the central government's financial resources and the trend of the economic center moving southward.

The Sui and Tang Dynasties are one of the periods in which the government's control policy on iron and salt changed a lot. That is to say, the government's control over iron was relaxed, while the control over salt was not relaxed, but had a trend of strengthening. There are many reasons for this change. Among them, salt is one-off consumption and indispensable for residents, while iron is a durable article for daily use and producer good, which, even if damaged, can be recast. So, it is increasingly difficult for the government to control its source and flow direction. This adjustment reduces the management cost of the government and passes through the government financial revenue, reflecting the continuous

1 Department of Finance, Central Institute of Finance and Banking, Ed.: *A Brief History of China's Finance*, China Financial and Economic Publishing House, 1980, p. 88.

2 *The Book of Tang Dynasty* Vol. 49 Shi Huo Zhi II.

maturity of the government in economic management in the late feudal society.

According to "The New Book of Tang Dynasty, Shi Huo Zhi", the government of the Tang Dynasty "set up Jian Yuan (Salt Supervision Organization) near the sea, well and boiling basin, and the salt farmers become Ting Hu, free from miscellaneous corvees". During this period, the government mainly focused on controlling the price of salt purchase. The government controlled the Ting Hu households as a merchant employer. After the implementation of the two-tax law in the first year of the Jianzhong years during Emperor Dezong's reign in the Tang Dynasty (780), Ting Hu households also paid two taxes according to the two-tax law. In general, the Ting Hu households produce salt according to the salt quota stipulated by the Jian Yuan (Salt Supervision Organization). Except for the salt paid in the form of the two taxes in the south of the Yangtze River, the rest of the salt produced is purchased by the Jian Yuan (Salt Supervision Organization) in packages. Then, the officials give it to the businessmen according to the official price[1], and the businessmen sell it all over the country. Because it was controlled by the government at that time, the price of salt rose from 10 Qian per bushel to 110 Qian per bushel, with a rise of up to 1,000%. In this way, salt tax became one of the important sources of financial revenue of the Tang government at that time. Historically, after Liu Yan's reform of salt law in the Tang Dynasty, the government's salt profit in the Jianghuai area increased from 4,000,000 Min to 6 million Min annually. It is said that salt profit accounted for about 1/2 of the total tax of the whole country[2]. As Han Yu commented:

---

1 *The Book of Tang* Vol. 123 Biography of Di Wuqi.

2 *Zi Zhi Tong Jian* (*A General Reflection for Political Administration*) Vol. 225, the 14th year (779 A.D.) of Dali during the reign of Emperor Daizong in the Tang Dynasty, the May article: "At the end of Dali years (766-779), the total revenue of one year is 12 million Min, while salt profit accounts for half of that." This shows that the proportion of monopoly income in the government's fiscal revenue is relatively high, and with the expansion of the scope of national monopoly, its role of boosting the national fiscal revenue is constantly increasing. This is one of the real reasons why the absolute deprivation of direct producers by the government is gradually decreasing in the late feudal society, while the power of the state, that is, that of the capital directly controlled by the state, is continuously strengthening.

> The government levies tax on salt, and add salt tax to salt price and sell it to merchants; the merchants pay the tax and sell the salt to the people. Therefore, the common people, rich or poor, have submitted money to the officials. So they don't have to deal with the government, but already give money to the officials. [1]
>
> Wang Fuzhi made the following comments on Liu Yan's contribution to the Tang Dynasty's economy in his "Du Tong Jian Lun (Comments about History as a Mirror)":
>
> The government closely watches the harvest situation in the whole country. If the harvest is good, the rice will be bought at a high price; if the harvest is poor, the rice will be sold at a low price. Thus, the government has extra supplies and the people can be exempt from tax so as to stay away from hunger. This part will be replenished by the profiteering merchants and corrupted officials. The government shows benevolence to people, but not harm them. The profit from salt tax is taken by the unscrupulous merchants, but not the people who buy salt. The profit of water transport does not benefit people who deliver the supplies. Liu Yan tries to prevent the taxes and corvees from being increased. And the military supplies are sufficient.

Today, we can say that this comment is in line with historical reality. As the prime minister in charge of the overall situation at that time, Liu Yan took effective measures such as stabilizing prices and attaching importance to water transport in the economy. Without increasing the burden of direct producers and consumers, the state's fiscal revenue was increasing, and the economic rights and interests of businessmen were safeguarded. It was a win-win economic policy. Liu Yan is a famous financier in history.

---

1 *Quan Tang Wen* Vol. 550 Han Yu On the Change of Salt Law

In the Song Dynasty, the monopoly system of salt, tea and wine, the three necessities of people's life, became one of the main sources of government revenue. There were many changes in salt law in Song Dynasty. On the whole, the sales of salt in the early Song Dynasty was divided into two situations: official selling and commercial selling. The so-called official sale means that it is sold directly by the government. The salt sold directly by the government is called official salt, while the salt sold by the merchants is commercial salt, which is taxed by the government. In the late Renzong Dynasty, the salt law of Song Dynasty changed the "banknote law" into direct sale of official salt by merchants. The main practices were: merchants bought salt certificates and "banknotes" from the government, and then took them to the designated salt producing areas to claim the salt. After that, they could freely transport and sell them. This is the earliest "Voucher Salt Law" in the history of our country, which has been used in the later feudal society and occupies a very important position in the history of salt monopoly in China. In order to stabilize the salt price of the capital, Du Yan Yuan (Capital Salt Institution) was set up in the Song Dynasty, which stabilized the salt price in the capital between 35 and 40 Qian per Jin. When the price of salt falls below 35 Qian per Jin, Du Yan Yuan would only buy in but does not sell; when the price of salt exceeds 40 Qian per Jin, Du Yan Yuan sells the salt in stock at a price lower than the market price, that is, below 40 Qian per Jin, thus ensuring the relative stability of the price of salt and protecting the economic rights and interests of consumers and businessmen.

Wang Anshi's reform in the Xining years during the reign of Emperor Shenzong (1068-1077) also included the reform of salt law. Its main spirit was to raise the price of salt on the one hand and to introduce salt voucher — Yan Yin — for the transportation and sale of salt on the other. With Yan Yin, businessmen can carry out salt transportation and sales in the designated monopoly area. It is illegal for other people to transport and sell salt here. The practice in Chongning years (1102-1106) was to divide the monopoly time into long term and short term. The time limit of long monopoly is one year and that of short monopoly is three months.

During the Southern Song Dynasty, there were some changes in the salt law, such as the promotion of contract farms first implemented in Sichuan, the collection of tax money on the monopoly by the government, and the purchase of the right to monopoly by merchants. Jing Hu (households of well salt production) produce salt in accordance with the quota set by the government and pay local taxes to the government. The salt tax levied by the government to Jing Hu keeps increasing.[1] The government of Song Dynasty spent 45,040 Wen a year to occupy 116,500 Jin of salt produced by Qi Hu (households of pond salt production). According to the famous expert of economic history, Mr. Qi Xia, in the Economic History of Song Dynasty, it was estimated that the income from exploiting Ting Hu households by the government in Song Dynasty was as high as 90%. It can be seen that salt profit is one of the important sources of finance and taxation of the government.

In addition, due to the needs of ethnic minority areas, the central government of Song Dynasty also included the exchange of iron and other metals with the surrounding ethnic minority areas into the scope of special management of the government. Among them, in the seventh year of Qiandao years during the reign of Emperor Xiaozong of Song Dynasty (1171), the salt profit and the income of tea, fragrance and alum obtained by the government accounted for about 40% of the national monetary income, and its proportion could not be underestimated.

The government monopoly of Yuan Dynasty was more abundant than that of Song Dynasty, including gold, silver, copper, iron, tin, lead, mercury, alum, salt, tea, vinegar, and even agricultural tools and bamboo and wood. In the Yuan Dynasty, salt tax alone accounted for more than 50% of the national financial revenue. For example, during the Tianli years of Emperor Wendi in the Yuan Dynasty (1328-1330), the amount of salt tax in one year was as high as 7,661,000 ingots.[2]

1 *Comprehensive Examination of Documents* Vol. 9 Coins II.

2 *The History of Yuan Dynasty* Vol. 94 Shi Huo Zhi · Salt Law.

During the Ming and Qing Dynasties, the monopoly of salt and iron was still one of the basic national policies. However, at that time, the government's monopoly content was significantly decreased, and the production scale of government-run handicraft industry was reduced. The government monopolized profits mainly by controlling the marketing rights of patented products. In the Ming Dynasty, Kaizhong Law was implemented, which stipulated that merchants who were recruited to transport state military supplies, grain, fodder and other materials to designated locations would be granted corresponding salt sales licenses by the government according to the quantity of transportation. [1] On the one hand, it increases the government's financial revenue, and on the other hand, it saves the transportation cost of military supplies. The main economic responsibilities of local officials in the Ming Dynasty were "planning the affairs of salt and iron, business tax, and opening up land"[2]. It can be seen that the implementation of salt and iron monopoly in the Ming Dynasty is still one of the most basic economic functions of the government.

The salt law of the Qing Dynasty "basically follows the system of Ming Dynasty"[3]. The basic practice of salt law in the Qing Dynasty was to determine the number of Yan Yin issued each year according to the production and sales of salt, and to compile it into a "compendium" for each year, so as to attract investment until all the Yan Yin are claimed. This means that the government has completely separated itself from the production, transportation and sale of salt, and the sales of Yan Yin is led by merchants. Even so, the Qing government did not relax the management of salt industry, which was related to the national economy and people's livelihood.

The Qing Dynasty continued to implement the salt and iron monopoly system on the basis of previous practices. According to "The history of the Qing Dynasty, Shi Huo Zhi, Salt Law", the salt law of the Qing Dynasty included official

---

1 *The History of Ming Dynasty*, Vol. 80 Shi Huo Zhi, Salt Law.

2 *The History of Ming Dynasty*, Vol. 203 A biography of Ouyang Zhong.

3 *The History of Qing Dynasty* Vol. 123 Shi Huo Zhi, Salt Law.

supervision and merchant selling, official transportation and merchant selling, commercial transportation and merchant selling, commercial transportation and civil selling, civil transportation and civil selling, official supervision and civil selling, among which "only official supervision and merchant selling is extensive and lasts long". In fact, the Qing government strictly controlled the production and distribution of salt.

During the Ming and Qing Dynasties, on the one hand, the government monopolized salt and iron to control the lifeline of the economy. On the other hand, with the relatively active social economy, especially the commodity economy, the control of monopolized goods by the Ming and Qing governments also took on different forms of management and operation than before. This is an important phenomenon worthy of attention.

2.2. The government directly controls the economic lifeline – Mintage

In China's feudal society, policy makers in different periods generally used money coinage as a supplementary means of finance, or the use of currency issuance to serve the government's finance. Therefore, the central government in feudal society always attached great importance to the coinage right, and often regarded it as the key to control the lifeline of social economy.

At the beginning of the Western Han Dynasty, there were some overcorrections to the practices of the Qin Dynasty in some places, among which the monetary casting was an obvious example. We know that the unification of the six currencies in the Qin Dynasty conformed to the historical trend. Unifying currency is one of the important functions of unifying the country. It is indispensable for stabilizing social economy, promoting commodity circulation and strengthening the economic control of the country. At the beginning of the Western Han Dynasty, however, the government ordered the people to cast Jia Qian (a kind of money with the shape of elm pods)[1]. So, the rich merchants took advantage of the opportunity to forge money in order to make huge profits. Bad

1 *Han Shu* (*The Book of Han Dynasty*) Vol. 24 Shi Huo Zhi Vol. II.

money flooded the market and the prices were high. This inevitably affected the normal order of economic life, the financial revenue of the country, and even the normal operation of social economy. This should has some relationship with the situation that the local forces attempted to stand up to the central government as a rival in the Han Dynasty. There should be a certain relationship. In the fifth year of Emperor Wendi of the Han Dynasty (175 B.C.), "Because the money was more in number and lighter in weight, it was replaced by four Zhu coins, with the word 'Half Liang' on the front." The government had to rectify the monetary order. Not only that, the central government also abolished the "prohibition on civil casting" and "allow the people to cast money".[1] The decision of Emperor Wendi of the Han Dynasty aroused heated discussion in the government and among the public. Jia Yi, a political commentator, criticized the abolition. He emphasized that:

> The government monopolizes copper reserves, regulates the currency circulation with copper reserves, and finally achieves price stability and commodity balance.[2]

Jia Yi pointed out here that the central government should hold firmly the seigniorage, which is the key to control the economic lifeline, in order to effectively control the economy and local forces, and safeguard the central authority. This is quite insightful. In fact, this theory persisted throughout all periods of the feudal society after the Han Dynasty. On the whole, the feudal state did not pass the coinage power to others' hands, but controlled the coinage power more and more strictly. The practice in the early Western Han Dynasty was only a special case of overcorrecting the policies of the Qin Dynasty.

It is precisely because the government-controlled metal smelting and casting, which is a key area of the national economic lifeline, that from the Han Dynasty,

1 *Han Shu* (*The Book of Han Dynasty*) Vol. 24 Shi Huo Zhi Vol. II.
2 Ibid.

"those who dare to secretly cast iron or boil salt" were severely punished by the government[1] and this crackdown never stopped. During the Spring and Autumn Period and the Warring States Period, "those who secretly cast iron tools and boil salt can be as rich as the king"[2], which was not permitted by authoritarian centralization after the Qin and Han Dynasties. With the continuous strengthening and consolidation of centralization and the relative weakening of the powerful clans in line with it, since the mid-Tang Dynasty, although private money-casting still exists, it has not been the same as before the mid-Tang Dynasty. Generally, only according to the circulation of money in the market and the specific situation of commodity prices, the government decides to melt coin to make tools, or melt tools to make coins, just to gain the market price difference. That is to say, when coins are more expensive than tools, the coins will be melt to make tools; when coins are cheaper than tools, the tools will be melt to make coins. But as Ye Mengzhu in the Qing Dynasty said, "The collapse of coin-casting law starts with private casting, and the situation is worse than previous dynasties."[3] Such a summary is in line with history. In the Han Dynasty, the merchants said it was convenient to use the Wu Zhu Qian to improve the living order of the residents with the development of social economy.

Since the Tang Dynasty, the so-called private casting has already been different from "the monopoly of mountain and river resources" in the Wei, Jin and Southern and Northern Dynasties. But under the historical conditions of the continuous strengthening of authoritarian centralization, speculative businesses of "melting coins to make tools" or "melting tools to make coins" emerged according to the amount of coins cast in the society. Even so, the government still adopts severe laws against people who secretly cast money, in order to maintain the normal operation of social economy. In the history of coinage in the Tang Dynasty, private coin casting was a serious and common situation. In some cases, it even affected

1 *Records of the Grand Historian*, Vol. 30 Ping Zhun Shu.

2 *Records of the Grand Historian*, Vol. 129 Biographies of Merchants.

3 Ye Mengzhu, *Yue Shi Bian* (*Book of Reading the World*), Vol. 7 Money Law.

the circulation of normal coinage. There was a tendency for bad coins to reject good ones. In fact, as long as there is coinage, there must be private casting. This seems to be a rule in the history of coinage, and Tang Dynasty is no exception. Compared with past dynasties in the history, especially with the Han Dynasty, Wei Jin, Southern and Northern Dynasties, although the private casting in Tang Dynasty was not very serious, it had a certain negative impact on the social economy and the lives of the people at that time.

Private casting was directly related to the economic and social environment at that time, especially the quality of official governance. Tang Dynasty plays a very important role in the history of coinage in China. After the Qin Dynasty, the coinage system in the feudal society of China experienced two stages: the monetary system with Jizhong copper coin as the main circulation means and the monetary system with Jiyuan copper coin as the main circulation means. The demarcation line was the official appearance of Kaiyuan Tongbao in the fourth year of Wude, Gaozu of Tang Dynasty (621). During the circulation of Jizhong copper coins in China, the casting of Jizhong copper coins basically adopted the mode of government monopoly casting. The government monopolized the mintage of copper coins, which strengthened the nature of copper coins as legal currency and enhanced the circulation nature of valuable metals. During this period, the so-called private casting mainly focused on the raw material composition of the coin, that is, to reduce the proportion of copper and increase the proportion of tin that has relatively low value. In the later stage, besides the previous characteristics of private casting, the weight of coins was also reduced. In fact, such a distinction is only based on common sense, and the actual situation is much more complicated than this.

In the Tang Dynasty, a series of measures were taken to restrict and crack down on the situation of private casting, but the actual effect was not obvious. As early as Emperor Gaozong's years in the Tang Dynasty, there appeared such cases that "private casting thrives day by day, and some people even cast coins in boats floating on the river". In the Yifeng years during the reign of Gaozong in the Tang

Dynasty (676-679), "Most of the people living near the river make money by private casting. The patrol officers are ordered to inspect the Yangtze River and arrest the private casters. If still people are found in boats carrying copper, tin and wax more than 100 Jin, the officer will be dismissed from his post." In the first year of Yongchun years (682), it was further stipulated that "private casters will be sentenced to death, and at the same time people in the same neighborhood, community, or village will also be punished". However, these severe laws did not alleviate the extent of private casting. By the time of Emperor Wu Zetian, "private casting mushrooms. People depend on rivers and seas nearby to secretly cast coins, and officials cannot catch them".

In the early Tang Dynasty, only a higher proportion of base metals, such as lead and tin, was added. In the late Tang Dynasty and the Five Dynasties, however, the private casters often used little copper and used lead and tin as the main raw materials. Thus, the quality of money was poor and its value was greatly reduced[1]. In "Ziqing, Taiyuan, and Weibo, people blend in lead and iron in their trade"[2]. The period of Emperor Xuanzong is a key period of social development and change in Tang Dynasty and even the whole feudal society, which is also clearly reflected in coinage. During the period of Emperor Xuanzong in Tang Dynasty, many politicians and people engaged in the management of economic departments held discussion over the issue of coinage many times, which also reflects this social change from one aspect.

There was no fixed number of minters in the Tang Dynasty. During the period of Emperor Xuanzong of the Tang Dynasty, peasants with few skills were recruited to mint coins, which not only failed to guarantee the quality of the coins, but also made the peasants suffer terribly. They were "all fed up with this kind of life" and had reached the stage of tiring the people and draining the treasury. In view of this, "Wei Lun, a court workshop official, hire minters at high salary. So

1 Zhang Zexian: *Industry and Commerce in Tang Dynasty*, China Social Sciences Press, 1995, p. 50.

2 Zi Zhi Tong Jian Vol. 242.

the labor and expenses were reduced, but the high quality products are increased". If there should have 30 workers to take care of each stove, no less than 3,000 coins minters are needed all the year round. During the period of Emperor Xuanzong in Tang Dynasty, the output of copper coins was about 327,000 Guan.

Minting is the key for the state power to grasp the lifeline of social economy, and private ownership is not allowed under normal circumstances. One of the important reasons for the crackdown on Buddhism in the period of Emperor Wuzong in Tang Dynasty was that the practice prevails for people to melt coins to make utensils, especially Buddha statues. As recorded in "The New Book of Tang Dynasty·Shi Huo Zhi IV", "Emperor Wuzong cracked down on Buddhism. Yongping Supervisor Li Yuyan requested that the bronze statues, bells...furnace be given to the inspection department. There are more copper in prefectures and counties. The prefecture inspectors could set up more coin minting workshops. Huainan Jie Du Shi Li Shen demanded that each prefecture make money in the name of the prefecture, so the capital makes the capital money. The size of the capital money is similar to Kaiyuan Tongbao, and the old money is forbidden to be used in trade". This was the first time in Tang Dynasty that prefecture money was allowed to be used in trade. Emperor Wuzong's destruction of Buddha can be said to have led to relatively obvious benefits in coinage materials. A large number of copper Buddha statues have been melted into coinage raw materials, meeting the needs of the government for coinage to a certain extent. From another point of view, it can also be regarded as an extreme act of the central government in the Tang Dynasty to crack down on private casting under the circumstances of financial difficulties. After Emperor Xuanzong came to power, he immediately ordered the restoration of Buddhism, and stipulated that Huichang "new money can be distinguished because of the words on it and should be used to recast Buddha statues". This obviously is overcorrection to some extent, so it is difficult to accomplish in practice. Therefore, we can still see Huichang money today.

The phenomenon of private casting in Tang Dynasty was quite serious. As early as when in the fourth year of Emperor Wude's years when Kaiyuan Tongbao started to be cast, it was strictly stipulated to crack down on private casting: "The private will be sentenced to death, and the property of his family members will be confiscated"[1]. The more stable punitive law is: "Private minters will be sent into exile. Those who already have tools ready and have not yet begun casting will serve two years in prison...". Among them, those who "make smaller and thinner money in order to get copper for profits will serve one year in prison".[2]

In order to control the coinage right effectively, the Tang government set up an inspector[3] in areas where copper production was concentrated. In general, the Tang Dynasty "the post of mintage inspectors was held by the prefectural governor".[4] It is also a fact that the central government entrusts or appoints local officials to manage it, and at the same time sends envoys from the central government to supervise and control it. [5] In Tang Xuanzong's imperial decree, at least such information was revealed: at that time, the phenomenon of private casting was serious, and even severe punishment could hardly reverse the situation; at that time, those who had certain wealth in society tended to hoard coins, and when prices reached the expected 100% rise rate, they were willing to end the hoarding of coins. At that time, there were a large number of money hoarders, and they are often those economically powerful, which further aggravated the currency shortage in the circulation field (the so-called money shortage at that time). At the same time, Emperor Xuanzong of Tang Dynasty attempted to prohibit the sale of copper and lead, the basic raw materials of coins, by the people. He reiterated the importance of manufacture of copper wares, so as not to compete

1 *The New Book of Tang Dynasty* Vol. 54 Shi Huo Zhi IV.

2 T*ang Lv Shu Yi* (*Commentary of Criminal Law of Tang Dynasty*) Vol. 26 Miscellaneous Laws.

3 Maps and Annals of Yuanhe County, Vol. 33 Jiannan Road, Zizhou.

4 *The Six Administrative Codes in the Tang Dynasty* Vol. 22 Mintage Supervisors .

5 *Quan Tang Wen* Vol. 23, Tang Xuanzong Reiteration of the Prohibition of Private Copper Casting: "Appointed supervisory officials should issue official documents, prohibiting the private trade of copper and tin, as well as the production of copper ware. After copper and lead are mined, the government shall purchase at market price. The government should not force the prices down, so as to benefit the people."

with the government for raw materials. In fact, this is hard to achieve. As for Tang Xuanzong's statement, it is feasible for the government to purchase newly mined copper and lead raw materials in the form of package purchasers, which are purchased by the government at the market price, rather than by officially forcing down the price. In the Tang Dynasty, private mining was allowed, but the iron ore mined by the private sector had to be sold to the relevant government departments. So, the government actually played the role of a package purchaser.

From the perspective of monetary evolution in the feudal society of China, it has undergone a process of gradual transformation from metal currency to nominal currency. China's feudal society completed the whole process from full value currency to under-value currency, and finally to nominal currency without its own value.

The output of copper coins in the Northern Song Dynasty exceeded that in the Tang Dynasty. Generally, the annual output was between 1 million and 3 million Guan, with a maximum output of 5.06 million Guan. "Feiqian" appeared in the Tang Dynasty, and the Song Dynasty began to issue "Jiaozi" - banknotes from the Renzong years. This is a very important economic event in the history of China. The appearance of Jiaozi is a very complicated process, which reflects a series of social changes, such as the development of social productive forces, the relative activity of commodity-currency relations, the relative reduction of direct producer's personal dependence and the increase of feudal exploitation rate. In addition, the Song Dynasty also carried out such taxes as "He Mai Juan Bo" and "Di Liang Mi" and so on. At the beginning of the implementation, mandatory acquisition amounts were apportioned according to the amount of land, but only a certain amount of money was paid. Shortly after its implementation, it gradually became an unpaid apportionment. Even later, this kind of textiles or grain was converted into money and ordered people to submit, which evolved into a regular burden for the people.

As in the late Northern Song Dynasty, the Southern Song Dynasty issued money indiscriminately. The difference is that unlike the Emperor Huizong period in the Northern Song Dynasty who mainly issued Dang Shi Da Qian, the Southern Song Dynasty government mainly issued paper currency. And its cost of issuing money was much lower than that in the late Northern Song Dynasty. In the first year of Qingyuan years of Emperor Ningzong in the Southern Song Dynasty (1195), as many as 30 million Guan notes were issued by the central government. At that time, instead of converting money with gold, silver and copper coins, only old Jiao Zi is exchanged for new Jiao Zi, and the old ones depreciated by 50%. The government usually uses Jiaozi to buys grain and other handicraft products. The government also uses Jiaozi to pay the salaries of officials and the reward money of the army. Thus, due to the monetization of tax and corvee, prices soared and the currency depreciated, and the burden of the common people increased exponentially. In short, the government accumulated a large amount of social wealth through the issuance and exchange of banknotes, which made the consumption of the upper class temporarily living in the south of the Yangtze River in the Southern Song Dynasty reach a very high level. Relatively speaking, the prosperity at that time was not real. It was based on the monetization of taxation and corvee, not on the basis of active commodity economy.

During the Ming and Qing Dynasties, the government's control over coinage was basically the same as that of other periods. Baoyuan Bureau, an institution affiliated to Gong Bu (the Ministry of Industry), was in charge of coinage affairs throughout the country. The government strictly controlled the issuance of money, and also took a severe crackdown on the situation of private casting. However, private casting always existed in the Ming and Qing Dynasties.

2.3. Wine Monopoly

Brewing industry is one of the most profitable industries. In feudal society where agricultural productivity is relatively low, the brewing industry is often heavily restricted by the government. Besides the consideration of economic interests, the government's concern is also based on the factors of saving grain. However, driven by interest and influenced by people's consumption habits, it is difficult to really restrict folk brewing in social reality.

China's brewing industry has been relatively advanced in the government from beginning to end. The "Xiao Nie Chen" in inscriptions on bones or tortoise shells of the Shang Dynasty is the official being in charge of brewing, whose responsibility is mainly to serve the royal family and its nobles. Therefore, the oracle bone inscriptions recorded that the king of Shang and his ministers personally went to the official brewing workshop to inspect: "In the year of Ding Chou,...the Emperor went to inspect the job of the Xiao Nie Chen". In addition to the consumption of royalty and nobility, the Shang Dynasty government also sold part of the wine brewed as a commodity in the market: "There are many markets in the cities. And wagons and horses are used for the transportation of wine and meat."[1] Wine-making is an industry with high economic returns. It is reasonable that wine-making ranks first among the more than 30 profit-making industries listed in "Biographies of Merchants" of *Records of the Grand Historian*, Volume 129. Since then, there has been no significant change in the situation of high returns on wine-making. Wine monopoly is the "Que Gu". Firstly, wine-making needs certain amount of grain as raw material, which is regarded as a waste of food and a consumption of luxury goods in feudal society when productivity is low. Secondly, the government controls the production of wine or the distiller's yeast to control the price of wine, so as to obtain higher profits. Moisten. Another reason is that in traditional society, there is often a concept that drinking, especially excessive drinking, is not conducive to maintaining a simple and honest folk custom, which is not conducive to the implementation of the ideals of statesmen and intellectuals in governing the country, the family and the world.

In the Han Dynasty, in order to effectively expand the government's financial resources and inhibit the development of non-governmental commodity economy, the sale of alcoholic drinks was also monopolized. According to "*Han Shu*·Biography of Emperor Wudi", the practice of "Que Gu (wine monopoly)"[2]

1 The Emperor's Century, cited in Vol. 83 of *Taiping Yu Lan*.

2 As quoted from Ying Shao in *Han Shu*, Vol. 6, Biography of Emperor Wudi: "The county officials monopolize the sale of wine, and the common people couldn't engage in this."

began in the Western Han Dynasty at the latest the third year of Tianhan Dynasty (98 BC). The government strictly controlled the production and sale of wine through the "Que Gu officials" assigned everywhere. It is an indisputable fact that the profits of wine-making are abundant in ancient and modern times. Therefore, the state power tries its best to control it, and its abundant economic returns become an important part of the government's financial revenue:

> Since Emperor Xiaowu in Han Dynasty started wine monopoly, people either submit self-reported tax to sell wine in the market, or open shops to make profits, or pay wine tax monthly, or pay silk tax every month. What's more, the officials made wine themselves and banned the private brewing of the people. The officials mainly brewed wine and levyied tax on people. Up to the Xining years of the Song Dynasty (1068-1077), the tax on wine could reach more than 400,000. There was forced apportionment on woodcutters and small employers. What is even worse, sometimes, the apportioned tax was more than the regular tax.[1]

The government of Han Dynasty directly controlled or managed brewing, and the economic benefits are self-evident. In fact, since the implementation of the wine monopoly in the Han Dynasty, "the relaxation of alcohol prohibition originated from this."[2] The government's management of wine production and sales is relatively relaxed, and its control is mainly achieved through tax policies.

In the period of Wang Mang's new dynasty, the information of wine-making cost accounting in the government-run handicraft workshop was relatively clear. The production situation described by Xihe (Da Si Nong) Lu Kuang at that time is here presented. The main idea was as follows: he believed that "if wine is absolutely forbidden, people cannot perform ceremony and show courtesy; if wine

1 *Comprehensive Examination of Documents in the Qing Dynasty*, Vol. 30, Commodity Tax and Government Monopoly · Que Gu (Wine Monopoly).

2 *Ri Zhi Lu*, Vol. 28, Wine Prohibition.

is allowed with no limitation, there will be a waste of man power and money". He therefore requested:

> Please follow the example of ancient times, allowing the government to make wine, with 2500 Dan as one Jun. First open a shop to sell wine, with 50 Niang as a benchmark. The first brewing uses 2 Hu of brown rice and 1 Hu of distiller's yeast, making 6 Hu and 6 Dou of wine. They use their own rice yeast, 3 Hu every month, and calculate the prices to divide them into three parts, using one of them as the average price of one Hu. Apart from the cost price of the distiller's yeast, the calculated profit is divided into ten parts. Seven parts are handed over to the government, the remaining three parts and the wine and charcoal pay for of the craftsmen's equipment and firewood[1].

The government-run handicraft workshop had obvious scale benefit when brewing wine. One of the reasons that could not be ignored was that the craftsmen at that time were composed of folk craftsmen and official slaves, whose cost was very low. The main cost was the raw materials such as rice and yeast. At that time, about 30% of the government's brewing profit was used as cost, and the remaining 70% as government revenue. It is not difficult to see that government brewing is an industry with very high economic returns, and the economic significance of the government wine monopoly is self-evident.

In the Chen Dynasty (557-589) of the Southern Dynasty, "Yuyao Yu Li, the subordinate official of Chen Dynasty's prince, and Kong Wan, the imperial governor, initiated the establishment of a tax on boiling sea salt and an official patent wine-selling agency because of the state's financial constraints. Emperor Wendi approved this suggestion by decree."[2] Chen Dynasty's salt tax and wine

1 *Han Shu* (*The Book of Han Dynasty*) Vol. 24 Shi Huo Zhi Vol. II.

2 *History of the Chen Dynasty* Vol. 3 Chronicles of Shizu

monopoly was one of the main sources of national financial revenue at that time, and occupied an important position in the gross national product. Not only in the Southern Dynasty, there was also wine monopoly in the Northern Dynasty. [1]

Another way to expand tax sources in the Tang Dynasty was to intensify wine monopoly. One of the basic facts we know is that in the early Tang Dynasty, the government took a laissez-faire attitude generally toward wine brewing, allowing folk production and generally did not levy taxes. Only in the second year of Guangde years of Emperor Daizong (764) in the Tang Dynasty did it begin to stipulate that the wine brewers should pay taxes on a monthly basis. During the Jianzhong years of Emperor Dezong (780-783) when tea tax was levied formally, the government banned people from making and selling alcoholic drinks by themselves, but the government made wine in its own shops. At that time, it levied a tax of 3,000 Qian per Hu. At the same time, it is stipulated that those who brew alcoholic beverages privately are subject to criminal punishment. But the cost of production and management for the government to make wine was high. Especially at that time, the alcoholic content of yellow rice wine was relatively low, the amount of alcohol consumed was relatively large, and the transportation of wine was relatively difficult. For rice wine, long-distance transportation often deteriorated the wine. So, the practice of official wine-making was stopped soon. Emperor Dezong's practice in the second year of Zhenyuan years (786) was to adopt a tax system. For the those who brew and sell wine, the government would draw 150 Qian per Dou. The government exempted these wine sellers from corvee. To the sixth year of Yuanhe years during the reign of Xianzong in the Tang Dynasty (811), the government set up wine shop in the capital, and began to levy taxes on wine. In Tang Dynasty, there were many changes in the policy of wine brewing and selling, but it was gradually placed in the system of government wine monopoly, and became one of the fixed taxes in government revenue. Like other dynasties, the Tang government, especially in the middle and late Tang Dynasty,

1 *History of Northern Dynasty* Vol. 7 Chronicles of Qi Dynasty.

the focus was fixed on the amount of tax revenue.

As we know, the wine-making industry in Tang Dynasty developed rapidly. In addition to the small-scale wine-making mainly used for their own consumption by ordinary peasant families, a considerable number of professional wine-making households emerged. In the Tang Dynasty and later on, the brewing industry was first restricted, but later brought into the government's tax revenue system. During the reign of Daizong in the Tang Dynasty, the government formally levied taxes on private wine sellers, and each state assessed the sellers, who were divided into three grades according to the amount of their assets and the scale of production. Huzhou Cishi Li Ying asked the central government to "allow the people to sell wine, and levy tax on it"[1]. This was approved by the government. While promoting the development of private brewing industry, it undoubtedly increases the government's financial revenue.

Many times in the Tang Dynasty, the government cancelled wine monopoly, which just shows that wine monopoly did exist throughout the Tang Dynasty, especially when the government ran into difficulty with its financial revenue.

In Song Dynasty, the system of official brewing and selling was implemented. The central government has set up Du Qu Yuan, the largest brewing institution in Bian Jing. Du Qu Yuan "is responsible for making the first-class yeast, providing for the court and sell to wine shops for profit". Every year, the mill of wheat in Qu Yuan alone amounts to 40,000 Dan. The stone mill used for grinding raw wheat in Quyuan was 30 and the donkeys used were 600. And 428 soldiers participated. [2] Du Qu Yuan makes use of the cheap labor of soldiers and a small number of technical craftsmen to produce distiller's yeast, which is provided to private winery in the capital and other cities for a fee. The government obtained high profits by monopolizing liquor yeast. In Song Dynasty, besides continuing with

1 *Tang Hui Yao* (*Historical Records of the Systems in the Tang Dynasty*), Vol. 88, Wine Monopoly.

2 *Edited Manuscripts of Song Hui Yao* (*Historical Records of the Systems in the Song Dynasty*), Officials, 26-33~34.

the tea monopoly since Tang Dynasty, there was also monopoly of vinegar, spice, alum and so on, and their contents were further increased. In the Northern Song Dynasty, there was an "imperial edict ordering not to increase taxes"[1]. It showed that the wine monopoly was not only one of the basic sources of the government's normal fixed financial revenue, but also had an irreversible trend of increasing. Therefore, the policy of "exempting the areas of Yangtze River, Huai River, Jing River and Zhejiang Province from increasing tax"[2] was regarded as a beneficiary policy implemented by the central government at that time. "Increasing taxes and monopolizing wine, increasing prices and collecting vinegar tax"[3] shows that in the Song Dynasty the government was increasing tax sources and the proportion of tax revenue. "The legislation of wine monopoly is very strict and the prisoners' property will be confiscated."[4] Although in the Song Dynasty these provisions were not fully implemented in actuality, the government has always attached great importance to increasing fiscal revenue.

Compared with the tea law, the alcohol prohibition in Song Dynasty was stricter. In order to control the wine-making industry fundamentally, the early Song Dynasty stipulated that all levels of cities should set up wine-making business, and the government should make wine yeast for sale. As for villages and towns, people are allowed to brew wine by themselves, but they must pay wine tax to the government. Since the second year of Qingli years during the reign of Emperor Renzong (1042), additional tax has been levied to "add profit and tax on salt and wine", which is the origin of "Tian Jiu Qian (Additional Tax on Alcohol Tax)". Zhao Kaiyu of Southern Song Dynasty reformed the alcohol law when he presided over Sichuan's finance in the third year of Jianyan years during the reign of Gaozong (1129). At that time, special wine-making institutions were set up in Sichuan, presided over by government officials. If the local people brew

1 *History of the Song Dynasty* Vol. 7 Chronicles of Emperor Zhenzong II.
2 Ibid.
3 *History of the Song Dynasty* Vol. 179 Shi Huo Zhi II-1.
4 *History of the Song Dynasty* Vol. 381 Biography of Hong Ni.

with their own grain, the government only charges processing fees, i.e. 52 Qian per Hu. The government no longer concerns itself with whether the wine brewed by local people will be for their own consumption or for sales. This method of "Ge Cao Fa" is simple and easy, which not only increases the government's financial revenue, but also facilitates the people's demand for brewing wine. Later, however, the government arbitrarily increased the amount of wine tax, and additional taxes were very common. In Song Dynasty, a strict wine monopoly system was implemented. There were "forbidden areas" between urban and rural areas and between cities, which could not be surmounted. So, there was basically no long-distance transportation. In addition, the wine produced in Song Dynasty was mainly yellow rice wine, which would turn sour and deteriorate easily, and was not suitable for long-distance transportation. As for Song and Jin, a certain amount of high-quality wine was brought to Jin as a gift in the diplomatic engagement of envoys of the two countries. It can be seen that wine is very important for both sides. After Emperor Zhenzong in Northern Song Dynasty, wine profits rose sharply, reaching 17 million Guan at the peak in the Renzong Dynasty. However, wine profits could not increase indefinitely, because it was restricted by many factors such as consumption level and food production. So, it basically maintained at about 1.3 billion Guan after the Shenzong Dynasty.

In the Jin Dynasty, the general situation of wine monopoly was that "the Jin Dynasty adopted the wine monopoly system, and followed the old system of Liao and Song Dynasties. In the third year of Tianhui years (1125), the government began to appoint official. In the third year of Dading years during the reign of Emperor Shizong (1163), the imperial decree required that the private brewers be interrogated and convicted".[1] The system of wine monopoly in Jin Dynasty followed that of Song and Liao Dynasties, but there were also changes. In the Yuan Dynasty, the wine monopoly system made great adjustments in the time of Yuan Shizu Kublai Khan:

1 *History of the Jin Dynasty* Vol. 9 Shi Huo Zhi IV.

> At the beginning, the folk people made wine by themselves, but they must pay 1 Guan for 1 Dan of rice used. Lu Shirong prepared 50,000 ingots of official banknotes, and set up the wine monopoly law, stipulating that people must pay 10 Guan for I Dan of rice used, which was ten times more than before. So far, the government stopped wine monopoly, allowing people to make wine by themselves freely, but the tax was increased from 1 Guan to 5 Guan[1].

Although the folk were allowed to brew freely in Yuan Dynasty, the tax on brewing was greatly increased and the government's financial revenue was greatly increased. It can be seen that although the Yuan Dynasty relaxed wine monopoly, it improved the economic efficiency of the government through the tax policy. In fact, the government controlled the whole country's brewing through tax. Especially in the Yuan Dynasty, the establishment of a "Da Du Jiu Ke Ti Ju Si (Capital Wine Tax Administration Office), being in charge of the wine and vinegar monopoly affairs"[2], which shows that the wine monopoly institutions are relatively sound, and wine monopoly is one of the basic sources of government revenue.

During the Ming and Qing Dynasties, with the development of commodity economy, the government gradually relaxed its monopoly over wine, and its position in the national financial revenue is far less important than before.

In a word, liquor was a highly profitable trade in feudal society. Although the government adopted a prohibition system for wine, the implementation of the system was far less thorough than that of salt and iron monopoly, mainly determined by wine as a special commodity. We all know that after the Southern Song Dynasty, distilled liquor was invented in China. Before that, rice wine and

1 *History of the Yuan Dynasty* Vol. 13 Chronicles of Yuan Shizu Kublai Khan
2 *History of the Yuan Dynasty* Vol. 85 Bai Guan Zhi (Notitia Dignitatum) I.

yellow rice wine were commonly consumed. Their alcohol content was not high. It was a very difficult problem for the storage and transportation of such wine. The cost of government brewing and direct selling was relatively high. In addition, at that time, the conditions for wine production were relatively low, and individual families could also complete it, which affected the possibility of monopoly by the government.

Some scholars believe that the frequent government adoption of the system of "monopoly (official industry) " since Emperor Wudi of Han Dynasty is the most important restrictive factor hindering the development of China's market economy in the long history of more than two thousand years. [1] In fact, this is only one aspect of the problem, because although the monopoly system of feudal society in China has the effect of restricting the development of commodity economy, it is not the main aspect. Monopoly and wine monopoly take into consideration national economic security, macro control and the role of preventing the rich businessmen from monopolizing the lifeline of the economy. At the same time, the government controls or directly manages industries related to national economy and people's livelihood, such as smelting industry also plays the role of gathering manpower, material and financial resources to engage in large-scale production in feudal society with relatively low productivity, which has scale benefits to a certain extent. In addition, from the perspective of the operation of the government-run handicraft industry in feudal society, monopoly is not necessarily the official industry. In some periods, the so-called prohibition is only over the production price, quality, tax, etc. for the stipulated products, but not necessarily the government's direct production. Sometimes, the government supervises the production, circulation and even consumption process, with government serving as a package purchaser. It is a common phenomenon.

In a word, the content of monopoly system in Chinese traditional society is

1 Looking at the Periodic Rise and Fall of Market Economy from the History of China - Professor Wei Sen's Speech at Fudan University, *Wen Hui Bao*, April 22, 2007, p. 6.

very complex, which cannot be underestimated.

2.4. Tea Monopoly

The content of government monopoly in Tang Dynasty has been expanded. Tea monopoly becomes part of government monopoly in Tang Dynasty.

Although literature record of tea was early in China, it really became a popular beverage for residents starting from Tang Dynasty. Tea became one of the monopoly contents of the Tang Dynasty, which had a positive correlation with the increase of tea consumption at that time. Historically, people in the Tang Dynasty "got obsessed with tea, drinking day and night, and it became a custom" [1]. Tea has become a necessity in people's daily life, as indispensable as firewood, rice, oil and salt:

> Tea is food, no different from rice or salt, and people share the same customs far and wide. Tea can both quench one's thirst and get one refreshed, therefore it is difficult to give it up. People especially love drinking tea in the field. [2]

This trend of tea drinking has gradually expanded from the mainland to the surrounding minority areas. [3]

Tea monopoly began in the ninth year of the Taihe years during the reign of Emperor Wenzong (835), when the central government first appointed Wang Ya as Tea Monopoly Envoy. [4] At that time, the practice was to "the tea will be classified into three grades and one out of ten of the cost will be taken as tax". At

1 *Feng Shi Wen Jian* Ji Vol. 6 Tea Drinking.

2 *Book of Tang* Vol. 173 Biography of Li Yu.

3 *Feng Shi Wen Jian Ji*" Vol. 6 Tea Drinking: The custom of drinking tea in Tang Dynasty "began from the inner land and spread beyond the Great Wall. In the past, after the Uighurs came visiting the emperor, they returned home with horse and tea".

4 *Book of Tang* Vol. 17 Emperor Wenzong of Tang II: "Wang Ya presented the profit from tea monopoly, so he was appointed as the tea monopoly envoy. Tea tax started from Wang Ya's rule".

the beginning, a commercial tax of about 10% was levied according to the grade of tea. In the ninth year of Taihe (835), the tax on tea reached as much as 400,000 Min. At the end of Tang Wenzong's reign, the mining and metallurgical tax of the whole country was more than 70,000 Min, but it "could not be compared with the tea tax of a county"[1]. Among them, in Fuliang County, Raozhou, which abound in tea, there are "seven million loads (carried by a pack-animal) of tea and 150,000 Guan taxes per year"[2]. It can be seen that the income of tea monopoly was very important in the financial revenue of the central government at that time. In Tang Wuzong period, the government increased tea tax in the Yangtze River and Huai River area, the main tea producing area. In order to ensure the full collection of tea tax, the relevant government departments of the Tang Dynasty set up special agencies — "Di" — in various places. The profit obtained was called Ta Di Qian.

In the Tang Dynasty, when the government imposed heavy taxes, the phenomenon of tea smuggling became more and more serious. In order to effectively curb the smuggling activities, the government has adopted severe laws to suppress it. Those who sell tea privately will face death penalty[3]. It should be said that the government's harsh law can hardly work in practice, because in the three-party game among the government, businessmen and tea farmers, the government in a dominant position constantly increases the tea tax, which greatly enhances the profits of the government. This was finally achieved at the expense of the interests of tea farmers and consumers, which provided a broad space for tea smuggling and will inevitably affect the production and sale of tea under the direct control of the government, especially the government's financial revenue. There is a special reason why the Tang government attaches so much importance to the tea tax and the tea tax is so extremely heavy. This is because after the formation of the separatist regime in the middle and late Tang Dynasty, the government's revenue and expenditure are often insufficient, and one of the important ways to expand

1 *The New Book of Tang Dynasty* Vol. 54 Shi Huo Zhi IV.
2 *Annals of Yuan He County* Vol. 28 Rao Zhou · Fu Liang County.
3 *The New Book of Tang Dynasty* Vol. 54 Shi Huo Zhi IV.

the sources of tax is to increase the tea tax. In other words, the traditional tax potential of the Tang Dynasty government has been very limited, and opening up new tax sources is the inevitable choice of the imperial court in the increasingly embarrassing financial revenue environment, and tea tax is the best choice of the government at that time.

Among the many nationalities and tribes in the Tang Dynasty, the Tubo (Tibentan) nationality was greatly influenced by tea drinking culture in the mainland. During the Kaiyuan period of Emperor Xuanzong of Tang Dynasty (713-741), Tubo and Tang exchanged goods in Chiling and Longzhou, mainly horses, tea and silk.

In the middle and late Tang Dynasty, tea drinking was very popular in the upper class of Tubo, and their understanding of tea was very comprehensive. According to records, in the Jianzhong years during the reign of Emperor Tang Dezong (780-783), Chang Yan, a high-ranking official, was sent to Tubo by the imperial court.:

> Chang Yan (Lu Gong)was sent to Tubo as an envoy. One day, he was brewing tea in the tent. The Zan Pu (Tubo king) asked, "What is this?" Lu Gong said, "This is tea, which can help one forget worry and quench thirst". Zan Pu said, "I have it too!" Then he ordered people to bring out his tea, and said:" This from Shouzhou. This is from Shuzhou. This is from Guzhu. This is from Qimen. This is from Changming. This is from Huhu".[1]

From this material, we can see that making tea was quite popular in the upper class of Tubo at least at that time. Zan Pu had a very rich knowledge of tea, and could tell the specific origin of tea. His tea storage basically included the main origin of tea in the mainland. In addition, this historical data is enough to show that the tea flowing into Tubo from the mainland is mainly via folk communication, not through official exchange or tribute. Because if the official tea

1 *Supplement to History of Tang Dynasty*, Vol. II.

exchange was smooth at that time, Zam Pu would not show off his tea produced in the mainland in front of Tang officials.

The situation with Tubo's tea is in line with the general circulation of commodities, first through folk channels rather than through official exchanges or tributes. The popularity of tea in Tubo area is not only related to its basic functions of helping digestion, quenching thirst and dispelling fatigue, but also to their widespread belief in Buddhism in Tubo area, since Buddhist meditators need to drink tea to expel drowsiness. With the prevalence of tea drinking in Tubo, the demand for tea sets has become increasingly urgent. According to Han Zang Shi Ji (the Records of the History of Han and Tibet), Chidusong Zanpu of Tubo, in order to obtain tea-drinking utensils, sent special envoys to Tang Dynasty to request tea bowls and so on. It is said that the emperor did not directly meet Zanpu's specific requirements, but sent a skilled craftsman to Tubo. When the craftsman arrived in Tubo, he made a rare tea bowl even in the mainland with the clay and other raw materials Zanpu took from the inner storehouse. The bowl has the characteristics of wide rim, thin texture, short feet, being smooth and fine, and showing blue luster. The first bowl is decorated with Tubo legends about the origin of tea, while the other bowls are painted with various animal patterns. Zanpu was very satisfied with the tea bowl made by craftsmen in the Tang Dynasty and named it himself.[1] This is a wonderful story about the cultural exchange between Tang Dynasty and Tubo Dynasty, which shows that the central plains dynasty had painstaking efforts to promote cultural and economic exchanges with Tubo. According to legend, Princess Wencheng played a positive role in promoting tea drinking in Tubo. The Appendix to Tibetan Political and Religious Inspection records that the first batch of tea in the mainland entered the Tubo area with Princess Wencheng. Chen Tao, a Tang Dynasty poet, wrote in his poem Longxi Xing: "Since our princess married your prince, your culture resembles the Han style", which seems to include

1 Cairang: Handicraft Industry in Tubo Society, *Journal of Northwest Institute for Nationalities,* No. 3, 1990.

the popular tea drinking in Tubo area.[1] It can be seen from the interaction and influence of Tang and Tubo in economy, culture and living customs. In particular, the contribution of the central plains dynasty to the dissemination of inner land culture, art and production technology is self-evident.

The tea monopoly system was further developed in the Song and Yuan Dynasties. According to "History of the Yuan Dynasty, Shi Huo Zhi", in the Yanyou years (1314-1320), the government collected 1 million Yin of tea tax. If we estimate each Yin at 120 Jin each, the annual tea output in China was about 120,000,000 Jin. Such a huge output of tea, even today, is no small number.

The control of tea in Song Dynasty was stricter than that of salt. Tea has become a popular beverage since the Tang Dynasty, and at the same time it has become a popular beverage and necessity of life comparable to firewood, rice, oil and salt in ethnic minority areas. The food of nomadic people is mainly meat and cheese, while tea has the functions of helping digestion, quenching thirst and dispelling fatigue. Therefore, the nomadic people are increasingly demanding for it. They depend on them in their everyday life. In order to stabilize and increase the government's financial revenue on the one hand, and to effectively control the economic exchanges with nomadic peoples on the other hand, the Song Dynasty was quite strict about the tea law. In the early Northern Song Dynasty, the government implemented the policy of official sale of tea. The government set up six "Que Huo Wu (institutions that regulate trade and taxation)" and 13 mountain farms in the core area of tea production. According to the regulations at that time, Yuan Hu, the tea planting professional household, should first give a certain amount of tea to the government as tea tax, and the remaining tea was purchased by the government according to the official price, and then wholesaled to merchants for further sale at a higher price. All kinds of taxes paid by Yuan Hu can be converted to tea. In order to ensure the production of tea, the Song

1 See Wei Mingkong, The Improvement of Handicraft Industry and Life and Food Structure of Residents in Sui and Tang Dynasties, *Journal of Capital Normal University*, No. 5, 1997.

government first gave the Yuan Hu a certain amount of tea money --- the capital, which is similar to today's deposit. This is conducive to the maintenance of production and life of tea farmers, and undoubtedly has a certain role in promoting the stability of tea production. Tea merchants in the capital usually practiced Cha Yin Zhi (licensing policy). Tea merchants first pay money or submit textiles at the Que Huo Wu in the capital, receive tea license, obtain tea in designated tea fields, and then sell them. When dealing with the surrounding minority nationalities, they should hold the certificates issued by the relevant government departments. For the sake of safety and convenience, tea merchants in southeastern China can pay money or textiles at the local Que Huo Wu for tea license.

From the above, it can be seen that in Song Dynasty, because the relevant government departments package purchased tea, the purchase price and the price of tea sold to businessmen were both determined by the government. The price difference was relatively large, and tea became one of the important sources of government revenue.

During the Jiayou years of Song Renzong (1056-1063), the above-mentioned tea-selling system was reformed and replaced by commercial law. The so-called commercial law is to stipulate that Yuan Hu pays tea mountain rent to the government and tea merchants pay tea tax to the government. In this way, Yuan Hu and tea merchants can trade directly, and the degree of marketization is relatively high. The Song Dynasty changed the tea monopoly system to the tea tax system, which reflected the active commodity economy and the further reduction of the direct producer's personal dependence at that time. At the same time, it also reduced the government's management cost of tea tax.

The monopoly system of salt, tea and wine was implemented in Song Dynasty, which played a very important role in increasing government revenue, preventing businessmen from monopolizing the market and strengthening central power.

The Ming Dynasty was a period of unprecedented prosperity when the government managed the tea-horse trade. There are two main reasons for this. First, in order to resist Mongolia, the Ming Dynasty urgently needed to obtain a large number of warhorses from the northwest and other areas. Second, influenced by the development of commodity economy in the inner land at that time, national trade was also active, and the tea and horse trade was one of the most important contents of national trade. The tea and horse market in Ming Dynasty changed a lot from before, which mainly manifested itself as a kind of economic policy with political strategy that matched the military defense at that time. In the early Ming Dynasty, the central government established Qiwei in Guanxi area, including Anding, Quxian, Aduan, Handong, Shazhou, Chijin and Hami, west of Jiayuguan, west of Qinghai Lake and Qaidam Basin, which facilitated the effective control of such nomadic nationalities as Mongolian and Saliwuer here. In the process of political rule of the Northwest ethnic groups, the Ming Dynasty paid special attention to the use of tea, their daily necessities, as a means of control, which was based on the further dependence of the Northwest ethnic groups on tea. At that time, "the minorities liked cheese, so if they could not drink tea, they would fall ill"[1]. Especially in the Qinghai-Tibet Plateau, where highland barley was the main food crop, while "the heat of barley can only be eased by tea".[2] At the same time, the horses needed by the inner land mainly depended on the supply of ethnic minorities in the Northwest region. In order to unify the complementarity of multi-ethnic economy in the country, the tea-horse market in the northwest of the Ming Dynasty flourished unprecedentedly. Therefore, the Ming Dynasty was the golden age of the tea-horse market, just as the history recorded, "Both official tea and commercial tea are provided to trade horses"[3]. The Tea-Horse exchange market in Ming Dynasty was mainly controlled and operated by the central government.

In the Ming Dynasty, the tea-horse exchange institutions were more complete than before. The central government set up a special agency for the government-

1 *History of the Ming Dynasty* Vol. 80 Shi Huo Zhi IV "Tea Law".

2 Wang Tingxiang, *Ming Jingshi Wenbian* Vol. 149: Wang's Collection of Tibetan Literature, Vol. 2 Yancha (Shucha), photocopy edition of Zhonghua Book Company in 1962, p. 1489.

3 *History of the Ming Dynasty* Vol. 80, Shi Huo Zhi IV "Tea Law".

run Tea-Horse exchange, Cha Ma Si (Tea-horse Department), to manage the tea-horse exchange between the inner land and the Northwest Ethnic groups. As early as in the period of Ming Taizu Zhu Yuanzhang, when the war in the whole country had not completely ended, in view of the huge and urgent demand for horses from the central government, officials were sent to the Northwest Tibetan region, where horses were abundant, to buy or exchange horses in kind. During the eighth year of Hongwu years (1375), Zhao Cheng, the Imperial Supervisor who conveys the Emperor's edict, took silk fabrics and Bacha tea to Hezhou (now Linxia, Gansu Province) for the horse trade. Because the price of official horse trade was obviously higher than the market price, the ethnic minorities who came to trade horses were still in an endless stream. Driven by interests, even the Tibetans in the area of Guide (now East Hainan of Qinghai Province) traveled long distances to trade horses. The horse trade in Ming Dynasty was a victory. Following that, the Ming Dynasty Hu Bu purchased 7,000 horses in Xining, Hezhou and Minzhou, the important bases of Tea-Horse exchange in Northwest China, with a huge sum of 600,000 Ding. In the twenty-fifth year of Hongwu (1392), more than 10,300 horses were exchanged for 300,000 Jin of tea. The large scale of horse trade in early Ming Dynasty indicates that the nomadic people in Northwest China are quite active in Tea-Horse exchange or horse trade, and the trade space between the supplier and the demander is quite large. With the consolidation of the rule of the Ming Dynasty over the Northwest regions, the tea-horse market was gradually determined to be under the direct control of the central government, and various Tea-Horse Divisions in Hezhou, Xining and Ganzhou were set up successively to serve as the main place for the Ming Dynasty to acquire war horses in the Northwest regions.[1] The settings of Tea-Horse Divisions have changed in the later history. Until Wanli years (1573-1620), there were six Tea-Horse Divisions in Hezhou, Taozhou, Minzhou, Ganzhou, Xining and Zhuanglang. Among them, Hezhou, Taozhou, Ganzhou and Xining had the longest settings and had not

1 *Gansu Annals Manuscript*, Vol. 37 Finance and Taxation, II, Taxes and Levies.

changed much till the end of Ming Dynasty.

The Tea-Horse trade system in the Ming Dynasty was relatively advanced, which was mainly manifested in the implementation of Jin Pai Xin Fu system (the gold tally system) in Hongwu years during the reign of Zhu Yuanzhang (1368-1398). As for the gold tally system, the history books record it as follows:

> Gold tallies were made. Cao Guo Gong Yang Jinglong was ordered to enter the minority area, and offered to make a pact for trade. The seal inscriptions said "Emperor's Imperial Decree". The left tally said "if the two tallies fit, the Chaifa duty should be fulfilled", and right tally said "those who do not believe should be killed". Altogether there are forty-one tallies: Taozhou, Huoba, Zangsi and Nangri nationalities were given 4 tallies, and they should offer 3,050 Chaifa horses; Hezhou, Bili, and Weixi and other nationalities, altogether 29, were given twenty-one tallies, and they should offer 7,705 Chaifa horses; Quxian, Aduan, and Handong in Xining, Bawa, Shenzhong, Shenzang and other nationalities were given 16 tallies, and they should offer 3,050 Chaifa horses. The gold tally can not only rule the ethnic minorities, but also used as contract in the imperial storehouse. Every three years, an official was sent to match it. There are two routes: one is via Hezhou, the other is beyond Diaomen. Long the way, more than 500,000 Jin of tea was transported, and 3,800 horses were traded in return. [1]

The implementation of the gold tally system enabled the central government to effectively control the tea-horse exchange market in Northwest China, which was not only the result of the national economic development at that time, but also the inevitable result of the highly intensified authoritarian centralization. At that time,

1 *History of the Ming Dynasty* Vol. 80 Shi Huo Zhi IV "Tea Law"; *The Record of Hongwu Years during the Reign of Taizu of the Ming Dynasty*, Vol. 256 "February of the thirty-first year during the reign of Hongwu (1398)" Article.

the gold tally had a legal effect, and no individual was allowed to get involved in the tea-horse trade. Private trade was among the strictly banned: "If private tea leaves the country, the smugglers and those who do not stop them at the pass will both be sentenced to death".[1] In the early Ming Dynasty, such regulations were strictly enforced and smugglers were severely punished, even for princes and nobles. For example, Ouyang Lun, the Emperor's sun-in-law was sentenced to death in Lanzhou for tea smuggling[2], which fully demonstrates Zhu Yuanzhang's firm determination and strong attitude to crack down on tea smuggling, especially in the process of law enforcement. This event has a far-reaching effect at that time. In order to ensure the smooth progress of the tea-horse market, in the early Ming Dynasty, the procurator was set up to inspect tea affairs, regularly dispatching capital officials to supervise the collection of taxes, and strictly suppress smugglers and traffickers. This was the prevailing tea inspection system at that time. In the Ming Dynasty, the so-called "annually send officials to inspect" refers to this. Zhu Yuanzhang, Taizu of the Ming Dynasty, "sent four Xing Ren officials every month from March to September to inspect Hezhou, Lintao, Diaomen, Li and Ya. Within half a year, twenty-four officials will be sent to the areas". In the Xuande's decade during the reign of Emperor Xuanzong (1435), it was changed to "dispatch every three months". Emperor Ming Xianzong especially appointed the Yu Shi (Imperial Censor) to "inspect tea affairs". In the third year of Chenghua (1467), the Ming government sent the Yu Shi "to inspect in Shaanxi, where the ethnic minorities didn't like Yu Shi and the horse trade decreased. So, the court recalled Yu Shi and re-dispatched Xing Ren officials as well as An Cha Si for inspection. However, when the inspectors are not specialized, Bing Bu (the Ministry of the Army) says that the harm is caused, so there was the repatriation of Yu Shi. The tax should

1 *History of the Ming Dynasty* Vol. 80, Shi Huo Zhi IV "Tea Law".

2 *The Record of Hongwu Years during the Reign of Taizu of the Ming Dynasty*, Vol. 256 "June of the thirtith year during the reign of Hongwu" Article; *History of the Ming Dynasty* Vol. 80 Shi Huo Zhi IV "Tea Law".

be paid every year, which was established by law".[1] The vast northwest area was one of the important defense lines against tea smuggling in Ming Dynasty. Since the gold tally system of tea trade was stopped in the fourteenth year of Zhengtong (1449), "one Xing Ren official was sent to inspect tea smuggling from west of Tongguan to Ganzhou".[2] Objectively speaking, this supervisory system restrained the persistent "private tea" smuggling, restricted the malpractices of officials playing favoritism, committing irregularities and seizing pastures in the process of Tea-Horse market exchange, and ensured that the government played an indispensable role in the acquisition of horses from the aspects of system and inspection. However, banning the normal ethnic trade among the people is not conducive to the normal development of the tea-horse market.

In fact, the harsh law did not and could not really prohibit the normal folk trade, because the folk exchange market in Northwest China has a certain social basis. By the early year of Yongle (1403-1424), it had been "whenever tea ban is slightly relaxed, smuggling would increase". At the same time, the Ming Dynasty adopted a tacit attitude towards the exchange of tea and horses among the people. Since then, the tea ban has been sometimes tight and sometimes loose, and there is no fixed system.[3]

In the third year of Hongzhi (1490), the Ming court accepted the suggestion of Li Luan, allowing the three Cha Ma Si — Xining, Hezhou and Lintao — to gather businessmen to transport tea. But it stipulated that each businessman should not carry more than 3,000 Jin of tea. The government seized 40% of the goods and allowed businessmen to sell the rest freely. In this way, the government can get about 400,000 Jin of tea to exchange for about 4,000 horses[4]. In fact, this is the central government's recognition of the legitimacy of non-governmental ethnic

1 *History of the Ming Dynasty* Vol. 80 Shi Huo Zhi IV "Tea Law".

2 The Republic of China (1912-1949), *Gansu Annals Manuscript*, Vol. 37 Finance and Taxation, II, Taxes and Levies.

3 *Records of Zhengtong Years, Ming Ying Zong*, Vol. 88 "the Seventh Year of Zhengtong (1442) Spring Lunar January Gengwu" Article.

4 *History of the Ming Dynasty* Vol. 80 Shi Huo Zhi IV "Tea Law".

trade. the "civilian market" in the tea and horse market has a justifiable place, and for the government it is also benefiting.

In order to monopolize the tea-horse market, the Ming Dynasty made great efforts, and all kinds of measures were so strict that they could not be surpassed. However, with the development and change of social environment, as a whole, the tea-horse market presided over by the government declined in the Ming Dynasty. Since the mid-Ming Dynasty, the increasingly prosperous folk tea-horse trade has become the mainstream of trade among all ethnic groups. The great changes between the two reflect the social and economic development at that time, which has a profound historical background.

Generally speaking, the tea-horse exchange market in the northwest of the Ming Dynasty received good economic and social benefits. Historically, tea is used to trade for horse, and "the profit is about ten thousand annually. Together with the income collected by Si and Jian, the profits are enough for the border use". This made a positive contribution to alleviating the border military pressure in Ming Dynasty[1]. Liu Liangqing, an imperial tea Yu Shi in Jiajing years (1522-1566), said that the establishment of three Cha Ma Si in Shaanxi area to collect tea and trade it for horses was "for the purpose of the frontier army's military expedition, but it is in fact to gain popularity among ethnic minorities".[2] That is to say, the "Appeasement policy" of "Tea-horse Market" in the northwest regions during the Ming Dynasty is a political strategy to "pacify the ethnic minority people ". Its significance is not limited to economic aspects. A comprehensive survey shows that the Tea-Horse exchanges in the northwest of the Ming Dynasty not only received the expected economic and social benefits, but also laid a solid foundation for the continued prosperity of Tea-Horse exchanges in the northwest of the Qing Dynasty.

1 *Records of Hongzhi Years*, *Ming Xiao Zong*, Vol. 194 "the Fifteenth Year of Hongzhi (1502) December Jihai" Article.

2 *Records of Jiajing Years, Ming Shi Zong*, Vol. 188 "the Fifteenth Year of Jiajing (1536) June Yiwei" Article.

After the establishment of the Qing Dynasty, with the continuous strengthening of authoritarian centralization and the consolidation and development of a multi-ethnic country, the system of Tea-Horse exchange market in the northwest region, with its historical tradition, became more perfect. Exchanges became more frequent, and the number of transactions expanded. At the same time, influenced by the development of commodity economy in the infancy of capitalism, this kind of national trade, which was once mainly monopolized by the government, gradually transited to the form of folk national trade. During this period, the scope of trade became wider, the form of trade became more flexible, and the economic and social benefits became more obvious. In particular, it is worth mentioning that the non-governmental trade activities in the Qing Dynasty were more active, making the government tea-horse trade less active. "The ethnic minority people trade horses for tea" [1], and horses for the Central Plains Dynasty is also very important. Tea-Horse market for the Ming and Qing Dynasties is a form of reciprocal and mutually beneficial economic exchanges between the farming and nomadic peoples, or between the central government and the local ethnic powers.

V. Cao Yun (Canal transport of grain to the capital)

One of the basic functions of the ancient canal was to organize the transshipment of grain by the government to meet the normal administrative expenditure and royal consumption of the state. This is the Cao Yun (canal transport) in its usual sense. Therefore, the Grand Canal was also called Caohe River in ancient times. [2] In the Sui Dynasty, the central government organized a large number of people to dig the Grand Canal, which further strengthened the economic ties between the North and the South. At the same time, it made full preparations for the southward shift of the economic center and the eastward shift of the political center, and laid the foundation for the high development of social

1 *History of the Ming Dynasty* Vol. 80 Shi Huo Zhi IV.

2 Cui Jianli and Ma Zhonggeng: Water Transport Governors and Canal Transport Governors in Ming and Qing Dynasties, *Guangming Daily*, 12 Edition History, March 17, 2009.

economy in the Tang Dynasty. In the Sui Dynasty, the capital of Guanzhong was built. Although it was known as fertile land, its production was not enough to meet the needs of the capital because of its narrow land and large population, so it had to rely on taxes from all parts of the southeast. The canal was often blocked because of the limited amount of water in Weishui River. So, in the fourth year of Kaihuang (584), Emperor Wendi of Sui Dynasty ordered Yuwen Kai to open another canal. The Weishui River was diverted from the capital, and generally traveled eastward along the old Caoqu canal in the Han Dynasty to Tongguan, until finally entering the Yellow River. This 300-mile-long canal is the Guangtong Canal. After the Guangtong Canal was completed, the transportation conditions in Guanzhong (the central Shaanxi plain) area were greatly improved, so Guangtong Canal was also called "Fumin (Prosperity) Canal ". Houguangtong Canal was renamed Yongtong Canal. In the seventh year of Kaihuang (587), the Sui Dynasty, in order to prepare for the pacifying of Chen Dynasty, opened Shanyang in the North (now Huai'an, Jiangsu Province) and Shanyangdu in the southeast through Sheyang Lake and Hangou, thus opening up the canal between Shanyang and Jiangdu (now Yangzhou) from the Huaihe River to the Yangtze River.

The period of Emperor Yangdi in Sui Dynasty was an important period in the history of canal excavation in China. In the first year of Daye (605), Emperor Yangdi of the Sui Dynasty used more than 1 million men and women labor from Henan and Huaibei to dig and open Tongjiqu Canal. The western section of Tongjiqu Canal diverts Gushui and Luoshui from Xiyuan, Luoyang, and flows eastward along the old canal of Yangqu in the Eastern Han Dynasty to the southeast of Yanshi, where it flows into Luoshui and then the Yellow River. The eastern section diverts the water from the Yellow River to the east from Banzhu (now Sishui Town, Xingyang, Henan Province), and the water flows along the old Bianshui Canal to the east of Junyi (now Kaifeng, Henan Province), then to the southeast through Chenliu and other places, southeast into the old Jishui Canal, and through Jixian and other places to southeast of Xucheng (now near Baoji, west of Hongze Lake, Jiangsu Province), and then into the Huaihe River from what is now Xuyi. At the same time, more than 100,000 workers were used to dredge and renovate the Hangou Canal excavated at the end of the Spring and Autumn Period to replace Shanyangdu. Tongjiqu Canal and Hangou Canal are the two most important sections of the Canals in Sui Dynasty. The canal is more than 40 steps wide. Emperor Yangdi traveled between Luoyang and Yangzhou by dragon boat many times. In the fourth year of Daye (608), the government used more than one million people in Hebei to open the Yongjiqu Canal to connect Qinshui with the Yellow River, and constructed canals to link up Qinshui with Qingshui and Qishui on the eastern bank of the Qinshui River to reach Zhuojun (now Beijing). Yongjiqu Canal is more than 2,000 miles long. In the seven years of Daye (611), Emperor Yangdi of the Sui Dynasty set out from Jiangdu by ship to reach Zhuojun directly via Hangou and Tongjiqu Canals and the Yellow River. In the sixth year of Daye, Emperor Yangdi excavated the Jiangnan River from Jingkou (now Zhenjiang in Jiangsu Province) to Yuhang (now Hangzhou), which opens up the Jiangnan River linking up the shipping between the Yangtze River and Zhejiang Province. The Jiangnan River is more than 800 miles long and 10 feet wide. The canal network excavated in the Sui Dynasty covers nearly 5,000 miles from the capital in the west, Zhuojun in the north and Yuhang in the south. It connects the five river systems of Weihe River, Haihe River, Yellow River, Yangtze River and Qiantang River, and strengthens the links of such big cities as the capital, east capital Luoyang, Zhuojun, Junyi, Liangjun, Shanyang, Jiangdu, Wujun and Yuhang. The strengthened social and economic ties in these areas have further advanced the central government's ability to regulate and control the national economy. We know that the Sui Dynasty government established a considerable number of granaries along the canal as places for the government to transport or store grain. At that time, the more famous granaries were: Liyang granary (now in Junxian County of Henan Province), Xingluo granary (later renamed Luokou granary, now in Gongxian County of Henan Province), Huiluo granary (north of Luoyang City of Sui and Tang Dynasties), Huajia grnary (north of Luoyang City of Sui and Tang Dynasties), Heyang granary (now south of Mengxian County of

Henan Province), Guangtong granary (later renamed Yongfeng granary, now the estuary of Weishui entering the Yellow River), Shanyang granary (now the East Bank of Huai'an Northwest Canal in Jiangsu Province). These granaries are very large in scale. For example, Xingluo granary covers more than 20 square Li, and there are 3,000 grain cellars, each of which can store 8,000 Dan of grain. Huiluo granary covers about 10 square Li, and there are 300 grain depots. Hnajia granary has a total area of 430,000 square meters, with more than 400 grain depots. Shanyang granary can store more than 1 million Dan of grain.

The section connecting Chang'an, Luoyang, Yangtze River and Huaihe River area is still the most important part of canal in the Tang Dynasty. Especially after the An Lushan Rebellion broke out, it became the economic lifeline for Tang Dynasty to maintain its rule. During the period of Gaozu and Taizong of Tang Dynasty, about 200,000 Dan of grain were transported from the Yangtze-Huaihe River region to Chang'an by water every year, and thereafter the amount increased continuously. In the first year of Xianheng years during the reign of Tang Gaozong (670), "in that year, more than 40 prefectures suffered from drought, frost and insects. People are hungry, especially those in the central Shaanxi plain. The imperial decree allowed him to go begging and the government transferred rice from south of the Yangtze River to relieve them." [1] In the Tianbao years during the reign of Emperor Xuanzong in Tang Dynasty, up to 2.5 million Dan of grain were transported by water every year. Especially after Tang Suzong, the Central Plains was destroyed by war, and the government's financial revenue basically depended on the southern region of the Yangtze River. The wealth of the southern region of the Yangtze River was continuously transported to Chang'an by way of the canal. Due to the influence of war and natural environment, the canal was often shut down in the Tang Dynasty. In order to solve the problem of grain and the normal cost of the state in Chang'an area, Pei Yaoqing made great contributions to the smooth canal transport during the Xuanzong period of the Tang Dynasty. The

1 *Book of Tang* Vol. 5 Emperor Gaozong of Tang.

important content was to change the land transport from Luoyang to Shaanzhou into canal transport. And a mountain road of more than 10 miles was excavated on the North Bank of Mount Sanmen for short-distance land transportation to bypass the dangerous river section. In addition, a warehouse was built at the estuary of the Bianhe River to the Yellow River. After the canal-transported rice and other materials in the south of the Yangtze River were stored here, the ship returned to the Yangtze and Huaihe River. The government hired private vessels to transport the granary grain to go along the Yellow River and Luoshui route. One warehouse was set up to the east and west of Mount Sanmen respectively. After the grain and other materials was directly stored in the East warehouse, they continue to be transported via land route to the West warehouse, and then by canal transport to the official warehouses in the central Shaanxi plain. Tang Xuanzong adopted Pei Yaoqing's suggestion, which made the canal transport in Tang Dynasty take flexible measures according to different conditions such as topography, water volume and season, improved efficiency, decreased expenditure, and reduced the labor intensity of the transporters to a certain extent. After just three years, the grain transported by canals has reached more than 7 million Dan, and the transportation cost has been saved up to about 400,000 Guan. Therefore, Pei Yaoqing was appointed by the central government as the transit envoy of Jianghuai and Henan province.

However, there were still some obvious problems in the canal transport at that time. The main problem was that wagon transportation was still needed along nearly 20 miles north of Sanmenxia Gorge. At both ends of Sanmenxia Gorge, goods had to be loaded and unloaded, which was inevitably time-consuming and laborious. From the 29th year of Kaiyuan (741) to the first year of Tianbao (742), Li Qiwu of Shaanxi County creatively excavated an artificial channel in the rocks east of the narrows of Sanmenxia Gorge. This is called Sanmenyunqu Canal or "Kaiyuan New River" and "Tianbao River", which greatly reduces the transportation cost and the labor intensity of the transporters. At the same time, road was cut on the top of the mountain, and when the river rose, the boat tracker pulled the boat through the canal successfully, thus creating a situation of canal transportation from the Yangtze and Huaihe River to the central Shaanxi plain area. In the first year of Tianbao (742), canal and land transshipment envoy Wei Jian further opened the central Shaanxi plain Canal, enabling the Yangtze-Huaihe River boats to reach Chang'an, the political center of the Tang Dynasty, and to transport 4 million Dan of grain and other cargo each year, creating the highest record of water transport in the Tang Dynasty.

After the Anshi Rebellion, the Yellow River Basin was ravaged by war, and the normal order of life and production was disrupted. The Tang government's tax dependence on the Yangtze and Huaihe River area was further strengthened, and the importance of canal transport became more prominent. Because the canal was blocked, the Zu Yong Diao collected in the Yangtze River and the Huaihe River area were diverted to be shipped upstream from the Yangtze River and Hanshui River, to reach Fengxiang via Hanzhong. This greatly increased the freight and difficulty of canal transport in Tang Dynasty. After the Anshi Rebellion was crushed, it was very difficult to restore the original canal. The Bianqu Canal was out of repair for many years and was silted up without water, so it was difficult to navigate smoothly. Until the second year of Guangde years during the reign of Emepror Daizong in Tang Dynasty (764), Liu Yanzuo, the transshipment envoy of Henan and Jianghuai, proposed a decree from the emperor to dredge the Bianqu Canal, and reformed the canal transportation. Its basic practice is to build 2,000 ships, each of which carries 1,000 Dan, with 10 ships in a team of 300 people, and be equipped with 50 boatmen. Part of the salt profit in the national treasury was used to hire boatmen, and people no longer served as forced labor. In the process of transporting grain and other materials along the canal, the central government dispatches officials to supervise the transportation. At the same time, from Yangzhou to Heyin, they are escorted by the army. To the north of Heyin, laborers are organized to pull boats. Liu Yan also creatively adopted the method of sectional transshipment according to the specific conditions of the Yangtze River, Bianhe River, Yellow River and Weishui River. That is, " boats on the Yangtze

River do not enter the Bianhe River; boats on the Bianhe River do not enter the Weihe River; and boats on the Yellow River do not enter the Weihe River. The cargo from the south of the Yangtze River is stored in Yangzhou; the cargo transported along Bianhe River is stored in Heyin; the cargo transported by means of boats on the Yellow River is stored in Weikou; and the cargo transported by means of boats on the Weihe River is stored in Taicang ". When Liu Yan presided over the canal transportation, about 1.1 million Dan of cargo were transported northward each year, of which about 400,000 Dan were stored in Heyin granary, 300,000 Dan were stored in Taiyuan granry in Shaanzhou, and 400,000 Dan were transported to Chang'an. Although this can no longer be compared with the time when Pei Yaoqing was in charge of canal transport, it is also worth noting in terms of efficiency and cost savings. The canal became the lifeline of centralized politics at that time. In the second year of Baoying years (763), Liu Yan wrote in his book Yiyuanzaishu: "The central Shaanxi plain is lacking in grain only because of the need of army provisions. The Canal draws water from Xiao, Xiang, and Dongting Lake. Boats sails on the water all the way to Chang'an, and can cover thousands of miles within days. The people and the army of the central Shaanxi plain depend on the canal for food." [1] We can see from Liu Yan's words that the grain supply in the south of the Yangtze River was still large in scale and directly related to the grain supply in the central Shaanxi plain area. The canal transportation that Pei Yaoqing presided over mainly transported the rice of from Wuxing , Wujin and Kuaiji, while the canal transportation Liu Yan mentioned was mainly the rice from Cao Xiao, Xiang and Dongting Lake areas. In the second year of Zhenyuan (786), when canal transported rice from the south of the Yangtze River was sent to Shaanzhou again after the rebellion of Li Xilie was squashed, Tang Dezong, who was anxiously waiting the rice to come, said to the prince, "Rice has arrived in Shaanxi, and we both can survice!" It can be seen that the social function and economic significance of the canal at that time were very great. As Li Jinfang in

1 *Book of Tang* Vol. 123 Biography of Liu Yan.

Tang Dynasty said in Bianhe ZhijinChuan Ship: "The canal linking Bianhe River and Huaihe River brings many conveniences , but at the same time leads to many disasters, which can be regarded as a balance of advantages and disadvantages. Forty-three counties and prefectures in the whole southeast of China depend on this river to collect all the people's wealth". [1]

In the Northern Song Dynasty, the population of the whole country could reach about 100 million. Only in Kaifeng, when the population was the largest, it was roughly between 1 million and 1.5 million. In the traditional era of farming and handicraft industry, a large population means a large total economy. At that time, the main way to supply for Kaifeng's life was to ship grain and commodities from the southeast by means of canal transport. Kaifeng itself became a commodity distribution center. The economic prosperity of the Northern Song Dynasty was inseparable from the unblocked flow of canal transport at that time. In the Northern Song Dynasty, the amount of canal transport was generally 6 million Dan, up to 8 million Dan at most. [2] The volume of canal transport was much larger than that of the Tang Dynasty.

During the Yuan, Ming and Qing Dynasties, the government paid more attention to the canal transport and standardized its operation and management. The canal transport really became the economic lifeline of the capital to link north and south, and played a very important role in the country's social economy. We know that one of the contributions of the Yuan Dynasty is to straighten the Beijing-Hangzhou Grand Canal, shorten the transportation distance and reduce the transportation cost.

On the basis of Yuan Dynasty, the Ming Dynasty built Nanwang Water Distribution Project in Shandong Province, which made the Grand Canal of Beijing and Hangzhou truly have the shipping value of connecting the north and

1 See *Encyclopedia of China, History of China, Sui, Tang and Five Dynasties*, Edited by Tang Changru, China Encyclopedia Press, 1988, pp. 345-348.

2 Wang Zengyu: Correct Evaluation of the Historical Position of the Song Dynasty, *Beijing Daily*, Dec. 10, 2007.

south. In this way, the Beijing-Hangzhou Grand Canal became the transportation lifeline for the Ming and Qing governments to maintain economic circulation and political rule. The central government guaranteed it from political, economic and military aspects, regardless of cost. In terms of institutional setup, in the period of Ming and Qing Dynasty, two sets of local administrative organs of Beijing-Hangzhou Grand Canal, namely, the canal transport governor and the river channel governor directly under the central government, were specially set up. This is a change from earlier practice of having canal administration department or canal transport officials to concurrently manage the river affairs. In the Ming Dynasty, the canal transport governor and the river channel governor sometimes had different functions, and sometimes had the same functions. And the institutions are also sometimes set up and sometimes removed.

In the Qing Dynasty, the management of the Grand Canal was further strengthened. The responsibilities of the canal transport management system and the river management system were clearer and more standardized. In the first year of Shunzhi (1644), one Governor of canal Transport and one Governor of River Courses were set up, with a ranking of Er Pin (Second Grade), and sometimes Yi Pin (First Grade). Under Governor of canal Transport, there is Xun Cao Yu Shi (imperial inspector of canal transport), Du Liang Dao (inspector of grain transport), and Guan Liang Tong Zhi (inspector of grain storage). There is also an army directly under his jurisdiction, namely, Cao Biao. After Emperor Qianlong, the responsibility of Governor of River Courses was divided into He Ku Dao, He Dao, Guan He Tong Zhi, Tong Pan, and so on. The army under his jurisdiction was He Biao. In the Qing Dynasty, the Governor of Canal Transport was in charge of the administration of Shandong, Henan, Jiangsu, Anhui, Jiangxi, Zhejiang, Hunan and Hubei provinces. He was specifically responsible for the canal transport, inspection and selection, escort, ship production and repair, inspection of haulback, and supervision and urging for arrearage. The inspector shall personally inspect the collection, departure and arrival of the canal transport, and shall report to the central government any important information in the course of the canal transport at any time. In the twenty-first year of Kangxi (1682), it was further stipulated that, after passing through the Huaihe River, the general director of canal transport should go north with the ship, lead his subordinates to inspect the condition of the transport riverway and dispatch the whole canal transport. When the grain ship passed through Tianjin, the general director of canal transport immediately went to the capital to report on his duties. After that, he returned to Huai'an to handle the collection and transportation of grain for the next year. Emperor Kangxi attached great importance to river engineering. He said:

> I always pay attention to river affairs. I read reports on river defense in the palace, and... The place names of river charts and dangerous projects and breaches are deliberated over in time. Knowing the difficulty of the construction, I have never witnessed in person, so I cannot fully understand the danger of the turbulent and overflowing rivers, and the distance and height of the embankments.

So, in the twenty-third year of Kangxi (1684), Emperor Kangxi personally inspected the northern bank of the Yellow River. Emperor Kangxi further realized that "the breach of the Yellow River concerns the people's livelihood" and that the construction of water conservancy projects is "imperative" and must "make every effort to carry out" in order to achieve the social benefits of "water conservancy preventing seedlings from being harmed by drought and flood"[1]. The Kangxi years (1662-1722) were one of the important periods in which river engineering was valued and a series of projects were carried out in the history of China. River course officials harnesses the riverway section after section, and the duties and settings of the governor of the riverway are complicated. In the fourteenth year of Emperor Qianlong (1749), the position of Governor Beihe was abolished and his functions were concurrently assumed by the Governor of Zhili. For hundreds

1 *Kangxi Chaosheng Xun*, Vol. 33.

of years in history, the Yellow River overflew the Huaihe River. During the Qing Dynasty, sedimentation led to frequent flood, which made the task of canal management very arduous and onerous. This also made the central government of the Qing Dynasty pay more attention to the position of governor of rivers, whose status gradually overtook that of the general director.

In short, during the Ming and Qing Dynasties, the governors of canal transport and that of riverways had different responsibilities, but they could cooperate with each other and support each other. As the Yellow River moved northward to flow into the Daqinghe River in Shandong Province and then flew into the sea in the Xianfeng years (1855), the channel of the Beijing-Hangzhou Grand Canal was blocked and the inland river transportation was of little significance. Governor of the South Yangtze River Course, Governor of East River Course, and Governor of Canal Transport were respectively dismissed in the ninth year of Xianfeng (1858), the twenty-eighth year of Guangxu (1902) and the thirty-first year of Guangxu (1905) [1]. Throughout the Qing Dynasty, great importance was attached to the dredging and water transport of the Yellow River and the canal transportation. This can be proven by Emperor Kangxi's words: "Since I ascended the throne, I consider three the three rebellious military governors, river affairs and water transport as the three major events. I so concerned about them that I once wrote them down and hung it on the palace pillar"[2].

The Grand Canal transportation almost run through the entire history of feudal society in China.

When we discuss the monopoly system and water transport in the feudal society of China, there is another problem that cannot be neglected. That is, under normal circumstances, the government has a concept and specific practice of enriching the people (by reducing the taxes and corvee). This concept of enriching the people and the measures taken by the central government to directly manage

1 Cui Jianli and Ma Zhonggeng: Governors of Water Transport and Governor of River Course in Ming and Qing Dynasties, *Guangming Daily*, History, March 17, 2009, p. 12.

2 *Donghua Record*, February 31 of the Thirty-first Year during the Reign of Kangxi.

and control the economic lifeline run through the entire feudal society. The general trend is that the state's control over the economic lifeline is getting stricter and stricter. Although civil participation is permitted to some extent in the mining and salt industry in the later period of the feudal society, it is conditional. It means that the government purchases raw materials or products as merchant employers, or controls the circulation field. As for whether the government adopted the policy of "governing by non-interference", i.e. enriching the people, or whether the government plundered much of the folk wealth, especially intensifying the government's direct management and control of the government-run handicraft industry, it often depended on the complicated relationship between the domestic and international social environment, relations with ethnic groups and so on, not just the working of the personal preferences of the highest decision-makers. Even when the whole country pursues the basic national policy of "enriching the people", it is the first thing to ensure the normal operation of state machinery and the normal progress of social and economic order. Especially, the state has never handed over to the wealthy businessmen and dignitaries the economic lifelines such as salt and iron, which are related to the national economy and people's livelihood. In fact, as far as the whole feudal society of China is concerned, the so-called "enriching the people" did not last long. Generally, it was only a temporary measure to restore social production after the change of dynasties, followed by activities such as building up civil engineering, engaging in the production of public goods and opening up territory. This seemed to be a rule at that time. As far as the whole feudal society is concerned, with the relative reduction of the direct producer's personal dependence and the relatively active commodity economy, the government-run handicraft industry gradually appears sluggish. So, the folk handicraft industry developed correspondingly. In fact, this is only a false impression, or the government's control or operation of the economy seems more mature, because the government in the late feudal society is more concerned about the control of key economic areas, as well as the collection of tax revenue.

In the history of China, the growth and decline of government-run handicraft industry and folk handicraft industry often reflect the development and change of social economy. However, the government-run handicraft industry, such as salt and iron monopoly, tea-horse trade and liquor monopoly, has not been decentralized in the key economic fields related to the national economy and people's livelihood. Even though the production of salt and iron allows private participation, the government has strict control over its circulation field. This control is different in form. Sometimes the government buys it as merchant employers. Sometimes the profit of the merchant is set within a certain range by price regulation. Sometimes the merchant has the right to engage in monopoly only after fulfilling the obligations stipulated by the government, such as the introduction of salt listening system[1] and tea licensing system[2]. In addition, the special policy adopted by the government to encourage businessmen to operate salt and iron in areas with inconvenient transportation. But this is not considered mainly for the economic benefits of the government.

Therefore, for the feudal society, the idea of enriching the people and the power to firmly control the economic lifeline, that is, the Seigniorage and the various monopoly systems, were actually two aspects of the government's regulation and control of economic policies, the balance of which were often determined by the social environment at that time.

3. Government Water Conservancy Construction

For agricultural production, water conservancy project mainly includes two basic functions: irrigation and drainage, which is an important guarantee for agricultural harvest. Therefore, water conservancy project has been attached great importance by the government throughout the feudal society in China.

Water conservancy is the lifeline of agriculture and a common understanding of ancient and modern society. The term "water conservancy" appeared first in "Xiao Xing Lan · Shen Ren" in "Lv Shi Chun Qiu (Lv's Spring and Autumn

1 *History of the Jin Dynasty*, Vol. 92 Biography of Mao Shuo; *History of Ming Dynasty*, Vol. 80, Shi Huo Zhi IV.

2 *History of Ming Dynasty*, Vol. 80 Shi Huo Zhi, IV.

Annals)" published at the end of the Warring States Period. However, the concept of "water conservancy" mentioned in the book is quite different from that of later water conservancy projects. The term mainly refers to the harvest of aquatic products, including fish. In the first official biographical history *Records of the Grand Historian*, a Book of Rivers and Canals is specially set up, which shows that the government attaches great importance to water conservancy. The Book of Rivers and Canals is undoubtedly the first extant water conservancy book. After describing a series of historical facts of river control and flood control, canal opening and navigation, and water diversion irrigation in the historical period from Dayu to Huzi blockage of the Yellow River by Emperor Wudi of Han Dynasty, this book comments, "Water is really formidable." It also points out that "after that, the political rulers are very much concerned about water conservancy." [1] Since then, the word "water conservancy" starts to have the meaning of flood control, irrigation, shipping and other irrigation-building and floods-preventing meanings, and has been given the general meaning of water conservancy in the true modern sense. With the development of social economy and the continuous progress of technology, the connotation of water conservancy is constantly expanding. The feudal government of China paid more attention to the full utilization of water. On the one hand, it diverted water for irrigation, prevented and controlled natural disasters such as floods and droughts, and developed agricultural production; on the other hand, in order to improve the unit yield, it changed traditional farming habits, developed farmland irrigation, and developed paddy fields in the arid northern areas.

Even in the war-torn period, the countries such as the Three Kingdoms still attached great importance to water conservancy construction, and even regarded it as the most important measure for self-protection and ultimately unification of the whole country under the situation of tripartite confrontation. For example, during the reign of Cao Cao, the Cao Wei Dynasty successively built the Water

1 *Records of the Grand Historian*, Vol. 29 Book of Rivers and Canals.

Conservancy Project in Pi, Gupi, Taishoupi in Huaihe River Basin, Linjinpi in the central Shaanxi plain area, and Yandeng in Beijing Liling area. After the establishment of the Cao Wei regime, many water conservancy projects continued to be built in the Yellow River Basin and the Huaihe River Basin, the most famous of which is the 300-mile-long canal opened in the north and south of Yingshui River, with an irrigate area of 20,000 hectares. [1] Similar to Cao Wei, Wu and Shu Dynasties also actively constructed water conservancy projects in varying degrees to restore and develop agricultural production and handicraft production.

During the Western Jin Dynasty, the Yangkou Water Conservancy Project hosted by Du Yu was comparable to the Baiqu Project in the Han Dynasty in scale. The project "opens Yangkou, and diverts Xiashui water to Baling, which ranges for more than a thousand miles. It discharges the flood of the Yangtze River, and links up with the Canals of Lingling and Guiyang"[2]. On the one hand, it dredged inland rivers and opened up distributary channels, which improved the flood control and drainage capacity of agricultural reclamation areas along the Yangtze River in Hunan Province. On the other hand, it also brought the water transportation of Lingling (with the prefecture office in Quanling, now north of Huling Lingxian county) and Guiyang (with the prefecture office in Zhichen, now Chenxian County, Hunan Province) into line with the Yangtze River. Thereby, the rivers of Jiang, Han, Yuan and Xiang are connected into a network, which connects the major cities and towns of Jiangling, Xiangyang, Xiakou, Baling and Linxiang, thus making the internal links of Jingchu area more closely. At the beginning of the Eastern Jin Dynasty, Wang Dun was appointed as the Jingzhou Cishi (prefectural governor), "dig canals to conncet the north and south dams of the Jianghan river. [3]" "In Du Shi Fang Yu Ji Yao (Essentials of Historical Geography)", the entry of Huguang Jiangling provides notes for it: "Caohe Canal

1 *The History of the Three Kingdoms* (*San Guo Zhi*)" Vol. 1 The History of Wei Dynasty, Emperor Wudi.

2 *Book of the Jin Dynasty* Vol. 34 Biography of Du Yu.

3 *Yu Di Ji Sheng*, Vol. 64 Jingzhou Prefecture ·Canals.

is four miles to the north of (Jiangling) County. The annals said: The canal was dug in the years of Emperor Yuan of Jin Dynasty. It ran from the Luoyankou to Dacaohe River, and then from the Lishexue to Mianshuikou, straight to Xianghan." The Caohe River Project presided over by Wang Dun is another large-scale water conservancy project built near Jiangling after the Yangkou Project presided over by Du Yu. Since Wang Dun, the project has been continuously improved. It gave consideration to shipping, flood discharge and irrigation. After that, the project has been continuously improved. During the Yuanjia years of Liu Song Dynasty, it was connected with Yangkou Project. It was recorded as "During the Yuan Jia years of Song Dynasty (424-453), it passed through Baihu Lake and poured into Yangshui River to help water transport"[1]. In the late years of Liu Song Dynasty, Shen Youzhi, the Ci Shi of Jingzhou, presided over the construction of Huohu Irrigation District in Zhijiang County. In "Taiping Huanyu Ji" Volume 146, the entry of "Zhijiang County of Jingzhou" reads:" When Shen Youzhi of Song Dynasty is the Ci Shi of Jingzhou, he dug up canals and diverted water from the river, so there was a good harvest for the nearby fields. That is why it is called Huohu Lake (Harvest Lake)." This is the reclamation of a low-lying marsh land. Through such engineering establishments as weirs and canals, the flood and drought problems were solved, and the marshlands were turned into fertile lands. Because "the harvest of the fields are good", it got the name of Huohu Lake (Harvest Lake)[2]. According to the previously quoted "Huanyu Ji", people still benefited from this comprehensive water conservancy project in the Tang Dynasty.

It can be seen that the water conservancy project was one of the important tasks of the central government and even the local government at that time. Even when there set up the southern separatist regime, it still remained the same.

1 *Shui Jing Zhu* (*Commentary on the Waterways Classic*), Vol. 28 Commentary on Mianshui River. See Fang Gaofeng's Six Dynasties Regime and Agricultural Economic Development in the Middle Reaches of the Yangtze River (Report of Post-doctoral Research Center, Institute of Economics, Chinese Academy of Social Sciences, 2009).

2 Wang Jialun and Zhang Fang: *History of Farmland and Water Conservancy in China*, Agricultural Publishing House, 1990, p. 208.

In Tang Dynasty, great changes took place in the irrigation system of the Jing River diversion. The two main canals used Zheng and Bai Canals as irrigation areas. After many times of reconstruction, the first section of Zheng Guo Canal gradually lost its effectiveness until the middle of Tang Dynasty, and its downstream rivers each formed an independent irrigation canal system. In the late Tang Dynasty, the irrigation system mainly diverted water for Baiqu Canal, and gradually developed into three main canals in the north, south and the middle part. The irrigation system tended to be perfect and brought enormous economic benefits[1].

Tang and Song Dynasties are an important period for the fast development of water conservancy and irrigation in China's history. The management of irrigation is becoming more and more mature, and the laws and regulations of water conservancy management are relatively perfect. In the Tang Dynasty, the central government promulgated the regulation of irrigation management with national significance --- Shui Bu Shi. "Shui Bu Shi" is very rich in content, involving almost all categories of water conservancy. Its basic contents concerning farmland water conservancy mainly include: the regulation of irrigation regional organization and management, the regulation of water resources utilization, the regulation of irrigation sequence, and the regulation of agricultural and non-agricultural water usage. These regulations, even today, are not outdated.

In the Xining years of Song Dynasty (1068-1077), Wang Anshi promulgated the "Agricultural Interest Treaty"[2] in the course of the reform under his leadership, which was a policy and regulation of the government to encourage local and non-governmental development of farmland and water conservancy. After the Tang and Song Dynasties, almost all large irrigation projects have specific irrigation management systems, including organization management, project management,

1 Li Lingfu: On the Change and Benefit Increase of the Water Diversion Canal System in Tang Dynasty, *Chinese Agricultural History*, No. 2, 2008.

2 According to the *Agricultural Interest Treaty* (also known as *Agricultural Water Conservancy Regulation*).

conditions of water usage, production management, rights and responsibilities, reward and punishment regulations, etc.

After Beijing became the capital of the Yuan, Ming and Qing dynasties, the governments paid special attention to the water conservancy here. Through the water conservancy projects in Beijing area, we can see that the w government ater conservancy construction at that time was really remarkable.

During the Zhongtong years of Kublai Khan of the Yuan Dynasty (1260-1264), Yongping Prefecture, located in the northeastern corner of the abdomen of Fuli, started to grow rice in the third year of Zhongtong years (1262). Planting rice requires sufficient water irrigation and a relatively advanced drainage system. At that time, canals had been built here, and local farmers could loan cattle and seeds from the government, with a maximum of two cattle for each person. [1] These measures of the government have played a positive role in promoting the development of rice cultivation in the capital region. The ministers of the Yuan Dynasty, including Guo Shoujing, Yu Ji and Tuo Tuo, all proposed that the northern part of the North China Plain and beyond and the coastal areas of the Bohai Sea should be transformed into rice planting areas, which is very strategic insight. During the Taiding years (1324-1327), Yu Ji, a Hanlin Academician, proposed to develop water conservancy in the capital region and plant paddy fields in the eastern part of Beijing. Yu Ji pointed out that in view of the fact that "to the east of the capital, there lie thousands of miles of coast line; to the north, there is the Liaohai Sea; to the south, there is the Qingqi, where lies the reed marshes. When the tide rises, the silt is brought up and becomes fertile soil. We should use the method of Zhejiang people to build dykes to harness water for the field." His specific approach is to appeal for people to reclaim wasteland, and encourage the rich to reclaim wasteland as the basis for their success in obtaining official ranks. According to the number of peasants controlled by each landlord, different areas

1 Huang Zongxi: *Tian Xia Jun Guo Li Bing Shu* (*Merits and Drawbacks of All the Provinces and Counties in China*), Vol. 2, p. 42.

of wasteland are awarded to the landlords, and also posts of Wan Fu Zhang, Qian Fu Zhang and Bai Fu Zhang respectively. The government does not levy taxes on newly reclaimed wasteland for two years, and in the third year it determines the amount of tax according to the harvest situation and the grade of the land; in five years, if there is a harvest, government post will be officially granted; in ten years, it will issue a seal, and the descendants will be hereditary officials. Yu Ji believes that this method of wasteland reclamation has several advantages: first, it can make use of the peasants who reclaim wasteland to "guard the capital and resist the barbarian tribes from the nearby islands"; secondly, it can reduce the volume of water transport to "relieve the burden of the worn-out people"; thirdly, it can "satisfy the rich people's aspirations for government positions and make use of them"; fourthly, it can make "river and sea pirates and thieves all have something to do". Yu Ji's idea was opposed by some people at that time. They mainly believed that "if there was such a system, the person in charge would accept bribery, and the system cannot be implemented."[1] Although Yuji's proposition has not been put into effect, it also shows from one aspect that there is a certain space for reclaiming land and developing water conservancy in the capital region. It also shows that some officials in the government have a profound understanding of the agricultural development in the capital region and the ways of development. In addition, Yuji's proposal to learn from Zhejiang's advanced water conservancy experience is also laudable. Thirty years later, in accordance with the design of Yu Ji, Tuo Tuo, the Prime Minister at the end of Yuan Dynasty, partially implemented its contents. By the 13th year of Zhizheng years (AD 1353), the peasant uprising in the South was surging, the sea and water transport were interrupted, and it was difficult for the grain in the South to reach the capital. In order to meet the food needs of the capital, Tuo Tuo proposed to develop the paddy fields in the north. "If we develop water conservancy near the capital, and recruit people from the South of the Yangtze River to farm, we could obtain millions of Dan of millet

1 *History of the Yuan Dynasty* Vol. 181 Biography of Yu Ji.

and wheat each year, and get sufficient food for the capital without sea transport."[1] Therefore, he personally managed the Da Si Nongoing Si (Administration of National Treasury), allocated cattle tools, farm implements, seeds and loans, and planned to recruit 1,000 skilled workers from Jiangsu, Zhejiang, east of Huaihe River and other places who were good at planting paddy fields and building coastal areas. Each of the skilled workers was given 10 bills, and was allowed to return to their hometown one year later. Under his vigorous implementation, "from Xishan (foothills of Taihang Mountains) in the west, Qianmin Town (now Linyu County) in the east, Baoding and Hejian in the south, and Tan (under the administration of Miyun), Shunzhou (under the administration of Shunyi) in the north, there introduced water conservancy and legislative tenants. After one year, there was good harvest".[2] In December of the fifteenth year of Zhizheng years (1355 AD), there established four Da Bing Nong Si in Baoding, Hejian, Wuqing, Jingxian and Jixian to promote water conservancy and farming. These practices play an active role in developing agricultural production in North China, guaranteeing grain consumption in capital areas and reducing the cost of grain transportation.

Zhu Yuanzhang, the founding emperor of the Ming Dynasty, was born in the lower strata of society, and he had a better understanding of the people's conditions and knew the important role of water conservancy projects in agricultural production. As early as when Zhu Yuanzhang was the leader of Hong Jin Jun (the Red Scarf Army), he attached great importance to the construction of water conservancy facilities. In 1358, he appointed Kang Maochai as Du Shui Ying Tian Shi (official supervising water conservancy and farming), and took the initiative to repair and build water conservancy projects in Hong Jin Jun-controlled areas, which showed a statesman's brilliant strategy. After the establishment of the Ming Dynasty, the construction of water conservancy projects

1 *History of the Yuan Dynasty* Vol. 42 Biography of Emperor Shundi.
2 *History of the Yuan Dynasty* Vol. 138 Biography of Tuo Tuo.

was brought onto the agenda of the national economy. "Talents from the Imperial College, the highest educational administration in feudal China, were sent to govern the prefectures and counties. Officials and common people were gathered to build and fix water conservancy projects during the slack season. [1] According to incomplete statistics, by the 28th year of Hongwu (1395), there were more than 40,000 irrigation (waterlogging prevention) projects in the whole country, such as dredging rivers and building lateral canals. [2] In addition, there are 4,162 large and small water conservancy projects in the Yellow River Basin and 5,048 "canals and embankments".[3] Moreover, the government has also drew on the Treasury and mobilized the public to make necessary repairs to important water projects in history. In the mid-Ming Dynasty, with the military and economic needs of the country, no less than 4 million Dan of grain were sent via water transport from the south to the north every year, and the flood disasters in the Haihe River basin in the north were more frequent than before. In the middle Hongzhi years (1488-1505), the peasant insurrectionary army led by Liu Liu and Liu Qi fought successively in Hebei and Shandong provinces. For some time, the transportation was blocked, and the grain supply of the capital became a very difficult problem. Therefore, the court began to discuss the development of water conservancy and waste land opening up in the capital region. During the Jiajing and Longqing years (1522-1572), the Yellow River overflowed 15 times successively. The North-South transport channel was frequently obstructed, and the financial crisis was more serious. Da Xue Shi (the grand secretary) Qiu Jun first brought up the old proposal of Yu Ji in Yuan Dynasty. He suggested constructing dams in the coastal areas of Eastern Beijing, dredging rivers and storing water, improving and utilizing coastal land, and developing agricultural production. Qiu Jun proposed in his "Da Xue Yan Yi Bu" that in the area of capital where terrain is flat, ditches should be excavated and rivers dug in order to build capital water conservancy

1 *Ri Zhi Lu*, Vol. 12 Water Conservancy.

2 *The Record of Hongwu Years during the Reign of Taizu of the Ming Dynasty*, Vol. 234.

3 *Ri Zhi Lu*, Vol. 12 Water Conservancy.

projects:

> It would be better we follow the examples from past. Each county centers on the rivers within boundary, and dig huge ditches based on the features of the landform. Ditches with a width of more than one Zhang will be connected to a river. Small ditches will also be dug along with the landform, and ditches more than four Chi wide will be linked to the big ditches. Narrow ditches will be dug with the landform, and ditches more than two or three Chi wide will be connected with small ditches.

The specific operation method is that "the big ditch is managed by the government, the small ditch is jointly managed by the government and people with lands, and the narrow ditch is managed separately by people in their own lands. Every year after February, the government sent people to supervise its digging, and often patrol along the ditches, so as not to make the ditches silted up." In this way, "even downpour will not cause disasters".[1] The government and farmers should both be mobilized to complete water conservancy projects. In the coastal area of east of the capital, he suggested promoting Yuji's idea of Tuntian (having garrison troops or peasants open up wasteland and grow food grain), and dispatching competent officials to conduct an investigation, and then recruiting people to reclaim waster land. "Land is granted according to the situation, and official posts should be conferred according to the amount of land, which is just like the design of Yu Ji." In terms of specific project implementation, Qiu Jun proposed that the coastal saline-alkali land should be harnessed by "building embankments to prevent saltwater from entering the ditches so as to divert in freshwater". Qiu Jun especially emphasized cutting off rivers in Zhigu area, digging a long river, then building long dikes around low-lying areas, and setting

1 Emperor Guangxu, *Jifu Tongzhi* (*Annals of the Capital*), Vol. 91 Rivers and Canals · Water Conservancy II; Qiu Jun, *Da Xue Yan Yi Bu*.

up water gates as appropriate to control water in and out, so as to prevent saltwater from entering the dike from outside, and also to prevent freshwater in the dike from overflowing everywhere. Qiu Jun believes that opening up paddy fields along the coast by this method will turn thousands of miles of brine-laden land into good fields, so as to achieve the social effect of "both people and the government depend on its use. In this way, the country enjoys prosperity, and it can support people from far and near"[1]. In the fourth year of Longqing (1570), Yang Jiaxiang, Xun An Yu Shi (the imperial supervisory governor) of Zhili Province, once again proposed the development of paddy fields in the provinces of Jingdong, Henan and Shandong.[2] Although these proposals were not fully implemented for various reasons at that time, it can be seen that some insightful ministers paid great attention and enthusiasm to water conservancy projects and land reclamation in the capital region.

During the Wanli years (1573-1620), Xu Zhenming also proposed to build water conservancy projects and reclaim paddy fields in the capital region. He put them into practice and made some achievements. In September of the 13th year of Emperor Wanli years (1585), Xu Zhenming was appointed Shangbaosi Shaoqing. He later concurrently held the positions of Jiancha Yushi and Kentianshi, and went to various parts of Jingdong to implement water conservancy and land reclamation. Xu Zhenming used the southern soldiers stationed in Jizhou who were familiar with farming to open up waste land and recruited southern farmers to open up paddy fields. In the second year, he reclaimed more than 39,000 mu of farmland more than 100 Li in the east and west and 180 Li in the north and south of Yongping Prefecture in the east of Beijing (under the administration of now Lulong County in Hebei Province)[3], and achieved obvious economic and social benefits.

1 *Ming Jingshi Wenbian*, Vol. 72 Qiu Jun Tun Tian and Ying Tian.

2 *Records of Emperor Muzong during the Ming Dynasty,* Vol. 43 March in the fourth year of Emperor Longqing.

3 *History of the Ming Dynasty*, Vol. 223 Biography of Xu Zhenming.

In July of the third year of Emperor Yongzheng years (1725), during the relief, Emperor Yongzheng summoned Yiqinwang Yun Xiang, carefully analyzed the floods caused by the incomplete field drainage system around the capital, and commented that "if the water couldn't flow into rivers but was retained in the field, it is not because the landform is different from the past, but because the water conservancy projects are not constructed." In Zhili, a flat land expands for thousands of miles, most of which is low-lying land, but few ditches for drainage. "If water gathers, it will wreak havoc, but if it is diverted, it will be beneficial; making good use of water will bring benefits, but giving it up will bring harm." Therefore, Emperor Yongzheng decided to "follow the example of the previous dynasties in order to increase rice crop yields, without haste, at no expense, and without being hampered by objections." [1] In the winter of that year, Prince Yiqin Yunxiang and Da Xue Shi (the grand secretary) Zhu Shi were sent to investigate the river origin, the flow of water and the degree of water damage in various parts of the capital area, and analyzed the causes of water damage. The river course in Zhili was harnessed, and water conservancy and farming were carried out at the same time. At that time, there was water everywhere, and it was difficult to distinguish the terrain in the open country. Yunxiang and others traveled all over the capital area to survey the terrain so as to make careful planning.

Emperor Yongzheng agreed with Prince Yiqin and Zhu Shi's views on water hazards in the capital region, and fully supported their measures to solve the water hazards problem.

On January 27 of the fourth year of Yongzheng (1726), Zhu Shi submitted memorials to the emperor, saying that the eastern part of capital was backed by mountains, facing the sea and having more springs. So, the irrigation conditions were much better than those in the southern part of Zhili. "If we open up canals and divert water to grow rice, it would be of great benefit to the

1 Emperor Yongzheng, *Jifu Tongzhi* (*Annals of the Capital*), Vol. 46 Water Conservancy and Field Management I.

people's livelihood." Emperor Yongzheng gave a comment of "Agreed".[1] A few days later, Zhu Shi submitted another memorial, saying that when he passed by Qian'an and Luanzhou villages, he found that "there are many springs and rice can be planted. And the terrain is high, so there is no concern for flooding." The emperor commented, "This really comforts my heart, and it is all because of the concerted effort of you and Yiqinwang to achieve this satisfactory effect for me. I'm so happy that let's all try out best."[2] On the second day of March, Yiqinwang and others submitted a memorial on Jingdong water conservancy and made several proposals about dredging up canals. Two days later, he received the imperial order: Approved and speed up the process. On April 21, a commissioner for water conservancy and farming was set up. After discussion, Li Bu made a reply to Yiqinwang Yun Xiang: The water conservancy and farming affairs in Zhili are very busy. Please set up a division with four members from both Manchurian and Han people and a water conservancy and farming envoy. The emperor ordered Prince Yiyiwang Yunxiang to be in charge of this. And every bureau keep a register of water conservancy and farming issues and report them to the water conservancy and farming division for record.[3] In that year (1726), Prince Yiqinwang also pointed out that "there must establish a hierarchy of the management of paddy fields" and that the state "takes the lead in the management of paddy fields, in order to advocate for farmers."[4] Then specific implementation plans were further put forward: opening up paddy fields and harnessing rivers at the same time, which complement each other and can turn harm into benefit;

1 Yongzheng Dynasty's Chinese Written Instructions, On January 27 of the fourth year of Yongzheng, Zhu Shi, Memorial of Surveying the Jingdong Water Conservancy Project accompanying Prince Yiqinwang and Proposing a Decree to Open Canals and Divert Water to Irrigate Rice Paddy. Note: Some were marked with a prior date because no dates were annotated.

2 Yongzheng Dynasty's Chinese Written Instructions, On Februry 2 of the fourth year of Yongzheng, Zhu Shi, Memorial of snow in Yongping Prefecture and Jing rice can be grown in Qian'an Luanzhou villages.

3 Pan Xi'en: The first case of *Capital Water Conservancy*.

4 Ibid.

giving full play to the positive role of human beings and reversing the situation of "having to rely on the weather for good harvest"; taking the quality of paddy fields management as a main condition for assessing officials. "The performance of water conservancy and farming will be recorded, and the Du Fu (governor) will determine the quality ... The success or failure of local water conservancy and farming can tell whether the local officials fulfil their duty." [1] In order to speed up the progress of rice paddy opening-up, Da Xue Shi (the grand secretary) Zhu Shi put forward four more suggestions on December 12 of the same year: first, common people till the land by themselves, and they will be granted Ding Dai (official cap showing various ranks by button of precious stone on top) of beyond Jiu Pin (rank 9) and below Wu Pin (rank 5) according to the amount of land, so as to encourage private reclamation; second, the workers who render service to the water conservancy and farming shall be recruited as officials of different positions according to the amount of work finished; third, those officials who have been demoted or dismissed can serve in the projects and are permitted to resume their positions after completion of the work; and fourth, those who are condemned to exile and beyond can serve in the projects and their penalty will be reduced. [2] This is mainly due to the positive policies adopted by the government to give full play to the initiative of the people in reclaiming land and developing water conservancy facilities. [3]

Water conservancy and field management began in the east of capital, where there was the trial implementation of rice planting in Luanxian, Yutian and Fengrun. According to Chen Yi's Ying Tian Zhi (Field Management Record), "in the fourth year of Emperor Yongzheng (1726), those who first went to such prefectures and counties as Luan and Yu to dredge rivers, build dams and open canals all were promoted to governing position. The cost of work was loaned

1 Pan Xi'en: The first case of *Capital Water Conservancy.*

2 *Biographies of the Qing Dynasty*, Vol. 14 Biography of Zhu Shi.

3 See Li Chengyan's East of Capital Water Conservancy and Field Management in Yongzheng Period of Qing Dynasty, *China Economic History Research*, No. 2, 2009.

to them and the annual tax was one tenth. In that autumn, the field yielded good harvest. Altogether there are one hundred and fifty hectares. ... So everybody dredge rivers and build water conservancy projects, and the establishment of four bureaus started since then."[1]

As early as January 24 of the fourth year of Yongzheng, Prince Yiqinwang submitted a secret memorial, making a proposal to divide the Zhili Hedao into four bureaus: the North Canal (Baihe) as one bureau, concurrently managed by Tongyongdao (Tongzhou and Yongping Prefectures); the South Canal and the Ziya River under the Zangjiaqiao Bridge, with the Dianhe River east of Yuanjiakou as one bureau, which will now be under the jurisdiction of Tianjin Dao. Yongdinghe River as one bureau, and the current subdivisions are shifted under river management; Jinan rivers and Xidian were transformed into one bureau, and Damingdao was relocated under Baoding Prefecture for management. In the fifth year of Emperor Yongzheng (1727), the Haihe River Basin was divided into four bureaus, namely, the East Capital, West Capital, South Capital and Tianjin bureaus, which were responsible for water conservancy and field management projects. Each bureau is headed by a special officer with a certain number of assistants, and the local officials are instructed to cooperate closely with the Bureau officials. In order to govern the four bureaus, a special water conservancy and farmland management office was set up. Because the northern peasants know little about tilling of the paddy field, Emperor Yongzheng ordered that 30 peasants familiar with paddy field cultivation in Jiangsu and Zhejiang provinces are selected and given food and salary each month to teach cultivation in Zhili. After the local people grasped the skills, they were allowed to return home. The paddy field farming tools and water conservancy tools needed were made by Jiangsu and Zhejiang craftsmen, and Zhili craftsmen were ordered to learn in order to master the skills themselves. The cost of paddy fields is high, and ordinary farmers

---

1 Emperor Yongzheng, *Jifu Tongzhi* (*Annals of the Capital*), Vol. 46 Water Conservancy and Field Management I.

cannot afford to grow rice. Prince Yiqinwang suggests that "those who can't afford should be funded with government expenditure, and they should pay one tenth of their harvest to make up the Treasury funds, which will stop when the full amount is paid; If those who can afford and are the first to follow can build dykes to surround low-lying fields of more than one Qing, they should be praised and rewarded, and those who violate the supervision will be held responsible and no loan should be granted to them. Those who could provide funding to run the business on behalf of others will be honored officially if they are common people, and will be considered for promotion if they are government officials, but still one tenth of the annual income from the harvest should be returned to repay the principal." [1] From the fifth year (1727) to the seventh year (1729) of Emperor Yongzheng, more than 6,000 Qing of paddy fields have been opened up. "Every year there is abundant harvest, ears of rice accumulate in the threshing ground, and Jingdao rice abounds in the market." [2] Rice production in the capital region has begun to take shape, which is an important period in the history of agriculture and water conservancy, especially in the history of Beijing. All these indicate that the government played an important role in planning and implementing farmland water conservancy projects at that time. Water conservancy projects in the Qing Dynasty not only promoted the development of water transportation, but also promoted the development and prosperity of cities, industry and commerce. [3]

4. Government Direct Management of Land

The land system is an eternal theme, which reflects the relationship between people and land and the relationship between people formed on the basis of it. The land system has distinct features of the times. In feudal society, especially in

1 Emperor Yongzheng, *Jifu Tongzhi* (*Annals of the Capital*), Vol. 94 Prince Yixianqinwang,A Request for the Establishment of Special Officials for Field Management.

2 Emperor Yongzheng, *Jifu Tongzhi* (*Annals of the Capital*), Vol. 46 Water Conservancy and Field Management I.

3 Guo Yunjing: *A Concise Edition of Economic History of Qing Dynasty*, Henan People's Publishing House, 1984, p. 36.

the early stage of feudal society, the land system typically embodies the personal dependence relationship between producers and land owners and its change, because "political power status is arranged according to real estate ownership".[1] The land system of feudal society in China adapted to the traditional agricultural production technology, which did not change much even when the dynasty was constantly changing. In China's feudal society, the landlord economy occupied a leading position, while the self-cultivating peasant economy also occupied a considerable proportion in different periods. Even so, the feudal government also managed a certain amount of land, which became agricultural resources directly used by the royal family or directly allocated by the central government. It played an important role in social and economic life, especially in the regulation and control of the economy by the government. In feudal society of China, government-controlled official farmland mainly includes Tun Tian (classified into military, management, civilian, commercial, prisoner farmland and so on), which is mainly for providing for military expenses; official farmland, administration farmland, in order to solve official salaries or official expenditure; school farmland, sacrificial farmland, mainly for solving special expenditure of government, school or Royal family; ranches and gardens, mainly for the government to set up working sites for horses and other livestock, or for royal hunting and recreational activities. In addition, the government also owns a certain number of wasteland and barren mountains, which are often gradually converted into official or civilian farmland. The continuous privatization of official farmland is an indisputable fact.

During the Three Kingdoms period, in order to survive and eventually unify the whole country, each political power spared no effort to develop agricultural production and handicraft production, and to a certain extent allowed the existence of commercial circulation. The greatest feature was that they mobilized resources within their jurisdiction and made full use of the separatist regime to

1 *Selected Works of Marx and Engels* Vol. 4, People's Publishing House, p. 169.

support agriculture, handicraft production and military supply. In 196 AD, Cao Cao accepted the suggestion of Zao Zhi and Han Hao to have garrison troops or peasants open up wasteland and grow food grain (Tun Tian) in the vast area of northern China. In that very year, they gained millions of Hu of grains only in Xuxia. Its economic benefits are self-evident. At the same time, officials in various places were set up to take charge of local grain production, which not only increases the revenue of Cao Cao's administration, but also saves the cost of long-distance transportation of grain and other materials. Its social benefits are also very obvious. After Cao Cao, the Cao Wei administration continued to implement a fruitful system of Tun Tian farming. Under the leadership of Deng Ai, as many as 20,000 people were engaged in farming in Huaibei and 30,000 in Huainan. At that time, the benefit of farming was relatively good. According to Deng Ai's estimate, after the normal cost or expenditure was removed, there were still 5 million Hu of grain surplus in the annual production. If they continue for several years, they can maintain the food supply of 100,000 troops for five years. This was a remarkable achievement at that time. The Cao Wei administration was strong in the Three Kingdoms period, and eventually had the economic strength to unify the whole country. This has very complicated and profound reasons. Tuntian played a vital role, which cannot be eradicated in any case.

During the period when the Three Kingdoms were having a tripartite balance of forces, the Sun-Wu government established in the lower reaches of the Yangtze River still placed the development of social economy in its jurisdiction in a very important position, although it had been in a state of war for a long time. One of the most important aspects was the implementation of large-scale Tun Tian farming. According to records, the large-scale farming of Sun-Wu government began in 226 A.D. The implementation of Tuntian not only promoted the development of agricultural production in the south of the Yangtze River, but also increased the national financial revenue of Sun-Wu government, which is one of the important economic bases for the Sun-Wu kingdom to keep a foothold on the south of the Yangtze River.

During the Three Kingdoms Period, the governments implemented the system of Tun Tian farming within their jurisdiction to varying degrees, which showed that this farming system was one of the important ways to achieve social and economic benefits, and was a rational choice to mobilize national resources to restore and develop social economy in the wartime economic environment. At that time, the development of agricultural production was based on the wartime economic environment, and Tun Tian farming may after all be accepted as a more obvious form of benefit under the leadership of national economy. The scale and benefit of Tun Tian farming became one of the preconditions for the prosperity of the government. The prosperity of Cao-Wei eventually became the basis of unification, which had a lot to do with the economic benefits of Tun Tian in Cao-Wei.

The government has opened up new approaches, and the setting of Gong Xie Qian (government money for lending) is one of the important contents. "The supply and expenditure are insufficient for government officials, and all levels of government agencies have set up Gong Xie Qian to collect interest."[1] That is, the government allocates a certain amount of special funds to lend money as principal and use the interest collected to solve the expenses problem. However, during the period of Emperor Wendi of the Sui Dynasty, this situation underwent a transformation from Gong Xie/Tian Qian (government money/farmland lending) to Zhi Tian (government land for official salaries), reflecting the decision-makers' choice in the respect of officials' remuneration at that time. Su Xiaoci, Gong Bu Shang Shu (the Minister of Industry), believes that Gong Xie/Tian Qian is the use of lending money to obtain government revenue. It is in fact to scramble for profits with the people, but not a good policy for nation-building. So, he strongly demanded its abolition. At the same time, Su Xiaoci's specific countermeasure is to "ask the government officials below Gong Qing (nobles) to give different amounts of Zhi Tian land to their employees". That is, government

1 *The Book of Sui Dynasty* Vol. 24 Shi Huo Zhi.

officials are given diffenerent amount of Zhi Tian farmland according to their positions as part of their salaries, in order to replace the Gong Xie/Tian Qian. Emperor Yangdi of the Sui Dynasty accepted Su Xiaoci's suggestion and carried out Zhi Tian[1]. Whether the Emperor Wendi of the Sui Dynasty implemented the Gong Xie/Tian Qian or the Zhi Tian, it alleviated the government's financial expenditure to a certain extent and lightened the burden of the direct producers. Under the special conditions at that time, the society urgently needed to restore and develop production after the long-term separatist regime of the Northern and Southern Dynasties, but the government could not afford to heavily exploit the direct producers. The two are good policies. In particular, Gong Xie Tian plays a certain role in restricting private usury capital. Since the small-scale peasant economy has become the main body of social production, the characteristics of peasant households as both consumption units and production units determine the borrowing and lending in the traditional Chinese custom society is mainly related with peasants. It is manifested in the life and production consumption borrowing of peasants, and the main debt relationship also occurs among peasants, or between peasants, landlords and businessmen, with private lending as the main body. The reason why peasants get in touch with loan capital in their daily life lies in the periodicity of agricultural production itself. Spring sowing takes more than half a year to get benefits after autumn, and within a few years, agricultural harvest will appear periodically in good years, normal years and disaster years. From the perspective of social relations, among peasant households with the same conditions, some may be in urgent need, others may have temporarily idle property. Private ownership of property leads to unequal possession of wealth, resulting in the rich and poor. This is the natural and social basis for the emergence and existence of rural lending relations. It is a well-known fact that the individual small-scale agricultural economy, with family as the unit, not only needs to pay the living expenses in advance, but also needs to make a large number of

1 *The Book of Sui Dynasty* Vol. 24 Shi Huo Zhi.

advances in production. Everybody knows about the fact of the unstable character of the individual economy. Its production scale is small and its ability to cope with economic turbulence is very weak. But even in the most disadvantageous situation, they should also make great efforts to maintain reproduction. When they go bankrupt, they can no longer compensate for production conditions with normal production, or even cannot maintain their livelihood, they can only borrow money. In establishing a lending relationship, the borrower can only preserve the capital in anticipation of repayment and has a nominal right to recover the principal and interest. In order to reduce the risk of debt lending, creditors must require the debtor to provide certain property as guarantee. This is the first prerequisite for establishing credit. The government's lending to the direct producers plays a certain role in preventing the infiltration of private usury capital among the common people and in preventing the bankruptcy of individual small-scale production agriculture.

In the fifth year of Kaihuang (585) during the reign of Emperor Wendi of Sui Dynasty, in order to restore and develop agricultural production as soon as possible, the government "bought more than 6,000 cattle and donkeys and distributed them to the poorest", and let these poor people "go to east of Shanhaiguan to make a living". The disaster victims in other areas were given preferential treatment of reduction or exemption of the tax of the year[1]. These measures have played an obvious role in restoring and developing social production as soon as possible, reflecting the important role of the central finance in this regard.

There were many innovations in the social economy in the Sui Dynasty, among which the establishment of She Cang (Civil Granary) in the Sui Dynasty was of certain typical significance. In the fifth year of Kaihuang during the reign of Emperor Wendi of the Sui Dynasty (585), the court accepted the proposal of Sun Ping, Gong Bu Shang Shu (the Minister of Industry), to set up She Cang for the

1 *The Book of Sui Dynasty* Vol. 24 Shi Huo Zhi.

relief of famine caused by natural disasters. Because of its good effect, it has been popularized throughout the country. The central government has required the encouragement and supervision of setting up of Yi Cang among common people and soldiers. At that time, the Yi Cang was set up in the most basic level of Li She (villages or towns), which was managed by the clever and capable people. Its specific operating procedures are: in the harvest season, local residents are persuaded to take out a certain amount of grain to the Li She, which is stored in a special granary, and the granary managers set up accounts to register and record the income and expenditure of She Cang. If natural disasters affect the basic livelihood of local residents, the granary will be opened for relief. According to the regulations, the specific payment standard of She Cang is "to pay taxes based on upper, middle and lower levels. Upper level household should pay tax of no more than one Dan, middle household no more than seven Dou, and lower household no more than four Dou." These taxes, for the residents at that time, are not heavy burdens, but for the disaster victims, it is timely help. Just after the implementation of She Cang, "Shandong has been suffering from continuous heavy rain. From such prefectures as Qi, Song, Chen, Bo, Cao, Dai, Qiao, and Ying to Canghai Sea, people all suffer from floods." For those seriously affected by the disaster, the "granary relief" has been adopted, and altogether more than 5 million Dan of grain have been used in the She Cang.[1] At that time, She Cang received good benefits, and "from then on all the prefectures began storing grains".[2] In the Sui Dynasty, the stock of the state and local governments was enriched, which was inseparable from the establishment of granaries at that time.

The focus of the state's control over land transactions changed during the Tang and Song Dynasties. The focus of control in the early Tang Dynasty was to examine whether land transactions were legal. After the mid-Tang Dynasty, the

1 According to *The Book of Sui Dynasty* Vol. 24 Shi Huo Zhi, there are more than 500 Dan, which is not correct. According to Lu Xixiong's Bing Zhu Ou Chao, it should be more than 5 million Dan, and the word "ten thousand" is left out. Indeed, it is.

2 *The Book of Sui Dynasty* Vol. 24 Shi Huo Zhi.

restrictions on land transactions were abolished, and tax delivery involving land became the focus. The Song Dynasty unified the deeds and government inspection of the late Tang Dynasty and formed the deeds of mutual covenant. From focusing on official documents submission to tax delivery, it reflects the trend that the state gradually strengthened its control over land transactions during the Tang and Song Dynasties.[1]

In the early Ming Dynasty, many economic policies were adopted, including: First, reclaim wasteland. In order to encourage wasteland reclamation, the Ming government stipulated that wasteland, whether or not there is original owner, would be owned by new reclaimers as long as it was brought under cultivation, and it would always be exempted from taxation. At the same time, the government provides the necessary cattle, seeds and farming tools for the reclamation, and the amount of reclaimed land was considered one of the important bases for the assessment of officials. In addition, the Ming Dynasty encouraged the displaced people in the late Yuan Dynasty to return to their homeland. For those who had no or little land among the returnees, the government allocated a certain amount of wasteland according to the size of the population. The Ming Dynasty organized the largest relocation movement in China's history, aiming at the situation of sparse population in some areas, and achieved the national balance of labor resources through state compulsory behavior. This reflects the centralized state's ability to mobilize and allocate resources, including labor resources. The allocation of labor resources, such as the large-scale relocation in the Ming Dynasty, has far-reaching social impact, and its impact on future generations cannot be ignored.

The second is to carry out all kinds of Tun Tian farming, including military, civilian, commercial and prisoner farming. Tun Tian is an agricultural production activity organized and implemented by the state power, which has played an important role under special historical conditions. Tuntian in Ming Dynasty

1 Wang Xueping and Wu Shuguo: On the Change of Land Transaction Control in Tang and Song Dynasties, *Journal of Heilongjiang Institute of Education*, No. 4, 2008.

is richer in content than that in history. Facing the economic depression and the border pressure from Mongolian aristocracy in the vast northern region, Zhu Yuanzhang regarded Tuntian as a "way of long-term stability" and mainly promoted it in the northern border areas. It is stipulated that the military field shall be cultivated by the garrison military households, with 30% of the frontier garrison soldiers guarding and 70% tilling the field; and 20% of the inland garrison soldiers guard and 80% till the field. The grain produced by the army is mainly used as the cost of the army. Civil Tun Tian is mainly that the government relocate people from Xia Xiang (a place with a large population and limited land) to Kuan Xiang (a place with large expanses of land and a small population), or the government recruit peasants for farming. Civil Tun Tian people are actually special tenants of the government. They pay land rent according to the sharecropping system. If they bring cattle and seeds themselves, the land rent is 30% of the total income; and if cattle and seeds are provided by the government, the land rent is 50% of the total income. Commercial Tun Tian is to use the role of economic leverage. The government stipulated that the merchants could exchange grain for salt license and transport it to a certain place. Therefore, the merchants creatively recruited people to open up fields at the government designated grain transporting places, paid grain locally and obtained salt license from the government, and traded freely after salt license was obtained. Criminal Tun Tian is a special form of farming. The main producers are those who violate feudal laws. One of the basic historical facts we know is that the laws of the Ming Dynasty were rather severe and the number of people sent into exile was huge. These prisoners became an important labor force in Tun Tian. In Records of the Grand Historian of the Ming Dynasty, prisoner and civil Tun Tian were often combined as one.

In the early Ming Dynasty, more obvious social and economic benefits were achieved in Tun Tian. The number of Tun Tian farming was more than 903,300 hectares, which exceeded 10% of the cultivated land area in China. In the 21st year of Emperor Hong Wu (1388), the income of military Tun Tian was more than 5 million Dan. Although the Ming Dynasty began to implement various types of Tun Tian, and in the 21st year of Emperor Hongwu (1388) promulgated the Tun Tian law, in fact, the Tun Tian was still in the exploratory stage at that time, and did not spread throughout the country. Later, the central government achieved relatively successful experience in Lintao, Minzhou, Lanzhou, Hezhou, Zhuanglang, Ganzhou, Suzhou, Shandan, Yongchang, Liangzhou and other places after five years of extensive experiments, which fully conforms to Zhu Yuanzhang's governing conception that "the foundation of rejuvenating the country lies in strong troops and sufficient food". Later, Ming Taizu accepted the suggestion of Hu Bu Shang Shu Zhao Mian , and popularized the Gansu Province operation of Tuntian throughout the country, and adjusted the proportion of troops engaged in Tun Tian farming and garrison personnel to 7:3. Since then, the basic requirement of self-sufficiency during the early Hongwu years (1368-1398) has been changed to be, and the principle of land reclamation has been implemented in which the state uniformly collects rents without grading. During the period of Emperor Hongwu (1368-1398), the garrison Tun Tian farming in Gansu and other places had achieved self-sufficiency. The living standards of the direct producers had improved to a certain extent, and about 20% of their annual income had been turned over to the state treasury. Zhu Yuanzhang once said that, because of the implementation of Tun Tian farming, "the state supports millions of soldiers, and does not need a grain from the people". In addition to producing a large amount of grain, Tuntian farming also saves a huge amount of long-distance transportation expenditure for the country.

The third is to build water conservancy projects. The Ming Dynasty formed a network system of irrigation and waterlogging drainage on a certain scale throughout the country, which made the agricultural production of the Ming Dynasty develop greatly, and laid a solid foundation for the development of industrial and commercial economy and even the emergence of capitalist.

In the late Ming Dynasty, the imperial court continuously appointed eunuchs as mine supervisors and tax supervisors, crazily depriving industry and commerce to exhaustion. Only in the twenty-ninth year of Emperor Wanli (1601), taxes sent directly to Beijing by eunuchs included more than 900,000 Liang of silver, 1575 Liang of gold, and diamonds, crystals, pearls, tulle, ruby and emerald, etc. Numerous eunuchs lined their pockets with public funds. This has aroused many struggles among the citizens against the mine supervisors and tax supervisors. As Zhao Yi said, "The perish of Ming Dynasty is not in the Chongzhen years (1628-1644), but started from Wanli yers (1573-1620) ".[1] This is a very insightful view.

After the Qing army conquered the Central Plain, there once issued a land enclosure order to satisfy the greed of the Manchu nobles. After being strongly opposed by the broad masses of scholars and common people, including the Manchu people, and combined with its relatively low economic benefits, in the Shunzhi period, an order to prevent enclosure had to be promulgated. In the Kangxi period, it was further stipulated that "no enclosure will ever be allowed thereafter". " The land policy of the Qing government returned to the track of the feudal society.

In agricultural production, the Qing government invested and mobilized the people to build coastal embankments. On the one hand, it stabilized the output per mu in coastal areas, but also increased the area of cultivated land. While giving preferential treatment to direct producers, in order to stabilize agricultural production and fundamentally solve the long-standing problem of population concealment, the Qing government promulgated a decree in the 51st year of Kangxi (1712) that "prosperity breeds population but taxes will never be imposed". That is to say, whether the number of people increases or not, the original tax quota will be maintained. In addition, in the fifty-fifth year of Kangxi (1716), the government announced the implementation of the Di Ding Yin system, which incorporated the original poll tax into the land tax. In the early years of Yongzheng (1723-1735), the method of poll tax merged into land tax was carried out nationwide, and about 3.35 million regular poll tax in the fifth year of Kangxi (1711) was allocated equally to the land tax in different places according to the

1 *Notes on Twenty-two History Books,* Vol. 35 The Harm of Mine Tax in Wanli Years.

original amount of poll tax, and was uniformly collected. The amount of poll taxed integrated varies from 1 Qian 2 Li to more than 2 Li. This kind of taxation system is also called the Di Ding (land and poll tax) system. "Poll tax merged into land tax" is the inheritance and development of "the Law of Uniform Taxation". This tax system incorporates the peasants' general corvee into the land, which abolishes the privilege of exemption of landlords and country gentlemen in the system. The implementation of the system of "poll tax merged into land tax" marked the further relaxation of the personal dependence of the direct producers, the further strengthening of the state power, the further expansion and stability of the sources of tax collection by the government, and also a certain degree of development of the commodity economy at that time. The abolition of the craftsman registration system in the Qing Dynasty[1] had a positive and far-reaching impact on improving the enthusiasm and autonomy of craftsmen and enhancing production and productivity. The abolition of the craftsman registration system made the craftsmen in the feudal society of China have the same political status as the general household people, and it also of great significance to the further development of economy of the folk handicraft industry economy.

Because of the state policy of a closed country in the Qing Dynasty, China's social economy, which had been in the leading position in the world, finally collapsed under the decadent rule from within and the attack of the imperialist guns from without. This led to defeat of China in the face of the imperialist attack in modern times. The decadent Qing Dynasty finally perished.

1 *Comprehensive Examination of Documents in the Qing Dynasty* Vol. 21 Corvee Law I records: In the second year if Emperor Shunzhi (1645), the Qing government announced, "besides the abolition of the craftsmen registration system in Zhili Porvince, there was also that of the Beijing craftsmen", and since then craftsmen "follow the same corvee law as the common people". In addition, there are similar records in Vol. 16 of the *Records of Shi Zu of the Qing Dynasty* and Shunzhi's *Complete Book of Taxation and Corvee System in Jiangxi · Revision.*

Part II

Evolution of State Capital Enterprises in Modern China(1840—1949)

The 1840 Opium War in 1840 changed the development trajectory of China. Imperialist warships and canons blew open China's door which had been closed and thus isolated China from the world for centuries. The old China's economic development path was cut off, throwing China into a period featured with brand new realities and turmoils. China was transiting from an independent feudal sovereign to a semi-feudal and semi-colonial society.

Because of the influx of foreign capital, the thousands of year old Chinese feudal socio-economic structure, unprepared and unwilling, was thrown into an age of modern machinery. The three basic forms of capitalism, namely foreign capital, state capital[1] and national capital, started to make their respective debut in Chinese history and play their different roles.

Moreover, unable to stand the blow from advanced production force of capitalist countries, the feudal structure underwent a period of transition "not seen in thousands of years". The biggest socio-economic change was the birth, development and dominance of machine-based manufacturing. This period is thus referred to, by researchers, as the early modernization period (1860-1949) in China.

Table 4-1 shows the distribution of foreign capital, state capital and national capital in machine-based manufacturing at different points in the early modernization period in China.

1 In the past, "bureaucrat capital" was used by the academia to refer to "state capitalism" and "state capital enterprises". But now, more and more researchers agree that "state capital" is more accurate than "bureaucrat capital". So, this books has replaced "bureaucrat capital" with "state capital" and "bureaucrat economy" with "state capitalism". Moreover, the authors believe "baron capital" of "bureaucrat capital" is also different from "state capital". More specific explanations will be made later. "State capitalism" and "state capital enterprises" took very complicated forms in modern China. In this book, modern state capital enterprises refer not just to those directly funded by the state, but also include those enterprises which are controlled by he state and whose positioning and direction served the goals set by the state sovereignty.

Table 4-1 Estimates of Capital in Machine-Based Manufacturing (Unit: 10,000 yuan)

Year	Capital in total	Foreign Capital		Chinese Capital					
		Volume	Percentage (%)	Volume	Percentage (%)	State Capital		National Capital	
						Volume	Percentage (%)	Volume	Percentage (%)
1894	12 155	5 406	44.5	6 749	55.5	4 757	39.1	1 992	16.4
1914	178 673	102 125	57.2	76 548	42.8	47 807	26.8	28 741	16.1
1920	257 929	133 000	51.6	124 929	48.4	66 952	26.0	57 977	22.5
1936	1355 039	927 841	68.5	427 198	31.5	222 454	16.4	204 744	15.1
1948	693 228	111 650	16.1	581 578	83.9	420 079	60.6	161 499	23.3

Notes: 1. For 1914, the figure of state capital is for 1911 and that of national capital for 1913.
The Chinese capital for 1936 includes that in Northeast China.
All figures are for industrial capital, not including financial and commercial capital

Source: Xu Dixin and Wu Chengming, ed., *History of Capitalism in China*, Vol. 2 The People's Publishing House, 1990.

As is shown in Table 4-1, foreign capital was dominating in Chinese capitalism all through the modern Chinese history. From 1894 to 1936, foreign capital accounted for more than a half of the capital of modern machinery, increasing by 7 times in 16 years from 1920 to 1936, and accounting for over 68% of all capital in machinery industries. In a way, this was a typical sign of semi-feudalism and semi-colonialism. With respect to Chinese capital, state capital was gaining momentum. For example, China's modern machinery industries originated in government enterprises and government-supervised and merchant-managed Enterprises in the Late Qing Dynasty, which secured an prominent dominance in the Chinese capital funded machinery industries, more than doubling national capital. Under the Beiyang Government and the Kuomintang Government, state capital continued to thrive , maintaining an unchallenged competitive edge over national capital. Later, with the development and increase in the percentage of machine-based manufacturing in socio-economic structure, state capital entered a new stage of robust development after 1936. As statistics show, the Resources Committee of the Kuomintang Government alone controlled the production of 63% electricity, 33% coal, 90% iron and steel, 100% tungsten and antimony,

70% tin, 45% cement, and 90% sugar.[1] By 1948, the total volume of state capital controlled by the Kuomintang Government had been 3.8 times as much as that of foreign capital and 2.6 times that of national capital.[2] State capital boasted an absolute dominance of accounting for 60% of national economy, with even more dominance in heavy industries, the development of which was regarded as the benchmark of economic modernization. All these laid the foundation for economic development of the People's Republic of China.

As a whole, the dominance of state capital during this period was no accident, but an inevitability. First all, foreign invasion and successive civil wars threatened the survival of the Chinese people. In the face of both foreign and domestic challenges, the old national defense and economic pattern proved impotent. State mobilization, organization and operation became the only choice. In the words of institutional economics, "state intervention can make up for sustained insufficiency of institutional supply".[3] As is repeatedly proven in history, in times of crisis, state power is the most responsive and effective way of reform, social resources mobilization and crisis management. Against the unique historic backdrop of modern China, only state power was capable of changing resource allocation and production mode in a straightforward, timely and effective way. The state has the potential to mobilize and organize various social classes and systems to remove historic and realistic obstacles, to reform and to achieve stated objectives. These are the root causes of the rise and sustained dominance of state capitalism.

Moreover, the robust performance of state capital in modern China also owed to

1 "The Percentage of the Resources Committee Controlled Industrial Production in the Kuomintang Controlled Regions", in Chen Zhen, ed., Historical Files of China's Modern Industry, Vol. 3, Sanlian Bookstore, 1961, p.1445.

2 Calculated with figures in Table 1.

3 Lin Yifu: Economic Theories on Institutional Change: Guided and Forced Change", in R.Kos, A.Alchian, D.Nors and others, The Evolution of Property Rights and Institutions: Property Right Economics and Neo-institutional Economics, Sanlian Bookstore and Shanghai People's Publishing House, 1994: p.394.

China's historic heritage. With thousands of years of centralized authority, China had always had a powerful central government, an outstanding feature of Chinese politics, economics and social management. The government had been directly operating handcraft and commercial industries, with state monopoly over those strategic resources[1] such as salt and iron, and government handicraft workshops had dominated manufacturing. As a result, the government enjoyed a secured control over economy.

The combination the traditional of government control in history and the need of crisis management in modern China created one particular feature of the early modernization of China; that is, state capital funded modern machinery industries became the first to breach the feudal system. Governments had successively endeavored as much as they could to secure the dominance of state capitalism. The socio-economic conditions after the outbreak of the Anti-Japanese War further strengthened the monopoly of state capitalism.

In the following chapters, we shall trace and explore the development and features of state capitalism at different stages in modern China and analyze the role played by state capital in the economic system.

1 "The centralized feudal government played three economic functions: first, construction and management of public works such as hydraulic engineering, transportation and national defense; second, intervention in reproduction through tax and economic policies; third, direct participation in the handicraft industry and commerce. Quoted in Wu Taichang, "Review of the Impacts of the Feudal Socio-Economic Structure on the Development of Capitalism in China", *Researches of Chinese Economic History*, Issue 1, 1990. "

Chapter 4

State-run Enterprises and Government-Supervised and Merchant-Managed Enterprises in the Late Qing Dynasty

Industrialization marked by the use of machinery started in the Westernization Movement initiated by the Qing government for self-help in the mid 19th century. Although western imperialist powers stimulated the start of industrialization from without, China's pursuit of strength, wealth and military power was the real drive from within.

The Westernization Movement started by purchasing western machinery and building such modern industries as military, shipbuilding, machine-based mining and railway before expand to civilian industries, and established a modern industrial structure with "machinery, shipbuilding, railway and mining" as the starting point. The prioritization of these industries on the one hand satisfied the government's need of resources to fight against foreign invasion and suppress the Taiping Rebellion 1851-1864 and on the other was determined by the political and economic structure of the Qing government. Back then, China was a closed and underdeveloped agricultural country rather than a capitalist market economy. Machinery-based industries constituted a direct challenge to feudalism and therefore must be authorized by the government for a legal status. In the meantime, it is pivotal to break the mindset of the "superiority of the Chinese culture in every way" and the worries about "barbarians changing China". Moreover, these westernized modern enterprises had to rely on the government for financial, technological and institutional support. Because of all these, at the starting-up period of big industries in China, the state inevitably dominated, in both military and civilian industries, and in State-run Enterprises and government-supervised and merchant-managed enterprises (hereafter as GSMM enterprises) alike. As a result, state capital was the initiator, main player and controller.

Following the chronological order, the following parts start by studying government military enterprises before turning to government civilian enterprises.

1. State-run Enterprises Industries for Military Uses

In the late Qing Dynasty, the machine industry started with government military enterprises funded by state capital before expanding to the civilian sector. Such a development path came into being because of the following reasons:

First of all, the foreign powers demonstrated their weaponry superiority during the two Opium Wars and deeply impressed the Qing Imperial Court. Shortly after the first Opium War, Wei Yuan proposed "beat(ing) foreigners by learning fro m their advantages" Other leading westernizationists such as Zeng Guofan, Li Hongzhang and Zuo Zongtang, who rose to power when suppressing the Taiping Rebellion, were exposed to the superior ships and weaponry of western powers and considered purchasing and copying.

Zeng Guofan's report to the emperor in August 1861 was typical. Zeng spoke highly of the speed and range of English and French ships and cannons, which were unseen in China before. Zeng suggested purchasing and possessing these weaponry so that China would no longer be surprised and England and France would lose their advantage. It was also recommended that after purchase, craftsmen shall be involved to learn how to use and copy. Zeng foresaw that "in one year or two, steam-driven vessel will be used for transportation by both officials and common people".[1] In 1863, Li Hongzhang echoed by saying that Russia and Japan, before learning how to use cannons, were waning and inferior to other people until they learned the secrets of English and French weaponry and ships, made their own copies and became equals to England and France.[2] In April the same year, Li asserted, "If China had cannons and steam-driven ships, westerners would have to back off."[3]

In his August 1864 reply to the inquiry of the Ministry of Foreign Affairs of the Qing Dynasty, Li Hongzhang first explained the rent of western ships at various trading posts and accepted and recommended Ding Richang's idea about building shipsyards and allowing Chinese merchants to buy western ships. Li attached Ding's private correspondence to his reply, with detailed explanations of the purpose and execution principles and measures of his recommendations. In the private correspondence, Ding Richang argued that the west's advantage in weaponry and shipsbuilding gave them an upper hand and recommended that China should make use of western technologies to sere Chinese interest. Ding analyzed the pros and cons of renting and buying by saying that bandits might take advantage of rented steamships and splint ships for robbery. Therefore, it is important for the government to register and number these ships for supervision, with the guarantee of the gentry at purchase and the inspection of the government when sailing out. The Chinese sailors might need the guidance of westerners at the beginning, but practice should enable them to navigate the ships themselves. Cargo ships would be exempt from tariff as a sign of favor and trust. During peacetime, these ships should be allowed to trade on their own

1 On the Priority Necessity to Buy Western Ships and Cannons, in Institute of Modern History, Taiwan Central Research Institute, ed., *Costal Defense: Purchase of Ships and Cannons (I)*, (hereafter as *Costal Defense*)1957, p.20.

2 Li Hongzhang, Messages to Grand Councilor Zeng (Dated March 17 of 2nd Year of Emperor Tongzhi), in *Complete Works of Li Hongzhang: Correspondents, Vol. 3*, Shanghai People's Publishing House, 1985.

3 Li Hongzhang, Messages to Grand Councilor Zeng (Dated April 4 of 2nd Year of Emperor Tongzhi), in *Complete Works of Li Hongzhang: Correspondents, Vol. 3*, Shanghai People's Publishing House, 1985.

but be expropriated when necessary. Twenty to thirty steamships and a hundred splint ships at each trading port would not only strengthen ourselves but also take back the power from imperialists, because we could then compete with westerners in speed. However, in terms of price and quality, Chinese merchants definitely were unquestionably more competitive than their western counterparts and consequently could be cost effective. So, westerners who came for lucrative profits would leave when the profit margin shrank. Great potentials were found in such business. There was no reason to doubt our advantages. In the end, on one hand he suggested that money be raised and a proper port be chosen to build a steamships factory and that Chinese craftsmen learn from western technicians. On the other, Chinese gentry should be allowed to buy steamships so that they could make money for future use when necessary. [1]

In May 1866, in his analysis on the conflict with the English, Zuo Zongtang argued, "In land battles, we are equals, if not necessarily more superior, to the English. However, when it comes to naval battles, they have steamships but we don't. How would we compete?"[2] He then presented a secret report to the emperor, asking for permission to build a shipyard in Fuzhou. His ideas had a lot in common with Ding Rizhang's. He emphasized that the key in the southeast did not lie on the land but in the sea. To the east of the coastline from Guangdong, Fujian, Zhejiang, Jiangnan, Shandong until Shengjing was sea. In peace, the sea connected different provinces and provided for people with its sea products. In time of war, the sea could enable quick mobilization and response by uniting coastal provinces. Analyzing the impact of foreign steamships trading along the coastline and rivers, Zuo Zongtang argued since western ships were allowed to carry northern products to trade at various trading posts, the prices of these

1 Bureau of Machinery, *Costal Defense (III)*, pp. 4-5

2 Zuo Zongtang, On Planning for Self-Strengthening Matters, in *Complete Works of Zuo Zongtang: Memorials to the Throne*, p. 10, quoted in Chinese History Society, ed., *The Self-Strengthening Movement*, Shanghai People's Publishing House and Shanghai Bookstore Press, 2000.

products had soared. As a result, merchants from Jiangnan and Zhejiang, who took the sea lanes, had to pay more for these products, only to find their goods slower but more expensive and thus less competitive than those traded on western steamships. If this situation continued, these merchants would lose profits and even go bankrupt. At the moment, there was a lack of ships in sea transport while the canal transport was lagging behind, too. So, the only solution is to build shipyards to build steamships. Emphasizing the emergency of such undertaking, Zuo said, "Both sides could benefit from the sea, but they have the advantage but we don't. It is like crossing a river. Others have boats, but we have only rafts. Or, they are riding horses, but we donkeys. How could we let it be?" and concluded, "Every thing which might cause troubles would bring benefit eventually. So, if steamships are built successfully, water transportation will flourish and the military, the government, the businessmen and the people could all benefit. Tariff revenues would increase, which shall benefit the generations to come."[1]

In its September 1864 replay to Li Hongzhang, the Ministry of Foreign Affairs spoke highly of Ding Richang's proposals as "ideas of unprecedented vision which hit the core of the issue and state the ministry's unspoken hidden dangers",[2] and commissioned Li Hongzhang to plan. In addition, Zuo Zongtang also received a favorable reply and authorization. This way, machine-based modern industry made the first breakthrough in shipbuilding and weaponry. Thus, the Westernization Movement characterized with the introduction of western machinery started. These cases demonstrate but for the proposal, the Qing government would not have agreed with the development of modern industry. This is the root cause for state capital enterprises to rise first.

These reports from leading westernizationists such as Zeng Guofan, Li Hongzhang and Zuo Zongtang show that their original plans attached equal importance to national defense and civilian industries. However, foreign

1 Zuo Zongtang, *Complete Works of Zuo Zongtang: Memorials to the Throne*, Vol. 18, pp. 1-5.

2 Bureau of Machinery, *Costal Defense (III)*, p. 6.

aggression forced them to put military enterprises before everything else. Therefore, the pursuit of power was the root cause to prioritize the military industry at the birth of state capital enterprises.

State capital military enterprises of the Qing Dynasty until 1894 were listed in Table 4-2:

Table 4-2 Military Enterprises in the Late Qing Dynasty:1862-1894

Name of Enterprise	Location	Date of founding	Founder	Number of workers	Capital		Remarks
					Amount (*Liang*[1] of silver)	Commencement date and deadline	
Anqing Arms Plant	Anqing	1862	Zeng Guofan	Unknown	Unknown	Unknown	Dissolved in 1864
Shanghai Western Cannon Plant	Shanghai	1863	Li Hongzhang	150-600	Unknown	Unknown	Of the three departments, one was integrated into the Suzhou Western Cannon Plant in 1863 and the other two into the Kiangnan Arsenal in 1865.
Suzhou Western Cannon Plant	Suzhou	1863	Li Hongzhang Zeng Guofan	60	179969 ①	1864-65	Integrated into the Jinlin Machine Mill in 1865.
Kiangnan Arsenal	Shanghai	1865	Li Hongzhang	2800	16981974 ①	1865-94	The largest arsenal in China then.
Jinling Machine Mill	Nanjing	1865	Li Hongzhang	700-1000	2430000 ② 182895 ① 520000 ②	1865-94 1881-84 1885-94	Large scale with the addition of the Jinling gunpowder plant by Liu Kunyi in 1881.
Fuzhou Shipyard	Fuzhou	1866	Zuo Zongtang	1730-2000	15422590 ①	1866-95	The largest shipyard.

contd.

Name of Enterprise	Location	Date of founding	Founder	Number of workers	Capital		Remarks
					Amount (*Liang*[1] of silver)	Commen-cement date and deadline	
Tianjing Machine Mill	Tianjin	1866	Chong Hou and Li Hongzhang	1400-2500	7252099 ① 540000 ③	1866-94 1893-94	Large
Xi'an Machine Mill	Xi'an	1869	Zuo Zongtang	Unknown	Unknown	Unknown	Integrated into the Lanzhou Machine Mill in 1872.
Fujian Machine Mill	Fuzhou	1869	Ying Gui	60	22655 ① 120000 ③	1885-86 1887-94	Small with intermittent operation until 1885.
Lanzhou Machine Mill	Lanzhou	1872	Zuo Zongtang	Unknown	Unknown	Unknown	Small and out of business in 1880.
Guangzhou-Machine Mill	Guangzhou	1874	Rui Lin	200	527320 ① 236000 ③	1874-94	Small when first founded but extended by Liu Kunyi and Zhang Zhidong after 1885.
Shandong Machine Mill	Jinan	1875	Ding Baozhen	250	186800 ① 648000 ②	1875-76 1877-94	Medium
Sichuan Machine Mill	Chengdu	1877	Ding Baozhen	250	77352 ① 164518 ① 804000 ③	1877-79 1880-82 1883-94	Medium. Operation stopped in 1879 until back in business in 1880.
Jilin Machine Mill	Jilin	1881	Wu Dacheng	300	420000	1881-94	Medium
Divine Engine Division Machine Mill	Beijing	1883	Yi Huan	Unknown	1000000 ①	1883-90	Large but burnt out in 1890.
Zhejiang Machine Mill	Hangzhou	1883	Liu Bingzhang	50	67299 ① 73100 ① 240000 ②	1883-84 1885-86 1887-94	Small
Taiwan Machine Mill	Taipei	1885	Liu Mingchuan	100	122466 ①	1885-86	Small
Yunnan Machine Mill	Kunming	1885	Ceng Yuying	60-100	Unknown	Unknown	Small

contd.

Name of Enterprise	Location	Date of founding	Founder	Number of workers	Capital		Remarks
					Amount (*Liang*[1] of silver)	Commencement date and deadline	
Hubei Gun and Cannon Factory	Hanyang	1890	Zhang Zhidong	1200	2100000 ①	1890-97	Large
Total				9100-10810	50319037		

Notes:

① The actual reimbursements or records;

② Calculated based on the recorded annual budget;

③ Calculated based on the actual reimbursements (annual or average).

Source: Xu Dixin and Wu Chengming, ed., *History of Capitalism in China*, Vol. 2, The People's Publishing House, 1990, pp.341-342.

Table 4-3: Fund Sources of Military Enterprises in the Late Qing Dynasty

Name of Enterprise	Initial Fund Sources		Regular Fund Sources	
	Source	Amount (*Liang* of Silver)	Source	Amount (*Liang* of Silver)
Suzhou Cannon Factory (1863-1865)	— Shanghai Tao-tai, Guangdong Commissioner	— 68 000	Military budget	110657
Kiangnan Arsenal (1865-1894)	Atonement Shanghai Customs Military budget HSBC loans	40 000 20 000 415 000 400 000	20% of the foreign tariff at the Jianghaiguan Customs (including a small amount of special allocation)	15027736
Jinlin Arsenal (1865-1894)	Foreign trade tariffs at Jianghai, Jianghan and Jiujiang Customs, Kiangnan De	110 000 182 895	Tariff of Nanyang and Beiyang, Jinlin Defense Finance Bureau	1870000 624000
Fuzhou Shipyard (1866-1895)	Tariffs of Fujian Customs	400 000	Tariffs of Fujian Customs, likin of Fujian Province	11870000 260000

contd.

Name of Enterprise	Initial Fund Sources		Regular Fund Sources	
	Source	Amount (*Liang* of Silver)	Source	Amount (*Liang* of Silver)
Tianjin Machine Mill (1866-1894)	General Office of Tax's stored ships in cash tariffs of Jinhai and Donghai Customs, Medicine tariff	80 000 100 000 33 333	40% of the tariffs of Jinhai and Donghai Customs (including Merchant Group ship taxes and allocations from the Ministry of Revenue)	
Shandong Machine Mill (1875-1894)	Government Repository, Food Rout Repository, Linqing Customs	94 000 72 800 20 000	Government Repository	684 000
Hubei Gun and Cannon Factory (1890-1897)	Military fines, donations from salt merchants and officials, loans from Arnhold Karberg & Co.	700 000 150 000 200 000 600 000	Medicine tax Extra Tax from Salt Tax of Szechwan, Jiangsu and Anhui Province	1 100 000 210 000

Source: Sun Liutang, ed., *Historical Data of Modern Chinese Industry*, Vol. 1, Science Press, 1957, quoted in Xu Dixin and Wu Chengming, ed., *History of Capitalism in China*, Vol. 2, The People's Publishing House, 1990, p.373.

In sum, the period from 1860 to 1894 was the first stage for machine based industries in modern China. The Qing government prioritized the military industry, as shown in Table 4-2 with 20 or so enterprises, 10,000 industrial works and a total investment of 50 million *liang* of silver. The main products from these enterprises included weaponry, ship and machinery. Most taproduction machines were purchased from England, France, Germany and the United States. Interms of training, in addition to school training and overseas study tools, foreign technicians were hired especially from the above mentioned four countries.[1] However, there was no overall planning for these military enterprises. Instead,

1 Zhang Yufa, Government-run Businesses in the Late Qing and Early Nationalist Government Period, in Institute of Modern History, Taiwan Central Research Institute, ed., *Collected Papers of the Symposium on the Self-Strengthening Movement*, Vol. 2, 1988.

local officials played a major role here, but for different purposes and with different levels of management. As shown in Table 4-3, funds for these enterprises came mostly from customs tariffs, allocation from the Ministry of Revenue, local funding, donations, military budget and loans from foreign companies. These military enterprises did not aim to make profits or sell in the market, but in nature were an expanded version of government funded handicraft workshops. However, against the backdrop of foreign invasion and domestic turmoil, these enterprises played a much bigger role in maintaining and prolonging the rule of the Qing government.

2. Government and Government-Supervision Machinery Enterprises for Civilian Uses

After the state capital funded government military enterprises, the westernizationists in the 1870s started to build modern civilian industrial enterprises such as shipyard, coal and metal ore mine, iron and steel plant, textile, railway and telegram. The enterprises on one hand provided much needed fuels and raw materials to military enterprises and one the other generate profits. When building these civilian enterprises, besides State-run Enterprises, a new operation model was created: the government-supervision merchant-management (GSMM) enterprises. Though different from State-run Enterprises, these GSMM enterprises are a special kind of state capital funded enterprises.

The real reason for the expansion into civilian industries is the urgent need of raw materials and fuels, especially coal and iron, by military enterprises established since 1860. Moreover, in the process, westernizationist officials started to realize the interconnection between the pursuit of power and that of fortune and the inseparability between military and civilian industries. Li Hongzhang said, "Fortune first, power comes. When the people are well-being, the state is built on a more solid foundation."[1] Li Zongxi reported, "After the Fujian Machine

1 Li Hongzhang, On the Establishment of the Textile Bureau (Dated March 6 of 8th Year of Emperor Tongzhi), in *Complete Works of Li Hongzhang: Memorials to the Throne*, Vol. 43, Shanghai People's Publishing House, 1985.

Mill, Shanghai, Jiangning and Tianjin followed suit. All these mills started with guns and cannons and then expanded to shipbuilding...China is blessed with rich resources of coal and iron. If mined, these natural resources would not only satisfy the needs of these mills, but also generate wealth."[1] In 1872, in his Report on Opinions on Shipyard Building, Li Hongzhang asserted, "Shipbuilding depends on iron and coal. England's unparalleled power originates from these two." Li pointed out the danger of dependency on imported coal, iron and other metal for military enterprises and purchased warships, by saying, "If trade were disrupted, mills would have to stop production without iron and ships could not sail without coal. This is the danger!" Therefore, in addition to his opposition to closing shipyards, Li recommended the use of western machinery and methods to mine coal and iron. He added, "These are also daily necessities. If mined efficiently, they would sell themselves in the market and generate great fortune. The fortune could be used to maintain ships and drill soldiers. Therefore, mining these resources means a lot to a prosperous country with a strong army."[2]

Later, in one of the letters to his associates, Li Hongzhang further elaborated his ideas about the interconnection between power and fortune by drawing lessons from the experience of western powers. "While China is weak and poor, western countries, though only hundreds or thousands of miles big, had billions in tax revenue each year from coal and iron mining, railway, telegram, post service and capitation. Such a situation mandates a change in policy by copying practices in those key industries. When the poor and weak fight the rich and poor, the outcome requires no analysis." [3]

In a memorial to the emperor in 1878, Cao Bingzhe, the censor, reported,

---

1 The Biography of Li Zongxi, in *The Draft of the History of the Qing Dynasty,* Vol. 213.

2 Li Hongzhang, On Canceling Part of the Shipbuilding Plan (Dated March May 15 of the 11th Year of Emperor Tongzhi), in *Complete Works of Li Hongzhang: Memorials to the Throne*, Vol. 19, Shanghai People's Publishing House, 1985.

3 Li Hongzhang, Reply on Ding Zhi Huang Gong Bao (Dated August 26 of 2nd Year of Emperor Guangxu), in *Complete Works of Li Hongzhang: Correspondences with Friends and Colleagues*, Vol. 16, Shanghai People's Publishing House, 1985.

"The newly established machine mills in different provinces have a large demand of coal and iron. The inland provinces should be encouraged to adopt western machines and methods to mine these much needed resources. This will not only save money in purchase but also general large revenues."[1] In 1890, Zhang Zhidong also reported, "Manufacturing weaponry and ships...depend on iron and coal. Sufficient fund could ensure the success of such mines. This is the foundation for power and wealth.[2] In a sense, the opinions and arguments of the westernizationists plant the seeds for the birth of civilian industries.

Another reason for the rise of civilian industries was to compete with westerners and solve the problems brought by foreign companies in China. Since the Opium War, foreign capital gradually seized the navigation right along the coast and the rivers and as a result the shipping business of western companies flourished in China. After the Treaty of Nanjing, foreign ships were allowed to do business at the trading ports from Guangdong to Fujian and Shanghai. With the Treaty of Tianjin after the Second Opium War, foreign ships sailed from trading ports to the Yangtze River. After English and French steamships and American Pacific liners started direct routes to Chinese ports, the first western shipping company with business only in China appeared in 1848; that is, the Hong Kong & Canton steam Packet Co. In the following decades, other foreign shipping companies such as Russell & Co., Guangdong, Hong Kong and Macao Co., Justice, Beiqing, Tai Koo, and Huahai were established.[3] These foreign shipping companies with abundant financial resources had branches in different trading ports and established a complete shipping system with docks, warehouses and insurance systems.

1 Li Hongzhang, On the Establishment of the Textile Bureau (Dated March 6 of 8th Year of Emperor Tongzhi), in *Complete Works of Li Hongzhang: Memorials to the Throne*, Vol. 43, Shanghai People's Publishing House, 1985.

2 Zhang Zhidong, On Establishing Iron Mill and Coal Mine (Dated November 6 of 16th Year of Emperor Guangxu), in *Zhang Wenxiang's Memorials to the Throne*, Vol. 29.

3 Fact Sheet of Big Foreign Shipping Companies, in Nie Baozhang, ed., *Documents on Navigation in Modern China*, Vol. 1, Shanghai People's Press, 1983, p.727.

New type foreign ships were characterized with large carrying capacities, fast speed, punctuality and less vulnerability to weather and current conditions. Moreover, covered by the unfair treaties, these foreign ships were exempt from tariffs and screening. Attracted by the convenience brought by foreign ships, merchants "all chose foreign ships and could not be stopped".[1] Naturally, foreign shipping companies harvested enormous profits in China. From 1867 to 1872, the American Russell & Co. which sailed only along the coast and the Yangtze River secured a total revenue of 4.68 million *liang*, with the profit rate reaching 64.5% in 1867.[2]

Shipping led to the building of ship building and maintenance factories by foreign capital. Three years after the Opium War, Couper, an Englishman, first built a dock in Huangpu. After the Second Opium War, five to six foreign companies were operating in Huangpu with each owning one to three docks. After it was open to foreign trade, Shanghai quickly became the most important hub of foreign trade. Since the 1860s, the tonnage of trading ships in and out of the Shanghai Port accounted for a quarter of the national total. In as early as the 1850s, English and American merchants started their ship building and maintenance factories in Shanghai. In the 1860s, two English docks, Boyd & Company and Farnham, were founded. With years of expansion and upgrading, by the 1890s, both were capable of building ships with a tonnage of over 2,000 tons and employed over 4,000 Chinese workers. Before the Sino-Japanese War 1894-1895, these two docks both enjoyed high profits with the net profit accounting for 17% to 21% of the total assets.[3]

The quick expansion and handsome profits of foreign shipping companies

1 Banister-T. Roger, translated by the Statistics Division of the Tax and Tariff Department of the Customs, *China's Foreign Trade in the Last Century*, 1931, pp.144-145.

2 Liu Guangjing, Translated by Qiu Xirong and Cao Tieshan, *Competition of English and American Navigation Companies in China, 1862-1874*, Shanghai Academy of Social Sciences Press, 1988, pp.119 and 129.

3 Sun Yutang, ed., *Historical Data of Industry in Modern China*, Vol. 1, Science Press, 1957, p.9 of the Preface.

attracted many Chinese merchants to invest in these foreign companies or sailed their own ships under foreign flags. As a result, the shipping business carried by old-fashioned wooden boats at trading ports was devastated with boats discarded and sailors losing their livelihood. The trade of Northeast China's pisolite and other traditional products was seriously disrupted and the once most important canal transport was endangered.

In order to satisfy the demand of foreign trade and seize profits, foreign entrepreneurs were building machinery factories in China. Incomplete statistics up to 1894 showed 103 foreign enterprises in China in such industries as silk, tea, tobacco, sugar, pharmaceutical and cotton grinning mostly in Shanghai.[1] These foreign factories violated China's sovereignty, challenged China's traditional economic structure and let serious rights leakage.

Foreign ships and enterprises led to drastic changes in China, which caught the attention of the Qing government. To compete for market and profits and redeem lost rights became a key reason for the expansion from military to civilian industries.

A number of factors contribute to the development and the transition of modern machine-based industries in China: to break through foreign powers monopoly in advanced weaponry, to acquire the tools to compete with them, to provide fuels, raw materials and transportation service needed by military enterprises, to share the profits in doing business in China and to satisfy the pursuit of power and wealth. Because of all these, top officials of the Qing government at the central and local level, such as Yiqin, Zeng Guofan, Li Hongzhang and Zuo Zongtang advocated and championed the development of machine and steam based government military enterprises and government and government and GSMM civilian enterprises which focused on transportation, fuels and raw materials.

In other words, the military enterprises needed the support of the fuel, mining

1 Sun Yutang, ed., Fact Sheet of Foreign-owned Modern Industry Companies in China, *Historical Data of Industry in Modern China*, Vol. 1, Science Press, 1957, p.234..

and transportation industries. This was the key reason for the rise of civilian industries. However, after the two Opium Wars and the Taiping Rebellion, the Qing government was financially on the verge of bankruptcy. Developing the military industry became an unbearable additional burden. In 1874, a report from the Ministry of Foreign Affairs said, "In addition to the seed money, more investment is expected in the future for salary, training, provisions, ship purchase, building and maintenance, arsenal and coal. The total is enormous. But for the allocation of a generous fund, such enterprises could not be possible. Sustained input is the key for future development. In our report in 1866, we proposed the Ministry of Revenue should put aside 40% of foreign tariffs as the special fund. However, in the last several years, continuous allocations and loans have stripped the fund. A calculation shows there is only enough money to cover 30% of the start-up investment..."[1] Li Hongzhang summarized the financial difficulties of the Qing government by saying, "Since the start of military industries, all means to raise money had been exhausted and so were merchants and people. The condition is dire already." [2]

Military enterprise, established with government fund to defend against foreign invaders, did not produce for market, which meant there was only investment but no profit. The expansion of such enterprises over time would definitely drain the financial capacity of the Qing government.

Against such background, the fuel, mining and transportation industries, which could generate inexhaustible revenue to support the government and the military industry, became a natural choice. However, having no more means to raise the money to build such civilian enterprises, the Qing government had to solicit

1 Chinese History Society, ed., The Zongli Yamen's Memorial to the Throne on September 27 of the 13th Year of Emperor Tongzhi, *The Self-Strengthening Movement*, Shanghai People's Press and Shanghai Bookstore Press, 2000. p.29.

2 Li Hongzhang, On Financing for Costal Defense (Dated May 11th of the 1st Year of Emperor Guangxu), in *Complete Works of Li Hongzhang: Correspondences with the Translation Agency*, Vol. 3, Shanghai People's Publishing House, 1985.

"private capital to compensate the deficiency of the imperial court".[1] As a result, the GSMM model came into being.

Table 4-4 shows the government and GSMM civilian enterprises and transportation enterprises during the late Qing Dynasty:

Table 4-4 Government and GSMM Civilian Enterprises: 1872-1894 Unit: silver dollars

Start Year	Name of Enterprise	Founder	Operation Model	Employment	Fund
Coal Mining					
1875	Zhili Cizhou Coal Mine	Li Hongzhang	government enterprise	Failed before operation	278 000
1875	Hubei Guangji Xingguo Coal Mine	Sheng Xuanhuai	government enterprise	Failed before operation	186 480*
1876	Taiwan Jilong Coal Mine	Shen Baozhen	government enterprise	1000	195 804
1878	Zhili Kaiping Coal Mine	Li Hongzhang Tang Tingshu	GSMM	3500-4500	2 055 944
1887	Shandong Zichuan Coal Mine	Zhang Yao	government enterprise	300-500*	Unknown
1891	Hubei Dayan Wang Sanshi Coal Mine	Zhang Zhidong	government enterprise	Stopped upon establishment	
1891	Hubei Jiangxia Ma'an Mountain Coal Mine	Zhang Zhidong	government enterprise	1500-2000*	
Metal Ore Mining and Metallurgy					
1877	Zhangjiakou the Outer Khorchin Mountain Lead Mine	Li Hongzhang	government enterprise	Unknown	6 950
1881	Rehe Chengde Pingquan Copper Mine	Li Hongzhang	GSMM	Unknown	333 600
1886	Guizhou Qingxi Iron Mill	Pan Lu Pan Wei	GSMM	300-500	417 000*
1887	Shandong Zichuan Lead Mine	Zhang Yao	government enterprise	Unknown	Unknown
1887	Rehe Tuzaozi-Bianshan Silver and Lead Mine	Li Hongzhang	government enterprise	300*	417 000
1887	Yunnan Copper Mine	Tang Jiong	GSMM	1 500-2 400*	Unknown

1 On Buying Ships and Cannons, *Costal Defence*, p. 866.

contd.

Start Year	Name of Enterprise	Founder	Operation Model	Employment	Fund
1889	Heilongjiang Mohe Gold Mine	Li Hongzhang Rong Tang	GSMM	2 800-3 600*	278 000
1890	Hubei Hanyang Iron Mill	Zhang Zhidong	government enterprise	3 000	5 560 000
1890	Hubei Daye Iron Mine	Zhang Zhidong	government enterprise	1 500-1 700*	
Textile					
1878	Lanzhou Machine Woolen Mill	Zuo Zongtang	government enterprise	Unknown	1 390 000
1879	Shanghai Machine Textile Mill	Li Hongzhang	GSMM	Unknown	1 418 203
1890	Hubei Textile Mill	Zhang Zhidong	government enterprise	2 500-3 000	1 342 700
1894	Hubei Spinning Mill	Zhang Zhidong	government enterprise	Unknown	834 000
1894	Hubei Silk Reeling Mill	Zhang Zhidong	Government and merchant joint venture	300	111 200
1894	Huangsheng Textile Mill	Li Hongzhang Sheng Xuanhuai	GSMM	4000*	1 118 900
Transportation					
1872	China Merchants Steamship Navigation Company	Li Hongzhang	GSMM	Unknown	2 780 000
1880	Shanghai Telegraph Administration	Li Hongzhang	GSMM	Unknown	2 247 352 2 009 342*
1885 1887	China Railways	Li Hongzhang	GSMM	3000*	1 868 855 125 100*
1890	Beiyang Official Railways	Li Hongzhang	government enterprise		417 000 2 446 400*
1891 1893	Taiwan Railways	Liu Mingchuan	government enterprise		1 800 050
合计				25 500-29 500	29 637 880

Notes from the original table:

1、* marks Sun Yutang's estimation. Mi Rucheng estimated the population of railway workers to be 3,000.

2、* in the "Fund" column marks estimated figures.

Source: Yan Zhongping and others, ed., *Selected Economic Statistics of Modern China*; Sun Yutang, ed., *Historical Data of Industry in Modern China*, Vol. 1; Mi Rucheng, ed., *Historical Data of Railways in Modern China*, Vol. 1; Mu Anshi, The Self-Strengthening Movement, quoted in Xu Dixin and Wu Chengming, ed., *History of Capitalism in China*, Vol. 2, The People's Publishing House, 1990, pp.380-381.

According to the table above, from 1872 to 1894, the Qing government established about 30 government or GSMM civilian enterprises, with a total employment of around 30,000 according to incomplete statistics and a total investment reaching 30 million silver dollars. In terms of number and employment, civilian enterprises surpassed military ones. Those more important civilian enterprises usually adopted the GSMM model.

The GSMM model was characterized with government supervision and government advance payment in the form of preferential treatments or partial allocation. In addition, the government would appoint people with official connections to raise money to fund and consequently support and supervise these enterprises. The GSMM model was first adopted by China Merchants Steamship Navigation Company, China's first new type civilian enterprise and later adopted by Kaiping Mining, Shanghai Machine Textile Mill, Shanghai Telegraph Administration and Hanyang Iron Plant. GSMM was the mainstream management model for civilian enterprises in the late Qing Dynasty. For a better understanding of this model, it is essential to analyze how it came into being and what its features are.

It was no accident for the GSMM model to develop first in shipping and navigation.

As mentioned above, after the two Opium Wars, foreign shipping companies developed rapidly in China with high profit rates and great impact on the Chinese economy and society, which caused a debate in China. Steamship transportation characterized with high safety and speed, low cost and high profit devastated China's wooden ship transportation and posed a serious challenge to canal transportation. In addition, men of insight in the ruling class in the late Qing Dynasty pursued power and wealth and tried to compete with foreign merchants. All these suggested that change and breakthrough were to happen first in shipping and navigation.

However, the Qing government did not allow or support the natural birth of this new type of business, which made it difficult for the shipping and navigation industry. Two factors are worth our attention. Firstly, the conservative faction were powerful in the government, holding onto the old practice. In addition, the society was still controlled by those deep-rooted traditional biases. Without the endorsement of officials, new enterprises were not likely to secure the authorization and support from the government, let alone bypassing social prejudice. History has proven, but for the support from top ranking officials such as Yixin, Wen Xiang, Zeng Guofan and Li Hongzhang, China Merchants Steamship Navigation Company could not have been funded at the end of 1872 and started operation in January 1873. Li Hongzhang, as the key figure for its success, regarded Chinese owned navigation business as "the key step to enrich the government and empower the military", and advocated it as "a must do in spite of every obstacle and every opposition"[1]. Secondly, at the moment, foreign shipping companies had monopolized navigation lanes over the seas and rivers and enjoyed the preferential treatments listed in those unfair treaties. Without government support, Chinese owned navigation companies would not have survived even after their establishment. In 1872, Li Hongzhang reported to the emperor, "Shipping business at trading ports have already been monopolized by foreign shipping companies, which took all necessary measures to destroy any new type Chinese shipping company which uses government ships. If a Chinese businessman start its own business with its own warehouses and insurance, which is complicated in nature, there could be no profit in it at least at the beginning. Profits would only come if such a business could survive and expand. Only those upright, capable and trustworthy government officials familiar with business could lead doubtful businessmen. Therefore, if any Chinese businessmen volunteer to work with the government, they shall be authorized to conduct canal transportation in addition so that they could survive the competition from foreign

1 Li Hongzhang, On Zhang Zhenxuan's Military Leadership (Dated November 11th of the 11th Year of Emperor Tongzhi), in *Complete Works of Li Hongzhang: Correspondences with Friends and Colleagues,* Vol. 12, Shanghai People's Publishing House, 1985.

companies." [1]

Li Hongzhang, by explaining foreign companies' dominance and Chinese companies' difficulties, proposed an active role by the government. In other words, his analysis elicited the necessity of "government supervision" of the newly established new type shipping enterprises.

In addition to the consent and support of the government, new type enterprises also needed the support of Chinese businessmen who had experience in the Westernization Movement, understood modern management and had sufficient capital. New type enterprises were something new to the westernizationists and the conservatives alike. It took time for Chinese enterprises to develop technical knowledge, management capabilities, business connections and credit systems. As a result, such enterprises had to be run by businessmen with "language proficiency", "business experience" and "down-to-earth spirit", especially those rich comprador businessmen with rich experience in dealing with foreign businessmen. For these reasons, "merchant management" became a must, which was proven true by the very different performances of China Merchants Steamship Navigation Company before and after compradors like Tang Tingshu and Xu Run took over. The development of other similar enterprises provided further proofs.

When the Westernization Movement turned from the "pursuit of power" to the "pursuit of wealth" and when entrepreneurship expanded from the military industry to new type civilian industries, it was necessary to change the old model of direct government sponsorship. Private capital had to be mobilized and utilized to build new type enterprises with government support, while the government used its power to provide resources and protection and to control the direction and scale of these enterprises. These were the preconditions for the rise of the GSMM model.

---

1 Li Hongzhang, ON Canceling Part of the Shipbuilding Plan (Dated May 15th of the 1st Year of Emperor Tongzhi), in *Complete Works of Li Hongzhang: Memorials to the Throne,* Vol. 19, Shanghai People's Publishing House, 1985.

The historical reality for new type enterprises was the combination of the powerful conservative faction and the advantages enjoyed by foreign companies in terms of timing and the preferential treatments. Therefore, the development of these enterprises depended on one hand the advocacy and support of prominent officials to conquer obstacles and symbolize government support and on the other businessmen with rich experience in foreign affairs and modern management and abundant capabilities to raise money and solicit talents to lead. Under these circumstances the government and the merchants joined hands and the GSMM model developed. This was the only mode that could be accepted by the government, westernizationists and conservatives alike and by compradors and regular businessmen. Zheng Guanying, a comprador, observed, "The government alone could not raise all the necessary money, but the concerted efforts of merchants made it possible. However, merchants alone would face a lot of obstacles from bandits, officials and policies. Therefore government supervision and merchant management must work together. Merchants who raise money to start business will not evade taxation while the government will treat enterprises foreign and Chinese on equal footings. This way, the problems are solved."[1] Of course, the enterprises established against such background must come under government control and serve government goals and therefore were state capital enterprises by nature.

From 1872 to 1895, many GSMM enterprises were established in some key civilian industries as shown in Table 4.4, including the first Chinese steamship navigation company--China Merchants Steamship Navigation Company, the first modern Chinese coal mine--Kaiping Coal Mining, the first machine textile plant--Shanghai Machine Textile Mill, the first civilian railway--China Railways and the first telegraph service--Shanghai Telegraph Administration. These top enterprises played a leading role among all modern civilian enterprises. Though with the

1 Zheng Guanying, *Warning Messages in Times of Prosperity: Mining*, Vo. 1, quoted in Xia Dong yuan, ed., *Collected Works of Zheng Guanying*, Vol. 1, Shanghai People's Publishing House, 1988, p.704.

rise of private capital funded enterprises after 1895, the GSMM enterprises were waning in influence, this did not negate the indispensable role and influence of these GSMM enterprises in the late Qing Dynasty.

Several other aspects of state capital enterprises in the late Qing Dynasty deserve attention:

First of all, since most GSMM enterprises were funded by equity-based private capital, how could they be categorized as state capital enterprises?

According to Lenin, "state capitalism is the direct state control of a capitalist enterprise in the capitalist system".[1] Put differently, the most important and basic feature of state capital enterprises is the "direct state control", which could take the form of either state capital holding the controlling share or the founder and manager with extensive official background having the absolute control over the operation and development. The common ground is that the enterprise is controlled and thus serves the government. In this sense, except the seed money from the private sector, these GSMM enterprises were indeed under "direct state control". Government supervision clauses explicitly stipulated state control over enterprises. For example the government management provisions for China Merchants Steamship Navigation Company read, "The government is responsible to make the charter, supervise operation and preside over the discussions of merchant share holders."[2] In addition, the government held the power to make personnel decisions. Liu Kunyi, viceroy of Jiangnan and Jiangxi Provinces, reported in 1881, "China Merchants Steamship Navigation Company is established with government authorization. Members of the Board are appointed by the government. It is more convenient for the company than the government to compete with other companies, because the latter faces a variety of constraints. Moreover, government fund raising may face a lack of enthusiasm by merchants and the market may not welcome direct government control. Though the company

1 *Selected Works of Lenin*, Vol. 4, The People's Publishing House, 1976, p.627.

2 Correspondence From Li Hongzhang, On Buying Ships and Cannons, *Costal Defence*, p.920.

is named as if it is a merchant business, the government chooses its board members and inspects its finance. Therefore, the company is in reality sponsored by merchants but controlled by the government."[1]

The Ministry of Foreign Affairs concluded, "China Merchants Steamship Navigation Company is proposed and controlled by Li Hongzhang, who understands the situation well. Tang Tingshu and others are actually appointed by Li Hongzhang. Therefore, Li shoulders the inescapable responsibilities to to take care of all affairs of the company and secure its operation."[2]

These remarks summarize the essence of GSMM enterprises. Such an official perspective was also accepted by merchants themselves. In Chinese, these enterprises were called "*ju*" (literally as "bureau" or "administration") instead of "*gongsi*" (literally as "companies") . Comprador Zheng Guanying explained, "According to western standard, government agencies for statecraft are called '*ju*' while business organizations for profits '*gongsi*'... These enterprises, though funded by private money, are authorized by the government for the good of the government, so they called '*ju*'...The controllers of these '*ju*' are mostly government officials."[3]

Secondly, until the demise of the Qing Dynasty, state capital was unquestionably dominating. After the Sino-Japanese War 1894-1895, as was stipulated in the Shimonoseki Treaty, foreign businessmen acquired the right to start manufacturing businesses in China. As a response, the Qing government had to relax the control over entrepreneurship by Chinese merchants. In its last decade, the Qing government even encouraged and supported private business, and thus created a golden age for new type enterprises in China, also called the new policy period. However, this did not change the domination by state capital, as proven by

1 Liu Kun's Memorial to the Throne on January 15th of the 7th Year of Emperor Guangxu, *The Self-Strengthening Movement*, Vol. 6, p.44.

2 Yi Xin and others' Memorial to the Throne on April 14 of the 7th Year of Emperor Guangxu, *The Self-Strengthening Movement*, Vol. 6, p.68.

3 Zheng Guanying, On Commerce, quoted in Xia Dongyuan, ed., *Collected Works of Zheng Guanying*, Vol. 1, p.612.

statistics. In 1894, the total assets of state capital enterprises reached 47.57 million silver dollars and further increased to 478.07 million in 1911, while private capital enterprises' total assets were 19.92 million in 1894 and 287.41 million in 1913, accounting for only 60% of the 1911 state capital volume.[1]

Monopolic and exclusive by nature, military enterprises enjoyed absolute dominance. In the civilian industry field, though private enterprises developed and multiplied fast with a bigger number than government and GSMM enterprises, most of these private enterprises remained small. Statistics show the dominance of military enterprises did not change before the final fall of the Qing government.

Thirdly, after the Sino-Japanese War 1894-1895, still unchallenged, state capital enterprises entered more industries, as shown in the following figures:

Table 4-5: State Capital in Different Industries Unit: 10,000 silver dollars

	1894	1911
Machinery and Weaponry	1071	1 394
Kiangnan Arsenal	340	231
Jiangnan Shipyard	——	142
Fuzhou Shipyard	96	140
Hanyang Arsenal	314	389
Six other enterprises	321	492
Textile	490	200
Huasheng Textile	280	——
Hubei Textile	210	——
Boli Wool and Leather	——	140
Hubei Carpet and Wool	——	60
Hydro-power		939
Eight enterprises from 1905 to 1911	——	939
Other Manufacturing		690
Six enterprises from 1905 to 1911	——	690
Coal Mining	820	588
Kaiping Coal Mining	800	——
Luanzhou Coal Mining	——	420
Six other coal mines	20	168

1 Xu Dixin and Wu Chengming, ed., *History of Capitalist Development in China*, Vol. 2, People's Publishing House, 1985, pp.1057 and 1065. .

contd.

Metal Mining, Metallurgy and Oil	682	4606
Five gold mines in Mohe and Kumar	28	56
Hanyeping Company	598	4000
Shuikou Mountain lead and zinc mine	——	84
Gejiu tin mine	——	177
14 other metal mines	56	248
Yanchang Oil	——	41
Transportation	1 694	39 390
Navigation	532	2 000
Railways	691	36 467
Telegraph	471	666
Postal Se	——	257
Sum of Industrial State Capital	4 757	47 807
Banking	——	4 489
Imperial Bank of China	——	490
Bank of China	——	2 200
Communication Bank of China	——	699
Local banks	——	1 100
State Capital Total	4 757	52 296

Source: Xu Dixin and Wu Chengming, ed., *History of Capitalist Development in China*, Vol. 2, People's Publishing House, 1985, p.1057.

According to Table 4-5, from 1894 to 1911, state capital total volume increased by about 11 times, with variations across industries. The machinery and weaponry industries increased by a unnoticeable margin and the textile and coal mining industries even decreased. Hydro-power and other manufacturing industries started from scratch but remained relatively small. The most rapid increase of state capital was found in Metal Mining, Metallurgy and Oil, and Transportation, with the former increased by 6.8 times and the latter 23 times in 15 years. Even more dramatically, state capital increased by 53 times in railways. These showed an obvious shift of focus of state capital in the last decades of the Qing Dynasty, from manufacturing to metallurgy, transportation and other major infrastructure industries. Such a shift is worth our attention.

Besides, after the Sino-Japanese War 1894-1895, new type financial organizations, especially government banks, came into being and developed unprecedentedly. State capital entered the finance industry and thus created modern banks, which played a more and more important social-economic role. The following part focuses on the development of state capital in the banking industry.

Before the Sino-Japanese War 1894-1895, foreign countries had established many banks and bank branches in various trading ports. Until the end of the Qing Dynasty, 15 foreign banks and their branches build built by England, Germany, Japan, France, Russia and the Netherlands were still operating in China, though with many changes.[1] Foreign banks in China served as a sign of financial invasion by foreign imperialist powers. After the Opium War, foreign banks started with foreign exchange business, expanded into other business lines and eventually monopolized China's international exchange and China's financial market. Later, by making large amounts of loans to the government, these foreign banks gradually controlled the fiscal policies of the Qing government. The activities of foreign banks convinced the westernizationists that China's old financial system could no longer satisfy the needs of social-economic development. The calls for Chinese banks kept getting louder. It was advocated that banks shall be established to ease fiscal difficulties, print money, fund railway projects and manage government fund. Sheng Xuanhuai made some of the most eloquent arguments for banks, by reporting, "In the west, banks serve as the hub to pool the wealth of the country and support commerce. We have to learn from them and thus prevent foreign banks from seizing profits from us." He also argued, "Chinese banks can grant credits to merchants, people and government alike. Banks could sell government bonds to replace loans from foreign banks, so as to free us from the control of foreign banks and the loss caused in foreign exchange. This way, banks

1 Ye Shichang and Pan Liangui, *The History of Finance in Ancient and Modern China*, Fudan University Press, 2001, pp.200-201.

can retain profits in China and enrich the country...Only the prompt establishment of Chinese banks can set Chinese businesses free from foreign control and promote rapid development."[1] Sheng Xuanhuai's proposal about establishing Chinese banks was approved by the Qing government, making the development of Chinese banks possible.

Imperial Bank of China: Founded in May 1897, Imperial Bank of China was the first Chinese bank with a total initial capital of 5 million *liang* and a first batch deposit of 2.5 million. China Merchants Steamship Navigation Company and Shanghai Telegraph Administration controlled by Sheng Xuanhuan invested 800,000 *liang* and 200,000 *liang* respectively and Sheng Xuanhuai invested another 730,000 *liang* as private investment. In addition, Sheng mobilized Li Hongzhang, Wang Wenshao, Zhang Zhenxun, Yan Xinhou and other prominent officials and businessmen to invest another 100,000 *liang.* A commercial bank by name, Imperial Bank of China was in fact "specially authorized by the emperor", entitled to a "2 million interest-making deposit by the Ministry of Revenue" and therefore a state capital bank by nature.

In the first few years, Imperial Bank of China received deposits mostly from the Qing government, followed by idol capital of GSMM enterprises, outstanding account of local governments and lastly private deposit of compradors and officials. The Qing government franchised the bank to issue money, the right reserved to a state bank. Imperial Bank of China borrowed HSBC's organization structure and management model, and at the same time carried with it the bureaucrat style of the imperial court. As a result, the bank was not particularly successful.

Bank of China: After Imperial Bank of China, the Ministry of Revenue proposed to the emperor about establishing the Ministry of Revenue Bank, the first attempt at an official state bank, because without a state bank, it is difficult

1 Chen Xulu, Gu Tinglong and others, ed., *Imperial Bank of China: Selected Works of Sheng Xuanhuai (Vol. 5)*, Shanghai People's Publishing House, 2000, p.3.

to finance government expenditure and guide the reform of the currency system.[1] Clearly, Bank of China aimed to fulfill two functions: 1) to supplement the empty treasury and 2) to execute the currency system reform. Provision I of the Bank Charter stipulated that the 4 million *liang* initial fund was divided into 40,000 shares with 100 *liang* per share. The Ministry of Revenue offered to buy 20,000 shares and the other 20,000 shares were to be bought by officials and people. Provision XX authorized the bank to issue to types of paper currencies in *liang* (silver) and (silver) *yuan*. In addition, the bank had the right to make coins, represent the treasury and issue government bonds. The president and vice presidents were appointed by the Ministry of Revenue.

In 1908, the Ministry of Revenue was restructured as the Ministry of Treasury and the Ministry of Revenue Bank restructured as the Qing State Bank under a new 24-provision charter. The 10 million *liang* capital was divided into 100,000 shares. The Qing government offered to buy 50,000 shares and the other 50,000 shares were restricted to Chinese buyers. By June 1911, the new bank had 21 branches and 35 sub-branches across China.[2] After the Revolution of 1911, the bank was renamed Bank of China.

Bank of Communications of China: in 1908, the Ministry of Communications of the Qing government authorized the establishment of Bank o Communications of China. In the proposal, the ministry stated, "The Ministry of Communications administers shipping, roads, electricity and postal service, with the mission to promote industrial development and reclaim sovereign rights. If the ministry has to rely on HSBC, Russo-Chinese Bank or Belgian Bank for deposits and loans, the division and ups and downs in their business make it difficult to make profits. Moreover, currency exchange was troublesome, and foreign banks benefit in

1 *Donghua Records of Emperor Guangxu's Reign*, Vol. 186, quoted in Zhang Yulan, *The History of the Banking Industry in China*, Shanghai People's Publishing House, 1957, p.25.

2 Xu Dixin and Wu Chengming, ed., *History of Capitalist Development in China*, Vol. 2, People's Publishing House, 1990, p.625.

the exchange process...Therefore, it is important to integrate the four services through a bank of communications."[1] Of the founding assets of 5 million *liang*, the Ministry of Communications offered to buy 2 million and the other 3 million were open for sale. Though Bank of Communication was a government-merchant joint venture in name, Provision 36 of its charter ruled, "With 20,000 shares, the Ministry of Communications is the biggest shareholder and therefore has the right to appoint the president.". Provision 20 further stated, "The president reports to the Ministry of Communications."[2] Government control was clear. With its headquarters in Beijing, Bank of Communications had branches in Tianjin, Shanghai, Hankou, Xiamen, Zhenjiang and Guangzhou. Until it stopped operation after the Revolution of 1911, the bank did not operate particularly well.

Local money houses and banks: During this period, many provincial governments also established some government money houses and provincial banks. For details before 1911, please refer to Table 4-6.

Table 4-6 Local Government Money Houses and Provincial Banks in the Late Qing Dynasty

Date of Establishment	Province	Location of Headquarters	No. of Branches	Location of Branches and Sub-branches
1889	Xijiang	Dihua (Urumchi)	3	Three branches at: Zhendi, Aksu and Kashgar; 32 sub-branches at: Kumul, Turpan, Shanshan, ZWAK City, ZWAK County, Xayar, Wushi, Kuqa, Bytown, Yanqi, Lunai, Kelpin, Shule, Shufu, Bachu, Jiashi, Engel, Shache, Karghalik, Alpilles, Hetian and Khotan.
1894	Shaanxi	Xi'an	3	Hanzhong, Xingan and Yan'an
1896	Hubei	Wuchang	6	Shashi, Ychang, Fancheng, Laohekou, Wuxue and Anlu

1 Bank of Communications Headquarters and the Second Historical Archives of China, ed., *Historical Data of the Bank of Communications,* Collection 1, Vol. 1, China Finance Publishing House, 1995, pp.7-8.

2 Bank of Communications Headquarters and the Second Historical Archives of China, ed., *Historical Data of the Bank of Communications,* Collection 1, Vol. 1, China Finance Publishing House, 1995, pp. 174 and 176.

contd.

Date of Establishment	Province	Location of Headquarters	No. of Branches	Location of Branches and Sub-branches
1896	Shandong	Jinan	4	Zhoucun, Jining, Linqingzhou, and Yangjiaogou
1896	Henan	Kaifeng	13	Beijing, Tianjin, Shanghai, Hankou, Woyang, Zhoukou, Luohe, Daokou, Qingua, Xiuwu, Weihui, Yongcheng and Zhengzhou
1896	Jilin	Jilin	10	Changchun, Harbin, Yingkou, Yushu, Yilan, Ningguta, Yanji, Mishan, Huichun and Tianjin
1900	Fujian	Fuzhou	unknown	According to *The History of Currency Systems* in China by Zhang Jiaxiang, sub-branches were found in all cities and counties.
1902	Zhili	Tianjin	8	Shanghai, Hankou, Beijing, Baoding, Zhangjiakou, Shunde, Luozhou and Tangshan
1902	Jiangxi	Nanchang	11	Jiujiang, Hankou, Shanghai, Ji'an, Ganzhou, Jindezhen, Hekou, Wucheng, Yiningzhou, Hangzhou and Shanggao
1902	Shanxi	Taiyuan	1	Hedong
1903	Jiangsu (Yusu)	Suzhou	4	Shanghai, Jinzhou, Wuxi, and Pingwang
1903	Jiangsu (Yuning)	Jiangning (Nanjing)	29	Remaining documents show 24 sub-branches.
1903	Guangxi	Guilin	8	Four branches in Wuzhou, Shanghai, Nanning and Longzhou with four additional branches in Xiangtan, Changde, Hengzhou and Hongjiang after it was restructured as a bank in 1909.
1896	Hunan	Changsha	4	Xiangtan, Change, Hengzhou and Hongjiang
1908	Heilongjiang	Tsitsihar	9	Suihua, Hulan, Bayan, Hailun, Harbin, Kuanchengzi, Yingkou, Tianjin and Fengtian
1896	Fengtian	Fengtian	6	Yingkou, Jinzhou, Liaoyang, Tieling, Andong and Changchun.
1896	Sichuan	Chongqing	8	Shanghai, Beijing, Hankou, Yichang, Shashi, Wanxian and Fuzhou.
1904	Guangdong	Fanyu (Guangzhou)	1	Shanghai (according to Jia Shiyi on Page 129 in Book II of *The Fiscal History of the Republic of China*, sub-branches were also found in Hong Kong and Shantou)

contd.

Date of Establishment	Province	Location of Headquarters	No. of Branches	Location of Branches and Sub-branches
1906	Anhui	Anqing	6	Zhengyang, Huaiyuan, Wuhu, Bozhou, Liuan and Linhuai
1906	Gansu	Lanzhou	1	Chifeng
1906	Rehe	Rehe (Chengde)	1	Chifeng
1908	Zhejiang	Hangzhou	unknown	
1906	Guizhou	Guiyang	9	Zunyi, Anshun, Bijie, Zhenyuan, Tongren, Guzhou, Chongqing, Hankou and Changde

Sources: 1. Documents of the Ministry of Finance (The Forbidden City Archives); 2. Provincial financial statements; 3. *Selected Works on Currency in Modern China*, quoted in Xie Hangsheng, A Study of Provincial Government-run Money Houses in the Late Qing Dynasty, in *Collected Works of the Institute of Economy of the China Academy of Social Sciences*, Vol. 11, China Social Sciences Press, p.1988.

Provincial money houses and banks came in different sizes with assets ranging from tens of thousands to hundreds of thousands. Most were funded by provincial treasury with partial private capital. In terms of jurisdiction, most of these money houses and banks were managed by relevant provincial departments while some had presidents or supervisors directly commissioned by the central government. In addition to regular businesses such as managing provincial treasury, registering cash flow, taking deposits, issuing loans and dealing with foreign exchanges, these money houses and banks also print local paper money to finance local governments. After the Revolution of 1911, many of them, trapped in credit crisis, stopped operation or were restructured as banks.

So far, we have depicted the trajectory of state capitalism in the late Qing Dynasty, from the military industry, to civilian industries and then the financial sector. Though variations existed in time and path, state capital's dominant position was unchallenged during this start-up period.

New type enterprises funded by state capital remained a minority when small agricultural production remained dominant. These enterprises, still feudal in nature, relied on foreign capital, technologies and equipment. Moreover, because the corruption and incompetence of managing officials, in addition to other constraints and difficulties, most of these enterprises performed poorly, failing to finish capital accumulation of scale and unable to promote the development of capitalist productive relations in China.

In practice, this primitive form of state capitalism and the dominance of state capital enterprises did play a role in resisting the invasion of foreign capital. On the other, from the historical materialistic perspective, in the economic restructuring period in modern China, the development of state capitalism was historically inevitable. In addition to the above mentioned factors, capitalist industries did not descend from workshop industries or developed as a result of breakthroughs in certain key industries. Instead, capitalism developed by learning from, introducing and transplanting advanced productive forces from the west, and therefore rose as a result of some external forces. The priority of the "pursuit of power" mandated a start in military-centered state capital heavy industry before the development of civilian industries.

State capital enterprises dominated in the late Qing Dynasty because of China's very slow primitive accumulation of capital and state capture of surplus products through taxation while private capital alone was too weak to start heavy industrial enterprises. Around 1895, the Qing government still could not go beyond the induction of production technologies and other materialistic things from the west. In order to prolong the feudal regime, the Qing government was not ready to change the regime from political, social and economical perspectives and to embark on western style capitalism. Accordingly, private capital could not have the freedom to start enterprises. Therefore, only the government had the right to start heavy industrial enterprises in machinery, shipping, railways and mining. The situation changed a little after 1895, but limited in scale and duration. Therefore, the sustained dominance of state capitalism was no surprise.

Chapter 5

State Capital Under the Beiyang Government[1]

The Revolution of 1911 overthrew the Qing government and the Beiyang government (also called the Beijing government) ruled China until the establishment of the Nanjing National government in 1927. However, the Republic of China under the Beiyang government was not different from the late Qing regime in nature. Yuan Shikai's restoration of the monarchy and the ensuing warlords' rule created a period of several feudal "emperors" in China. With years of wars and turmoils, the Beiyang government was politically weak. For these reasons, state capital during this period was different from that of the late Qing Dynasty and of the Nanjing National government. Economically, sate capital was not as weak as the government. The death of Yuan Shikai in 1916 marked a turning point. In addition, state capital performed differently in different industries. Moreover, state capitalism took up a new form where government officials invested as individual entrepreneurs, or state capital took the form of bureaucrat private capital.

1 Also known as the Northern Warlords Government of China from 1912-1928. Translator's note.

1. State Capital Enterprises Under a Weak Government

Politically unstable with constant warfare, the Beiyang government continued the capitalist industrial and commercial policies since the Sino-Japanese War 1894-1895. During as early as the Nanjing Provisional government, Sun Yat-sun emphasized, in his Interim Presidential Inaugural Speech and many other documents, that "construction must not wait" and that "only industrial revitalization and financial reform could benefit the state and the people."[1] One of the announcements of the Ministry of Industry stated, "Industry is the lifeline of the Republic...Industrial revitalization is the way to enrich the state and the people...therefore is a matter of urgency."[2] These statements and guidelines satisfied the needs of social-economic development and coincided with, promoted the movement of developing industries to save the country and laid the foundation for social-economic policies in the future.

After assuming power, while taking many political measures which went against history in order to restore monarchy in China, Yuan Shikai understood that industrial and commercial revitalization was desired by the people and that supporting such endeavors could consolidate his rule and enrich the treasury. Therefore, Yuan Shikai took several measures to promote capitalism development. In his inaugural speech, he claimed, "The republic would prioritize industrial development". Later in many government orders, he reiterated "respect for free business as is stipulated in the Constitution", and urged provincial governments to "take practical measures to promote industry to enrich the country" and to "protect operating private companies and take measures to help those non-operational and start-up companies."[3]

While encouraging private capital to revitalize industry and commerce, Yuan

1 The Institute of Modern History of the China Academy of Sciences, ed., *Historical Documents of the Revolution of 1911*, Zhonghua Book Company, 1961, pp.3 & 217.

2 Huang Yiping and Yu Baotang, ed., *Economy of the Beiyang Government*, Shanghai Academy of Social Sciences Press, 1995, p. 1.

3 *Collected Works of Yuan Shikai*, Vol. 1, pp. 3 & 53-54, quoted in Huang Yiping and Yu Baotang, ed., *Economy of the Beiyang Government*, p.2

Shihai, in order to maintain economic control, closed certain economic sectors to private capital and even repealed some rights once granted to private investment. State capital monopoly was most typical in railways.

Private railways were the products of the "right recovery movement" in the late Qing Dynasty. After assuming power, Yuan Shikai put forward the policy of "unified road (including railways) administration", and proclaimed "the state-people unity in the republic" and "state ownership equals people ownership". The government forced shareholders to "offer and return" their shares to the state and bribed the top management of railway companies to take over. From August 1912 to January 1915, the government retrieved the road rights in Sichuan, Hunan, Anhui, Hubei, Henan, Jiangsu and Shanxi and many private railway companies went out of business. According to the agreements between the Beiyang Ministry of Communications and provincial railway companies, the Beiyang government would pay 51 million yuan for shares and 17 million yuan for interests. However, in practice, only Henan where Yuan Shikai was originally from received 4 million in cash, but other provinces had nothing but Beiyang government bonds, which stopped cashing in 1924. Statistics showed in total only half of the shares and a third of the interests were actually paid for.[1]

Table 5-1 Timetable for the Nationalization of Provincial Railway Companies

Province	Date
Sichuan	Nov. 2, 1912
Hunan	June 3, 1913
Jiangsu	June 12, 1913
Henan	Aug. 15, 1913
Shanxi	Sept. 9, 1913
Anhui	March 3, 1914
Zhejiang	April 11, 1914
Hubei	Jan. 1 1915

Source: Mi Rucheng, *Imperialism and China's Railways*, Shanghai People's Publishing House, 1980, p.225.

1 Mi Rucheng, *Imperialism and China's Railways*, Shanghai People's Publishing House, 1980, pp. 224-225.

In the meantime, the Yuan Shikai government denied all application for railway construction by private capital, accusing them of impertinence and rashness. It was claimed by the government that private businesses were actually accumulating wealth by unfair means in the name of building railways and that such practice would do no good to transportation, business and credit. In the end, the government outlawed private capital in the railway business[1] and therefore realized the state capital's monopoly of railways.

Such a policy did not change with the step-down of Yuan Shikai, but sustained all through the Republic of China period.

Because of political turmoil, constant warfare and exhausted finance, railway construction under the Beiyang government lagged far behind the late Qing government before and the KMT government later. China's railway mileage increased by 319 km a year on average during the late Qing Dynasty, and only 212 km a year under the Beiyang government. If railways constructed by foreign companies were calculated, the figures would be 552 a year and 229 a year respectively. Fortunately, main line railways such as Beijing-Fengtian, Beijing-Hankou, Tianjin-Pukou, Lanzhou-Lianyungang, Beijing-Hangzhou and Shanghai-Hangzhou-Ningbo lines were finished or almost finished and railway equipment was added and upgraded. Statistics showed the number of locomotives increased from 600 in 1912 to 1,131 in 1925, passenger trains from 1067 to 1803, cargo trains from 8335 to 16718. Table 5-2 details the in crease in railway carrying capacities.[2]

Table 5-2 Increase in Railway Carrying Capacities 1912-1925

Year	Mileage (km)	Tractive Force (ton)	Passenger Train Capacity (seats)	Cargo Train Capacity (ton)
1912	9 468	5 619	45 177	183 224
1925	12 302	11 966	101 101	452 272

1 Mi Rucheng, *Imperialism and China's Railways*, Shanghai People's Publishing House, 1980, pp. 226-227.

2 Yan Zhongping and others, ed., *Selected Economic Statistics of Modern China,* Science Press, 1955, pp.194 &196. .

contd.

Year	Mileage (km)	Tractive Force (ton)	Passenger Train Capacity (seats)	Cargo Train Capacity (ton)
Increased by	2 834	6 347	55 924	269 048
Increase rate %	29.9	113.0	123.8	146.8

Notes: 1. Figures for tractive force in 1912 is unavailable. The 5,619 was the figure for 1915.
2. "Increased by" and "Increase rate %" are the authors' calculation.

Sources: 1. Mileage quoted in Mi Rucheng, *Imperialism and China's Railways*, Shanghai People's Publishing House, 1980, p. 679.
2. Tractive Force, Passenger Train Capacity and Cargo Train Capacity quoted in Yan Zhongping and others, ed., *Selected Economic Statistics of Modern China,* Science Press, 1955, p. 196.

Besides railways, the military industry was another key industry under state capital control during the Beiyang government. In addition to take-overs from the Qing government, many new military enterprises and local government sponsored military enterprises were established.

The Beiyang government inherited a dozen of military enterprises from the late Qing government, including Hubei Gun and Cannon Plat and Jiangnan Shipyard which developed further during the Beiyang period while most of the others were on the wane. During the Revolution of 1911, Yuan Shikai attached and captured Hanyang and the destroyed machines at Hubei Gun and Cannon Plant were worth 300,000 yuan. After the founding of the Republic of China, Hubei Gun and Cannon Plant was renamed Hanyang Arsenal, with a government investment of 1 million yuan under the leadership of Liu Qing'en. In 1913, the government threw in another 2 million yuan to expand the production of self-made gun moulds, iron and steel and machine cannons. In addition, to the south of the Dabie Mountain, four branch plants were built, which purchased production machines from Krupp in Germany. During the late Qing Dynasty, Hubei Gun and Cannon Plant with 500 or so works could only manufacture 10,000 bullets, 100 or so cannonballs, 72 rifles and 4-5 mountain cannons every day and 1 land cannon over several days. The introduction of new machines in 1913 greatly enhanced it production capacity and efficiency. With only 300 workers, the figures increased to 200,000, 2,000,

150, 10 and 3-4 every day respectively.[1]

In addition to enhanced productivity, new products were introduced and produced, including Krupp Type 75 land cannons in 1913, Maxim machine guns in 1915, Krupp Type 14 howitzers in 1918, Japan's Taisho 6 Type 75 mountain cannon, Browning M1917 and Mauser pistols in 1921, trinitrotoluene in 1922, TNT and Type 75 mortars in 1924, Krupp Type 75 mountain cannons and Bergman portable machine guns in 1925, 20-120 pound airborne bombs in 1926, and grenades in 1927.[2] The asset value of the arsenal was estimated to be 3.14 million in 1894, 3.89 million in 1911 and 6.39 million in 1920.[3]

In 1912, Jiangnan Dockyard was restructured to be Jiangnan Shipyard under the jurisdiction of the Ministry of Navy. From 1912 to 1912, Jiangnan Shipyard built 369 ships, with a tonnage of 144,093 in total or 9,606 per year. 50 out of the 369 ships were over 500 tons each, making a total of 99,987 tons. The World War I period was the peak of its development, especially when it was contracted by the United States in 1918 to build four 14,000 ton transport ships. To build these four ships, Jiangnan Shipyard doubled its size with the addition of 4 major docks, a new turbine plant, 76 sets of new machines and new wharves and warehouses. The new investment equaled the total assets of Jiangnan Dockyard when Jiangnan Dockyard, with an estimated assets of 773,000 *liang*, became an independent enterprise from Jiangnan Arsenal in 1905. The total employment increased from 3,000 to 7,000~8,000. By then, Jiangnan Shipyard boasted a production capacity larger than the new Farnham & Company, making itself the largest shipyard in the Far East outside Japan.

In addition, Jiangnan Shipyard also had a large ship maintenance business, servicing 2,198 ships from 1912-1926 or 146 ships per year. Accordingly, its

1 *Eastern Times*, May 3, 1913, quoted from Chen Zhen, ed., *Historical Files of China's Modern Industry*, Vol. 3, Sanlian Bookstore, 1961, p.258.

2 Da Gong Bao, August 13, 1917, quoted from Chen Zhen, ed., *Historical Files of China's Modern Industry*, Vol. 3, Sanlian Bookstore, 1961, p.259.

3 Arsenal Outline of JinLing and Hanyang, Chen Zhen, ed., *Historical Files of China's Modern Industry*, Vol. 3, Sanlian Bookstore, 1961, pp.234-236.

turnover jumped, securing an annual net profit of 700,000 yuan with a peak volume reaching 2 million yuan.[1]

However, besides railways and Jiangnan Shipyard, state capital was on the way in other industries. Political instability and military conflicts drew the warlords' attention to military production, even when faced with fiscal difficulties. As a result, many arsenals and military plants developed well. However, instability also victimized these military plants and increased the uncertainty in their development. The rise and fall of these military plants were determined by the battle ground. The expansion of military plants in Shanxi and the Northeast was attributed to the relative stability under the rule of Yan Xishan and Zhang Zuolin respectively, while military plants in Sichuan and Guangzhou suffered from constant wars. Most government military enterprises were not built on the basis of well developed industries but depended on warlords for development. For example, Hanyang Arsenal, funded by government investment, was supported by Li Yuanhong's support. Gongxian Arsenal was built because Gongxian County was Yuan Shikai's birth place and was part of Yuan's scheme for restoration. Jiangnan Shipyard developed with the support of the Ministry of Navy in addition to commercialization, foreign management and opportunities created by WWI. Military enterprises without such support were hardly surviving. Besides military enterprises, many government mines started operation[2] but with limited success. So was the government financial organizations. For example, from 1912 to 1914, the government controlled 100% shares of the Bank of China, but the percent of government shares kept decreasing to 40.7% in 1917, 11.13% in 1922 and 2.53% in 1923.[3] Upon the founding of the Bank of Communications, the Ministry of

1 Xu Dixin and Wu Chengming, ed., *History of Capitalist Development in China*, Vol. 2, People's Publishing House, 1990, p.1057.

2 *History of the Jiangnan Shipyard*, 1983, pp.107&111, quoted in Xu Dixin and Wu Chengming, ed., *History of Capitalist Development in China*, Vol. 2, People's Publishing House, 1990, pp. 795-796 & 798. .

3 Huang Yiping and Yu Baotang, ed., *Economy of the Beiyang Government*, Shanghai Academy of Social Sciences Press, 1995, pp. 232-233. .

Communications was the biggest shareholder, holding 2 million yuan in shares out of the total of 5 million yuan. However, the ministry's shares were also decreasing until 10% out of the total of 7.715 million yuan in 1928 when the KMT government announced the new charter for the Bank of Communications.[1]

The main reason for the decline of state capital enterprises during the Beiyang government was political turmoil and warfare between warlords when the Anhui Clique controlled Anhui, Shandong, Zhejiang and Fujian, the Zhili Clique controlled Jiangsu, Jiangxi, Hubei, and Zhili, the Fengtian Clique in the three northeast provinces, Yan Xishan reigned Shanxi, Zhang Xun controlled Xu Zhou, the Yunnan Clique led by Tang Jiyao took Yunan and Guizhou, the Gui Clique seized Guangdong and Guangxi, and warlords in Sichuan split the province into several "defense zones"of several counties. These warlords constantly fought against each other, while the head of the government was shifting hands as if it was a game from Yuan Shikai, to Duan Qirui, Li Yuanhong, Zhang Xun, Feng Guozhang, Cao Kun and Zhang Zuolin. In the 16 years from 1912 to 1928, the Beijing government saw 47 administrations, with the shortest lasting for only 6 days.

2. Enterprises with State Capital as Individual Investors [2]

In addition to government funded and controlled enterprises, a new and unique type of state capitalism developed; that is, enterprises invested by government officials and warlords as individual investors. This kind of dual identity practice was very typical under the Beiyang government. These enterprises enjoyed special rights and preferential treatments unimaginable by private enterprises and played unparalleled roles. According to Lenin's definition of state capital enterprises,[3]

1 Deng Xianhong, Relations between the Bank of China and the Beiyang Government, *Collected Works of the Institute of Economy of China Academy of Social Sciences*, Vol. 11, China Social Sciences Press, 1988.

2 Weng Xianding, A Study of the Governmental Involvement of the Bank of Communications, in *Collected Works of the Institute of Economy of China Academy of Social Sciences*, China Social Sciences Press, 1988.

3 Sun Jian, *The History of Chinese Economy: Modern China*, Renmin University Press, 1989, p.263.

these enterprises had very close relations with state capital. This dual identity became the breeding ground for corruption and gave rise to bureaucrat capital.

After the Revolution of 1911, advocated by the government and supported by social enthusiasm, industries developed quickly. Business opportunities in WWI further promoted their growth. During this period, bureaucrats and warlords were particularly active in starting business with large investments. Wang Zhanyuan, a warlord, invested a total of 2.9 million in 32 enterprises.[1] Liang Shiyi, the leading figure in communications, boasted a total investment of over 20 million yuan.[2] Warlord Ni Sichong had investment in various industries in Anhui, Suzhou, Shanxi, Beijing and Tianjin. In Tianjin alone, Ni invested a total of 8 million yuan, making him the No. 1 warlord investor in Tianjin.[3] During WWI, many flour mills were built in Jinan, Shandong Province, such as Fengnian, Huifeng, Huaqing, Minqing and Chengfeng, with investment coming from people like Shandong Military Commander and Governor Zhang Huaizhi, Vice Minister of Communications Lao Zhichang, Shandong Military Commander Tian Zhonghe, Shandong Finance Department Director Zhou Xiaoru, Hubei Military Commander Wang Zhanyuan and Shandong Civil Affairs Department Director Cheng Yi'an.[4]

In addition to these enterprises invested by individual bureaucrat and warlord investors, a more important and typical category of state capital enterprises were enterprise groups in the form of government-merchant joint venture and

---

1 Lenin defines state capitalism as a form of capitalism in which the government directly controls capitalist enterprises, *Selected Works of Lenin*, Vol. 4, The People's Publishing House, 1976, p.627.

2 *Selected Historical Documents of the History of Tianjin*, Vol. 4, quoted in Huang Yiping and Yu Baotang, ed., *Economy of the Beiyang Government*, Shanghai Academy of Social Sciences Press, 1995, p. 339.

3 Archives of the Ministry of Agriculture and Commerce of the Beiyang Government, and statistics of The Agriculture and Commerce Report and Government Report, quoted in Huang Yiping and Yu Baotang, ed., *Economy of the Beiyang Government*, Shanghai Academy of Social Sciences Press, 1995, p. 340.

4 *Selected Historical Documents of the History of Tianjin*, Vol. 4, quoted in Huang Yiping and Yu Baotang, ed., *Economy of the Beiyang Government*, Shanghai Academy of Social Sciences Press, 1995, p. 340.

government-support and merchant-management.

When Yuan Shikai was still Governor of Zhili, Zhou Xuexi was working for Yuan on government industries, founding a silver mint, a government money house, Queyechang Iron Mill, Zhili Handicrafts Bureau, Qixin Cement and Luanzhou Coal Mining. Zhou not only directly managed some important enterprises, but also supervised industrial development in Zhili Province. After the founding of the Republic of China, Zhou Xuexi took over Luanzhou Coal Mining (renamed Kailuan Coal Mining) and Qixin Cement, started many new industrial enterprises such as Huaxin Textile, Tangshan Electricity, Yaohua Glass and Xinghua Cotton, and founded the Industrial Bank of China and Huaxin Bank. This conglomerate of industry and finance had a total assets of over 40 million.[1] The Zhou Group was funded by government capital, warlord capital and a marginal amount of business capital. Government capital, though not the majority and gradually brought out, played a disproportionately important role. At the very beginning, Qixin Cement was short of capital. With Yuan Shikai's authorization, the Huai Army fund allocated 500,000 yuan with interest payable and Qixin Cement could also receive loans (accumulatively 400,000 yuan in total) with interest payable from the "cash flow" of Tianjin Government Money House. When Qixin Cement issued another 1.5 million in shares, "half were bought by shareholders and the other half by the Ministry of Communications and the Post Service".[2] Other backbone enterprises in the Zhou Group also received government capital support in like manners.

Even in commercial fund raising, government support was prominent. Typically, the government would forces some social elites to buy shares. For example, when Kailuan Mining offered share buying, "commercial shares were allocated to county chiefs and other government personnel".[3] In 1909 and 1914,

1 Lin Zhu'an, Flour Industry in Jinan and Huaqing Flourmill, *Selected Documents of the History of Shandong*, Vol. 8.

2 Sheng Bin, Monopoly of the Zhou Xuexi Capital Group, *Historical Research*, Issue 4, 1986.

3 Institute of Economics of Nankai University, ed., *Historical Documents of Qixin Cement Company*, Sanlian Bookstore, pp.38-39 & 88-89.

Qixin Cement offered twice, the Beiyang government, through the Ministry of Communications and the Post Service, instructed provincial commercial railways to buy.[1] For the Industrial Bank of China, "the Beiyang government salt dealers in Changlu, Donggang and Lianghuai must invest". When fund raising ran into difficulties, these salt dealers asked for refund, but the Beiyang government ruled "bought shares could not be refunded freely and measures should be taken to buy the unpaid shares."[2]

In the enterprises in the Zhou Group, operation and management was all controlled by official merchants. A study of the board members, presidents and vice presidents showed 18 people controlled the four most important enterprises in the group, namely Qixin Cement, Huaxin Textile and the Industrial Bank of China. Nine of the 18 people were official merchants like Zhou Xuexi and Sun Duosen, who used to have or had official titles with business experience before ore after their officialdom. These people occupied such posts as presidents, manager, managing director and board chairman and thus had the actual control of these enterprises. The other nine were warlords, serving as board members. These people in the management enabled the Zhou Group to pull strings in both the government and the business world to maximize profits.

In terms of operation, enterprises founded by bureaucrats and warlords enjoyed various privileges. For example, Qixin Cement had the exclusive right to build cement plants in Zhili Province and was franchised to set up branches in the northeastern provinces and the Yangtze River Basin. In its early years, Huaxin Textile had the exclusive right to build textile plants in Zhili, Shandong and Henan Provinces for 30 years. Secondly, these enterprises enjoyed tax exemption. Products of Qixin Cement, "no matter where they were sold, had to pay one a 5% tax once and therefore were exempt from all other taxes". Kailuan Coal Mining

1 Wang Jingyu, ed., *Historical Data of Modern Industry in China*, Vol. 2, Science Press, 1957, p.922.

2 Institute of Economics of Nankai University, ed., *Historical Documents of Qixin Cement Company*, Sanlian Bookstore, pp.88-89

enjoyed similar preferential treatment while only two fifths of booked production from its Chenjialing Mine were subject to tax. At its preparation stage, the Beijing Water Supply Company could buy any machines free of tax. With Yuan Shikai's authorization, Huaxin Textile could buy raw materials free of tax while its products was exempted from all repeated taxes other than regular taxes. Thirdly, these enterprises enjoyed further privilege in transportation. Qixin Cement's products were prioritized by various railways and China Merchants Steam Navi gation Company and enjoyed a 30~40% discount. Fourthly, the government also stepped in to promote products of these enterprises. For example, Yuan Shikai personally instructed railway companies such as Guanneiwai, Jingzhang, Jinghan, Zhengtai, Bianluo, Daoqing and Huning to buy cement produced by Qixin. The Agriculture and Industry Ministry once promoted the Beijing Water Supply Company. The transportation, post service and taxation ministries of the Beijing government once demanded their subordinates to use paper money printed by the Industrial Bank of China. These privileges put the Zhou Group at a unequaled favorable position in operation.[1]

Clearly, enjoying all these privileges granted by the government, the Zhou Group should not be classified as regular private enterprises. Shortly after the establishment of Luanzhou Coal Mining, it was argued that" Luanzhou Coal Mining was funded by private capital only in name"and that "a study of its share configuration and founding procedure showed it was the same with Kaiping Coal Mining by nature and therefore a government enterprise." People pointed out that Luanzhou Coal Mining's fund raising was operated by Tianjin Government Money House and that "besides the shares bought by the Beiyang government, other shares were apportioned to county chiefs and other government personnel." "Out of the 2 million *liang* worth shares open to purchase in 1906, the Beiyong government bought 500,000 *liang*, the Zhili Salt Administration 500,000 *liang*

1 Yu Heping and Xia Liangcai, ed., *Works of Zhou Xuexi*, Central China Normal University Press, 1999, pp.9-10.

and the education fund 300,000 *liang;* that was 1.3 million *liang* in total. The so-called "private" shareholders held only 700,000 *liang*." "There was doubt about who these 'private' shareholders were."

It was argued back then that Yuan Shikai appointed Zhou Xuexi to build Luanzhou Coal Mining for two purposes: firstly, "to supply coal to the Beiyang navy under his command so as to build up his own military power"; and secondly, "to gain profits" because Yuan invested in it. Therefore, "before the merger of Kaiping and Luanzhou, Yuan managed to have his son to serve as the Director of the Mining Administration." [1]

In spite of the private face, these enterprises, eligible for preferential treatments from the government, were state capital enterprises in nature. For this reason, these enterprises did not have to assume the responsibility for the losses in case of poor performance. Wutong Shipping Company founded in 1919 in Harbin was a case in point.

Wutong Shipping Company was proposed in 1918 and started to operate in March 1919 in Harbin with a total authorized capital of 2 million yuan. The company had a fleet of 29 Russian ships and 20 tugboats with a total tonnage of 29,300 tons, far surpassing the combined tonnage of all Chinese ships then sailing in the Heilong River, the Songhua River and the Wusuli River in 1917. Shortly after its foundation, the company built a four-story headquarters building in the Daowai No. 12 Street in Harbin, in addition to machine factories, shipyards, warehouses, docks, ticket boxes and staff residence buildings. Branches and offices were built along the Songhua River and the Heilong River. By 1920, Wutong Shipping's routes had covered all of the three rivers and even unprecedentedly reached Khabarovsk and the Russian Temple Street. Wutong Shipping became the largest Chinese navigation company in Northeast China and the second largest in China just behind China Merchant Steamship Navigation

1 Yu Heping and Xia Liangcai, ed., *Works of Zhou Xuexi*, Central China Normal University Press, 1999, pp.10-11.

Company.

The rapid rise of Wutong Shipping was primarily attributed to the 1917 Revolution in Russia, as a result of which dominating Russian shipping countries had to sell their ships to protect themselves from the revolution. As was ruled in the Aihui Treaty[1], they were treaty bound to sell their ships to Chinese merchants, which created a golden opportunity for Wutong to take over the monopoly. For another important factor, the founders and main shareholders such as Liang Shiyi, Cao Rulin, Ye Gongchuo and Meng Zhaochang were all figures of importance in the Ministry of Communications, the Bank of Communications or local governments in Northeast China. These put Wutong on an advantageous footing financially and politically compared with other private businesses.

These founders and main shareholders also created a special connection between Wutong and the Ministry and the Bank of Communications, which benefited Wdutong in various ways. First of all, the Bank of Communications provided great financial support. Though with an authorized capital of 2 million yuan, Wutong only had 500,000 in reality. Money used to buy Russian ships and to build headquarters, docks, shipyards and machine factors all came from loans from the Bank of Communications.[2] From its founding to November 24 1920, Wutong borrowed 3.74 million yuan from the Bank of Communications and 40,000 yuan from other banks in loan, and had another 100,000 yuan debt in form of suspended deposit, cash deposit, saving deposit and unpaid service charge. Its total debt reached 4,385,000 yuan.[3]

With the excuse of inability to pay debts, Wutong Shipping filed for nationalizations in 1920 under the Ministry of Communications while its real

1 A Survey of the Kailuan Coal Mine, quoted in Chen Zhen, ed., *Historical Files of China's Modern Industry*, Vol. 3, Sanlian Bookstore, 1961, p.538.

2 According to The Aihui Treaty of 1858, the Heilong River, the Songhua River and the Wusuli River were exclusively reserved for Chinese and Russian ships and ships of other nations could not navigate the rivers. Quoted in Wang Tieya, ed., *Collection of Treaties between China and Foreign Countries*, Vol. 1, Sanlian Bookstore, 1957, p.85.

3 Xie Lin, *Reports on the Harbin Wutong Navigation's Business*, 1919, p. 1.

intention was to require further financial support from the ministry. Eventually, the Ministry of Communications restructured Wutong as a government-merchant joint venture in 1921 with the ministry injecting another 1.5 million yuan in shares to the original share structure. As for Wutong's debts, "the Ministry of Communications shall investigate into the issue before subsidizing or sharing the debts"[1]. In addition to using the 1.5 million yuan injection to pay the Bank of Communications, Wutong signed a loan contract of a 2.5 million in installment with the bank with the Ministry of Communications as the underwriter. According to Clause No. 10, "at the due date of the loan, in case the Company fail to repay, the Underwriter is legally bound to repay in full"[2], which meant the ministry had taken full responsibility for Wutong's debts. Ye Gongchuo, alternate board member and Minister of Communications, admitted, "With the excuse of accidents, Wutong claimed to be in financial difficulty and applied for nationalization. As the Minister of Communication then, I have to take measures. Eventually, the government decides to share its debts."[3] For the 2.5 million yuan loan from the Bank of Communications, the Ministry of Communications paid for the first batch interest of 174,315 yuan.[4] For the 500,000 yuan private shares, the Ministry of Communications promised "an annual interest rate of 6% or more".[5] In addition, since "many of the shareholders are actually high-ranking employees of the Bank of Communications"[6], the Ministry of Communications allocated another 2 million in guaranteed mortgage to the Bank of Communications." Such

1 Zhang Xinzheng and Zhang Zhu's Report to the Ministry of Communications, Compilation Commitee for the History of the Ministries of Communications and Railway, ed., *Chronology of Transportation and Navigation*, Vol. 1, p. 407.

2 Proposal of the Ministries of Communications and Agriculture and Commerce to the State Council Conference, *Chronology of Transportation and Navigation*, Vol. 1, p. 413.

3 Loan Contract between Wutong and the Bank of Communications, *Chronology of Transportation and Navigation*, Vol. 1, p. 464.

4 Ye Gongchuo, Postscript to the Account on Wutong, *Collected Works*, Vol. 2, 1946.

5 *Chronology of Transportation and Navigation*, Vol. 1, pp.464-465.

6 Minister Gao Enhong's Proposal to the State Council Conference, *Chronology of Transportation and Navigation*, Vol. 1, p. 465.

preferential treatment owed to the fact that the shareholders of Wutong were actually important figures in the Bank and the Ministry of Communications. However well the company performed, "the Ministry of Communications would take responsibilities, so profits was guaranteed."[1]

In addition, they also used their powers to seek advantages for Wutong, for the example the transportation of government salt. In the past, government salt was transported by Russian ships, but was then "exclusively contracted to Wutong".[2] This alone promised a net annual profit of 200,000 yuan. Wutong's contract to transport Mobil kerosene added another 100,000 yuan every year.[3] Wutong, taking advantage of its special status, also signed a water-land transshipment contract with Middle East Railways.[4] Other navigation companies had no access to such privileges. Wutong even was entitled to tax exemption for fuel use, which saved "tens of thousands every year".[5]

It is fair to conclude that Wutong was founded against a very historical context while the founders and shareholders took advantage of their access to preferential treatment unavailable to their shipping companies. However, in spite of all these favorable conditions, corruption and other problems dragged Wutong to bankruptcy in the spring of 1925, only 7 years after its founding. The biggest shareholder, the Bank of Communications took over the remaining assets and then sold it to the Government of the Northeast at the price of 1.6 million yuan in August 1925. The later restructured the company to the government company of

1 The Inside Story of Wutong Becoming State-owned, *Eatern Times*, December 6,1920.

2 "Qian Dayong's Plan to Restructure Wudong", *Chronology of Transportation and Navigation*, Vol. 1, p. 419.

3 "Instructions on Wutong", *Chronology of Transportation and Navigation*, Vol. 1, p. 412.

4 "Report on the Combined Transportation of Shandong Railway and Wutong Shipping", *The Far East*, November 5, 1920.

5 "Instructions on Wutong", *Chronology of Transportation and Navigation*, Vol. 1, p. 416.

Northeast Navigation Corporation.[1]

From the macro-political-economy perspective, the state may intervene in national production in two ways: 1) loan, subsidy, tax exemption, make for order or government purchase; 2) direct investment or joint ventures.[2] In the last Qing Dynasty, the imperial court preferred the second way, that is direct state investment, in the development of military industries, but the first in the form of GSMM for civilian industries. However, as is analyzed above, the Beiyang Government favored the second way for both civilian and military industries.

During the Beiyang period, corporate groups in the form of government-private partnership or GSMM, such as Zhu Xuexi's corporations or the Wutong Shipping, were hardly private enterprises, taking into account the preferential treatments they enjoyed and their management models. These are state-controlled and state capital funded corporations. It was a special manifestation of state capital under a weak Beiyang government.

1 Jin Ruixin, *An Overview of Navigation in Northeast China*, unspecified publisher and date, p. 6.

2 Xu Dixin and Wu Chengming, ed., *History of Capitalist Development in China*, Vol. 1, People's Publishing House, 1985, p.19.

Chapter 6

State Capitalism Under the Kuomintang Government

Compared with the Beiyang government, the Nanjing Kuomintang Government (hereafter as Nanjing Government) was much more dominant. The Nanjing Government went through very different development before and after the Anti-Japanese War. In general, state capitalism gained further momentum characterized with consolidation and new development as a result of multiple factors and actual development within and without.

First and foremost, Sun Yat-sen and his legacies could not be overlooked. During his formative and revolutionary years, Sun Yat-sen closely studied and reflected on the development of capitalism overseas. His theories were embodied in his idea of "People's Livelihood", featured with his plans to curb the negative side of capitalism. He saw with his own eyes the social and class conflicts in the capitalism west when he was living there. To prevent China from falling into the same trap, he argued "prevention is better than a cure".[1] Accordingly, he believed

1 People's Livelihood and Social Revolution, *Collected Works of Sun Yat-sen*, Vol. 1, The People's Publishing House, 1956, p.85.

China must "restrict private capital but develop state capital" by nationalizing railways, electricity, mines and other monopoly industries. This way, on one hand, productivity would quickly develop with state power so as to enrich the people and the government and on the other, state-ownership of production means could "prevent the corrupt practices of monopoly private capital."[1] As for industries that could be left alone to private capital, he advocated government support and protection while the government should regulate with progressive income and inheritance taxes and such progressive measures as social welfare and corporate legislation.

Because of Sun Yat-sen's prestige and influence, the Nanjing Government, which proclaimed to be a follower of Sun, inherited his theories. In fact, Sun's theories were widely accepted by scholars, celebrities and economic practitioners. Weng Wenhao, then director of the largest state capital corporate group, the National Resources Commission, also believed "the priority (of industrialization in China) must be state owned business". Weng argued that the success of China's industrialization relied on planning and prioritizing heavy industries. Moreover, the development of heavy industries depended not on weak and profit-driven private capital but on state-operated government endeavor. Monopoly businesses such as electricity, transportation, communications and energy at the foundation of national economy must be state owned so as to prevent "private monopoly and capitalist corrupt practice". [2]

Such an approach was further consolidated by the political and economic development within and without in the 1930s. .

First, beginning with FDR's New Deal in America in response to the 1929 world economic crisis, the role of government involvement in economy was heightened. Second, the rapid economic development in the socialist Soviet Union

1 People's Livelihood and Social Revolution, *Collected Works of Sun Yat-sen*, Vol. 1, The People's Publishing House, 1956, p.88.

2 Quoted in Li Xuetong, *Vanishing Dreams: Weng Wenhao and Early Industrialization in China*, Tianjin Ancient Works Publishing House, 2005, pp.182-183.

and the Fascist Germany achieved as a result of state control served as a model to other countries. Third, the real threat posed by Japan after Japan controlled China's Northeast in 1931 stimulated the development of state capital business in China. For example a typical example is the former National Defense Planning Committee being restructured as the National Resources Commission in the 1930s as an economic response to the possible full-fledged invasion by Japan. The National Resources Commission which gradually became the controller of dozens of agencies and over a hundred companies became the largest state capital corporate group in modern China and the largest group in heavy industry, energy and transportation. It continued growing even during the Anti-Japanese War period. War usually invites government control and centralization of economy. As a result, during the Anti-Japanese War, in both the Kuomintang-controlled areas and the border regions under the CPC's leadership, state capital enterprises were growing both in number and strength.

The confiscation of Japanese and Japanophile assets after the war led to a further explosive development of state capital enterprises. Such a development was challenged by private capital, led to the debate on "whether state capital was contending with the people for profits" and gave rise to such failed reforms as "restructuring of state-operated enterprises"and "reducing state-operated shares" by selling shares to private capital. However, the dominance of state capital became a reality of Chinese economy, whose development was inevitable as a result of China's tradition and social-economic context.

An overview of the development trajectory of state capitalism under the Nanjing Government shows that since 1927, the Nanjing Government had been taking over the Beiyang Government's state enterprises in railway, highway, post service, banking and industry and laid the foundation for state capitalism in the new age.

Prior to the Anti-Japanese War, the Nanjing Government had taken various measures to forcefully incorporating private capital into the path of state controlled economy, starting with the financial sector. At the same time, some state-controlled enterprises were established. State capitalism further strengthened and developed during the war and eventually dominated national economy with monopoly state capitalist corporate groups after the war.

In general, in addition to confiscation of the Beiyang Government assets, the Nanjing Government developed state capitalism mainly in three ways: forceful acquisition and share-holding of private enterprises, direct investment for new establishments and confiscation of Japanese and Japanophile assets.

This chapter shall analyze how each of these three ways worked.

1. Forceful Acquisition and Share-holding of Private Enterprises

The Nanjing Government started state capitalism by forcefully acquiring and nationalizing private share-holding companies. A case in point is the nationalization of China Merchants Shipping Group (hereafter as Merchants Group) by the Nanjing Government.

Before 1927, Merchants Group had gone through two stages: GSMM and merchant management while affiliated to the government under the late Qing government and the Beiyang Government. As the first and largest shipping company, Merchants Group had always been at the central stage in the conflict and competition between government and merchants. Attempts for "government management" and "nationalization" of the group never ceased,[1] thus highlighting the conflict between government and merchants.

In this respect, the Nanjing Government was no exception, but only more urgent. After taking over railways, highways and post services, the Nanjing Government inevitably tried to control the shipping business, with the take-over of Merchants Group as a key step. The decade from 1927 to 1937 witnessed the Nanjing Government making various efforts to nationalize Merchants Group to

1 Li Zhigang, Issues Concerning the State-Ownership of the Merchant Group 1878-1881, *Collected Works of the Institute of Modern History of the Central Research Institute*, Vol. 17, 1988. Also seen in, Zhu Yingui, *State Intervention and Modernization in China and Japan: A Comparative Study of the Merchant Group and Mitsubishi Shipping*, Oriental Press, 1994.

integrate it into the state capitalist system, which spotlighted the government's determination to expand state capitalism. This decade fell into two stages: nationalization from 1927 to November 1932, and strengthened control in the following years.

However, it was no easy business to nationalize the biggest shipping company which had survived "government management" and "nationalization" reforms in previous decades. Therefore, it was no surprise that the group's management and institution changed constantly and bewilderingly under the Nanjing Government around the nationalization of the group.

For a better understanding of the evolution of such change, the author has worked out a chronology of the nationalization of Merchants Group: [1]

In early January 1927, before the revolution of Shanghai and establishment of the Nanjing Government, Chiang Kai-shek assied Yang Quan to work on the business of Merchants Group. Yang "did not take the position on the grounds of unspecified responsibilities and authority".

On March 15, the Fourth Political Meeting of the Central Executive Committee appointed Jiang Zungui and Qian Yongming to negotiate with the management of Merchants Group.

On March 30, the 85th Kuomintang Central Committee Political Meeting established Merchants Group Liquidating Committee made up of Zhang Renjie, Jiang Zungui, Yu Hede, Guo Taiqi, Chen Huide, Song Hanzhang, Qian Yongming, Yang Quan, Pan Yizhi, Yang Duanliu and Li Gufan. At the 110th Meeting, He Huansan was added to the dommittee.

On May 20, the Liquidating Committee started operation and produced 16 liquidating reports and directives and 26 statistical charts. Upon fulfilling its obligations at the end of September, the Liquidating Committee was dissolved. Relevant "settlement business" was transferred to the Ministry of Communications

1 Merchant Group, ed., Memorial Vol. of 75th Anniversary of the Merchant Group, *Chronology of the Merchant Group*, 1947, pp. 74-84.

on the grounds that "Merchants Group was in communications business".

In November, the Nanjing Government stipulated the 7-Item Merchant Group Supervision Guidelines. Accordingly, a Merchants Group Supervision Office affiliated to the Ministry of Communications was established to be staffed with one supervisor and one director. These two posts were filled by Wang Boqun, the Minister of Communications and Zhao Tieqiao, a ministry dispatched counsellor who outspokenly advocated nationalization.

In January 1928, Wang Boqun threw out the board and suspended all board members. At the same time, an Executive Management Office was established to overlook Merchant Groups. Zhao Tieqiao and Li Guojie were appointed to run the office, with the latter turning down the appointment with the excuse of illness.

On February 22, the Executive Management Office started operation, by re-formulating the organization charter, reforming the management and restructuring the Inland River Company, the Jiyu Real Estates, and Renjihe Insurance.

On August 10, Executive Director Zhao Tieqiao and Merchants Group President Li Guojie attended the National Transportation Conference organized by the Ministry of Communications. At the meeting, "it was stipulated that Merchants Group be an interim government-merchant joint venture before eventual nationalization."

In February 1929, someone tattled on Zhao Tieqiao for "poor management and duty dereliction". The Ministry of Communications, the Ministry of Industry and Commerce and the Control Yuan launched a joint investigation. But the one-month investigation "produced no definite conclusion."

On June 17, at the Second Plenary Session of the Kuomintang Central Committee, the jurisdiction over Merchants Group was transferred from the Ministry of Communications to the Nanjing Government directly. According to the government order, Wang Boqun became the director of Merchants Group Committee and Zhao Tieqiao served as the commissioner. By then, "Merchants Group, merchant managed in name, had become a de facto state-operated enterprise".

In February 1930, Zhao Beiqiao, through a court action, confiscated the Jiyu Real Estatas for the Executive Management Office and took over officially in April.

On July 24, "because of jealousy of his role in restructuring Merchants Group, Commissioner Zhao Tieqiao was assassinated." Cai Pei, Director of Shipping of the Ministry of Communications, served as general commissioner in adjunct. "The Nanjing Government then commissioned Chen Xizeng, who turned down the assignment."

In September, Deputy Minister of Communications, Li Zhonggong was assigned to serve as the Director of the Executive Office and General Commissioner. At the same time, Merchants Group Restructuring Committee was established with seven appointed committee members including Zhang Qun as the Director and Li Zhonggong as the Restructuring Commissioner. However, "because Zhang Qun did not take his position, the Committee became an abortion."

In May 1931, Li Zhonggong resigned from his post as Restructuring Commissioner, only to be succeeded by Guo Waifeng.

In the spring of 1932, the Kuomintang Central Political Conference decided to return Merchants Group to the Ministry of Communications.

In March, Guo Waifeng resigned. The Ministry of Communications established Merchants Group Supervision Committee to replace the Executive Management Office and appointed Chen Fumu as the General Supervisor and Li Guojie as the general manager of Merchants Group.

In October, at the 331st Meeting of the Kuomintang Central Committee, Merchants Group became a state enterprise. The government would pay 50 *liang* of silver for each set (made up of 2 shipping shares and 2 industrial shares) of Merchants Group shares and "inherit all assets and legal liabilities of Merchants Group". The Supervision Committee was canceled while new offices such as the Board of Directors, the Board of Supervisors and the General Manager were established. The Interim Organization Charter and the Interim Charter for the

Board of Directors and the Board of Supervisors were stipulated. Seven were appointed as managing directors including Ye Zhuotang and Liu Hongsheng and eight as directors including Qian Yongming. Nine supervisors including Lu Xuepu were appointed. Liu Hongsheng served as the General Manager.

On November 11, all the above-mentioned people took office and started to operate under the new name of National Merchants Group.

In February 1036, "all supervisors and General Manager Liu Hongsheng resigned on the ground of inability to fulfil duties."

On February 4, the Executive Yuan approved their resignation and "appointed Cai Zengji as General Manager and Tan Boying and Lao Mian as Deputy General Manager".

On February 8, the Ministry of Communications revised the National Merchants Group organization charter and thus canceled the Board of Supervisors. The office of General Manager was sustained and two more deputy general managers were appointed.

In January 1937, Deputy General Manager Tan Boying resigned and was replaced by Shen Zhongyi appointed by the ministry.

This chronology constitutes a sketch of the major developments of Merchants Group from 1927-1937, in an effort to picture the complexity of the Nanjing Government's effort to control Merchants Group.

However, the real reason behind this complexity was that the persons in charge of Merchants Group were strongly against nationalization, which was not reflected in the chronology. For example, at the beginning of 1927 when the North Expedition Army seized Wuhan and before the liberation of Shanghai and the establishment of the Nanjing Government, Chiang Kai-shek, in his effort to restructure Merchants Group, the largest shipping organization in China, nominated Yang Quan to work on the group.[1] However, Yang "did not take the position on the grounds of unspecified responsibilities and authority".

1 Merchant Group, ed., Memorial Vol. of 75th Anniversary of the Merchant Group, *Chronology of the Merchant Group*, p. 74.

However, the reality was much more complicated. The records of a special meeting of the Board of Directors read, "The chairman reported that Yang Quan and others came to the Group with the order of General Chiang and the Ministry of Communications to took over, only to be given a flat refusal..."[1]Therefore, there were good reasons to believe Yang did not took office because of a lack of authority and the refusal. Then, when the Fourth Political Meeting of the Central Executive Committee appointed Jiang Zungui and Qian Yongming to negotiate with the management of Merchants Group, the Board of Directors responded by arguing, "The group is a merchant operation...The decision on reform rests with the group itself and concerns the right of shareholders. The Board of Directors shall draft relevant plans and present the plans to the general meeting of shareholders." [2]

However, the Board of Directors could hardly resist the Nanjing Government which was determined and powerful enough to nationalize Merchants Group. In April, according to the resolution of the 85th Kuomintang Central Committee Political Meeting, Merchants Group Liquidation Committee was established to handle restructuring. Merchants Group was forced into concession. To send a mission, the Nanjing Government arrested and prosecuted Fu Zongyao, Director of Merchants Group, Person-in-charge of shipping business and Manager of Jiyu Real Estates, with "providing financial support to enemies"and "standing in the way of the army of justice", and confiscated Fu's 200 shares as "government shares operated by the Ministry of Finance".[3] Although the opponents of nationalization took revenge by assassinating Zhao Tieqiao, the nationalization of Merchants Group was already meat on the table.

Another point worth attention was that the Nanjing Government nationalized

1 Special meeting on April 12, 1927, Archives of the Merchant Group No. 468(2)/ Minutes of the 308th Board of Directors.

2 Special meeting on April 18, 1927, Archives of the Merchant Group No. 468(2)/ Minutes of the 308th Board of Directors. .

3 Special meeting on December 5, 1927, Archives of the Merchant Group No. 468(2)/ Minutes of the 308th Board of Directors.

Merchants Group at a minimal cost. When Merchants Group was acquired by the Nanjing Government in October 1932, the Nanjing Government only paid 50 *liang* of silver for each set (made up of 2 shipping shares and 2 industrial shares) of Merchants Group shares, making a total of 2,126,340.45 *liang* when the acquisition ended in 1934.[1]However, at the moment, Merchants Group had a capital fund of 8.4 million *liang* and a total assets of 25,288,062 *liang* according to the 55th Annual Balance Sheet in 1928. According to Atkinson&Dallas's estimation, the Group's real estates and docks around China were woth 26,752,005 *liang* and all its ships were valued at over 4,264,900, making a total assets of over 31.01 million *liang*.[2] Moreover, the value of real estates was bound to go up. Even when the appreciation of real estates was not counted, Merchants Group had a total assets of no less than 26 million *liang* in the forms of real estates and ships in 1934. The Nanjing Government's acquisition plan greatly undervalued Merchants Group, which would not have been possible without the use of state power.

In its effort to establish the state capitalist system, The Nanjing Government adopted another approach to deal with regular private share-holding companies; that is to forcefully participate in , control and nationalize these companies.

In 1935, Bank of China started to have government shares and in no time changed from private share majority to government share control. This is a typical case of merchant companies being share controlled by the government.

As mentioned earlier, Bank of China could be traced back to the Ministry of Revenue Bank established in the 31st year of Qing Emperor Guangxu's reign (1905). It was the second Chinese bank, next only to the Imperial Bank of China. The Ministry of Revenue Bank was renamed the Qing Imperial Bank in 1908 and restructured as Bank of China in 1912. In 1928, the Nanjing Government injected 5 million yuan in government shares and restructured the bank to be the Charted

1 Zhang Houquan, ed., *History of Merchants Group (Modern History)*, China Communications Press, 1988, p.407.

2 General Management Division of the Merchant Group, *Reports of the General Management Division*, pp.313-314 & 311.

Foreign Exchange Bank. In fact, by then, government share accounted for only 1/5 of the Bank's total assets of 25 million yuan. Although Bank of China did played the role of the central bank for a considerable period, in terms of its capital portfolio, private capital had always been the majority from 1917 when Zhang Jia'ao became a director and served as Vice President of the bank until 1935 when the Nanjing Government imposed government shares on the bank. [1]

Bank of China played a unique and critical role in the development of banking in Modern China, not just because of its history, size and strength or because of its decision to ignore Yuan Shikai's order to stop foreign exchange service which built the credit basis in China and won the bank a leading role in the banking sector. More importantly, ever since Zhang Jia'ao, its managers had been adhering to its principle of independent operation and social responsibility. All these made Bank of China a leader of Modern China's banking industry and the most successful national capital share-holding bank. As Zhang Jiaao pointed out, "During the 16 years from the refusal to Yuan Shikai to the restructuring into the Charted Foreign Exchange Bank, we have worked diligently to expand business domestically and stand up against foreign aggression. Fortunately, we have managed to protect the independence of the bank. In a sense, Bank of China,China Customs and China Post should be regarded as the three soundest organizations in China. It is no exaggeration to say that Bank of China is the largest and most successful national capital share-holding company."

Bank of China being the largest and most successful national capital share-holding company, which Zhang Jia'ao took pride in, was the result of various

1 According to Deng Xianhong's work, under the Beiyang Government, merchant shares in the Bank of China accounted for 59.29% in 1917, 72.64% in 1921, 88.87% in 1922 and 97.47% from 1923 to 1926. Deng Xianhong, "Relations between the Bank of China and the Beiyang Government", *Collected Works of the Institute of Economy of China Academy of Social Sciences*, Vol. 11, China Social Sciences Press, 1988 pp.355-356. After the the injection of government shares by the Nationalist Government, government shares accounted for only one fifth of all shares. In this sense, the Bank of China was a merchant share dominated private corporation.

factors working together. However, after the Najing Government consolidated its rule, the situation started to change.

In the 1930s, China was haunted by crises from within and without. The financial crisis as a result of the world economic crisis and American silver purchase frenzy, the Yangtze River flood, the September 18 Incident in Northeast China and the bankruptcy of the rural areas made things even worse. In 1935, China's financial sector and economy in general were on the verge of crisis. These offered the Nanjing Government a chance to control the banking industry and created a new channel for the establishment of state capital enterprises.

In mid March 1935, Kong Xiangxi (Minister of Finance) and Song Ziwen had a meeting with Chiang Kai-shek in Hankou. "It is decided the government will issue 100 million yuan worth government bonds, of which 30 million will be handed over to the Central Bank, 20 million to Bank of China and 10 million as government shares to Bank of Communications. Zhang Jia'ao, then General Manager of Bank of China will be transfer to Deputy Governor of the Central Bank and Song Ziwen will serve as President of Bank of China." [1]

On March 28, 1935, the Nanjing Government sent to instructions to Bank of China in the form of Ministry of Finance directives. The first one reads, "Mr. Zhang Jia'ao is appointed as Deputy Governor of the Central Bank". In Yao Songling's *Draft Chronicle of Mr. Zhang Gongquan's Life*, this appointment was recorded as follows: "In November of the 22nd year of the Republic of China, Kong Xiangxi succeeded Song Ziwen as Minister of Finance. Kong worked to raise money and had to take loans from the Central Bank, Bank of China and Bank of Communications to make up for the imbalance. The Central Bank, though controlled by the Ministry of Finance, was not competent enough, while Bank of China, rich in resources, did not dance to the government's tune. At the moment, the price of silver kept climbing, creating further financial gap. The government

1 Yao Songling, *Twenty-four Years of the Bank of China*, Taiwan Biographic Literature Publishing House, 1976, p. 194.

decided to reform the monetary system and centralize the issue of currency, which necessitated the Ministry of Finance's control of the three banks. To make things easy, the government injected capital into and accordingly restructured each bank. Mr. Zhang Jia'ao was transferred to Deputy Governor of the Central Bank while Song Ziwen served as President of Bank of China."[1]

The second instruction reads: "The Ministry of Finance instructed Bank of China to increase government shares from 5 million to 25 million yuan, as a result of which the total capital stock of Bank of China would reach 45 million from 25 million yuan." [2]

The original instruction reads: "Your bank has a capital of 25 million yuan including 5 million yuan in government share. The new injection will be 20 million yuan, which comes from government bonds issued in the 24th year of the Republic of China. The new injection has been proposed and approved by the Ministry. Attached to the instruction is the booking certificate for 20 million yuan government bond. Upon receiving the certificate, please file the receipt of share capital to the Ministry. Within the increase of government shares, your bank's old charter is subject to revision accordingly. I recommend a meeting of the Board of Directors for a proposal to be sent to the shareholder's meeting on the 30th of this month for approval. Your cooperation is appreciated. Kong Xiangxi."[3]

It is noteworthy that this round of capital injection involved three banks not just one. The Central Bank was established as a government bank while Bank of Communications, to become a government holding company after the injection, was not subject to personnel adjustment. Only the management of Bank of China changed. Why so?

One of Chiang Kai-shek's telegrams to Kong Xiangxi might shed light. On

1 Yao Songling, ed., *Chronology of Zhang Jia'ao*, Vol. 1, Taiwan Biographic Literature Publishing House, 1982, p. 140.

2 Bank of China Headquarters and The Second Archives of China, ed., *Historical Documents of the Bank of China*, Vol. 1, Archives Publishing House, 1991, p. 383.

3 Yao Songling, *Twenty-four Years of the Bank of Chin*a, Taiwan Biographic Literature Publishing House, 1976, p. 194.

March 22, 1935, that is, less than one week after the instructions from the Ministry of Finance, Chiang Kai-shek sent a first-class priority telegram to Kong Xiangxi, which reads: "The government and the social are both on the verge of bankruptcy. In a final analysis, it is because of the lack of unity in the monetary system and the issue of currency. The major obstacle comes from the outdated old policies of Bank of China and Bank of Communications which have been exploiting the people and ignoring the needs of the country and the society...In view of the risky circumstances and in the interest of the government and the society, the three banks have to be absolutely subjected to government control for cooperation, which is the only hope of the country and the people..." For such an end, Chiang believed that Zhang Jia'ao had to leave Bank of China. "I intend to persuade him to take a clean cut from Bank of China and appoint him to other government positions or Deputy Governor of the Central Bank..."[1]

Besides the rude tone and leaving no room for argument about removing Zhang Jia'ao from Bank of China, this telegram is evidence of the difference between Zhang, and Chiang and Kong over how to run the bank; that is, the irreconcilable conflict between Zhang Jia'ao's adherence to "traditions" and Chiang Kai-shek's plan of "absolute subjugation". Before this uninvited injection of government shares, Bank of China was "a benchmark of banking with the most abundant assets, longest history, most stable credit system and most flexible business". By the end of 1934, Bank of China's total assets reached 975.75 million yuan while Bank of Communications had 425 million yuan. These two banks accounted for "one third of the total assets of all Chinese banks" and "tripled the Central Bank in size". [2]

As a leader in the financial sector, Bank of China under Zhang Jia'ao's leadership was operating in conflict with the Nanjing Government's policy of issuing government bonds and taking bank loans to make up for fiscal deficit.

1 *Historical Documents of the Bank of China*, Vol. 1, p.385.

2 Economic Research Office of the Bank of China, ed., *Almanac of the Banking Sector in the 26th Year of the Republic of China*, 1937, pp.818-823.

Zhang Jia'ao believed that the resources of banks should be used to help Chinese economy devastated by recession to recover rather than pay government debts. He argued, "Government bonds are built on credit. Capital raised from such bonds, if not used to stimulate production, would led to rising prices and inflation".[1] It was not right to stimulate the financial market with government bonds and therefore not right for banks to rely on government bonds. Therefore, the government should change policies for political stability and production growth and "come to realize the importance of enabling the people". He also advocated, "The government must make good judgment about priorities and cut all unnecessary and non-urgent expenditure." Zhang was also sincerely concerned with the decline of rural economy and pointed out, "The decline of rural economy is manifested in the outflow of cash. Farmers are leaving the land uncultivated and agriculture products are getting cheaper...Farmers have used up their money...It has become a major threat to society and economy." Accordingly, "the government must enact a program to stimulate rural economy." He told his shareholders, "If the rural economy collapses, Shanghai won't survive alone. Without the deposits coming from the rural area, Shanghai cannot continue to prosper...With this understanding of the critical impact of rural economy on national economic prosperity, we have to find appropriate ways to use our money to stimulate rural economy."[2] He was severely dissatisfied with the government's policy of issuing government bonds for military purposes. He pointed out, "Government bonds capture the already limited social capital while people are lamenting a lack of capital for production." Therefore, he called on the government, "The only solution is to cut military expenditure by large margins and non-urgent expenditure, so as to reduce government bonds and increase capital for production and construction."[3]

1 The 1932 Annual Business Report of the Bank of China, in *Historical Documents of the Bank of China*, Vol. 1, pp.2055-2056.

2 Ibid., pp.2094 & 2076-2077

3 The 1933 Annual Business Report of the Bank of China, in *Historical Documents of the Bank of China*, Vol. 1, pp.2129-2130.

However, the Nanjing Government turned a deaf ear to Zhang Jia'ao's call, only to move further in the opposite direction. Instead for investing in agriculture, the Nanjing Government spent more money fighting the Communist led forces. Bank capital was not used to recover economy but to buy government bonds and make government loans.

In face of the conflict between the Nanjing Government and Bank of China under Zhang Jia'ao's leadership, Bank of China took a clear standing by distancing itself from government bonds, as shown in Table 6-1, which shows the change in investment securities in the hands of some of the major banks in Shanghai from 1931-1934.

Table 6-1: Change in Investment Securities in the Hands of Major Banks in Shanghai

Unit: Million Yuan

Bank	1931	1932	1933	1934
Bank of China	72.0	64.5	32.0	25.4
Bank of Communications	21.4	26.0	29.9	29.3
Other Members of the Shanghai Banks' Union	145.8	148.4	212.9	265.5
Central Bank		0.3	0.2	155.4
合计	239.2	239.2	275.0	475.6

Source: Liu Dajun, *Study of Industrialization in Shanghai*, The Changsha Commercial Press, 1940, p. 300; Xu Nong, An Overview of China's National Economy, *The New China*, Item 4, May 1936, p. 2, quoted in Parks M. Coble, Jr., *The Shanghai Capitalists and the Nationalist Government*, translated by Yang Ximeng, China Social Sciences Press, 1988, p.210.

As shown in Table 6-1, while other banks were buying more government loans, Bank of China had been reducing its holding of government loans. When the Nanjing Government was issuing and promoting new government bonds, Bank of China, instead of buying more, had reduced its holding of government loans by 46 million yuan from 1931 to 1934.

Clearly, before the forceful injection of government shares and restructuring, Zhang Jia'ao had adhered to the principle of "merchant operation and independence", running against and further away from the government requirement of "absolute subjugation and cooperation". In fact, there existed only a "conditional cooperation" between the government and the bank.[1] However, after consolidating its rule, the Nanjing Government could tolerate no longer the independence of the leading Bank of China, which intentionally disobeyed Chiang and Kong's instructions and run against government economic policies. This should be the real reason why Zhang Jia'ao was expelled from Bank of China and why government shares and eventually restructuring were imposed on the bank, rather than "anything personal" as Zhang Jia'ao believed. [2]

Moreover, the Nanjing Government did not consult private shareholders or General Manager Zhang Jia'ao about the uninvited injection of government shares. On this, Zhang Jia'ao commented, "We were not notified of the injection of government bonds and the ensuing personnel change until Kong and Song came back from Hankou in mid March."[3] This kind of non-negotiable mandate was clearly backed by state power.

Under the weight of state power, Bank of China had no other option but concede to the fact of "nationalization after government injection". "At the shareholders' meeting on March 30, in accordance with the ministerial instruction, it was announced the resignation of Li Ming, Chairman of the Board and Zhang Jia'ao, General Manager and the appointment of Song Ziwen as Chairman and Song Hanzhang as General Manager. To ease the opposition from private merchant shareholders, the Ministry of Finance reduced the injection from 20 million yuan to 15 million, which, combined with the existing 5 million, made a

1 Mao Zhili, *Zhang Jiaao and the Operation and Development of the Bank of China*, Taipei National History Office, 1996, pp. 462 &435.

2 Zhang Jia'ao said, "During the 23 years in the Bank of China, personnel matters have caused much trouble...When Minister Kong assigned Song Ziwen as the Chair of the Board and me as the Deputy President of the Central Bank, no personnel rearrangement was made in the Bank of Communications. It was clear personal connections played a role..." quoted in Yao Songling, ed., *Chronology of Zhang Jia'ao*, Vol. 1, Taiwan Biographic Literature Publishing House, 1982, p. 142.

3 Yao Songling, *Twenty-four Years of the Bank of Chin*a, Taiwan Biographic Literature Publishing House, 1976, p. 195.

total of 20 million yuan government share."[1]

By then, Bank of China had been nationalized. Although the revised charter still read, "Bank of China is a share-holding limited liability company with shareholders' liabilities limited by their shares,"[2] government shares accounted for only 50% of all shares. However, taking into account that it was one government versus many private shareholders and that Song Ziwen, dispatched by the Ministry of Finance, served as the leader, Bank of China was clearly no longer its old self under Zhang Jia'ao's leadership.

Taking advantage of the financial crisis in June and November 1935, the Nanjing Government repeated this "injection+restructure" model and forcefully dragged other big banks into its orbit, including Commercial Bank of China, Siming Bank, National Industrial Bank of China and Canton Provincial Bank. Thus, the government cleared the way for the national financial system spearheaded by Central Bank, Bank of China, Bank of Communications, Agricultural Bank of China, Postal Remittances and Savings Bank and Central Trust of China.

The only explanation for these moves of the government is that the Nanjing Government had consolidated its rule and embarked on the road "from financial to industrial monopoly".[3]

In spite of everything, government injection was imposed on Bank of China and Song Ziwen arrogated all authority to himself with the revision of the bank charter.[4] With the forceful injection of government shares into Bank of China and

1 Yao Songling, *Twenty-four Years of the Bank of China*, p. 195.

2 Clause 2 of the *Interim Regulations of the Bank of China*, on the record of the Ministry of Finance dated May 2, 1935, *Historical Documents of the Bank of China*, Vol. 1, p. 170.

3 Xu Dixin and Wu Chengming, ed., *History of Capitalist Development in China*, Vol. 3, People's Publishing House, 1993, p.12.

4 According the Clause 27 of the *Interim Regulations of the Bank of China*, on the record of the Ministry of Finance dated May 2, 1935, "The Chair of the Board of the Bank of China is the chair of the Board of Directors, the General Administration and the Shareholders' Conference. The Chair will be full-time position in charge of the comprehensive business of the bank.", quoted in *Historical Documents of the Bank of China*, Vol. 1, p. 173.

Bank of Communications, the Nanjing Government formulated the first way of developing state capital enterprises.

2. New State Capital Enterprises Directly Funded by Government Investment

State enterprises funded by government investment fall into two categories: 1) those as represented by China Development Finance Corporation (hereafter as CDFC) which were structured and masked as private shareholding companies to attract foreign investment and facilitate international business; 2) state capital enterprises in iron and steel, chemical and electricity to satisfy energy need.

In the form of shareholding companies, the first category of companies are directly invested by the government or government representatives or agencies. Such practice was common after the establishment of the Nanjing Government. The establishment of CDFC was a typical case .

As for the history of CDFC, Dr. Zheng Huixin of the Chinese University of Hong Kong has published several papers and a monograph, titled *From Investment Corporation to "Official Business": The Founding and Operation of China Development Finance Corporation.* This book constitutes an extensive study on CDFC based on rich historical documents and publications, with the focus on how CDFC changed from an investment corporation into an "official business". It argues, "The integration of government and business under the Nanjing Government is a result of the society's need of the positive functions played by such integration."[1] In fact, though presenting itself as a private holding companies, CDFC was a typical state capital enterprise with all the basic features upon birth in terms of its purpose, organization and business operation.

First, in term of its purpose, CDFC was built to serve government policies and objectives by Song Ziwen. When CDFC was founded in 1934, Song Ziwen had just recently stepped down as Deputy Chair of the Executive Yuan and Minister of Finance. However, this by no means proved that he had step out of the political

1 Zheng Huixin, *From Investment Corporation to GSMM: Founding and Operation of the CDFC*, The Chinese University of Hong Kong Press, 2001, p. 5. (hereafter as Zheng Huixin or *From Investment Corporation to GSMM*).

circle. In fact, as Dr. Zheng Huixin argues, Song Ziwen did not leave the political circle, but only "temporarily drifted from the center of political power". In fact, he still enjoyed unparalleled political resources and high-level connections as a result of his special identity.

Zong Ziwen's motives for CDFC were reflected in his explanation of "Funding the China Development Finance Corporation". According to Song Ziwen and other founders, one of the major reasons for the economic and policy failures was that "banks and financial institutions could not operate independently to fulfil their policy roles under the current organization system," either because "such policies were two extensive for any single institution and therefore necessitate cooperation" or because when public investors were expected to play a role, no institution was capable of finishing relevant professional and technical investigation and carrying out investment and management responsibilities." Accordingly, CDFC identified itself as a platform which "units but also surpasses various financial institutions". Its main businesses including: "to facilitate cooperation and mutual investment between banks and other corporations, to issue company bonds and to research and investigate for major projects", so as to "promote connection and cooperation between Chinese and foreign investment and attract foreign investment into various industries in China". The key was that "bankers and investors of various countries"would regard CDFC as "the only agency through which they could invest in Chinese industry".[1]

The CDFC Charter specified its business as: "The Corporation will facilitate and collaborate with various government agencies, Chinese and foreign banks and other institutions to support the development of agriculture, industry and commerce companies, governmental and private alike, and deal in relevant investment, management and trust issues."[2]

Clearly, CDFC aimed to "collaborate with government agencies and Chinese

1 Selected Works on the Founding of the CDFC, *Files and History*, Item 6, 1998.

2 *Shun Pao*, June 3, 1934, Quoted from Chen Zhen, ed., *Historical Files of China's Modern Industry*, Vol. 3, Sanlian Bookstore, 1961, p. 1023.

and foreign banks", to "support the development of various companies", to "promote agricultural, industrial and commercial development", to became the "only agency" recognized by foreign bankers and investors, and to "unite but surpass various financial institutions". None of these could be possible, short of a very favorable status, rich resources and government support. In other words, only a company of a particular kind could play so many roles at the same time, which was not for any regular businessman. Therefore, as one of the Nanjing Government's efforts to gain control over economy, many professional companies were established in a planned way. In appearance, these companies were jointly funded by both government and private shares as shareholding companies to gain control over production and circulation. It was against such a background that CDFC came into being. Therefore, it was no accident that Song Ziwen, as a retired government official, was in a right position to lead CDFC.[1]

Besides, in terms of the configuration of shareholders and its organization, CDFC differed great from regular private shareholding companies. Table 6-2 lists the background of CDFC's founding directors and supervisors.

Table 6-2: Background of CDFC's Founding Directors and Supervisors (June 1934)

Name	Age	Shares	Position	Social Roles
Kong Xiangxin	54	20 000	Chair of the Board	Vice President of the Executive Yuan, Minister of Finance, President of the Central Bank
Song Ziwen	40	25 000	Executive Director	State Councilor of the Nanjing Government, Standing Member of the National Economic Committee, and later Chair of the Board of Bank of China
Bei Zuyi	41	30 000	Executive Director	Manager and Director of Foreign Exchange of Bank of China's Shanghai Branch,
Ye Xun	55	5 000	Director	Director Manager of the Continental Bank

1 CDFC was founded as a private corporation to attract foreign investment. However, Song Ziwen's official role would not only facilitate the investment of European countries and America, but also avoid Japanese suspicion and obstruction. Quoted from Zhen Huixin's book.

contd.

Name	Age	Shares	Position	Social Roles
Cheng Xing	44	10 000	Managing Director	Managing Director and Vice President of the Central Bank
Tang Shoumin	43	30 000	Managing Director	General Manager of Bank of Communications and Managing Director of the Central Bank
Hu Bijiang	53	35 000	Managing Director	General Manager of Central South Bank and Chair of the Board of Bank of Communications
Zhou Zuomin	50	15 000	Managing Director	General Manager of Golden City Bank
Xu Liuxin	44	10 000	Managing Director	General Manager of the National Commercial Bank of Zhejiang
Song Ziliang	35	15 000	Managing Director, General Manager	Director General Manager of China Guohuo Bank and resigned from General Manager of CDFC in 1936
Zhang Jia'ao	45	30 000	Managing Director	General Manager of Bank of China, Standing Member of the Supervisor
Xu Kan	46	10 000	Director	Director of the Currency Department of the Ministry of Finance, Director of China Guohuo Bank and promoted to Executive Deputy Minister of Finance
Li Ming	47	10 000	Managing Director	General Manager of the National Commercial Bank of Zhejiang and Chair of the Board of Bank of China
Ye Zhuotang	59	10 000	Managing Director	Managing Director of the Central Bank and later General Manager of Siming Commercial Bank and Director of the Central Trust of China
Yang Dunfu		5 000	Director	Managing Director and Deputy General Manager of Shanghai Commercial Deposit Bank
Li Yuying	53	25 000	Managing Director	Chair of the Board of China Agricultural and Industrial Bank, Member of the Central Political Conference, Standing Member of the Supervisor
Liu Tizhi	56	5 000	Director	General Manager of National Industrial Bank of China
Chen Guangfu	53	10 000	Managing Director	General Manager of Shanghai Commercial Deposit Bank, Managing Director of the Central Bank
Xi Demao	42	50 000	Director	General Manager of the Business Division of the Central Bank
Xie Qi	48	25 000	Managing Director	Former Director of the Consolidated Tax Administration of the Ministry of Finance
Qian Youming	49	10 000	Director	General Manager of the Four Bank Deposit Association and later Chair of the Board of Bank of Communications

contd.

Name	Age	Shares	Position	Social Roles
Zhang Hancheng		70 000	Director	Managing Supervisor of the National Industrial Bank of China and General Manager of Yuhua Bank
Song Hanzhang	62	20 000	Director	Chair of the Board of China Insurance Company, Managing Director of Bank of China and later General Manager of Bank of China
Zhang Shouyong	58	10 000	Director	Managing Director of China Women's Commercial Deposit Bank, Counselor to the Ministry of Finance and former Vice Minister of Finance
Qi Zhi	41	10 000	Director	General Manager of Agriculture and Industry Bank of China
Zhang Jingjiang	57	25 000	Supervisor	State Councilor of the Nanjing Government, Chair of the Supervisor
Song Zi'an		15 000	Supervisor	Supervisor of China Guohuo Bank, Inspector and later General Manager of Songjiang Salt Administration
Zhang Weiru	46	5 000	Supervisor	Director General of Shanghai Chinese Merchants Stock Exchange
Qu Zuhui		5 000	Supervisor	Managing Director of Guohua Bank
Xu Busun		10 000	Supervisor	Director General of Shanghai Gold Exchange and Chair of the Board of Zhonghe Commercial Bank
Wang Huaizhong	41	15 000	Supervisor	General Manager of China Reclamation Bank
Sun Hengfu	59	6 000	Supervisor	Chair of the Board and General Manager of Siming Commercial Deposit Bank
Fu Yaozong	62	15 000	Supervisor	General Manager of Commercial Bank of China
Wang Baolun			Supervisor	Managing Director of the Central Bank

Source: Zheng Huixin, *From Investment Corporation to GSMM*, pp.69-70.

As reflected in this list, with a registered capital of 10 million yuan, CDFC involved all the leading banks and financial institutions in China back then with two former Vice Presidents of the Executive Yuan and Ministers of Finance serving major roles. It is unparalleled in terms of prestige and influence.

The registered capital of 10 million yuan was divided into 1 million shares, that is, 10 yuan per share. The above-mentioned directors and supervisors took 591,000 shares, accounting for 59.1% of the total. However, they bought these shares not as private investors but representatives of other banks,[1] which made CDFC all the more unique.

The swiftness from preparation to establishment was also unprecedented. The preparation of CDFC was first reported in March 1934 in a newspaper in Shanghai. On April 18, the fund raising plan was put on records. Six days later, that is on April 24, its registration application was approved by the Shanghai Social Affairs Bureau. On May 28, the Ministry of Finance examined and approved the establishment of CDFC. On May 31, CDFC organized the first founders' meeting. Two days later, the Inaugural Meeting on June 2 announced the establishment of CDFC.[2] This is a record-making procedure for the establishment of a major shareholding company in modern Chinese economic history.

In terms of its operations, CDFC focused on the following sectors. First, to cooperate with foreign capital. Song Ziwen recalled, "In the 25th[3] year of the Republic of China, CDFC, in collaboration with Britain's Sino-British Bank and HSBC, made the British-CDFC loan to finance the construction of the Hangzhou-Ningbo railway. Later, before the beginning of the Anti-Japanese War in the next year, two additional such loans were made for the Pukou-Xiangyang railway and the Guangzhou-Meixian railway respectively. In addition, "CDFC, on behalf of the Jiangxi Provincial Government, borrowed from British banks to build the Nanchang Hydro Power Plant." In terms of cooperation with France, CDFC "made greater achievements". First, CDFC "collaborated with the French bank consortium made up of BNP, Banque de I'IndoChine, Rothschild & Co and Sino-French Bank for railway construction and mine development." In December 1936, CDFC, the French bank consortium and the Ministry of Communications

1 According to Zheng Huixin's research, "Though only Song Ziwen, Li Yiying, Zhang Jingjiang and Xie Zuokai were listed as private investors in theory, there is good reason to doubt whether their investments were private...Shares are decided by the scale of the bank and people's relations with the founders.", Zheng Huixin, *From Investment Corporation to GSMM*, pp.326-327.

2 Zheng Huixin, *From Investment Corporation to GSMM*, pp.64-67.

3 1936, translator's note.

"signed a loan treaty to finance the purchase of construction materials of the Chengdu-Chongqing railway," while the Nanjing Government would cover "other domestic cost". Upon the outbreak of the Anti-Japanese War, "land acquisition, tunnel construction and the building of bridges and rail-beds have finished". After Shanghai and Nanjing fell into enemy hands, CDFC cooperated with French companies to "build the railway from Nanning to Zhennanguan so as to open connections with Vietnam". in 1939, "an even more extensive project plan" was signed " to build the railway connecting Kunming and Xufu (Yibin) to reach the Yangtze River and develop mineral mines along the railway, subject to further discussion". With respect to cooperation with American companies, because of "America's strength in industry rather than railway construction, CDFC focused on the development of industries such as the manufacturing of "rayon, paper, fertilizer, trucks and rubber".[1] Second, to penetrate into the stock market, handle government stamp tax and undertake corporate securities. Third, to invest in energy development and mining. In December 1943, CDFC published a business report, describing its business before the Anti-Japanese War. According to the report, in the energy development and mining sectors, CDFC operated "many big companies such as the Capital Power Plant and Qishuyan Power Plant affiliated to the Yangtze Electric, Huainan Railway and Coal Mine, Hankou Jiji Hydro Power Plant, Jiangnan Railway, Chengdu-Chongqing Railway, Guangzhou-Meixian Railway, China Cotton, China Wood, China Mines, Xijing Power Plant, Nanchang Hydro Power Plant, Lushan Mountain Cable Bus, and Xianyang Ethanol Plant.[2]

Among this projects before and during the war, some involved tremendous investment, some necessitated government guarantee,[3] and some were major railway and power projects. Most of these projects were implemented during the

1 Song Ziwen's report on donating the assets of CDFC, in *Northeast China Daily*, September 19, 1947, quoted in Chen Zhen, ed., *Historical Files of China's Modern Industry*, Vol. 3, Sanlian Bookstore, 1961, pp. 1024-1025.

2 For more details of CDFC, please refer to Chapters III-V in Zheng Huixin.

3 For example, loans for the Chengdu-Chongqing Railway was sponsored by the Nanjing Government, in Zheng Huixin, p.112.

three years between the establishment of CDFC in June 1934 and the outbreak of the Anti-Japanese war in July 1937. It was common sense that no regular private enterprise was capable of carrying out all these projects. After securing control over Yangtze Electric and Huainan Coal Mine, Song Ziwen, CDFC's actual controller proclaimed, "With electricity from Yangtze Electric and coal from Huainan and Fanle, it is easy to connect Shanghai, Nanjing and Hankou with a power network of cheap electricity, so as to promote industrial development in Central China."[1] Clearly, Song did not speak like the boss of a "purely private business" here.

Against such background, CDFC enriched its assets at an appalling speed. According to the balance sheet dated December 31, 1936, that is, two and half years after its establishment, CDFC secured a total assets of 32.8 million yuan, more than doubling the 10 million total capital. The annual net profit in 1936 reached over 1.91 million yuan.[2]

Some might argue that it is inappropriate to categorize CDFC as a state capital enterprise on the ground that the capital portfolio showed no government share. Then, why so? As argued above, during the Nanjing Government period, the nature of a company was decided by "whether the company was controlled by the government". That's the key. Government might secure control by various means. As long as a company shows the basic features of a state capital corporation in terms of its purpose, organization and business and its management have background in government, this company is categorized as a state capital corporation. The existence of government shares, that is officially government shares, is not critical.

With respect to the nature of CDFC, the Hokkaido University library has an

1 Economic Information Association, ed, *Inside Stories of T.V. Song's Family Wealth*, Chen Zhen, ed., *Historical Files of China's Modern Industry*, Vol. 3, Sanlian Bookstore, 1961, p.1034.

2 Chen Zhen, ed., *Historical Files of China's Modern Industry*, Vol. 3, Sanlian Bookstore, 1961, p.1034.

investigation report on CDFC compiled by the Investigation Department of the Korean Bank of Japan in July 1934. This report provides further evidence.

According to the report, CDFC was the joint effort of "international alliance, western powers and pro-west Chinese". "People in the financial and banking sector who usually tended to hate each other...worked together to build this new investment institution for mutual benefits." Japan "had to watch it closely". CDFC was established against the background where after Japan supported Manchukuo, "western powers encircled and isolated Japan". CDFC became a channel for "close cooperation" between China and western powers in an effort to "contain Japanese development". Therefore, "close supervision"was necessary. With such an analysis of CDFC, the report drew its conclusion about CDFC, claiming it as "a designated agency of the government". On the surface, it was "a Chinese company, but controlled by the west". The record ended with some policy recommendations: "If the Chinese could not realize that Japan is the keeper of peace in the Orient and thus drag in the political and economic power of a third party to contain the prosperity of the Orient, our best defense is to strike back resolutely...Proper methods should be taken to drive home this point to the Chinese".[1] It is clear in the report that Japan, regarding CDFC as an obstacle to Japanese occupation of China, was very concerned about the establishment of CDFC and CDFC's connections with western powers, Moreover, the Japanese investigation drew a definite conclusion that CDFC was "an designated agency of the government", serving as further evidence to our evaluation that CDFC was a state capital enterprise in nature.

In terms of its purpose, CDFC, under the disguise of a private company, could circumvent international laws and treaties to accomplish many purposes which the government could not and should not do while minimizing Japanese intervention. Its business portfolio was beyond the scope of any non-state capital enterprise.

1 CDFC and Its International Business, published by Korean Bank Investigation Department in July 1934, pp.2-3, 16-17.

For these reasons, as early as during its preparation, CDFC had been regarded as "a quasi-governmental enterprise or a branch agency of the Economic Committee".[1] In the 1940s, CDFC was regarded as an "official business" equal to the Yitong Enterprise, the Fuzhong Enterprise and Yangtze Construction and severely criticized by Kuomintang high-level personage. The evaluation of "official business" did shed light on its state capitalist nature.

After the founding of the Nanjing Government, the National Resources Commission (hereafter as the Resources Commission) directly funded many new state capital enterprises in heavy industry, energy, fuel and communications. The Resources Commission played an eye-catching role in the economic development of modern China. When its predecessor, the National Defense Design Commission was first established in November 1932, there were only 31 in the staff. Upon the victory of the Anti-Japanese War, the Resources Commission, by then a ministerial agency directly under the Executive Yuan, had jurisdiction over several hundred large-and medium-sized enterprises with a total employment of over 300,000 across China (including Taiwan Province). Most companies in oil, mineral mining and melting, iron and steel, electricity, coal, chemical and machinery were controlled by the Resources Commission. Companies affiliated to the Resources Commission were typical cases of state capitalism prior to 1949.

Upon its establishment in November 1932, the National Defense Design Commission was affiliated to the General Staff Office of the Nanjing Government and commissioned to conduct economic and resource investigation and research. Chiang Kai-shek was the Director while Weng Wenhao and Qian Zhaochang as Secretary General and Deputy Secretary General respectively. The commission was composed of established scholars, financial practitioners and government technical and management officials. In history, the Resources Commission went through several stages of rapid development.

1 The Future of CDFC, *Social News*, Vol. 7, Item 22, June 6, 1934, quoted in Zheng Huixin, p. 94.

In April 1935, the National Defense Design Commission was renamed as the National Resources Commission. From this moment until March 1938 when it was transferred from the General Staff Office to the Ministry of Economy, the Resources Commission, besides sustained efforts in doing economy and resource related investigation, calculation and research, had two additional focuses, namely 1) to control mineral resources and monopolize the export of wolfram and antimony and 2) to promote the development of heavy industries. In 1935, the Resources Commission developed the Five Year Plan for the development of heavy industries, namely the metallurgical, fuel, chemical, machinery and electrics industries. In the summer of the same year, with the 10 million yuan allocation from the Nanjing Government, the Resources Commission started to prepare for the following businesses:

- Metallurgical: Central Iron and Steel Plant, Chalin Iron Mine, Lingxiang Iron Mire, Jiangxi Ferrotungsten Plant, Pengxian Copper Mine and Yangxin Daye Copper Mine
- Fuel: Gaokeng Coal Mine, Tianhe Coal Mine, Wanxian Coal Mine, Sichuan Oil Development, Plant-based Light Oil Refinery and Gas Car Promotion Agency
- Machinery: Machinery Plant
- Electrics: Electrical Appliance Plant, Wireless Electric Motor Plant, Electroceramics plant and Sichuan Hydro Power Plant.

With 20 million yuan additional allocation from the government in 1937, the development of these businesses continued with “minor adjustments”. In practice, 1936 saw the establishment of 12 businesses including Antimony Administration, Tungsten Administration, Central Iron and Steel Plant and Chalin Iron Mine. Eleven new businesses came into being in 1937 such as Xiangtan Coal Mine, Tianhe Coal Mine, Sichuan Oil Development, Lingxiang Iron Mine, Shuikoushan Lead and Zinc Mine, Central Copper Plant and Chongqing Temporary Steel Works. In addition, “the Foreign Business Division was established in charge of the export of wolfram and antimony”. The investment into these projects came "mostly from treasury allocation and partly from the profits of wolfram and antimony export".[1] However, because of a lack of capital and the outbreak of the Anti-Japanese War, most projects did not achieve the expected effects.

After the outbreak of the Anti-Japanese War, the political and economic demands created a second development opportunity for the Resources Commission. According to *The Evolution of the National Resources Commission*, in March 1938, the Resources Commission was transferred to the Ministry of Economy and its responsibilities also "changed from economic planning and industry development to state-operated industry development". The organization charter stipulated by the government specified the four main responsibilities of the Resources Commission: "1) found and manage basic industrial enterprises; 2) develop and operate strategically important mines; 3) found and manage fuel related businesses; 4) handle other government designated businesses". Thus the Resources Commission changed from an official state capital industrial and mining monopoly to a designated agency of state capitalism.

After transferred to the Ministry of Economy, the Resources Commission took over several enterprises from the former Ministry of Industry and the former Construction Commission. By the end of 1938, the Resources Commission controlled 63 companies in total.[2] During the 8-year Anti-Japanese War, the Resources Commission focused on two businesses: 1) to manage the barter trade with the Soviet Union and the United States through the export of tungsten, antimony, tin and mercury; 2) to manage the development and operation of industrial, mining and electric businesses. By the end of the Anti-Japanese War, the Resources Commission held jurisdiction over 130 businesses, including 115 manufacturing companies while others were service and management agencies including the Telegraph Service and the Tungsten Administration. Among the

1 Resources Commission, ed., *History of the Resources Commission*, quoted in Chen Zhen, ed., *Historical Files of China's Modern Industry*, Vol. 3, Sanlian Bookstore, 1961, p.839.; Wu Taichang, Review of Monopoly Activities of the Resources Commission of the KMT Nationalist Government, *Researches of Chinese Economic History*, Issue 3, 1986.

2 Ibid, pp.840 842-844.

115 manufacturing companies, 57 were solely invested by the Commission, accounting for 50.9%, 41 were joint-ventures between the Commission, private investors or other agencies, accounting for 34.7% and the other 17 were partly invested by the Commission.[1]

During the war, the Resources Commission invested mostly in heavy industries characterized with capital intensive, slow economic return and high technical requirement. Statistics show, by 1941 state-operated enterprises in the Kuomintang-controlled region made an actual investment of 800 million yuan, 600 million of which were made by the Resources Commission.[2] Over 95% of the Commission's investment went into heavy industries such as electricity, oil, iron and steel, machinery, mineral mining and coal mining.[3] As a result, in the Kuomintang-controlled region, the Resources Commission had full control over the production of gasoline, kerosene, diesel, natural gas, tungsten, antimony, tin and mercury, and produced 68.3% of iron and steal, 46.5% of cast iron and 35.9% of electricity. [4]

During the Anti-Japanese War, taking advantage of the favorable conditions in the home front and state power, the Resources Commission expanded quickly. "In 1942, the National Resources Commission's assets reached 800 million yuan, accounting for 40% of modern capital and 55% of state capital in the home front."[5] By concentrating on the production of energy and raw materials, the Resources

1 Zheng Youkui, Cheng Linsun and others, *Resources Commission in Old China: History and Evaluation*, Shanghai Academy of Social Sciences Press, 1991, p.107.

2 Chen Mingyuan, On Improving Government Businesses, *Financial Review*, Vol. 11, Item 4, April 1944, quoted in Chen Zhen, ed., *Historical Files of China's Modern Industry*, Vol. 3, Sanlian Bookstore, 1961, pp.1419-1420.

3 Resources Commission, ed., *The Work of the Resources Commission Since Liberation*, quoted in Xue Yi, *A Study of Resources Commission*, Social Sciences Academic Press, p. 297.

4 Special Report on Industry and Mining in the Eight Years of the Anti-Japanese War, quoted in Xue Yi, *A Study of Resources Commission*, p. 295.

5 Wu Taichang, Formation of the KMT's State Monopoly Capital, quoted in Jian Rui, An Overview of the Development of KMT Bureaucrat Capital, *Researches in Chinese Economic History*, Item 3, 1986.

Commission, controlling national economy, became the most important economic monopoly agency of the Nanjing Government and established the monopoly of state capital in the industrial and mining sectors.

3. Province-owned Enterprises on the Home Front during the Anti-Japanese War

After the outbreak of the Anti-Japanese War, state capital enterprises on the home front entered a period of development.While the military, the Ministry of Communications, the Ministry of Economy and the national banking system were investing and building new enterprises, different provincial governments were playing a major role in the development of state capital enterprises by founding province-owned enterprises. Before the war, province-owned enterprises had rather common, especially in inland provinces. Because of separatist warlord regimes were rather common under the Beiyang Government, some local government and warlords enjoyed a relatively high level of fiscal independence. To develop economy and strengthen military power so as to consolidate their rule, these local governments and warlords invested heavily in modern industries. Province-owned enterprises in Guangdong, Guangxi, Shanxi and Yunnan were very typical. Whether solely funded by the provincial government, jointed invested by government and private capital, or franchised to bank consortium, these enterprises took very diverse forms.

In August 1933, the Shanxi provincial government established the Northwest Industrial and Commercial Company, a comprehensive, all-embracing company in charge of various economic matters within the province. "With the company, under the General and Assistant Managers were four divisions including textile, local produce, mining and chemical and the Machinery Management Office. It managed all major province-owned mines."[1] In a sense, from the Beiyang Government to the outbreak

1 Yang Jixuan, Chuangkang Industrial and Commercial Company in the Context of Provincial Enterprise Development, *Sichuan Economic Monthly*, Vol. 1, Item 4, quoted in Chen Zhen, ed., *Historical Files of China's Modern Industry*, Vol. 3, Sanlian Bookstore, 1961, p. 1151.

of the Anti-Japanese War, "in the development of capitalism in inland provinces, state capital of a lower level played a dominant role". [1]

After the outbreak of the Anti-Japanese War, China's economic center moved inland. State capitalism grew in an unprecedented way when the central government joined hands with local governments. Established in Guizhou Province in June 1939 as advocated by the provincial government, the Guizhou Enterprise Group was the first government company in charge of the operation of province-owned businesses. Since then, provincial government companies developed rapidly across China. By early 1942, similar companies or preparation organizations had been established in 16 provinces, including Guizhou, Yunan, Sichuan, Xikang, Guangxi, Guangdong, Fujian, Jiangxi, Hunan, Hubei, Shaanxi, Gansu, Ningxia, Shanxi, Shandong and Anhui; that is, "in over half of the provinces in China with increasing market shares". "Such companies and organizations inevitably played a uniquely important role in the development of new economy."[2]

The following table lists the development of provincial enterprise groups by 1943:

Table 6-3: Provincial Enterprise Groups on Home Front During the Anti-Japanese War

Unit: thousand yuan

Provincial Enterprise	Date of Establish-ment	Total Assets	Local Government Share	Central Government Share	Private Share	Date of Capital Verification	Remarks
Guangdong Provincial Enterprise Group	1 941.9	40 000	20 000		20000	1941.9	

1 Wu Taichang, Monopoly of KMT State Capital in Industrial and Mining Industries and a Comparison with Private Capital, *Researches in Chinese Economic History*, Issue 3, 1987.

2 Resource Commission Reports, Vol. 2, Item 2, quoted in Chen Zhen, ed., *Historical Files of China's Modern Industry*, Vol. 3, Sanlian Bookstore, 1961, p. 1155.

contd.

Provincial Enterprise	Date of Establish-ment	Total Assets	Local Government Share	Central Government Share	Private Share	Date of Capital Verification	Remarks
Others		11 000	8 500	2 500		1942	Joint ventures with the Resources Commission
Shanxi Northwest Industrial and Commerical Group	1 932.1	10 000	10 000				
Guangxi Provincial Enterprise Group	1 941.9	100 000	69 000		31000	1942.7	Founding Capital of 50 million yuan
Enterprise Bureau and Economic Committee affiliated companies of Yunan		275 000	110 00	16 500		1942.6	Economic Committee affiliated enterprises invested 350 million yuan, Enterprise Bureau invested 220 million. The left column refers to industrial and mining businesses invested by the two government agencies. Local government share was estimated to account for 40%.

contd.

Provincial Enterprise	Date of Establish-ment	Total Assets	Local Government Share	Central Government Share	Private Share	Date of Capital Verification	Remarks
Dianxi Provincial Enterprise Group	1939.9	20000	20000			1939	Founding capital of 50 million yuan with 30 million yuan invested by the Enterprise Bureau and therefore not double counted.
Guizhou Provincial Enterprise Group	1939.3	20000	3500	16500		1942.5	Founding capital of 6 million yuan.
Sichuan-Xikang Industrial Group	1942.3	70000	15000	50000	5000	1942.3	
China Industrial Group of Sichuan	1939.7	60000	6000	48000	6000	1942.3	Founding capital of 12 million yuan.
Others		200000	50000	150000		1942	Estimate of the Ministry of Economy
Fujian Provincial Enterprise Group	1940.7	15000	15000			1940.7	Merger with the pharmaceutical company and the trading company increased the total assets to 50 million yuan.
Anhui Provincial Enterprise Group	1941.10	10000	6000	2000	2000	1941.10	
33 Government-owned companies in Zhejiang		80000	50000	30000		1942	Estimate of the Ministry of Economy
Jiangxi Provincial Enterprise Group	1940.12	30000	13000	17000		1942.12	

contd.

Provincial Enterprise	Date of Establish-ment	Total Assets	Local Government Share	Central Government Share	Private Share	Date of Capital Verification	Remarks
Association of Heavy Industries	1942	20000	10000	10000		1942	Joint ventures with the Resources Commission
Hunan Provincial Enterprise Group	1943.11	60000	30000	30000		1942	Authorized capital of 600 million yuan. Actual assets evaluated at 360 million yuan upon establishment, that is 60 million yuan adjusted according to currency value in 1942.
Hubei Provincial Enterprise Group	1941.1	50000	30000	20000		1941.1	Shares are estimated.
Gansu Development Group	1941.5	10000	3000	7000		1941.12	Joint ventures with the Resources Commission and the Ministry of War
Others		43000	23000	20000		1942	
Shaanxi Provincial Enterprise Group	1940.12	20000	20000			1940.12	Founding capital of 30 million yuan, including 10 million yuan private capital
Suiyuan Provincial Enterprise Group	1941	5000	5000			1941	
Xikang Provincial Enterprise Group	1942	12000	6000	6000		1942	
合计		1161000	523000	574000	64000		

Notes: Local government shares refer to the investment by local and provincial governments; Central government shares are the investment from the Resources Commission, the Ministry of Economy and government banks.

Source: Chen Zhen, ed., *Historical Files of China's Modern Industry*, Vol. 3, quoted in Wu Taichang, Monopoly of KMT State Capital in Industrial and Mining Industries and a Comparison with Private Capital, *Researches in Chinese Economic History*, Issue 3, 1987.

According to this list, by 1943, there had been dozens of enterprise groups jointly share held or invested by local governments and central government shares on the home front. Out of the total assets of 1.161 billion yuan, local governments invested 523 million yuan, accounting for 45%, central government shares reached 574 million yuan, accounting for 49.4% and private shares added up to 64 million, or just 5.5%. In the process, the Central Government as the backbone grew by the largest margin while local government capital was strengthened and became an important part of state capital of the Nanjing Government. In this sense, of all the state capital enterprises, besides those funded by various ministries and the Resource Commission, provincial enterprise groups played a most significant role as a relatively comprehensive large-scale state capitalist enterprise system.

Most provincial enterprise groups were managed by local governments and organized as share-holding companies in charge of various economic affairs within their respective provinces. They constituted an important part of state-operated enterprises and state capital during the War and became the economic pillar on the home front. Some scholars have commented on their importance as: "In different provinces, these provincial enterprise groups formed the backbone of new economy. For example, of the 100~150 million yuan industrial capital in Guizhou, its provincial enterprise group accounted for 25 million yuan with its total assets reaching over 67 million yuan. Guangxi Provincial Enterprise Group controlled 17 industrial companies with a total capital of 18 million yuan; that is, 11 times as much as the total capital of 1,733,995 yuan of all the 36 registered private industrial companies. Guangtong Provincial Enterprise Group invested in 8 industrial companies with a total capital of 16 million yuan, five times as much as the total of 3.29 million yuan of 42 register private companies. Though we lacked the figures for other provinces, there were good reasons to believe similar conditions in other provinces, taking into account the relatively weak and immature development of government-private joint ventures. Therefore, it was clear that provincial enterprise groups played a disproportionately important role in economic development."[1]

Provincial enterprise groups usually controlled several to tens of sole invested, holding or joint-venture companies. The investigation of the Province-owned Enterprise Supervision Administration of the Ministry of Economy showed the following conditions in the beginning of 1942. 1) Jiangxi, Hunan, Guangxi, Yunnan and Shanxi had built metallurgical businesses while Shaanxi and Ningxia were building, making a total of 81 plants; 2) Jiangxi, Fujian, Guizhou, Shanxi and Shaanxi had machinery plants, Anhui and Ningxia were planning while Henan and Hunan were preparing, making a total of 10; 3) two motor works had been established in Zhejiang and Guizhou ; 4) Anhui, Hubei, Guangdong, Yunnan, Guizhou, Shandong and Shanxi had build chemical factories, Gansu, Shanxi, Henan, Fujian, Xikang and Hunan were preparing while Jiangxi was planning, making a total of 31; 5) Jiangxi, Hubei, Fujian, Guangxi, Yunnan, Guizhou, Shandong and Shanxi had textile mills, four mills were planned while preparations were made for six, making a total of 24; 6) there were 66 companies in other fields. "There were altogether 141 plants, including 25 in Shaanxi (many still in planning or preparation), 20 in Jiangxi , 14 in Guizhou, and 9 in Hubei. Qinghai had the fewest plants." [2]

These provincial enterprise groups did business in very diverse fields and generally fell into two categories. 1) joint ventures in collaboration with the Resources Commission and other government agencies were most in mining, electricity and other basic industries. During the War, there were over 40 such

1 Wu Lianyan, On the Development of Provincial Enterprises and Economic Construction, *Guangxi Enterprise Quarterly*, Vol. 2, Item 1, Jan. 1944, quoted in Zhang Zhongmin, *State-owned Enterprises During the Nanjing Nationalist Government*, Shanghai University of Finance and Economics Press, 2007, pp.199-200.

2 Resource Commission Reports, Vol. 2, Item 2, quoted in Chen Zhen, ed., *Historical Files of China's Modern Industry*, Vol. 3, Sanlian Bookstore, 1961, p. 1156.

joint ventures between provincial governments and the Resources Commission. In general, these joint ventures were operated and managed by the Resources Commission or other government agencies. 2) Companies solely funded by provincial governments or joint investment by government banks, other government agencies and local governments did business mostly in civil industries such as food, textile, leather, chemical, construction materials and household appliances. In these companies, local government funded companies played a major role, serving as supplementary to the first category. These two categories of state capital enterprises greatly expanded the Kuomintang's state capital and consolidated its dominance in the economic field on the home front. Their development was the epitome of the robust growth of state capital during the Anti-Japanese War.

4. State Capital Enterprise Groups After the Anti-Japanese War

After the victory of the Anti-Japanese War in 1945, the Executive Yuan established the National Confiscation Commission, in charge of the confiscation and handling of Japanese and Japanophile assets. With such confiscation, state capital reached the peak of its development in modern China.

To confiscate the businesses in the Japanese-controlled region, the Nanjing Government established the Confiscation Bureaus and Confiscation Supervision Commission in the Jiangsu-Zhejiang-Anhui, Guangdong-Guangxi-Fujian, Hebei-Beiping-Tianjin, Shandong-Qingdao regions, established the Confiscation Commissioner Offices in Henan and Wuhan, and the Confiscation Commissions in Northeast China and Taiwan. Since Japanese assets were limited in Hunnan and Jiangxi, no special agencies were established and relevant matters were to be handled by the respective provincial government. Different ministries also set up their own agencies to assist the above mentioned organizations to confiscate, holding and transporting assets relevant to the field of responsibility of different ministries. The Ministry of Economy dealt with factory and mine machinery, raw materials and finished products; the Ministry of Communications with railways, highways, air transportation and post service; the Minister of Finance with money shops; and the Central Trust with real estates. By the end of 1946, except in Northeast China, confiscation and taking-over were over in general. Not counting communications related assets, the Nanjing Government confiscated a total assets of 2,324.56 million yuan (adjusted according to local price) in the forms of plants, businesses, real estates and furniture, warehouses and docks, gold, silver and foreign exchanges and vehicles (not including national defense and other military supply). [1]

During the period, building on the foundation of wartime economic basis and through the confiscation of enemy assets, the Nanjing Government established several national and local state-operated enterprise groups, as a result of which state capital greatly increased its role in the national economy and further strengthened its monopoly in various sectors of economy. The percentage of state capital in national new industrial economy jumped from 50.5% in 1944 to 80% in 1946. If the development index of state capital in industrial and mining sectors was assigned as 100 in 1945, the index reached 1,054 in 1946 and 2,137 in 1947, making a increase of 20 times in three years.[2] The Resources Commission and Merchants Group expanded greatly while China Textile Industries Inc. (hereafter as China Textile was a new state capital enterprise group built on confiscated enemy assets. In the post-Anti-Japanese War state capital system, these three groups were very representative.

The following constitutes a sketch of the development of these three groups:

After the victory of the war, the Resources Commission had already monopolized industrial and mining sectors in the Kuomintang-controlled region. Confiscation of enemy assets and relevant businesses promoted the further development of the Resources Commission. This became the third development opportunity for the Commission, making it the largest state capital monopoly group in industry and mining.

1 Jian Rui, An Overview of the Development of KMT Bureaucrat Capital, *Researches in Chinese Economic History*, Item 3, 1986.

2 Zheng Youkui, *China's International Trade and Business*, p. 167, quoted in Huang Yifeng, Jiang Duo and others, *Compradors in Old China*, Shanghai People's Press, 1982, p.203.

Before the end of the war, the Resources Commission had sent several investigators to the occupied territory to collect information on enemy economy and compiled reports as "reference to the rejuvenation program". In March 1945, the Commission drafted and submitted to the Executive Yuan the *Confiscation Plan for Industries and Mines in the Occupied Territory.* According to the plan, confiscated enemy industry and mining businesses would be handed over to the Resources Commission to "build the foundation for state owned businesses". Accordingly, the Commission established the Preparatory Committee for the Take-over of Industrial and Mining Businesses in an effort to prepare for confiscation. In October 1945, proposed by Song Ziwen, then President of the Executive Yuan, and approved Chiang Kai-shek, the National Commission of Confiscation and Reclamation (hereafter as the Confiscation Commission) was established under the leadership of Weng Wenhao, then Vice President of the Executive Yuan and Director of the Resources Commission. In the same month, *Enemy Assets Confiscation Methods in Reclaimed Areas* was enacted, according to which the Ministry of War would take over military supply, the Ministry of Communications land vehicles, Merchants Group boats and ships, Central Trust real estates and the Resources Commission industrial and mining businesses. For that matter, the Resources Commission, as instructed, sent over 2,000 management personnel and 800 middle and above level professionals to deal with confiscation matters.[1]

By June 1946, the Resources Commission had taken over 2,401 businesses, the region and number of which are shown in Table 6-4.

Table 6-4 Enemy Industries and Mining Confiscated by the Resources Commission

	Jiangsu-Zhejian-Anhui	Hunan-Hubei-Jiangxi	Guangdong-Guangxi-Fujian	Shandong-Henan-Shanxi	Hebei-Chahaer-Rehe-Suiyuan	Northeast China	Taiwan	Total
Metallurgical	28	4	4	1	20	15	8	86
Machinery	82	18	12	25	54	32	45	269

1 Xue Yi, *Study on the Resources Commission of the Nationalist Government*, Social Sciences Academic Press, 2005, pp. 347, 352 and 353.

contd.

	Jiangsu-Zhejian-Anhui	Hunan-Hubei-Jiangxi	Guangdong-Guangxi-Fujian	Shandong-Henan-Shanxi	Hebei-Chahaer-Rehe-Suiyuan	Northeast China	Taiwan	Total
Hardware	23	1		3	49	18	6	100
Electric Appliances	29				21	5	11	66
Chemical	173	39	50	55	110	51	111	598
Textile	149	27	8	26	27	7	17	261
Garment	26	2		2	8		2	40
Catering	81	63	17	22	40	1	29	259
Print and stationery	1	1		1	12		16	31
Other Industries	37	10	4	17	25	3	31	127
Mining	2	15	4	23	6	11	16	71
Electrics	19	6	10	2	5	2	1	45
Finance	43	32		37	285		38	435
Executive and Academic Institutions	7					3	2	13
总计	700	218	109	214	677	148	335	2 401

Source: *Take-over of Enemy Economy*, Archives of the Economy Department of the Nationalist Government, November 1946, in the archives of the Second Archives Center, quoted in Xi Baotang, *The Nationalist Government and National Economy*, East China Normal University Press, 1998, pp.403-404.

By September 1946, the Resources Commission took over a total of 3,255 industrial and mining businesses. On the basis of industrial and mining businesses under its control on the home front, the Resources Commission strengthened it monopoly in these two sectors in the Kuomintang-controlled region after the war. In the region in 1946, the Commission controlled the production of 100% oil, 70% of steel, iron, antimony, tin, locomotives and motors, 40% of electricity, voltage transformers and light bulbs, over 30% of acid and coal and over 20% of tungsten ore, power machines, ethanol, sugar, cement and paper. "Its industrial production was enough to affect the whole country". However one year later, in 1947, these market shares further expanded: 63% electricity, 33% coal, 90% iron and steel,

100% tungsten and antimony, 70% tin, 45% cement and 90% sugar.[1]

The Resources Commission had a monopoly counterpart in the textile industry: China Textile, the largest monopoly industry agency established by the Nanjing Government in modern China after the Anti-Japanese War. It was first founded in December 1945 in Chongqing upon the victory of the war and then relocated back to Shanghai in January the next year. With its headquarters in Shanghai, China Textile have three branches in Tianjin, Qingdao and Shenyang, and offices in Xi'an, Shashi, Hankou, Guangzhou, Nantong, Hangzhou, Shantou and Zhengzhou. China Textile was built on the basis of 85 confiscated textile companies of various kinds which used to be controlled by eight Japanese textile corporations in China, namely Neiwaimian, Tongxing, Yuhua, Rihua, Toyota, Dakang, Shanghai de Dagong textile corporations, in addition to some other textile mills.

As to why China Textile was established, Minister of Economy, Weng Wenhao explained, "The government confiscated quite a lot of Japanese textile plants. To promote the recovery of the textile industry and supply the market, the government founded China Textile to take charge of relevant businesses."[2] In a confidential documented submitted by the Textile Business Administration to the Ministry of Economy, the purpose of China Textile was put as: "The government is eager to develop the textile industry...Only when the government controls the means to produce textile products can it subside the panic over the lack of textile products, curb the rise of prices and solve the problems with the national economy and people's livelihood...China Textile aims to control to stabilize the price of textile products."[3] As a result, China Textile, the first large state capital textile corporation, was founded.

1 *Take-over of Enemy Economy*, Archives of the Economy Department of the Nationalist Government, November 1946, in the archives of the Second Archives Center, quoted in Xi Baotang, *The Nationalist Government and National Economy*, East China Normal University Press, 1998, pp.403-404.

2 Quoted in Chen Zhen, ed., *Historical Files of China's Modern Industry*, Vol. 3, Sanlian Bookstore, 1961, p. 1445.

3 *The Central Daily*, December 8, 1945.

Focusing on the cotton textile business, China Textile was dominant in China in terms of machinery and production capacity. In 1947, China Textile boasted 1.77 million spins, 330,000 wire bars and 40,000 loom machines, accounting for 39.26%, 70.7% and 60.9% of the total in China then respectively. It produced 426,000 and 745,000 units of cotton yarn and 9.55 million and 16.12 million units of cotton cloth in 1946 and 1947, accounting for 32% and 39%, and 29% and 40% of the total respectively. In addition, half of the 60,000 wool spins and 10,000 silk spins, China textile controlled a half. China Textile employed 85,000 people at its peak and 60,000 people at its low. As a large scale corporation group, China Textile was capable of producing cotton, wool and silk products and of spinning, weaving and dyeing.[1] China Textile's role in Kuomintang's state capital corporation groups was more than clear.

China Textile was also entitled to various government preferential treatments and privileges. First, it had priority access to raw materials at low pries. China Textile took over the raw material stock of Japanese textile plants and could access government imported cotton from the United States and India at low price, before finished products were sold by a general profit margin. Second, it had monopoly in the market. With considerate strength, China Textile controlled the cotton yarn market and was the exclusive supplier of military cotton and cloth. In 1946, it provided 320,000 units of military cloth, the figure of which jumped to 3.5 million units in 1947. Moreover, it was the sole cloth supplier to governments and schools at about 360,000 units in 1946.[2] China Textile also participated in and controlled the silk yarn futures market. All these privileges made China Textile a specialized monopoly, which could harvest vast profits in its business. Moreover, China Textile had a very close relationship with government banks. Its General Manager Shu Yunzhang had long work experience in Bank of China and was a

1 Annual Report of China Textile Management Board 1946, The Second Archives Center, No. 76-279, quoted in Jin Zhihuan, *Study of China Textile Constructions*, Fudan University Press, 2006, p.35.

2 Jian Rui, An Overview of the Development of KMT Bureaucrat Capital, *Researches in Chinese Economic History*, Item 3, 1986.

personal friend of Song Ziwen. As a result, China Textile had the support of the Central Bank in a way impossible to private enterprises.[1]

Merchants Group suffered great losses during the Anti-Japanese War and came out of the war with only 18 ships with a total tonnage of just 20,000 tons.[2] By confiscating enemy boats and ships, Merchants Group quickly expanded its fleet in tonnage and number.

These confiscated boats and ships came most from Japanese invested shipping companies and some State-run Enterprises of the Wang Jingwei regime. In 1945, the Group took over 1,335 boats and ships with a total tonnage of 129,510 tons. Such confiscation did not stop in 1946. By July 1946, Merchants Group had taken over a total of 2,158 boats and ships with a total tonnage of 239,141 tons. The following table shows the details.

Table 6-5 Enemy Boats and Ships Confiscated by Merchants Group

Type of Vessel	September to December 12, 1945		September 1945 to July 1946	
	Number	Tonnage	Number	Tonnage
Oceangoing Vessel	3	1 095	10	18 685
River Steamer	32	32 759	31	42 251
Tugboat	260	9 167	431	22 135
Motor Sailer	135	9 229	235	19 039
Iron Barge	307	60 867	368	101 947
Wooden Barge	317	13 602	698	26 971
Vessel for Special Purposes	281	2 792	385	8 113
Total	1 335	129 510	2158	239 141

Source: 1. Archives of Merchants Group, "Take-over of Enemy Ships by the Merchant Group", dated Dec. 21, 1945.

2. Archives of Merchants Group, "Take-over of Enemy Ships Handled by the Merchant Group", dated August 28, 1946.

Quoted from Zhang Houquan, ed., *The History of the Merhant Group (Modern History), China Communications Press*, 1988, p.512.

1 Commerce and Industry Historical Records, Vol. 4, Cultural and Historical Records Publishing House, 1984, p.153, quoted in quoted in Xi Baotang, *The Nationalist Government and National Economy*, East China Normal University Press, 1998, p 422.

2 Wang Ju, *Final Glory of Shanghai's Textile Industry in Modern China*, Shanghai Academy of Social Sciences Press, 2004, p.52.

Enemy vessels confiscated by Merchants Group were also handled by it. Besides those detained for use by the itself, Merchants Group returned some to their original owner, priced some for sale, transferred some to other government agencies and rented some to other shipping companies. By 1947, the Group had had 314 boats and ships for use with a tonnage of 81,297 tons and another 39 (1,550 tons) vessels waiting to be handled. Moreover, Merchants Group also purchased a great many of vessels from other countries. By June 1948, the Group had a fleet of 490 vessels with a total tonnage of 409,200 tons, including 108 (315,184 tons) large ocean going ships or river steamers. That was the peak of the Group in terms of number of vessels since its founding. The total tonnage was 4.74 times as much as that on the eve of the war (early 1937), and 17.2 times as much as that shortly before the end of the war (early 1945, while the tonnage of large ocean going ships or river steamers was 5.76 times and 13.8 times as much as that on the eve and the end of the war respectively. In addition to vessels, Merchants Group also reclaimed 34 docks, 162 warehouses, 4,390 mu of real estates and many ship yards.[1]

Thanks to the privileges bestowed by the Nanjing Government, Merchants Group's capital swelled. With 2.97 million yuan on the eve of the War, its assets quickly reached 1,669.51 million yuan in 1945, an increase of 561 times and further to 600 million as adjusted in "golden yuan" notes.[2]

The rapid expansion of Merchants Group was just a typical case of the rapid growth of state capital corporate groups in the transportation and communication sector, as shown in Table 6-6.

1 Zhang Houquan, ed., *History of Merchants Group (Modern History)*, China Communications Press, 1988, p.523.

2 Archives of Merchants Group, Operations of Merchants Group from Reoperation in Chongqing to 1947, quoted in Zhang Houquan, ed., *History of Merchants Group (Modern History)*, China Communications Press, 1988, pp.512-513.

Table 6-6 State Capital and Private Capital Shipping Companies, 1935-1948

Index: the tonnage of 1935=100

Year	National Total			State Capital			Private Capital			Percent of State Capital	
	Number of Vessels	Tonnage		Number of Vessels	Tonnage		Number of Vessels	Tonnage		Vessels	Tonnage
		Tons	Index		Tons	Index		Tons	Index		
1935	3895	675173	100	28	71117	100	3867	604056	100	0.7	11
1946	2351	669474	99	533	302418	425	1818	367056	61	23	45
1947	3615	1032305	153	612	450670	634	3003	581635	97	17	44
1948	4032	1092217	162	464	477086	671	3568	615131	102	12	44

Source: Yan Zhongping and others, ed., *Selected Economic Statistics of Modern China,* Science Press, 1955, p. 233.

Statistically, the national tonnage in 1948 was only just 1.5 times as much as that of 1935 while the total state capital tonnage had increased by 6 times. In terms of percentage of total number of vessels, state capital shipping companies' share increased from 11% in 1935 to 44%. Therefore, taking into account state capital's monopoly of big shipping companies and large ships, state capital enterprises had an unchallenged dominant advantage in the shipping industry.

These were just some of the high-profile state capital corporate groups. The development of these groups highlighted the rapid growth of state capital of the Nanjing Government after the Anti-Japanese War. In fact, statistics of the percentage of state capital in national economy in the Kuomintang-controlled region further proved its overall sweeping strength was not limited to certain sectors or corporate groups.

Table 6-7 Percentage of State Capital Enterprises' Production in the Kuomintang-controlled Region in 1947

Products	Percentage in the KMT-controlled Region%	Products	Percentage in the KMT-controlled Region%
Iron and Steel	98	Caustic soda	65
Machinery (capital in 1942)	72	Sulfuric acid	80
Electricity	78	spin	60

contd.

Products	Percentage in the KMT-controlled Region%	Products	Percentage in the KMT-controlled Region%
Coal	80	Machine-made sugar	90
Tungsten, antimony, tin, mercury, copper and oil	100	Bleaching powder	41
Cement	67	Fertilizer	67
Machine-made paper	50	hydrochloric acid	45
Exported plant oil	70		

Source: Chen Zhen, ed., *Historical Files of China's Modern Industry*, Vol. 3, Sanlian Bookstore, 1961, p. 1445.

Notes: The original table used "bureaucrat capital". However, more scholars know prefer "state capital" as a more accurate term. So, adjustments have been made accordingly.

There was another note to the original table: "Not including industrial products manufactured by provincial enterprises, the Ordinance-affiliated plants, companies operated by various ministers and other bureaucrat capital companies in the disguise of 'private business'". This means, if products manufactured by these government sponsored or similar companies were taken into account, the market share of state capital product will be even higher. All these figures show that with the confiscation of Japanese assets after the Anti-Japanese War, state capital of the Nanjing Government expanded drastically, and thus gained greater control over the national economy.

The old concept of "bureaucrat capital" actually referred to two parts:state capital and baron capital championed by the Four Families. Since the reform and opening up, with the emphasis on "seeking truth from facts" and "freeing the minds", scholars have had different opinions on the concept of "bureaucrat capital". It is argued that "bureaucrat capital" was a common sense concept without a clear definition. "In politico-economy terminologies, it is, in essence, state capitalism under different regimes".[1] From the perspective of economics, "bureaucrat capital" is just a popular political term with neither its connotation or

1 Xu Dixin and Wu Chengming, ed., *History of Capitalist Development in China*, Vol. 1, People's Publishing House, 1985, p.18.

denotation specifically defined.[1] It is also argued that it is "inappropriate" to take both private investment of bureaucrats and state capital as "bureaucrat capital". Therefore, it is recommended "to replace 'bureaucrat capital', an ambiguous and problematic term, with 'state capital' or 'state monopoly capitalism'".[2] The lack of clearly defined connotation and denotation has made "bureaucrat capital" a problem in the study of modern Chinese economic history.[3] For these reasons, more and more scholars prefer "state capital" or "state capitalism" to "bureaucrat capital".

In fact, a study of the origin of the concept of "bureaucrat capital"and the reasons for the use of this highly political but condemned and hated term shows how those baron families had been taken advantage of their political power, intelligence and monopoly of resources to feather their own nests with public goods. Prof. Wu Chengming pointed out that the term of "bureaucrat capital" gained popularity in 1940 when Kuomintang bureaucrats were exploiting the people and monopolizing industry and commerce. When reported, these problems became widely known.[4] After the victory of the Anti-Japanese War, confiscation of Japanese assets became "plundering" to a certain extent. By using the political power, bureaucrats joined hands with business tycoons who controlled the financial sector to build privileged corporations under the disguise of private businesses, each with a monopoly of a certain resource, for their own benefits. These many privileged corporations, especially those registered as private, were particularly powerful, especially those corporations with close connections with those baron families. Because of their special background and lucrative business

1 Wu Li, The Concept of 'Bureaucrat Capital' and How to Define It During Confiscation, *Journal of Chinese Communist Party History Studies*, No. 2, 1991.

2 Ding Richu, Issues of Bureaucrat Capital and Bureaucrat Capitalists, in *Modernization and Capitalists in Modern China*, Yunnan University Press, 1994, p.137.

3 Du Xuncheng, *National Capitalism and the Old Chinese Government 1840-1937*, Shanghai Academy of Social Sciences Press, 1991, p.4.

4 Wu Chengming, *Chinese Capitalism and Domestic Market*, China Social Sciences Press, 1985, p.116.

operation, these corporations were referred to among the public and in the media as "official businesses". Some of the most typical cases included Fuzhong Industry, Yangtze Construction and CDFC controlled by the Kong and the Song families.[1] In terms of their operations, these corporations took advantage of their political power and intelligence for the benefit of some small groups. These corporations and their operation made "bureaucrat capital" an infamous public condemnation.

Shortly after the Anti-Japanese War, the Nanjing Government implemented a series of fiscal policies, the most obvious change of which was to replace foreign exchange control with an open gold and foreign exchange market and to cancel the policies of strict trade control and procurement and distribution control by canceling the Trade Commission and its affiliated trading companies and adopting more open trade policies. Against the background of inflation and currency depreciation, the Nanjing Government adopted the tagged low exchange rate policy, which inevitably benefited those dealing with import business. "Because of high price, low exchange rate, the value of yuan differed greatly from domestic market to foreign market. Importers could use cheap foreign exchange to buy products and sell them at high prices in China at a 300% profit margin". "Take the import of sulfur black as an example. According to the recollection of a business insider, the cost of importing sulfur black from the United States to Shanghai was about $40 per 50 kilograms. However, if sold in Shanghai in yuan, the money could exchange for $500. Then this $500 could import another 600 kilograms of sulfur black. This way, in 4~5 months, besides tariffs and other cost, the fortune of

1 After the Anti-Japanese War, the state shares of the CDFC were sold to private owners (mostly government officials including those from the Kong and Song families and financial barons) at low cost, the company changed it nature and business and became a typical case of "bureaucracy+baron capital". Zheng Huixin, *From Investment Corporation to Official Business: Founding and Operations of CDFC*, The Chinese University (of Hong Kong) Press, 2001.

the dealer could multiply by tens of times." [1]

Thanks to their unique political position and special relations with the government, corporations controlled by the Kong, Song and other baron families were particularly active. On one hand, they served as exclusive sales agencies of American corporations and thus monopolized automobile, electric appliances, pharmaceutical, luxury products and other non-productive products. On the other, with their privileges, they fraudulently purchased a large amount of foreign exchange and applied for big import quotas and harvested excessive profits by taking advantages of favorable foreign exchange rates.

These corporations are characterized with privilege, monopoly and self-interest. When exposed, they became the focal target of concern and criticism. Fu Sinian, who enjoyed high prestige among the academia and the political circle, published a series of articles, condemning the economic policies advocated by Kong Xiangxi and Song Ziwen and arguing that baron family corporations were "destroying Chinese economic by sweeping Chinese industries and workers off their feet and causing major outflow of national fortune". In his article titled "Baron Capital Must Be Eliminated", Fu Sinian criticized Song Ziwen for his "insatiable and insane desire to dominate" who bought and turned to 'Song family businesses", through CDFC, Qishuyan Power Plant, Capital Power Plant, Jiji Hydro Power Station, Huainan Coal Mine and Bole Coal Mine.[2]

When limited constraints were imposed on the privileged, this baron corporations had caused very serious damage to their own reputation and to the society. Featured with the combination of power and interest, personal-family-small group-interest orientation and exemption from law and regulations, baron capital was the worst of all capital. The development of baron capital meant the

1 Shanghai Academy of Social Sciences Institute of Economics and Shanghai International Trade Association Academic Committee, ed., *Shanghai's Foreign Trade*, Vol. 2, Shanghai Academy of Social Sciences Press, 1989, p.171.

2 Quoted in Wu Jingping, *Biography of Song Ziwen*, Fujian People's Publishing House, 1998, p.505.

suffering of the society. In his reasoning for the confiscation of the monopoly capital of the Chiang, Song, Kong and Chen families in his three economic guidelines of new democratic revolution, Mao Zedong argued, "Monopoly capitalism, foreign imperialism, land lords and old-style rich peasants combined makes comprador-feudal state monopoly capitalism...which has a popular name in China as 'bureaucrat capital'."[1]

The authors find three core factors in the old version of "bureaucrat capital", namely power, self-interest and exemption from law and regulations. Therefore, in the discussion about replacing "bureaucrat capital" with state capital and state capitalism after reform and opening-up, it is argued that "bureaucrat capital" has two components:1) state capital enterprises, including not only large state capital corporate groups like the Resources Commission, its affiliated companies and Merchants Group, but also local government-owned corporations; 2) baron capital enterprises, the real bureaucrat capital, including Fuzhong Group, Yangtze Group and CDFC, and local baron capital. In a sense, baron capital based on power and self-interest was essentially different from state capital corporations in terms of purpose and social function. Therefore, it is necessary to differentiate the two; that is, state capital does not include baron capital. Only when "state capital" is used this way can the research into modern Chinese economic history be better targeted.

1 Mao Zedong, Current Situation and Our Tasks, in *Selected Works of Mao Zedong*, Vol. 4, People's Publishing House, 1960, p.1253.

Part III

Development of State Capital and State Capital Enterprises 1949—1978

Chapter 7

Establishment and Development of State-Operated Economy of the People's Republic of China

In its early years, the People's Republic of China (hereafter as the PRC or China), by confiscating bureaucrat capital and enemy assets, inheriting the public operated economy of the liberated region and procuring foreign enterprises, established its state-owned economy system, which was directly operated by the central and local governments, and therefore called "state-operated economy"[1]. Stated operated economy played a leading role among the various economic elements during the new democratic period. Therefore, it was the basic economic guideline of the PRC government to prioritize the development of state-operated economy. *The Common Programme* stipulates, "State-operated economy was socialist in nature. Any business which is of significance to and capable of controlling national economy must be operated by the government in a unified way. State-owned

1 To differentiate state-owned enterprises operated by the Central Government and local governments, those operated by the Central Government were referred to as "state-operated economy" while those by local governments as "local state-owned economy".

resources and enterprises are all public property shared by all people and therefore are the material foundation for the prosperity of the People's Republic and the leader of social economy as a whole."

1. Establishment of State-Operated Economy[1]

The founding of the PRC on October 1, 1949 marked the beginning of a new stage of state capital in China. However, state capital went through a major change in accordance with the change of state system. State capital was no longer controlled by big landlords and big capitalists, but became socialist "state-operated economy" which belonged to all the people and was managed by the people government.

1.1. Socialist State-Operated Enterprises Based on Confiscation of "Bureaucrat Capital"

Upon the founding of the PRC, bureaucrat capital was confiscated and later managed and operated by the government. This was a major source of state-operated economy. Here, bureaucrat capital included both state capital of the Kuomintang Government, and confiscated assets of traitors, war criminals and anti-revolutionaries.

"To confiscate bureaucrat capital for the new democratic country"was one of the three economic guidelines of the new democratic revolution. Before 1949, during the over 20 years rule of the the Nanjing Government, state capital and bureaucrat capital developed in different ways and controlled national economy. According to the statistics published by the Nanjing Government in 1947, in the national total output, industrial enterprises affiliated to the Resources Commission alone accounted for 66% electricity, 33% coal, 90% iron and steel, 100% tungsten and antimony, 70% tin, 45% cement and 90% sugar. In 1947, while loans made by all private banks amounted to about 1 trillion yuan, banks controlled by the

1 China Academy of Social Sciences and the Central Archives, ed., *Selected Economic Archives of the PRC 1949-1952*, Comprehensive Vol., China City Economy Press, 1990, p.198.

Nanjing Government made 17 trillion yuan loans, not including loans made by provincial and municipal government banks. Meanwhile, modern communications and international trade were monopolized by bureaucrat capital. The concentrated and enormous bureaucrat capital served as a foundation for the establishment of state-owned economy of the PRC.

Bureaucrat capital refers to state capital owned by the Kuomintang Government and private capital owned by high-level officials (above county or regiment level), in forms of solely invested enterprises or joint ventures. During the confiscation process, a major issue was to decide which private capital was bureaucrat capital. It started to get urgent when the People's Liberation Army was on strategic counter-offence and started to liberate cities in 1947. In April 1948, the Central Committee of the Communist Party of China (hereafter as the CPC Central Committee), in its response to problems arising from the confiscation of bureaucrat capital in Louyang, developed detailed policies and guidelines. Four different approaches were signed to handle four different types of bureaucrat capital. 1) Government capital of the Kuomintang Government and official assets of Kuomintang party organizations and systems would be directly confiscated; 2) Kuomintang government officials' and military officers' private assets would be directly confiscated if clearly defined or be put into supervision if further clarification was needed to avoid the loss or damage of assets; 3) Investment in private industrial and commercial businesses by Kuomintang's party, government and military organizations and officials would be left untouched for the time being, subject to future confiscation after verification; 4) For private investment in bureaucrat capital enterprises, its ownership, if not illegal encroachment or underbuy, was recognized. On April 25, the CPC Central Committee and the Central Military Commission jointed issued the Proclamation of the People's Liberation Army, reading, "Bureaucrat capital will be confiscated. The people's government will confiscate factories, shops, banks, warehouses, ships, docks, railways, post service, telegraph, electricity, telephone, water supply, farms and pastures operated by the reactionary government or bureaucrats of Kuomintang.

Private investment if verified still belong to its rightful owner." Put differently, confiscation targeted at enterprises owned by the central, provincial and county governments of the Kuomintang regime and those owned by high-level Kuomintang bureaucrats, but not those by low-ranking bureaucrats and small landlords and national capitalists' private investment in bureaucrat enterprises.

Accordingly, bureaucrat capital were confiscated along three stages:

Stage One: During the War of Liberation, the focus was on the confiscation of state capital and State-run Enterprises. Starting with the liberation of Harbin in 1946, such confiscation rolled out after the liberation of Shenyang and Northeast China in November 1948. To ensure smooth transition, the CPC Central Committee developed some concrete policies to properly deal with organizations and people subject to take-over. When Shenyang was liberated in November 1948, Chen Yuan, as the Director of the Military Management Committee of the city, developed the approach characterized with "system for system, from top to bottom, left intact, and take-over first, division later". "In reality, this approach not only prevented chaos but also ensured promptness (with connections built in two days). If not so, there would have been great loss and very negative impact." The take-over endeavors in Beiping, Tianjin, Nanjing and Shanghai all took reference from Shenyang's experience. The Guidelines on Confiscation Bureaucrat Capital Enterprises issued by the CPC Central Committee on January 15, 1949 stipulated the policy of old position, old salary and old system. Directors of confiscated enterprises "if not saboteurs, could retain their old positions" and they were entitled to their "old salaries, bonuses and security policies". "The old organizations and systems shall remain intact while caution must be taken in case of reform or cancellation." Based on the experience of Shenyang, Beiping and Tianjin, a three-step procedure, namely transfer, clearing and confiscation, was proposed to avoid disruption to regular business.

Stage Two: During the take-over of cities and the campaign to crack down on counterrevolutionaries around the founding of the PRC, private assets of enemies, namely traitors, war criminals and counterrevolutionaries, were confiscated.

Limited in amount, these assets laid the foundation for local state-operated enterprises and state-owned assets at the municipal and county levels.

Stage Three: During the campaign to sort out state shares and state assets which started in 1951, bureaucrat assets in the disguise of private investment in private enterprises were confiscated. Through self application, investigation and verification, and registration, national capitalists' shares were set apart from bureaucrat capital, in an effort to solve the remaining questions of the previous two stages. Though bureaucrat capital was limited in confiscated private enterprises, the handling of the issue was rather complicated and of great influence. To avoid regional difference in policy implementation, the CPC Central Committee assigned the right of final verification to the Financial and Economic Committee of the Government Administration Council. In case of un-confiscated private bureaucrat capital and enemy assets, reports should be reported to the People's Government of the Greater Administrative Area and then transferred to the Financial and Economic Committee for approval before implementation. Thanks to such caution and care, great achievements were made at this stage.

The whole bureaucrat capital confiscation process from confiscation of bureaucrat capital to sorting out state shares and state assets lasted about four years. According to incomplete statistics, confiscated bureaucrat capital enterprises concentrated in the following sectors:

The Financial Sector: the Central Bank, Bank of China, Bank of Communications, Farmers Bank of China, Central Trust, Postal Remittances and Savings Bank and Joint Treasury at the national level and over 2,400 provincial and local government banks; government and private joint-venture banks such as Commercial Bank of China, Industrial Bank of China, Siming Bank and Sin Hua Bank, which continued to operate under the leadership of government sent supervisors and with its government shares confiscated; bureaucrat private banks like Yuhua Bank in Shanxi and Yadong Commercial Bank; overseas branches of Bank of China.

The Industrial Sector: the Resources Commission affiliated enterprises; China

Textile, enterprises funded by the ordinance system and the military logistics system of the Kuomintang Government; enterprises funded by the Ministry of Communications, the Ministry of Food and other government ministries; "private" enterprises funded by the Song and Kong families and other high-level bureaucrats; party enterprises funded by the Central Club system; provincial and local bureaucrat capital enterprises. In total, there were 2,858 industrial enterprises with a total employment of 1.29 million, including 138 power plants, 120 coal and oil mines, 15 ferromanganese mines, 83 nonferrous metals mines, 19 steel works, 505 metal works, 107 chemical plants, 48 paper making plants, 241 textile factories and 844 food businesses.

In the Transportation Sector: all transportation enterprises affiliated to the Ministry of Communications and Merchants Group, including 20,000 kilometers of railway, 4,000 locomotives, 4,000 passenger coaches, 47,000 cargo trucks, 30 locomotive and ship maintenance plants, and vessels of various kinds with a total tonnage of 200,000 tons. In addition, the people government also confiscated the bureaucrat capital shares of the Zheng Family Shipping Company, Continental Shipping and Sanbei Company. Because of the revolt of employees of the former Air China and Central Airlines , the 12 planes hijacked by the Kuomintang to Hong Kong were came back on November 9, 1949. As a result of crew revolt, the Hong Kong Branch of Merchants Group and 13 ocean-going ships in the Hong Kong Harbor plead allegiance to the people's government.

The Commercial Sector: the Kuomintang Government operated companies such as Fuxing, Fuhua, China Tea, PetroChina, China Salt, China Silk and China Plant Oil; high-leve bureaucrat owned monopoly trading companies such as Fuzhong, China Import and Export, Gold Mountain, Litai, Yangtze Construction, and Yangtze Industries.

By confiscating bureaucrat capital, socialist state-owned economy had already had a leading role in the financial, modern industrial, communications and trading sectors when the PRC was founded in 1949. In terms of industries, state-operated enterprises had played a major role in national economy, namely 73% installed power capacity, 70% coal, 60% iron, 90% steel, 60% cement, 50% machine tools and 43% cotton spins. In general, state-operated economy accounted for about 50% of the output of major modern industries. In finance, railway, harbor and aviation, state-operated economy had a more dominant advantage.

Local state-operated enterprises large in number but small in size were also established based on confiscated bureaucrat capital and counterrevolutionaries' assets. By the end of 1952, there were over 7,000 local state-operated enterprises across China. 80-90% of these enterprises were medium- and small-sized enterprises confiscated after liberation, less than 10% were newly built and the rest were confiscated government and organization production facilities during the period from 1950 to 1952.

1.2. State-Operated Enterprises Built on the Basis of Public Economy in the Liberated Areas

Although upon the founding of the PRC, most industrial and communications state-operated enterprises were built upon confiscated bureaucrat capital, the financial sector was based on banks in the liberated areas in addition to taken-over and restructured bureaucrat capital banks. Large state-operated commercial banks were also developed from public-operated trade companies in the liberated areas.

A. State-owned Financial System

The People's Bank of China (hereafter as PBOC) originated from banks in the liberated areas. During the Anti-Japanese War and the Liberation War, different liberated areas started to build their own banks, which were constantly merging, dismantling and rebuilding. Upon the end of the Liberation War, there were over 30 banks in the liberated areas. With the liberation of cities, in line with the guideline of "taking over and building banks simultaneously", the PBOC had been taking over bureaucrat capital banks and at the same time establishing PBOC branches across the country. In line with administrative division, the PBOC established a four-layer system made up of the headquarter bank, regional banks at the greater administrative region level, branches at provincial, autonomous region and municipal levels and sub-branches in counties. In cities, branches or sub-branches were built according to the scale and business requirements of the city, with affiliated agencies and offices. Township offices were also built to hand grass-root business.

After restructuring, Bank of China and Bank of Communications also adopted the system of headquarters, branches and sub-branches. Branches affiliated to the headquarters were simultaneously under the jurisdiction of the headquarters and the local PBOC In December 1949, Bank of China Headquarters was relocated in Beijing from Shanghai and so was Bank of Communications Headquarters in January 1950.

On October 20, 1949, the People's Insurance Company of China (PICC) was founded with branches set up across the country. Vice Governor of the PBOC, Hu Jingyun also served as the General Manager of PICC.

By December 1949, the PBOC had established the East China, Mid-South, Northwest and Southwest regional banks, 40 provincial and municipal branches and 1200 sub-branches and offices at the county and city levels. On April 1, 1951, the Northeast Bank was restructured the PBOC Northeast Regional Bank and the Inner Mongolian People's Bank restructured as the Inner PBOC Mongolian Branch. In November 1951, the Xijiang Provincial Bank was restructured as the PBOC Xinjiang Branch. By then, except for Tibet, Hong Kong, Macau and Taiwan, all provinces had established their own branches of the PBOC. In August 1951, as approved by the Government Administration Council, the central government established the Rural Cooperative Bank, with branches across the country

B. State-Operated Commercial and Trading System

Before the founding of the PRC, public-operated commerce developed quickly to guarantee war supply and manage the market. For example, after the North China Trade Company set up by the North China People's Government was dismantled on September 17, 1949, eleven national professional trade companies were established to deal with the trading of coal, local produce, food, articles of daily use, cloth etc. respectively. These companies demonstrated their strength in their efforts to stabilize prices in April 1949, which proved that with government support, these companies were already capably of controlling the market and main commodities in North China. After the founding of the PRC, trade companies of the liberate areas became state-operated and quickly expanded. Major state-operated trade companies came into being during the half year from the fourth quarter of 1949 to the first quarter in 1950.

State-operated foreign trade companies originated in the foreign trade companies in the Northeast and North China liberated areas, whose businesses continued to expand. These old foreign trade companies were restructured as state-operated trade companies after the founding of the PRC. In early 1950, according to the requirements of the Government Administration Council, shops affiliated to government agencies, the military and schools were transferred to these state-operated trade companies.

By early 1951, the Central Government had established 17 trade companies dealing in salt, articles of daily use, cloth, local produce, food, coal, bristles, eggs, tea, import, leather and fur, grease, silk, oil, mines, and export, in addition to 5,519 package companies, retail companies and trust companies. The total employment reached 195,027 people. Products of strategic importance to national economy and people's livelihood, such as food, cotton, cloth, cooking oil, coal, salt, steel, cement, oil and export and import trade, were generally controlled by state-operated enterprises, which provided the PRC government with market control.

1.3 State-Operated Enterprises Handed Over from the Soviet Union, Transferred by Foreign Companies and from Others Sources

According to the Treaty of Yalta signed by the American, British and Soviet heads of state in February 1945, China would protect the Soviet Union's "priority interest and right" in the Dalian Harbor, the Middle East Railway and the South Manchurian Railway and the Soviet Union leased the Lvshun Harbor as a naval base. On August 14, 1945, the Kuomintang Government and the Soviet Union signed the Sino-Soviet Treaty of Friendship and Alliance, recognizing the Treaty of Yalta. According to the Sino-Soviet Treat, all Soviet assistant should go to the

Kuomintang Government; the Soviet Union recognized China sovereignty over and the territorial integrity of North East China; Out Mongolia would became independent; the Soviet Union and the Kuomintang Government shared the ownership and management of the Middle East and South Manchurian Railways; the Dalian Harbor would be open to free trade; and the Soviet Union had the right to station naval and air forces in Lvshun. After the founding of the PRC, Mao Zedong visited the Soviet Union in December 1949 and signed the Sino-Soviety Treat of Friendship, Alliance and Mutual Assistance on February 14, 1950 in Moscow and the Agreement on the Changshun Railway, Lvshun and Dalian. According to the Agreement, the Soviet Union would forsake its privileges in China and transfer the Changchun Railway and relevant properties back to China at no cost; the Soviet military forces would withdraw from Lvshun while the Chinese Government would compensate the Soviet Union for the construction there; the Chinese government had administrative jurisdiction over Dalian and the Soviet Union would transfer all temporarily managed and leased assets to the Chinese government before the end of 1950 (the transfer went smoothly). According to the Agreement and the change of notes between the two countries on the same date, the Soviet Union would, at no cost, hand over Soviet temporarily managed and leased assets, confiscated Japanese assets by Soviet economic agencies and all the assets of the Beijing Barracks back to the PRC government. Such transfer involved altogether 302 property items, including 47 factories, 11 cinemas, 188 residence buildings, 33 warehouses and 23 real estates. Of all these properties, 260 previously were controlled by Soviet economic agencies, of which 24 used to be properties of the Qiulin Corporation and its trade branches. In 1952, the Soviet Union handed over the Changchun Railways and relevant assets, including: the rails from Manzhouli to Suifen and from Harbin to Dalian and Lvshun and their affiliated land, buildings and equipment; vehicles, locomotives, and cargo and passenger carriages, and maintenance stores; power plant, telephone and telegraph services, telecommunication equipment and lines; railway auxiliary lines, office and technical buildings, and residence buildings; economic facilities, affiliated plants and organizations; newly built, restored and procured assets during the joint management period. All these assets became part of state-owned economy.

After the founding of the PRC, many concerned and suspicious foreign companies withdrew their investment and left. This was especially serious after the outbreak of the Korean War when the America-led west imposed economic sanction and embargo on China, which made it difficult for companies in western countries to invest in China. Many foreign companies were taken over by or handed over to the Chinese government. For example, Standard Oil Company China and Shanghai American Commercial Electric Company were taken over as state-operated enterprises while Kailuan Coal and Yizhong Tobacco were handed over to become state-operated enterprises.

1.4 Asset Accounting and Democratic Reform

After the establishment of state-operated enterprises, these enterprises, either confiscated, handed over or inherited, had a major change in its ownership and therefore it became necessary for asset accounting and structural reform. For example, for those confiscated bureaucrat capital enterprises and enterprises and stock shares confiscated from traitors, war criminals and counterrevolutionaries, because of diverse sources, complicated affiliation, sabotage before confiscation (such as personnel flee, incomplete booking and direct asset loss), different dates of confiscation, lack of major reform for the sake of stability in people's life and production, there was a mess in terms of ownership and asset inventory, which needed to be verified as soon as possible. At the same time, since public-operated enterprises of the liberated areas were first built to provide war supply, they were usually small in size, operated in a military or planned fashion and lacked economic accounting (mostly because of too many uncertainties during the war). As commented back then, "meat rots in the pot" and "accounting or not, all profits go to the Treasury". It was urgent to emphasize accounting. When the war ended and the nation regained peace and embarked on economic recovery, it was high time for asset accounting and democratic reform.

1.4.1 Straighten out government shares and assets and clearly define government and private ownership

Mostly confiscated through revolution, most state-operated enterprises, because of diverse sources, different dates of confiscation, and different handlers of confiscation, faced various problems. Some enterprises and assets eligible for confiscation were left out or concealed while some ineligible ones were confiscated. This problem was particularly serious an complicated with respect to government shares and assets in private enterprises. In response, on February 4, 1951, the Government Administration Council issued the Methods for Straightening out Government Shares and Assets in Enterprises, focusing on public-private joint operations and private enterprises with government shares and assets.

According to the Methods, government shares and assets referred to: 1) shares and assets (including loans, and advance money, the same below) owned by the Kuomintang Government and its national economic and financial institutions; 2) shares and assets owned by enemy governments (Japan, Germany and Italy) and their residents in China; 3) confiscated or to-be-confiscated shares and assets owned by war criminals, traitors, bureaucrat capitalists and their enterprises; 4) investment of the people's government, government economic institutions and state-owned enterprises after liberation. In addition, the Central Government should control and own most enterprise shares of Bank of China and Bank of Communications. These enterprise shares would be counted as government shares but their ownership still belonged to these banks. Since Item Three was particularly vulnerable to mistakes, the Government Administration Council issued the "Instructions on the Confiscation of Assets Owned by War Criminals, Traitors, Bureaucrat Capitalists and Counterrevolutionaries", which required: 1) Confiscation of the shares and assets owned by war criminals, traitors, bureaucrat capitalists and counterrevolutionaries was subject to the Government Administration Council's approval of the report from the Greater Administration Area Government. 2) Confiscation of shares and assets of ordinary bandits, special agents, bullies and counterrevolutionaries was subject to the approval of the provincial government (or designated agency) or the provincial people's court and was to be implemented by county (city) people's courts. 3) For assets of the previous two types which were already confiscated, if there was no doubt, no change would be made. Records showed that though accounting for a relatively small share of state-owned capital then, these shares and assets accounted for a major part of government shares and assets that needed to be straightened out, especially for the second category. Fortunately, the Government Administration Council had designed detailed guidelines for the confiscation of counterrevolutionary assets.

The Central Financial and Economic Committee, in accordance with ownership and size of enterprises, assigned local responsible institutions or commissioned local financial and economic commissions to designate responsible institutions to carry out the clearing-up procedure. The designated responsible institution, in collaboration with other relevant institutions (such as business and investment management institutions), would confer with representative private shareholders on the principles and actual plans for share and asset accounting and restructuring of the boards of directors and supervisors. Relevant agreements should be reported to the Central or Local Financial and Economic Committee for approval or for record. For public-private joint operations, the main task was to straighten out government and private shares and assets and to restructure boards of directors and supervisors. For private enterprises with government shares and assets, after being straightened out, one of the three approaches would apply: 1) restructured as government-private limited companies or share-holding limited companies; 2) restructured as private enterprises after the withdrawal of government shares; 3) untouched temporarily with Bank of Communications controlling government shares or local governments commissioned to manage.

Three months after the Methods to Straighten out Government Shares and Assets was issued on February 9, 1951, according to the statistics of Bank of Communications Headquarters, out of the 2,000 public-private joint operations, only 1,252 companies had filed report and only 98 had finished straightening out and became joint-ventures officially with boards of directors and supervisors or state-operated or private enterprises with one party withdrawing its shares. Clearing-up work was still in process. Accordingly, the Central Financial and Economic Committee postponed the deadline and designed supplementary measures accordingly, such as On How to Handle Encroachment in public-private joint operations, On How to Designate Responsible Institutions to straighten out Government Shares and Assets, Supplementary Instructions on Leadership and Share Division in Government-Private Enterprises, and Supplementary Instructions on Leadership Responsibilities in Straightening out Government Shares and Assets.

In this endeavor, the principles of fair, justice and no encroachment aimed to straighten out public and private property right. For example, at first, the government planned to waive the debts between debts between bureaucrat capital enterprises and government and military institutions which existed before liberation. However, after the work started, it became clear that Bank of China and Bank of Communications with their private shares were different from state-owned enterprises. Therefore, it was necessary to liquidate the debts between the two banks and those confiscated enterprises owned by government and military institutions and bureaucrat capital. Accordingly, relative policies were implemented.

1.4.2. Appraise fixed assets and current assets

In the early years of the PRC, the Party and the Government, lacking experience in managing state-operated enterprises, turned to the Soviet model of planned management and accounting. To do so, the first step was to appraise fixed assets and current assets of each enterprise. In April 1951, when politics became stabilized and inflation was brought under control, a relatively stable external environment was created for the operation of businesses. The Central Financial and Economic Committee of the Government Administration Council decided to appraise fixed assets and current assets of state-owned enterprises. From May to

July in 1951, the Central Financial and Economic Committee issued a series of instructions, including On Appraisal of Fixed Assets and current assets of State-Operated Enterprises, Interim Measures to Appraise Fixed Assets and current assets of State-Operated Enterprises, and Interim Measures to Verify current assets of State-Operated Enterprises. According to this instructions, "enterprises operated by the Central Government and Greater Administrative Region Governments must all carry out inventory taking, registration, appraisal and verification of fixed assets and current assets".

To carry out this endeavor, the National Asset and Fund Appraisal Committee (NAFAC) was established with affiliated local institutions. The NAFAC's plan for appraisal became the main tasks of state-operated enterprises and relevant departments in charge from September to December in 1951.

This appraisal campaign applied to all actual assets (including ledge asset and unlisted asset), which would be revalued in renminbi (RMB). Actual assets would be divided into fixed assets and current assets. In addition to raw materials, main materials, purchased semi-finished products, auxiliary materials, fuels, products being processed, spare parts for minor maintenance, packaging equipment, low-value and perishable articles, advance payment, receivables and cash in stock, current assets also included articles with a utility life of less than a year, articles with a utility life of over a year but a value of less than RMB 100 yuan, and fragile articles (for example glassware).

Fixed assets were revalued according to their "complete replacement value" in the end of June 1951. "Complete replacement value" referred to all the cost of replacing a certain asset in the end of June 1951, including invoice price, tax, commission fee, and freight and miscellaneous charges. After deduction of depreciation, the net value could be decided. Current assets would be revalued according to their "complete replacement value" in the end of 1951, including current price, tax, commission fee and freight and miscellaneous charges. As for the valuation of land, state-operated enterprises controlled mines, forests, ponds, oil fields, salt fields, farmlands, pastures, railways and highways, if not specified otherwise and if procured or having gone through relevant financial procedures after the land had been taken-over by the people's government, the actual investment or the original book value would be taken as the value of the land . Otherwise, the land (while the surface constructions were categorized as construction assets) would not be valuated. House sites and attached land, if procured or already appraised and booked after the land had been taken-over by the people's government, would be valued at its original book value or otherwise would be appraised according to the standard specified by local governments. Government bonds and securities, if having current prices, would be valued at the current prices and if not having current prices, would be appraised according to actual situations.

In order to avoid differences in appraisal, the Central Financial and Economic Committee stipulated: As for the price standard for fixed and current assets in the end of June 1951, relevant responsible institutions should organize technical and financial experts and insiders to apply multiple computing methods and make sound appraisals. Relevant central government authorities should specify the price and utility life standards of major equipment while the appraisal of fixed and current assets must comply with approved standards for different regions. These standards developed by different ministries in theory applied to all, subject to local interpretations.

Enterprises must report revalued assets as well as categorized debts by the end of June 1951. After reappraisal, in case of depreciation or appreciation between revaluation and book value, adjustments should be made in asset accounts, depreciation reserve and balance of appraisal. After final verification, government fund transfer could be made accordingly.

As for the appraisal of funds, the Central Financial and Economic Committee stipulated: state-operated enterprises' funds subject to computing and verification included fixed and current funds. Since fixed funds had been appraised, the focus was on current funds. The following categories of current funds were subject to appraisal:1) raw material, material, fuel and supplementary material quotas;

2) spare part quota; 3) low-value and fragile article quota; 4) quota of products being processed; 5) finished product quota; 6) advancement payment quota; 7) cash in stock. In accordance with their respective production, financial plan and assets and liabilities at the end of June 1951, computing and verification should be carried out seriously at different levels so as to decide the minimum government investment. Irregular current funds as a result of seasonal production and operation or other special causes would be secured with short-term loans from state banks. After appraisal, the system of independent accounting would be implemented and the enterprise coffer system would be replaced by bank settlement. The Central Financial and Economic Committee demanded enterprises to hand in surplus current funds after appraisal and different ministries should develop their installment plans.

Fixed and current asset appraisal started in April 1951 and completed by the end of 1952. During this 20 month period, the appraisal at the central and ministerial level was accomplished within only 4 months. Before the Movement Against Corruption, Waste and Bureaucracy (hereafter as the Movement Against Three Evils), enterprises directly affiliated to the Ministries of Heavy Industries, Fuel, Textile, Light Industries, Railway and Communications and state-operated enterprises in the Northwest and Southwest Administration Region had finished the appraisal of 70-80% assets. After the beginning of the Movement, appraisal work was suspended until June and July 1952, when reexamination was carried out in those ministries and great administration regions where appraisal was already over and enterprises affiliated to the military logistics system and in North East Administration Region started to plan the appraisal of their assets. Asset verification was finalized in the 1953 economic plan. Before appraisal, state-operated enterprises showed a book value of 4.533 billion yuan, a depreciation of 372 million yuan and a residue value of 4.161 billion yuan and the figures after appraisal were 19.161 billion, 6.175 billion and 12.986 billion respectively; that was, an additional residue value of 8.825 billion yuan.

The appraisal had taken a general inventory of the assets and operation of state-operated enterprises (with a 112.08% increase in book residue value) and solved the problems of chaotic asset management and law-breaking in accounting, which improved the management of state-operated enterprises. However, the campaign also revealed the difficulties in appraising assets of state-operated enterprises: how to reconcile the different profit motives of the state as the owner and enterprises as the user of the assets, how to reconcile the conflict between standards and reality, how to determine fixed asset depreciation, major maintenance funds and current asset valuation and how to scientifically calculate current asset quotas. However, since conflicts were not acute in the early years of the PRC, the appraisal had in general achieved its goals.

1.4.3. Democratic Reform of State-Operated Enterprises

To restructure enterprises from confiscation and other sources as socialist state-operated enterprises, the people's government started democratic reform since early 1950s and established new management systems.

1. To cleanse state-operated enterprises of feudalism, counterrevolutionaries and redundant personnel. Democratic reform started in those state-operated enterprises which were confiscated and taken-over from bureaucrat capital but remained untouched in 1950. The reform focused on the following areas: to abolish "body search" and foremen in textile enterprises; to abolish labor contractor in coal mines; to implement personnel adjustment and remove redundant personnel. When the Campaign to Suppress Counterrevolutionaries started in October 1950, state-operated enterprises also worked to remove reactionary gang organizations and counterrevolutionaries both in history and in reality. To promote democratic reform, the CPC Central Committee issued "Instructions on Suppressing Counterrevolutionaries and Carrying out Democratic Reform in Factories, Mines and Transportation Enterprises" on November 5, 1951. According to the Instruction, by the end of 1952, counterrevolutionaries inside state-operated enterprises should have been systematically cleansed and remaining old systems should have been democratically reformed properly. The Instruction came with detailed methods and guidelines. After the launching of the Movement Against

Three Evils and the Movement Against Five Evils,[1] the state-operated enterprises started to report and self-check illegal economic practice (mainly corruption, embezzlement and stealing).

2. To establish democratic management systems. A key tenet of democratic reform was to establish new democratic management systems, as captured in the slogan of "corporate operation and democratic management". Democratization was achieved mostly through the establishment of factory management committees and congress of workers and staff.

On February 7, 1950, *The People's Daily* published an editorial titled "Learn How to Manage an Enterprise". According to the editorial, "All state-operated enterprises must change the old bureaucrat management system and democratize management by establishing factory management committees to involve workers in management so as to enhance their awareness of being the master of themselves and to mobilize their enthusiasm for work. This is the basic step to reform old enterprises and improve management of people's enterprises."Accordingly, the Central Financial and Economic Committee instructed enterprises to establish their respective factory management committees and congress of workers and staff and reprinted the August 1949 "Implementation Regulations on the Establishment of Factory Management Committees and Congress of Workers and Staff in State- and Public-Operated Enterprises" by the North China People's Government.

According to the Implementation Regulation, the Enterprise Management Committee (hereafter as Management Committee) was an administrative organization under the leadership of the superior department in charge and was to be made up of manager, deputy managers, chief engineer, chairman of the labor union, other leadership personnel and the same amount of worker and staff representatives. Besides natural members such as manager, deputy managers,

1 The the Movement Against Five Evils (corruption, tax evasion, embezzlement of state assets, cheating on workmanship and materials, and theft of national economic intelligence) against the capitalists was launched by the CPC Central Committee in big and medium-sized cities in 1952.

chief engineer, and chairman of the labor union should serve, the candidacy of other leadership personnel should be reported by the manager to the superior department in charge for approval. The Management Committee was responsible to discuss major production and management issues and conduct regular check and review in accordance with the plan and instruction of the superior department in charge. The manager should serve as the Chair of the Management Committee and the Management Committee's resolutions would be announced and implemented as Manager Directives. In case of disagreement between the manager and the majority members, the manager's opinion should triumph and reported to a superior department for approval.

Worker and staff representatives to the Management Committee would be elected at the Congress of Workers and Staff every half a year or every year. Each representative could serve more than one term while incompetent representatives were subject to impeachment and replacement. The size of the Management was decided by the size of the enterprise and usually was made up of 5~17 members. The Congress of Workers and Staff review and discuss the reports of the Management Committee, examine the management and working style of the Management Committee and offer criticism and suggestion to the Management Committee. However, any resolution by the Congress of Workers and Staff had to be approved by the Management Committee and the resolution would not take effect until issued as a Manager Directive. The Congress of Workers and Staff was also the representative conference (or general assembly) of the labor union. The labor union was responsible for the implementation of resolutions of the Congress of Workers and Staff. Unless a superior labor union decided otherwise, the labor union would not change the resolution.

After the above-mentioned confiscation, take-over, appraisal and democratic reform, socialist state-operated enterprises were established and played a leading role in national economy.

2. Socialist Reform of Capitalist Industry and Commerce

After the founding of the PRC, China established a new democratic economic system of diverse labor-capital relationships. The basic economic policy was the coordination of various economic sectors under the leadership of the state-operated sector. The policy of "use, restrain and reform" applied to private capitalist businesses which came in large numbers.[1] After 1953, the CPC announced the "general guideline during the transitional period" to transit to socialism solely on the basis of public ownership. According, the "government-private joint adventure" mechanism was applied to turn all private capitalist businesses into state-owned and state-operated enterprises. The reform ended in the end of 1956. As a result, China's new democratic economic system of diverse labor-capital relationships were generally replaced by the socialist public-ownership economic system of state-operated and joint-venture enterprises.

During the process, socialist public ownership and planned economy in the form of state capitalism was a success model of peaceful transition to socialism based on the combination between Lenin's ideas of "procurement" and "state capitalism" and Chinese realities. Back then, industrialization had just started in China, traditional agriculture, handicraft and commerce still occupied a large portion of the national economy. At a low level, national economy was still far from socialization and troubled with extreme imbalance between regions, rural and urban areas and sectors. Because of these, planned public-ownership economy could not realize its expected advantage, especially in medium- and small sized enterprises with outdated technologies and scattered production while most public-private joint operation enterprises fell into this category.

Moreover, after socialist reform in 1956, these small and scattered private enterprises joined the rank of state-operated enterprises, causing additional challenge to management. Because of the abolition of the market mechanism's role in resource allocation, planned management was faced with various challenges while mistakes were made in macro-economic decision making. All

1 Before 1953, "reform" referred to reorganization, merging and restructuring, and public-private joint operation of individual enterprises. After 1953, "reform", in essence, aimed to "eliminate" private economy.

these deteriorated the difficulties facing state-operated enterprises from 1956 to 1978. Because of the absence of market mechanism, the reform of state-operated enterprises was caught in the trap of "control=death, laissez-faire=chaos".

2.1. Public-private Joint Operation from Management Model to Reform Approach

Government-private cooperative enterprises could be dated backed to the Self-Strengthening Movement in the late Qing Dynasty. During the late Qing and the Nationalist China period, such enterprises played a major role in controlling national capital and in bureaucrats' embezzling of state capital and profits.

After the founding of the PRC, during the confiscation of bureaucrat capital and enemy properties, state enterprises with substantial private shares and private enterprises with substantial state shares, if check and return was impossible, were restructured as public-private joint operations. Meanwhile, some large private enterprises which were in need of help or aimed for great development also pursued state investment (or turning loans into investment) for joint operation. Accordingly, during the recovery period, Premier Zhou Enlai pointed out, "Public-private joint operations are state capitalism lead by the government and can create the necessary conditions for socialism. Capitalists also aspire to public-private joint operation to ensure the supply of raw materials and credits. However, we have to be selective and prioritize enterprises which are significant to national economy and the people's livelihood. In a word, the development of public-private joint operations should be paced with priorities." [1] In accordance, the Financial and Economic Commission specified the three preconditions for public-private joint operation: 1) conforming to the national economic development plan; 2) completely voluntary on the part of private entrepreneurs; 3) enterprises with a bright future and high investment efficiency. Therefore, during the recovery period, the government was cautious with the public-private joint operation in the

1 *Selected Works of Zhou Enlai on the United Front*, People's Publishing House, 1984, pp.170-171.

transportation sector, focusing on restructuring and managing extant public-private joint operations. In order to attract tourism and investment from overseas Chinese to improve national economy and the people's livelihood, local government established some public-private joint investment companies since 1950, with government shares accounting for no more than 25% in general.

From 1949 to 1953, the number of public-private joint operations increased from 193 to 997, an increase of four times, while the output value increased by 5.2 times. The percentage of public shares decreased from 70.7% in 1949 to 60.7% in 1952. A survey of 695 public-private joint operations showed that 62.18 of public shares came from confiscated bureaucrat capital and enemy assets, while 31.14% were new investment made by the P.R.C. government.

Since most public-private joint operations were joint-equity corporations, they practice the manager responsibility system under the leadership of the board of directors and supervisors. The management of public shares fell under the jurisdiction of relevant government agencies while the Bank of Communications was designated to manage finance. Drawing lessons from the inequality, dominance or manipulation of the old GSMM system, the Bank of Communications recommended that public-private joint operations should be managed not exclusively by the government but jointly by the board of directors and supervisors filled by representatives from both the public and the private sectors.

In terms of management style, the government exercised its leadership role not through administrative orders but through public representatives in the boards who implemented government policies through negotiations which led to joint decisions on management, finance and personnel matters. Public representatives came from the Bank of Communications, the Industry and Commerce Administration and the corresponding industry administrative agencies, in charge of finance, management and taxation, and planning respectively. To ensure public representatives agree with each other, a chief representative was designated among public representatives to ensure consensuses before board meetings. If only one public representative was in the board, the representative would appointed by the Bank of Communications. The General Management Office of the Bank of Communications developed interim regulations concerning the selection of board representatives, their responsibilities and salaries, and financial arrangement.

As for the deployment of materials between the government and public-private joint operations, the Financial and Economic Commission ruled: in case of emergency, the government could purchase public-private joint operations' materials at market prices with the consent of the joint operations; when the joint operations applied for materials, the allocation of materials would be made at market prices with government approval. As for revenue, after taking out reserve funds and public welfare funds, dividends would be allocated according to shares. Public share dividends would be collected and then transferred to the Ministry of Finance by the Bank of Communications. The relevant government agencies in charge would decide whether to increase investment or use public share dividends as investment; that is, local financial and economic commissions sent their respective applications to the Central Financial and Economic Commissions.

Before the CPC Central Committee took public-private join operation as the main channel for peaceful reconstruction of private capitalist enterprises in June 1953, the government adhered cautiously to the three principles of joint operation. As Chairman Mao commented in 1953, concessions were necessary. The reasons for such polices include: 1) because of the limited capital available, state-owned economy was prioritized to enhance efficiency; 2) The KMT once controlled and possessed national industries through state-private cooperation, so the CPC must take necessary measures to avoid misunderstandings and unease.

In June 1953, based on his research, Li Weihan, Minister of the United Front Work Department of the CPC, advocated public-private joint operation as a good method to promote the transition from capitalism to socialism, and his advice was taken by the CPC Central Committee. Since it had already been decided that the socialization of private agriculture and handicraft would most take the form of cooperatives, the decision in fave of joint operation became the key policy in the transitional period. Chairman Mao decided to eliminate capitalism through public-private joint operation for mainly three reasons: 1) when designing guidelines for the transitional period, Chairman Mao and the CPC Central Committee decided that it was pivotal that a "peaceful redeem" approach that fit Chinese realities was adopted; 2) within enterprises, because of the "Five Antis" Campaign, capitalists were afraid to enforce management rules while workers did not respond to management (because capitalists could not fire workers), which created the conditions for joint operation through shareholding (instead of share-based decision making); 3) because of the mass economic construction programs, raw materials and capital became strained, especially after state monopoly of purchase and sale of agricultural products, as a result o which private enterprises, faced with difficulties, had no other choice but accept the state planning of material allocation. Compared with external control measures like production order and unified purchase and sale, joint operation enabled internal control and facilitated the integration of enterprises into state planning, so as to reach the balance between production, supply and demand.

On September 7, 1953, Chairman Mao invited representatives of other democratic parties and the commerce and industry sectors for discussion. At the meeting, Chairman Mao unfold his plans for the reform of capitalism: firstly, "to achieve the socialization of capitalism through state capitalism"; secondly, "Take steady steps and avoid hasty decisions. The socialization of private commerce and industry may take 3-5 years, to avoid turmoil...The transitional period, including industrialization and the socialist reform of agriculture, handicraft and capitalist commerce and industry, is not the matter of 3 or 5 years, but several five-year periods. For this matter, both defeatism and rashness must be avoided."; thirdly, "State capitalism must be oriented to reality and based on voluntarism of capitalists. This is a joint operation endeavor and therefore coercion must be avoided. Capitalists are different from landlords". [1] On October 27, at the national

1 *Selected Works of Mao Zedong*, Vol. 5, People's Publishing House, 1977, pp.98-100.

congress of the federation of industry and commerce, Li Weihan, on behalf of the CPC Central Committee, further elaborated on the above-mentioned visions of Chairman Mao.

2. Public-Private Joint Operation of Individual Enterprises

Back then, public-private joint operations, which were directly under state planning, had secured accesses to credits, raw materials and markets and benefited from capitalist capital and talents, greatly enhanced their economic performance, especially since the first few public-private joint operation enterprises all had a promising future. As a result, both the public and the private sectors welcomed the policy, which was the decisive factor in the CPC's final decision. This part analyzes the economic performance of public-private joint operations and its reasons before the joint operation of all industries in 1955.

In early 1953, the Bank of Communications transferred the public shares to local government agencies. In the middle of the year, the Central Party Committee decided to achieve public-private joint operation in a planned way, which started in 1954. But because of the start of mass economic construction, raw materials and capital became limited. According to Li Weihan's investigation in Shanghai in early 1953, if the state banks tightened credits, many capitalists would get into trouble. If the government stopped placing orders, many manufacturing enterprises would go bankrupt. If the government cut the supply of copper materials, 37 private industries in Shanghai would suffer and even die out.[1]

For private enterprises, the "Five Antis" Campaign in 1952 stressed labor relations and more internal and external difficulties kicked in. Externally, because raw materials and markets were state-controlled, accesses to both became were limited. Internally, stressed labor relations, lack of autonomy and shortage of capital made operation difficult. Against such a background, public-private joint operation promised to solve three problems: 1) improve labor relations; 2)

1 General Office of the CPC Central Committee, ed., *Collection of Central Committee Documents 1953*, Vol. 4, p221.

integrate into state planning, so as to ensure equal treatment; 3) legitimize for state investment. The following part illustrates the features of public-private joint operations before the joint operation of all industries in 1955.

1) Government shares accounted a big share in join venture companies. Emphasizing investment, the state gained control and reformed and expanded the enterprises accordingly.

Table 7-1 Capital Portfolio of public-private joint operations, Unit: million yuan [1]

Year	1949	1952	1953	1954	1955
Total capital	130	537	693	1 400	1 875
Government shares	87	282	402	634	761
Private shares	36	182	210	640	930

2) Private enterprises restructured as public-private joint operations were mostly large enterprises with a promising future.

In terms of size, most private enterprises which were restructures as joint ventures were large private enterprises with good conditions and promising future (with products which were much needed but in short supply). The following shows the size and development conditions of these private enterprises before joint venture reform:

Table 7-2: Average Employment and Capital of Private Enterprises Before Joint Venture Reform, 1950~1954

	1949	1950	1951	1952	1953	1954
Number of Enterprises	193	294	706	997	1036	1746
Employment (1000 people)	105.37	130.89	166.33	247.76	270.11	533.27
Average	545.9	445.2	235.6	248.5	260.7	305.4
Gross Output (100 million yuan)	2.2	4.14	8.06	13.67	20.13	51.10
Average (10,000 yuan)	113	140	114	137	194	292
Net Asset Value (100 million yuan)	2.01	3.07	4.75	8.27	10.92	20.78
Average (10,000 yuan)	104	104	67	83	105	119

1 National Bureau of Statistics, *Statistics of Socialist Construction*, October 1956, p.59.

contd.

Fixed Assets (100 million yuan)	1.37	2.37	3.44	4.53	6.81	12.84
Average (10,000 yuan)	71	80.6	48.7	45.4	65.7	73.5

Table 7-3 Development of Public-Private Joint Operation Enterprises 1949-1954

	1949	1952	1954
Coal Mining	18	32	45
Iron and Steel	1	15	45
Machinery	9	42	141
Chemical	7	41	99
Rubber	1	4	21
Wood processing	6	13	28
Matchstick	6	22	32
Paper	5	26	49
Textile	15	103	334
Sewing	-	-	3
Leather	-	2	4
Food	30	164	286
Salt	4	2	5
Total	193	997	1746

In terms of employment, joint operations were usually based on large former private enterprises. In comparison, in 1953, only 2,048 private enterprises had an employment of over 100 people, accounting for 1.36% and the figures dropped to only 1,646 and 1.23% respectively. In terms of net assets, joint operations also took the lead by a large margin than large private enterprises with an employment of over 100 people (which was 770,000 yuan in 1953 and 460,000 yuan in 1954). Moreover, joint operations concentrate on rapidly developing industries: 1) promising industries that promoted industrialization, such as iron and steel, machinery and chemical; 2) industries with a lack of raw materials but of importance to national economy and people's livelihood, such as textile, and food (including grain and cooking oil).[1]

1 *Socialist Reform of Capitalist Commerce and Industry in China: Central Government* Vol., CPC Party History Press, 1992, p. 754.

(3) Joint operations were more efficient than enterprises of other labor-management relationships Since joint operations were mostly large enterprises with a bright future and managed by experienced management personnel. After the injection of state investment and being incorporated into the national plan (which means guaranteed supply and sales), joint operations greatly improved their economic efficiency, higher than private enterprise before and after joint operation restructuring and even state-operated enterprises.

Table 7-4 Workers' Productivity in Various Types of Enterprises 1949-1954 [1]

Unit: yuan/person/year

	1949	1950	1951	1952	1953	1954
Total	4 839	6 037	7 087	8 049	9 016	103 72
State Operated	4 933	6 218	7 118	7 919	8 894	10 218
Cooperative	6 436	7 003	7 671	8 415	8 557	9 165
Joint Operation	3 515	4 257	6 553	9 297	10 880	13 401
Private		4 357	5 928	6 801	7 848	7 222

Before 1951, the productivity of joint operations was lower than that of state-operated and cooperative enterprises, mostly because joint operations, based on confiscated bureaucrat capital enterprises and enterprises owned by traitors, were weak and faced with major restructuring. After the joint operation restructuring in 1952, with improved management, join operations greatly improved their productivity and surpassed state-operated and cooperative enterprises. Newly established joint operations after 1952 had no such problems. After solving labor-management conflicts and with equal access to raw materials, credits and market in addition to government capital injection, joint operations were able to take advantage of their clearly defined ownership, rich experience of management and profit-based salary to win a competitive edge. Joint operations before 1955 were

1 *Socialist Reform of Capitalist Commerce and Industry in China: Central Government* Vol., CPC Party History Press, 1992, pp.1332&1335; National Bureau of Statistics, Basic Statistics of Public-private Joint Ventures and Private Industrial Prodction in the Seven Year since the Foundation of the PRC, August, 1956.

quite similar to Chinese-foreign joint ventures after reform and opening-up, where both focused on promising industries and improve efficiency by capital injection and management improvement, though the former relied on the government while the latter on foreign investors. Moreover, at the early years of the PRC, because of war damage and immature management, state-operated enterprises had a productivity lower than cooperatives. However, with restoration and management improvement in 1953, state-operated enterprises quickly demonstrated the advantage of economies of scale.

According to the Report on Profits and Distribution of Private Enterprises in 1953 issued by the Administrative Bureau for Industry and Commerce (ABIC) in November 1954, out of the 220,000 private enterprises in Beijing, Tianjin, Shanghai, Wuhan, Guangzhou, Xi'an, Chongqing and Shenyang, 96.9% made a profits at a profit rate of 12.33% (compared with 15.4% in 1951 and 10.51% in 1952). Another investigation by the ABIC into 904 joint operations in June 1954 showed that 716 made a profit and that over 50% joint operations secured a profit rate of 30%. [1]

3. Public-Private Joint Operation in All Industries

In 1954, because of serious natural disasters, the agriculture sector failed to realize the preset goals, as a result of which industries, because of the lack of raw materials, did not finish their plan either. Since the government-controlled agriculture products which were in short supply, the government had to guarantee the supply of capital and raw materials to state-owned enterprises and joint operations. As a result, private enterprises, especially those small enterprises with backward technologies, were in big trouble. After the end of 1954, private enterprises faced the following four types of difficulties:

First: a lack of raw materials. Besides agricultural raw materials, because of tightened supply of industrial raw materials and stricter supply plans, private

1 *Socialist Reform of Capitalist Commerce and Industry in China: Central Government* Vol., CPC Party History Press, 1992, p. 1331.

enterprises were constantly faced with a lack of raw materials in 1955. According to the State Statistics Bureau's investment from May to August 1954, for private enterprises of 10 or more people, because of a lack of raw materials, their equipment utilization rate was: 60% for everyday rubber (Chongqing), 60% for textile (Shandong), 70% for knitting, 50% for sewing, 40% for wood processing, 25% for flour, 80% for rice milling, 80% for machine-based food oil, 25% for tobacco and 15% for matchstick making. Most private enterprises dealt with light industries.[1] According to another investigation into key industries in the first half of 1955, compared with normal production, the equipment utilization rate was 66% for machinery manufacturing, 30% for drillers and millers, 49% for dyejiggers, 26% for hand hosiery machines and 35% for circular saws, and the productivity utilization rate was 57% for cotton cloth, 51% for cooking oil, 37% for tobacco, 20% for rubber footwear, rice milling and soap, and only 6% for bare copper wire. Taking into account the three-shift system, the equipment utilization rate was even lower.

Second: a shortage of capital. After the socialist reform of private financial institutions in late 1952, the short-term capital market was completely controlled by the government. The "deposit-based loan"system applied to private industrial and commercial enterprises; that is, loans must not exceed deposits. However, because the government (especially local governments) still had a serious shortage of capital, it hardly had the necessary means to take care of private enterprises. In 1953, the deposit of private enterprises in the PBOC increased by over 800 billion yuan compared with that of 1952 (before the currency reform in 1955, the same below), but loans by private enterprises decreased by 1.9 trillion yuan, a decrease by two thirds. The percentage of loans to private enterprises in the PBOC's total loans dropped from 2.6% in 1952 to only 0.7%. According to the State Statistics Bureau's investment from May to August 1954, private enterprises of 10 or more

1 National Bureau of Statistics, "Survey of Private Industrial Businesses with Over 10 Employees", February 22,1955.

people faced a serious shortage of capital, especially small enterprises. Out of the 559 private plants with over 10 people, only 13.5% had an adequate supply of capital, 28.2% had just enough capital to maintain production while 54.6% were troubled. The production of most enterprises depended on bank loans, receivable in advance for government works and down payment.

Third: a disruption to the old supply and sales system. Small in size, most private enterprises did not take government orders for processing. They used to purchase raw materials in the market and rely on commercial channels for sales. After the restructuring of private commercial businesses in 1954, most private whole-sale companies were restructured. As a result, the commercial channels changed and private industrial enterprises lost their old supply and sales channels. At the same time, state-operated businesses and cooperatives were reluctant to purchase or promote the products of small private enterprises because of their low standardization, small production and high transaction cost. As result, sales became difficult for most private enterprises in 1954.

Third, after two years of "apple eating" (public-private joint operation restructuring), most remaining private industrial enterprises were small with low technology and efficiency which did not have too much of a future. Statistics showed in 1954 there were altogether 133,962 private industrial enterprises with an average employment of 13.40 people and an average output value of 77,200 yuan. Of these enterprises, only 31.3% had over 10 people and 3.74% have over 50 people. In those enterprises with over 10 people, 60% still relied on hand tools for production while most small plants with fewer than 10 people had no modern equipment, thus incapable of producing standardized products or in a large scale. State-operated enterprises and joint operations had an advantage not only in technology and production scale, but also in terms of capital and raw material supply and sales. In the end, private industrial enterprises, unable to give full play to its flexibility, were at a disadvantage in competition.

According to the investigation of troubled private industrial enterprises in the first half of 195 in Shanghai, 28% were troubled by poor product quality, 22% by a lack of raw materials, 20% by overproduction as a result of blind expansion, 18% by the general difficulty faced by the industry and 12% by difficulty in sales.[1]

The Central Government demanded local governments to make overall plans and take into account the needs of private industrial and commercial enterprises in the first half of 1955. However, because of the remaining private enterprises' small scale, backward equipment and low standardization, and because of the general shortage of raw materials and capital, local governments and state-operated commercial enterprises were reluctant to invest or sell raw materials to these companies. In comparison, joint operations enjoyed government support in raw materials, capital and sales. Therefore, medium- and small-sized private enterprises, workers and owners a like, were willing to accept joint operation reform as a way out of trouble.

To solve these problems, in April 1955, the CPC Central Committee endorsed the Report on the Conference on Expanding Public-Private Joint Operation in Industry and on Convening the Forum on Difficulties Faced by Private Industrial and Commercial Enterprises. The report proposed the principle of "overall planning and comprehensive arrangement". During the joint operation reform, with an overview of development of an industry as a whole, large and advanced enterprises would provide assistance to medium- and small-sized enterprises. Restructuring and merging should be organized according to actual situations before joint operation reform. Such arrangement marked the beginning of industry-wide public-private joint operation reform.

In the second half of 1955, promoted by Mao Zedong, the socialist reform of agriculture reached its peak in rural China. On one hand, the reform eliminated private economy in rural areas and further isolated private capitalist businesses which were brought to feel the general trend of socialism. On the other, the reform gave rise to impatience for prompt socialist reform in the CPC and the

1 National Bureau of Statistics, "Report on the Production of Private Industrial Enterprises in the First Half of 1955", August, 27, 1955.

government. In October 1955, Mao Zedong called a forum of the executive members of the All-China Federation of Industry and Commerce and expressed his hope that private industrial and commercial enterprises could understand the law of social development, accept socialist reform and control their own fate by integrating personal fortune with national future. Later, at a Conference of the All-China Federation of Industry and Commerce, Vice Premier Chen Yun gave further explanations about industry-wide joint operation reform and fixed interest on capital. In the Letter to National Industrial and Commercial Community which got passed at the conference, industrial and commercial enterprises were called on to accept socialist reform. In November, the CPC Central Committee called the Forum on Socialist Reform of Capitalist Industry and Commerce and the 7th Plenary Session of the 7th CPC Central Committee made decisions on the guidelines, policies and plans for industry-wide joint operation reform. Accordingly, starting from January 1956 came a new wave of socialist reform of capitalist industry and commerce. On January 1, 1956, private enterprises in Beijing started to apply for industry-wide joint operation reform and then on January 10, the reform was accomplished. The same practice quickly spred to other cities in China. By the end of January 1956, industry-wide joint operation reform had finished in Shanghai, Tianjin, Guangzhou, Wuhan, Xi'an, Chongqing, Shenyang and over 50 medium-sized cities. By the end of March, except Tibet, industry-wide joint operation reform had finished across the country. By the end of 1956, 99% private industrial enterprises and 82.2% private commercial companies became joint operations or cooperatives.

Against the background of operation difficulties and the socialist reform wave in the latter half of 1955, private enterprises, in view of the advantages of joint operation reform, became enthusiastic about industry-wide public-private joint operation reform, which kind of caught the government unprepared (as the original plan to implement such reform by stages and in groups during a two year period). As Chen Yun commented, "They were very earnest for joint operation; as a result, we have to recognize joint operation first and then organize appraisal of assets, arrange production, restructure enterprises and adjust personnel arrangement".[1] This formed a sharp contrast with agriculture cooperative reform.

Agriculture cooperative reform aims to increase agricultural production to satisfy the need of industrialization, rather than as a result of low efficiency or difficulty in survival of household agriculture (especially for rich and middle peasants). The 1955 cooperative reform was imposed from the outside in the eyes of most peasants. Industry-wide joint operation reform reached its peak in 1955 because large private enterprises, under political and social pressure, participated enthusiastically because they realized they had to do so sooner or later and the earlier the better. For small and troubled private enterprises (small in assets and output but large in terms of people involved), joint operation was an economic, political and psychological relief. In other words, most private enterprises which accepted socialist reform were caught in trouble first and and then accepted reform.

Industry-wide public-private joint operation not only improved the organization of private enterprises and greatly reduced the cost of the government because of reduced investment and government shares. Statistics back then showed, in every single enterprise joint operation, the government invested 1,273 yuan in every 10,000 yuan and appointed one government represent for every 63 employees, while in every industry-wide joint operation, the figures were 86 yuan and 160 employees respectively.[2]

Although private enterprises were restructured as state-operated enterprises though joint operation and fixed interest for investors (an 5% annual interest rate for 10 consecutive years), these enterprises accounted for a very small portion of state-operated economy. State-operated economy came mostly from government investment. In the joint operation reform, private shares were valued at 2.4 billion

1 Quoted in Li Weihan, *Meetings and Research*, Vol. 2, CPC Historical Documents Publishing House, 1986, pp. 766-767.

2 The State Econmic and Trade Commission, ed., *Fifly Years of Chinese Industries*,Vol. 2, Part II ,China Economic Publishing House, 2000, p.1804.

yuan in total. During the First Five-Year Plan period, state budgetary investment reached 53.12 billion yuan. If state extra-budgetary investment were included, total state investment reached 58.85 billion yuan, or 24.5 times as much as private shares in joint operations. Therefore, this extensive socialist reform of capitalist private ownership of production means was not the main source of state-owned enterprises and assets. However, the reform laid the foundation for state concentration of surplus value and centralized resource allocation; that is, the institutional conditions for the expansion of state-operated enterprises.

3. State Investment and Additional Capital (1949-1978)

From 1949 to the eve of reform and opening-up in 1978, the overall economic development goal was industrialization and socialism. Therefore, both the 2nd Plenary Session of the 7th CPC Central Committee in March 1949 and the First Chinese People's Political Consultative Conference (CPPCC) in 1949 prioritized the development of state-operated enterprises. After the completion of socialist reform in 1956, China's pattern of ownership was made up state-operated economy and collective economy. State-operated enterprises dominated those basic industries such as finance, heavy industry, foreign trade and modern communications and played a major role in the accumulation for industrialization (resources).

3.1 Establishment of Government Investment System

After the founding of the PRC, faced with the conflict between a shortage of capital and the need for development, and in line with the basic policy of prioritizing state-operated economy, a key component of economic system establishment was to optimize the use government investment. Before the founding of the PRC, different liberated areas had different economic policies in a scattered way without a centralized management. After the founding of the PRC, government basic investment was also managed by different ministries and local governments.

After the centralization of finance and economy, the fiscal power of local government and the depreciation and profit of large state-operated enterprises were all handed over to the Central Government. To optimize government investment in capital construction, it was necessary to establish an investment distribution and management system and relevant regulations. In March 1951 and January 1952, the Central Financial and Economic Committee issued the Interim Regulations on Work Procedure for Capital Construction and the the Interim Regulations on Capital Construction, which established a primary management system in terms of investment distribution and construction project management.

3.1.1 Investment Distribution System

After the founding of the PRC, the following government investment distribution system was established:

1. In accordance with the annual state fiscal budget and overall planning, the Central Financial and Economic Committee would allocate central government investment to various ministries and specify the planned target of capital construction for each ministry. Ministries then would decide the planned targets of their affiliated construction units.

2. Construction units would report their capital construction work plans to their superior department in charge.

3. The Central Financial and Economic Committee would approve the capital construction work plans of different ministries and then different ministries would approve the capital construction work plans of their affiliated construction units.

Local government investment (from fiscal revenue) was organized and managed by local governments. Major projects must report to relevant ministries for record.

This investment management system based on top-down government investment distribution was tailored to handle the conflict between a shortage and a great demand of government capital, which necessitated effective centralized capital management. Meanwhile, since investment was comparatively small and centralized, the Central Government was capable of managing government investment. However, this administration-based top-down government investment system, especially when capital was allocated at no cost, led to the practice of "eating from the same pot"; that is, enterprises share the pot with the government and construction companies with construction projects regardless of their work performance. Under this system, although government investment allocation institutions were charged with investment decision making, they were not responsible for investment risks, while construction projects (future enterprises) though used money were not held accountable for their investment decisions. Consequently, different ministries, local governments and enterprises all competed for government investment for new projects, but did not care much about opportunity cost or investment efficiency, which gave rise to "investment thirst" and "fishing projects". When competition for investment was fierce at lower levels, information reported to higher levels was more likely to be twisted. As a result, the cost for departments in charge at the central level to get real information would go up while mistakes were more likely in investment decision making. When banks and the financial system realized investment problems and low efficiency and even loss in projects, it was already too late.

To solve the problems of investment thirst and competition for investment, after 1953, the Central Government gradually withdraw back to its hand the rights to make investment decisions and to allocate capital construction investment. Top-down investment allocation was implemented through administrative means. Investment would be allocated along administrative lines (with the ministry in charge) and ministries and local governments were responsible to only pass on investment quotas in accordance with the allocation plan imposed by the central government but had no authority to adjust investment. Enterprises and construction units were just grass-root units to carry out state investment projects. Since the Central Government was responsible for investment decisions and overall balance, right and responsibility were united. Except under special circumstances (for example political disturbance), centralized investment decision making was capable of suppressing investment thirst and irresponsibility.

3.1.2 Capital Construction Project Management System

A classified management system was established to manage capital construction projects. According to investment scale, construction projects were classified as "above quota" projects and "below quota" projects. For any single construction unit, either newly built, restructured or restored, if its total investment was above quota, it was an "above quota" construction unit, while a "below quota" construction unit if the total investment was below quota. Quotas were specified according to different standards for different industries and sectors.

Before 1952, the Central Financial and Economic Committee only established the Division of Capital Construction under the Planning Bureau to be in charge of capital construction, urban construction and geological work. With such limited resources, the Central Financial and Economic Committee was responsible to issue the annual capital construction quota, manage major construction works and make decisions about projects of importance to national economy. Decision making for most above quota projects which were under the jurisdiction of the Central Government was shifted to ministries and greater administrative region governments. After greater administrative region governments were restructured as administrative committees, a lot of cadres were promoted to work in ministries in the Central Government and the State Planning Commission was established to take charge of project-related decision making in a centralized way. When greater administrative regions were abolished in June 1954, the State Construction Commission was established and thus decision making and design plan approval for above quota projects became centralized.

This investment volume based categorized management system was able to focus on investment at the central level so as to ensure the best use of investment against the background of limited government capital and relatively small investment.

3.1.3 Procedure for Capital Construction Projects

In general, the implementation of a capital construction project followed a five-stage procedure, namely feasibility study, survey and design, construction and acceptance check. In the early years of the PRC, because of a lack of experience and impatience about success, this procedure was not followed strictly, which led to waste and rework. To solve the problem and put capital construction on the right track, since the end of 1950, the Central Government had been strengthening institutional development. In December 1950, in Decision on Final Accounting, Budget Auditing, Government Construction Investment and Currency Management, the Government Administration Council emphasized all construction investment must be approved by the government with caution taken in planning design and construction. In March 1951, the Central Financial and Economic Committee issued the Interim Regulations on Procedure for Capital Construction Projects, which mandated a five-stage procedure, namely plan drafting and verification, design, construction and allocation, report and inspection, final accounting and acceptance check, thus formalizing the practice of survey before design and design before construction. On June 16, 1951, *The People Daily* carried a featured editorial titled "No Design, No Construction". On January 9, 1952, with additional revision, the Central Financial and Economic Committee issued the Interim Regulations on Capital Construction and thus established formal institutional constraints of capital construction projects.

3.1.4. Monitoring and Management of Capital Construction Funds

In terms the monitoring and management of capital construction funds, a bank (Bank of Communications) was designated to manage government investment. Before 1950, the Ministry of Finance allocated government capital construction funds to other ministries, which then further allocated to their affiliated capital construction units. Such practice led to embezzlement or waste. Learning from the Soviet experience, in February 1951, the PBOC designated Bank of Communications to allocation government capital construction investment and thus established the system of designating a professional bank to allocate and manage government investment. However, many ministries and local governments were afraid that another agency in charge might affect the use of construction funds, the new system faced major resistance. At first, Bank of Communications only took over allocation in 10 ministries, 2 greater administrative regions and 20 provinces and municipals. Since 1952, Bank of Communications had done a lot of work to take over at the ministerial and greater administrative region level until the Ministry of Trade handed over capital construction fund allocation to the bank in 1953. Bank of Communications took over all local level allocation in 1954 and allocation in military-industrial complexes and advanced industry. Thus, the monitoring and management of capital construction funds was centralized.

3.2. Government Investment During National Economic Recovery

After the found of the PRC, according to the Common Programme's guideline of prioritizing state-operated economy while drawing lessons from Soviet experiences, governments at the central and local levels alike had actively prioritized the development of state-operated economy. However, during this national economic recovery, the state still had only limited financial resources. Therefore, after "centralization of financial and economic authority"in March 1950, the limited government investment was all handled by the Central Government.

The beneficiaries of government investment fell into two groups. The first group was made up of financial and trading companies. Government investment enriched the capital of these state-owned banks and trading companies so as to expand their business and control. During the recovery, in addition to expanding the PBOC system, socialist reform also realized industry-wide public-private joint operation in the financial sector.

In terms of trade, state-operated trading companies expanded quickly with the establishment foreign trade companies which controlled important and export and the establishment and expansion of state-operated commercial enterprises, which controlled the market and the supply of main products.

Industrial and water conservancy capital construction projects constituted the second group of beneficiaries of government investment. Capital construction allocation into these projects was 1.04 billion yuan in 1950, 1.88 billion yuan in 1951 and 3.71 billion yuan in 1952, making a three year total of 6.633 billion yuan, accounting for 17.7% of the total fiscal revenue of the same period. If local government investment was counted, the total investment reached 7.84

billion yuan. If adjusted according to the price level of the time, budgetary capital construction investment was worth 46.93 million liang gold or 3.31 billion silver yuan,[1] or more than the total capital construction investment of the 10 years under the Kuomintang Government before the Anti-Japanese War. This investment focused on the following three fields:

① Water conservancy projects, for example the Jinjiang River Flood Diversion Project;

② Communications restoration projects. In 1952, investment in railways accounted for 11.6% of the total capital construction investment. During the three year recovery period, in addition to the restoration of existing railways, the government invested to build the Laimu Railway, the Chengdu-Chongqing Railway and the Tianshui-Lanzhou Railway. As result, the total railway traffic mileage reached 24,518 kilometers, very close to the high point before liberation. Highway, shipping and civil aviation also recovered quickly. The total highway traffic mileage reached 126,675 kilometers, higher than the high point before liberation while inland shipping mileage and civil aviation flight mileage reached 95,025 km and 13,123 km respectively. Moreover, the international flight route to Moscow via Ulan Bator started to operate and the Sino-Soviet joint operation airline was established.

③ Recovery industrial construction projects. In industrial investment, besides recovery investment, new establishment investment prioritized heavy industries. For example, out of the total capital construction investment in 1952, industrial investment accounted for 38.8% with 29.5% into heavy industries and 9.3% into light industries. One of the reasons was that heavy industries were indeed a bottleneck in economic development and mattered directly to the strengthening of national defense power. During this period, investment in heavy industries was clearly recovery construction investment, focusing on utilizing old plants and

1 Quoted in Zeng Peiyan, ed., *Fifty Years of Investment and Construction in China*, China Planning Press, 1999, pp. 46-47.

equipment. Capital construction projects focused more on recovery and reform than on new establishment, with an emphasis on bring old industrial bases' potential into full play. For example, the Northeast took 24.8% of the national total capital construction investment. In light industries, in view of excessive production capability, government investment focused on improving regional balance and reducing the out and back haul between manufacturing, raw material and sales. During the three year recovery period, the government invested 350 million yuan in textile to build three new textile mills in Xianyang, Handan and Wuhan, to balance the concentration of the textile industry in the coastal regions, especially Shanghai, Qingdao and Tianjin. In addition, Shenyang Textile Machine Plant, Zhenzhou Textile Machine Plant and Harbin Flax Mill were established besides cotton and flax textile projects in Xinjiang, Hunan, and Zhejiang.

Capital construction investment also achieved high efficiency during the 3 year recovery. With a total budgetary capital construction allocation of 8.621 billion yuan, newly increased fixed assets were valued at 5.9 billion yuan, with the percentage of fixed assets being delivered for use reaching 75.3%. The coefficient of investment yields reached 2.9; that is, every yuan of fixed assets investment could increase national revenue by 2.9 yuan.[1]

3.3 Government Investment During the First Five-Year Plan

By the end of 1952, national economy had generally recovered. Accordingly, 1953 saw the beginning of the First Five-Year Plan and large-scale economic construction. During this five-year period, government investment came mostly from the Central Government. In terms of the implementation of the First Five-Year Plan, government capital construction investment reached 58.85 billion yuan, with the annual average surpassing the total investment during the three-year recovery. Government budgetary investment was 3.12 billion yuan, accounting for 90.3% of the total. 82% of government budgetary investment was central

1 Quoted in Wang Haibo, ed., *Study of China's Economic Efficiency*, Economy and Management Publishing House, 1991, p.427.

government directly managed investment and 18% came from local governments. During the First Five-Year Plan, the national fiscal revenue reached 135.49 billion yuan, with budgetary capital construction investment accounting for 39.2%, a rather high rate against the background of low industrialization level and low surplus.

During this period, government industrial investment continued to prioritize heavy industries, especially machinery and national defense industries. The investment focused on the 156 key projects with Soviet assistance.

The 156 Industrial Construction Project (hereafter as the 156 Project) involved 156 industrial projects to which the Soviet Union committed support from 1950 to 1955, which became the core of industrial development during the First Five-Year Plan. Though categorized as projects of the First Five-Year Plan, these 156 industrial projects actually marked China's industrialization efforts during the 1950s, starting from the recovery period and connecting the first two Five-Year Plans.

These Soviet Assisted Projects were established gradually during continuous negotiation; that is, 50 projects were established in 1950, 91 projects in 1953 and 15 projects in 1954, making a total of 156 projects. In 1955, 16 additional projects were agreed upon and later oral agreements were reached for two more projects. At these five rounds of negotiation, the two sides reached 174 assistance agreements. After verification and adjustment, including cancellation, postpone, combination, division and disqualification for above-quota projects, 154 projects stayed. Because the "156 Industrial Construction Project" was already announced, the umbrella name for these projects also remained. In fact, only 150 projects were actually implemented, 146 of which kicked off during the First Five-Year Plan.

The 156 Project focused on the introduction of advanced technologies in national defense, machinery, electronics, chemical and energy. These projects either filled in gaps in industries or greatly improved technological levels. Traditionally, industrial construction based on the 156 Project in the 1950s was regarded as laying the foundation for industrialization in China. These efforts not only filled in many industrial gaps, laid the basic foundation for industrial development, but also improved regional balance, especially industrialization in central and western regions.

To understand the industrial structure of the 156 Project, three factors must be taken into account. 1) The Korean War and China's weak national defense industry prioritized national security; 2) The weak heavy industry foundation had become the bottleneck of industrialization; 3) In addition to the use of existing industrial bases, efforts were needed for war preparation and regional balance. Accordingly, the 156 Project had projects in mainly five sectors: 1) 44 national defense projects; 2) 20 metallurgical projects; 3) 52 energy projects, 4) 24 machinery projects and 5) 10 chemical and light industry projects.[1]

In terms of regional distribution, the 156 Project, especially energy and machinery projects, was rather balance with sufficient attention to inland region development. 70% of the limited industrial facilities of the Old China concentrated in costal regions. The limited industrial construction in inland provinces concentrated in several big cities. To change this imbalance, the 156 Project put more emphasis on Northeast, Central China and Western China. Out of the 150 implemented projects, a majority of the 44 national defense projects situated in inland provinces, including 35 projects in Central China and Western China and 21 projects in Sichuan and Shaanxi. Of the 106 civilian projects, 50 projects were in Northeast and 32 in Central China. In the electric sector, besides 7 projects in Northeast, other projects were scattered in provinces with a weaker electric industry such as Beijing, Hebei, Shanxi, Shaanxi, Inner Mongolia, Gansu, Henan, Hubei, Hunan, Sichuan, Yunnan and Xijing. According to Bo Yibo's recollection, then Deputy Chair of the Central Financial and Economic Committee, such a distribution was the result of careful consideration. "Back then, the key

1 National Bureau of Statistics, *Fixed Asset Investment in China 1950-1958*, China Statistics Press, 1987, pp.196-205.

considerations included:1) Energy, iron and steel, nonferrous metal and chemical plants should be located in regions rich in resources; machinery plants be close to raw materials...2) To promote the development in backward regions...3) military considerations."[1]

In terms of industries, the metallurgical industry finished a total investment of 4.661 billion yuan with a newly increased fixed asset of 3.813 billion yuan, the chemical industry 1.361 billion yuan and 875 million yuan and the machinery industry 3.847 billion yuan and 3.025 billion yuan. The coal industry finished a total investment of 3.555 billion yuan, built or started to build 194 new mines and secured a designed production capacity of 75.37 million tons. As for the building materials industry, six new cement plants were build in Dadong of Shanxi Province, Yongdeng of Gansu Province, Urumuqi of Xinjiang Autonomous Region, Kunming of Yunnan Province, Jiangyou of Sichuan Province and Luoyang of Henan Province besides the two glass plants in Zhuzhou of Hunan Province and Luoyang of Henan Province. For the textile industry, the government planned an investment of 1.556 billion yuan while the actual total investment reached 1.705 billion yuan, newly building or expanding 68 cotton mills (with a capital construction investment of over 5 million each), 6 printing and dyeing mills, 3 woolen mills, 7 flax mills, 4 silk mills, 4 chemical fibre mills and 1 textile machine plant.

In transportation and communications, 33 railway lines were newly built and 3 railway lines restored. The total mileage of newly built and restored trunk railway, multiple tracks, branch tracks and enterprise lines reached 10,000 kilometers. The Baoji-Chengdu and the Yingtan-Xiamen railways were completed and put into operation. In 1957, the Wuhan Yangtze River Bridge was completed, which marked the completion of the railway from Beijing to Guangzhou. Civilian aviation developed quickly. By the end of 1957, the total milage of air lines reached 26,400 kilometers, an increase of 101.5% compared with that of 1952.

1 Bo Yibo, *Review of Major Decisions and Issues*, Vol. 1, Publishing House of the Party School of the Central Committee of the CPC, 1991, p.298.

The flight fleet increased from 29 to 118 planes.

In a sense, with state investment and restructuring of capitalist commerce and industry during the First Five-Year Plan period, state-operated economy had become the backbone of industrialization in China.

Investment efficiency was rather high during the First Five-Year Plan with four prominent features. First, high application rate of fixed assets investment. During the period, the capital construction investment of state-owned units reached 58.85 billion yuan and the total newly increased fixed assets investment reached 49.22 billion yuan, making a fixed assets investment application rate of 83.6%. Second, short construction cycles and high operation rates. Among the over 10,000 construction projects during the period, 921 were above-quota major projects. During the five-year period, 595 above-quota major projects started operation, making a annual operation rate for major projects of 15.5%, or an average construction cycle of 6.44 years. Third, high investment efficiency for key construction projects. For the 156 Project, the total designed investment reached 20.27 billion yuan (which after adjustment involved 150 projects with a total designed investment of 18.78 billion yuan) and the total actual investment reached 19.63 billion yuan. By 1957, 146 projects had started construction work with 68 completed or partly completed for operation. Accordingly, for the 156 Project, the average construction cycle was just 3.6 years. Fourth, high investment effect coefficients. During the 5-year period, state-owned units finished a total fixed assets investment of 51.158 billion yuan and generated a total national revenue of 31.9 billion yuan, making an investment effect coefficient of 0.52, which was rather high compared with those of developed countries during the similar period, for example 0.41 in the United States, 0.45 in Japan, 0.49 in West Germany, 0.44 in Britain and 0.25 in the Soviet Union from 1956 to 1978.[1]

IV Government Investment during the "Great Leap Forward" and the National Economic Adjustment Periods

1 Quoted in Wang Haibo, ed., *Study of China's Economic Efficiency*, Economy and Management Publishing House, 1991, p.430.

After 1956, Mao Zedong started to take lessons from the excessive centralization and the lack of autonomy for local governments and enterprises. Since 1958, China launched the Great Leap Forward Movement, characterized with decentralization and the pursuit of high economic targets. During the Great Leap Forward from 1958 to 1960, the total state capital construction investment was 100.7 billion yuan, 80% more than that of the First Five-Year Plan period. In the Great Leap Forward mania, a large number of projects were implemented in a hasty way. In 1958, 1,587 major projects were implemented, 595 more than 1957. The number reached 1,361 in 1959 and then 1,815 in 1960. In terms of small projects at the county and above levels, 1959 saw the completion of 50,000 projects and 1960 witnessed the construction of over 70,000 projects. Small projects at the sub-county levels were even more. In addition, unplanned projects also multiplied. In 1960, 380 unplanned major projects were constructed, accounting for over 20% of all constructed projects. Unplanned small projects were just larger in number and higher in percentage. [1]

Against the background of emphasis on production, small blast furnaces and rolling mills were built in large numbers using both Chinese and western technologies. However, such efforts did not turn into productivity. For example, in the Cherry Orchard and the Gongchangling Mine regions, the Anshan Iron and Steel built quite a few 100-cubic meter blast furnaces and another converter steel-making plant in Lingshan. Taiyuan Iron and Steel, Wuhan Iron and Steel and Baotou Iron and Steel also established similar works, which took up much a lot of capital, equipment and materials and distracted the attention of the management. The low quality iron and steel production installations were later dismantled or used for other purposes. Many of these installations also face challenges in production. The cost was also much higher, a high as RMB 600 yuan per ton, that was, 4-5 times higher than that of big blast furnaces. [2]

1 Editorial Department of *Modern China*, ed., *Iron and Steel Industry in Modern China*, China Social Sciences Press, 1989, p.125.

2 Editorial Department of *Modern China*, ed., *Iron and Steel Industry in Modern China*, China Social Sciences Press, 1989.

The three-year Great Leap Forward did not bring the expected healthy economic growth, but created new difficulties in national economy. In 1961, the government had to readjust national economy according to the principle of "adjustment, consolidate, enrich and improve". During this period, investment power was centralized while capital construction investment was greatly reduced. After the four rounds of adjustment in 1961, fixed assets investment was 62.54% lower than that of 1960 and another 44.07% reduction in 1962, that is an actual fixed assets investment of 8.728 billion yuan in 1962. Because of these, the average annual investment from 1961-1963 was 12 billion yuan, accounting for only 28.8% of the 41.65 billion yuan in 1960. By the end of 1963, national economy recovered substantially, followed by an increase in government fixed assets investment in 1964 and 1965 reaching 16.589 billion and 21.69 billion respectively, realizing a year-on-year increase of 42.2% and 30.7% respectively.

During the Great Leap Forward period, the number of state operated enterprises increased rapid. With the adjustment in 1961, many wasteful, high-cost and low quality enterprises were closed, stopped, merged or transformed. On other hand, many collective-owned enterprises which had been "upgraded and transited into"state operated enterprises regained their collective ownership. As a result, the number of state operated enterprises decreased. Take industry as an example. There were 318,000 industrial enterprises in 1959, 197,000 in 1961 and 158,000 in 1965. Meanwhile, the initial asset value of state-owned industrial enterprises grew by a large margin. By the end of 1965, the total initial asset value of industrial enterprises owned by the whole people reached 104 billion yuan, doubling that of 1957. Industrial productivity also enhanced greatly from 1957 to 1965: oil extraction increased by 6.5 times, coal mining increased by 74%, iron 69%, steel 100%, installed capacity of electricity 2.25 times, cement 1.38 times, sulfuric acid 3.2 times, knitting spindle 29%, machinery and cardboard 57.9%, machine made sugar 84%, sewing machine 3.2 times, and bicycle 100%. In terms of machinery equipment, the number of machine tools increased by 1.4 times and forging equipment by 1.1 times. [1]

Investment fluctuated drastically and so did investment efficiency. In general, investment was reducing while investment efficiency was improving. During the Second Five-Year Plan period, the rate of capital construction fixed assets put into operation among enterprises owned by the whole people was 71.5%, about 8 percentage point lower than that of the First Five Year Plan period. The average annual completion and operation of large and medium capital construction projects was 8.1%, much lower than 15.5% in the First Five Year Plan. In this sense, the average construction cycle of medium and large capital construction projects was 12.4 years during the Second Five-Year Plan period, twice as long as the 6.5 years during the First Five-Year Plan period. A drastic dive was also found in terms of the fixed asset investment efficiency. During the Second Five-Year period, the total fixed asset investment in enterprises of people ownership was 130.7 billion yuan, or a 114% increase over that of the First Five-Year. However, GDP recorded an increase of only 1.6 billion yuan during the five years. As a result, the investment efficiency was as low as only 0.01; that is, every 100 yuan investment could only increase GDP by 1.23 yuan. During the adjustment from 1963 to 1965, investment efficiency started to improve. Fixed asset investment operation rate grew from 71.5% during the Second Five-Year plan to 87.2 % during the period from 1963 to 1965 (with that of 1965 reaching 93.6%, the peak before 1978). Investment efficiency recovered quickly. From 1963 to 1965, the total fixed asset investment in enterprises of people ownership was 49.945 billion yuan, which added 46.3 billion yuan to GDP, with the investment efficiency reaching as high as 0.93, as high as that during the economic recovery period.

3.4 Government Investment (1966-1976)

After the economic adjustment from 1963 to 1965, China entered the Third-Five Year Period in 1966. During this period, the development of government

1 Zeng Peiyan, ed., *Fifty Years of Investment and Construction in China*, China Planning Press, 1999, p. 78.

investment and state-operated enterprise focused on the development of heavy industries and industrial development in inland regions. Geographically, government investment favored inland regions, especially Southwest China.

From August to September 1963, when revising the first draft of "On Industrial Development", Mao Zedong added, "During the 105 years from the 1840s to the mid-1940s, China was invaded and bullied by various imperialist powers and lost almost all the wars which ended with humiliating unfair treaties , except the Anti-Japanese War. Such humiliations came as a result of corrupt social systems and backward economy and technology. Now, China's social system has changed, thus in general removed the former, though not completely so with class struggle still a social reality. The latter factor was also changing, but it may take several more decades to eliminate its impact. Unless we completely reverse our disadvantage in terms of economy and technology in the next few decades, we remain vulnerable to attacks. Of course, imperialism is on the wane, while China, the socialist camp and the anti-suppression nationalist revolutions are flourishing. It is possible to avoid another world war. However, wars are still possible though it is possible to prevent them from happening. For us, our vulnerability to attacks should remain the starting point of our work. Therefore, we shall endeavor to end our lagging in economy and technology in the near future. Otherwise, we are making mistakes."

In April 1964, the State Development Planning Commission was about to distribute state investment according to the order of agriculture, light industry and heavy industry according to the original Third Five-Year Plan[1]. Mao Zedong, in accordance with his analysis of the international situation, proposed "One Butt plus Two Fists" as the guiding principle for the Third Five-Year Plan; that was: "Agriculture and national defense as the two fists while basic industry as the butt".[2] Mao Zedong also advocated the Dazhai Spirit, namely self-reliance and

1 Bo Yibo, Policy Issues in Drafting Long-term Plans, in *Selected Works of Bo Yibo*, People's Publishing House, 1992.

2 Mao Zedong's Comment During the State Development Planning Commission's Reporting on the Third Five-Year Plan, *Party Literature*, No. 3, 1996.

hard work, for agricultural development. In May 27, Mao Zedong emphasized the Third Five-Year Plan must deal with the imbalance in industrial development.[1]

Investment efficiency headed downward after rejuvenating from 1963 to 1965. During the Third and Fourth Five-Year Plan periods, the average operation rate of fixed asset investment in people ownership enterprises was only 60.7% while the large and medium-sized project operation rate remained at about 10%. Investment efficiency hit the lowest point and stayed there for the longest period since the founding of the PRC.

3.5. Government Investment in the New Leap Forward 1977-1978

In March 1977, the State Development Planning Commission hosted the National Planning Conference to discuss the annual economic development plan for 1977. At the conference, it was argued that three key issues were to be addressed in 1977. Firstly, agriculture and light industry was incapable of satisfying the demand of economic development and people. Secondly, fuels and raw materials were insufficient to support national economic development. Thirdly, capital construction projects were far beyond national capacity in terms of finance and resources. Accordingly, the following targets were set for 1977: 4.6% increase in agriculture, 8% growth in industry and basic construction investment down by 23% to 25 billion yuan. The efforts in 1977 revived national economy in certain ways, with industry total output value reaching 372.8 billion yuan, increasing by 14.4% and basic construction investment totaled 33 billion yuan. The total agriculture and industry output value reached 505.5 billion yuan, 4.4% higher than the target.

On November 24, 1977, the National Planning Conference was convened in Beijing. The Key Points in Economic Development Planning, produced at the conference, pointed out that in the last 23 years of the 20th century, national economy shall develop along three phases while conquering same major obstacles.

1 Mao Zedong's Talk at the CPC Central Committee Work Meeting on May 27, 1964, in Jin Chongji, ed., *Zhou Enlai's Biography*, pp.1768-1769.

Phase I: During the last three years of the Fifth Five-Year Plan period, the focus was on agriculture and such industries as fuels, power and raw materials, which were expected to grow at 4-5% and 10% per year respectively, so as to lay the foundation for the Sixth Five-Year Plan. Phase II: During the Sixth Five-Year Plan period, production would reach a new level in terms of all indicators. By 1985, grain output would have reached 400 billion kilos, steel 60 million tons and crude oil 250 million tons. To achieve the production targets, an extensive basic construction plan was developed. For industry, 20 projects were newly developed or expanded, including 30 big power plants, 8 large coal mines, 10 oil fields, 10 steel big iron and steel plants, 9 nonferrous production bases, 10 chemical fibre plants, 10 petroleum plants, 10 fertilizer plants, 6 new trunk railways, 9 upgraded railways, and 5 harbors namely Qinhuangdao, Lianyungang, Shanghai, Tianjin and Huangpu. In February 1978, the Political Bureau of the Central Committee of the CPC approved the "Key Points" for implementation. The "Key Points" was also incorporated into the report on government work of the Fifth NPC.

To achieve such economic goals, domestic capital and technologies were insufficient. Therefore, the government turned the focus to extensive importation of foreign technologies in 197.

China sped up the introduction of foreign equipment and technologies in this period. In 1977, the State Development Planning Commission submitted a plan for introducing new technologies and equipment. According to the plan, in the following 8 years, 6.5 billion U.S. dollars were needed in foreign exchange while the supporting construction would take 40 billion U.S. dollars. A theory-discussion meeting at the State Council in 1978 restated the need to realize the "Four Modernizations" ahead of time. Accordingly, China started 22 large and medium-sized projects to import iron and steel, oil and petroleum, chemical fiber and fertilizer equipment and technologies from Japan, the U.S. and the Federal Republic of Germany at a total cost of 7.8 billion U.S. dollars, which meant a need of 1.17 billion U.S. dollars in foreign currency in that year. In 1977, with an export volume of USD$7.95 billion and an import volume of USD$7.21 billion,

China had a small trade volume and an even smaller trade surplus. Still under the influence of the idea that socialist countries must not borrow money (let alone receiving direct foreign from capitalist countries), in order to raise money to pay for imported equipment, the Bank of China raised USD \$5.1 billion by receiving U.S. dollar deposit overseas and taking loans from the European financial market. However, the interest rate of European loans was as high as 15-16%. Moreover, since every dollar spent required 4~5 yuan in RMB as counterpart, these projects required a total investment of over 50 billion yuan, which went far beyond the fiscal capacity of the government.

In accordance with the plan to introduce new technologies and equipment complexes in March 1978, the Central Government set the quota at USD \$8.56 billion. That year, the volume of transaction reached USD \$5.92 billion and the actual total usage was USD \$1.17 billion. After listening to the report of the Chinese delegation to Europe on June 30, Hua Guofeng commented that the last 22 years of the 20th century was actually longer than expected. The study tour showed that Japan started its modernization only 13 years ago while modernization in Germany and Denmark had a history of only dozens of years. China's modernization started with a production of 30 million tons of steel, compared with Japan's 220 million tons. So, it was possible for China to catch up. France had loan more than 2 billion in USD to China and more loans, up to USD \$5 billion, were possible, while West Germany proposed USD \$20 billion and Japan was thinking about even more. It was important for negotiations to proceed faster if projects could be specified as soon as possible before projects could be implemented batch by batch. In July, at the theory-discussing meeting at the State Council, it was argued that it was imperative to start a New Leap Forward of national economy, to realize the "Four Modernizations" ahead of schedule, to achieve a higher level of modernization at the end of the century and to use foreign capital to introduce advanced technologies and equipment. In 1978, the contract value of technology and equipment introduction projects reached USD \$7.8 billion, all to be paid in cash. The total volume of the technology and equipment introduction program was originally set at USD$6.5 billion, but increased to USD$18 billion, which was also beyond China's capacity then. Moreover, some project contracts were signed in a hasty way without duel scrutiny, even at a dinner party. For example, in the last 10 days of 1978, ten chemical project contracts were signed at a total volume of USD$3.1 billion, without any feasibility study or overall planning, which laid down the seeds for future problems.

Chapter 8

Formation and Reform of the Operation and Management System of State-Owned Enterprises (SOE)

It has always been the hope of CPC since the foundation of PRC that socialist SOEs could be the main drive for China's industrialization with better effectiveness and more attention to social equity than private economy. Unfortunately, SOEs fell far behind such expectations, as at the macro-economy level SOEs were never separated from the government and they were "stagnate when managed, and chaotic when given power", while at the micro-management level SOEs lacked a proper mechanism for constraint, supervision and stimulation, with the "soft budget constraint" and a tendency for egalitarianism, that is, "employees eat from the same pot of the enterprise, and enterprises eat from the same pot of the government". To solve this problem, from 1949 till the reform and opening-up policy in 1978, China had been exploring an operation and management system of SOEs which not only conformed to its national conditions, but also could realize the superiority of socialism.

1. Formation and Development of the Internal Management System of SOEs

As discussed in previous chapters, one of the three economic programs in CPC's democratic revolution was to confiscate and nationalize bureaucrat capital, and it was clearly stipulated in the Resolution of the Second Plenary Session of the Seventh CCCPC and the Common Program that the state-owned economy should be the leading component in the economy and should be given priority for development. Nonetheless, it remained a tough challenge for the system as well as for the government's capacity and experiences, especially for CPC who fought its way to power through years of war and from the rural areas, to bring into play the expected "superiority" of the state-owned economy and to manage the investment and operation of SOEs in such a democratic and effective way that could both fully execute the plan of the country and motivate to the full the initiatives of the enterprises and employees. In addition, the Chinese economy was underdeveloped and extremely unbalanced, and SOEs varied greatly in scale and industries as they were formed by confiscated assets from bureaucrats, traitors, war criminals, and counter-revolutionaries. PRC was confronted with the issue of establishing a socialist system of operation and management for SOEs from the very beginning.

1.1. Co-existence of multiple leadership systems in the early years of PRC

CPC had years of experience of operating and managing public enterprises in revolutionary base areas before the foundation of PRC. As early as during the Land Revolution, the Central Soviet Area promulgated the Regulations on the Management of Soviet State-owned Factories in April 1934, which stipulated that the person in charge of the state-owned factories was the factory director, who was appointed by the factory's superior Soviet organs, had the final decision on all matters in the factory, and was absolutely responsible to the Soviet government. Under the director was the managing committee of the factory to solve the major issues of the factory, composed of 5 to 7 people including the director, representatives of the Party branch, the Trade Union, the Youth League branch, and employees, and other persons in charge of the factory, with the director chairing meetings of course. Further, a "three-person group" was set up within the managing committee with the job to coordinate and deal with daily issues of the factory, composed of the director and representatives of the Party branch and the Trade Union. Such a leadership system was actually influenced by the "one leader" system of the Soviet Union. As factories grew with the base areas in number, scale and complexity of management in the last few years of the Sino-Japanese war, the "three-person group" was replaced by the "factory affairs board" under the new "unified" leadership headed by the factory director, as disagreements could easily occur between the three persons under the old system. The new system granted more power to the director, who was in charge of the operation and management of the factory on behalf of the government with the help of the Party branch, the Trade Union and all employees of the factory. This was in nature a "one leader" system.

However, after the implementation of the "factory affairs board" system, in some factories the power of the Party branch was weakened and the independence of the Trade Union was impeded and hampered, resulting in the failure to motivate the employees to participate in factory management. In response to this situation, CCCPC issued in May 1946 Directive on Policies of Industrial and Mining Enterprises, emphasizing that the enterprises should be managed in a democratic way with workers participating in management; further, in January 1948 CCCPC demanded that factory management committees and employee representative meetings be set up in public enterprises in revolutionary areas after successful trials of setting up the committee in some area. The factory management committee took unified charge of the factory's production and was made up of the director, engineer, chairperson of the Trade Union, and workers' representatives, with the director as the committee chair as before, while the employee representative meeting would check, criticize, and advise on the administrative work of the factory. This system was fully and most specifically stipulated in Regulation on the Implementation of Establishing Factory Management

Committee and Factory Employee Representative Meeting in National and Public Factories and Enterprises (Draft) issued by People's Government of North China in August 1949.

Per the Regulation, (1) the factory management committee is composed of the director, deputy director, chief engineer, chair of the Trade Union (all of them *ex officio* members), other persons in charge of production (nominated by the director to the superior and appointed by the latter), and employee representatives in equal number as the previous members (*ex officio* members from the employees are elected by general employee meeting or employee representative meeting). (2) The factory director is appointed by superior departments. (3) The factory director is the *ex officio* chair of the factory management committee. The director has the right to stop the execution of any decisions passed by a majority vote of the committee should he consider it inconsistent with the interests of the factory or directives from superiors, but should report immediately to superiors for instructions; the majority members of the committee can also report their opinions to superiors at the same time should they find the above measure taken by the directive inappropriate or disagree with his report. However, the director's decision should be carried out before instructions from superiors are received.

It is clear that the factory management committee system was a combination of the "one-leader" system from Soviet Union and the democratic management long upheld by CPC. Inherently it was predominantly a "one-leader" system supported by the employee representative meeting; the status and function of the Party organization in enterprises, however, was missing in the system, which could be explained by the imperfect Party organization in enterprises and the proven effectiveness of the "one-leader" system in Soviet Union and in China during war times.

After the foundation of PRC and in the early stages of reforming and rectifying SOEs, CCCPC promulgated in the famous editorial "Learning to Manage Enterprises" that the factory management committee system should be universally established in SOEs, following which came Directive on Establishing Factory

Management Committee in National and Public Factories from the Finance and Economics Committee of the Government Administration Council, demanding the same thing and attaching as reference Regulation on the Implementation of Establishing Factory Management Committee and Factory Employee Representative Meeting in National and Public Factories and Enterprises (Draft) issued by People's Government of North China in August 1949.

Nevertheless, there were considerable difficulties in establishing the factory management committee system which was actually a "one-leader" system in nature. First of all, most of the SOEs were established through confiscating bureaucrat capital during whose takeover and reform the Party played an important role, and army representative system was in place before the new leadership system (factory management committee) was set up. As the administrative personnel were mostly old staff who were unfamiliar with Party policies, unable to lead the democratic reform in the enterprise, and hadn't earned the full trust of superior departments, the Party organization was the *de facto* leader of the SOEs relied on by both superior departments and army representatives and responsible for the enterprise reforms. This would inevitably affect the implementation of the leadership system of the factory management committee. Secondly, the factory director must have both high political quality and outstanding professional ability since the management committee was a one-leader system; however, in reality it would be hard to find both in most managers of SOEs in the early years of the PRC. Generally speaking, old administrative staff of the enterprises had professional knowledge and ability, yet lacked political quality and awareness as they were just out of the old society; new managers sent by the Party and the government for the takeover or just retired from the army, on the other hand, were insufficient in professional knowledge and ability as they were new on the job. The lack of senior managers for SOEs who were both politically and professionally proficient was an important reason why the factory management committee system could not be established within a short time.

For the above two reasons, the leadership system of factory management committee was not established universally in SOEs in the early years of PRC. In most of the areas inside the Shanhaiguan Pass, the Party committee leadership system was adopted as the democratic reform was yet to be completed, which some considered to be more suitable for China's national conditions and the management of SOEs at that time.

Several factors contributed to the *de facto* leadership of the Party in many SOEs, namely, the increasingly important status and function of the Party in enterprises through leading political campaigns like the democratic reform and the campaign to suppress counterrevolutionaries, who strengthened its organization construction in enterprises as the reform progressed, and the lack of politically and professionally proficient cadres to be factory directors as requirements for their political status became higher and higher after the campaign to suppress counterrevolutionaries and the war to resist the US and aid Korea. Consequently, how to define, coordinate and straighten out the Party-government relationship within enterprises became an urgent issue and was put on both the Party and the government's agenda, which became a top concern of both the central government and major administrative areas on SOE management in 1951.

In July 1951, the Northeast Bureau of the CCCPC drew up a "Resolution on the Party's Leadership of Enterprises", which was essentially a decision to implement the "one-leader system". The Resolution stipulated that: (1) The director responsibility system is implemented to manage the production and administration work of factories and mines. The director should be appointed by the economic departments of the government, acquire necessary production materials and funds from the government, and take charge of the administrative work of the enterprise, while the management committee under the leadership of the director serves as a democratic mechanism for the employees to take part in the management of the enterprise. (2) The Party is an independent organization, taking full responsibility for the political and ideological work of the enterprise while guaranteeing and supervising its administrative and production work. The Party committee of the enterprise should unify the ideas of the Party, the government, the Trade

Union and the Youth league within the enterprise and ensure the consistency in their actions by political and ideological methods according to the laws and regulations of the country, the plans of superior departments and the instructions of superior Party committees. In addition, the Resolution criticized the Party committee leadership system, saying that it could easily confuse the boundaries between the Party and the government and prevent the Party from carrying out the political and ideological work in the enterprise as well as its role to guarantee and supervise. The draft Resolution was highly valued by leaders in the CCCPC after it was reported, and Comrades Li Fuchun, Chen Yun and Liu Shaoqi put forward the following opinions: much as the director responsibility system was an ideal management system for SOEs, it still needed to be based on the actual conditions of China; the director responsibility system should be allowed to be first piloted in the Northeast, and the draft Resolution could be promulgated and implemented after certain amendments (deleting the criticism on the Party committee leadership system, etc.).

While the Northeast was eager to implement the director responsibility system, the East and North were talking about the Party committee leadership system at their urban work conferences. Eventually the North China urban work conference decided after heated discussions to implement the Party committee leadership system for the following reason: currently in most of the big factories and mines in North China the directors were old staff who could not actually unify the Party, the government, and Trade Union and the Youth League, while even though the directors in many small enterprises were Party members, they did not know how to manage production, which meant that neither type of directors were qualified as politically and professionally competent managers who could unify the ideas and coordinate the work rhythm of the enterprise; at the same time, the unified leadership of the Party proved effective by its long line of successful experiences from the Sino-Japanese War, the People's Liberation War, the land revolution and the leadership of the Army. Considering the current lack of both politically and professionally qualified cadres, the Party committee leadership system should be the choice. In fact, both North and East China decided to adopt this system, that is, all instructions from the superiors of the Party, the government, the Trade Union and the Youth League and the plans and measures for their implementation must be discussed, decided and assigned as tasks by the Party committee of the enterprise, who also had the final decision for all important matters of the enterprise and to whom the director should be responsible. The Party committee became the *de facto* decision-making and managing organization of the enterprise.

The SOEs in the Central South and Southwest China also advocated the Party committee leadership system, as they were then going through comprehensive democratic reforms with a great many political tasks to fulfill, which highlighted the necessity and benefits of this system. As for the Northwest, due to the low competence (mostly transferred from rural cadres in northern Shaanxi province) and small number of cadres in SOEs, they could only do jobs such as recruiting and educating Party members and had little say in production, hence the unified leadership of the Party was for now out of the question.

CCCPC agreed with the opinions of North and East China. Comrade Liu Shaoqi wrote a letter on this matter (reviewed by Mao Zedong) to Gao Gang, secretary general of the Northeastern Bureau, on May 16, 1951, in which he said the following: since we do not have enough cadres now who know not only economic work and technology but also the Party and people work, the one-leader system would be a bad choice for managing factories, while collective leadership in the form of the Party committee can make up for the weaknesses of the director and unify leadership from all fronts, just like in the Army. The Party committee leadership system, therefore, is now a better management for the factories, while the one-leader system will have to wait until conditions mature. [1]

In December 1951 the Policy Research Office of the CCCPC gathered representatives from the major regions, departments and industry ministries

1 *Selected Documents from PRC's Economic Files 1949-1952·Industrial and Commercial Systems*, China Social Sciences Press, 1993, p195-196.

directly under the Central Government, the All-China Federation of Trade Unions and industry unions to discuss Decision of the Central Committee of the Communist Party of China on the Management of State-Owned Factories (Draft). A consensus was reached at the meeting on the Party-government relationship within enterprise – the director responsibility system in the Northeast was a good system and the inevitable direction for factory management, but there must be a transitional period for the areas within the Shanhaiguan Pass whose conditions were not mature enough for it, which meant that the Party committee leadership system was more appropriate while the director responsibility system had to wait until the democratic reform was completed and the production reform had some foundation. According to the experiences of the Northeast, conditions for transition to the director responsibility system included: (1) basic completion of the democratic reform; (2) implementation of planning management and economic accounting system in the factories; (3) establishment of specialized administrative agencies and regulations for technical management; (4) foundations established for the Party-people work and managing experiences acquired by the cadres. In addition, East China Bureau contributed one more, that is, coordinated pace of the external leadership of the enterprise that would overcome multiple-leadership.

1.2. Resistance to the implementation of the "one-leader" system after 1953

China turned to large-scale economic construction and began its First Five-Year Plan in 1953. To meet the needs of the Plan, the Party and the government gradually strengthened centralization and "vertical" management of economic sectors, and put more emphasis on responsibility system and standardization in enterprise management. This serves as the background for the nation-wide implementation of the "one-leader" system by CCCPC in light of its original plan and the current needs.

The experiences of the "May 3" factory in implementing the "one-leader" system and properly handling the Party-government relationship was promoted throughout the country in 1953 in the name of the All-China Federation of Trade

Unions, approved by CCCPC after successful trials. In April 1954, the North China bureau issued "Decision on Implementing the Director Responsibility System in State-Owned Factories and Mining Enterprises, saying that in order to eliminate the confusion of no responsible persons and unclear responsibilities and establish normal working order in industrial and mining enterprises the director responsibility system was implemented in place of the director responsibility system under the leadership of the Party Committee, whose job afterwards would be "to be fully responsible for the political and ideological leadership; be responsible for the supervision and guarantee of administrative and production work, and for leading people's organizations such as the Trade Union and the Youth League." [1]

In May 1954, CCCPC circulated the North China Bureau's Decision on Implementing the Director Responsibility System in State-Owned Factories and Mining Enterprises with comments that as the country moved into planned economic construction and central ministries and regional governments strengthened their leadership on state-owned industrial and mining enterprises, "it is now necessary and also possible to implement the director responsibility system in state-owned factories and mines across the country (including local state-owned factories and mines) to further improve the leadership of industrial enterprises and better carry out the plans of the country."[2] It was also hoped that relevant regions and departments report all problems and experiences in the implementation of the director responsibility system to CCCPC so that nationwide experiences could be accumulated.

However, no consensus was reached within the Party on the leadership system of SOEs, and disagreement intensified after the Gao and Rao incident and the criticism of individualism at the Fourth Plenary Session of the Seventh CCCPC.

On January 21, 1955, CCCPC approved and circulated Opinions on the Current

1 *Historical Documents on the leadership Systems of Chinese Enterprises*, edited by Policy Research Office of the All-China Federation of Trade Unions, Economy and Management Pablishing House, 1986.

2 Ibid., p. 198.

Conditions and Problems of the Party Organization and Thoughts of the Cadres in Northeastern Industrial and Mining Enterprises and Solutions to the Problems drafted by Comrade Qian Ying from the Commission for Discipline Inspection. According to the report, many enterprises in the Northeast demonstrated more or less a tendency to ignore the political and ideological leadership of the Party, as they were influenced by Gao Gang's individualism which wrongly exaggerated the function of the individual and accepted wrongly his slogan "the Party, the Government, the Union, and the League unified in management". This tendency could be seen in the following aspects: (1) The political and ideological leadership of the Party was weakened during the implementation of the one-leader system, to the point that the Party committee was subordinate to the management. (2) In terms of the leadership personnel allocation, the rank of the director was usually two or three levels higher than that of the Party secretary with some even higher, and many Party secretaries were groomed and promoted by the directors, or used to be their subordinates; the Party secretary often paled in comparison with the director. (3) As the cadres of the Party were weak, the Party did not have much authority among the people, and many cadres dealing with Party-people work had been long unsettled at their work. In addition, this tendency suggested that some Party committees and secretaries were so involved with administrative work that they ignored Party affairs. The report proposed that the relationship between the Party committee and the one-leader system must be properly solved and strong Party committees and secretaries must be established and appointed in industrial and mining enterprises. Considering the weakness of the Party secretaries in the Northeastern industrial and mining enterprises, adjustments must be made so that the secretary and members of the Party Committee should not be lesser than the director and deputy directors in political capacity and seniority.

On February 11, CCCPC issued Notice on Adjusting Cadres for the Party Committee and Management of State-Owned Factories and Mining Enterprises, and circulated with approval Request Report of the Northeast Bureau for Instructions on Adjusting and Strengthening Cadres for Party Affairs in State-

Owned Factories and Mining Enterprises. According to the Notice, the tendency to ignore the political and ideological leadership of the Party and remove the Party's supervision on the administrative work of the enterprises was in fact a reflection of capitalist thoughts in the Party, and would damage immensely the socialist construction if not overcome in an effective and timely manner. The Notice instructed provincial (municipal) Party committees to conduct an investigation into the allocation of Party committee secretaries and factory directors of state-owned factories and mining enterprises in the region, and to adjust the inappropriate personnel for Party committee secretaries according to the principle that the two should be roughly equivalent in qualifications.

The above measures showed CCCPC's misgivings about and dissatisfaction with the weakening of the Party's role in enterprises by the one-leader system, as they emphasized the political leadership of the Party committee and the appointment of Party secretaries with strong qualifications even though they did not deny the one-leader system. However, despite the request for more powerful Party secretaries, these measures failed to solve the problem of "who has the final say" in enterprises, the practical power issue that needed urgent clarification, for "political leadership" had to be reflected in the actual decision-making.

In April 1955 the Third Office of the Secretariat of CCCPC invited twenty-four representatives from the National Party Representative Conference to attend the "Forum on the Issue of Leadership of Industrial and Mining Enterprises", so that the experiences from the one-year implementation of the director responsibility system could be summarized and the leadership system in enterprises improved. Three opinions were formed on the forum on the Party-government relationship in SOEs. The first, mostly represented by comrades from the Hubei Provincial Party Committee, advocated the director responsibility system under the leadership of the Party committee. It was believed that the core of enterprise leadership must be the Party organization instead of the director himself, as collective leadership by the Party committee was the basic principle of the Party and must be followed in the Party organizations of industrial and mining enterprises. They referred to experiences of the implementation of assigned responsibility system under the leadership of the Party committee in the army to prove that the same could be applied in these enterprises. The second opinion, mostly represented by some comrades from Hebei, Shanxi, Beijing and the Northeast, disagreed with the first one and advocated the director responsibility system, that is, the director was fully responsible to the government for the production management of the enterprise while the Party should only supervise and guarantee such work. It was believed that the Party committee leadership system had a number of weaknesses from multiple leadership, no proper person in charge, disorder in production, and weak political work, and that in light of the demands for unity featured in the planned economy and industrial production, individual responsibility system, rather than collective responsibility system, must be adopted top-down in industrial management. The third opinion, mostly represented by comrades from the cities of Shenyang and Anshan, disagreed with the previous two. It was believed that the one-leader system and the Party committee system were systems for different organizations, with the former suited for production management while the latter for the Party as a democratic collective system. The job of the Party organization in enterprises should be the supervision and guarantee of production management instead of unified leadership; however, the supervision of the Party should be comprehensive and should not be reduced to only advices or loss of decision-making power on certain matters. As a Party member, the director must obey and carry out the decisions of the Party organization, and could meanwhile report his own opinion to superiors for instruction should he disagree with such decisions.

After discussions, most comrades present disagreed with the implementation of the one-leader system under the leadership of the Party committee in industrial and mining enterprises, and yet no consensus was reached on the extent of the Party's supervision and on whether the director should obey the Party's decisions concerning production management. It was agreed, however, that no rash changes should be made to the different leadership systems implemented in different regions, and that the director responsibility systems and other responsibility systems in industrial and mining industries should be strengthened by overcoming their shortcomings, while the political and ideological work of the Party should be improved by strengthening where it was weak.

In May 1955, Comrades Bo Yibo and Huang Jing consulted the leaders of the Soviet Union in charge of the economic work on the one-leader system during their visit there (attending the All Soviet Union Industrial Workers' Conference). The Soviet Union introduced the history of the implementation of the one-leader system in their country, and pointed out that the system was demanding of the quality of the cadres.

On June 4, 6, and 13 of the same year, the Third Office of CCCPC invited fifty factories directors and Party secretaries for three separate forums, whose opinions were quite the same in three aspects. First, the leadership systems in factories were rather disordered. Second, although it had been two years since the first implementation of the one-leader system in the second half of 1953 (1951 in the Northeast), it was not really carried out in many factories, as the directors were not familiar with their business, dared not take responsibility, and had to consult the Party committee should anything happen. Third, the political and the ideological work of the Party needed to be strengthened, and its supervision and guarantee of the economic work was also weak. On October 24, 1955, CCCPC circulated with approval "Report of the Third Office of CCCPC on the Forums on the Issue of Leadership in Factories and Mining Enterprises", stating "Party organizations in enterprises must endeavor to help the enterprises establish and consolidate the one-leader system management, making sure there is no rashness, and educate all employees to abide by strictly the administrative disciplines and rules of the enterprises. Party organizations must take the establishment of the one-leader system as a basic political task, as only when such a strict system is set up in enterprises can an effective economic order and work order be established, which is indispensable for the smooth running of enterprises, while having no one in charge is a worst scenario." [1]

On December 26, 1955, the Second Office of the Secretariat of CCCPC issued Report on the Situation, Problems, and Opinions of the Implementation of the One-Leader System in Factories in Jinan and Qingdao which summarized the situation of implementing the one-leader system in Shandong Province. The Report listed both the advantages and problems after the director responsibility system was implemented. For the advantages, responsibilities were clearly defined for the functional departments and personnel at different levels, and there were few cases of procrastination, lack of proper person in charge, and multi-leadership; in addition, the cadres and professionals had better sense of responsibility and more initiative to learn and research on the business, while the production was more balanced (compared with before when production was "slack in the beginning and rushed in the end", always speeded up to meet production quotas in the month-end or year-end) and the Party organizations were more focused on their own affairs. For the problems, there were also a few – commandism was somewhat developed, the Party-government relationship remained inharmonious (worse than before), there was no clue as to how to carry out political and ideological work, and the directors were less than qualified in management and technical capabilities.

Even though at that time the one-leader system could better assign responsibilities to personnel than the Party committee leadership system and could reduce multi-leadership, buck-passing and trifle disputes, it had intrinsic weaknesses that prevented it from achieving the expected effects. First, the relationship between and work of the Party, the government, the Union, the League, and the Women's Federation could not be effectively coordinated in the one-leader system. Second, it was difficult to link the one-leader system of SOEs with the Party committee leadership system of their superior departments as well as other departments in the country. Third, the one-leader system was to

1 *Historical Documents on the Leadership Systems of Chinese Enterprises,* edited by the Policy Research Office of the All-China Federation of Trade Unions, Economy and Management Publishing House, 1986, p. 202.

some extent conflicting with the goal of democratic management of enterprises long pursued by the Party, and did not facilitate the employees' participation in management or motivate their initiatives. Moreover, as CPC had just come to power after the war and from the rural areas and the SOEs were developing too fast, there was a lack of not only politically and professionally competent managers, but also refined operation and management systems for enterprises. It came as no surprise that there were many cases or errors made at work after the implementation of the one-leader system either because the directors dared not take responsibility since they did not know the business, or because they were incompetent.

1.3. "One-leader system" replaced by the Party committee leadership system

If it could be said that CCCPC chose the "one-leader" system before 1955 because of its own explorations and blind faith in the Soviet Union experiences, in the beginning of 1956 when China broke away from the Soviet Union superstition and began to look for it own road of construction, it was only natural that whether to continue using the one-leader system based on the Soviet model became an issue on its agenda. At that time Chairman Mao Zedong began to listen to reports from relevant departments of the Government Administration Council, carefully investigated and summarized the lessons and experiences in the previous few years, and formed as an outcome CPC's exploration of China's road of socialist construction represented by his work "On the Ten Major Relationships". Mao discovered quite a number of drawbacks in the economic system of the Soviet Union, and it was around this time that CCCPC found that the one-leader system from the Soviet Union, with all its drawbacks, was ill-suited for the national conditions of China and would be better replaced by the director responsibility system under the leadership of the Party committee. Mao's speech at the Second Preparatory Meeting for the Eighth National Congress proved this point. Mao said, "As for the one-leader system, the Central Committee did consider it implementable and circulated some experiences of certain regions with approval.

That's because we had no experience in this and couldn't come to the conclusion that it was not good. It was only before long that we finally decided it was not good, and a system that combines collective leadership with individual responsibilities is much better." [1]

In September 1956, Liu Shaoqi formally announced the implementation of the director responsibility system under the leadership of the Party committee in SOEs in his political report at the Eighth National Congress. He said, "a leadership system that combines collective leadership with the Party at the core and individual responsibilities should be established in enterprises. All major issues should be discussed and decided collectively, while all daily work responsibilities should be assigned to specific individuals."[2] Deng Xiaoping quoted the decision of CCCPC on perfecting the Party committee leadership system in September 1948 when emphasizing the democratic collectivism of the Party in his Report on Modifying the Party Charter, saying that the Party committee system had great significance in ensuring collective leadership and preventing individual authority, and that "the experiences of the People's Liberation Army in years of wars have proven the system beneficial for the work of the Army without impeding its military leadership. In light of experiences in recent years, the Central Committee has decided to implement the same collective leadership of the Party committee in all enterprises, that is, the director/manager responsibility system under the leadership of the Party committee."[3]

At the Congress, Li Xuefeng, Minister of Industrial and Transportation Work of CCCPC, made a special report on the implementation of the Party committee leadership system in enterprises. Wang Rengzhong, Party Secretary of Hubei Province, and Ouyang Qin, Party Secretary of Heilongjiang Province, also introduced experiences and lessons in this respect.

1 *Literature of the Communist Party of China,* Issue No. 3, 1991.

2 *Literature of the Eighth National Congress of the Chinese Communist Party*, People's Publishing House, 1957, p.36.

3 Ibid., pp.87-89.

Li Xuefeng said, "the state-owned industrial enterprises have made great achievements in their work under the correct leadership of the Party, but also made many mistakes and errors as large-scale management of modern industrial enterprises is a new task after the victory of the Revolution. It is worth noting that in state-owned industrial enterprises a tendency to neglect the leadership of the Party and a style of subjectivism and bureaucracy that is divorced from reality and the people have developed. Therefore, strengthening the Party's leadership over enterprises and implementing the Party's mass line have become a very important task to improve the work of industrial enterprises at present." The director responsibility system under the leadership of the Party committee "is adopted after summarizing experiences and lessons in all aspects of the Party's work in enterprises." He also said that in implementing the one-leader system "all enterprises that have adopted the one-leader system have to some extent obscured the Party members' and people's understanding of the leadership role of the Party, eroded the Party spirit of the cadres, especially some cadres responsible for administrative management, given rise to bureaucracy, commandism as well as pride, complacency, and an arbitrary style of work as the capitalist management ideas grow, and increased the cases of buck-passing, estrangement, and disunity between cadres, cadres and the people, and enterprises."[1]

Wang Renzhong, on the other hand, believed that the one-leader system "is wrong and conflicting with both the Party's principle of the combination of collective leadership and individual responsibilities, which has been effective for many years, and the mass line approach to work which has been developed through long-term revolutionary struggles." Wang also quoted the failure of the one-leader system in the state-owned Jiang'an Locomotive and Rolling Stock Factory and the success of the Party committee leadership system in the state-owned Wuhan No.1 Cotton Textile Mill, Zhongnan Construction No.1

1 *Literature of the Eighth National Congress of the Chinese Communist Party*, People's Publishing House, 1957, pp. 457-458.

Engineering Company and the public-private jointly owned Wuhan Yuhua Textile Mill to demonstrate the superiority of the latter over the former.[1]

There were mainly two reasons why CCCPC decided in 1956 to give up the one-leader system for the Party committee leadership system.

First, politically speaking, CCCPC was learning from the mistakes Stalin made in his last years and emphasizing collective leadership and democratic collectivism in the Party. It was pointed out in CCCPC's "On the Historical Experiences of the Proletarian Dictatorship" that "when the workers' class and the Communist Party have become the leading class and party of the country after the success of the Revolution, the leaders of the Party and the government are faced with grave dangers of using state organs to act arbitrarily, alienate from the masses and collective leadership, implement commandism and undermine the democratic system of the Party and the state as they are attacked on many fronts by bureaucracy."[2] The Gao and Rao incident seemed to have proven this point, and that is why one of the main issues of the Eighth National Congress was to emphasize collective leadership and strengthen the construction of a democratic system in the Party. As important components of the country and important locales for the grassroot organizations of the Party, enterprises must have leadership systems politically in line with the unified leadership of the Party and the requirements of its collective leadership and mass line.

Second, from the respect of reducing management costs and improving management efficiency, problems like bureaucracy, estrangement from the masses, low efficiency and concealing from both superiors and subordinates must be overcome in the running of government institutions even though it would be difficult to do so, as the socialist transformation had brought the economic life of the whole society onto the track of the state's administrative planning and management. For CPC, the soundness and operational efficiency of government

1 Literature of the Eighth National Congress of the Chinese Communist Party, People's Publishing House, 1957", pp. 172-177.

2 *People's Daily*, April 5 1956.

institutions were far less mature and effective than that of Party organizations. In terms of the operation and management of SOEs, it was difficult to straighten out the management system of SOEs, as under the traditional full public ownership and planned economic system there lacked the supervision of the external property right owners and the constraint of the market, as well as a mechanism for stimulation and elimination due to the unclear definition of responsibilities, rights, and benefits inside the enterprises. As for the enterprise-government relationship, bargaining and "reversed transmission of pressure" from the enterprise to the government were prevalent due to insufficient and distorted information and the limited management capacity of relevant government departments, so that the government had a tough time urging the enterprises to improve their efficiency even though they resorted to administrative measures. Furthermore, inside the enterprises, organization systems like the Party, the government, the Union, and the League were all entangled together and the employees were in name masters of the enterprises, making it impossible for the enterprises to clear personnel conflicts and barriers by removing them. Consequently, under the traditional planned economic system and especially in light of the lack of both politically and professionally competent managers for enterprises, the Party committee leadership system could indeed do better than the one-leader system in strengthening the government's control of enterprises, easing the conflicts between enterprise workers and managers, and helping democratizing management of enterprises.

After the anti-rightest movement in 1957, the denial of the one-leader system was further identified as a struggle in the Party's political line, and criticisms on the system were launched in many regions as it was considered a breakaway from the Party's leadership. Mao Zedong wrote in his 1959 notes on the Soviet Union textbook *Political Economics* that since the socialist management principles for enterprises should be inherently different from those of the capitalist state-owned ones, all of whom adopted the one-leader system, the director responsibility system under the Party committee leadership implemented now strictly differentiated us from the management system of capitalist enterprise.

Nonetheless, since the Eighth National Congress in 1956 decided on the implementation of the Party committee leadership system in enterprises, the old drawbacks of the system surfaced again, for example, no proper person in charge, rough management, and slack discipline. Even though democratic supervision and management of the enterprise was strengthened through the establishment of the employee representative conference, the enterprise's responsibility to the state was slackened instead of strengthened under the new system. The Party committee in the enterprise, after all, was only a first-level organization of the Party, not an enterprise manager appointed and authorized by the state, whose responsibilities were only to the superior Party committees and the Party members in the people and who had as its first motive for action instructions from the superior Party organizations while also influenced by the demands of the Party members. Such a leadership system turned out to be the micro-institutional foundation for the 1905s.

After the 1959 Lushan Conference, the national economy fell into a predicament and forced Mao Zedong to further explore the management of socialist enterprises. Between December 1959 and February 1960, he researched in some length the issue of management after the establishment of the socialist public ownership while reading the Soviet Union textbook *Political Economics*. He said, "the most important issue is management after private ownership is basically abolished", and "management of enterprises should be a combination of collective leadership and mass movement, with the cadres participating in labor and the workers participating in management, so that inappropriate rules and systems can be continuously reformed and the workers, the cadres, and the technical personnel can be united."[1] Here the enterprise management theory of "two participations, one reform, and three unity" was quite clearly defined.

It was around that time, on March 11 1960, that the Party committee of Anshan

1 Selected Conversation Records of Mao Zedong's readings of Political Economics (Textbook) from the Soviet Union (V), *Literature of the Chinese Communist Party*, Issue No. 3, 1994.

Municipality submitted to CCCPC through Liaoning Provincial committee Report of Anshan Municipal Party Committee on the Development of Technical Innovation and Technical Reform on the Industrial Front. This report of fewer than ten thousand words was divided into four parts. The first part summarized the basic situation of technical innovation and technical reform movement in the Anshan region with three features. First, "the employees are greatly motivated with extensive participation in technical innovation and technical reform, and the movement is progressing very fast"; second, "the employees have demonstrated great innovative spirit, and many new and advanced technologies are created within a short time"; third, "production keeps leaping forward with the promotion of the movement." The second part summarized five experiences for technical innovation and technical reform. "First, ideological revolution must be carried out constantly, and political leadership must be insisted, so that superstition will be removed and the mind be emancipated." "Second, the masses should be fully mobilized and all innovations and reforms should be experimented." "Third, comprehensive planning should be made with focus on production as the key." "Fourth, self-reliance should be combined with extensive coordination." "Fifth, technical reform should be combined with technical competitions." The third part reported the plans for the continued leap of Anshan in 1960 and approaches to complete the tasks. The fourth part emphasized strengthening the leadership of the Party. Mao Zedong read the report "with increasingly enlightened mood", and on the 22nd of the same month wrote a comment of more than 700 words on the report to be circulated by CCCPC as follows:

Shanghai Bureau, Cooperative District Committees, Provincial, Municipal and Autonomous Region Party Committees, Ministries and Leading Party Groups at the Central Level:

The report from Anshan Municipal Party Committee is a good one. I grow happier reading it and don't feel it is long; in fact, I'd rather it was longer as it is based on facts and reasons and is very intriguing. As the first and largest enterprise of China with more than a hundred thousand employees, Angang (Anshan Iron and Steel Company) used to consider itself already modernized with no need for the so-called technical reform. They were against the mass movements, against the principle of "two participations, one reform, and three unity" and the political leadership, and believed that only few people could be trusted to do the business; many in the company believed in the one-leader system, and stood against the director responsibility system under the leadership of the Party committee, holding the Magang Constitution (a set of authoritative methods from a big steel company in the Soviet Union) scared and inviolable. This is the first stage, before 1958. The second stage came in 1959, when people began to think, to believe in mass movements and doubt the one-leader system and the Magang Constitution. In July 1959 during the Lushan Conference, the Central Committee received a good report from them, which advocated the great leap, the anti-rightest movement and the drive forward with enthusiasm, and proposed an implementable high index. The Central Committee was very happy with the report, and circulated it to the comrades, who then sent it to the provinces, municipalities and autonomous regions on the phone. It was then a great help to the struggle against the rightest opportunism. This report now (March 1960) is more advanced, as it has created an Angang Constitution to replace the Magang Constitution, a new one in China, in the Far East. This now is the third stage. We now circulate the report to you, and ask that you send it to large and medium enterprises under your charge, and the Party committees of all big and medium municipalities, and of course prefectures and cities, as a study document for the cadres. I hope the cadres can be inspired and think more about their work after studying this report, and that throughout the year of 1960 waves after waves of the great Marxist-Leninist economic and technical revolution can be carried out in both urban and rural areas under the leadership of the Party.

In 1962, CCCPC restored the director responsibility system under the leadership of the Party committee after formulating "Forty Articles for the Industrial Sector". Between 1961 to 1865, during the adjustment period of the national economy, explorations were made on the strengthening of management and improvement of efficiency in the respects of economic accounting and responsibility system.[1] In the academia, economic accounting was proposed by scholars such as Sun Zhifang, while the Central Committee had trials of the Trust system in enterprises led by the State Economics and Trade Commission.

1.4. Mistaken estimations of the leadership in SOEs and the "takeover of power" in the 1960s &1970s

Regarding SOEs, CCCPC issued on March 22 1964 the Directive on Continuing to Carry out the Five-Anti Campaign, proposing that "we should strive to complete or basically complete the campaign in 1964".[2] According to Bo Yibo, in 1964 the national industrial and transportation sectors organized work teams of more than 130,000 people and carried out the Five-Anti Campaign in 1,800 SOEs, and 45 ministers and deputy ministers from 18 ministries and commissions with more than 22,000 cadres were stationed in the SOEs. The campaign was also launched in 730 collectively owned enterprises by provinces, municipalities, autonomous regions and the Second Ministry of Light Industry.[3]

On December 5 1964, Mao Zedong commented on the Report on Various Measures of Capitalist Operation and Management in Shenyang Smelting Works submitted by Xie Fuzhi, Minister of Public Security. He wrote, "how much of our industry has been capitalized in operation and management, one third, or half, or even more? We need to find out by checking the enterprises one by one." Xie listed eight "capitalist measures of operation and management" in the report: (1) falsify records and deceive the government; (2) benefit the factory at the cost of the public with a disregard for the whole society; (3) benefit oneself by exploiting

1 Ma Wengui,Functional Problems in the Management of Socialist State-Owned Industrial Enterprises, *People's Daily*, March 28, 1964.

2 The Five-Anti Campaign is the socialist educational movement promoted by CCCPC in cities after the Four Cleans Movement in the countryside in 1964. The five antis imposed were "corruption and theft, speculation, extravagance and waste, decentralization and bureaucracy."

3 Bo Yibo, *Reflections on Some Major Decisions and Events*, Vol. 2, Central Party School Press, 1993, p.1127.

others; (4) buy cheap and sell dear for the sole purpose of making profits; (5) buy on margin and sell short to speculate on the market; (6) lead with bonuses as the material incentive; (7) carry out scientific experiments for the sake of fame and profits; (8) spend extravagantly and cause huge waste. Xie also analyzed the roots of these problems as follows: (1) the framework of old Soviet enterprises and the impact of Revisionism; (2) the influence of the old forces of capitalism (including feudalism); (3) the influence from superiors to some extent. Mao remarked on the last one: "not just to some extent, but the primary root."[1] It could be seen that Mao considered the drawbacks of SOEs under the planned economy and even their normal operation and management as being "capitalized", and thought its primary root was from "superiors". On December 7 CCCPC circulated Xie's report with Mao's comments.

On December 12, in his comments on the report of Chen Zhengren on his stay and work in Luoyang Tractors Factory Mao said that a "class of bureaucrats" had formed who "have become or are becoming capitalists that suck the workers' blood" and should be "target of struggle and revolution".[2]

As Mao Zedong overestimated the severity of the problem, he had some serious disputes with Liu Shaoqi on the nature of the socialist education movement when it was discussed at CCCPC's work meeting in December of the same year. While Liu thought that the conflict between the "Four Cleans" and "Four Uncleans" was the main conflict, and the internal conflicts of the people and conflicts between the enemy and ourselves were entwined together, Mao insisted that in nature the movement was a conflict between socialism and capitalism and proposed that "the key is to rectify the incorrect style of work of the cadres in power who take the road of capitalism", quoting a poem from the Tang Dynasty poet Du Fu – "The bow should be drawn strong, and the arrow should be long; to catch a

1 *Works of Mao Zedong since the Founding of the People's Republic of China*, Vol.11, Central Literature Publishing House, 1996, pp. 256-257.

2 Quoted from Bo Yibo, *Reflections on Some Major Decisions and Events*, Vol. 2, Central Party School Press, pp. 1128-1129.

man his horse must be shot first, and to catch the gang the leader must be seized first."[1] Mao's opinions were adopted in the meeting's "Seventeen Articles" (later modified to be "Twenty-Three Articles" and issued on January 14 1965), which mistakenly proposed that the key of the movement was to "rectify the incorrect style of work of the cadres in power who take the road of capitalism".

By the first half of 1966, the Four Cleans movement was completed in 694 counties and cities (including some where it was only partially completed), accounting for 32% of the total number of counties and cities; Liaoning and Hebei provinces had completed more than 40% of the movement, while Beijing and Shanghai almost finished it. Adding the units that carried out the movement later, over one third of the country were key areas for the Four Cleans, while other areas carried out a simpler form of the movement, that is, the "Small Four Cleans". The same went for industrial and mining enterprises in China.[2]

In short, after the national economy entered the adjustment period in 1961, due to the limitations in understanding the socialist economic system reform and its problems as well as CCCPC's adoption of the "class struggle" method to solve the problems in economic management represented by Mao Zedong, explorations launched in the beginning of the adjustment were blocked which looked into diversified operation and management methods, multiple ownership structure and the use of the market mechanism, and the dangers of the so-called "capitalism" and "revisionism" were gravely overestimated, with more and more leftist prevention measures.

In May 1966, based on these mistaken estimates, the campaign of "taking over power" to overthrow the "power-holders who take the capitalist road" was carried out in the SOEs as well as in government and public institutions throughout the country, and the Revolutionary Committee established subsequently replaced the

---

1 Quoted from *Biography of Zhou Enlai (1949-1946)* (II), edited by Jin Chongji, Central Literature Publishing House, 1998, p. 834.

2 Bo Yibo, *Reflections on Some Major Decisions and Events*, Vol. 2, Central Party School Press, 1993, p.1134.

director responsibility system under the leadership of the Party committee, which went on until 1977 when the Revolutionary Committee was abolished in China.

2. Relationship Between State-Owned Enterprises and the Government in the Early Years of the People's Republic of China

In the twenty-nine years between the founding of the People's Republic of China to the Third Plenary Session of the Eleventh CCCPC which adopted the reform and opening-up policy, the SOEs of China were in name and in fact state-owned and government-operated. The SOEs were divided into state-owned enterprises and local state-owned enterprises. The former were enterprises directly under the central government, operated by central ministries and their headquarters, while the latter were operated by provincial, municipal and county governments. The government's direct operation and management of enterprises can be seen in the following aspects.

2.1. Direct management of enterprises by the government

In terms of asset ownership, all assets of SOEs were owned by the government (central or local government) as their sole investor, with no assets belonging to the SOEs themselves. Except for some assets acquired through confiscation and takeover, all newly-added assets were invested by the government, and all depreciation funds from the SOEs' fixed assets were handed over to the government.

In terms of operation and management, the government, as the owner of the SOEs, had unlimited liability. To prevent the loss of state-owned assets and profits and to use the limited financial resources collectively, the most cost-effective and simplest way for the government was to implement planning management in SOEs featured by administrative management. Accordingly, administrative departments were set up to directly manage the production and operation of SOEs. The following is an organization chart for the management system of industrial and mining enterprises in the early years of the PRC.

The government's direct management of SOEs can be found in the following aspects. (1) The government had the right to appoint and remove the leaders of SOEs, decide their production and operation (such as production plans and business activities) and the distribution of wages; (2) all profits were turned over to the government except for the retained rewards as stipulated; (3) the government examined and approved the revenue and expenditure plans of the SOEs and supervised their implementation; (4) the government decided on the SOE's construction and development, and managed their depreciation and major repair expenses, leaving no investment rights in the hands of the SOEs. The government issued twelve mandatory planning targets[1] to SOEs to ensure that they complete the government's economic plans.

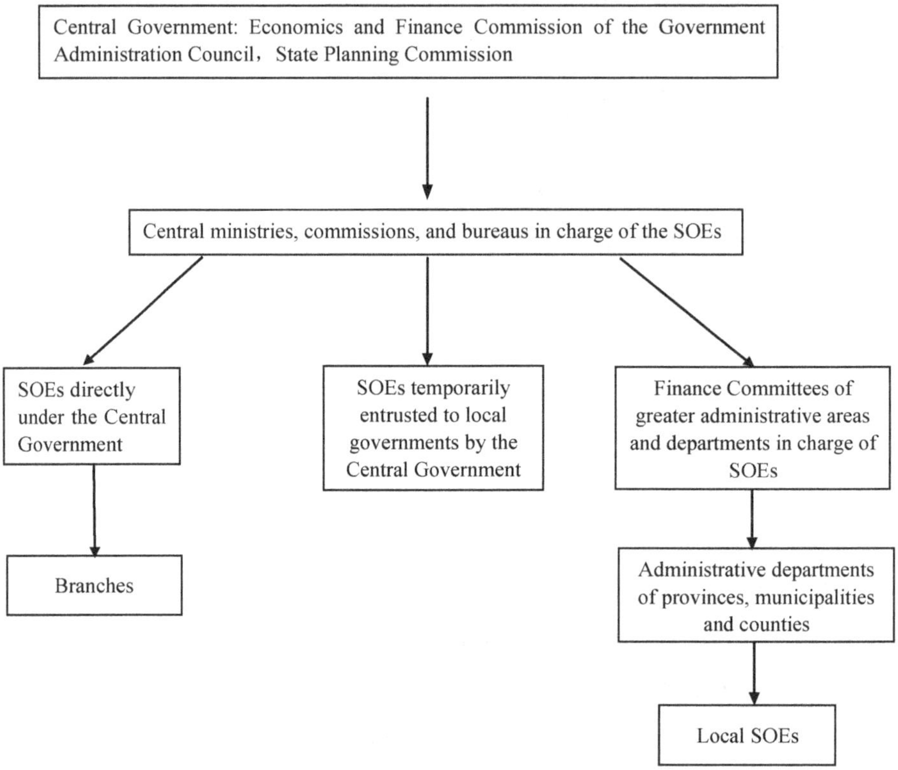

Chart 8-1

The reward funds for industrials SOEs were divided into two parts, one for

1 These include: total turnout, production Vol. of main products, trials on new products, important technical and economic quotas, cost reduction rates, cost reduction Vol., total number of workers, total number of workers reached at the end of the year, total wages, average wages, labor productivity and profits.

completing the plans and the other for exceeding the plans. It was stipulated in 1952 that SOEs in different sectors could retain 2.5% to 5% of the profits according to plans and 12% to 25% of the profits in excess of the plans as their reward funds.[1] The amount of loss reduction of a loss-making enterprise approved by the state should also be regarded as excess profits. Standards of retaining reward funds differed across sectors, but the total amount should not exceed 15% of the enterprise's annual basic salary, and enterprises in finance, commercial and foreign trade, agriculture, forestry, and water conservancy were forbidden from retaining reward funds. In that year, it was decided that state-owned trust companies should turn over 80% of their net profit to the Central Ministry of Trade and retain the remaining 20% for expanding business, which was an exception among commercial and trade enterprises at that time.

2.2. A management system that combined "vertical" and "horizontal" management but was mostly vertical

The government adopted a system that combined "vertical" and "horizontal" management at different levels for all SOEs except for the rail and financial sectors which were directly managed by the administrative departments of the central government. In the industrial sector, SOEs were classified into three categories: SOEs directly under the central government, SOEs entrusted to local governments by the central government, and enterprises under local governments, with the former two labeled "state-owned enterprises", while the latter two "local SOEs" to show the differences. Generally speaking, enterprises of considerable scale or significance were managed by administrative departments of the central government, while small-scale ones were managed by local governments. In May 1951, based on experiences and problems of the year after "unified finance", the Government Administration Council formulated Decision on Dividing Management Rights between the Central and Local Governments on Financial

1 State Economics and Trade Commission of the People's Republic of China, ed., *Fifly Years of China's Industry*, Part Ⅱ, China Economic Publishing House, 2000, p. 89.

and Economic Work, requesting that local governments supervise, guide and assist SOEs located in their jurisdiction directly under the central government and be in charge of all political work in these SOEs. As for SOEs entrusted to local governments and some important local enterprises, local government should report regularly to relevant departments in the central government on their business and work, and obey the departments' leadership in business policies and technology decisions, while the enterprises' important production plans and construction plans should be approved by the Central Finance and Economics Committee or administrative departments of the central government. Local governments were allowed to invest in local state-owned retail companies (branches of specialized central enterprises) with an investment amount of no more than 50% of the company's total investment, and should share with the company its profits and losses according to respective investment amounts.

After the implementation of "unified finance" in March 1950, state-owned trade enterprises were also managed collectively by the central government in order to control the market and guarantee supplies. Starting from February 1950, on the basis of the trade companies in large regions, provinces, municipalities and autonomous regions and the confiscated bureaucrat capital commerce, the central government established specialized headquarters for industries including grain, gauze, department stores, salt, coal, local products, oil, industrial equipment, livestock, export, oil, import and mineral products to operate respectively domestic commerce and foreign trade under the direct leadership of the Ministry of Trade. These specialized national headquarters could set up branches in large regions, provinces (municipalities), prefectures, cities and counties according to their business needs, while being managed, operated, and accounted collectively by the headquarters nationwide. Not only was their business directly managed by the headquarters, their capital was controlled and adjusted by the Ministry of Trade and their turnover was to the central government, while the local governments were only responsible for the supervision and guarantee of business, personnel and Party relationship.

During the adjustment period of the national economy, as the SOEs were small in number and concentrated in sectors important for the national economy and people's livelihood, the central government took into its own hands the operation and management of large and medium enterprises and enterprises in some important sectors to ensure its power to adjust the national economy. According to statistics, of the 9517 industrial SOEs in 1952, 2,254 were turned over to the central government, accounting for 23.59% of the total number yet with 71.61% of the production volume. As for commerce and foreign trade, the statistics in May 1951 showed that the number of branches and employees of commercial and foreign trade headquarters directly under the Ministry of Trade accounted for 56.84% and 66.49% respectively of the total number of branches and employees in this sector.

2.3. "Level management" that divided the management of SOEs into different levels

In the early years after the founding of PRC, SOEs were managed by local governments together with their investment and profits, as the time of liberation differed between areas. In March 1950, after "unified finance", the central government took back the management of sectors and enterprises concerned with the national economy and people's livelihood, putting them under direct control of administrative departments, and stipulated the following regulations for the jurisdiction, operation, and management of common SOEs. All state-owned industrial enterprises were classified into three categories and managed in three different ways, the first directly manager by ministries and departments of the central government, the second entrusted temporarily to local governments or military institutions while still under the central government's jurisdiction, and the third managed by local governments or military institutions. For the first category of SOEs, the central government was responsible for their investment, operation, and management, and should take over their profits and also subsidize their losses. For the second category, the central government was responsible for their investment, profits and losses, but in terms of operation and management the administrative departments of the central government should approve their policies and guidelines, appoint or remove their management, or plan overall the allocation and distribution of products and material resources when necessary, while the rest fell under the management of local governments. For the third category, the local governments were in control of their investment, operation, management and profits. During the categorization, most large and medium enterprises were taken over by the administrative departments in the central government or entrusted to local governments, while the small ones went to local governments (whose production volume accounted for only 25% of the total volume of SOEs, a small percentage despite their large number).

In 1951, however, the problem of the lack of initiative on the part of local governments became increasingly serious with the recovery of the national economy from wartime, as they had very limited authority in economy after "unified finance", while at the same time the problems of unclear leadership and responsibilities surfaced in the management of SOEs, with either multi-leadership or no proper person in charge. In response to these problems, the Government Administration Council issued on May 24, 1951 Decision on Defining Management Responsibilities of the Central and Local Governments in Economic and Finance Work. According to the Decision, in enterprise management local governments were asked to supervise, guide and assist SOEs directly under the central government which were scattered across the country to ensure the implementation of the state's unified policies, guidelines, plans, and important systems. All political work of these SOEs fell under the leadership of local governments, to whom they should report regularly on their business and work. For SOEs entrusted to local government and some important local SOEs, on the other hand, local governments should report to relevant departments in the central government on their business and work, and obey the leadership of the central government in business guidelines and technical decisions, while the important production plans and basic construction plans of these SOEs should be approved by the Central Finance and Economics Committee or other administrative departments in the central government.

In the industrial sector, considering local government's limited authority and lack of initiatives (as the scope of local industry was not defined, and large enterprises were taken over by the central government, they feared that the small ones would face the same fate if developed), the Government Administration Council defined the development direction and operation scope of local state-owned industry, mainly light industries with abundant local resources to draw on, small-scale enterprises for production materials and public utilities. In addition, the Government Administration Council stipulated that the development of local state-owned industry should rely on their own accumulated capital, and the central government would only help in the following aspects if possible: (1) Spare production equipment of the central government could be allocated to the industrial construction of local governments according to their basic construction plans, and an annual depreciation fee must be paid to the central government or counted as investment from the central government. (2) Relevant central departments in charge of the industrial sector should offer technical guidance and help to local industry. (3) Trade department and banks should support local industry to the extent possible. (4) Profits of local state-owned industry could be exempt from being turned over to the Treasury for a limited period of time so that they could be used to expand local industry. (5) Local industrial leadership systems should be established to strengthen the management and assistance of local industry.

In the commerce and trade sector, the central government allowed local governments to invest in local retail SOEs with an investment amount of no more than 50% of the company's total investment, who should share with the company its profits and losses according to respective investment amounts. As for the management of these SOEs, the central government was only in charge of operation guidelines, business scale, pricing standards, and accounting system, and all the rest was the responsibility of local governments. Further in May 1952, the Ministry of Trade approved local governments' investment in state-owned trust companies in big cities, who should have full control and use of all the profits from their investment; the Ministry would only decide the operation guidelines and business scope of the trust companies, and all daily operation and management was the responsibility of the municipal bureaus of commerce.

2.4. Centralization of enterprise management from 1953 to 1956

After three years of recovery of the national economy after its foundation, PRC entered a period of large-scale economic construction and started the First Five-Year Plan. Local governments all had a strong demand and urge for a rapid economic development, yet at that time the economy was underdeveloped with a weak foundation; also, limited funds needed to be pooled to "support key constructions and make steady progress" and give priority to heavy and national defense industries. Therefore, since the end of 1952, the central government gradually strengthened centralization to meet the demands of the First Five-Year Plan.

In December 1952, the State Planning Commission was established in the central government which strengthened its capacity on planning and implementing planning management and highlighted the authority of central planning management agencies. In 1953, the central government removed the economic management responsibilities of the governments of the greater administrative areas (military and political committees), took back most of the power and transferred the cadres in charge to the central government. Thus, the central-local relationship turned from that between the central government and the greater administrative areas to that between the central government and provinces, with more control on the national economy on the part of the central government. In the meantime, nine new ministries were set up in the Government Administration Council, six of which were in charge of the economy, that is, the First Ministry of Machinery Industry, the Second Industry of Machinery Industry, the Ministry of Geology, the Ministry of Construction Engineering and the Ministry of Food, while the Ministry of Trade was divided into the Ministry of Commerce and the Ministry of Foreign Trade.

In 1954, the State Council was established according to the decision of the First National People's Congress. The number of working departments increased from 42 in the original Government Administration Council to 64, with 12 of them on economy, namely, the Third Office of the State Council (heavy industries), the Fourth Office of the State Council (light industries), the Fifth Office of the State Council (finance and trade), the Sixth Office of the State Council (transportation), the Seventh Office of the State Council (agriculture, forestry, and water conservancy), the Eighth Office of the State Council (reorganization of private economy), the State Planning Commission, the State Construction Commission, the Ministry of Local Industry, the National Bureau of Statistics, the Central Administration for Handicraft Industry, and the Central Administration for Industry and Commerce. Within two years, that is, by the end of 1956, 17 more departments were set up in the State Council, again with most of them on economy, namely, the State Economics and Trade Commission, the State Technology Commission, the Third Ministry of Machinery Industry, the Ministry of Electric Manufacturing, the Ministry of Forestry Industry, the Ministry of Product Procurement, the Ministry of Agricultural Reclamation, the Ministry of Fishery, the State Bureau of Material Supplies, while the Ministry of Heavy Industries was divided into the Ministry of Metallurgical Industry, the Ministry of Chemical Industry, the Ministry of Construction Material Industry, and the Ministry of Fuel Industry was divided into the Ministry of Coal Industry, the Ministry of Oil Industry, and the Ministry of Power Industry. Meanwhile, corresponding departments were set up in provincial governments, and in most lower-level governments. A highly centralized system of economic management institutions had been set up with a focus on department management (the "vertical" management) and an allocation of agencies according to industries and products.

In terms of government finances (including investment), the highly centralized financial system in the early years of PRC was adjusted during the First Five-Year Plan to guarantee key constructions and tap local initiatives, reducing the degree of centralization and adopting a measure with the focus on centralization and an allowance for certain decentralization and flexibilities in many places after the Greater Administrative Areas were dissolved. The specific methods were as follows: (1) Implement a three-level management where the finances of the country was divided into the central government, province (municipality directly under the central government), and county (city) levels. (2) The national fiscal expenditure was divided into central and local expenditures according to the jurisdiction and business scope of enterprises, public enterprises, and administrative institutions. (3) The national revenue was divided between central and local governments by percentages according to different categories. (4) Local budgets were approved by the central government and divided into revenue and expenditure. Local fiscal expenditure was first paid by local fixed revenue and fixed national revenue percentage, and any differences were made up by adjusted national revenue allocated by the central government whose percentage was decided annually. After the implementation of this system, 75% of financial resources were controlled by the central government and 25% by local governments during the First Five-Year Plan. Local governments had fixed financial resources and some mobile ones, and they all had considerable surplus even though their budgets were approved by the central government. On the other hand, the national fiscal revenue grew at an average annual speed of 12.3% between 1953 and 1957.

In terms of commerce and trade, to guarantee the supply-demand balance (market stability) under shortage of goods and key constructions, the government began to monopolize and plan the purchase and sales of main staple and non-staple agricultural products such as grain, cotton, and oilseeds, and divided the production materials in industrial products into three categories – state-allocated materials, ministry-managed materials and local-managed materials (also named "three materials"), with the first two (materials allocated by the central government) at 227 kinds in 1953 (112 state allocated, and 115 ministry-managed) and increased to 532 in 1957 (231 state-allocated and 301 ministry-managed). To take steel as an example, the percentage of steel supplied by the market was reduced from 25.9% in 1953 to 8.2% in 1956.[1]

In terms of the jurisdiction over SOEs, a clear trend of centralization could be discerned in this period. During the recovery of the national economy, as SOEs were small in number and concentrated in important sectors concerned with the national economy and people's livelihood, the central government took over control of the operation and management of large and medium enterprises and some important sectors to ensure its power to adjust the national economy. According to statistics, of the 9,517 industrial SOEs in 1952, 2,254 were taken over by the central government, accounting for 23.59% of the total number, yet with a production volume that accounted for 71.61% of the total and 67.31% of all the employees in industrial SOEs in China. As for commerce and foreign trade, the statistics in May 1951 showed that the number of branches and employees of commercial and foreign trade headquarters directly under the Ministry of Trade accounted for 56.84% and 66.49% respectively of the total number of branches and employees in this sector.[2] However, in 1957, the number of enterprises and public enterprises directly under the central ministries exceeded 9,300.

3. First Adjustment of Relationship between SOEs and the Government

China's SOEs (including a large number of new "public-private partnership" enterprises) expanded rapidly after the basic completion of socialist transformation in 1956, and consequently the government was faced with the urgent issue of how to effectively manage such a great number of enterprises without damaging their flexibility and initiative in operation.

3.1. Reform plans formulated in 1957

The flexibility and initiative of local governments in economic construction were suppressed with increasing centralization, of which CCCPC had been aware

1 *Reform of the Economic System in Modern China*, China Social Sciences Press, 1984, p. 503.

2 *Selected Documents from PRC's Economic Files 1949-1952·Industrial and Commercial Systems*, China Social Sciences Press, 1993, pp. 280-285.

since the beginning of 1956.

In April 1956, Comrade Mao Zedong discussed in detail the central-rural relationship in "On the Ten Major Relationships" after investigation and research. He said, "It should be noted that at present, on the premise of consolidating the unified leadership of the central government, more power and independence should be given to local governments so that they can do more.", that "We cannot centralize everything like the Soviet Union, leaving no room at all for local governments to maneuver.", and that "Local governments need to develop industry, just like the central government; even industry directly under the central government needs support from local governments, and it is even more so for agriculture and commerce. In short, local initiatives must be brought into full play so as to develop socialist construction, and local interests must be taken into consideration so as to consolidate the central government." On the issue of how to reduce over-centralization, Mao proposed the following solution: "Central departments can be divided into two categories. The first should manage the enterprises directly, and their local managing branches and enterprises should be supervised by local governments; the second are responsible for drawing up guidelines and work plans, leaving the actual business to local governments."[1]

On the Eighth National Congress of CPC in September 1956, Comrade Zhou Enlai made an important speech on the division of central-local responsibilities and proposed seven principles as follows. (1) It shall be clearly stipulated that the provinces, autonomous regions, and municipalities directly under the central government have jurisdiction within a certain scope on planning, finances, enterprises, undertakings, materials, and personnel. (2) All enterprises and undertakings pertaining to the whole national economy which are global, critical and centralized in nature shall be managed by the central government, while other enterprises and undertakings shall be handed over to local governments as much as possible, and the relevant planning, financial management and personnel

1 *Selected Works of Mao Zedong*, Vol.5, People's Publishing House, 1977, pp. 275-277.

management shall be handed over too under normal circumstances. (3) A dual-leadership system shall be improved and implemented in the management of enterprises, with the central government as the main responsible body and local governments as assistants, or the other way around, so that leadership can be effectively strengthened. (4) Major planning and financial indicators under the central administration shall be issued by the State Council in a unified manner instead of being issued by different ministries vertically. (5) Some room for adjustment and maneuver shall be left to local governments in some planning indicators and personnel quota. (6) Specific provisions shall be made for the implementation of various autonomous rights in ethnic autonomous areas, so as to help the political, economic and cultural development of ethnic minority areas. (7) System reform shall be carried out gradually, and major changes shall be made steadily by preparing in the first year, having pilot runs in the second year, and implementing fully during the Second Five-Year Plan.[1] These principles reflected the ideas of centralization of major responsibilities and decentralization of minor ones, and of unified leadership coupled with flexibilities under local conditions. In order to change the "separated vertical management", major planning and financial indicators under the central administration were issued by the State Council in a unified manner, while guidelines of steady progress after pilot runs were applied in the reform process.

To reform the economic system, the State Council held a national conference on systems between May and August 1956, and further to that, issued three documents at the end of 1957 after over a year of deliberations and with approval from CCCPC, the State Council and the Standing Committee of the National People's Congress, namely, Regulations on Improving Industrial Management Systems (Draft), Regulations on Improving Commercial Management Systems (Draft), Regulations on Improving Financial Management Systems (Draft),

1 *Selected Works on Economics of Zhou Enlai*, Central Literature Publishing House, 1993, p.314.

which came into effect in 1957. The documents aimed in general to adjust the relationship between central and local governments and between the state and the enterprise by delegating certain management power in industry, commerce, and finances to local governments and enterprises so that their initiative and enthusiasm could be brought into fully play and the unified plan of the central government could be implemented in accordance with local conditions. The main policies delineating the relationship between central and local governments are as follow:

1. Adjust the present jurisdiction of enterprises and delegate some enterprises directly managed by central ministries to local governments. According to the documents, of the enterprises directly managed by the heavy industry ministries, large mines, large metallurgical enterprises, large chemical enterprises, important coal bases, large power grids, large power stations, petroleum refining enterprises, large and precision machinery factories, military industries and other industries with complex technology would remain in the jurisdiction of the ministries, and all other enterprises should be delegated gradually to local governments in accordance with their conditions; the enterprises managed by the ministries of light industry, food industry, and commerce should all be delegated to local governments except some large ones difficult to manage by local governments; the civil construction enterprises in the construction industry should be delegated gradually to local governments in many districts.

2. Expand the financial power of local governments. Should revenue exceed expenditure in implementing local budgets, local governments could arrange for its use and retain the year-end balance for use in the next year. The central government would also give local governments a percentage of the foreign exchange earned to encourage them to actively implement the national export plans.

3. Expand the local governments' power in materials allocation. local governments could make adjustments in the volume, types, and time of use of materials allocated to SOEs, local enterprises and local commercial organizations

within their jurisdiction, as long as they could ensure that the enterprises complete the national plan.

4. Expand the local governments' power in planning management. Of the indicators in commercial planning, the State Council would only issue yearly purchase plan, sales plan, total number of employees, and profit targets, and would allow local governments a 5% difference in the total volume of purchase and sales plans while implementing them.

5. Manage prices of commercial products by category. The purchasing and selling prices of farm produce and sideline products in the third category, and the selling prices of secondary markets and secondary industrial products shall be set by the local authorities on their own according to the pricing principles stipulated by the commercial departments of the central government.

6. Expand the personnel management power of local governments. The personnel management of all enterprises delegated to local governments from central ministries should be handled in the same way as local enterprises; local governments could make adjustments to cadres in enterprises still managed by central ministries, provided that such adjustments do not weaken the enterprises.

The documents also imposed certain restrictions on the power of local governments while expanding it. For example, in finances, it was stipulated that "there should be an upper limit on the extra revenue local governments can get from improving financial systems, which should allow them an appropriate amount of mobile financial resources, while at the same time guarantee the needs of key national construction." The cumulative amount of such revenue in three years should not exceed 2 billion yuan. In terms of materials management and commercial circulation, it was stipulated that for materials allocated by the central government or managed by central ministries which were produced in enterprises managed by governments of provinces, municipalities, and autonomous regions, local governments could retain and arrange for use a certain percentage of the part of production in excess of the national plan, but could not change the types of products in the national plan; also, the requests of the local governments for production of certain products in excess of the national plan, for example, in a mechanical factory managed by the central government, should be approved by the central government if the said products were allocated by the central government or managed by central ministries, to avoid blind excess production. In personnel management, transfers of cadres managed by the State Council made by local governments should be reported to and approved by the State Council, and transfers of cadres managed by the central ministries made by local governments should be consulted with the ministries.

Despite their seeming effectiveness, the decentralization of power did not serve its intended purposes, as such reforms in the economic system failed to change the unitary public ownership and the planned management system that did not separate the government from the enterprises.

3.2. Decentralization of power in 1958

In 1958, however, the above reforms were hastily and rashly implemented amid the irrational atmosphere of the period, and within a very short time the following power of economic management was delegated from the central government to local governments.

1. The majority of SOEs were handed over to local governments. In 1958, the number of enterprises and institutions directly managed by central ministries was reduced from 9,300 in 1957 to 1,200, with 88% delegated to local governments, while the percentage of industrial output of SOEs in the total national industrial output also dropped from 39.7% to 13.8%.

2. Planning management was decentralized, and a "planning management system based on comprehensive regional balance and combining specialized departments and local governments" was implemented. Local governments' management power was excessively expanded so that they could form their own system. In 1959, the types of industrial products managed by the National Planning Commission was reduced from over 300 in 1957 to 215, the proportion of central revenue directly collected by the central government dropped from 40% to 20%, and the types of materials allocated by the central government or

managed by central ministries were reduced from over 500 to 132, a 75% cut, and the organization of supply and sales was also handed over to local governments.

3. Examination and approval of capital construction projects were delegated to local governments. For local construction projects over the capital limit, only a brief proposal needed to be reported to the central government for approval, and all other design and budget files were examined and approved by local governments; for projects over the capital limit which had no coordination with SOEs and whose products did not need to be balanced nationwide, local governments could approve after filing for record to the central government; for projects below the capital limit, local governments had full approval power. In July 1958, the central government put forward a contract system for local capital construction investment, which meant that within the scope of contracting, the investment in capital construction was decided and its proliferation enjoyed by local governments.

4. Financial and taxation management was decentralized. The financial resources of the central government decreased from 75% in the first Five-Year Plan period to only about 50%, and the extra budgetary funds of local governments and enterprise increased from 8.5% of the budget income in 1957 to 20.6% in 1960.

5. Labor management was decentralized. In June 1958, the central government decided that local labor recruitment plans could be implemented after confirmation from provincial (municipal) governments and needed no approval from the central government.

6. Management of commercial and banking industries was decentralized. In commerce, national specialized companies were abolished, specialized bureaus (offices) were set up at local administrative levels to integrate government and enterprises, and commercial outlets with different economic components were merged. In finance, changes were made to "decentralize deposits and loans, implement contract responsibility system in planning, manage balances locally and unify capital movement". As a result of decentralization of credit management, the

credit funds in use reached 95.44 billion yuan in 1960, an increase of 2.35 times over those in 1957.

7. Education management was decentralized. 60 higher education institutions and 143 secondary vocational schools were handed over to local governments, while at the same time examination and approval of new higher education institutions was delegated to provinces, municipalities and autonomous regions, with a request that they promote education.

This re-allocation of power between central and local governments happened under the premise that unitary public ownership and the economic system with administrative planning should remain untouched. Despite its intention to motivate both central and local governments so that local governments could make scientific decisions based on a full grasp of local economic information and the central government could be less rigid in decision-making, the outcome was quite to the contrary. Local governments were reluctant to shoulder the responsibility of maintaining an overall balance nationwide, and their leaders aimed to enhance their personal prestige through establishing a comprehensive industrial system and achieving a high economic growth rate locally;[1] in addition, too much power was decentralized without necessary restriction, and there was a general impatience in economic construction formed in the "anti-rightist" and anti-"anti-rash advance" movements. As a result, local governments blindly pursued local economic expansion, leading to a breakdown of the overall balance, a serious decline in product quality, and an unprecedented economic chaos.

Furthermore, decentralization also means that power was delegated from specialized agencies and experts (referred to as "technocrats" abroad) to non-specialized agencies and bureaucrats. As economic management of the country began to be centralized in 1953, outstanding and specialized personnel were also centralized and housed in specialized management institutions as mentioned

1 Refer to *The Socialist System* by Kornai for analysis on classic investment hunger in socialist countries, published in 2007 by Central Compilation and Translation Press, pp.153-156.

before (the so-called "vertical departmental management"), while at the same time local governments (mostly party committees at different levels) did not intervene much with economy. The decentralization in 1958, however, put economic management in the hands of the party committees, whose members knew nothing or next to nothing about economy and could only think and act blindly, leading to the prevalence of high indicators and blind command. It can be said that the decentralization of power in 1958 was one of the important reasons for the rashness of the period and its serious consequences.

4. Re-Adjustment of the Relationship between SOEs and the Government

China entered a period of economic adjustment in 1961 due to the disorder and imbalance of the national economy in the late 1950s, and correspondingly the relationship between the government and the SOEs also entered a period of re-adjustment. Enterprise operation and management were centralized between 1961 to 1965, and were decentralized again in 1966. The government-enterprise relationship began a cycle of change, where enterprises were "stagnant when centralized, but chaotic when decentralized".

4.1. Re-centralization of financial, trade and economic management in industry

The change in industry management system was necessitated by the recovery and development of the national economy under the guideline of "adjustment, consolidation, enrichment and improvement". The principle behind such change was to stress the coordinated economic management of the country and implement a high degree of centralization and unification in order to overcome the state of decentralization and disorder in industrial production. In January 1961, the central government officially issued Some Provisional Regulations on the Adjustment of Management System, emphasizing centralization and unification to overcome current economic difficulties. The Regulations stipulated that economic management should be concentrated to the central government, regional bureaus, and provincial (municipal or autonomous regions') committees, and within the next two or three years be more concentrated to the central government and regional bureaus. All personnel, financial, commercial, and industrial management improperly delegated to prefectures, counties, communes, and enterprises by provinces, municipalities, autonomous regions and central ministries must be taken back; the power of administrative management, production command, material dispatch, and personnel arrangement of enterprises directly under the central ministries should be concentrated in administrative departments in the central government; all national defense enterprises should be led directly by the Commission of Industry for National Defense and all decentralized national defense enterprises should be taken back; all railways nationwide should be managed and all railway transportation commanded by the Ministry of Railways; all important materials that needed to be organized and balanced nationwide should be managed and allocated uniformly by the central government, and the materials uniformly allocated or managed by central ministries which were distributed to different "sectors" based on the industry they belong should be arranged by these sectors. Approvals must be obtained from administrative departments if regional bureaus and provinces (municipalities and autonomous regions) wanted to adjust material allocation of enterprises directly under the central government while guaranteeing completion of the national plan; financial management must be centralized, with no deficit budget allowed on any levels and the power to issue currency rested with the central government; no departments or local governments should violate the labor plans made by the central government; all work tasks, including production, construction, purchase, finance, culture and education, and labor, must be implemented according to the national plan and no addition to the plan was allowed at any level. Based on these policies, the central government centralized and unified industry management, which could be seen in the following aspects.

First, a number of improperly delegated enterprises were centralized. During the late 1950s, some large key enterprises with production, supply, and sales across the country were delegated to local governments, who were unable to ensure their normal production conditions, while the coordinating relationship formed between enterprises before was also sabotaged. As a result, materials and capital were misappropriated, enterprises were unable to complete the national plan, and financial revenue of the central government was greatly reduced.

In view of the above situation, in 1961 some industrial departments adjusted the jurisdiction of certain enterprises and institutions. The Third Ministry of Mechanical Engineering took under its direct management 26 national defense enterprises. All railways nationwide were managed and railway transportation commanded uniformly by the Ministry of Railways. The Ministry of Transportation also claimed jurisdiction over key ports on the seaside and along the Yangtze River. The Ministry of Metallurgical Industry took under its direct management Shenyang Flotation Reagents Factory, Jinzhou Ferroalloy Plant, Fankou Aluminum-Zinc Mine in Guangdong Province, and likewise the Ministry of Petroleum took back Fushuan No. 3 Petroleum Plant, and the Ministry of Geology took back Tianjin Offset Printing Plant, Shanghai Geological Mining Machinery Plant, Shanghai Geological Instrument Factory, Wuxi Diesel Engine Parts Factory and the two Geological Schools located in Nanjing and Kunming. The Departments (Bureaus) of Geology in provinces, municipalities and autonomous regions were re-directed under the dual leadership of central and local governments, with the Ministry of Geology as the main administrative body. Significant changes were also made in the jurisdiction of local state-grid and electric power bureaus. Further to this, more enterprises were centralized after 1962. By 1963, 110 of the 120 key mechanical engineering enterprises had been taken under direct management of the First Ministry of Mechanical Engineering, while the Ministry of Metallurgical Industry had under its direct leadership 24 major iron and steel companies, including Anshan, Wuhan, Baotou, Benxi, Shijingshan, and Taiyuan. In 1966, the steel output of these companies amounted to 65.5% of the total national output, and that of pig iron amounted to 86.8%. In light industry, a total of 308 enterprises were centralized between 1961 and 1965, of which the tobacco industry took back all of its 61 enterprises, and the salt industry took back 39, whose output accounted for more than 70% of the national output. At the same time, supply and marketing enterprises in 24 provinces, municipalities and regions were centralized, whose sales volume accounted for over 90% of the national total. In 1963, the Ministry of Textile Industry reclaimed all of the 10 textile machinery factories and their subsidiaries and put them under direct management of the Textile Machinery Manufacture Bureau. The number of enterprises and institutions directly under the central government fell to merely 1,200 after decentralization of management in 1958, but surged to 10,533 in 1965, including new enterprises built by central ministries during and after the late 1950s. The total industrial output of these enterprises amounted to 42.2% of the national total, of which the output of production materials accounted for 55.1%.[1]

Second, centralized and unified management of planning was strengthened. Several tasks in this respect were prioritized in this period. (1) Stress the unified plan of the nation and strengthen overall balance. The guideline of unified national plan and one account at both central and local levels was followed, which changed the "two accounts" situation during the late 1950s and overcome the increasing upgrading of the indicators at different levels and hence the loss of control of the national plan. (2) Restore the planning-making procedure to the "two-down, one-up" one. During the late 1950s planning was made from bottom-up, while according to the restored procedure, the State Council would first issue control figures top-down, then planning drafts were compiled bottom-up, and finally the State Council approved and promulgated the plans top-down. (3) Add more planning indicators. During the adjustment, national planning not only restored most of the set of planning indicators in the First Five-Year Plan period, but further refined some of them. (4) Expand the scope of planning. In this period the central government directly managed a major percentage of the indicators for various economic activities. For example, the number of industrial

1 *Economic System Reforms in Contemporary China*, Editorial Board of the Contemporary China series, China Social Sciences Press, 1984, pp. 99, 100, 295, 341, 390, 417, 418.

products managed by the State Planning Commission recovered and increased from 215 to 400, whose value amounted to 60% of the gross industrial output; 30 kinds of major products in agriculture, forestry, husbandry, and fishing were directly managed by the central government, whose value amounted to 70% of the gross agricultural output. In addition, the central government managed directly 90 major retail goods, with retail sales worth 70% of the total retail volume of social goods, 50 kinds of import goods, with import volume as high as 90% of the total, and 80 kinds of export goods, with export volume at 85% of the total. The central government was also responsible for unified allocation of 200 kinds of major production materials and 10 materials for livelihood.

Third, centralized and unified management of capital construction was strengthened. Further to Some Provisional Regulations on the Adjustment of the Management System in January 1961, the central government issued a series of detailed regulations to restore a centralized and unified management system for investments. On May 31 1962, after CCCPC approved the Report on the Issue of Strengthening Management of Capital Construction from the State Planning Commission, the State Council issued three documents, namely, Several Regulations on Strengthening Management of Capital Construction, Regulations on Compiling, Examining, and Approving Design Proposals for Capital Construction, and Several Regulations on the Methods of Compiling, Examining, and Approving Design Documents for Capital Construction. These documents mostly aimed to: (1) take back the examination and approval rights for capital construction projects; (2) take back management of investment planning; (3) implement a stricter procedure for capital construction; (4) strengthen supervision of capital allocated for the construction.

The above measures proved very effective. The adjustment goal of scaling down capital construction and shortening its front was realized, making its scale more compatible with the financial and material resources of the country at that time.

Fourth, centralized and unified management of finance and credit was strengthened. The first step was to centralize financial power and strengthen financial management. On January 15 1962, CCCPC approved and circulated the Ministry of Finance's Report on Improving the Financial System and Strengthening Financial management, and issued on 20th of the same month Some Regulations on the Adjustment of Management Systems, both of which stressed centralization of financial power and strengthening of financial management. The second step consisted of improving the financial management system of enterprises, restoring and perfecting their cost and capital management systems, and enhancing economic conversion.

Centralized and unified management was also implemented in taxation system. Reduction of and exemptions from the unified industrial and commercial tax for trial products, products manufactured with substitute raw materials, or products affected by disasters should be approved by provinces, autonomous regions, and municipalities directly under the central government.

The centralized and unified management of finance in this period was not just a repetition of the centralized system in the beginning years of the People's Republic of China or during the First Five-Year Plan. This system highlighted and upheld what was rational in the old system, and strengthened centralization and unification according to current needs with improvements and additions, so that the fiscal revenue directly controlled by the central government increased from 50% to 60%, ensuring that the limited funds of the country go to developing and enriching the weak links, and thus promoting the adjustment of the national economy.

The centralized and unified management of credit mostly lied in implementing rigorously the "six rules" for the banking industry in coordination with the "six rules" of the financial sector. In March and April 1962 CCCPC and the State Council issued Decision on Effectively Strengthening the Centralization and Unification of the Banking Work and Controlling Rigorously the Issue of Currency (in short "six rules" for the banking work). During the late 1950s and the initial stages of the adjustment period, many local governments violated financial disciplines, asking the banks to increase loans arbitrarily, maintaining the many enterprises operating at a loss with bank loans, and misappropriating bank loans for fiscal expenditure, which resulted in fiscal deficits, currency overdraft, serious shortage of commodities, and soaring prices, driving the national economy into a very severe situation. Under such circumstances, the measures to strengthen centralized and unified management of financial and banking work, tighten control on the state capital and issue of currencies, and implement strict financial disciplines no doubt proved extremely effective.

The promulgation and implementation of the "six rules" for financial and banking work served successfully to perfect necessary rules and regulations, improve management and supervision, and effectively strengthen centralization and unification; it proved especially helpful in making necessary adjustments to enterprises (close, suspend, merge, and transfer) and turning loss-making ones to profit-making ones by putting a stop to the high /indicators in industrial production and overcoming the anarchy in fund allocation.

Fifth, centralized and unified management of commerce and materials (production materials for industrial products) circulation was implemented.

During the adjustment of the national economy, the most prominent feature of the adjustment of commerce was to rectify the "over-decentralization" during the late 1950s, especially that of management of state-owned commercial enterprises, which played a crucial role in overcoming economic difficulties and stabilizing the market.

4.1.1. Recover and establish specialized commercial companies

During the late 1950s, the top-down leadership, i.e., the so-called "vertical management", in the specialized company system was abolished. Admittedly this served to facilitate the local governments' leadership over the commercial industry and motivate their initiative, it also caused a series of problems, including local trade protectionism, provincialism, and severing of normal economic ties. To better organize the nationwide circulation of commodities and restore the principle of "unified leadership and leveled management", the State Council issued on May 5 1962 Decision on Restoring Different Levels of Specialized Companies within the System under the Ministry of Commerce. According to the Decision, the restoration fell into three categories. The first category included enterprises in hardware machinery, power equipment, and chemical raw materials, whose business should be mainly managed by the headquarters. The second category comprised enterprises in textile, general merchandise, sugar, tobacco, alcohol, food, medicine, petroleum, coal, and construction equipment, whose business should be managed by the headquarters and the Departments (Bureaus) of Commerce of provinces, municipalities and autonomous regions, and whose company organization was similar to those in the first category. The third category ranged from ethnic trade, vegetable trade, catering, and service to labor protection appliances, warehousing and transportation, for whom specialized management bureaus were set up by the Ministry of Commerce in place of headquarters, and for whom the decision on whether to set up provincial head offices or specialized management departments lied with the provincial governments. Enterprises in the third category were entirely managed by local governments, and the Ministry of Commerce would only make necessary unified arrangement for operation guidelines, policies and commodities planning, and monitor, examine, and direct their business operations. By 1965, the Ministry of Commerce had established 10 specialized headquarters, namely, general merchandise, textile, hardware and power equipment, chemical raw materials, petroleum, coal construction, food, sugar, tobacco and alcohol, medicine, and traditional Chinese medicine, and set up specialized management bureaus for catering services, vegetable trade, ethnic trade, labor protection appliances with corresponding offices in local commercial departments at different levels.

4.1.2. Adjust management jurisdiction and strengthen centralization

As mentioned above, out of the concern to motivate the initiative of local governments, the central government decided to decentralize power in 1958, and apart from the management of many specialized companies, the right to set up local commercial institutions, to purchase industrial and agricultural products, to lower the prices of unpopular, unmarketable, defective and substandard products, and to allocate production materials was also delegated to provinces, municipalities and autonomous regions, who in turn delegated it further down the chain of command. This resulted in not only extremely loose management and operation of state-owned commerce but also provincialism and the mixing of the governments with enterprises, with neither willing to take responsibility for business.

Following the guideline of the central government, the Ministry of Commerce also made adjustments to the management system of the entire commercial industry. Starting from 1961, the examination and approval of commercial enterprises' financial plans, together with their main financial rights, were managed by the Ministry of Commerce and the departments (bureaus) of commerce in provinces, municipalities, and autonomous regions. Starting from 1962, the funds of enterprises at different level within the commercial industry were controlled and managed by the Ministry of Commerce, and their profits were split between the central and local governments with 70% going to the former and 30% to the latter except as expressly stipulated otherwise; the guidelines for other issues, such as planning, statistics, accounting, pricing, labor wages, and capital construction, were also uniformly stipulated by the Ministry of Commerce, while the departments (bureaus) of commerce in provinces, municipalities, and autonomous regions could specify the specific measures for their implementation according to local conditions without making any arbitrary changes. Also starting from 1962, the central government decided to change the management of food supplies from contract production at different levels and unified allocation of differences in production to unified purchase, sales, and allocation by the central government coupled with leveled management.

4.1.3. Implement centralized and unified management of materials circulation

During the late 1950s, conflicts between supply and demand of materials were intensified and normal economic order was disrupted due to provincialism, inefficient dispatch, scattered location, and disordered management in materials administration. To improve the situation, CCCPC decided to implement the policy of centralized, unified, and comprehensive management for materials circulation, according to which the following changes were made. First, a unified national system of vertical leadership was established for materials management; second, sales of goods allocated by the central government was managed in a unified way; third, transfer warehouses were set up and managed in a unified way; fourth, the scope of materials management was expanded.

Explorative reforms were also carried out in the methods of organizing materials circulation during the adjustment period, for example, having trials on unified supply of materials based on economic regions instead of on administrative departments or districts, organizing fixed-point supply and direct delivery with trials on specialized chemical companies (i.e., trusts) on pilot run, setting up supply stations and service teams responsible for local supply of materials of small quantities, establishing production materials service companies, unifying charging standards, and strengthening management of economic contracts.

The above measures served to strengthen centralized and unified management of materials and effectively prevent the disruption of the national plan by using materials outside the plan, thus ensuring the implementation of the allocation plan and fulfillment of the need for materials of industrial production and construction.

Sixth, centralized and unified management of labor wages was strengthened. In 1962, after CCCPC decided to reduce the number of staff and the urban population, examination and approval of labor employment in industrial enterprises became increasingly stricter. On February 7 1967, Mr. Zhou Enlai said at the expanded Central Work Conference, "no more staff should be employed after the staff size, number of permanent staff and the contingent staff number reserved for local governments are decided. Even a single addition to the staff must be approved by the central government. Food and wages will be distributed according to the staff size and number of permanent staff."[1] In March 1963, CCCPC and the State Council emphasized again that any increase in staff number

1 *Literature of the Communist Party of China*, Issue No. 3, 1993.

must be managed by the central government in accordance with the system and disciplines, and further stipulated that the staff numbers provided in the national plan must be adhered to most rigorously and that no local governments, departments, or institutions should exceed those numbers. Staff additions outside the national plan by local governments and departments must be reported case by case to central administrative departments for examinations and approval, and then transferred to the central government for final approval. Punishments would be handed out to institutions and individuals who recruited new staff and increased the staff number in violation of the national plan and the disciplines.

In the same period, apart from strengthening centralized and unified management of industrial production and construction in terms of its system, such management was also implemented in the political work of industrial and transportation sectors. Following the guidelines of Chairman Mao, it was decided on the National Industry and Transportation Work Conference held at the beginning of 1964 that political work institutions should be set up in these two sectors from top to bottom to strengthen ideological and political work and ensure the Party's absolute leadership of these sectors. Accordingly, CCCPC established for this purpose the Central Political Work Department for Industry and Transportation, and soon after political work departments were set up in the 15 ministries and two bureaus of the industrial and transportation sectors.

4.2. Problems in state-owned enterprises and trial runs of trusts

As the government took back the power delegated to enterprises, old problems of SOEs re-emerged, such as multiple bodies for management and stagnation once centralized. As discussed in a 1965 forum organized by the State Economics and Trade Commission, "a major problem in current industrial management is multiple leadership and decentralized operation. The factories and mines in the same industry are managed by many ministries, departments and bureaus at central, provincial, municipal, prefecture and township levels, while they operate by themselves." For example, the 222 factories in the automobile industry were managed by 10 central ministries, namely, the First, Third, Fifth, and Eighth

Ministries of Mechanical Industry, and Ministries of Transportation, Metallurgical Industry, Construction Industry, Health, Public Security and General Logistics, and 25 provinces and municipalities. Also, of the 11 enterprises in the rubber industry in Shenyang City, 2 were managed by the central government, 2 by Liaoning Province, and 7 by the City. It was agreed on the forum that, "such multiple leadership and decentralized operation make it difficult to rationalize labor division and coordination in the production and construction of the same industry, resulting in unnecessarily repetitive production of the same product by many factories, and sparse use of equipment and technology which should have been used in sets. This proves very detrimental to adopting new technology, improving quality, increasing product varieties, reducing cost, enhancing labor productivity and developing production."[1]

Mr. Liu Shaoqi had a relatively more profound understanding of this problem. On December 26 1963, he interrupted when Bo Yibo and Yu Qiuli were reporting on the National Industry and Transportation Work Meeting held by the State Council, "We must take into consideration the fact that China is a huge country, and more and more factories will be set up in the future. What kind of management is best for the country?" "All in all, we have to solve the problem. Neither the Soviet Union nor the other socialist countries nor we can solve it now, but we've got to solve it in the future. We only talk about "vertical" or "horizontal" when it comes to the issue." He proposed, "Wouldn't it be better if the party committees and governments just go beyond? We should stand beyond enterprises and conflicts; we should be the judges when problems occur, not players. Some bureau and department chiefs, and party secretaries in industry, commerce and coal got so involved that they overlooked the whole picture. Wouldn't it be wiser not to involve themselves? You see the whole picture if you can go beyond just a little. It's not a problem of whether the Party and the government should manage

1 Bo Yibo, On Some Problems in the Trial Runs of Trusts, June 21, 1964. *Selected Works of Bo Yibo*, People's Publish House, 1992, pp. 238-239.

it, but how they should do it. They should manage planning, balance, arbitration, supervision, and ideological and political work, and leave production and operation to factories and companies." [1]

4.2.1. Formation of the idea on trial runs of trusts

In the spring of 1960, Liu Shaoqi began to sense that some adjustments in superstructure and production relations were needed while he was discussing the plans for the last three years of the Second Five-Year Plan with other leaders of CCCPC. The issue of setting up trusts came into their discussion on reforms in the organization and management methods of production.

On March 24 and 25 of 1960, CCCPC held a meeting in Tianjin, at which Deng Xiaoping said: we agree that product relations must be reformed, which actually means that superstructure must be reformed. After research, we think that we might need to try trusts. We discussed trusts in Beijing recently, to speed up industrial development, and also to integrate resource usage. The primary problem in setting up trusts is product relations and superstructure. Setting up trusts means having one industry as the base while in the mean time managing other industries. For example, in South Anhui Province there are coal, iron, and chemical industries; when a trust is set up, it can be managed by either the Ministry of Coal Industry or the Ministry of Metallurgical Industry. Another example is Shijingshan Iron and Steel Plant. It has right next to it West Beijing Coal Mine as well Qian'an and Longyan Iron mines. We can set up some iron and steel bases and chemical bases there, and then set up a trust to manage them all.

Although setting up trusts had been proposed, the specific measures were not planned as the national economy was in the process of adjustment. In 1963, as the national economy began to turn for the better, the central government decided to reform the industrial management system, gradually reducing administrative management measures and increasing economic ones, and establishing trusts in

1 *Liu Shaoqi on the Economic Construction of the People's Republic of China*, Central Party Literature Press, 1993, pp. 530-531.

industrial and transportation enterprises.

In the summer of 1963, a work team was sent by the State Commission of Economy and Trade to investigate in Shenyang. At that time Shenyang had 463 state-owned industrial enterprises, of which 102 were directly managed by the central government, 54 by the provincial government, and the rest by the municipal government, and these enterprises at the same time were under the jurisdiction of 38 bureaus of 17 central ministries, 18 provincial departments, 20 municipal bureaus or companies, and other economic departments. The institutions responsible for managing the enterprises were intertwined in their complex relationships, with vested interests for each and every one of them. Under the circumstances the enterprises had no choice but to go down the "all-inclusive" road in production no matter whether they were big or small, resulting in serious waste and disuse of resources and equipment. Many enterprise officials strongly demanded that such management system be changed, and specialized companies like trusts be set up.

In September of the same year, CCCPC drafted documents on industrial development, acknowledging that setting up trusts was an important measure for the industrial management system. It was pointed out that: "Economic measures should be adopted in managing industrial enterprises instead of relying entirely on administrative measures." "Trust, an organizing form that integrates production, exchange, and scientific experiment, should be considered as a means to serve socialism, an economic way to manage industrial enterprises."[1] For some reasons this document was not officially approved, but the idea of setting up trusts began to be deliberated and trials were discussed in some industrial departments.

On October 21, 23, and 24 of the same year, Liu Shaoqi, while listening to Bo Yibo's reports on the industrial situation, stressed that the current administrative measures of economic management, i.e., administrative institutions at different

1 Quoted from Bo Yibo, *Reflections on Some Major Decisions and Events*, Vol. 2, Central Party School Press, 1993, p. 1174.

levels were responsible for managing the economy, caused either over-unification or decentralization and led to bureaucracy in economic work. Liu further pointed out that: "Currently all central ministries and provincial and municipal departments and bureaus intervene with the economy, which is actually a supra-economy measure, not even a capitalist one, but a feudal one."[1] He proposed once again that industry-specific specialized companies be set up and administrative intervention be reduced, saying that: "To organize a unified domestic market means to organize unified production",[2] which would be "better managed by companies than administrative institutions", i.e., economic organizations like trusts should replace administrative organizations in managing the economy, and administrative institutions such as the departments and bureaus of central ministries and provinces should be re-structured into enterprise organization, so that they could "be closer to production and enterprises".[3]

In December of the same year, the National Industry and Transportation Work Conference was held by the State Commission of Economy and Trade, where discussions and comments were made on the trial runs of trusts. On December 26, Liu Shaoqi listened to Bo Yibo and Yu Qiuli's reports on the meeting, and once again gave instructions on how to organize trusts.

On January 7 1964, during Bo Yibo's reports to Mao Zedong and Liu Shaoqi on the National Industry and Transportation Work Conference, Liu reiterated systematically his opinion on setting up trusts to improve China's industrial management. Mao also said, "We have to change the current administrative measures of economic management if they are not good. For example, what do enterprises need all those people for … it violates economic laws."[4]

On Feburary 26, the leading Party Group of the Ministry of Coal Industry

1 *Liu Shaoqi on the Economic Construction of the People's Republic of China*, Central Party Literature Press, 1993, p.528.

2 *Literature of the Communist Party of China*, Issue No. 2, 1993.

3 Ibid.

4 Quoted from Bo Yibo, *Reflections on Some Major Decisions and Events*, Vol. 2, Central Party School Press, 1993, p.1175.

submitted to the State Commission of Economy and Trade and the Secretariat of CCCPC a request report on the organizational and leadership relationship of East China Coal Industry Company. The report said, "According to Comrade Liu Shaoqi's instructions on organizing trusts and managing industry with economic measures, we are prepared to set up East China Coal Industry Company in Xuzhou this year as a trial, which has been approved by the State Council." The report was approved by CCCPC on April 30, and the first trial trust was officially set up in China.

Following the decision of CCCPC and the State Council, the State Commission of Economy and Trade began to work immediately on the specific plans for trials of trusts in conjunction with departments of industry and transportation.

In June 1964, after repeated investigations and studies, the State Commission of Economy and Trade drafted Report on Opinions on Trials of Trusts in Industry and Transportation (Draft), which was officially submitted to CCCPC on July 17. Zhou Enlai gave special attention to this report and chaired the discussions in person, where he put forward opinions on principles: first, the central-local relationship must be dealt with properly in the process of organizing trusts; second, after their establishment, trusts should handle well their coordination with others, including with local governments and in production and sales, and avoid doing everything by themselves; third, the future for their development must be made clear; fourth, trusts must be organized in accordance with economic laws and with economic measures. On August 17, CCCPC and the State Council circulated with approval this report and requested that it be referred to and implemented as such by the Central Bureau, the Party committees of provinces, municipalities, and autonomous regions, central ministries and departments and their Party committees and leading Party groups.

4.2.2. Trial runs of trusts

Trusts were officially set up after the State Commission of Economy and Trade promulgated its plan, and they had different characteristics due to varying conditions. Of the first 12 trusts approved, the tobacco company and the medicine company were industry-wide trusts, managing all tobacco and medicine factories in the country, the geomechanical instruments company managed only enterprises previously directly under the central government, while the other 6 national trusts, apart from managing enterprises previously directly under the central government, also took over a varying number of local enterprises. To name a few, the salt company pooled all big saltworks and salt sales agencies in the country; the automobile company took over 42 of the 169 local auto parts factories, occupying 39% in the national production of auto parts; the rubber company took under its management 103 of the 205 local rubber enterprises, the tractor and internal combustion engine parts company took 23 out of 122 and the textile machinery company 3 out of 36; and the aluminum manufacturing company chose two large ones from local factories. Altogether over 300 local enterprises were handed over to trusts. In the mean time, some provinces and municipalities also set up local trusts, for example, Sugar Industry Company in Heilongjiang, General Factory of Glass and General Factory of Plastics in Beijing, Machine Tool Industry Company, Paper Mill Company and Dye Chemistry Company in Tianjin, Light Industrial Machinery Company, Standard Parts Company and Silk Company in Shanghai, Sugar Industry Company in Zhejiang, and Leather Industry Company in Chongqing. In 1965, the State Council set up three more trial trusts, namely, Petroleum Industry Company, Instrument Industry Company and Wood Processing Industry Company. In October of the same year, it was decided on the National Capital Construction Work Conference that the professional installations teams and specialized civil engineering teams in ministries of industry and transportation should be combined industry-wise or near-industry-wise into several national construction trusts. In July 1966, several more local trial trusts were approved by the State Commission of Economy and Trade, i.e,. the knitting and plastic trusts in Tianjin, East China Power Machinery Company organized by the First Ministry of Machinery Industry, Fushun Petroleum Company set up by the Ministry of Petroleum Industry, Provincial Instrument Industry United Company in Heilongjiang, and Provincial Instrument Industry Company in Hunan.

Right after their establishment, the trial trusts set about restructuring production organization, improving the management system, and applying operation and management measures suitable for socialized mass production and specialized division and coordination, leading to better utilization of equipment and improvement in production technology. Even though the trial runs were rather short, they achieved impressive economic results. The following trusts can serve as examples.

China Tobacco Industry Corporation was established in July 1963, and was officially listed as a trust in August 1964. The Corporation managed all tobacco industry enterprises in China in a centralized and unified manner, including the purchase, redrying, allocation and dispatch of tobacco. It then adjusted all the enterprises in the tobacco industry on principles of optimal layout and professional coordination, effectively promoting the development of production. The number of cigarette factories was reduced from 104 to 62, and the number of staff reduced from over 59,000 to 41,000, while the cigarette production capacity increased from 3.3 million boxes to 4.8 million boxes, and the number of cigarette brands was reduced from the messy figure of over 900 to 274. The labor productivity in 1964 went up by 42.4% from 1963, and the processing costs for cigarettes dropped by 21%. Moreover, the Corporation coordinated with the agricultural departments in managing tobacco production, conducting researches, expanding higher-grade tobacco production bases, sending technicians to provide technical help to stimulate farmers' enthusiasm in planting tobacco, so that the production volume of tobacco surged and its quality was also improved. In 1966, 12 million barrels of flue-cured tobacco were purchased, an increase of 1.7 times over that in 1963, and the percentage of middle- and higher-grade tobacco increased from 23% to more than 30%. With more higher-grade tobacco, the quality of cigarette products improved significantly, with grade-A cigarettes increasing by over 100%. A total of 5.6 billion yuan profits was turned over to the state between 1963, when the Corporation was established, and the end of 1965.

China Automobile Industry Corporation was established in October 1964 to organize and manage the country's automobile industry. The Corporation had 78 factories directly under its management, including the existing ones and the 38 local factories it newly took over, amounting to 42% of the 180 automobile manufacturing factories and key parts factories in China. The Corporation set up 4 regional subsidiaries in Changchun, Beijing, Nanjing and Chongqing, two general manufacturing works in Jinan and Wuhan, and a specialized coordination network centered around the subsidiaries in Changchun, Beijing and Nanjing which also covered local factories. The Corporation implemented unified leadership and planning, adjusted and restructured the enterprises on the principle of specialized coordination, and achieved a rapid increase in automobile production. In 1965, over 40,000 automobiles were produced in China, an over 40% increase from that of 1964, and 15 new models were successfully trial-manufactured. The supply of parts also turned for the better after the Corporation managed the sales of automobile parts in a unified way.

The medicine company reduced the number of pharmaceutical companies in China from 297 to 167, with redundancies of 4,700 staff members. In the first quarter of 1965, the output of the six major APIs (active pharmaceutical ingredient) was 29% higher than that of the same period of the previous year, and at the same time quality was improved and varieties increased.

Despite a 50% reduction in output due to natural disasters in 1964, Salt Industry Corporation managed to ensure domestic supply and achieved an export volume that exceeded the highest record in history, thanks to trust management. Besides, as transportation was organized in accordance with economic laws, over 100 million ton-kilometers of transport capacity and 3 million sacks were saved in 1964, while profits almost doubled that of the original plan.

After its establishment, the aluminum manufacturing company pooled funds to expand Shandong and Lanzhou Aluminum Factories and unified supply and allocation of materials. During the two months these measures were implemented in Shandong Aluminum Factory at the beginning of 1965, more than 50 tons of equipment, 140 tons of steel, 140 tons of copper, and 17,000 tons of aluminum and other materials were allocated accordingly.

East China Coal Industry Company improved its operation and management after unified management, and in the first quarter of 1965 began to reverse four consecutive years of losses, making a profit of 5 million yuan.

Problems also emerged in the trial runs of trusts, notably in the following three aspects:

First, conflicts arose between national or trans-regional trusts and local governments, which mainly lied in: (1) Taking over enterprises. Of the 12 trial trusts, some took over all enterprises in the same industry, while others took over major enterprises. However, local governments might have different opinions; some would not hand over certain enterprises, and some even transferred the equipment and staff, or converted the enterprises to other business. (2) Restructuring production and adjusting enterprises. Again, as local governments held different opinions, some adjustment plans had not been implemented, and some faced problems even though implemented. For example, Shanghai hoped to organize specialized production and coordination locally as it had a strong industrial foundation, and deemed it unnecessary when the medicine and rubber trusts were restructured. Jiangsu, Shandong, and Beijing had similar worries that local interests would suffer if the trusts carried out unified management. For another example, the medicine trust cut certain small varieties due to improper overall arrangement and affected the supply of some medicines. (3) External coordination. Some trusts gave too much priority to coordination within the industry and overlooked coordination with local governments.

Second, conflicts existed between unified operation within the trust and leveled management of the enterprises. In the early stages of the trials, some trusts only had two levels, company and factory/mine, as they did not have many enterprises directly under their management; some others with a large number of enterprises, on the other hand, had three levels – corporation, subsidiary, and factory/mine. For unified operation and management, some trusts set out to centralize to the subsidiary or corporation level business rights that used to be controlled by factories and mines separately, including planning, accounting, supply and sales, and labor, so that production, supply, sales, personnel, funds, and materials were all aligned. This naturally created frictions with factories and mines who used to have independent accounting, and was not conducive to understanding and solving problems in production in a timely manner.

Third, there were also conflicts between trusts and the existing economic management system. Trial trusts were new in China, a fresh attempt in the history of reforms of China's industrial and economic management system, and inevitably conflicts arose with the existing system in the trial run, mostly in three aspects: (1) Financial management system. At that time, local fiscal revenue relied mainly on industrial profits and taxes, which were necessarily reduced as most of the enterprises the trusts took over were the more profitable ones. This was an important reason why many local governments opposed handing over the enterprises. (2) Material management system. At that time materials were allocated according to the jurisdiction of the enterprises, and the trusts were only responsible for planning, but not materials supply for local enterprises under their management. Without an unobstructed channel for materials allocation, it was very hard for the enterprises to complete the plans. (3) Price management. The product prices of some enterprises were still decided by local pricing authorities even after they were taken over by the trusts, which was quite disadvantageous to the unified operation of the trusts.

After a year of trial run, the trusts had on the one hand made achievements by managing production and transportation with economic measures, and on the other hand encountered problems in the trial. It was therefore necessary to summarize the experiences and find solutions to cope with the problems. Between May 10 and June 7 in 1965, the leading Party group of the State Commission of Economy and Trade held a symposium on the trial of trusts, and present at the symposium were persons in charge of the trusts, of industry and transportation departments and economic departments in the central government, and of Party committees and economic committees of 9 provinces and municipalities. Liu Shaoqi and

Deng Xiaoping listened to the reports and gave instructions. Liu said that trusts should be organized so as to achieve specialization and standardization, increase production, improve quality and develop new varieties, and that there should be more than a few trusts, for which we should look in the long run and at the global picture. Deng pointed out the issue of a charter for trusts.

Nevertheless, just as the central government decided to continue trials of trusts and use it as an opportunity to gradually reform the economic system where development of productivity was restricted due to overcentralized economic management, put an end to this exploration with possibly profound and far-reaching significance in 1996.

4.3. Re-expansion of local governments' power in the later stages of the adjustment

To change the unorganized and disordered situation in industrial economic management in the late 1950s, to suppress the overheated atmosphere, rationally adjust the severely damaged industrial structure, and to put the entire industrial production on the normal track of development, CCCPC had resolutely adopted emergency measures of highly centralized and unified management, which was essential at that time. Now that industrial production and construction was recovered and developing at the later stages of the adjustment, certain management power of local governments and enterprise was expanded to motivate the initiative of all parties.

On August 27 1964, Mao Zedong commented on related documents that "Changes must be made within two years to the methods of planning work, otherwise the current Planning Commission has to be abolished and replaced by other institutions."[1] Between September 21 and October 19, the National Planning Meeting was held, which focused its discussions on the improvement of planning

1 *Selected Economic Files and Documents of the People's Republic of China 1958-1965: Comprehensive Vol.*, compiled by China Academy of Social Sciences and the State Archives Administration of China, China Financial and Economic Publishing House, 2011, p. 564.

work. Principles of "centralization of big power, and decentralization of small power" and "unified leadership with leveled management" were proposed at the meeting, together with suggestions on specific measures.[1]

On November 30 1965, the State Council issued to governments and enterprises three documents drafted by the State Planning Commission, State Construction Commission, Ministry of Finance and Ministry of Materials, namely, Several Regulations on Improving Planning Management in Capital Construction (Draft), Several Regulations on Retaining for Local Uses Materials Allocated by the State (Draft) and Several Regulations on Financial Management in State-Owned Industry and Transportation Enterprises (Draft). These Regulations were actually specific measures to implement the principle of "unified leadership with leveled management" put forward in 1964.

Based on the above principles and regulations, the central government expanded the management power of local governments and enterprises in the later stages of the adjustment, which mainly consists in the following aspects.

First, expand the planning management power of local governments. While the planning indicators of enterprises and institutions directly under the central ministries were still arranged by the ministries, the indicators for local enterprises and institutions were now arranged by provinces, municipalities, and autonomous regions according to the policies of the central government and local conditions. Now that local governments had some flexibility with controlling figures in planning, they could first make suggestions on these figures, which would be incorporated into the national plan after being balanced at different levels. For products outside the production plan, the administrative regions could retain some according to a prescribed percentage to fulfill local needs. The number of products

1 Refer to Letter from Comrade Bo Yibo to Chairman Mao, September 28 1964. *Selected Economic Files and Documents of the People's Republic of China 1958-1965: Comprehensive Vol.*, compiled by China Academy of Social Sciences and the State Archives Administration of China, China Financial and Economic Publishing House, 2011, pp.568-570.

and balance sheets managed by the State Planning Commission declined greatly, with the sheets reduced by more than half from 1963 to 1964 and the varieties of industrial products reduced from 340 to 63 in the same period.

Second, expand the management power of local governments in capital construction. Arrangement for investments in 18 local sectors was returned to local governments, namely, agricultural and husbandry, agricultural machinery stations and repair networks, agricultural reclamation, forestry, water conservancy, meteorology, aquatic products, transportation, commerce, banking, higher education, health, culture, broadcasting, sports, science, and urban construction, and the central governments would no longer stipulate construction projects or investment targets in these sectors. Utilities fees for agricultural water facilities and investment in local water infrastructure could be combined and arranged as a whole. As for local industrial capital construction, large and medium-sized projects would be arranged by the central government, and small projects arranged jointly by the central departments concerned and local governments, the capital saved from which could be retained for use by local governments. Local capital construction with self-financing funds should be arranged by provinces, municipalities and autonomous regions themselves, and large-scale projects should be submitted to the State Planning Commission for approval.

Third, expand the material allocation power of local governments. The products in excess of the national plan produced by small local iron and steel enterprises should be split equally between the central and local governments in the case that the main raw materials and fuel were supplied jointly by both governments, while in the case that the main raw materials and fuel were allocated by the central government, only 20% of these products should be retained by local governments. The iron ores and pig irons in excess of the national plan produced by local enterprises would be converted at half their volume into steel supplied by the central government. The waste, substandard, and scrap materials created in local production should be allocated locally. As for the waste iron and steel recycled locally, after reserving a certain amount to use as fuel for steel-making and foundry in local enterprises according to the national plan, 70% of what was left should be handed over to the central government and 30% retained by the local government. The coal in excess of the national plan produced by locally managed mines should be split equally between the central and local governments. Small-size and substandard timber produced by forestry enterprises should be retained by local governments. Products of local enterprises using raw materials bought with local foreign exchange or retrained funds should be allocated by provinces, municipalities, and autonomous regions on their own. In addition, basic depreciation expenses were singled out from the fiscal revenue and retained in full by local governments and enterprises. The number of temporary staff could be decided by departments and local governments, provided that the total wage did not break through the cap.

While expanding autonomy for local governments, the central government also expanded operational autonomy for enterprises. In September 1961, CCCPC officially issued 70 Rules for Industry, and soon afterwards rectifications were made to the messy enterprise management orginating in the late 1950s with no regard for profit-making and accounting. Further improvements were made in both enterprise management and economic efficiency through national movements such as making stock inventories, verifying assets, clearing delayed payments, turning losses to profits, increasing production and economizing. As the tasks for adjustment were completed one by one, it became imperative to expand enterprises' autonomy in operation, and hence new regulations were made in this regard.

First, a certain percentage of the expenses for technical organization, purchase of sporadic fixed assets and labor safety protection were allocated to enterprises for their own use, and these funds could be combined with funds for fixed assets renewal.

Second, the expenses needed for small-scale technical measures could be recorded as costs, provided that the national fiscal and cost plans were completed and that no additional allocation of materials were required, with the maximum expense for each measure set at 1,000 yuan for large and medium-sized enterprises and 500 yuan for small ones.

Third, in addition to the purchase of major production equipment being recorded as fixed assets, the purchase expenses of auxiliary production tools and other low-value consumables could be recorded as costs, with the maximum expense for each variety set at 200 yuan for small enterprises, 500 yuan for medium-sized ones, and 8,000 yuan for large ones. Expenses over these amounts could be recorded as low-value consumables with approval from relevant departments.

Fourth, the expenses of constructing sporadic, small, and simple buildings with an area of no more than 20 square meters could be recorded as costs, provided that it did not affect the completion of the enterprise's cost and financial plans of the year.

Fifth, the large repairs fund and small and medium repairs expenses were combined (called repair expenses), which could be used for no other purposes except as part of the cash flow temporarily or for necessary technical renovations to support overhaul projects.

Sixth, the measures enterprises used to adopt to retain funds from revenue in excess of the national plan were abolished, and a higher percentage was given to such funds, i.e., 5% of the total wages of the enterprise instead of the previous 3.5%.

The above measures expanded the management power of both local governments and enterprises and were instrumental in bringing their initiative into full play.

4.4. The second decentralization

Between 1969 and 1972, great changes took place in China's economic management system, mainly in three aspects: the streamlining of state institutions and decentralization of enterprises and management power, decentralization of financial, material and capital investment power, and simplification of taxation, credit and labor wage systems. These changes had their complex historical roots, and were also necessitated by realistic political concerns.

In the end of 1950s, similar changes features by decentralization of economic management power took place in China's economic management system. In the ensuing adjustment period, however, more emphasis had to be put on centralization and unification due to the serious challenges posed by the failure of the Great Leap Forward and the natural disasters. The delegated power was taken back, and centralization of power became increasingly severe in the system. In 1957, the ministries of the State Council had under their direct management 9,300 enterprises and institutions, with industrial output accounting for 39.7% of the national total; after the decentralization in 1958, the number was reduced to 1,200, and the percentage of industrial output reduced to 13.8%; in 1965, however, the number rose to 10,533, greater than that in 1957.

Mao Zedong had been advocating reforming over-centralization. On March 12 1966, he wrote in a letter to Liu Shaoqi: "It is not a good thing that everything is centralized and too rigid." [1]On March 20th, he said at the Expanded Meeting of the Political Bureau of CCCPC held in Hangzhou that: The central government had better be a "constitutional monarchy" in that it should deal only with the superstructure, i.e., policies and guidelines, and should not get involved in actual businesses at all, if maybe just a little. He criticized the central ministries for taking over so many enterprises, asking them to return the enterprises to local governments, together with the staff and equipment.

In 1969, the "struggle, criticize, and transform" movement began in China, and under the slogan "transform unreasonable rules and regulations", transformations in the economic system were brought up again, with the additional motive of preparing for war apart from the old ones of reforming over-centralization and over-rigidity in management. As estimates were made that a new world war could break out at any moment, independent and complete systems of national defense industry must be built locally as soon as possible so that they could all fight their

1 *People's Daily*, December 26 1977.

own battle. In February 1970, it was proposed at the National Planning Meeting that the country was divided into 10 major coordinating regions with respective industrial systems so that they could arm themselves. The Lin Biao group, on the other hand, attempted to take advantage of war preparations to merge more institutions into the military system and consolidate the power they had acquired since 1966.

In February 1969, it was proposed at the National Planning Meeting that enterprises should be mostly managed by local governments, while those directly under the central government could be managed by the central or local government or by them both. Mao Zedong personally decided that on May 1 1969, Anshan Iron and Steel Company, the largest enterprise in China, should be handed over to Anshan City, Liaoning Province,[1] which started a wave of delegating enterprises to local governments. On March 5 1970, the State Council promulgated Notice on Delegation of Enterprises Directly Under the Ministries of Industry and Transportation of the State Council to Local Governments (Draft), demanding that most of the enterprises and institutions directly under the ministries be handed over to local governments, with a few put under the dual leadership of both central and local governments, and a very few large and key enterprises under the dual leadership still managed mostly by the central government. Capital construction projects in process which were directly managed by the ministries were also handed over to local governments. The Notice stipulated further that such delegations had to be completed within the year. On the same day, CCCPC decided to delegate over 2,600 central enterprises and institutions to local governments, including Daqing Oilfield and Changchun Automobile Works.

Ministries went on with the delegations. Take the Ministries of Machinery Industry as an example. In April 1970, the First and Eighth Ministries of Machinery Industry were merged, and 277 of the 310 enterprises directly under them were delegated, including large key enterprises that could impact the

1 Accounts vary as to the specific time of the event. Here reference is made to a lecture made by Yuan Baohua at the Institute of Contemporary China Studies on April 14 1995.

overall national economy such as the First and Second Automobile Works, the First and Second Heavy Machine Tool Plants, and Luoyang Tractor Factory. Another example is the Ministries of Metallurgical Industry. With the exception of Panzhihua Iron and Steel Company and the Great Wall Steelworks, all 70 large joint enterprises and key factories directly under them were handed over to and mostly managed by local governments, including 24 large enterprises such as Anshan, Wuhan, Baotou and Taiyuan Steel Companies. The Ministries of Coal Industry delegated all the 72 mining affairs bureaus.

After these delegations in 1970, including the 22 mining affairs bureaus already delegated in 1968, a mere 500 enterprises and institutions remained under direct management of the central ministries, a 86.5% reduction from that in 1965, with an industrial output only accounting for 8% of the national total. Some enterprises delegated to provinces, municipalities and autonomous regions were further handed over to prefectures or even counties and cities.

Under the political environment of that time, such delegations were rather blind and caused chaos in management. After being delegated, some large key enterprises fell into a state of no central planning and no local management even though supposedly they should have dual leadership, as local governments could not handle production planning and supply of raw materials and equipment. The complementary chemical fiber products in Beijing, for example, were within the jurisdiction of 9 ministries, including ministries of metallurgical industry, first machinery industry, water resources and electric power, fuel and chemical industry, and first light industry, a typical "too many chiefs, not enough Indians" situation, which was mocked at the grassroots as "the government above has no ideas, while the ideas below have no right to govern."[1] The excessively rapid and far-reaching delegation of central enterprises, on the other hand, disrupted the existing coordination and caused further decline in economic efficiency.

1 Briefing on the Situation of the Symposium on the Issue of Systems, Files of the State Planning Commission, January 24 1972.

While the delegations were going on, ministries and departments directly under the State Council also went through streamlining, merger, or dissolution. On June 22 1970, CCCPC approved the State Council's report that reduced the number of ministries from over 80 to 27 and retained only 18% of the staff. For departments related to economic management, the State Planning Commission, Commission of Economy and Trade, Industry and Transportation Office of the State Council, State Commission of Materials, Ministries of Materials, Geology, and Labor, State Statistics Bureau, and the Central Relocation Office were merged into the State Planning Commission; the State Construction Commission and Ministries of Construction, Building Materials and Ministry of Political Work in Capital Construction were merged into the State Construction Commission; the First and Eighth Ministries of Machinery Industry were merged into the First Ministry of Machinery Industry; the Ministries of Chemical Industry, Petroleum Industry and Coal Industry were merged into the Ministry of Fuel and Chemical Industry; the Ministries of Railways and Transportation and the post transportation departments of the Ministry of Posts and Telecommunications were merged into the Ministry of Transportation; the Ministry of Textile Industry and the First and Second Ministries of Light Industry were merged into the Ministry of Light Industry; the Ministry of Finance and the People's Bank of China combined to form the Ministry of Finance; the Ministries of Commerce and Food, the All-China Federation of Supply and Marketing Co-operatives, and the Central Bureau of Business and Commerce were merged into the Ministry of Commerce; the Ministry of Foreign Trade and the China Council for the Promotion of International Trade combined to form the Ministry of Foreign Trade; and, lastly, the Ministries of Agriculture, Forestry, Land Reclamation, Water Products, the Office of Agriculture and Forestry of the State Council, and the Central Ministry of Political Work in Agriculture and Forestry were merged into the Ministry of Agriculture and Forestry.

Prior to these mergers, as part of the preparations for war, the telecommunication departments of the Ministry of Post and Telecommunication, State Administration of Surveying and Mapping, Meteorological Administration and Civil Aviation Administration were already handed over to the PLA as part of its General Political Department or the Air Force. Influenced by the leftist guidelines, some non-economic government institutions were dissolved, including the Supreme People's Procuratorate, Ministries of Culture and Education, National Ethnic Affairs Commission and Overseas Chinese Affairs Commission.

Part IV

Changes and Development of State Capital since Reform and Opening-up (1978—2015)

State-owned enterprise is the major realization form of state-owned capital. For over 20 years of planned economy spanning from 1952 to 1977, state capital had been expanding at an excessively fast speed, while state-owned enterprises, affiliated to the government as its means for direct allocation of resources and promoting economic development, were practically operated in the same mechanism as the government. Consequently, state capital not only gained increasing volume, but became more and more politicized in its operations, until the Third Plenary Session of the Eleventh Central Committee of CPC sounded the trumpet for China's reform and opening-up in 1978. Looking back now at the history of reforms in enterprise systems and state capital since 1978, three stages can be discerned: the early stage of granting enterprises autonomy in operation, the middle stage of changing and clarifying property ownership, and the late stage of strategic restructuring and strengthening of supervision of state-owned assets. The reform polices and guidelines at each stages were constantly adjusted to cope with the changes in political, economic and social environment, but it is an indisputable fact that state capital has been gradually upgraded, state enterprises are integrated more and more into the market, and the functions of state capital are gradually working and showing superiority. Still, how to deepen the reform on the management system of state capital and make the state-owned enterprises bigger, better, and stronger remains a challenge for China.

Chapter 8

"Decentralization of Power and Transfer of Profits" and the Marketization of State-Owned Enterprises

Generally speaking, the reforms of SOEs that began in 1980s happened against the backdrop that the national economy was struggling with survival and that the efficiency of enterprises was on a sharp decline since 1966. The basic principle at the early stage of the reform was to adjust the division of decision-making power over operation and of economic interests between the government and the enterprises through "decentralization of power and transfer of profits" and "contracted management system". This has far-reaching significance in ideology and system innovation, as the reform acknowledges as a premise the interests for enterprises and individuals, a fundamental negation of the dominant idea of the planned economy that only takes into consideration public interests, and also lays an important foundation for the further marketization of SOEs and state capital in the late stage. Nevertheless, reality proved that SOEs could not become really independent players in market competition simply through "decentralization of power and transfer of profits" and "contracted management system". As is shown in history, only through a fundamental reform in property ownership of SOEs can increase in their operation efficiency be guaranteed, and only through a gradual separation of the state capital from SOEs in such reform can it play its designated role.

1. Review of Background for Reform of SOEs

In mid-1960s to mid-1970s, the government concentrated state capital on heavy industry at all cost, which did increase the output of some heavy industry products, but at the same time led to serious imbalance in the industrial layout of state capital and reduced greatly its overall macro-efficiency. In 1976, the decline of China's total economic output and the conflicts within the industrial structure had come so far that they were neither bearable nor reconcilable. Most people felt strongly that reforms and adjustments must be made to such inefficient system and development strategy.

1.1. High centralization of state capital and its achievements

From 1966 to 1976 was a period of high centralization of state-owned capital in China's planned economy. It must be admitted that in this period state capital did, as a strong impetus to some industries, serve to some extent to promote the increase of the output of some industrial products, building a number of large and middle-sized SOEs, and expand the scale of state-owned economy.

1.2. Prices paid for high centralization of state capital

The Chinese government continued to adopt high accumulation as a way to promote industrialization, only to see it reduce drastically both micro- and macro-efficiency instead of improving them, as such extreme measure violates the laws of economy as well as the laws of nature and technology.

First, the economic efficiency declined drastically and on a full scale for enterprises owned by the whole people which represented the will of the state. As can be seen from the following table, the profit per 100 yuan fixed assets for such enterprises with independent accounting dropped by 42.1% from 1965 to 1976, the taxes for profits per 100 yuan capital dropped by 35.2%, the taxes for profits per 100 yuan net value of fixed assets dropped by 27.1%, the output per 100 yuan industrial output dropped by 40.8%, while within the same period the cash flow per 100 yuan output increased by 44.7%, and the cost per 100 yuan sales revenue increased by 8.4%. In 1976, 31.5% of industrial enterprises in China made a loss, with the total loss reaching 7.69 billion yuan.[1]

Table 9- 1 Major Fiscal Indicators of Industrial Enterprises Owned by the Whole People with Independent Accounting

	1965	1970	1973	1976	1976 to 1965 年（%）
profit per 100 yuan fixed assets	20.9	21.3	15.9	12.1	-42.1
taxes for profits per 100 yuan capital	29.8	30.6	22.7	19.3	-35.2
taxes for profits per 100 yuan net value of fixed assets	39.8	45.7	34.0	29.0	-27.1
output per 100 yuan industrial output	21.3	18.2	14.2	12.6	-40.8
Output per 100 yuan original value of fixed assets	98	117	105	96	-2
cash flow per 100 yuan output	25.5	29.9	33.4	36.9	+44.7
cost per 100 yuan sales revenue	69.0	69.0	73.6	74.8	+8.4

Source: *Statistics on the Development of Chinese industry 1949-1989*, compiled by the Department for Industry and Transportation Statistics of the National Statistics Bureau, p90, China Statistics Press, 1985.

Secondly, the efficiency of energy consumption was reduced. The national income produced by each ton of energy (calculated at current prices) dropped from 734 yuan in 1965 to 507 yuan in 1976, while the energy consumed for each 10,000 yuan of national income increased from 13.4 tons in 1965 to 17.9 tons in 1976.

Third, the efficiency of equipment usage was low.

Fourth, construction costs were greatly increased. The investment needed for a ton of steel-making capacity rose by 80% from 1,342 yuan in the First Five-Year Plan to 2,452 in the Fourth Five-Year Plan, while over the same time span the

1 *Statistics on the Development of Chinese industry 1949-1989*, compiled by the Department for Industry and Transportation Statistics of the National Statistics Bureau, China Statistics Press, 1985, p.88.

investment for a ton of coal-mining capacity rose by 112% from 56 yuan to 119 yuan.

Fifth, construction time was extended. The construction time for key enterprises in the machinery industry was over 8 years, while in the First Five-Year Plan period it was only around 3 years. This led to a sharp decline in the formation rate of state capital, which dropped from 83.7% in the First Five-Year Plan to 59.5% in the Third Five-Year Plan and 61.4% in the Fourth Five-Year Plan.[1]

And lastly, in terms of industrial structure, the industrial layout of state capital was worsened.

2. Expanding the Autonomy of State-Owned Enterprises (1978-1992)

The high decentralization of state-owned capital did not prove effective; instead, it led directly to overall decline in economic growth and efficiency, making it a top priority to increase supply through improving enterprise efficiency and alleviate the economic crisis caused by economic shortage. Expanding the autonomy of SOEs is the logical and historical starting point for improving their operational efficiency and implementing market-oriented reform. Even though no predictions about current outcomes could have been made at that time, "decentralization of power and transfer of profits" was the government's most pressing and most practical choice to motivate the enterprises' initiative and improve economic efficiency.

2.1. Trials in expanding the autonomy of SOEs

In October 1978, Sichuan Province took the lead in granting certain autonomy to some of the SOEs in industry and transportation, including setting a target for increases in output and revenue, allowing a small percentage of the profits to be retained by these SOEs after meeting the target, and allowing bonuses for employees. These measures proved quite effective in motivating the initiative of both the SOEs and their employees after three months' trial. The Third Plenary

1 Li Debing, A Brief Economic History of the People's Republic of China 1949-1985, Hunan People's Publishing House, 1987, p.481.

Session of the Eleventh CCCPC officially put forward guidelines for reforms of the economic management system, including granting more autonomy in operation and management to local governments and industrial enterprises, and solving problems like no clear division between the Party, the government, and the enterprise, having the Party working in place of the government, or the government in place of the enterprise.[1] These guidelines served as theoretical and policy bases for trials in expanding the autonomy of SOEs in Sichuan Province.

In February 1979, Sichuan Province summarized the experiences of 6 trial enterprises and drafted after investigation Opinions on Trials in Expanding Enterprise Autonomy and Speeding up Production and Construction, whose key message was "decentralization of power and transfer of profits". For example, enterprises should be allowed to retain a percentage of the planned profits as enterprise fund, provided that they had completed all targets in the national technical and economic plans of the year and all supply contracts; enterprises should be allowed to tap into their potentials and increase production and revenue or do materials processing business according to the needs of both domestic and international markets, provided that they guaranteed timely completion of the national plan; enterprises should be allowed to export their products after approval and retain a percentage of the foreign exchange earned to import new technology, equipment in urgent need and raw materials and to further enhance their competitiveness in overseas markets; all enterprises who had completed the national technical and economic targets and all supply contracts could retain for bonuses a volume equal to10-20% of the total standard wages; enterprises could also recruit workers from society on their own and implement contract labor system. These measures were carried out in 100 industrial enterprises and 40 commercial ones in Sichuan Province, whose performances in that year indicated

1 *Selected Important Documents of the Central Plenary Sessions of All National Congresses of the Communist Party of China since the Third Plenary Session of the Eleventh Central Committee* (Vol.1), compiled by the Party Literature Research Center of the CPC Central Committee, Central Party Literature Press, p.23.

an elevated enthusiasm on the part of both the enterprises and employees, and outshone non-trial enterprises in output, profits relegalized, and turned-in profits.

2.2. Promotion of trials in expanding the autonomy of SOEs

In April 1979, the State Economics and Trade Commission, following the guidelines of the Third Plenary Session of the Eleventh CCCPC, held a symposium on expanding trials for more autonomy for SOEs, which proposed granting more autonomy to SOEs in production operation, finance, materials, foreign trade, recruitment, awards and punishments, establishment of agencies and appointments and dismissals of cadres. In May, trials were carried out in 8 SOEs in Beijing, Tianjin and Shanghai, including the Capital Iron and Steel Company, Tianjin Bicycle Factory, and Shanghai Diesel Engine Factory, under the joint leadership of the State Economics and Trade Commission, Ministry of Finance and other four departments. The trials gained support from many enterprises and employees, and were piloted by many local governments and departments with measures made on the basis of experiences gained from the 8 trials.[1] On July 13 1979, the State Council issued 5 documents on expanding the autonomy of SOEs and demanded trials be carried out by local governments and central ministries in a small number of enterprises in industry and transportation: Some Regulations on Expanding the Autonomy in Operation and Management for State-Owned Industrial Enterprises, Regulations on Implementing Profit Retention in State-Owned Enterprises, Interim Regulations on Levying Fixed Assets Taxes for State-Owned Industrial Enterprises, Regulations on Improving the Fixed Depreciation Rate and the Use of Depreciation Cost in State-Owned Industrial Enterprises, Interim Regulations on Implementing Full Credit for Cash Flow in State-Owned Industrial Enterprises.[2] On January 20 1980, the State Council

1 Ma Jiaju ed., *Historical Investigations on China's Economic Reform*, Zhejiang People's Publishing House, 1994, p.195.

2 *Ten Years of Reforms in Chinese Enterprises*, complied by the Enterprise System Department of the State Commission of Economic System Reform and Office of the Enterprise Management Steering Commission of the State Council, Reform Press, 1990, p.634.

circulated with approval Interim Measures for Profit Retention in State-Owned Industrial Enterprises drafted by the State Economics and Trade Commission and the Ministry of Finance, which stipulated the specific measures for "transfer of profits".

2.3. Effects of trials in expanding the autonomy of SOEs

Shortly after the State Council issued the 5 documents, trials were carried out in 1,590 industrial enterprises by 26 provinces, municipalities, and autonomous regions, and the total number of trials reached 2,100, adding those implemented with self-made measures by some provinces, municipalities and autonomous regions. By June 1980, the number grew to 6,600, accounting for 16% of all industrial enterprises on the national budget, with 60% of the national output and 70% of profits.[1] Great economic effects were achieved in these enterprises. Compared with 1978, in 1979 the total industrial output increased by 11.6%, realized profits increased by 15.9%, and turned-in profits increased by 12.6%; overall, the increases in production volume, output, and turned-in profits in the trial enterprises exceeded not just their pre-trial years but also those of non-trial enterprises. According to statistics from 4,200 enterprises, the profit retention rate of trial enterprises amounted to 8.5% of all realized profits, and, minus the two fiscal items of employee benefits and bonuses fund which were retainable before the trial, to 40.8% of the increased profits.[2] In the first half of 1980, the output and profits of these enterprises surged once again.

The reform in expanding the autonomy of SOEs at the early stage of the reform and opening-up brought about significant changes in enterprises through its trials focusing on motivating enterprises' initiative in operation. The most prominent change lies in the fact that enterprises, with autonomy in operation and management, began to become economic entities with internal motivations

1 Zhao Dexin ed, *Economic History of the People's Republic of China*, Henan People's Publishing House, 1989, p.580.

2 Hu Jinglin ed, *Theories and Ways for Reforms of State-Owned Enterprises*, Economic Science Press, 1995, p.36.

and stress more the adjustments of market as well as strategies in operation. Nonetheless, a series of problems emerged that reflected conflicts between the trials and the old system, among which several were more serious. 1. Planned targets for production volume, output, profits, labor and material were still issued separately with no connection in between, making it hard for enterprise operators to cope and to adjust to the market. 2. Power granted to enterprises was still quite limited, who did not have full autonomy in using retained profits or allocating bonuses, or real autonomy in personnel arrangement.

In response to these problems, the State Economics and Trade Commission issued in August 1980 specific opinions on solving the problems during the expansion of enterprise autonomy to push forward the expansion.

2.4. Deepening the reform of expanding the autonomy of SOEs

As the reform of expanding the autonomy of SOEs deepened, the government further promoted and expanded it. In May 1984, the State Council issued Interim Regulations on Further Expanding the Autonomy of State-Owned Industrial Enterprises,[1] granting the enterprises more power in the following ten aspects and further loosening the state's control on them: plans for production and operation, sales, pricing, selection and purchase of materials, use of funds, disposal of assets, establishment of agencies, personnel and labor management, wages and bonuses, and collaborative operation.

In October 1984, the Third Plenary Session of the Twelfth CCCPC passed Regulations of the Central Committee of the Communist Party of China on Economic System Reform, which pointed out that "enterprises should truly become relatively independent economic entities, become socialist producers and operators who have autonomy in operation and take full responsibility for profits and losses and who are capable of self-transformation and self-development,

1 *Ten Years of Reforms in Chinese Enterprises*, complied by the Enterprise System Department of the State Commission of Economic System Reform and Office of the Enterprise Management Steering Commission of the State Council, Reform Press, 1990, p.129.

and become legal persons with certain rights and obligations." A few years later, the government promulgated a number of specific measures aimed to perfect the rights of SOEs. In 1986, Some Regulations of the State Council on Deepening the Enterprise Reform and Enhancing Enterprise Vitality was issued, and Enterprise Bankruptcy Laws of the People's Republic of China (for Trial Implementation) was put into effect; in April 1988, the State Council promulgated Law of the PRC of Industrial Enterprises Owned by the Whole People,[1] based on which Provisional Regulations on the Change of Operating Mechanism of Industrial Enterprises Owned by the Whole People was made in July 1992. Through these laws and regulations, 14 rights were granted to SOEs, namely, decision-making in production and operation, pricing of products and labor services, sales of products, selection and purchase of materials, export and import, investment decisions, use of retained funds, disposal of assets, collaborative operation and merger, labor recruitment, personnel management, allocation of wages and bonuses, establishment of internal departments, and rejection of apportionments, which further specified the 13 rights stipulated in Law of the PRC of Industrial Enterprises Owned by the Whole People and ensured the legal basis for SOE's operational and management rights. In a word, although more rights were granted to SOEs after the 1980s, the reform of decentralization of power and transfer of rights mostly happened in the early 1980s.

2.5. Comments on the reform of "decentralization of power and transfer of rights"

The reform that continued to expand the enterprises' autonomy in operation and management was in fact an acquiescent acknowledgment that enterprises were the main interest bodies, and that enterprise directors and managers were the main persons controlling the enterprises (Mao Tianqi, Zhu Ling, 1997). This was in line with the basic reform strategy to groom the SOEs as main entities

---

1 *Ten Years of Reforms in Chinese Enterprises*, complied by the Enterprise System Department of the State Commission of Economic System Reform and Office of the Enterprise Management Steering Commission of the State Council, Reform Press, 1990, pp.219-223.

for market operation, and also with the inherent need that arose from the SOEs being the main decision-making bodies, hence achieving quite some effects. However, as at the early stage the reform was only a contingent solution to solve the government's pressing financial difficulties and its measures never touched the fundamental system of the enterprises–property ownership, it would never solve the essential problems such as the enterprises' over-dependence on the government and the government's over-intervention in the enterprises.

First of all, the government remained the main operator of enterprises, and power granted to enterprises was limited. Despite its promotion of the reform, the government still had the ultimate power in deciding the allocation of various resources including basic decision for enterprises such as what to produce, how much to produce and for whom, as can be seen from the basic principles and specific measures of "decentralization of power and transfer of profits". The enterprises still needed to carry out production according to planned targets handed down from above, and based on the completion of these targets the government awarded or punished the enterprises accordingly. Of course, the government did allow the enterprises certain extra profits in addition to successful completion of the planned targets, and the enterprises did acquire some claim over surplus and certain control in operation and management compared with the planned economy period, stimulating their awareness of autonomy. According to the conclusions of the empirical research conducted by the Economic Research Group of the Chinese Academy of Social Sciences (1995), through the reform of decentralization of power and transfer of profits in the 1980s, both the autonomy concerned with the management of daily operational activities (the first type of autonomy) and the autonomy concerned with investment, output and allocation (the second type of autonomy) expanded for SOEs, although the first type grew at a faster speed.[1] Great differences existed between the objectives of the government,

1 Dong Furen, Tang Zongkun, and Du Haiyan eds, *Studies on the Changes in the Enterprise System of China's State-Owned Enterprises*, People's Publishing House, 1995, p.127.

who controlled the operation and management of enterprises to a large extent, and those of the enterprises, who had acquired some power in the same respect, and such disparity reflected the limitations of this reform.

Secondly, decentralization of power and transfer of profits only provided limited incentives to the operators and employees of the enterprises. According to regulations of the reform, the awards for enterprise operators and employees were directly related to the completion of planned targets, which were set through the game between administrative departments of the government and insiders of the enterprises (even though the latter cannot be counted as economic persons at that time). Considering that the enterprises had the advantage of information, the administrative departments often resorted to an egalitarian way of granting awards in an attempt to avoid losses to the government due to deceptions of the enterprises, as they were aware that it was quite impossible for them to have accurate information regarding the actual production capacity of the enterprises. This often resulted in a mismatch between awards granted and the efficiencies of enterprises, reducing greatly the effects of such incentives.

Thirdly, the "intermediate government" had become the "bowel obstruction" in decentralization of power. The central government was the leading power behind delegating rights to SOEs, but for some "intermediate government" departments and officials, this meant giving away some of their rights, and out of concern for their own interests (rent-seeking being a major reason) they would create all kinds of obstructions (Ju Jinwen, 1998). Even though they were forced to give up some rights under pressure from the central government, they clung to the crucial ones for as long as they could and at the same time resorted to all means to influence and intervene in enterprises' use of delegated rights with those not delegated, for example, long-term control over personnel appointment and dismissal at top-level management of enterprises.

Lastly, the non-normative division of interests between the government and enterprises constituted a game of interests between them. After acquiring certain rights, the enterprises became more or less independent entities of operation, and entered into the game of interests with the government, as the division of interests between them had not been normalized. The enterprises often adopted the strategy of "going all out for big interests, halfway for small interests, and nowhere for no interests", and what's worse, they were only concerned with the division percentage between the government and enterprises and immediate benefits, overlooking the enterprises' profitability in the future and the proliferation of state-owned capital. Due to insufficient information, the government, on the other hand, could not make accurate judgements as to how much interest it took for enterprises to go all out, or whether their operators and employees conspired to erode the expected turn-in profits, and had to take back to different degrees the delegated rights in the next around of contract adjustment, reducing greatly the efficiency of "decentralization of power" (Yi Zhixiong, 1997). These directly caused the subsequent "tax for profits" reform in SOEs.

To conclude, "decentralization of power and transfer of profits" during the early stage of the reform and opening-up had broken the old enterprise management system where the government controlled everything and granted some operational and management power to enterprises, which was an important step towards deeper reforms of SOEs. However, as only part of the operational and management power was decentralized and the issue of property ownership at the heart of the SOEs was left untouched, there was still a long way to go to establish an enterprise system that can adapt to market needs and operate efficiently. Deepening the reform of SOEs, therefore, became the common request of both enterprises and the government.

3. Full-Scale Promotion of Economic Responsibility System and "Tax for Profits"

In the reform of "decentralization of power and transfer of profits", there was a short period when the economic responsibility system and "tax for profits" were implemented in SOEs. Despite its brief time span, it served a transitional role in the reform of SOEs and acquired a unique position, considered by many scholars as a distinct stage in the reform of SOEs.

3.1 Proposal of the Economic Responsibility System

In as early as April 1981, the central government officially put forward at the National Industry and Transportation Conference that the economic responsibility system in industrial production should be carried out in trial enterprises, i.e., the contract system for the enterprises' profits. The proposal and quick implementation of the enterprise economic responsibility system was a direct result of the deteriorating situation of the government's fiscal revenue and expenditure. From 1979-1980, for two consecutive years China had faced huge fiscal deficits, and the central government made it a task to increase fiscal revenue and reduce deficits. To complete the task, local governments adopted measures to implement "contract profit targets and awards" in their enterprises, i.e., the contract responsibility system.

In October 1982 the State Council circulated with approval Opinion on Implementing Economic Responsibility System in Industrial Production drafted by the State Economics and Trade Commission and the System Reform Office of the State Council, which defined economic responsibility system as first enterprises' economic responsibility to the state, and second an internal system within the enterprises. The enterprises must first of all complete all plan targets issued by the state, secondly ensure the quality of their products, thirdly do their best to reduce production costs, fourthly guarantee a year-by-year increase of the national fiscal revenue, fifthly improve the overall level of staff income, and lastly carry out an evaluation system with clear awards and punishments. The economic responsibility system could take the following forms according to the condition of the enterprises: retention of part of both base profits and increased profits, retention of part of full profits, retention of part profits in excess of the targets, retention of profits in excess of the agreed target, retention of losses reduced from the agreed target, and taxes for profits with enterprises taking sole responsibility for profits and losses.

On November 11 1981, the System Reform Office of the State Council, the State Economics and Trade Commission, the All-China Federation of Trade

Unions and four other national departments jointly held a conference on economic responsibility system for five provinces and municipalities, including Beijing and Liaoning, on which the Interim Regulations on Some Problems in Implementing Economic Responsibility System in Industrial Production (hereafter referred to as the Regulation)[1] was formulated. The Regulation pointed out a series of problems that needed attention in further implementing and perfecting the economic responsibility system. Soon after its issuing, the system was carried out in full scale in SOEs in provinces, municipalities and autonomous regions across the country. By the end of 1982, the economic responsibility system was in place in over 80% of SOEs, and consequently the pressure on the government's fiscal revenue was alleviated. Take 1982 and 1983 as an example. The national fiscal revenue in 1982 [2] reached 112.397 billion yuan, growing by 3.2% from the year before, and the fiscal revenue in 1983 went up to 124.899 billion yuan, a 11.1% increase from 1982. In addition, over-centralization of the management of enterprises was relaxed, and enterprises gained some autonomy in operation and management. At its early stage the economic responsibility system aimed to solve the problems in the distribution of interests between enterprises and the state, but since 1983 it began to deepen towards the transformation of interest allocation within the enterprises.

3.2. Economic responsibility system in the taxes-for-profits period

Between 1983 and 1984, reform of the interest allocation system in enterprises was carried out gradually in China, with taxes-for-profits at its core. As regulated in the Interim Measures for Taxes-for-Profits in State-Owned Enterprises issued by the State Council in April 1983, the SOE's turned-in profits should be converted to taxes paid in categories and rates promulgated by the state, and profits after

1 *Ten Years of Reforms in Chinese Enterprises*, complied by the Enterprise System Department of the State Commission of Economic System Reform and Office of the Enterprise Management Steering Commission of the State Council, Reform Press, 1990, pp.65-67.

2 Department of Comprehensive Planhing, Ministry of Finance, ed., *Statistics of China's Finance 1950-1988*, China Financial and Economic Publishing House, 1989, p.12&14.

taxes would be entirely at the discretion of the SOEs, so that the distribution between the state and SOEs could be normalized through taxes. Before taxes-for-profits, it was very difficult to ascertain the base and percentage of retained profits for enterprises, as the vastly diversified internal and external conditions of the enterprises and the continually changing situations during the reform required a one-by-one check of the enterprises to arrive at a reasonable figure, which was not only impractical but also liable to cause imbalance between enterprises. It was believed that taxes-for-profits was an applicable solution to the problem.

3.2.1. Main contents of taxes-for-profits

On April 12 1983, the State Council issued Interim Measures for Taxes-for-Profits in State-Owned Enterprises from the Ministry of Finance,[1] starting the first stage of taxes-for-profits. The measures were listed below. First, all profit-making large and medium-sized SOEs (including finance and insurance enterprises) should pay income tax at a rate of 55% according to realized profits. For profits after income tax, part of it should be turned in to the state, while another part retained by the enterprises according to a percentage approved by the state. Second, all profit-making small SOEs should pay income tax at the 8-level excess progressive tax rate according to the realized profits. After paying taxes, the enterprises should be fully responsible for their own profits and losses, with no funds allocated by the state. However, for enterprises with more after-tax profits, a certain contracting fee might be charged by the state or a fixed amount of the profits be turned in to the state. Third, loss subsidies for loss-making enterprises should be handled in the following ways: (1) Any losses allowed by the state policy should continue to be covered by quota subsidies or planned subsidies, with no compensations for losses over the limit and a retainable percentage for losses below the limit, the percentage set for a period of three years. (2) Any enterprises

1 *Ten Years of Reforms in Chinese Enterprises*, complied by the Enterprise System Department of the State Commission of Economic System Reform and Office of the Enterprise Management Steering Commission of the State Council, Reform Press, 1990, pp.107-109.

with losses caused by poor operation and management should be ordered by administrative departments to rectify the losses within a specified period of time. Appropriate subsidies should be granted, with examination and approval by the financial department, should the enterprises managed to rectify the losses within the prescribed period, and no subsidies should be compensated if the rectification exceeded the prescribed period. Fourth, SOEs should make reasonable use of their profits after taxes in establishing funds for new products trials, production development, reserve fund, staff welfare and staff awards. Fifth, after taxes-for-profits the administrative departments could still pool some funds from the SOEs' retained profits to cover expenses in key technological innovation, setting up new commercial outlets, and constructing simple buildings. The percentage or amount of profits to be pooled should be decided by the administrative departments and reported to the financial departments for filing. Sixth, the income tax paid by SOEs should be turned in to the central and local governments respectively according to the jurisdiction of the enterprises. The central government should make no changes to the retention percentage of the fiscal base of the provinces, municipalities and autonomous regions.

On September 18 1984, the State Council issued Interim Measures for the Second Stage of Taxes-for-Profits in State-Owned Enterprises from the Ministry of Finance[1] , which means a full-scale replacement of profits with taxes. The measures included: First, the industrial and commercial tax was divided into product tax, value-added tax, salt tax and business tax according to the object of taxation. Different tax rates were drawn up according to different situations of production and operation, so that such activities could be carried out by SOEs under the guidance of national plans and strategies. Second, the rate of regulatory tax should be determined with the SOEs' realized profits in 1983 as the base.

1 *Ten Years of Reforms in Chinese Enterprises*, complied by the Enterprise System Department of the State Commission of Economic System Reform and Office of the Enterprise Management Steering Commission of the State Council, Reform Press, 1990, pp.137-140.

For large and medium-sized SOEs whose profits left after deducting income tax calculated at 55% from the approved base-period profits did not meet the bottom line for reasonable tax retention in 1983, no regulatory tax should be levied and a certain amount of income tax should be reduced after approval and within a period of time. Third, profit-making small SOEs, after paying income tax at the new 8-level excess progressive tax rate, should be fully responsible for their own profits and losses, with no funds allocated by the state. For those whose profits after tax did not meet the bottom line for reasonable tax retention in 1983, a certain amount of income tax should be reduced after approval and within a period of time. Fourth, certain tax subsidies, reductions and exemptions should be granted to SOEs with losses or little profits. Fifth, SOEs should make reasonable use of their profits after taxes in establishing funds for new products trials, production development, reserve fund, staff welfare and staff awards.

3.2.2. Promotion of the economic responsibility system during taxes-for-profits

As taxes-for-profits was carried out in SOEs in two stages, the economic responsibility system was further promoted and strengthened. On the one hand, an investment restraint mechanism was initially formed. One important aspect of the taxes-for-profits reform was that loans should be paid after tax rather than before tax, which means that SOEs, instead of the financial departments, became the party responsible for paying back investment loans, defining clearly responsibilities for investment. This could to some extent help solve the old problem of SOEs' blind competition for investments and loans. On the other hand, the operational mechanism of SOEs was transformed. The SOEs' duties and responsibilities to the state were defined clearly through taxes and profits, so that the division of interests between the enterprises and the state was normalized and stabilized, effectively motivating the enterprises to continually improve their economic efficiency.

(3) Outcome of taxes-for-profits

Great hope was attached to taxes-for-profits when it began to be implemented. It was believed to be the way to go for SOE reform, as the normalization of interest division between the state and the enterprise could solve the problem of bargaining for more interest, the government's fiscal revenue could increase steadily as it could get the majority of the profits with 55% income tax and regulatory tax, and the enterprises could be greatly motivated as they would aim to make more profits so that more profits after taxes could be retained. The results of the reform, however, turned out to be a great surprise. Immediately after the measures for the second stage of taxes-for-profits were issued, credit, investment, and consumption funds all expanded overwhelmingly, deteriorating the government's fiscal revenue and expenditure. For example, the total amount of bank loans in 1984 increased by 28.9% from 1983, with 48.4% of the increase coming from December 1984, the third month in the second stage of taxes-for-profits. The total amount of staff wages in China in 1984 increased by 19% from 1983, with the growth rate reaching 38% in the fourth quarter when taxes-for-profits began.[1] Enterprises employed a number of ways to expand expenses on wages, including using more retained profits and using year-round balances for bonuses, and some loss-making enterprises even resorted to falsification to pay bonuses. In terms of fixed-asset investment, in 1985 the investments by enterprises owned by the whole people surged by 44.6%, and extra-budget investment loans of SOEs reached a rare growth rate of 54.7%. Credit, investment and consumption funds all spun out of control, leading to a 8.8% increase in prices in 1985. Following that, starting from the second half of 1985, the government's fiscal revenue lapsed into a consecutive 22-month decline and landed in a fiscal deficit for 1987. This forced the government to reflect on the taxes-for-profits reform and explore new alternatives.

3.3. Comments on the economic responsibility system and "taxes-for-profits"

Despite its short time span, the economic responsibility system for SOEs served

1 Chen Guoheng, *Studies on State-Owned Property System Reform*, China Social Sciences Press, 2004, p.203.

as an exploratory trial of SOE reform and some of its measures did promote the deepening of reform in SOEs.

First, the relationship between the government and the enterprise was clarified. Compared with "decentralization of power and transfer of profits" implemented earlier, the economic responsibility system made some changes in the government-enterprise relationship, mostly reflected in the government's control over enterprises which began to shift from the earlier physical indicators to monetary indicators, signifying a switch from arbitrary policy plans to systematic plans for "decentralization of power and transfer of profits".

Second, neither the economic responsibility system nor taxes-for-profits touched upon the essential system of SOEs. With the economic responsibility system, the government's control over the enterprises by orders was not abolished, with the former still having control power over the latter, and the ownership structure of enterprises remained unchanged; it was, therefore, rather difficult for enterprises to arrange production and operation according to the needs of the market, whose enthusiasm and initiative were yet to be motivated. However, the promotion of the economic responsibility system laid a foundation for the later pervasive contract responsibility system carried out in SOEs, making it in essence a transitional enterprise system. On the other hand, with taxes-for-profits, the ownership of state-owned assets was made completely abstracted, while the enterprises were not granted legal ownership, leaving their ownership system hanging in the air. This was the underlying reason why taxes-for-profits could no longer proceed.

Third, SOE reform began to be associated with the government's fiscal conditions. Some researchers argue that the government's fiscal difficulties were the most direct drive for SOE reform, as can be seen from the government's intention in promoting the economic responsibility system and taxes-for-profits. Emphasizing the SOEs' economic responsibility means ensuring that the government's fiscal revenue could materialize; otherwise the reform had to go on. This promotion mechanism for reform actually played an important role in later

SOE reforms.

4. Full-Scale Implementation of Contract Management Responsibility System

The separation between the ownership and management of enterprises was confirmed in the Decision of the Central Committee of the Communist Party of China on Economic System Reform passed at the Third Plenary Session of the Twelfth CCCPC in 1984, which then became the main theory for SOE reform. In December 1986, the State Council promulgated Some Regulations on Deepening the Reform of Enterprises and Strengthening the Vitality of Enterprises, which proposed that "various forms of contract management responsibility system shall be promoted, allowing full operational autonomy for managers". Contract management responsibility system emerged as an innovation by some SOEs during the implementation of "decentralization of power and transfer of profits", and became a model for SOE reform with Chinese characteristics. Following the principle of separation between ownership and management, this operation and management system delineated the responsibilities, rights, and interests between the state and the enterprise through a management contract so that the enterprise could operate independently and take full responsibility for its profits and losses without altering its ownership structure. Compared with the reform of "decentralization of power and transfer of profits", the contract management responsibility system involved issues at the root of the SOE system, for example, separation between the government and the enterprise and legal acknowledgement of the enterprise's autonomy.

4.1. History of the contract management responsibility system in SOEs

In as early as 1982, the Capital Iron and Steel Company started to implement a system where profits in excess of the growth targets were retained. According to the contract, the Company should ensure a 7.2% year-by-year increase of its profits, and could retain all profits in excess of this target, which was divided into development fund, welfare fund, and award fund according to a 6:2:2 ratio, while the depreciation fund were retained in total by the Company with no further funds allocated by the state. The total amount of staff wages was pegged to the realized profits in that the wage amount should increase 0.8% for every 1% increase in profits.[1] The nation-wide promotion of contract responsibility system did not start until the beginning of 1987. With the national finance facing new difficulties, some provinces and municipalities combined increasing production and saving costs, increasing income and saving expenses with the deepening of SOE reform, and various forms of contract management responsibility system were carried out in SOEs. In March 1987, the government's work report passed at the Fifth Session of the Sixth National People's Congress proposed that the key for reform should be perfecting the management system of enterprises, and that various forms of contract responsibility system should be implemented under the principle of separation between ownership and management so that enterprises could truly become economic entities that could operate and manage independently and autonomously and take full responsibilities for their profits and losses.

In April 1987, entrusted by the State Council, the former State Economics and Trade Commission held a symposium on contract management responsibility system in enterprises across China, and arranged all work concerning the implementation of the system. Since then, contract responsibility system began to be promoted in SOEs all over the country. In 1987, only 6% of industrial SOEs adopted the system, but in the first half of 1988 it became pervasive and by the end of that year the system was implemented in over 80% of industrial SOEs with independent accounting and 90% of industrial SOEs on the national budget, among which 95% large and medium-sized enterprises adopted the system.[2]

To ensure the smooth implementation of the contract responsibility system, relevant government departments and legislative bodies formulated and issued a

---

1 *Contract Responsibility System in Capital Iron and Steel Company*, compiled by the Research and Development Center of Capital Iron and Steel Company, Economics and Management Press, 1987, p.114.

2 Hu Jinglin (ed), *Theories and Ways for Reforms of State-Owned Enterprises*, Economic Science Press, 1995, pp.55-56.

series of policies, regulations and laws since 1987. On August 31 1987, the State Economics and Trade Commission and the State System Reform Commission circulated Opinions on Deepening the Reform of Enterprises and Perfecting the Contract Management Responsibility System, based on which the State Council drafted and issued on February 27 1988 Interim Regulations for Contract Management Responsibility System in Industrial Enterprises Owned by the Whole People.[1] On April 13 1988, the First Session of the Seventh National People's Congress passed Law of the People's Republic of China on Industrial Enterprises Owned by the Whole People. In February 1990, the State Council re-issued the new version of Interim Regulations for Contract Management Responsibility System in Industrial Enterprises Owned by the Whole People with modifications made to Article 21. These policies, regulations and laws legalized and normalized the contract responsibility system in SOEs.

4.2. Main content of the contract management responsibility system

In the Interim Regulations for Contract Management Responsibility System in Industrial Enterprises Owned by the Whole People issued by the State Council in February 27 1988, it was stipulated that the contract management responsibility system in SOEs, while insisting on the socialist ownership by the whole people, aimed at an organic integration of responsibilities, rights, and interests with responsibilities at the core, an interest mechanism that served as a restraint to adjust the interest relationship between the state, the enterprise, and the staff, and the separation between ownership and management that could guarantee the enterprise's status as an independent legal person. The main measures of the contract responsibility system included contract targets for turned-in profits, contract tasks for technological reformation, and pegging between the total amount of wages and economic efficiency. Innovations were carried out in

1 *Ten Years of Reforms in Chinese Enterprises*, complied by the Enterprise System Department of the State Commission of Economic System Reform and Office of the Enterprise Management Steering Commission of the State Council, Reform Press, 1990, pp.215-217.

promoting the contact responsibility system and models with distinctive features were formed. The following are a few examples:

1. "Two contracts and one pegging", i. e., contract targets for turned-in profits, contract tasks for technological reformation, and pegging between the total amount of wages and economic efficiency.

2. Contract targets for year-by-year turned-in profit increases;

3. Contract targets for base turned-in profits and part retention of the excess profits;

4. Contract fixed-amount turned-in profits for enterprises with little profits;

5. Contract targets for reduction in losses (or subsidies) for loss-making enterprises;

6. Contract overall targets for industry input and outcome.

The base for turned-in profits was set at the amount of profits turned in the previous year (the income tax and regulatory tax paid by enterprises at the second stage of taxes-for-profits). For enterprises whose profits fluctuated due to influences of external factors, the base could be set at the average of the turned-in profits of the two or three years before the contract system. In the meantime, the base could be adjusted with reference to the average capital profit margin of the area or the industry. The year-by-year profit growth rate and the retention percentage of excess profits should be set in consideration of the enterprises' potential for production increase and with reference to their tasks for technological reformation. The contract period should be no less than three years. The contract management responsibility system should be implemented through deciding the managers or managing groups of the enterprises by way of competition through open tendering, or in the form of risk mortgage contract. Trials of separate fund accounts should be carried out in enterprises with contract management responsibility system with the state funds and the enterprise funds separated and written under different accounts.

The basic principle for the contract responsibility system is "fixed base for contract, guarantee of turned-in profits, retention of excess profits, and self-compensation for insufficient profits", which could serve to sort out the relationship of responsibilities, rights, and interests between the state and the enterprise, motivate the SOE's initiative for increasing production and profits, and allow more autonomy for enterprises in operation and management by restraining to a certain extent the government's intervention. Therefore, the contact responsibility system was in essence the continuation and deepening of the earlier reform of "decentralization of power and transfer of profits" in SOEs.

4.3. Effects of the implementation of the contract management responsibility system

The contract management responsibility system in SOEs was more stimulating than previous systems and achieved better effects in the early stages of its implementation, as it related the enterprise and its economic efficiency more closely to the personal contributions of managers and staff and reduced the government's administrative intervention.

First, the system ensured a continual increase of the government's fiscal revenue and growth of the enterprises' operational efficiency. According to statistics, for industrial SOEs on the national budget, realized taxes and profits in the four years (1987-1990) after the contract responsibility system increased by 27.8% compared with the four years (1983-1986) before the system, turned-in profits and taxes (including pension and unemployment insurance funds) increased by 26.3%, profits of the SOEs went up by 27.6%, and average per person income for the staff went up by 79%. However, it was suggested by other researches and statistics that in the later stages of the contract responsibility system the efficiency of SOEs took a turn for the worse after an initial period of growth. In 1987, the total profits of the industrial enterprises owned by the whole people with independent accounting increased by 14.5% from 1986, total profits and taxes increased by 12.9%, and general labor productivity by 7.8%, but the year 1988 saw a gradual decline in these figures. In 1989 the total profits decreased by 16.6% from the previous year, the total losses of the loss-making enterprises were 120% of those of 1988, and the general labor productivity only went up by 0.5%.[1] In 1991, one third of SOEs made a loss, and another estimated one-third either had a hidden loss or made a loss even though making a profit on the books.[2]

Second, the system handled properly the restraints of rights, responsibilities, and interests between the state, the enterprise, and the staff through a contract, and improved the enterprise's awareness of competition as well as its competitiveness by pushing it gradually towards the market. Compared with the earlier "decentralization of power and transfer of profits", the contract responsibility system was after all a contractual relationship between the government and the managers of enterprises, even though it was far from being normalized. With rights and responsibilities of the government, the enterprise, and the mangers stipulated in the contract, the managers had much more room in making decisions according to market changes, hence improving the operational efficiency of the enterprise.

Third, the system promoted a reformation in the management system of the enterprise where the main body of investment began to change. Statistics show that between 1987 and 1992 the contract management responsibility system was adopted to different degrees in 98% of large and medium-sized industrial SOEs. During the planned economy, the government was the only investor of SOEs, but things began to change with the contract responsibility system. According to statistics, during the Seventh Five-Year Plan, the cost of newly added fixed assets of industrial SOEs on the national budget increased by 168.6% compared with that of the Sixth Five-Year Plan, with one-third of the new fixed assets bought with the SOEs' retained profits and accumulated depreciation, and the other two-thirds renewed or transformed with bank loans. This changed the previous situation where the SOEs depended entirely on the government as the sole investor.

1 National Bureau of Statistics, *China Statistics Almanac (1991)*, China Statistics Press, 1992, pp.410-411.

2 Chen Guoheng, *Studies on State-Owned Property System Reform*, China Social Sciences Press, 2004, p.209.

4.4. Comments on the contract management responsibility system

The contract management responsibility system of SOEs was indeed an innovative enterprise system, and did contribute to promote the separation between ownership and management of the SOEs and motivate the initiative of enterprises and individuals. However, the contract responsibility system did not touch the ownership system essential to the enterprises, and had in itself some insurmountable weaknesses which prevented it from meeting the needs of the SOEs to participate in market competition. It was precisely because of these fundamental weaknesses that the contract responsibility system could not sustain.

First of all, the contract responsibility system was in essence a profit-sharing contract that reformed the apportion of the enterprises' surplus income. Through the contract, the government and the enterprise decided how to allocate the surplus income so as to motivate the managers and the staff. However, as the principal, the government was not a shareholder in the full sense of the term, and when a contract was signed, the enterprise, i.e., the agent pursuing maximum interests, would usually exploit its information advantage and encroach on the interests of the principal through, for example, less mention of depreciation, more on-the-job consumption to embezzle state-owned assets, and especially short-term predatory business practices. Besides, due to information disparity, the government found it very difficult to determine the base of the contract and had to pay more transaction cost for the contract, which did not give it the promised interests.

Secondly, the contract still maintained a hierarchical administrative relationship between the government and the enterprise. The enterprise had to obey the government's will and follow its arrangement in important management decisions in investment, asset disposal, income apportion, and personnel appointment; the enterprise had never truly become an independent market player, as it never had the property rights as a legal person. The enterprise, as the agent, was not on an equal footing with the government, i.e,. the principal, in negotiating the contract; the agent had to always "beg", while the government could arbitrarily modify the content of the contract or even terminate it for no reason, giving the contract little legal credibility and also contributing an institutional reason for the agent's short-sighted practices. On the other hand, the one-to-one negotiation of the contract responsibility system could easily induce the agent to employ improper means to collude with the representative of the principal in order to change the profit-sharing ratio. There were also cases where the agent took responsibility only for profits and not losses so that the contract responsibility system could not punish the enterprises with poor performance even though it did award those with good performance. As can be seen from a large number of cases, in the first round of contracts only very few were signed with managers chosen through competitive bidding or peer review while most were signed through one-to-one negotiations between the government and the managers, where the process lacked fairness, transparency and binding force.

Lastly, in terms of incentive mechanism, the contracts were usually of a short term and pegged with enterprises' annual profits, which induced the managers' severely short-sighted practices of blindly pursuing maximum interests within the contract term while overlooking long-term development of the enterprises, depending mostly on upgrading equipment, reducing cost or increasing short-term cost while ignoring technological advancement and long-term investment. Due to these inevitable weaknesses of the contact responsibility system, in the three years between 1987 and 1989, only 88% of the contracts were completed; in 1990, when China was faced with severe economic conditions, the completion rate dropped to 69%, with the number of loss-making enterprises increasing by 92% from the previous year. In 1992, 36.7% of SOEs made a loss. Under the circumstances, the contract responsibility system began to turn into mere formality. Flexible methods were adopted in determining the base of the contact, competitive mechanisms such as tendering and bidding were canceled, and in many provinces and municipalities almost 100% of the contracts were signed with the enterprises' team of leaders of the Party, the government, the Workers' Union and the Youth League; contract periods were shortened, and an increasing number of contracts had its targets appraised and approved each year. The contracts were leaning towards soft restraint, low responsibility, and zero risk, and the enterprise system was showing a tendency of regression to the old system. It was this decline in the marginal effects of the contract responsibility system that to a large extent urged the government to change its policy. At the beginning of 1991, 90% of the enterprises with completed contracts turned to the second round of contracts, and the central government's policy was on the one hand to continue and perfect the contact management responsibility system and on the other hand to create favorable conditions for trials of share-holding system in SOEs. This signals that the contract management responsibility system had completed its historical mission in the reform of SOEs.

Chapter 10

Ownership Reform and System Re-Construction in State-Owned Enterprises

The reform path of state-owned enterprises in China in the 1980s, generally speaking, was to adjust the control power of management decision-making and the economic interest relationship between the government and the enterprise through decentralization of power and transfer of profits. Such measure alone, however, failed to make SOEs truly independent players in market competition despite the innovations in management contract responsibility system, as the drawbacks of SOEs were not overcome structurally. Practices have proved that SOEs cannot maintain long-term management efficiency or competitiveness without a fundamental reform in their ownership system.

At the beginning of 1992, Deng Xiaoping's Southern Tour Talks set off a new round of reform upsurge in China, thus providing a favorable political and economic environment for further deepening the SOE reform. On October 12 1992, the Fourteenth National Congress of CPC was held, which clearly put forward that the goal of China's economic structural reform is to establish a socialist market economic system, in which enterprises are the basic economic units and the main competitors of the market, thus linking the dominant position of enterprises in the market with the establishment of a socialist market economic system. In June 1993, an investigation and research team, led by the State Economics and Trade Commission in concert with thirteen ministries and commissions assigned and entrusted by the Central Leading Group on Financial and Economic Affairs, was sent to Shanghai, Guangdong, Fujian, Shandong, Heilongjiang and other provinces, where they conducted interviews and seminars with over 100 enterprises and 200 people and sought extensively views from all walks of society. In July 1993, four months later, the team produced a report titled Establishing a Modern Enterprise System Befitting the Socialist Market Economic System, which later played an instrumental role in deepening the reform of ownership system of SOEs and promoting the modern enterprise system.

1. Ownership System Reform in SOEs

After the mid-1980s, the issue of ownership began to become a concern of SOE reform with the implementation of decentralization of power and transfer of profits as well as management contract responsibility system. Under the vigorous promotion of the government, some enterprises began to explore diversified ownership reform with the aim to establish a modern enterprise system, the most important form of which was the shareholding system.

1.1. Early explorations of shareholding system in SOEs

In as early as 1980s, i.e., the early stages of the reform and opening-up, some collective enterprises in counties and townships began to explore the shareholding system,[1] whose innovation stimulated the same attempt in some small-scale SOEs. Between 1984 and 1986, municipalities such as Beijing and Shanghai selected a few large and medium-sized SOEs as trials for the shareholding system. In July 1984, Beijing Tianqiao Department Store Company had its initial semi-public

1 China Securities Regulatory Commission, *Report on the Development of China's Capital Market*, China Financial Press, 2008, p.4.

offering (mostly within its social network), and formed a diversified shareholding structure with 50.67% state shares (composed of the assets of the original Tianqiao Department Store), 25.89% bank shares, 19.69% enterprise shares, and 3.46% individual shares for the staff.[1] In December 1986, the State Council issued Some Regulations on Deepening Enterprise Reform and Strengthening Enterprise Vitality (Regulations for short), in which it was stated that "Local governments can choose a few large and medium-sized enterprises owned by all people with favorable conditions and carry out trials for the shareholding system." Following the Regulations, some provinces and municipalities began to select large and medium-sized SOEs for trials of the shareholding system. Shanghai officially approved Shanghai Vacuum Electronic Devices Company as the trial enterprise after shortlisting 8 large and medium-sized SOEs, and had its IPO in January 1987, which formed a diversified shareholding structure with 74.5% state stocks, 1% organization stocks (shares subscribed by legal entities such as enterprises and administrative institutions apart from the Company), and 24.5% individual shares after three issues.[2] By the end of 1988, according to statistics from the State Commission for Structural Reform, there were altogether 3,800 shareholding enterprises in China, of which 800 were transformed SOEs with 60 having issued shares, and the other 3,000 used to be collective enterprises. In terms of regional distribution, most of the shareholding enterprises were located in more developed areas in East China, of which 1,255 were in Shanghai, 707 in Shenyang, 290 in Guangdong, and 133 in Wuhan.[3]

Between 1989 and 1991, the shareholding system reform was briefly

1 Zheng Zhenlong ed., *A Brief History of the Development of China's Securities*, Economic Science Press, 2000, pp.173-174.

2 State Commission for Structural Reform ed. *Almanac of China's Economic Structural Reform (1989)*, Reform Press, 1989, p.126.

3 *Ten Years of Reforms in Chinese Enterprises*, complied by the Enterprise System Department of the State Commission of Economic System Reform and Office of the Enterprise Management Steering Commission of the State Council, Reform Press, 1990, p.318.

influenced by political reasons and economic austerity policy, but it maintained its momentum. According to incomplete statistics on 34 provinces, municipalities and autonomous regions from the State Commission for Structural Reform, by the end of 1991 there were altogether 3,320 shareholding enterprises of different types (excluding township enterprises with a shareholding cooperative system, Sino-foreign joint ventures, and jointly operated domestic enterprises), of which 63% used to be collective enterprises, 22% SOEs, and 15% other types of enterprises.[1] The number of standardized shareholding enterprises in Shanghai and Shenzhen increased to 11 and 108 respectively. According to a 1991 investigation in Shanghai, the total share capital of the 20 approved trial shareholding enterprises amounted to 2.01 billion RMB, among which 50% were state shares, 29.5% were legal person shares, 15.4% individual shares, and 5.1% foreign capital shares. The state shares and legal person shares, mostly subscribed by publicly owned enterprises, combined to make 79.5%,[2] an absolutely controlling status for state-owned shares.

1.2. Promotion of the modern enterprise system in SOEs

In November 1993, the Third Plenary Session of the Fourteenth CCCPC passed Decision on Several Issues Concerning the Establishment of the Socialist Market Economic System, which stated clearly that the SOE reform should be oriented towards establishing a modern enterprise system that befit requirements of the market economy with "clear ownership structure, distinct rights and responsibilities, separation of government and enterprise, and scientific management". The Decision also pointed out that the corporate system for SOEs was a worthwhile exploration in establishing the modern enterprise system; large and medium-sized SOEs with favorable conditions could be transformed into wholly state-owned company, limited liability company or limited shareholding

1 State Commission for Structural Reform ed, *Almanac of China's Economic Structural Reform (1992)*, Reform Press, 1992, p.322.

2 Zheng Zhenlong ed, *A Brief History of the Development of China's Securities*, Economic Science Press, 2000, p.183.

company based on their own situations, while small SOEs could be contracted or leased, re-structured into shareholding cooperative enterprises, or sold to organizations or individuals. In December 1993, the Fifth Session of the Standing Committee of the National People's Congress passed the Company Law of the People's Republic of China, which stipulated that the company should operate independently in accordance with law with all its corporate property and take sole responsible for its own profits and losses. When an SOE is transformed into a company, it must transform its operating mechanism according to law and take steps to liquidate its assets, define its property rights, liquidate its creditors' rights and debts, evaluate its assets, and establish a standardized internal management system, etc. This marks that China's SOE reform entered a new phase in 1994, a phase of establishing a modern enterprise system according to law and implementing ownership structural reform on a full-scale.

1.2.1. Trials of establishing a modern enterprise system

In November 1994, after the Third Plenary Session of the Fourteenth CCCPC clearly pointed SOE reform in the direction of planned corporatization, the State Economics and Trade Commission and the State Commission for Structural Reform jointly held a work meeting on trials for the modern enterprise system, at which leaders of the State Council were present. Several documents were discussed and passed at the meeting, including Standard Opinions on Deepening Enterprise Reform and Improving Large and Medium-Sized State-Owned Enterprises (Draft) and Plan for Selecting Some Large and Medium-Sized State-Owned Enterprises for Trials of the Modern Enterprise System (Draft for short), officially beginning the trials for the modern enterprise system. Following this, the State Economics and Trade Commission and the State Commission for Structural Reform first selected 100 large and medium-sized SOEs and 3 holding companies for such trials, with the State Commission for Structural Reform in charge of 30 SOEs and one holding companies, and the State Economics and Trade Commission in charge of the other 70 SOEs and two holding companies. In addition, the provinces, municipalities and autonomous regions also selected

2,000 local SOEs for trials,[1] allowing them a head start in establishing a modern enterprise system.

The Draft issued by the State Council stipulated specifically the objectives, [2] principles, content, measures, implementation and steps in establishing the modern enterprise system.

(1) Objectives and principles for the trials

The following objectives were expected to be achieved through selecting some enterprises for trials of establishing a modern enterprise system. First, Seek an effective way of combining publish ownership with market economy so that the enterprises' operation and management system could be transformed, their economic efficiency improved, and productivity further liberated and developed; Second, Explore ways to separate the government from the enterprise and change the role of the government so that the government should no longer interfere directly with the production and management of the enterprise and the enterprise could be completely rid of its affiliation to administrative institutions and become the main player of the market, operating independently according to principles of the market economy. Third, Straighten out ownership structure and gradually set up an operation and management system for state-owned assets that would establish the legal property rights of the enterprise and make it a true legal person with independent civil rights and liabilities and unified capacity for civil rights and capacity for action so that the enterprise can indeed assume sole responsibility for profits and losses and self-development. Fourth, Perfect the leadership system and management system inside the enterprise and make them more standardized and scientific so that a system could be formed with clear demarcation of rights and responsibilities, high efficiency, and mutual restraints.

The principles for the trials were first of all to give full play to the leading role

1 Zou Dongtao, *Innovations in China's Economic System: Explorations in the Reform Years* Vol. Ⅱ, People's Publishing House, 2003, p.499.

2 Wu Jie ed., *Operational Manual for the Modern Enterprise System*, Reform Press, 1995, p.202.

of the state-owned economy to ensure the preservation and appreciation of the value of state-owned assets; secondly, to separate the ownership of investors from the property rights of corporate entities; third, to focus on institutional innovation and standardized operation; fourth, to start from the national conditions and learn useful experience from abroad, combining tradition with innovation; fourth, to promote relevant supporting reforms; and lastly, to guide by classification, move forward steadily and mobilize the enthusiasm of all parties.

(2) Main contents of the trials

First, perfect the legal person system in enterprises so that they could enjoy the property rights of legal persons. A series of actions were carried out to get a clear picture of the assets and capital of SOEs in accordance with relevant provisions of the state, including defining property rights, sorting out creditors' rights and liabilities, evaluating assets, verifying the percentage of property owned by the legal person, determining the amount of capital, and registering the property rights of state-owned assets. State-authorized investment institutions and departments, as well as other investors, should enjoy legal shareholders' rights according to the percentage of their shares, including rights in acquiring stock returns, implementing important decisions, and selecting mangers, and should bear limited liabilities for the enterprise up to the amount of their capital contribution. The investors could not participate directly in the operation and management of the enterprise or control directly the property of the legal person. The investors were not allowed to withdraw their capital contribution, nor was the enterprise allowed to withdraw shares, but its property rights could be transferred legally. The enterprise would enjoy civil rights and bear civil liabilities independently based on all its legal person property, operate in accordance with the law, assume sole responsibility for profits and losses and take responsibility to the investors in maintaining and appreciating the values of assets (capital). The enterprise, as an independent legal person entity and the main player in market competitions, had shaken off their dependence on the administrative departments and got rid of the administrative hierarchy that it had adopted.

Second, establish the status of state-owned assets as the main investment in the trial enterprises. As per the principle that the government's role as manager of social economy should be separated from its role as owner of state-owned assets, state-authorized investment institutions could act as both the investor and the manager of state-owned assets and implement equity management over state-owned assets in enterprises. Such investment institutions include state-owned holding companies as special legal persons and special operating departments authorized by the state, the former mostly taking the form of state investment companies, state-owned asset management companies and large group corporations.

Third, determine the organizational forms of the companies that enterprises transformed into. A few enterprises of special industries or producing certain special products could be restructured into wholly state-owned companies, while most enterprises should be made into limited liability companies; those with favorable conditions could be transformed into joint stock limited companies, of which only a few could become listed companies; of the existing national industry headquarters, those with favorable conditions could be transformed gradually into state holding companies, but not one giant monopolizing the industry; group corporations should be restructured according to the headquarter-subsidiary system.

Fourth, establish a scientific and standardized organization structure within the companies. Board of directors should be established in wholly state-owned companies, with members appointed by state-owned asset managing institutions. Shareholders' meeting, board of directors and board of supervisors should be established in other companies with multiple investors in accordance with the provisions of the Company Law, where members of the board of directors and the board of supervisors should be appointed according to the decision of the shareholders' meeting, and part-time directors and supervisors should be subsidized.

Fifth, reform the labor and personnel wage system in enterprises. The management of enterprises was no longer identified as government cadres, the identity boundary was broken between employees of different ownership systems, and a two-way selection system was established between enterprises and employees. The government would only exercise an indirect control over the total wages of the enterprises, stipulate a minimum wage, and guide, supervise and check their wage levels.

Sixth, improve the financial and accounting systems of enterprises. General Rules on Enterprise Finance, Accounting Standards for Enterprises, and other relevant regulations of the state were implemented on a full scale so that the financial and accounting systems of enterprises could meet the requirements of the company system and conform to international standards.

Seventh, improve the work of the Union and strengthen democratic management by the staff. For wholly state-owned companies and limited liabilities companies set up by more than two SOEs or more than two state-owned investors, democratic management should be achieved through employee representative meeting and other forms; for other limited liabilities companies and limited joint-stock companies, such management could be achieved either through employee representative meeting or by the Union on behalf of the staff. The Union should, on behalf of the staff, conduct balanced consultation with the enterprise on wages, working hours and other labor conditions, sign collective contracts and establish an effective mechanism for stabilizing labor relations in enterprises. The company should listen to the opinions and suggestions of the Union and staff when studying major issues concerning production and operation and formulating important rules and regulations, and should seek their opinions in advance when deciding on issues concerning the staff's vital interests, and invite their representatives to attend relevant meetings.

1.2.2. Supporting policies, laws, and regulations issued by the government

To support the ownership system reform in SOEs, relevant departments of the government formulated and promulgated in a timely manner a number of laws, regulations, and policies, mostly in the following three areas:

First, perfecting the micro enterprise system. In as early as June 1992, the State Planning Commission, Ministry of Finance, People's Bank of China, and the Production Office of the State Council jointly issued Measures for Trials on Joint Stock Companies, which stipulated that the purpose of the trials was to convert the operational mechanism of enterprises, open up new financing channels for them, promote reasonable flow of production factors, and improve the operational efficiency of state-owned assets. The principle for the trials was to protect state-owned assets from infringement and uphold equity equality, risk sharing and benefit sharing. The Measures also made detailed stipulations on the organizational forms, stock right definition, employee stocks, scope and approval of trials, as well as the government's management of such joint stock companies. In December 1993, the State Commission for Structural Reform formulated Opinions on Trials on Wholly State-Owned Limited Liabilities Companies, which defined wholly state-owned companies as part of the modern enterprise system and required that such companies verify state capital contribution and establish legal person property and governance structure. In June 1994, the State Council issued Regulation of the People's Republic of China on Administration of Registration of Companies, further emphasizing the legal norms for operations of corporate enterprises.

Second, managing state-owned assets. In August 1992, the State Bureau for State-Owned Asset Administration and the State Commission for Structural Reform jointly issued Interim Regulation on Administration of State-Owned Assets in Joint Stock Companies, which put forward for the first time the concepts of state shares and state-owned legal person shares. It pointed out that both shares were state-owned and stressed that no attempts to carve up state-owned assets or infringe upon national interests would be tolerated in the joint stock trial companies. Management of these trial companies should follow the principle of separation between the government and the enterprise, and separation between ownership and operation. In July 1994, the State Council issued Regulations on Property Management in State-Owned Enterprises, which stipulated that the purpose of establishing a clearly defined ownership structure was to clarify the responsibilities of relevant government departments and other supervisory institutions as well as rights and responsibilities of the enterprises, and sort out the relationship between the state-ownership, hierarchical management, division of supervision of enterprise property and enterprise operation. Enterprises should operate independently and in accordance with the law the property authorized by the state to be operated and managed by them. The State Council should authorize relevant departments or institutions to supervise the operation and management of property of enterprises designated by or affiliated to the State Council, and the principle for supervision emphasized preservation of capital and maintenance of owners' interests. In November 1994, Interim Measures for Equity Management of Joint Stock Limited Companies was issued by relevant departments of the government, which stipulated that in restructuring into joint stock companies SOEs could restructure the whole enterprise or restructure enterprise property according to their conditions. Restructuring of enterprises must be to the benefit of their own development, their profitability, as well as the development of specialization and social services. Definition of property rights must be conducted in accordance with state regulations when SOEs were restructured into joint stock companies.[1] In January 1996, the State Council promulgated Measures for Management of Property Registration of State-Owned Assets in Enterprises, aiming to strengthen the management of property registration of state-owned assets in enterprises, perfect the basic management system for state-owned assets, and prevent loss of these assets. In August 1997, the State Bureau for State-Owned Asset Administration and the State Commission for Structural Reform jointly issued Opinions on Standardizing the Exercise of Equity Rights by State-owned Shareholders of Joint Stock Limited Companies, aiming to regulate the exercise of equity rights by state-owned shareholders in joint stock limited companies, protect

1 Wu Jie ed, *Operational Manual for the Modern Enterprise System*, Reform Press 1995, p.289.

the interests of state-owned shares, and promote the healthy development of joint stock limited companies.

Third, protecting the interests of the staff of enterprises. In October 1994, the State Council issued Notice on Some Questions Concerning Trials of Bankruptcy of State-Owned Enterprises in Some Cities, which pointed out that the first priority of bankrupt enterprises was to settle their staff. In March 1993, the State Council issued Notice on Deepening the Reform of the Pension System for Employees of Enterprises, aiming to guarantee the basic requirements of life for retired staff in enterprises.

Fourth, managing the leadership and leading group of enterprises. In May 1995, the Central Commission for Discipline Inspection issued Opinions on Implementing and Handling the "Four Provisions" of Integrity and Self-discipline for Leading Cadres of State-owned Enterprises; in September of the same year, the Central Commission of Organization, State Economics and Trade Commission, and Ministry of Personnel jointly issued Opinions on Strengthening the Construction of Leading Groups in State-Owned Enterprises, emphasizing that priority should be given to large and medium-sized SOEs in strengthening the construction of leading groups, and that guidance should be provided according to classification of SOEs[1]. In March 1997, the Central Commission of Organization, State Economics and Trade Commission, Ministry of Personnel, and All-China Federation of Trade Unions issued a notice that required a full-scale, thorough examination of the leading groups of SOEs in 1997 so that the leading group construction in SOEs could be strengthened.

2. Promotion and Achievements of the Modern Enterprise System

The modern enterprise system, which CCCPC officially began to promote in SOEs in 1993, made impressive progress with cooperation from all levels of local

1 All the above documents are quoted from Summary of *Major Events in the Reform and Development of State-owend Enterprises since the 14th National Congress* compiled by the fourth editing office of the Party Literature Research center of CCCPC, Central Party Litereture Press, 1999.

governments and enterprises, and marked an important stage in adapting SOEs to the market economy.

2.1. Trials of the modern enterprise system and their achievements

Trial for implementing the modern enterprise system at both the central and local levels after more than three years of careful organization (see the table below) made considerable achievements. From the beginning of the trials to the end of 1996, of the 100 enterprises listed as trials by the State Economics and Trade Commission and State Commission for Structural Reform, 98 completed restructuring, with the exception of one enterprise disintegrated, and another merged. The restructuring happened in four ways: (1) 17 enterprises were restructured directly into joint stock companies with multiple shareholders, among which 11 became joint stock limited companies and 6 limited liabilities companies. (2) 69 enterprises were restructured into wholly state-owned companies, among which 29 were first turned into wholly state-owned companies, and then their production entity was further restructured into limited liabilities companies or joint stock limited companies with multiple investors. (3) 10 industry administrative departments were restructured into pure wholly state-owned holding companies. (4) Two enterprises had their assets restructured on the principle of restructuring followed by system reform. By the end of 1996, these trial enterprises had a total capital of 360.08 billion yuan, an increase of 99.45 billion yuan and 27.6% from before the trials; their total owners' equity reached 123.18 billion yuan, increased by 38.3 billion and 31.3% compared with before the trials; their asset-liability ratio, on the other hand, dropped from 67.95% before the trials to 62.28%, a decrease of 5.31%. 117,000 surplus personnel were diverted from these enterprises, accounting for 65% of the total number of surplus personnel, among whom 8,566 were diverted to society, 10,544 were retrained after being laid-off, 45,359 were re-employed by expanding enterprises, and over 50,000 were retired. Some enterprises also transferred to local governments certain business that should fall within their jurisdiction, and thereby reducing their social burdens. In addition, the State Economics and Trade Commission and the

State Commission for Structural Reform oversaw 3 trials for holding companies, restructuring them according to standard requirements of holding companies. Apart from the 100 trial enterprises managed by the central government, 2,343 enterprises were selected by local governments for trials, with a total number of employees at 10.04 million and total capital at 194 billion yuan. The local trials also made impressive progress. By the first half of 1997, 540 enterprises were restructured into limited companies, accounting for 23% of the total number, and an equal percentage of enterprises, i.e., 540, were turned into limited liabilities companies; 909 enterprises were restructured into wholly state-owned companies, 38.8% of the total number; the remaining 307, i.e., 13.2%, had not completed their restructuring. The asset-liability ratio of all trial enterprises in 1996 was 65.8%, decreasing by 2.4% from the previous year; the asset appreciation rate was 26.5%, and the liquidity ratio was 1.056%, 1% higher than that of the previous year; and the quick ratio was 0.722, which was 2% higher than that of the previous year. The trial enterprises diverted 2,265 social service institutions with 117,000 personnel; they also diverted 611,000 surplus personnel from their own staff, accounting for 6% of the total number of employees, among whom 131,000 were re-assigned to other institutions, 115,000 entered into retraining after being laid-off, 154,000 retired early, and 211,000 were awaiting re-employment.[1]

Table 10-1 Overview of Trials for Establishing the Modern Enterprise System

	CCCPC	Nationwide
Enterprises	100	2 343
Number of staff (ten thousand)		1 004
Total capital (a hundred million yuan)	3600.8	13 783
Ways of restructuring		
joint-stock limited companies	11	540
Limited liabilities companies		540
Wholly state-owned companies	6	909
Others	69	47
	10	

1 Institution of Industrial Economics of the Chinese Academy of Social Sciences, *Report on the Development of China's Industry: System Innovation, Structural Changes, and Policy Adjustment*, Economics and Management Press, 1998, p.20.

contd.

	CCCPC	Nationwide
Not restructured, bankrupt, or merged	4	307
Changes in assets and debt Increases in total assets (a hundred million yuan) Increases in owners' equity (a hundred million yuan) Decreases in debt ratio (%)	 994.5 383 2.31(62.28)	 2.4(65.8)
Diverting surplus personnel (ten thousand) Into society Retraining after being laid-off Re-employed by expanding enterprises Early retirement Awaiting re-employment	11.7 0.8566 1.0544 4.5392 5.0000	61.1000 13.1000 11.5000 15.4000 21.1000
Diverting non-production institutions		2 265

Source: Jin Pei ed, *Comparisons of Enterprise Reforms in China and the United Kingdom*, Economics and Management Press, 1999, p.143.

2.2. Nationwide promotion of the modern enterprise system in SOEs

The establishment of the modern enterprise system with the ownership system reform at its core began to sweep across China, despite the many obstacles encountered in the trials, such as the heavy debt of enterprises, overstaffing, overburden in carrying out social duties, difficulties in bankruptcy and unclear definition of ownership (Zou Dongtao, 2003). According to statistics, by the end of 1997 over 10,000 SOEs were restructured into joint stock companies, of which 745 were listed on Shanghai and Shenzhen Stock Exchanges. Of the 512 national key enterprises, 36% were listed; of the 120 trial corporate groups, 42% were listed; and of the 100 trial enterprises for the modern enterprise system, 48% were listed.

The non-trial small SOEs are especially worth mentioning, as they broke the existing SOE system model through a number of reform forms such as bankruptcy, auction, lease, contractual management and joint-stock cooperative system. By the first half of 1997, over 50% of small SOEs had privatized, and in some provinces with faster paces the percentage reached over 75%. In a number of prefectures and cities all small SOEs had become privatized, such as in Shunde City of Guangdong Province, Zhucheng City of Shandong Province, Yibin City of Sichuan Province, Luohe City of Henan Province, Xinle City of Hebei Province, Binxian County of Heilongjiang Province, and Lanxi City of Zhejiang Province.

The nationwide SOE system reform made substantial progress in the 21st century. According to statistics from the Committee for Supervision and Administration of State-Owned Assets of the State Council, by the end of 2003 2,541 of the 4,223 large and medium-sized key SOEs were restructured through different ways into joint stock companies with multiple shareholders, amounting to 60% of the total number.[1] Of the 2,524 state-owned and state-controlling enterprises in the key national enterprises, 52.7%, i.e., 1,331 enterprises were restructured into joint stock companies with multiple shareholders. Over 80% of small SOEs were restructured, of which the highest percentage went to county SOEs, reaching over 90% in some counties. Some central SOEs promoted corporate governance structure, with 19 enterprises carrying out trials on Board of Directors and a total 66 of external directors dispatched, and the number of external directors reaching half or more than half of the number of board members in 14 trial enterprises. The percentage of joint stock companies in central enterprises and their subsidiaries increased from 30.4% at the end of 2002 to 64.2% in 2006.[2]

2.3. Diversified financing for enterprises and further expansion of their autonomy in investment

First of all, after reform and development most SOEs had some retained funds, which on average was 14% of their realized profits and over which the enterprises had independent control. Secondly, the enterprises could acquire from banks loans necessary for production and operation. Thirdly, the enterprises

1 Insisting on SOE Reform and Promoting SOE Restructuring in a Standard Manner, *People's Daily*, September 29, 2004.

2 Zhang Zhuoyuan, *A Collection of Zhang Zhuoyuan's Reform Theories*, China Development Press, 2008, p.125.

could, with approval from relevant departments, raise funds through measures such as joint ventures, introducing foreign capital, and issuing bonds and stocks, thus breaking their dependence on the government for funding and diversifying their means and channels for financing. According to statistics, in 1996 the total investment on fixed assets in state-owned economy was 1,205.624 billion yuan, among which 55.695 billion came from the national budget, accounting for 4.5%, 285.123 billion from bank loans, accounting for 13.6%, 81.107 billion from foreign investment, accounting for 6.7%, and 614.225 billion were raised by the enterprises themselves, 50.8% of the total, with the rest 14.4%, i.e., 173.149 billion, from other investments. The enterprises had also gained greater autonomy in determining projects for technological transformation, expansion and other investments. These measures allowed some well-operated enterprises to raise funds through multiple channels and develop businesses according to the needs of the market.

2.4. Establishment of new financial and accounting systems nationwide and tightened restraints on SOE's finances

As mentioned earlier, a new financial and accounting system began to be implemented in China's SOEs on July 1, 1993. This new system was applicable to all types of enterprises and also conforming to international conventions; it could provide not only more financial and accounting information to the government but also necessary financial and accounting information for owners, legal person organizations and individuals with investment intentions, as it could reflect in a more comprehensive way the long-term operational conditions of the enterprises, especially their assets and liabilities. The new accounting system, in addition, was more scientific in accounting entries setup, methods of cost calculations, and accounting statements system, which could both improve the management of the enterprises and facilitate the work of their accounting personnel. The implementation of this new financial and accounting system in SOEs further promoted their turn to the modern enterprise system.

2.5. Changes in the labor personnel system and income distribution system of SOEs

First, the enterprises had great autonomy in recruitment, and most carried out reforms in their employment system. By the end of 1996, over 200,00 SOE had adopted the labor contract system for all staff, and 5.549 million employees had signed labor contract, accounting for 50.7% of the total number of employees in SOEs across China. Some enterprises had also optimized their labor structure and improved labor organization. Second, as SOE employees' income was generally pegged with the economic returns of the enterprises, and the state set limits only on the extent of income increases, the income gap between enterprises widened. On the other hand, the income gap between employees of the same enterprise also widened, as the enterprise now decided the income distribution among its employees and the state adjusted individual income with measures such as income tax. Both changes served to motivate the initiative of the enterprises as well as the employees. Third, a preliminary pension guarantee scheme was established in SOEs. According to statistics, a total of 28 provinces, autonomous regions and municipalities and 5 industry coordinating departments introduced pension reform plans based on the principle of social-pool-plus-personal-accounts, with over 200,00 employees collecting their pensions according to the new scheme and basic pension scheme covering all industrial enterprises. By the end of 1996, 8.8 million employees and 2.3 million retirees had joined the pension social pool scheme. Trials of reforms in unemployment and medical insurances were also carried out in a number of cities.

2.6. Progress in debt reduction of SOEs

First, the government adopted different measures to increase the capital of SOEs. Through increasing capital investment from the state, "loans-to-investment", returning profits, and allowing the issuance of bonds and stocks, governments at different levels managed to reduce the debt ratio of SOEs and thereby reduce their financial expenditure. By the end of 1996, 2.42 billion yuan of principal and interest of "state-allocated-funding-to-loans" was converted to state capital, reducing the asset-liability ratio by 2.5% in the 131 enterprises concerned. For SOEs in coal, military industry, and hydropower with policy-oriented deficit, all the balance of the principal and interest of "state-allocated-funding-to-loans" was converted to state capital. A large number of SOEs had increases in their capital through increased retainment of depreciation funds, income tax returns, and issuance of bonds and stocks. In 1996, the asset-liability ratio was 65.25% for industrial enterprises with independent accounting, a decline from the previous two years. Second, social duties were removed from the enterprises. The measure of "removing auxiliaries and streamlining core businesses" was adopted universally in SOEs, with many of them separating social duties from the enterprises, including production support departments, logistics and life service departments, schools, and hospitals. This reduced not only the enterprises' social burden but also surplus personnel. By the end of 1996, statistics showed that 5,908 non-production departments and 1.23 million surplus personnel were removed in cities with trials for optimizing capital structure alone.

2.7. Promotion of merger and bankruptcy of SOEs and optimization of capital structure

Trials for "optimizing capital structure" began in 18 cities in China in 1994, and were expanded to 50 cities in 1996, with 8 more cities serving as the control group. In 1997, the trial cities were further expanded from 58 to 110, and provisions for bad debts in the mergers and bankruptcies in these cities increased from 20 billion yuan to 30 billion yuan. Considerable efforts were made to promote mergers and bankruptcies of enterprises in these cities. By the end of 1996, 1,192 enterprises were merged involving 1.13 million employees, with a total capital of 29.2 billion yuan and a total debt of 27.8 billion yuan, among which balance of principal and interest of bank loans accounted for 19.7 billion yuan, and suspended loans with interest exemptions accounted for 1.13 billion yuan. 1,099 enterprises declared bankruptcy, with a total capital of 24.98 billion yuan and a total debt of 42.99 billion yuan, and involving 680,000 employees.

3. Further Deepening of the SOE Reform[1]

In October 2014, the Third Plenary Session of the Eighteenth CCCPC passed Decision of the CCCPC on Some Major Issues Concerning Comprehensively Deepening the Reform, which made important strategic plans for comprehensively deepening the reform of SOEs and state capital and proposed a series of new ideas, new tasks, and new measures. In August 2015, CCCPC and the State Council jointly issued Guiding Opinions on Deepening State-Owned Enterprise Reform, which defined the guidelines of SOE reform as "to improve the modern enterprise system that is characterized by clear property rights, well-defined powers and responsibilities, separation between government and business, and scientific management according to the standards of liberating and developing social productivity, and by centering around the core missions of raising the efficiency of state capital and enhancing the vitality of SOEs, to fine-tune the state-owned assets regulation framework to prevent the loss of state-owned assets, to make comprehensive progress in managing and governing enterprises by the rule of law and strengthen and improve the Party's leadership over SOEs, to develop stronger, better and larger SOEs, constantly enhance the vitality, controlling power, influence and the ability to withstand risks of the state-owned economic sector, and let SOEs proactively adapt to and lead the 'new normal' of economic development, thus actively contributing to promote the sustained and healthy development of the economy and the society at large, and realize the Chinese dream of the great rejuvenation of the Chinese nation."

The document also proposed five basic principles for the SOE reform: (1) The basic economic system shall be upheld and improved. (2) The direction of socialist market economic reform shall be adhered to. (3) The principle of combining the efforts to enhance vitality and those to reinforce regulation shall be upheld. (4) The Party's leadership over SOEs shall be upheld. (5) The reform of SOEs shall always proceed in an active, steady and coordinated manner.

1 All references in this section are from government websites of China.

The document defined the main objectives of SOE reform as: "by 2020: to make decisive achievements in the key fields and aspects of SOE reform; to form a state-owned asset management system, a modern enterprise system and a market-oriented business operation mechanism that are more in line with China's basic economic system and the requirements on the development of socialist market economy; to develop a more reasonable layout and structure for state capital; to nurture a large number of outstanding entrepreneurs of upright character who are capable, competent at operations and vibrant; to develop a legion of key SOEs with innovation capability and international competitiveness; and, to significantly enhance the vitality, controlling power, influence and the ability to withstand risks of the State-owned economic sector." More specifically, the objectives were: (1) "The corporate-style reform of SOEs shall be largely completed. The following objectives shall be achieved in this regard: to make positive progress in developing the mixed ownership economy; to perfect the corporate governance structure; and, to fine-tune the market-oriented mechanisms featuring the survival of the fittest under which SOEs engage in autonomous and flexible business operations, and promote and demote internal management personnel, employ and let go staff members, and increase and cut remunerations according to market practices." (2) The state-owned asset regulation framework shall become more mature, with relevant laws and regulations that are more robust, regulatory means and methods that are continuously optimized, and regulatory operations that are more scientific, targeted and effective. For-profit state-owned assets shall be placed under centralized and unified regulation, and the responsibilities for preserving and increasing the value of state-owned assets shall be fully assigned to the parties concerned." (3) "The efficiency for the allocation of state capital shall be significantly raised, and the layout and structure of state-owned economy shall be continuously optimized to effectively play its leading role. SOEs shall fully display their leading and exemplary role in enhancing the capability of independent innovation, protecting resources and the environment, accelerating transformation and upgrading, and performing social responsibilities." (4) "The Party building of enterprises shall be comprehensively strengthened, and their anti-corruption frameworks and work systems shall become more robust. In addition, the Party organizations of SOEs shall enjoy a more solid statutory position in corporate governance, and fully display their core political role." According to the above arrangement, a series of reform policies and measures were promulgated by the State Council and relevant ministries and departments, leading the SOE reform to a new stage.

1. Change from "managing assets" to "managing capital" in state capital supervision

As pointed out in the Decision of the CCCPC on Some Major Issues Concerning Comprehensively Deepening the Reform passed at the Third Plenary Session of the Eighteenth CCCPC, it is a basic policy to "improve the State-owned assets-management system and strengthen state-asset supervision by focusing on capital management, establish a number of state capital operating companies and back the transformation of qualified state-owned enterprises into state-owned investment companies". Based on this policy, Guiding Opinions on Deepening State-Owned Enterprise Reform jointly issued by CCCPC and the State Council in August 2015 proposed that the function of regulatory institutions for state capital would be changed from managing enterprises to managing capital. In October 2015, the State Council issued Several Opinions of the State Council on Reforming and Improving the State-Owned Asset Management System, which defined the guideline for reforming and improving the state-owned asset management system as the following: "the basic economic system of socialism shall be upheld and improved, the reform direction of socialist market economy shall be adhered to, the pattern of market economy and the pattern of enterprise development shall be respected, the relation between the government and the market shall be correctly handled, the regulation of state-owned assets shall be strengthened with capital management as the main content, the authorized operation system of state-owned capital shall be reformed, the status of state-owned enterprises as market participants shall be really established, and the transformation of the functions of state-owned assets supervision and administration institutions shall be advanced, so as to adapt to the new situation of market orientation, modernization, internationalization, and the new normal of economic development, and continue to heighten the dynamism, dominance, influence, and capability of risk resistance of the state-owned economy."

This document also stipulated four basic principles for reforming and improving the state-owned asset management system. (1) Adhering to well-defined rights and responsibilities. The separation of the government administration from enterprise management, the government's socioeconomic management function from its function as the owner of state-owned assets, and ownership from business management rights shall be achieved, and the capital contribution relationship between the government and state-owned enterprises shall be straightened out according to the law. Government functions shall be transformed practically, the status of state-owned enterprises as market participants shall be established according to the law, and a modern enterprise system shall be established and improved. The separation of the public administration functions of the government from the functions of state-owned asset contributors shall be adhered to so as to ensure that state-owned enterprises operate lawfully and independently and to trigger the dynamism, creativity, and inherent motives of enterprises. (2) Adhering to highlighting priorities. As required by the market economy rules and the modern enterprise system, with prominence given to capital management, with capital as the bond, with property rights as the foundation, effective administration of the layout of state capital, well-regulated capital management, raising returns on capital, and maintenance of capital safety shall be the priorities. Attention shall be paid to the lawful exercise of the rights by the state as a shareholder through the corporate governance structure. (3) Adhering to the combination of decentralization with appropriate control. According to the requirements of well-defined rights and responsibilities, efficient regulation, and standard and transparency, the transformation of the functions and regulatory modes of state-owned assets supervision and administration institutions shall be advanced. The power that should be delegated to enterprises shall be delegated by law so as to practically enhance the dynamism of enterprises and raise the efficiency of state capital management; and what should be controlled shall be scientifically and effectively controlled so as to strictly prevent the loss of state-owned assets and ensure the preservation of and increase in the value of state-owned assets. (4) Adhering to soundness and order. The relation among reform, development, and stability shall be effectively handled, the systematisms and synergy of the reform and improvement of the state-owned asset management system shall be highlighted, with priority fields to make breakthrough in, pilot programs shall be conducted, implementation shall be conducted step by step, and overall plans shall be made, so as to advance the relevant supporting reform collaboratively.

In the future China's supervision and administration of state capital will switch from "managing assets" to "managing capital". In the past, the state-owned asset management system has been centering on "managing assets", which made it inevitable for the government to manage the SOEs' personnel and business, and resulted in problems such as no clear separation between the government and the enterprise, or between the government and its role as investors, multiple management, and dispersed rights for investors. Under the "managing capital" model in the future, SASAC will eventually return to its role as an investor following the principles of streamlining administration and decentralization of power, which means that state-owned asset management institutions must acquire certain rights and shoulder certain responsibilities in accordance with The Company Law and charters of the enterprises and based on the amount and percentage of their capital contribution. In the meantime, senior executives of SOEs will be hired on the market instead of being appointed by administrative departments, and professional mangers will play a major role in operating and managing enterprises.[1] Trials for state-owned investment companies have been

1 Li Chang'an, SOE Reform Needs to Change from "Managing Assets" to "Managing Capital", *Economic Information Daily*, August 19 2015.

carried out in State Development and Investment Corporation and COFCO.

2. Diversified ownership reform in SOEs

As pointed out in the Decision of the CCCPC on Some Major Issues Concerning Comprehensively Deepening the Reform passed at the Third Plenary Session of the Eighteenth CCCPC, "diversified ownership integrated by state capital, collective capital and private capital is the prime method for materializing the basic economic system." Developing diversified ownership economy serves to further optimize the equity structure of SOEs, with multiple forms such as wholly state-owned, absolute state controlling, relative state controlling, and state equity participation. Diversified ownership was defined for the first time as the main direction for SOE reform in a CCCPC document at this Plenary Session. In September 2015, the State Council issued Opinions of the State Council on Development of an Economy of Mixed-Ownership of State-Owned Enterprises, stipulating four basic principles for developing an economy of fixed ownership in SOEs, namely, (1) government guidance and market operation; (2) systemic improvement and property rights protection; (3) making the relevant procedures strict and standardizing operation; (4) carrying out reform where it is feasible, and making promotion steadily. It is also proposed in this document that mixed-ownership reform in SOEs should be promoted by classification and implemented level by level, that all types of capital should be encouraged to participate in the reform, and that a healthy and sound governance system should be established for mixed-ownership enterprises, together with operational regulations in accordance with the law and relevant rules, so that a favorable condition can be created for the mixed-ownership reform. In October of the same year, NDRC, SASAC, and the Ministries of Finance, Human Resources and Social Security jointly released Notice on Issuing the Guiding Opinions on Encouraging and Regulating the Introduction of Non-State-owned Capital into Investment Projects of State-owned Enterprises. The general requirements for this work are stated as such: "Introducing non-state-owned capital into investment projects of state-owned enterprises should be helpful to improve the structure of property in the investment projects of state-owned enterprises, and improve project management and efficiency of fund utilization; it should be helpful to magnify the functions, preserve and increase the value, and improve the competitiveness of state capital; it should also help capital of all kinds of ownerships make up each other's deficiencies, promote each other and grow together. Non-state-owned capital shall abide by the requirements of the market access negative list and the foreign investment negative list if it wants to hold or control shares in investment projects of SOEs." The basic principles are: (1) government guidance and market operation; (2) equal rights and interests, and mutual development; (3) compliance with the laws and regulations, openness and transparency; (4) improving the system and optimizing the environment. The improvement of relevant systems and supporting polices shall be accelerated so that prominent conflicts will be solved and capital introduction can be conducted in a standardized and orderly manner, with a fine-tuned system, scientific standards, and effective operations.

According to incomplete statistics, in July 2014 SASAC of the State Council launched the pilot projects of mixed ownership economy in China Pharmaceutical Group Corporation and China Construction Materials Group Corporation, followed by implementation plans for mixed ownership reform in SOEs in Beijing, Taijin, Shanghai, and Chongqing.[1]

China Construction Materials Group Corporation, one of the pilot enterprises, deals in the fully competitive area of construction materials, and has built in the 21st century a mixed ownership industry platform, including companies listed overseas, by integrating over a thousand private enterprises in the competition. In the process of capital restructuring, China Construction Materials Group implemented the shareholding system through equity financing, leaving about 30% of the shares for private entrepreneurs; it also integrated talent, capital, technology and other elements to produce impressive results. In the cement

1 Ju Jinwen, Contracting Analysis on Promoting Mixed Ownership Reform in State-owned Enterprises, *Tianjin Social Sciences*, Issue 1, 2016.

industry, for example, China Construction Materials Group has restructured over 900 cement and concrete enterprises, with a production capacity of 400 million tons that ranks first in the world.[1]

To further deepen the SOE reform, the government has also carried out trials in Xinxing Cathay International Group, China Energy Conservation and Environment Protection Group, China Pharmaceutical Group Corporation and China Construction Materials Group Corporation, where the Board of Directors exercise its power in the selection and employment of senior executives, performance appraisal and salary management. In addition, to avoid corruption in the SOE reform, two to three central SOEs whose management is under the charge of SASAC are selected for trials of stationing discipline inspection teams in enterprises.

1 Song Zhiping, Win-Win for the Country and the People: Developing Mixed-Ownership Enterprises Vigorously, *China Enterprise News*, December 24 2013.

Chapter 11

Strategic Restructuring of State-Owned Enterprises and the Increased Control Power of State Capital

Based on the basic connotations of the theory of the primary stage of socialism, it is necessary not only to maintain the dominance of public ownership but also to provide space for development for non-public ownership. A new strategic guideline for SOE reform has been gradually formulated after discussions at several important CCCPC meetings, that is, to strengthen control on the big SOEs and give more autonomy to the small ones, and make advances or withdrawals when necessary so as to achieve overall development of the national economy. More specifically, with regards to scale, the policy of "reforming, restructuring, transformation, and strengthening management" shall be adopted in large SOEs and corporations for their development, while more flexible policies shall be applied to open up and invigorate small and medium-sized SOEs; with regards to industry, the control power and influence of state-owned economy shall be enhanced in key industries and areas, and can be either advanced or withdrawn in other industries and areas with a focus to improve the overall performance of the national economy.

1. Historical Background for the Strategic Restructuring of the State-Owned Economy

Despite considerable progress made in stabling the modern enterprise system in SOEs, there has not been any fundamental change to turn the tables for the state-owned economy. Industrial SOEs with independent accounting continued to make more losses on a greater scale, while at the same time non-state-owned economy showed a momentum for rapid development. In November 1993, CCCPC officially announced its decision to establish a socialist market economy, and it was against this backdrop and after careful deliberation that CCCPC decided to strategically restructure the state-owned economy.

1.1. Continued increases in the loss of SOEs

The SOEs' efficiency was on a continued decline between the beginning of the marketization reform of the state-owned economy and the mid-1990s. The losses of SOE kept increasing, and the loss rate kept going up, rising from 7.6% in 1978 to 44.8% in 1995 (see table 11-1). The net profits of SOEs increased from 50.88 billion yuan in 1978 to 66.56 billion yuan in 1995, a poor 13.8% growth, which was actually a big drop in net profits over the decade if considering inflation. In addition, state-owned industry suffered an overall net loss between January and April of 1996 and January and March of 1997.[1] In the meantime, the original value of fixed assets in industrial SOEs with independent accounting expanded from 37.3 billion yuan in 1980 to 309.36 billion yuan in 1995, growing by 7.3 times, and the net value of fixed assets increased from 25.28 billion yuan in 1980 to 174.74 billion yuan in 1995, growing by 5.9 times.

It was in light of the increases in the losses of SOEs and the sharp decline in the operational efficiency of the state-owned economy that the decision-makers at CCCPC had to consider strategic reform plans for the state-owned economy.

1 Wu Jinglian et al, *Strategic Restructuring of the State-Owned Economy*, China Development Press, 1998, p.25.

Table 11- 1 Losses and Profits of Industrial SOEs with Independent Accounting

Year	Losses of SOEs making a loss (1) (100 million yuan)	Profits of SOEs making a profit (2) (100 million yuan)	Net profits(2)-(1) (100 million yuan)	Loss rate(1)/(2) (%)
1978	42.06	550.86	508.8	7.64
1980	34.30	619.70	585.4	5.53
1985	32.44	770.64	738.2	4.21
1990	348.76	736.87	388.1	47.33
1991	367.00	769.17	402.2	47.71
1992	369.27	904.37	535.1	40.83
1993	452.64	1269.90	817.3	35.64
1994	482.59	1311.60	829.0	36.79
1995	540.41	1206.01	665.6	44.81

Source: *Almanac of Chinese Statistics (1996)*, China Statistics Press, 1996, p.429.

1.2. Proposal of strategic restructuring of the state-owned economy

Inspired by Deng Xiaoping's speech during his southern China tour at the beginning of 1992, the Fourteenth National Congress of the Communist Party of China held on October 12 1992 clearly defined the establishment of a socialist market economy system as the goal for China's economic system reform. The Fifth Plenary Session of the Fourteenth CCCPC proposed for the first time the task of reforming the state-owned economy at a macro level, and made the following requirements while discussing the Ninth Five-Year Plan for Economic and Social Development and long-range objectives for 2010: "Focus should be placed on improving the whole state-owned economy and carry out strategic restructuring of state-owned enterprises through the flow and reorganization of stock assets."[1] The report of the Fifteenth National Congress of CPC released in September 1997, while continuing to stress "focusing on improving the whole state-owned economy by strengthening control on large SOEs, granting autonomy to and

1 *Selected Important Documents of the Central Plenary Sessions of All National Congresses of the Communist Party of China since the Third Plenary Session of the Eleventh Central Committee* Vol.Ⅱ, compiled by the Party Literature Research Center of the CPC Central Committee, Central Party Literature Press, 1997, p.350.

invigorating small ones, and implementing strategic restructuring of SOEs", put forward for the first time that "the layout of the state-owned economy should be readjusted strategically. The State-owned economy must dominate in key industries and areas concerning the lifeline of the national economy, while in other areas asset restructuring and structural adjustment can be adopted to reinforce priorities and improve the overall quality of state-owned assets." [1]

In September 1999, the Fourth Plenary Session of the Fifteenth CCCPC passed The Decision of the Central Committee of the Communist Party of China on Major Issues Concerning the Reform and Development of State-Owned Enterprises, which further stipulated that the control power of the state-owned economy over the national economy must be strengthened and that the layout of the state-owned economy should be readjusted and the SOEs restructured strategically. The meeting defined "key industries and areas" as: "industries that are related to national security; industries that are naturally monopolized; industries that supply major products and services for the public; and pillar industries and backbone enterprises in high and new technology sectors"; it also made the requirement that "the strategic readjustment of the layout of the state economy should be combined with the optimization and upgrading of industrial structures and the readjustment and improvement of the structure of ownership, while adhering to the principles of developing what should be developed, withdrawing what should be withdrawn, doing what should be done while leaving others alone."

In November 2002, the report of the Sixteenth National Congress of CPC proposed that re-adjustment of the layout and structure of the state-owned economy should speed up. In October 2003, the Third Plenary Session of the Sixteenth CCCPC passed Decision of the Central Committee of the Communist Party of China on Some Issues concerning the Improvement of the Socialist

1 *Selected Important Documents of the Central Plenary Sessions of All National Congresses of the Communist Party of China since the Third Plenary Session of the Eleventh Central Committee* Vol. Ⅱ, compiled by the Party Literature Research Center of the CPC Central Committee, Central Party Literature Press, 1997, p.426.

Market Economy, which further pointed out that "We should improve the mechanism for the entry-withdrawal and rational movement of state capital, encourage more state capital to go to the important industries and key fields that have a bearing on national security and the lifeline of the national economy, and enhance the controlling power of the state-owned sector. The state-owned enterprises in other industries and fields should adopt assets restructuring and structural adjustment, and prosper or perish through fair market competition." On December 18, 2006, the General Office of the State Council forwarded the Guiding Opinions of the SASAC about Promoting the Adjustment of State Capital and the Restructuring of State-owned Enterprises (Guiding Opinions for short), which stipulated that: For central SOEs in the military industry, important resources exploitation such as oil and natural gas, and infrastructure such as the power grid and telecommunication, state capital must have sole proprietorship or absolute controlling shares; for important subsidiaries and central enterprises in civil aviation and shipping, state capital must hold absolute controlling shares; for central enterprises in downstream products management in the petrochemical industry and value-added services in the telecommunication industry, further steps should be taken in the reforms to attract non-public and foreign capital and promote diversity in investors and ownership. Meanwhile, for key enterprises in fundamental and pillar industries, the state-owned economy should maintain strong control, including equipment manufacturing, automobile, electronic information, construction, iron and steel, nonferrous metals, chemical industry, survey and design, and science and technology, where the percentage of state capital should be reduced while the influence and pull of the state-owned economy should be strengthened. Among these industries, in mechanical equipment, automobile, electronic information, construction, iron and steel and nonferrous metals, central enterprises need to become the key enterprises and leading models with state capital holding absolute controlling shares or conditional controlling shares; for central enterprises in the science, technology and design industries responsible for important tasks such as common research for the industry and conversion of technological achievements, state capital should hold controlling shares. The Guiding Opinions was obviously consistent with the principle of the CCCPC and also lent more practicability to previous policies.

The purpose of SOE reform is to enhance their competitiveness on the market so as to maintain the dominance of public ownership and give full play to the control power and leading role of state capital and the state-owned economy. It is through establishing the modern enterprise system that SOEs change their operational mechanism and become legal entities as well as the major market player that take responsibilities for their own operation and management, bear their own losses and profits, self-direct their development and exercise self-restraint. It is through changing the operational mechanism of SOEs that the market competitiveness of SOEs and enterprises of collective ownership can be enhanced, which in turn ensures the dominance of public ownership in the national economy and the leading role of the state-owned economy. Such dominance and leading role is demonstrated in three aspects: the advantage of assets of state and collective ownership in the total social assets, the control of state-owned economy over the lifeline of the national economy, and the guiding role of state-owned economy in the development of the national economy. The SOE reform should focus on improving and invigorating the entire national economy, placing individual enterprises in the global picture of the national or regional economy and determining their development goal and direction within the context of structural optimization of the layout of stock state-owned assets. In other words, as long as strategic restructuring of SOEs is carried out through the flow and reorganization of stock assets following the development trend of the whole national economy and under a competition mechanism featuring the survival of the fittest, SOEs can be improved and invigorated and the operational efficiency of all state-owned assets enhanced.

2. "Strengthening Control on the Big SOEs and Giving More Autonomy to the Small Ones" and the Corporatization of Large and Medium-sized SOEs

Large and medium-sized SOEs play a crucial role in the national economy even though they are small in number as the majority of SOEs are small ones. The 500 biggest industrial SOEs have 37% of the total assets of all industrial SOEs, 46% of sales revenue, and 63% of realized profits. It is therefore vital to control and develop these "key minorities" by improving their quality and benefits of scale through establishing the modern enterprise system, optimizing their capital structure, speeding up technological transformation and enhancing enterprise management, so that they can play an essential role in strengthening the dominance of public ownership and bringing into full play the leading role of the state-owned economy, and in the meantime influence and stimulate the development of small and medium-sized enterprises as well as providing more room for adjusting enterprises in distress. As for small and medium-sized enterprises vast in number and dispersed across industries and regions, more open and flexible reform measures should be adopted, for example, merger, lease, joint ventures, restructuring into joint stock companies, or putting up for sale. This is what is later called "strengthening control on the big SOEs and giving more autonomy to the small ones".

2.1. "Strengthening control on the big SOEs" and the concentration of state capital on large and medium-sized SOEs

In 1993, the Third Plenary Session of the Fourteenth CCCPC announced that the goal of SOE reform in China was to establish the modern enterprise system. Following that, the State Council decided to select a number of large and medium-sized SOEs for trials of the modern enterprise system. In 1995, 1,000 key enterprises were selected, and the first group, i.e., 300 enterprises with advantages in their industries (later expanded to 512), were given appropriate supporting policies, that is, "strengthening control on the big SOEs".

2.1.1. More operational autonomy granted to trial enterprises

Apart from establishing the modern enterprise system, some wholly state-owned enterprises and corporations were authorized as investors of state-owned assets and allowed to set up their financial companies. In addition, autonomy was granted in export and import, and some enterprises were authorized to conduct international business.

2.1.2. Priority in entry into the capital market and the establishment of stable bank-enterprise relationship

Priority was given to these enterprises in issuing bonds and stocks domestically. They were encouraged and guided to control and mobilize more social capital with their limited state capital so that their development and expansion could be accelerated. The government selected 300 large enterprises and arranged a one-on-one partnership between each enterprise and a sponsoring bank, by which the bank signed an agreement with the enterprise, promising priority in the supply of credit funds in accordance with the credit rating within the approved scope. Priority was also given to projects of technological transformation and scientific development, with increased investment and exemptions of interest. Technology centers were set up in qualified enterprises to enhance their capacity for independent research and development. Besides, the government helped the enterprises with arrangement for their surplus personnel. [1]

2.1.3. Establishment of a new management system for large SOEs

In December 2003, SASAC (State-owned Assets Supervision and Administration Commission) of the State Council was established, continuing to exercise property rights management over the 187 mega-enterprises directly under the CCCPC. State-owned assets supervision and administration commissions were then established in all provinces, autonomous regions, and municipalities to manage in a unified way the large SOEs within their jurisdiction. A connected and relatively

1 Yang Shujin, *China: Reform, Development, and Stability*, China Development Press, 2000, p.89.

complete supervision and administration system of large SOEs was thus formed.

After a few years of efforts to strengthen and support the large SOEs, a number of large enterprises and corporations emerged victorious in market competition through replacing non-performing assets, improving their "blood-making capacity", regulating leadership and organization systems, carrying out specialized restructuring internally, and accelerating technological development and transformation. Some large state-owned corporations became strong competitors on both domestic and international markets, such as Changhong Group, Baoshan Iron and Steel Corporation, Yanshan Petrochemical Company, and the First Automobile Works, while others developed into multi-business corporations dealing in industry, trade, science and finance by taking full advantage of state policies and focusing on business development.

2.2. Outstanding achievements of "strengthening control on the big SOEs"

Large SOEs are the key to economic development. By focusing its attention on the system reform and operation of these large or mega-SOEs, the government has undoubtedly grasped and satisfied the needs of SOEs to survive and develop under increasingly fierce market competition, and fulfilled the requirements of the goal to establish a socialist market economy. Impressive achievements ensued as a matter of course.

2.2.1. Establishment of a number of large state-owned corporations

A number of state-owned corporations were established during the implementation of "strengthening control of the big SOEs". Most of the over 10,000 sate-owned holding companies were established in a bottom-up way and restructured from the parent companies of corporations, such as Dongfeng Motor Corporation, China Heavy Duty Truck Group, the First Automobile Works Group, Tianjin Bohai Petrochemical Group, Guizhou Aviation Industry Corporation, and China Textile Machinery Group. These parent companies were usually restructured into joint stock limited companies or limited liabilities companies, with a few into wholly state-owned companies. During the restructuring, the corporation was granted full authority from the state to operate and manage in a unified way state-owned assets occupied and used by its members, and in turn shoulder the responsibility to the state of maintaining and increasing the value of these assets.

Trials of state-controlled industry corporations started in 1994. Many state holding industry corporations had been established before, but they were only "government-body-turned" companies, and had never formed a parent-subsidiary bond with their subsidiaries. To meet the requirements of the reform of state-owned assets management system, in November 1996 the State Council officially approved the establishment of three national industry corporations as trials of state controlling corporations, namely, China Petrochemical Corporation, China Non-Ferrous Metal Industry Corporation, and China Aviation Industry Corporation. The trial went on for over a year, and then the three national industry corporations were restructured into wholly state-owned companies to manage the assets of their subsidiaries. In the trials a parent-subsidiary operation and management system bonded by assets was established in all three holding corporations, which improved the operation, management, and supervision system of state-owned assets; as state-authorized institutional investors, the corporations adjusted the organization structure, product and industry structures and strengthened their responsibility in maintaining and increasing the value of state-owned assets.

While these trials were carried out, explorations were being made in restructuring SOEs into holding companies by other departments or divisions of departments, such as China National Petroleum Corporation and China North Industries Group Corporation. In the meantime, trials of local holding companies progressed even faster. In as early as 1987, Shenzhen Investment Management Company was established in Shenzhen, and in 1995 Shenzhen Construction Investment Holding Company and Commerce and Trade Investment Holding Company were established to deal in investment and property rights operation of state-owned assets. Between December 1993 and April 1996, Shanghai authorized over 30 institutions to operate and manage state-owned assets through cancelling administrative bureaus, carrying out structural reform, and authorizing large corporations, with the value of state-owned assets authorized for operation reaching over 270 billion yuan, accounting for 60% of the total value of for-profit state-owned asset of Shanghai. Generally speaking, there were two types of local state-controlled companies, the first being multi-business companies to operate state-owned assets established by local governments, and the second industry companies to operate state-owned assets restructured by the enterprise administrative departments of local governments. The establishment of state-controlled companies at both the central and local levels promoted the separation of the management from the operation of state-owned assets, and helped establish a responsibility system for state-owned assets through level-by-level authorization.

State-owned and state-controlled corporations went further in their development in the 21st century, especially during the Tenth Five-Year Plan period. By 2005, 50.8% of all corporations in China were state-owned corporations and state-controlled corporations, down by 14.6%; in terms of asset size, their total year-end assets accounted for 85.5% of those of all corporations, a drop of 8%; and in terms of business scale, their business revenue accounted for 79.6% of the total revenue of all corporations, decreasing by 9.6%. Despite these relative decreases, state-owned and state-controlled corporations gained significant growth. During the Tenth Five-Year Plan, the year-end total assets of these corporations increased at an annual rate of 14.6%; in terms of asset concentration, their average asset scale amounted to 13.7 billion yuan by the end of 2005, a 22.9% increase from 2004; in terms of business scale, the annual growth rate of their business revenue reached 21.2% during the Tenth Five-Year Plan, not to mention that 84.4% corporations of state ownership made a profit. [1] By the end of 2006, 42 state-owned corporations had an asset scale of over 100 billion yuan, and 398 had a scale o f over 10 billion yuan, whose total assets amounted to 21,737.45 billion yuan, 74.9% of the total

1 Calculated according to relevant statistics in *2005 Annual Report of Statistics of Enterprise Corporations* by the State Statistics Bureau.

assets of all SOEs.[1] According to statistics reported by *Shanghai Securities News*, from 2002 to 2007 a total number (times) of 95 central SOEs participated in 47 restructurings. By the end of 2007, there were 151 central SOEs, among which 26 had main business revenue of over 100 billion yuan, and 19 had profits of over 10 billion yuan.[2]

2.2.2. Improved asset operational efficiency of large and medium-sized SOEs

During the corporatization process of SOEs', the scale economy of the enterprises continued to grow and the economic efficiency kept improving. By the end of 2005, the central SOEs had made historical records in all the following aspects, with realized sales revenue of 6,7312.9 billion yuan, increasing by 19.8%; profits of 627.65 billion yuan, increasing by 27.9%; net profits of 336.16 billion yuan, going up by 24.5%; rate of return on net assets at 9.7%, a 1.2% growth, and added value of 197,55 billion yuan, a 20.8% increase.

Following the considerable progress made in 2005, in 2006, the 159 central SOEs in China realized profits of 754.69 billion yuan, with a year-on-year growth of 18.2%, and the 1,031 provincial and municipal SOEs realized profits of 209.72 billion yuan, with a year-on-year growth of 38%. In 2006, the 159 central SOEs realized sales revenue of 8,166.88 billion yuan, with a year-on-year growth of 20.1%, profits of 754.69 billion yuan, with a year-on-year growth of 18.2%, turned-in tax of 661.1 billion yuan, with a year-on-year growth of 20%. The central SOEs in military industry, power industry, machinery, construction, commerce and trade industries all had a profit growth rate of over 20%, while those in communication, metallurgical industry, mining industry, and petrochemical industry maintained stable growth. By the end of 2006, the total assets of central SOEs were valued at 12,266.34 billion yuan, with a year-on-year increase of 16.2%, and their net assets valued at 5,348.9 billion yuan, with a year-on-year increase of 15.2%. In 2006, the state-owned economy maintained a rapid

1 *Almanac of Supervision and Administration of State-Owned Assets of China (2007)*, China Economics Press, 2007, p.48.

2 *Shanghai Securities News*, May 22 2008.

and healthy development nationwide, with the production and operation of SOEs growing at a faster rate and with better quality. The 1,031 state-owned and state-controlled enterprises in China had realized profits of 209.72 billion yuan, with a year-on-year growth of 38%, and turned in taxes of 237.53 billion yuan, with a year-on-year growth of 20.4%. By the end of 2006, their total assets and net assets had a year-on-year growth rate of 18.5% and 13.1% respectively. According to statistics reported by *Shanghai Securities News*, by the end of 2007, the SOEs in China had realized a total sales revenue of 1.8 trillion yuan, with a year-on-year increase of 20.1%, and realized profits of 0.162 trillion yuan, with a year-on-year increase of 31.6%. [1]

2.2.3. More reasonable product structure of large SOEs

Takes as an example the central SOEs. In 2005, these SOEs invested 104,5.38 billion yuan in fixed assets, an increase of 21.2%, and launched a number of key projects of great significance to structural adjustment and optimization. Sinopec officially put into operation the Yangtze-Basf integrated petroleum base, with an additional ethylene capacity of 600,000 tons; the 900,000 tons ethylene project of Shanghai Secco was also launched formally, which has become the ethylene production unit with the largest line capacity in China. CNPC launched 5 million tons refining reconstruction projects in Changqing, Dagang, North China and Karamay, and ethylene reconstruction projects in Jilin, Lanzhou and Daqing. China National Offshore Oil Corporation (CNOOC) started several LNG projects in Guangdong, Fujian, Zhejiang, and Shanghai. New progress had been made in offshore crude oil exploration; newly discovered geological reserves in the Bohai Bay amounted to about 200 million cubic meters of petroleum and about 150 million cubic meters of natural gas, and the Lufeng 13-2 oilfield in the eastern South China Sea was successfully put into operation, with a test productivity of as high as 30,000 barrels per day. In the meantime, the State Grid brought online the model project of 750 KV transmission and distribution, filling the gap of

1 *Shanghai Securities News*, May 22 2008.

transmission and distribution lines with over-500KV voltage in China.

The product structure of central SOEs were now more adapted to the changing needs of the market. The Baosteel Group completed all planned technical transformations in the Tenth Five-Year Plan, including the wide and heavy plate rolling mill and its supporting continuous casting, 1800 cold-rolled strip, stainless steel and carbon steel hot-rolled coil and Meishan steel hot-rolled sheet, which allowed it to become the largest production base in China for quality steel, including seamless steel for automotive and household appliances, stainless steel, steel for ship and pipeline, special seamless pipes for petroleum and power industries, and new construction steel. The automobile industry maintained a relatively high market share by accelerating the introduction of new models and expanding the production and sales of marketable and in-demand models while faced with rapid market change, slow growth of demand and high oil price. The mechanical and electrical equipment manufacturing enterprises developed a number of high-tech products, greatly improving their manufacturing capacity. Harbin Electric Equipment Group increased significantly the proportion of 600 MW supercritical and ultra-supercritical units in its product structure, and had begun to manufacture 1,000 MW ultra-supercritical units. Dongfang Electric Group began to take on large orders after successfully putting into operation 600 MW supercritical units, and its thermal power product structure would leap from 600MW to 1000 MW with the 600 MW large air-cooled units being developed and the 1000 MW supercritical units being manufactured. China First Heavy Industries completed the technical transformation for the capacity of casting 700 tons of molten steel in a joint casting process and built a new free forging hydraulic press of 15,000 tons so that it comprehensively improved and expanded the variety, quality and scope for large-scale production of large forgings, forming an annual production capacity of 220,000 tons of molten steel, 100,000 tons of forgings, 30,000 tons of castings and 150,000 tons of various heavy machinery products.

The structural adjustment of central SOEs continued in 2006 and produced further progress. The petroleum and petrochemical enterprises stepped up efforts to prospect oil and gas. CNPC reported newly prospected geological reserves of 570 million tons of petroleum and 357.6 billion cubic meters of natural gas, with the reserve replacement ratio of petroleum at over 1 and oil-gas valent weight accounting for 62% of the national total. The product structure of iron and steel enterprises was further optimized. Four iron and steel enterprises produced 56.07 million tons of steel, an increase of 11% over the previous year, with the output of cold-rolled, hot-rolled and galvanized sheets increasing by 40.7% and 18.5% respectively and that of wire rod and threaded steel decreasing by 8.1% and 14.1% respectively. The proportion of special materials in Anshan Iron and Steel Group reached 77%, and the proportion of high-tech content and high value-added products in Wuhan Iron and Steel Corporation reached 77.3%, a year-on-year 20.5% increase. The commercial and trade enterprises actively adjusted their business structure and developed their domestic trade. Domestic trade now accounted for 60% of China Minmetals Group's business revenue. The electric power enterprises strengthened the integration of stock and optimization of growth in accordance with the national energy development strategy and the requirements of industrial restructuring, China Electric Power Investment Group shut down 486,000 KW of small thermal power units, and in China Huaneng Group, 75.3% of the total installed capacity was now large thermal power units with a capacity of more than 300,000 KW, and 21.9% was 600,000 KW units.

2.2.4. Improved scientific and technical innovation in large SOEs

Take as an example the central SOEs. By the end of 2005, national-level research and development institutions were established in almost all such enterprises, with 476 institutions and 276,000 research staff working on technical innovation. According to incomplete statistics, in 2005 17 central science and technology enterprises won 8 second-class awards of the National Science and Technology Progress Award and 137 provincial and ministerial science and technology awards; 745 patents were applied for and 361 patents were authorized, of which 569 and 231 were invention patents; 14 software copyrights were obtained; and 33 international standards, 215 national standards and 230 industry standards were formulated. In the construction of the Three Gorges Project, Harbin Electric Equipment Group and Dongfang Electric Group made great strides in promoting the design and manufacture technology of super-large hydroelectric generating units in China by introducing technology, digesting, absorbing and re-innovating. In the bidding with foreign first-class power equipment manufacturers, they successfully obtained the Design and Manufacture Contract of some hydroelectric generators on the right bank of the Three Gorges Project. Anshan Iron and Steel Group successfully developed a steel plate for spiral case which could meet the requirements of hydroelectric generating units of the Three Gorges Hydropower Station. Wuhan Iron and Steel Group made significant breakthroughs in the development of low-temperature-oriented silicon steel with advanced international-level quality; its high-durability low-temperature pressure vessel steel passed the national evaluation and became the only domestic steel used in the national petroleum strategic reserve. The Aerospace Science and Technology Group focused on independent innovation and integrated system innovation of key links and overcame many technological difficulties commonly recognized in the international Astronautics field in manned space engineering.

The scientific and technical innovation capacity of the central SOEs was further promoted in 2006. The machinery and equipment manufacturing enterprises strengthened their research and development on advanced manufacturing equipment and made significant achievements. China First Heavy Industries successfully completed the hot test of the 15,000 tons hydraulic press independently developed by the group and began to put it into use. Independent intellectual property rights on the production of 600 MW subcritical units, the main product of power plant equipment manufacturers, was obtained, and the production capacity of 1,000 MW supercritical units was also achieved. China Eastern Electric Group reached first-class international level in its power plant equipment production technology and capacity, with its output ranking first in the world for three consecutive years. The military enterprises adhered to the integration of the military and the civil, and developed a number of products and technologies with independent intellectual property rights in the fields of aerospace, aviation and shipbuilding industries. The automobile manufacturing enterprises put on the market an increasing number of self-owned brand products, including HQ3, Pentium, Weizhi and the Junwei series of heavy-duty trucks developed by China First Automobile Corporation, and commercial vehicles such as EQ1141 lorry, and Tianlong heavy-duty truck developed by Dongfeng Automobile Corporation, which won 6 awards for independent innovation achievements in China's automobile industry. The central science and technology SOEs developed a series of world-leading new technologies and products based on the needs of industry development and the market, which won them 7 second-class national awards for scientific and technological progress, and one second-class national award for technological invention; in addition, 406 patents were granted, a 36.2% increase from 2005. The "TD-SCDMA Third Generation Mobile Communication Standards and Product Development Project" of the Institute of Telecommunications Science and Technology, checked and accepted by the Ministry of Information Industry, achieved an annual production capacity of tens of thousands of system equipment and would provide mobile phone solutions, laying the foundation for large-scale commercial use.

By the end of 2012, SOEs across China owned 292,000 independent intellectual property patents, 187,000 of which belonged to central SOEs. Large enterprises became the major force in scientific and technological innovation. By 2012, 219 academicians of the two academies (Chinese Academy of Sciences and Chinese Academy of Engineering) worked in central SOEs, together with 1.33 million personnel engaged in scientific and technological businesses and 304,000 in R&D, accounting for 12.5% and 2.85% respectively of the total number of employees of the central SOEs. The central SOEs persisted in perfecting and improving the scientific and technological innovation system under the guidance of the strategy of scientific and technological innovation, increased investment and sped up the improvement of such innovation capacity. Breakthroughs were hence achieved in a number of key technologies. To name a few, Shenzhou 9 completed China's first manned spacecraft rendezvous and docking with Tiangong 1, Jiaolong accomplished the 7,000 meters test dive and its scientific exploration tasks, China's aircraft carrier was officially put into use and the take-off and landing of domestically-made carrier-based aircraft was successfully tested, and the Beidou regional navigation system was fully completed. [1]

2.2.5. Increasingly significant status of large and medium-sized SOEs in the national economy

The status of large and medium-sized SOEs in the national economy was enhanced through their corporate re-structuring. Take as an example the central SOEs under the management of SASAC. In 2005, the output of the main products of these SOEs reached a historical level. According to the SOE production briefing of SASAC, two coal enterprises (Shenhua Group Co., Ltd. and China Coal Energy Group Co.) produced together 225.828 million tons of raw coal, increasing by 25.4% and accounting for 10.5% of the total output; the sales of coal reached 270.347 million tons, increasing by 16%. Seven power enterprises (Three Gorges Corporation, China Huaneng Group, China Datang Group, Guangdong Nuclear Power Corporation, State Grid, State Power Investment Corporation, and China Huadian Corporation) completed 1,056.49 billion kilowatt-hours of power generation, an increase of 20.5% and accounting for 42.7% of the country's total. Two power-grid enterprises (State Grid and China Southern Power Grid) achieved total sales of 1,814.1 billion kilowatt-hours, an increase of 13.4%. Three petrol and chemical enterprises (CNPC, SINOPEC, and CNOOC) had their total output of crude oil both inside and outside the country at 197.111 million tons, increasing by 4.1% (in 2005, the total output of crude oil inside China was 180.84 million tons)[2]; their total output of natural gas reached 52.88 billion cubic meters, an increase of 20.5%; their output of product oil came together at 164.307

1 *Almanac for the Supervision and Management of China's State-Owned Assets (2013)*, China Economics Press, 2013, p.28.

2 *China Statistical Abstract (2006)*, China Statistics Press, 2006, p.136.

million tons, an increase of 6.7%, and their sales of product oil 183.893 million tons, an increase of 10.1%; the total output of their five major chemical products reached 27.33 million tons, a 7.7% increase. Three air transport enterprises (China Aviation Group, China Eastern Airlines Group and China Southern Airlines Group) completed a transport turnover of 21.03 billion ton-kilometers, an increase of 10.8%, of which passenger turnover reached 14.19 billion ton-kilometers, an increase of 12.1%. Three shipping enterprises (COSCO, China Shipping Group and Changjiang National Shipping Group) completed a transport turnover of 2170.23 billion ton-miles, an increase of 15.2%. Four automobile enterprises (China FAW Group, Dongfeng Automobile Corporation, AVIC II, and China South Industry Group) produced 2.708 million vehicles, an increase of 10.5% and accounting for 47.5% of the national total. Among them, the production of cars reached 1.345 million, increasing by 30.1% and accounting for 48.6% of the national total, while the sales of cars reached 1.339 million, increasing by 28.7%. Four iron and steel enterprises (Baosteel Group, Anshan Iron and Steel Group, Wuhan Iron and Steel Group, and Panzhihua Iron and Steel Group) had a total steel output of 51.402 million tons, increasing by 7% and accounting for 14.6% of the national total; their total output of rolled steel reached 48.146 million tons, increasing by 4.9% and accounting for 12.1% of the national total.

The central SOEs continued to make significant contributions in the key industry areas in 2006 according to relevant reports. Shenhua Group and China Coal Energy Group had a combined output of raw coal of 2,930 million tons, an increase of 18.1%, with the former's output and sales of coal both exceeding 200 million tons and the latter's sales exceeding 100 billion tons. There was also a significant increase in power supply. The five major central power SOEs had a total installed capacity of 2.43 trillion kilowatt-hours at the end of the year, doubling from the end of 2002 and their total power generation reached 1.13 trillion kilowatt-hours, an increase of 17.1% from 2005. In the production and supply of petrol and natural gas, the three major petrol SOEs had a total output of crude oil over 200 million tons both inside and outside China, increasing by

4.3%, with that of natural gas reaching 64.08 billion cubic meters, an increase of 21.1%, and that of product oil reaching 172 million tons, an increase of 4.8%; 272 million tons crude oil was processed domestically, increasing by 5%. In the meantime, the capacity of transport SOEs was improved. The shipping enterprises completed a transport turnover of 2.32 trillion ton-miles, increasing by 9%, while the air transport enterprises completed 23.63 billion ton-kilometers, increasing by 12.4%. In addition, the production and sales of automobiles grew substantially. China FAW Group, Dongfeng Automobile Corporation, AVIC II, and China South Industry Group produced in total 3.229 million vehicles, increasing by 19.2%, and their sales combined to reach 3.209 million, increasing by 17.9%. The total amount of shipbuilding also made history. China State Shipbuilding Corporation and China Shipping Industry Corporation completed 8.71 million dead weight tons of shipbuilding, an increase of 4.2%, while China State Shipbuilding Corporation completed 6.02 million dead weight tons, accounting for 43% of the national total and making it the third largest shipbuilding group in the world.[1] On top of that, a number of SOEs made it to the Global 500 and kept moving up the list (see Table 11-2). For instance, CNPC ranked 54 in 2003, and moved up to 5 in 2012.

Table 11- 2 Number of SOEs from the Chinese Mainland on the Global 500

	2003	2005	2009	2012	2015
Number on the Global 500	14	15	35	73	94
Number of Central SOEs among them	7	10	24	42	47
Number of SOEs	14	15	34	68	88
SINOPEC	54	31	9	5	2
CNPC	52	46	13	6	4
State Grid	46	40	15	7	7
ICBC	243		92	54	18

Source: statistics from *Fortune* magazine.

1 How Central SOEs Achieved High Growth in Economic Indicators, *Economics Daily*, February 13 2007.

Despite its effectiveness in promoting the development of SOEs, the strategy of "strengthening control on the big SOEs" failed to solve some more deep-seated problems of the SOEs, for example, there were too many wholly state-funded enterprises, especially large and mega-SOEs which were mostly wholly state-funded. On the other hand, most of the SOEs strengthened by the government were in industries of natural monopoly or administrative monopoly, and the true reason behind their fast growth in profits in recent years was more the monopoly than the technological and systematic efficiency of the enterprises; so the strategy did not actually fulfill the purpose of motivating the SOEs to improve their operational efficiency. Diversified shareholding system of SOEs and the restriction of monopoly on competition remain the key problems we should strive to solve in the future.

2.3. The strategy of "giving more autonomy to small SOEs" and the withdrawal of small and medium-sized SOEs form competitive areas

Considerable achievements were made in "strengthening control of the big SOEs" after the proposal of the strategy of "strengthening control of the big SOEs and giving more autonomy to the small ones". By the end of 1998, there were 2,472 enterprise groups in China with a total asset of 6,699.4 billion yuan, which marked a step-up in scale of China's enterprise corporations.[1]

"Giving more autonomy to the small SOEs" was another important measure adopted in the SOE system reform in the 1990s, just like "strengthening control of the big SOEs", and was actually carried out in greater strides. Local governments at all levels made active explorations and adopted multiple ways to reform focusing on constructing a diversified ownership structure and transforming the operation mechanism. Small SOEs with relatively good operation and competitive products but not enough funding were restructured into shareholding companies through "capital responsibility shares", after defining the property rights, to

1 *Reference for Leadership Decisions*, compiled by the Party School of CCCPC, issue 26, 2000, p.29.

attract employees, natural persons and legal persons as shareholders. For those SOEs with difficulties in productions and operation, a variety of approaches were adopted. Some were turned into joint-stock cooperatives by setting aside a part of the net assets to exchange for the status of employees; some were restructured into enterprise corporations through merger, transfer and merger, share investment, share controlling, and transfer; multiple forms of leasing were adopted in some SOEs, where the managers turned in a certain amount of fees to the financial administrative departments for occupying state-owned assets, provided that they offered as risk collateral negotiable securities or real estate and helped to employ old staff. Some SOEs were "grafted" through attracting capital, technology and management both domestic and overseas by exploiting their advantages in location, technology and products. For others, the property rights of all or some of the enterprises' assets were transferred (through auction, sale or bankruptcy) so that the state-owned assets could be revitalized and the burdens of debt and personnel could be alleviated. Through these bold and drastic reforms, a large number of small SOEs regained vitality, among which those from Zhucheng City, Shandong Province emerged as outstanding examples.

In October 1992, Zhucheng municipal government approved the joint-stock trial in its electric motor factory, marking the beginning of reforms of its small SOEs. The trial went as follows: all the employees of the factory bought the entire 2.7 million yuan production and operation assets of the factory as internal shares, and established Zhucheng Kaiyuan Motor Co. Ltd., which turned the original SOE into a joint-stock cooperative owned by 277 shareholders. The new company officially started its business on January 1, 1993, and within four months it began to show great vitality with significant growth in all economic and technological indicators. The success of Zhucheng Kaiyuan Motor Co. Ltd. prompted the municipal government to expand the joint-stock trials to more enterprises in the beginning of 1993, which turned out to be even smoother and more transformative than Kaiyuan. In May 1993, the enterprise restructuring reform campaign was launched on a full scale in Zhucheng, with limited liability company and joint-stock cooperative as the major approaches. Fifteen months later, in July 1994, 274 enterprises above the township level (of which 37 were SOEs) were restructured into seven different forms, with 210 adopting the joint-stock cooperative approach.

The effects of small and medium-sized enterprises reform in Zhucheng proved substantial. Before the reform, 68.7% of the enterprises made a loss, with the total loss amounting to 147,000 million yuan, while in 1994, one year after the reform, the enterprises realized 400,000 million yuan of profits and taxes, increasing by 114% from 1993, the fiscal revenue of the government reached 210,000 million yuan, an 50% increase, and the state-owned assets had 8 million yuan in interest, with their value maintained and appreciated. The wage income of the employees in the ten enterprises with earlier restructuring averaged at 3,223 yuan, increasing by 36.3% from 1993, and the average bonus was 522 yuan. In 1997, industry at and above the township level realized 720,000 million yuan of profits and taxes, increasing by 26.1% from 1996, and its fiscal revenue reached 430,000 yuan, doubling that in 1994.[1]

The number of SOEs continued to decrease from the end of 1990s to 2006. In 1998, there were 238,000 SOEs in China, and the number was reduced to 119,000 in 2006, decreasing by 50% at an annual rate of above 8%.[2] Statistics show that in 2005 local SOEs were reduced by 11,489, among which county-level SOEs were reduced by 8,211, accounting for 76.8% of the total reduction in that year, with 96.3% being small and medium-sized SOEs and 79.4% making a loss; in particular, SOEs in storage, wholesale and retail, and food and catering was reduced by 7,918 from the previous year, accounting for 74.1% of the total

1 *Compilation of Enterprise Reform Regulations and Policies* (internal document), compiled by the Office of the Leading Team for Deepening the Reform in Provincial SOEs of Shandong Province, September 2003, p.711.

2 *Exploration & Research: Research Report on the Reform of State-Owned Assets and State-Owned Enterprises (2007)*, compiled by the Research Office of the State-owned Assets Supervision and Administration Commission of the State Council, China Economics Press, 2008, p.165.

reduction.[1] The trend continued in 2006, with a further 8,156 reduction in local SOEs, decreasing by 8.4%, and a net reduction of 7,581 in small SOEs, decreasing by 12.8% from 2005, along with a 7,797 reduction in SOEs in competitive industries, decreasing by 8.3%.[2]

Problems were likewise triggered in the process of "giving more autonomy to small SOEs", the most serious among which were the loss of state-owned assets and the infringement upon employees' interests. According to statistics from Job-Related Crime Department of the Supreme People's Procuratorate, 63% of cases filed in Beijing were corruption and bribery cases in SOEs between 1997 and October 2000, and the number of such cases kept rising since 1998 at a level higher than the national average. Between January and November 2000, Liaoning Provincial Procuratorate investigated and prosecuted 754 SOE personnel in accordance with law for job-related crimes such as corruption, bribery, and embezzlement of public funds by, amounting to 51% of all people prosecuted. In Guizhou, the number of suspects investigated and prosecuted for economic crimes such as corruption, bribery, and embezzlement of public funds in SOEs and institutions between 1997 and August 2000 reached 2,243, among which 670 were prosecuted in 1997, accounting for 50.83% of the total prosecuted cases of that year, 584 in 1998, 57.76% of the total cases, 556 in 1999, 58.04% of the total cases, and 433 between January and August in 2000, 55.71% of the total cases.[3]

The huge risk of loss faced by state-owned assets and state-owned capital indicate that there are still flaws in the current management system of state-owned property rights, which we believe are rooted in the multipolar agent chain of state-owned property rights and the "abstraction" of their owner. State-owned property

1 *Almanac for the Supervision and Management of China's State-Owned Assets (2006)*, p. 48, China Economics Press, 2006.

2 Ibid.

3 *Establishing a Working Mechanism for Prevention of Job-Related Crimes in Chinese Procuratorates with Chinese Characteristics: Explorations and Practices of Prevention of Job-Related Crimes by Procuratorates*, compiled by the Job-Related Crimes Department of the Supreme People's Procuratorate, Law Press, 2001.

rights have to be actualized if the huge risk of loss of state-owned assets is to be avoided.

3. Strategic Industrial Restructuring in the National Economy

Strategic restructuring of the industries in the national economy became inevitable as the SOE reform policy changed from "decentralization of power and transfer of profits" to innovations in the enterprise system, and from improving each SOE to invigorating the entire national economy. Against this backdrop, the focus of the reform turned to strengthening the control of the state-owned economy, i.e., state capital, on the national economy and implementing industry restructuring of state capital with more concentration in key industries.

3.1. Implementation of industrial restructuring in the state-owned economy

As the SOEs took the initiative to restructure industries, the central government officially announced industry restructuring in 196 industries of the state-owned economy at the beginning of 2001 with the following principles. First, state-owned industry must monopolize or mostly monopolize 15 industries, including three categories: those related to national securities, such as military industry, minting, and aerospace; the important natural resource extraction industries, such as oil, natural gas exploitation, and forest harvesting; and public utilities with natural monopoly or public welfare, such as tap water, gas, and electricity. Second, state-owned industry must maintain control power, albeit no monopoly, in 35 industries, also including three categories: the mining of important natural resources apart from those to be monopolized by the state, such as coal, oil, iron, and other mineral resources; the high- and new-tech industries related to the comprehensive competitiveness and power of the nation, such as aerospace, new materials, computer technology, and biomedicine; and pillar industries with increasing potentials for economic growth, such as electronics, petrol chemical and automobile, which should be key competitive industries encouraged by the state instead of being labeled common competitive industries, as they had advantages in high added value, strong industry relevance, and rapid growth in production efficiency and were featured by economy of scale and concentration of capital. Third, state-owned industry should gradually withdraw from 146 common competitive industries, including again three categories: clothing and textile industries with severe excess production capacity; food, beverage, and daily commodity industries serving to fulfill common consumption needs; and those industries which could complete centralization and improve competitiveness on their own through the market mechanism, such as some home appliances manufacturing industries and other manufacturing industries with relatively low technical demands. It was calculated that in these 146 industries 39,231 industrial SOEs would need to be restructured or re-organized, 13.765 million employees would be laid off, transferred or unemployed, and 750.99 billion yuan of net assets would be sold or transferred.[1]

In 2004, SASAC further divided the industries into three categories and seven areas based on the current condition and adjustment orientation of central SOEs. The first category was important industries and key areas related to national security and the lifeline of the national economy, including (1) industries related to national security, such as military industry, important materials reserve, and trade of military products; (2) monopolized industries with either regulatory or natural monopoly, such as communication and power grid; (3) industries providing important public products and service, such as power generation and civil aviation; (4) industries engaging in exploitation of important natural resources, such as oil, petrochemical, natural gas, coal, gold, and salt. The second category was industries indirectly involved in national security, national economy and people's livelihood, including (1) important and key enterprises in pillar industries, such as metallurgy, technical equipment, automobiles, construction, real estate, building materials, and chemical industry; (2) scientific and technical industries, such as electronic information, biomedicine, and research. The third

1 Li Chang'an, SOE Reform Should Change from "Managing the Assets" to "Managing the Capital, *Economic Reference News*, August 19 2015.

category included other industries, mostly domestic and foreign trade, investment, design, consulting, transportation, agriculture, and service.[1]

On December 18, 2006, the General Office of the State Council forwarded the Guiding Opinions of the SASAC about Promoting the Adjustment of State Capital and the Restructuring of State-owned Enterprises, which further stipulated that seven major industries must be controlled by the state-owned economy. State capital should maintain full funding or absolutely controlling shares in central SOEs in military industry, industries dealing with exploitation of important resources such as oil and natural gas, and infrastructure industries such as power grid and communications. State capital should have absolutely controlling shares in the important subsidiaries in the above mentioned industries and central SOEs in civil aviation and shipping, while non-public economy and foreign capital could be introduced to central SOEs in areas such as downstream petrochemical products business and value added communication services to strengthen the restructuring reform and diversify investment and property rights. In the meantime, the state-owned economy should maintain a powerful control on important and key enterprises in basic and pillar industries, including equipment manufacturing, automobile, electronic information, construction, steel, non-ferrous metals, chemical industry, survey and design, and science and technology, where its pull and influence should be strengthened while the percentage of state-owned capital reduced. Central SOEs in the industries of equipment manufacturing, automobile, electronic information, construction, steel and non-ferrous metals should serve as key enterprises and industry pioneers with state-owned capital holding absolutely controlling shares or conditional controlling shares, while central SOEs in science and technology industry responsible for converting achievements in industry-common technology and research should be controlled by state capital.

China quickened its pace of SOE reform since the 19th National Congress of

1 Ju Jinwen, Analysis of Contracting in Promoting the Mixed-Ownership Reform in SOEs, *Tianjing Social Sciences*, Issue no. 1, 2016.

CPC in 2012. Based on the policies of Decision of the CCCPC on Some Major Issues Concerning Comprehensively Deepening the Reform passed at the Third Plenary Session of the 18th CCCPC, in December 2015 SASAC, the Ministry of Finance, and NDRC jointly issued Guiding Opinions on the Function Definition and Classification of State-Owned Enterprises, classifying the SOEs into two categories – commercial and public welfare. It was pointed out in the document that "as independent market entities, both commercial and public welfare SOEs must have operational mechanisms befitting the requirements of the market economy; as SOEs under the conditions of a socialist market economy, they must conscientiously serve the national strategy and actively fulfill its social responsibility." It was required that commercial SOEs should "engage in commercial operations in accordance with market requirements, and independently carry out production and business activities pursuant to the law primarily for the purposes of enhancing the vitality of the state-owned economic sector, amplifying the functions of state-owned capital, and preserving and increasing the value of state-owned assets, so as to achieve the survival of the fittest and orderly market entry and exit. Specifically, commercial SOEs whose primary business concerns major industries and key fields concerning national security or national economic lifeline, or that are mainly responsible for major special project tasks shall, with the aim of safeguarding national security and national economic operation, focus on developing forward-looking strategic industries and achieve the organic unity of economic, social and safety benefits." It was required that public welfare SOEs should "aim to guarantee the people's livelihood, serve the society and provide public products and services, with prices of necessary products or services regulated and controlled by governments. Market mechanism shall be introduced to continually enhance the efficiency and capabilities of public services."

Different policies were adopted to promote the development of these two categories of SOEs. For commercial SOEs, "allocation of resources should be optimized, restructuring and integration efforts and R&D investment should be stepped up, and innovations in science, technology and management should be sped up, so that transformation and upgrading can be continually promoted and a number of key SOEs with innovative capabilities and international competitiveness can be cultivated. Specifically, commercial SOEs whose main businesses are in fully competitive industries and areas must be supported and encouraged to develop businesses with a competitive edge and improve their competitiveness on the market through optimizing the investment of state-owned capital, pushing the transfer of state-owned property rights and disposing of non-performing assets with low or no efficiency; commercial SOEs whose main businesses are in important industries and key areas concerning national security and the lifeline of the national economy and who undertake important special tasks shall ascertain their main business scopes in a reasonable way and increase the investment of state capital according to industry characteristics so as to play a better role in serving the state's macro-control, safeguarding national security and the operation of the national economy, and completing special tasks." For public welfare SOEs, "state capital investment shall be increased according to the enterprises' responsibilities and the requirements of social development so as to improve the quality and efficiency of public services. The enterprises' main business scopes must be strictly delineated and their main businesses better managed, focusing on making greater contributions to the provision of public products and services."

3.2. Industrial restructuring in the state-owned economy and its effects

Strategic industrial restructuring in the state-owned economy is an objective requirement of establishing a socialist market economy in China. After years of efforts, the state-owned economy has seen transformative changes in its industrial layout, while its control and influence has been strengthened.

3.2.1. Preliminary achievement of "making advances and withdrawals as appropriate" of the state-owned economy

Under the guiding principle that state capital should "make advances and withdrawals as appropriate, and know what they can and cannot do", SOEs began to withdraw from competitive industries and areas while strengthening their influence in basic industries and industries with significant bearings on the national economy and people's livelihood. The State-owned economy needed a stronger presence in industries pertaining to national security, industries of natural monopoly, industries providing important public products and services, and important and key enterprises in the pillar and high- and new-tech industries. The industrial layout of for-profit state capital changed significant after this strategic policy was implemented.

First of all, the number of SOEs, which had been on the decline, began to increase since 2009, especially the central SOEs (see Table 11-3). In 1997, there were altogether 262,000 SOEs in China, of which 23,000 were central SOEs and 236,000 local ones. In 2008, the number of SOEs dropped to 110,000, of which 22,000 were central SOEs and 88,000 local ones. In 2014, the total number increased to 161,000, of which 54,000 were central SOEs and 107,000 local ones.

Table 11- 3 Total Number of SOEs Ten thousand

Year	National Total	Central	Local
1997	26.2	2.6	23.6
1998	23.8	2.3	21.5
1999	21.7	2.2	19.5
2000	19.1	1.5	17.6
2003	14.6	1.9	12.7
2005	12.6	2.0	10.6
2006	11.6	2.1	9.6
2007	11.2	2.2	9.0
2008	11.0	2.2	8.8
2009	11.1	2.5	8.6
2010	11.4	2.7	8.7
2011	13.6	4.2	9.4
2012	14.7	4.8	9.9
2013	15.5	5.1	10.4
2014	16.1	5.4	10.7

Source: calculated by the authors according to *China Financial Almanac* over the years.

Secondly, the asset scale of SOEs kept expanding and continued to concentrate in basic and pillar industries. In 1998, the total assets of SOEs reached 13.5

trillion yuan, which increased 20.1 trillion yuan the end of 2003, growing by 6.6 trillion at an average annual rate of 26.4%. In 2005, the number further increased to 26.7 trillion yuan, a 97.8% growth from 1998, and the total value of state-owned net assets increased from 5,037.07 billion yuan in 1998 to 7,676.32 billion yuan, growing by 52.4%; in the same year the total output of state-owned and state-controlling industrial enterprises reached 8,374.992 billion yuan, 25.5 times of that in 1978. In 2006, state-owned assets in China were valued at 30,440.5 billion yuan, with revenue from main businesses reaching 16,196.9 billion yuan, total profits reaching 1,224.2 billion yuan, and the total volume of state-owned capital amounting to 4,645.5 billion yuan.[1] The total assets of sate-owned and state-controlling industrial enterprises in 2014 reached 37,130.884 billion yuan, 9,459.979 billion yuan higher than that in 2003, and their total profits reached 1,450.802 billion yuan, 383.63 billion yuan higher than that in 2003.

As the total asset scale of SOEs kept expanding, the capital strength of basic and pillar industries in the national economy was enhanced. The percentage of the eight major industries, including electric and thermal power generation and supply, coal mining and washing, ferrous metal smelting and plating, chemical raw materials and chemicals manufacturing, oil and natural gas extraction, non-ferrous metal smelting and plating, petroleum processing, coking and nuclear fuel processing, and equipment manufacturing for railways, ships, aviation and aerospace, and other transportations, increased from 64.94% in 2003 to 76.06% to 2010, although it declined slightly to 67.17% in 2014 (see Table 11-4).

Table 11- 4 Total Assets and Operation Situations of Stat-Owned and State-Controlled Industrial Enterprises **100 million yuan**

	2003			2005			2008		
Industry	Total Assets	Revenue from Main Businesses	Total Profits	Total Assets	Revenue from Main Businesses	Total Profits	Total Assets	Revenue from Main Businesses	Total Profits

1 Song Zhiping, Win-Win for the Country and the People: Vigorously Developing Mixed-Ownership Enterprises, *China Enterprise News*, December 24, 2013.

contd.

	2003			2005			2008		
Electric and thermal power generation and supply	22828.34	10038.06	531.64	34362.42	16670.86	985.68	55742.58	27780.23	424.63
Coal mining and washing	4929.5	1930.92	88.31	7244.15	4101.55	335.36	14696.76	9279.06	1351.96
Ferrous metal smelting and plating	8827.52	6227.6	420.22	11651.49	10537.21	677.69	21011.33	20054.03	329.58
Chemical raw materials and chemicals manufacturing	5936.3	3628.39	113.66	6551.8	5108.08	264.61	9686	8017.02	156.02
Oil and natural gas extraction	4802.28	3225.37	1150.07	6434.96	5780.3	2743.75	12351.86	10731.37	4491.73
Non-ferrous metal smelting and plating	2491.13	1502.64	85.09	3278.5	2791.74	226.27	6293.1	6507.38	211.21
Petroleum processing, coking and nuclear fuel processing	3174.45	5436.5	76.78	4515.04	9654.34	-197.17	7609.64	16452.71	-1341.86
Equipment manufacturing for railways, ships, aviation and aerospace, and other transportations	8391.05	6987.84	513.11	9741.07	8071.35	302.36	16450.96	15070.67	968.36
Total of eight industries	61380.57	38977.32	2978.88	83779.43	62715.43	5338.55	143842.23	113892.47	6591.63
National total of all industries	94519.79	58027.15	3836.2	117629.61	85574.18	6519.75	188811.37	147507.9	9063.59
% of the eight industries in the national total	64.94	67.17	77.65	71.22	73.29	81.88	76.18	77.21	72.73

contd.

	2010			2012			2014		
行业	Total Assets	Revenue from Main Businesses	Total Profits	Total Assets	Revenue from Main Businesses	Total Profits	Total Assets	Revenue from Main Businesses	Total Profits
Electric and thermal power generation and supply	68024.78	37419.85	1717.32	83147.25	49302.72	2457	100872.16	53219.08	3717.81
Coal mining and washing	21907.33	13960.1	1969.39	31443.48	20157.53	2026.81	37113.43	17734.6	418.66
Ferrous metal smelting and plating	26143.83	22837.64	501.49	29769.62	24132.48	-213.33	33717.75	23260.33	40.81
chemical raw materials and chemicals manufacturing	12194.97	9526.72	449.68	15867.47	12455.94	267.33	19341.59	13285.58	85.31
oil and natural gas extraction	16125.41	10131.47	2896.11	16625.04	10432.25	3699.48	19064.81	9973.94	2779.06
non-ferrous metal smelting and plating	8762.48	9267.35	407.32	12068.18	13962.55	247.92	14101.86	16670.29	32.59
petroleum processing, coking and nuclear fuel processing	9336.42	20930.5	733.98	11945.8	27452.74	-147.44	13395.91	27226.9	-283.69
equipment manufacturing for railways, ships, aviation and aerospace, and other transportations	25950.35	26134.64	2261.09	10621.02	6188.19	267.7	11815.55	7216.1	329.58
Total of eight industries	188445.57	150208.27	10936.38	211487.86	164084.4	8605.47	249423.06	168586.82	7120.13
National total of all industries	247759.86	194339.68	14737.65	312094.37	245075.97	15175.99	371308.84	262692.28	14508.02
% of the eight industries in the national total	76.06	77.29	74.21	67.76	66.95	56.70	67.17	64.18	49.08

Source: calculated by the authors according to Chinese statistics almanacs over the years.

It was through increasing investment in these areas that state capital concentrated in basic monopolized industries. Take as an example the central SOEs. Between 2003 and 2006, the investment of central SOEs concentrated in petrochemical, communication and power industries, with the amount of investment reaching 559.8 billion yuan and 613.8 billion yuan and accounting for 74.5% and 75.8% of their total investment in 2003 and 2004 respectively. In 2005, the investment of central SOEs was more concentrated, with 868.9 billion yuan invested in 26 important enterprises in these three industries, accounting for 83.6% of their total investment,[1] and the percentage rose further to 86.3% in 2006.[2] According to documents released by SASAC of the State Council in 2013, the percentage of SOE assets in common manufacturing and processing industries such as food production, textile and timber procession dropped to 11.9%, while the percentage of SOE assets in basic and pillar industries rose to 50.6%, and the percentage of assets of central SOEs in military, energy, communication, and transportation industries amounted to almost 70% of their total assets. State-owned capital is clearly increasingly concentrated in industries and areas concerning national security and the lifeline of the national economy.[3]

Third, the industrial layout became more reasonable. The percentage of state-owned assets decreased on a national scope, dropping from 55.99% in 2003 to 38.81% in 2014, but in terms of specific industrial layout the state-owned economy still dominated (with over 50% percentage) 12 of the 41 industries involved in national statistics in 2014 (see Table 11-5).

1 *Reference for Leadership Decisions*, compiled by the Party School of CCCPC, Issue No. 1, 2001, p.15.

2 *Almanac for the Supervision and Management of China's State-Owned Assets (2004)*, China Economics Press, 2004, p.42.

3 *Guiding Opinions on the Function Definition and Classification of State-Owned Enterprises*, http://www.mof.gov.cn/zhengwuxinxi/zhengcefabu/201512/t20151230_1638704.htm

Table 11- 5 Percentage of SOEs in Some Industries **100 million yuan**

Industry	2003		2008		2012		2014	
	State-owned assets	%	State-owned assets	%	State-owned assets	%	State-owned assets	%
National total	94519.79	55.99	188811.37	43.78	312094.37	40.62	371308.84	38.81
Tobacco products	2764.07	98.73	4389.77	99.13	7027.99	99.20	8385.85	98.84
Oil and natural gas extraction	4802.28	97.11	12351.86	96.45	16625.04	94.50	19064.81	94.07
Electric and thermal power generation and supply	22828.34	89.00	55742.58	89.56	83147.25	90.31	100872.16	90.02
Other mining	43.59	97.39	0.14	3.44	2237.17	87.97	2272.35	85.35
Water production and supply	1894.53	88.16	3514.05	79.97	5238.29	80.78	7080.39	81.22
Coal mining and washing	4929.50	90.73	14696.76	75.53	31443.48	70.18	37113.43	70.94
Repair of metal products, machinery and equipment	-	-	-	-	645.48	55.13	615.09	56.11
Manufacturing of transport equipment	8391.05	70.42	16450.96	52.82	10621.02	56.81	11815.55	55.96
petroleum processing, coking and nuclear fuel processing	3174.45	79.78	7609.64	65.05	11945.80	57.05	13395.91	54.31
Gas production and supply	720.39	87.99	1261.39	57.29	2543.51	56.88	3403.74	53.12
Ferrous metal smelting and plating	8827.52	73.43	21011.33	59.70	29769.62	51.17	33717.75	51.68
Automobile manufacturing	-	-	-	-	19292.64	47.75	24825.99	47.07
Ferrous metal mining and processing	279.03	59.04	1195.24	37.59	3963.42	48.49	4721.41	46.21
Non-ferrous metal mining and processing	388.89	63.32	942.23	41.14	1818.16	43.72	2378.15	44.76

Source: calculated by the authors according to Chinese statistics almanacs over the years.

3.2.2. Improved control and influence of state capital

According to statistics of the first national economic census, by the end of 2004 the total paid-in capital of the 3.25 million enterprise entities in the second and third industries amounted to 18.2 trillion yuan, of which there was 8.7 trillion state-owned capital, accounting for 48.1% of the total, 1.4 trillion collective capital, accounting for 7.9%, 5.1 trillion private capital, accounting for 28%, 1.3 trillion capital from Hong Kong, Macao and Taiwan, accounting for 7.3%, and 1.6 trillion foreign capital, accounting for 8.7%. State capital clearly played the most significant role. In addition to that, it was found after analysis of the statistics that state capital now was widely dispersed in all types of economies instead of simply concentrating in SOEs, which demonstrated its influence and control over and wide participation in other economic organizations. (Please refer to Table 11-6.)

Table 11- 6 Sources of Paid-in Capital of Enterprises %

	Paid-in Capital(100)				
	State capital	Collective capital	Private capital	Capital from HK, Macao, and Taiwan	Foreign capital
SOE	98.9	0.7	0.3	0	8.7
Collective enterprises	3.3	88.2	7.8	0.5	0.2
Joint-stock cooperatives	12.1	24.9	62.1	0.6	0.3
State joint-ownership enterprises	93.9	3.6	2.9	0.1	0.1
Collective joint-ownership enterprises	5.5	74.2	19.8	0.3	0.2
Joint state-collective enterprises	45.6	50.2	4.2	0	0
Other joint-ownership enterprises	19.8	26.9	48.4	1.2	3.7
Wholly state-funded enterprises	98.5	0.7	0.3	0.3	0.2
Other limited liabilities companies	36.2	15.1	47.2	0.5	1.0
Share-holding companies	52.0	8.4	32.5	2.6	4.5
Other domestic-funded enterprises	10.7	27.1	57.6	2.7	1.9
Private enterprises	0.4	1.8	97.3	0.3	0.2
Enterprises funded by HK, Macao, and Taiwan	10.3	3.8	3.7	73.9	8.3
Foreign-funded enterprises	7.6	4.3	3.2	14.5	70.4
Total	48.1	7.9	28.0	7.3	8.7

Source: main data bulletin of the first national economic census

By the end of 2008, the total paid-in capital of enterprise entities in the second and third industries in China (excluding administrative institutions and self-employed businesses) amounted to 34 trillion yuan, of which 11.4 trillion was state-owned capital, accounting for 33.5% of the national total.[1]

3.2.3. Increased economic efficiency of SOEs

The efficiency of SOEs on the whole continued to increase. The total profits of SOEs in 1998 were valued at 52.514 billion yuan, which scored to 383.62 billion in 2003 and then to 1,450.802 billion in 2014. The percentage of SOE profits in the total profits of all enterprises above the designated size increased from 36.02% in 1998 to 46.01% in 2003, and then dropped to 21.29% in 2014 (see Table 11-7).

Table 11- 7 Profits and Value-Added Tax of SOEs **100 million yuan**

Year	Total profits of all enterprises above the designated size	Total profits of SOEs	Percentage of SOE profits in total profits of all enterprises above the designated size
1998	1458.11	525.14	36.02
2000	4393.48	2408.33	54.82
2002	5784.48	2632.94	45.52
2004	11929.30	5453.10	45.71
2006	19504.44	8485.46	43.51
2008	30562.37	9063.59	29.66
2010	53049.66	14737.65	27.78
2012	61910.06	15175.99	24.51
2014	68154.89	14508.02	21.29

Source: calculated by the authors according to Chinese statistics almanacs over the years.

SOEs gained rapid growth in total assets contribution rate, increasing from 6.51% in 1998 to 11.32% in 2014, while in the meantime current assets turnover times and the ratio of profits to total industrial costs rose significantly and the debt-to-asset ratio kept decreasing. The per capita main business revenue of SOEs

1 *Exploration & Research: Research Report on the Reform of State-Owned Assets and State-Owned Enterprises (2007)*, compiled by the Research Office of the State-owned Assets Supervision and Administration Commission of the State Council, China Economics Press, 2008, p.162.

reached 1.4256 million yuan, compared with the national average of 1.1096 million yuan. It should be noted, however, that the economic efficiency of SOEs still lagged a little behind the overall national level, with the 2014 total assets contribution rate 2.37% lower than the national average and the current assets turnover times lower than 0.46 time/year (see Table 11-8). The authors believe that the SOE system reform certainly enhanced the system efficiency of SOEs, but their operation efficiency needs to be further improved, as most of the current SOEs gained their high profits from the excess benefits through monopolizing their industries.

Table 11- 8 Operational Efficiency of Enterprises

	Total assets contribution rate (%)	Debt-to-asset ratio (%)	Current assets turnover (time/year)	ratio of profits to total industrial costs (%)	Per capita main business revenue (ten thousand yuan/ person)
National Total					
1998	7.12	63.74	1.41	2.35	
2000	9.00	60.81	1.62	5.56	
2002	9.45	58.72	1.80	5.62	
2004	12.26	59.17	2.16	6.52	
2006	12.74	57.46	2.5	6.74	
2009	13.44	57.88	2.43	6.91	
2012	15.11	57.96	2.57	7.11	
2014	13.69	57.17	2.53	6.52	110.96
State-owned & state-controlled					
1998	6.51	64.26	0.93	1.61	
2000	8.43	60.99	1.34	6.15	
2002	8.71	59.30	1.47	5.93	
2004	12.13	59.35	1.86	8.23	
2006	12.92	56.24	2.28	9.35	
2009	11.29	60.3	2.05	6.73	
2012	12.77	61.31	2.21	6.52	
2014	11.32	61.98	2.07	5.82	142.56

Source: calculated by the authors according to Chinese statistics almanacs over the years.

It was pointed out at the Third Plenary Session of the 18th CCCPC that "we must unswervingly consolidate and develop the public ownership economy, insist on its dominant position, give full play to the leading role of the state-owned economy, and constantly strengthen the vitality, control and influence of the state-owned economy." It remains to be explored further in both theory and practice how state capital can better serve the strategical national goals under the new economic normal and grow to be stronger, better, and greater.

This book is the result of a co-publication agreement between China Social Sciences Press (China) and Paths International Ltd (UK)

This book is published with financial support from Chinese Fund for the Humanities and Social Sciences.

Title: The Historical Analysis of China's State Capital
Author: Wu Taichang, Wu Li et. al.
Translated by Song Ying, Chen Juebin, Li Zhaohui
ISBN: 978-1-84464-666-1
Ebook ISBN: 978-1-84464-667-8

Copyright © 2021 by Paths International Ltd, U.K. and by China Social Sciences Press, China

All rights reserved. No part of this publication may be reproduced, translated, stored in a retrieval system, or transmitted in any form or by any means, electronic, mechanical, photocopying or otherwise, without the prior permission of the publisher.

The copyright to this title is owned by China Social Sciences Press, China. This book is made available internationally through an exclusive arrangement with Paths International Ltd of the United Kingdom and is permitted for sale outside China.

Paths International Ltd
www.pathsinternational.com

Published in the United Kingdom

CPSIA information can be obtained
at www.ICGtesting.com
Printed in the USA
LVHW100851050821
694100LV00006B/7